Northern Renaissance Art

Oxford History of Art

Susie Nash is senior lecturer in Northern Renaissance Art at the Courtauld Institute of Art in London. She has published widely on painting, manuscript illumination, textiles and sculpture of the period, including most recently a book on André Beauneveu and a study of the famous *Well of Moses* by Claus Sluter.

Oxford History of Art

Titles in the Oxford History of Art series are up-to-date, fully illustrated introductions to a wide variety of subjects written by leading experts in their field. They will appear regularly, building into an interlocking and comprehensive series. In the list below, published titles appear in bold.

WESTERN ART

Archaic and Classical Greek Art
Robin Osborne

Classical Art From Greece to Rome
Mary Beard & John Henderson

Imperial Rome and Christian Triumph
Jas Elsner

Early Medieval Art
Lawrence Nees

Medieval Art
Veronica Sekules

Art in Renaissance Italy
Evelyn Welch

Northern Renaissance Art
Susie Nash

Art in Europe 1700–1830
Matthew Craske

Modern Art 1851–1929
Richard Brettell

After Modern Art 1945–2000
David Hopkins

WESTERN ARCHITECTURE

Roman Architecture
Janet Delaine

Early Medieval Architecture
Roger Stalley

Medieval Architecture
Nicola Coldstream

Renaissance Architecture
Christy Anderson

Baroque and Rococo Architecture
Hilary Ballon

European Architecture 1750–1890
Barry Bergdoll

Modern Architecture
Alan Colquhoun

Contemporary Architecture
Anthony Vidler

Architecture in the United States
Dell Upton

WORLD ART

Aegean Art and Architecture
Donald Preziosi & Louise Hitchcock

Early Art and Architecture of Africa
Peter Garlake

African-American Art
Sharon F. Patton

Nineteenth-Century American Art
Barbara Groseclose

Twentieth-Century American Art
Erika Doss

Australian Art
Andrew Sayers

Byzantine Art
Robin Cormack

Art in China
Craig Clunas

East European Art
Jeremy Howard

Indian Art
Partha Mitter

Islamic Art
Irene Bierman

Japanese Art
Karen Brock

Native North American Art
Janet Berlo & Ruth Phillips

Polynesian and Micronesian Art
Adrienne Kaeppler

WESTERN DESIGN

Twentieth-Century Design
Jonathan Woodham

Design in the USA
Jeffrey L. Meikle

Fashion
Christopher Breward

PHOTOGRAPHY

The Photograph
Graham Clarke

American Photography
Miles Orvell

WESTERN SCULPTURE

Sculpture 1900–1945
Penelope Curtis

Sculpture Since 1945
Andrew Causey

THEMES AND GENRES

Landscape and Western Art
Malcolm Andrews

Portraiture
Shearer West

Eroticism and Art
Alyce Mahon

Beauty and Art
Elizabeth Prettejohn

REFERENCE BOOKS

The Art of Art History: A Critical Anthology
Donald Preziosi (ed.)

Oxford History of Art

Northern Renaissance Art

Susie Nash

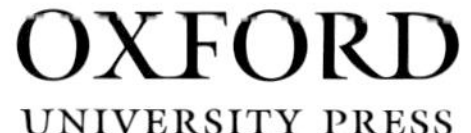

OXFORD
UNIVERSITY PRESS

Oxford University Press, Great Clarendon Street, Oxford OX2 6DP

Oxford University Press is a department of the University of Oxford.
It furthers the University's objective of excellence in research, scholarship,
and education by publishing worldwide in

Oxford New York

Auckland Cape Town Dar es Salaam Hong Kong Karachi
Kuala Lumpur Madrid Melbourne Mexico City Nairobi
New Delhi Shanghai Taipei Toronto

With offices in

Argentina Austria Brazil Chile Czech Republic France Greece
Guatemala Hungary Italy Japan Poland Portugal Singapore
South Korea Switzerland Thailand Turkey Ukraine Vietnam

Oxford is a registered trade mark of Oxford University Press
in the UK and in certain other countries

Published in the United States
by Oxford University Press Inc., New York

First published 2008

British Library Cataloguing in Publication Data

Data available

Library of Congress Cataloging in Publication Data

Nash, Susie.
Northern Renaissance art / Susie Nash.
p. cm.—(Oxford history of art)
Includes bibliographical references and index.
ISBN 978-0-19-284269-5
1. Art, Renaissance–Europe, Northern. 2. Art, Northern European.
I. Title.
N6370.N37 2008
709.02'4—dc22

2008015113

Picture Research by Elisabeth Agate
Typeset by Sparks Publishing Services, Oxford – www.sparkspublishing.com
Printed in Great Britain
on acid-free paper by C&C Offset Printing Co Ltd

ISBN 978–0–19–284269–5

3 5 7 9 10 8 6 4 2

Contents

Preface and Acknowledgements

Any historian who has to survey a large region or period is acutely aware of the difficult choices they must make about what to include and what to leave out. In some respects, the decision to eschew a chronological or geographical narrative in this book has made these choices harder still: I was not obliged to select evenly from every region or moment, and have instead sunk deep shafts at certain points where the evidence of various sorts—physical, technical, documentary, or literary—is notably rich. In making my choices I have also tried to let the contemporary record guide me, pausing on works that observers in the period judged to be worthy of comment, on objects that consumers regarded as desirable, powerful or valuable, and on images that artists viewed as imitable or marketable, insofar as it is possible to establish such things.

This book has taken much longer to bring to completion than I (or my long-suffering colleagues, friends, and family) ever could have envisaged. In part this was because I set out to write a text that took a broad view yet was rich in detail, an introduction with sufficient depth of evidence and academic apparatus to stimulate further enquiry and research, and this was a much harder balancing act than I had foreseen. But it was also because seeing everything I was to write about, and many things that I would not in the end include, in as close proximity as possible, and usually more than once, naturally took both time and resources, especially given the wide geographical scope. Often this also entailed special access and I am deeply grateful to those many curators, conservators, and custodians who have allowed me to view or handle objects and documents, who provided technical information, high quality images, and even on occasion ladders, and who allowed me to photograph works in their care. This brief list cannot acknowledge all the help I have received in this respect over many years, but special thanks go to Maryan Ainsworth, François Avril, Rachel Billinge, Till-Holger Borchert, Bodo Brinkmann, Gabriele Finaldi, Susan Foister, Beatrix Graf, Sophie Jugie, Philippe Lorentz, Mark McDonald, Scot McKendrick, Joachim Sander, Marika Spring, Griet Steyart, Lieve Watteeuw and Rowan Watson. Hildegard Vogeler and the staff at the St Annen museum in Lübeck deserve special mention for providing the memorable experience of the opening and closing of their altarpieces on a visit there in 2004.

Given the richness of experience I have been surrounded by at the Courtauld and the opportunities to examine works both alone and in the company of those with greater insights, I feel the book should be much more than it is.

Without this research culture and the collegiality of my fellow teachers and students there and in the wider academic and art historical community, it would be so much less. These include Stephanie Buck, Georgia Clarke, Elizabeth Cleland, Caroline Campbell, Paul Crossley, Peter Dent, Susan Foister, Bart Fransen, John Goodall, Bridget Heal, Melena Hope, Susan Jones, Stefan Kemperdick, Joseph Koerner, Meg Koster, Robert Maniura, Jim Marrow, Mark McDonald, Paula Nuttall, Zoe Opacic, Jenny Stratford, Jan van der Stock, Hugo van der Velden, Lieve Watteeuw and all my students who have asked the questions and made the observations to which this book is in part a response. Particular debts, of which friendship and support are not least among them, are due to Joanna Cannon, the late Caroline Villers (who is sorely missed), John Lowden, Patricia Rubin, Alixe Bovey, Beth Williamson, Douglas Brine, Jim Harris, Kim Woods and Sam Fogg, in whose company I have learnt to look ever more closely, critically or differently, on many memorable study trips, and who have made the travelling so much more enjoyable; Joanna Cannon, John Lowden, Patricia Rubin, and Caroline Villers have also instigated many stimulating and inventive opportunities for academic exchange, such as the 'Prado Conversations', held in Madrid in 2002 and the Lille-Leuven-London triangle; Jo Kirby and Claire Richardson have in recent years continued my education in matters technical and scientific where Caroline Villers left off, which have included several memorable practical sessions in painting in oil and egg. Last, but not least, Catherine Reynolds and Lorne Campbell have provided over many years a model for how to look, write, and research on this field. Needless to say, mistakes or misunderstandings which remain are there in spite of their input, not because of it.

Many have supported this project in practical ways. For help in gathering references I am grateful for the assistance provided at various points by Douglas Brine (who also expertly helped footnote and correct errors), Hanna Wimmer (who also helped with translations of some of the more tricky German material), Elizabeth Cleland, Delphine Cool, Ursula Weekes and Andreas Puth. A grant for research leave from the AHRC allowed much needed time to write; the Research Committee of the Courtauld Institute provided the funds for a camera (which enabled me to provide a number of the photographs used in this book myself), travel, and research assistance; the Central Research Fund of the University of London also provided travel funds. I acknowledge their vital assistance here most gratefully. My colleagues, especially Christopher Green and Joanna Cannon, took over administrative duties for me at certain crucial moments when deadlines were looming. Douglas Brine, Kim Woods, Jim Harris, Elizabeth Cleland, Mark McDonald, John Lowden and Claire Richardson all read and commented on all or parts of the text, often at short notice and always with care; Jim Harris provided a great deal of last minute help, in particular regarding processing my images for print and compiling the index. At OUP, Matthew Cotton has been a most patient and understanding editor; Lisa Agate has worked magic obtaining images; Nancy Marten and Kate Hind expertly saw the text though to production; and John Duggan at Sparks has done wonders with the design, responding to the visual needs of such a book with patience and care. I am grateful to OUP for their willingness to publish a larger volume than many in the series, something that for me was symbolically important in redressing the balance of attention given to northern Europe at a period that is unhelpfully, but here unavoidably, termed 'the Renaissance'.

Finally I owe a special debt to Amos Miller, for all his support and for the efforts he made over a long period to help me carve out writing time while we were juggling two demanding careers and the care of two small boys, and to the friends and family who rallied round to look after those boys when I was travelling. It is to those boys, Sam and Linus, who have had a mother distracted by this project for all their lives, that this book is dedicated.

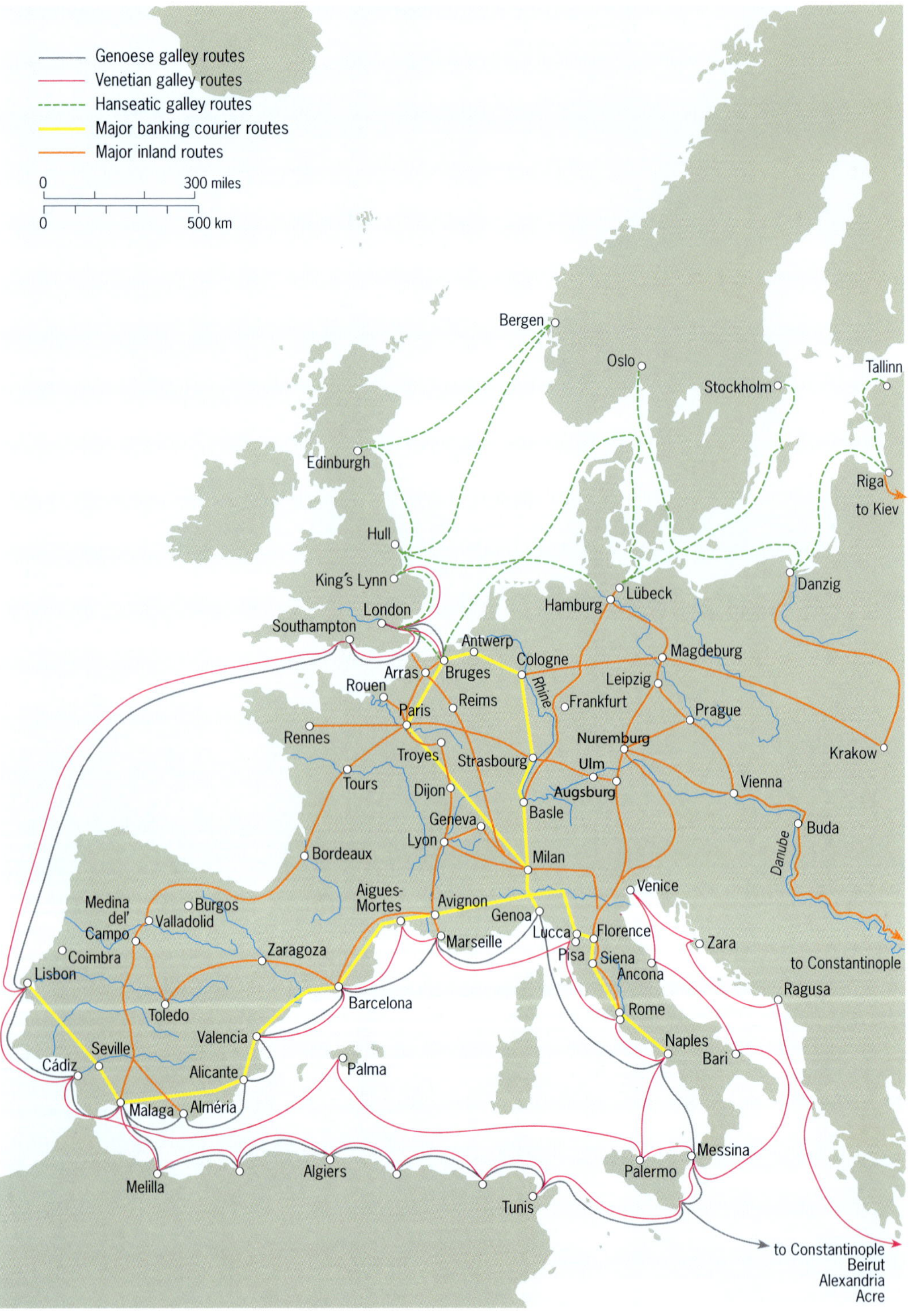

Map 1: Major Sea and Land Trade Routes

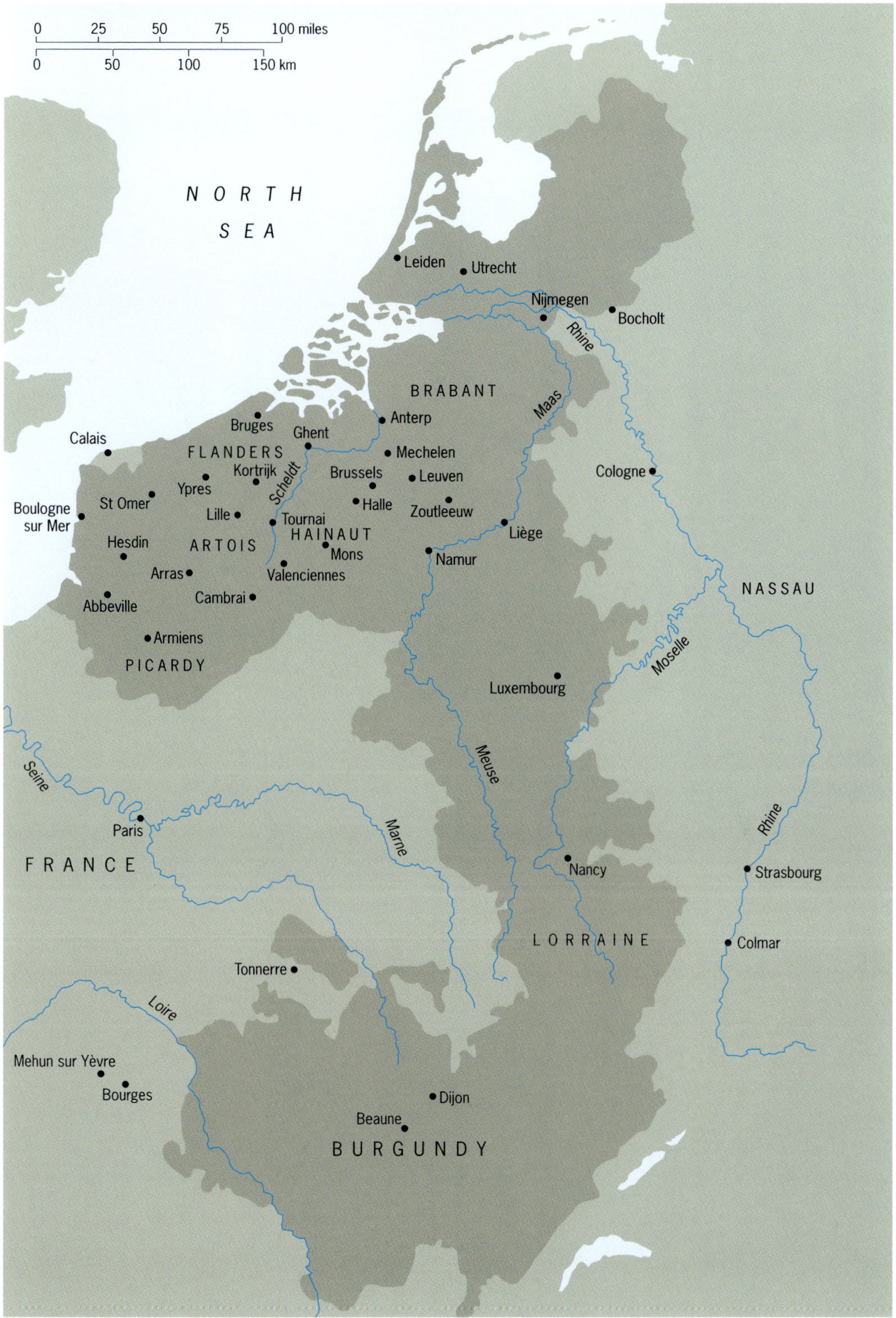

Map 2: The Burgundian Netherlands

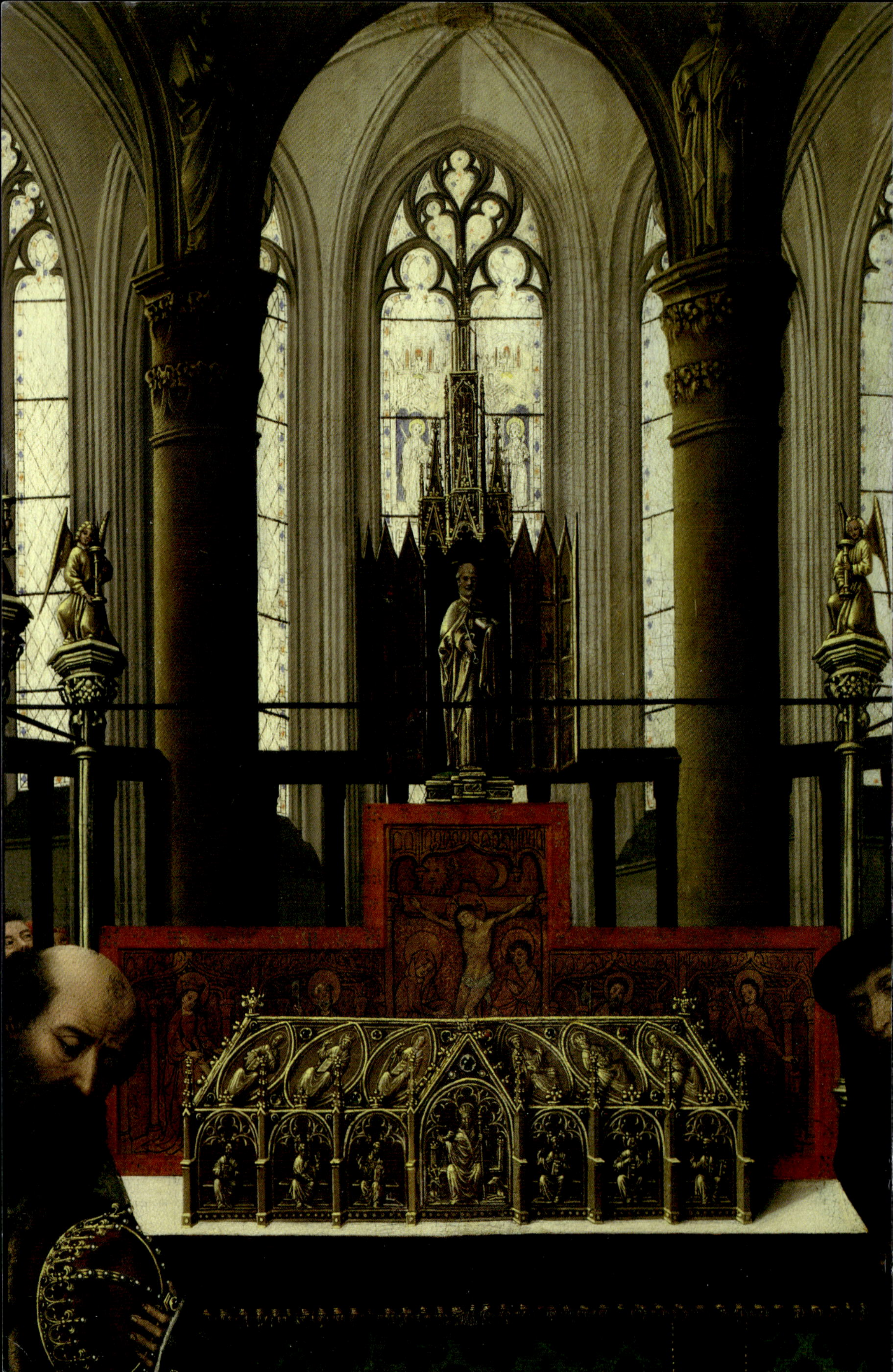

Introduction

One must begin somewhere. And yet, the point at which one begins assumes inordinate importance, for it tends to be regarded as the point from which everything flows, like the spring of a great river—and this it cannot be.

Max J. Friedländer, *Early Netherlandish Painting, I: The Van Eycks and Petrus Christus*

1

This book considers the artistic production of northern Europe from the middle of the fourteenth century to the turn of the sixteenth. Of course, any chronological boundaries are by their nature artificial, cutting across continuities and creating a starting point where none may have existed. In this case the choice of where to start, and where to stop, has been governed by reasons which are primarily art historical or cultural, and they are necessarily fluid: some objects and documentary material from outside this period are included because they shed important light on earlier or later practices.

Although there are many continuities which can be drawn between our period and the preceding centuries,[1] the last decades of the fourteenth century arguably present an artistic sea-change in many ways: they saw the beginning of a boom in the level, range, and scale of artistic production, as the number of artists active in the towns of northern Europe, and particularly in Paris, the Burgundian Netherlands and southern Germany, began to increase dramatically, a pattern which was to continue throughout the fifteenth century and into the sixteenth (see Part II). This increase reflected, and helped fuel, a burgeoning demand for images of all kinds from a wider range of the population than ever: by *c.*1500 we have extensive documentation for the private ownership of images of all sorts by a broad cross-section of society: merchants, craftsmen, clergy, lawyers, doctors as well as members of the nobility; this is much harder to find prior to 1350. In the church as well as in the home, the desire for commemoration and the needs of salvation were increasingly met in visual terms: memorials, tombs, private chapels, and their furnishings proliferated in ecclesiastical interiors, which were much more densely adorned with images around 1500 [**168**] than they would have been in around 1350, and indeed than at any point in their later history given the tumultuous events of the following centuries, the implications of which are discussed in Part I.

The latter half of the fourteenth century was also a period when the emphasis on the visual in many realms became more intense and widespread: ritual events began to utilize figurative props in a more marked way, be they the coronation ceremonies of the kings of France, the glorious entries of the Burgundian dukes into their towns, the celebration of New Year and other festivities at the courts of Europe, or liturgical dramas enacted most intensely around Easter and Advent (discussed in Part V). It is this period, too, which is charted by historians of dress as a key moment in the development of fashion in the modern sense, as clothing became more complex in construction,

Detail of 6

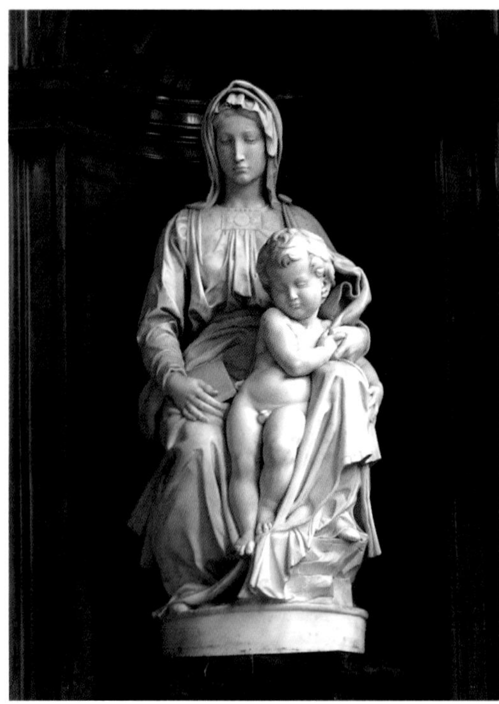

1 Michelangelo
The Virgin and Child (the 'Bruges Madonna'), marble, 1503–6.

more frequently subject to change in its forms and shapes, and more nuanced as an indicator of status. Because of this, perhaps, dress at our period is a particularly vivid and vital tool in visual imagery, where it could convey complex meanings and a range of subtle associations, aiding narrative construction as well as creating emotional and dramatic impact.[2]

This period was also witness to great technical innovation and virtuosity. In the late fourteenth century new art forms, or refinements in already established ones, were developed (although not, as is sometimes supposed, in the realm of oil painting, which was a well-established method in every sense, see pp. 30–31). The boundaries of what was possible in metal, stone, wood, glass, and wool were pushed to its limits. These developments were, in large part, prompted or precipitated by the enlightened patronage of the European courts: the French royalty in Paris and the regional capitals of Dijon, Angers, and Bourges; the Holy Roman Emperor Charles IV in Prague; Sigismund of Luxembourg in Budapest; and the court of Richard II in London. These patrons had the money and the desire to commission monumental, ambitious, expensive, and innovative projects. The level of technical achievement and visual invention in works like the *Parement de Narbonne* for Charles V of France (d. 1380, **194**), the *Goldenes Rössl* for his son Charles VI (d. 1421, **24**), the *Well of Moses* for Philip the Bold, Duke of Burgundy (d. 1404, **146, 147, 148**), the Angers *Apocalypse* tapestries for Louis, Duke of Anjou (d. 1384, **143, 144, 145**), or the *Très Riches Heures* [**74, 75, 76**] for Jean, Duke of Berry (d. 1416), is extraordinary, and in some respects reached a peak in these objects. Technical experimentation and a different prerogative, that of speeding up the production processes involved in image making, lay behind the most influential of new media of the period: printmaking. Early prints were of a modest nature,

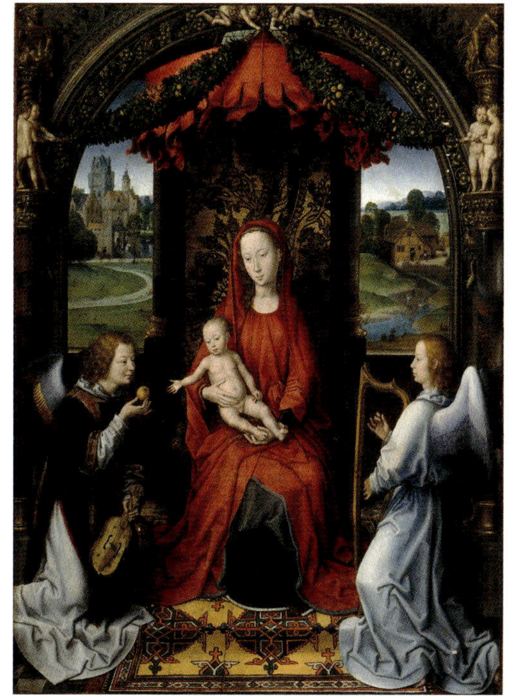

2 Hans Memling

The Virgin and Child with Angels (the 'Pagagnotti Triptych'), oil on Baltic oak, *c.*1480.

This panel is the centre part of an altarpiece made for Benedetto Pagagnotti, a Florentine Dominican and bishop. He never visited the Netherlands, and must have commissioned or been given this work through an agent there. It was well known to Florentine painters in the 1480s and 1490s, who copied elements of its landscape with precision.

simple woodcuts aimed at the lower end of the market [**46**], spurred on by the need for reasonably priced religious images. By the end of our period, with the development of intaglio printing from engraved metal plates, prints had the potential for a level of sophistication quite beyond this, with the complex engravings of Martin Schongauer (*c.*1435/50–1491, **91**, **96**) and Albrecht Dürer (1471–1528, **84**). These were displays of artistic invention and technical mastery, designed for a different consumer and budget, and they were hugely influential Europe-wide (see Part III).

Our period closes around 1500 when an artistic tide starts to turn: the Burgundian Netherlands, for over 100 years the dominant force in Europe in terms of its artistic output and influence (see Part II), begins to give way to Italy, and particularly to the towns of Florence, Venice and Rome. Northern products continued to dominate the international market for some years, but Italian art became increasingly influential and desirable, particularly following the arrival in Brussels of Raphael's tapestry cartoons from Rome in 1517. It is, however, the arrival in Bruges in 1506 of the marble *Madonna* by Michelangelo [**1**], sent there by a Flemish merchant, Alexandre Mouscron, which represents our symbolic turning point: the muscular child, so typical of Michelangelo, is a stylistic direction which many artists in the north as well as the south were to follow in the next century and beyond, dictating taste for the next few hundred years and becoming by far the most admired object in Bruges (a position it maintains to some extent to this day). Yet it is simultaneously representative of the impact northern art had had throughout Europe in the preceding century: the Virgin is a type that surely alludes to those of Hans Memling, whose paintings were well known in Florence [**2**]. This is both visually evident and historically plausible (see Chapters 7 and 10), even if we are slow to accept an artist like Michelangelo learning from northern ideas.

The geographical boundaries of this study are perhaps more artificial than the chronological ones, in a Europe which had such a fluid political map, and where trade routes by land and sea dictated relationships and contacts as much as the physical proximity of countries and natural borders like the Alps: Genoa, Lucca, Milan, Florence and Venice arguably had as much commercial contact with Paris, Bruges, Cologne, and Nuremberg as they did with each other (see Map 1). Moreover, in treating the north (an entity encompassing everything north of the Alps and west of Krakow and Vienna) as distinct from the south (which is basically for our purposes the Italian peninsula), we reinforce a long tradition in art historical literature which implies that Italy was a homogenous and discrete society from its northern neighbours. That neither of these ideas is entirely or even partly tenable is widely recognized, yet we continue to separate out the two regions in how we teach and write about their artistic production. We mostly specialize in one area or the other, rarely crossing the Alps to consider the continuities, despite concerted and accelerating interest of scholars in particular artistic relationships between these regions.[3] While it would be preferable to try to dissolve the boundary of the Alps (which proved relatively easy for most travellers and traders of the period to overcome, either by sea route or land), the scope of this study does not permit it, given that Italy has been covered admirably in another book in this series.[4] The juxtaposition with Italy is, however, fundamental in other ways: we have historically viewed northern achievements of this period though the lens of Italy (or more properly Florence), mostly to the detriment of northern works. We still are prone to assuming Florentine superiority and dominance at the period, a particularly deep-seated belief in Anglophone countries, and one rarely challenged sufficiently. This issue is addressed in Part I.

Even without Italy the range of this book as implied by the generic term 'northern' is potentially vast. Although this study encompasses examples of objects made as far east as Krakow (image heading chapter 16), as far north as Stockholm [**127**], and as far south as Zaragoza (**134**; Spain for our purposes is also northern, given its political affinities and artistic leanings), such a range can only be attempted with a thematic approach, which makes no attempt at a balanced coverage of all regions at this period. Without doubt, and unashamedly, the bias in this study is towards works made in Paris and Dijon (mostly before 1420), in the towns of the Burgundian Netherlands (Bruges, Brussels, Ghent, Tournai and Antwerp) and Germany (such as Lübeck, Colmar, Cologne, Ulm and Nuremberg after *c*.1450). These centres and regions were, at varying points, the most commercially and culturally successful, and the areas of greatest industrialization. Their importance is vividly conveyed in the travel account of Pero Tafur (*c*.1410–*c*.1484), a nobleman from Castile, who in the 1430s undertook an extensive journey across Europe. Setting out from Gibraltar, Tafur had sailed to Genoa and travelled through Italy, stopping in Florence, Rome and Venice, from where he took a ship via the Greek islands to the Holy Land. From there he travelled to Egypt and Constantinople, returning westward across the Alps to Germany, reaching the Low Countries in 1438. In all these places he saw and recorded many marvels, such as the pyramids and bazaars of Cairo, and miraculous images in Constantinople.

However, it was the towns of Bruges, Antwerp, Ghent and Brussels which seem to have impressed him most. Here, in northern Europe, were the most cosmopolitan cities he had seen anywhere, where one could buy the greatest range of luxury goods, including works of art. Bruges, he thought, was 'one of the greatest markets in the world', and he witnessed greater commercial activity there than in Venice, since, he said, in Bruges all the nations of the world could be found engaging in trade. Tafur was particularly astounded by the range and quality of the produce: he noted that 'anyone who has money and wishes to spend it will find in the town alone everything which the whole world produces'. The sheer scale of the trade which took place fascinated him: with awe he recounts that he has been told that, at certain times, 700 ships a day sailed from Bruges. Antwerp, Bruges' rival as the commercial centre of Europe, left him lost for words: 'I do not know how to describe so great a fair as this. I have seen others at Geneva in Savoy, at Frankfurt in Germany and at Medina in Castile, but all these together are not to be compared to Antwerp.'[5] The reasons why we no longer perhaps see these centres quite as Tafur did are explored in Part I. Places such as Bruges and Antwerp specialized in the making and selling of goods rather than in the production of raw materials, and these centres were also the most geared up for the exportation of their products. Tafur, commenting on the lack of local agricultural produce in Bruges, noted that its 'extraordinarily industrious' inhabitants exchanged 'the work of their hands' for the 'products of the whole world ... so that they have everything in abundance'. Many of the exported goods manufactured in the cities of the north were luxury items; the range and nature of these exports are considered in Part II.

The geographical scope of this book is one reason why it is not structured chronologically or around artists' biographies; the thematic approach selected here is also beneficial for other reasons. Although there are some famous artists whose careers we will investigate (Part III), a biographical structure privileges the artist as the context for the work and can sideline other contexts (such as media, location, use, and processes of production). Moreover, it does not easily encompass works made by artists whose names have not, for many reasons, come down to us. With northern art this is a high proportion of surviving production, particularly in media like metalwork and tapestry, and a more acute problem, on the whole, than for Italian works of the period (the reasons for this and their implications are explored in Chapter 2). This book also does not attempt to chart evolutions of style or follow developments in the visual exploration of space and form. Although northern painters, in particular, excelled in the creation of spatial, and other, illusions, it is only one of the many visual strategies which these sophisticated artists wielded, and the idea that this period witnessed a progressive advance towards greater naturalism or that this was the aim of any farsighted Renaissance artist is one that should not be encouraged. Rather than artists or style, this book therefore takes as its point of departure the physical evidence of the objects themselves: their scale, materials, technique, condition, and what is represented and how. Some of this evidence comes from technical methods of examination, which have been used with great success on Netherlandish paintings in particular (see Chapter 5), but it mostly comes from close, extensive, detailed looking, a procedure which can be followed by all. Our other key point of departure is primary sources, which may be documentary evidence concerning particular works, but can be more tangential like guild regulations, legal disputes, wills, inventories, or poetry (these sources are discussed in Chapter 4). In many cases objects have been chosen for discussion because the evidence of either or both these sorts is particularly rich, allowing us to consider questions such as how they were made, used, and viewed.

Also at the heart of the approach of this book is that it concerns itself with a wide range of media, and is not limited to painting. Indeed, our modern tendency to separate out the work of painters in galleries devoted to their art alone, and to write histories of art that look only at painted works, is particularly anachronistic. The period that this book covers valued the works of goldsmiths, sculptors, embroiders, and weavers more highly, in most cases, than painting. That is not to say that painters did not play a crucial part in much of the production of the period: indeed, they were often the designers of metalwork, stained glass, sculpture, and tapestries, and as such they continue to have a starring role in this book. However, like any viewer of the period, our horizons must encompass images in many different media, from metalwork to parchment and ivory, polychromed wood to carved limestone and alabaster, sometimes combined on the same object [**155, 156, 163**], referred to visually from one medium to another [**174**] or seen in tandem, used together or in sequence in liturgical and devotional rituals [**6, 168, 191**].

This book, then, looks not just at a representative range of different types of art in different materials, but considers some of the technical, practical, social, economic, and functional relationships between these different media, the craftsmen who worked in them, and the meanings of the materials they used. This was clearly something central to the makers and consumers of the works we are concerned with here. Indeed where we have evidence of what was important to contemporary audiences, it tends to indicate that materials, their quality, and the skill of the artist in their manipulation and deployment were more current considerations when images were made, used, viewed, and valued than the more modern interest in style. This is not to say that contemporaries did not recognize artistic difference or quality in terms other than material ones: both Margaret of Austria and Catherine of Aragon could make judgements concerning the works and skill of Michel Sittow (see p. 108, 237), and a sensitivity to different hands and an appreciation of the ability to invent are threads which can be picked up through the period, but patrons' expressions of value nevertheless insistently centred in some manner around technical skill. Thus the town council of Barcelona, when commissioning their altarpiece [**27, 28**], wanted 'the best and most able painter to be found',[6] while the mayor of Nördlingen recommended two craftsmen, the painter Friedrich Herlin (*c.*1425/30–1500, see **153**) and the carpenter Hansen Waidenlich, to another city on the basis that they had completed 'two beautiful and masterfully crafted pieces of work',[7] and Philip the Good wanted the cartoons for his tapestries of the story of Gideon painted by 'Bauduin de Bailleul or by another better painter that they may find'.[8] Even the famous encomium of this same patron concerning his court painter Jan van Eyck, which praises that artist's 'science', should be read as referring to the craft of painting, not science as we might understand it.[9] What we come back to is that the best artists were invariably those who could work their materials in extraordinary ways, as is most startlingly evident from the way van Eyck handled oil paint (detail heading chapter 5), Claus Sluter (*c*.1360–1406) and his team constructed stone monuments [**146, 147, 148**], or Veit Stoss (*c*.1445/50–1533) carved wood [**149, 150, 152**]. This book is necessarily, then, concerned in large part with these matters of materials—and why materials mattered: the relative challenges, advantages, expense, and difficulties of working different media. In this we can start to understand artistic choices as well as patronal desires, driven, in most cases, by practical and technical considerations: cost, availability, time, durability, visibility, and decorum.

Finally some notes on terminology. Because Europe at this period was rather differently distributed to how it is today, our modern names for countries and regions cannot always be applied: Belgium, Spain, Germany, and Italy did not properly exist as distinct entities, and large parts of France were actually ruled by England for much of this period. Although Italy is used here as a term for the whole peninsula, it was in fact a group of city states and principalities, not a monolithic or even remotely homogenous whole until the nineteenth century; the same is largely true of Germany. Spain was a set of five kingdoms until the end of the fifteenth century; Belgium was both split into several territories but part of a larger whole—the Burgundian Netherlands—which stretched from Zeeland in the north to Burgundy in the south (see Map 2), a centrally administered state which was created, enlarged, and ultimately dissolved during our period. Because of this, wherever possible, precise regional terms are used: Castile, not Spain; Brabant, not Belgium; Florentine, not Italian. Flemish, strictly speaking, only refers to works made in towns in Flanders (which includes Bruges and Ghent, but not Brussels or Leuven, which are in Brabant), so Netherlandish is preferred when a wider region is implied, encompassing the area indicated on Map 2. In a book of this scope the broader geographical terms are, however, impossible to avoid and without them the text would become rather unwieldy. When the all-encompassing 'north' and northern art' are resorted to, which is necessary at times, they refer to Western Europe north of the Alps: anything not Italian.

Secondly, we have the problem of how to refer to the period in general. In the title of this book Renaissance has been used; this is intended as a shorthand, but its implications and appropriateness need to be considered. The fact that it is a French term conveys a false sense of universal validity, but it is arguably not applicable to works from northern Europe from this period, having been developed and applied primarily in relation to Italian art and culture, or to a later period of northern history, from *c*.1500 onwards.[10] As a consequence, it tends to bring with it assumptions and criteria proper to Italian art and its achievements and aims, which were demonstrably different, on the whole, from northern art. Despite the implications of the adoption of 'Renaissance' for northern art of this period, it is used here in the title of this book since it is the best available term. So long as we do not seek what was valued by Italian eyes, especially Florentine sixteenth-century eyes (this is harder than it might seem, see Chapter 3), we can use this label as a convenient one, and one which does evoke the rich boom in production, the new media and ideas, technical feats, imagery, and imagination which we see in this period in northern Europe.

Part I

Problems and Perspectives

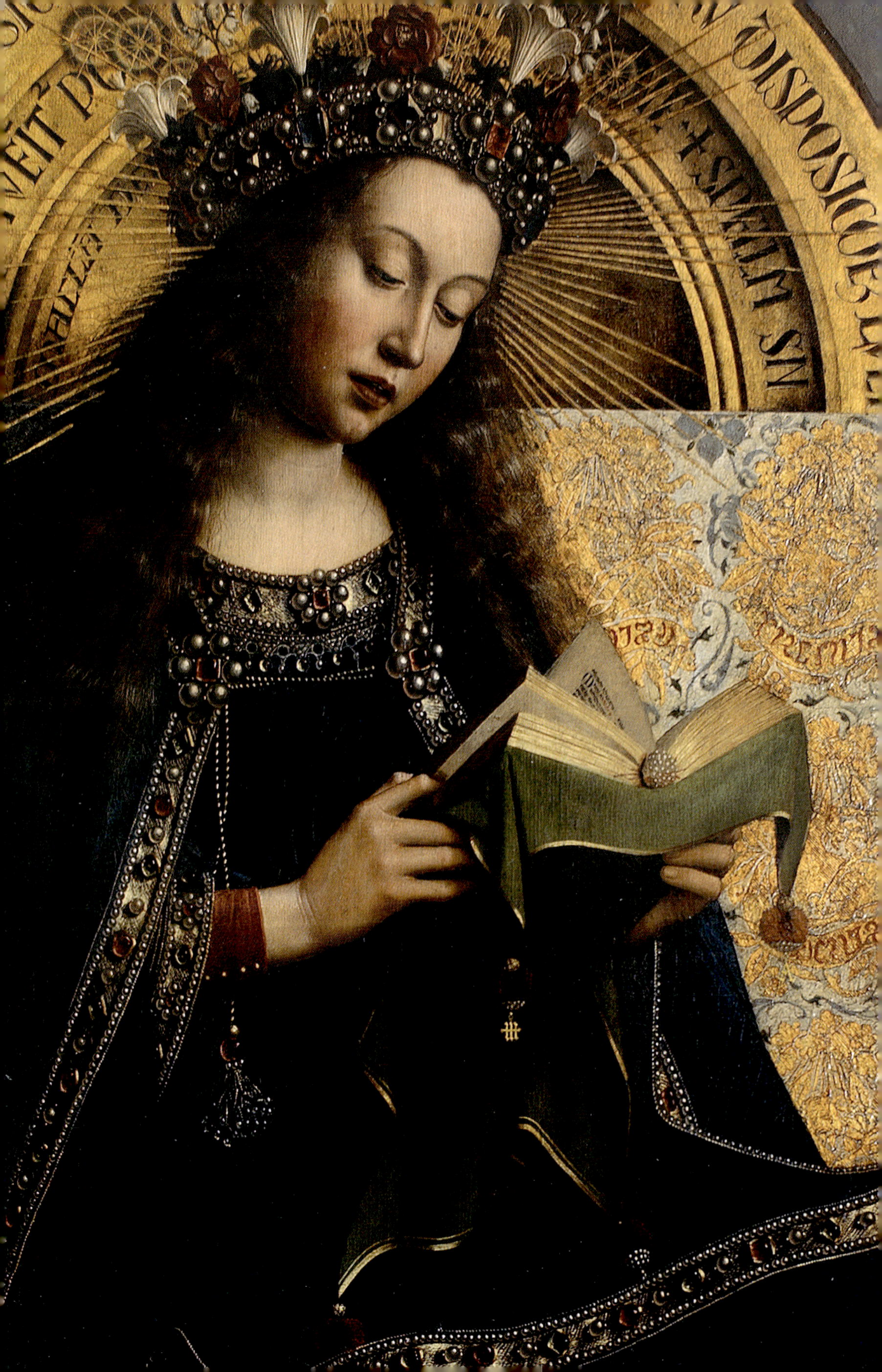

Dispersal and Destruction

It would be close to impossible to enumerate all the works of sculpture, ornaments, statues and others destroyed by the wars.

Marcus van Vaernewijck (1516–69), on the destruction of images in Ghent in 1566[1]

2

The Ghent Altarpiece, begun by Hubert and completed by Jan van Eyck, is perhaps the most famous and most debated work of the northern Renaissance [**3a, 3b**].[2] As such it often stands at the beginning of surveys of this period. Indeed, it is where the earliest historians of Netherlandish painting, such as the Italian Ludovico Guicciardini (1521–89) and the Netherlander Karel van Mander (1548–1606), writing in the sixteenth and early seventeenth centuries, began their narratives; it is also where the great twentieth-century art historian, Max J. Friedländer (1867–1958), began his magisterial fourteen-volume study on the subject.[3] This is unsurprising since there is no Netherlandish painting as monumental or visually so arresting which is demonstrably earlier than this work: bearing the date 6 May 1432, it measures over 5 metres across when open, making it also one of the largest surviving panels from this period.

The richness and complexity of its subject matter and the brilliance of its oil technique, the illusionism of passages such as the figures of Adam and Eve or the fictive stone sculptures of the two Saint Johns, and the skill with which the effects of fabrics, jewels, hair, tiled floors, polished armour, or flowers are evoked, astounded observers in the fifteenth and sixteenth centuries and continue to do so today. Albrecht Dürer was among the many to admire it; Antonio de Beatis, secretary to the Cardinal of Aragon, in 1517 on a visit from Naples declared it 'the finest painting in Christendom'; in the later sixteenth century a lengthy ode was composed in its honour by the Ghent painter and poet Lucas de Heere, and it was the only painting outside of Italy that was specifically cited by Giorgio Vasari in 1568.[4] It was also the first painting on which a full technical investigation was undertaken in the late 1940s, the start of a vital new way of investigating works of art, the results of which play an important role throughout this book.[5]

The Ghent Altarpiece is a starting point here, too, but not because it marks the beginning of something. Indeed, it is likely that if more works from the southern Netherlands in the century before this was made survived, we would find this was certainly not the case: in terms of technique and form it was undoubtedly part of a long tradition of oil painting and altarpiece design that we can now only glimpse, literally, fragments of. It is these very issues of survival, and the patterns of destruction and dispersal, which open our discussion here and make this altarpiece such an apposite choice with which to begin, since its fame, and its consequently well-documented history, provide a dramatic illustration of the potential fragility of the visual culture of this period. Arguably, the range and extent of our

Detail of 3b

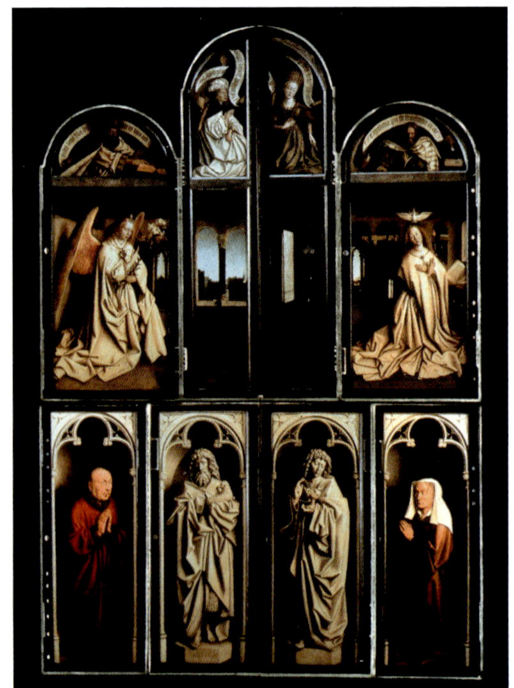

3a Hubert and Jan van Eyck

The Ghent Altarpiece (closed), oil on Baltic oak, dated 1432.

This work was made for the chapel founded by Joos Vijd in the church of St John the Baptist, now St Bavo's, in Ghent. Its much disputed Latin inscription, painted across the lower edge of its frame, can be translated as: 'The painter Hubert van Eyck, a greater than whom cannot be found, began this work; Jan, his brother, second in art, completed the heavy task at the request of Joos Vijd. On the sixth of May [1432] he invites you by means of this verse to look at what has been done.' The year is given as a chronogram, made up of the roman numerals in the last line.

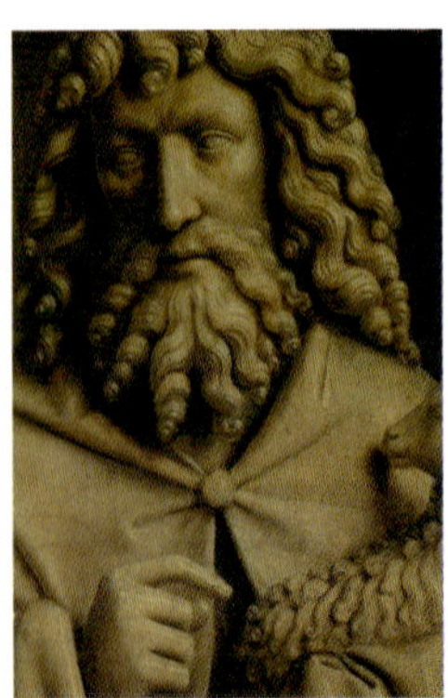

losses and their patterns are more important to detail in a survey of this type than a potted history of the period itself, because what has survived, why, and where has had undeniable impact on how we have understood, studied, and evaluated Renaissance art in general.

On 19 August 1566, during a wave of iconoclasm which swept the Netherlands, an eye witness account by the Ghent historian Marcus van Vaernewijck (1516–69) recorded how the Ghent Altarpiece was 'taken to pieces and lifted, panel by panel, into the tower' to preserve it from the rioters.6 It was again nearly destroyed just ten years later, in another outbreak of image-directed violence, this time preserved only by a special guard placed on the work. Fame and value can, of course, also bring their own dangers: in the late eighteenth century, following the French Revolution, the altarpiece was a prime candidate for the museum that Napoleon was creating in Paris; the four central panels were looted by his troops and taken to the French capital. While the display of these panels in the Louvre gave them important publicity and, in effect, began the modern phase of the study of early Netherlandish art, the taste of that period on the whole did not favour works of this type. The panels were returned to Ghent in 1815, but in another twist to the altarpiece's fate, the wing panels (except those of Adam and Eve) were promptly sold off by one of the canons to an art dealer. Defending this move, the vicar-general of the cathedral could claim that the panels were dirty, useless objects, 'just a piece of old furniture' with worm-eaten frames, their only interest being their age and the name of the painter.7 This deeply unappreciative view is depressingly not untypical: as many northern works of art were simply discarded in the eighteenth and nineteenth centuries because they were unfashionable and old as were deliberately destroyed in the six-

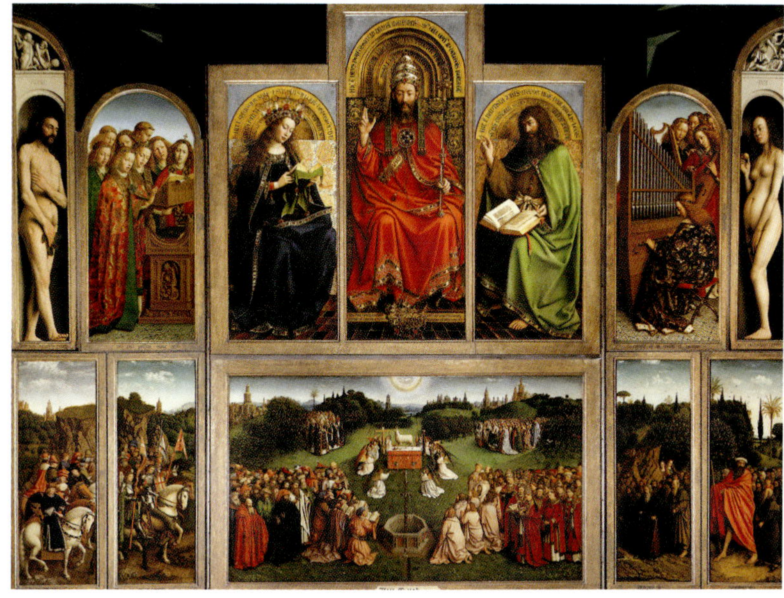

3b Hubert and Jan van Eyck

Interior of the Ghent Altarpiece [**3a**].

Art historians have long debated, with no resolution, what parts of this work might be by the elder, little-known brother Hubert and what might be by the younger Jan, who had Europe-wide fame. Since we have no other documented work by Hubert from which we might assess his style, separating out the two brothers is perhaps an impossible task. Technical examination has revealed only similarities with Jan's known oeuvre rather than differences which might indicate the hand of another artist. The results of recent dendrochronology on the wing panels suggest that these, at least, are unlikely to be the work of Hubert, who died in 1426, since some of the planks have a probable felling date of 1421; with a likely seasoning time of 10–15 years this gives a creation date well after his death.

teenth. Although the Ghent Altarpiece was returned to Saint Bavo's following an outcry over the sale, two panels were stolen in 1934 (one of which has yet to be found) and during the Second World War it was looted again, this time taken by the Germans to Pau, and recovered eventually by the American forces from the Alt Aussee mines in 1945, an event captured in [**4**]. Amazingly, having survived its many journeys around Europe, it can still be found, mostly intact, in the church for which it was intended; until relatively recently it was even in its original, if somewhat remodelled, chapel. This is a rare circumstance for much northern art: frequently, if the setting remains the objects are lost; if the objects remain the setting has been destroyed, or, in many cases, we simply have no way of establishing where and for whom many images were made. Consequently, one of the problems we will be grappling with in this book is that of original context, which sometimes can only be evoked rather than reconstructed.

The Ghent Altarpiece survived: literally thousands of other works, mostly anonymous and certainly not so famous, were not so lucky. Van Vaernewijk,

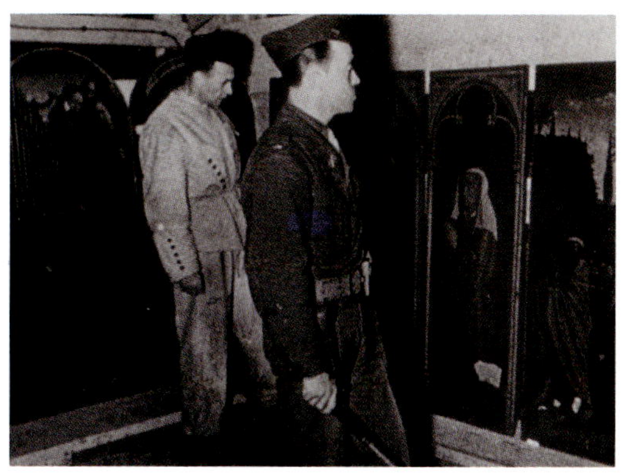

4

The discovery of panels from the Ghent Altarpiece by American troops in the Alt Aussee mines in 1945

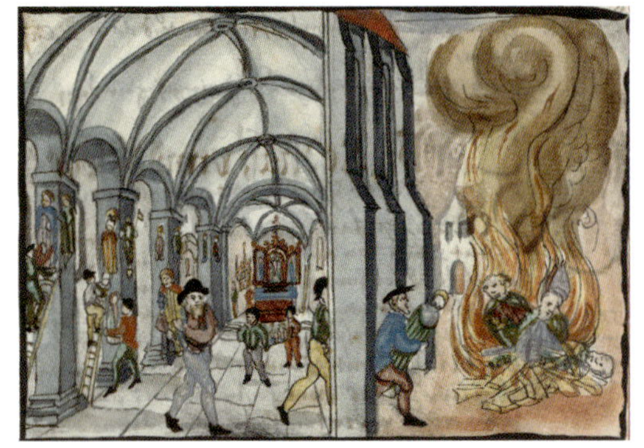

5 Heinrich Thomann

How the Mass and Images were suppressed in Berne, copy of Heinrich Bullinger's *Reformationgeschichte* (History of the Reformation), pen and watercolour on paper, 1605–6.

The removal of images from churches and their destruction are vividly displayed in this illustration to an account of Reformation activities in Berne; note how ubiquitous polychromed sculpture was in such interiors, providing almost all the imagery depicted here.

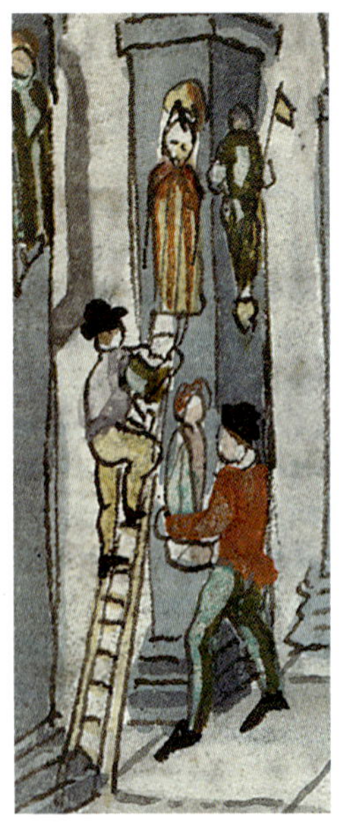

along with his description of the saving of the van Eycks' painting, recorded that the reformers' destruction of images in Ghent in the summer of 1566 alone was on such a scale that at times the fires in which they were burnt could be seen from over 10 miles away. He described the smashing of stained glass windows, alabaster altarpieces, carved wooden retables, painted panels set on the pillars of the church, sculpted statues of the Virgin and saints in wood and alabaster, metalwork shrines, rood screens with crucifixes and images of the apostles, liturgical furnishings in brass and bronze such as angels flanking the high altar, embroideries and silk curtains on and around the altar—anything which had imagery on it or was overtly luxurious which was seen as idolatrous [**5**].

One consequence of this is that it is very hard today to register what visually rich ensembles the interior of a church in this pre-Reformation period tended to be, and how images could resonate and work with other images. Rogier van der Weyden's (*c*.1399–1464) depiction of a church interior in his *Exhumation of St Hubert* [**6**], made for a chapel in the church of St Gudule in Brussels, gives some sense of the range of imagery evoked by van Varnewijck's descriptions, and shows how any one image would necessarily be seen in relation to other images, repeating, enlarging, or diversifying the chosen themes and the most important religious figures.[8] In Rogier's painting, on the altar, is a metalwork *châsse* containing the relics of St Hubert, with an image of that saint in raised relief in its centre. Reliquaries of this type would only be visible at a few special feasts during the year, and at this point it sits in front of, partially obscuring, the embroidered altarpiece, with a central Crucifixion scene and other saints, including Peter, with his key, the patron of the church (the exhumation was meant to have occurred in St Peter's in Liège). Set atop the altarpiece, Peter is found again, clearly indicating the dedication of the altar, this time in the form of a gilded and painted wooden statue in a tabernacle, its wings open to reveal thirty-two small painted scenes, probably detailing events from the saint's life. Visible behind this, one level further back and up, are stained glass windows, with yet another image of Peter, this time with St Paul. Stained glass was a dominant feature of most churches and chapels founded at this period but rarely does the original glass remain, allowing us to see how it would work visually and iconographically with the rest of the decoration, as it does here. Moving upwards, on the columns of the choir there are stone statues of the twelve apostles, which of course include yet more images of Peter and Paul, who are set in prime position either side of the central arch framing the

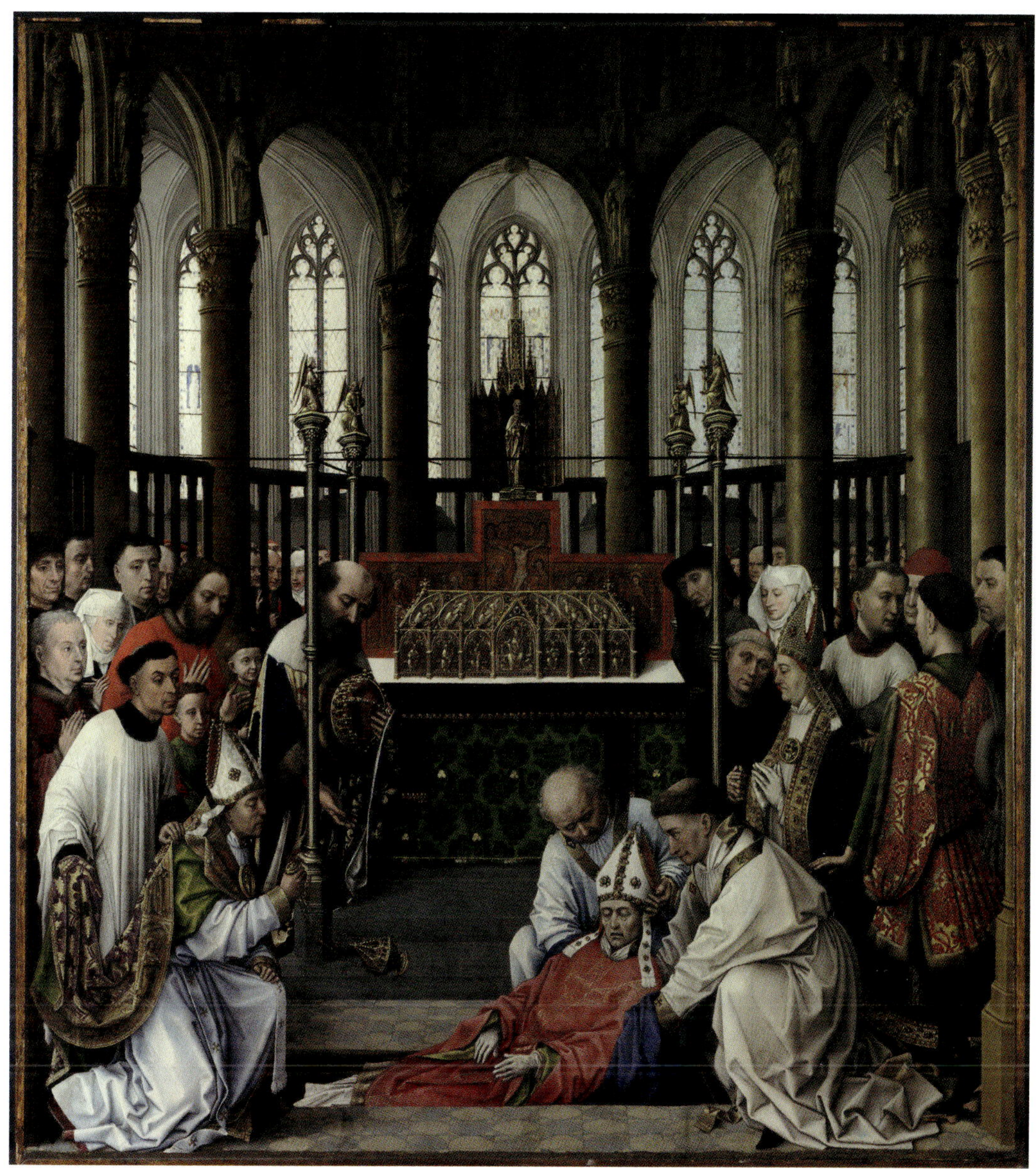

6 Rogier van der Weyden and workshop

The *Exhumation of St Hubert*, oil with some egg tempera on oak, *c.*1435–40.

Note the importance of textiles, metalwork, sculpture and stained glass in church interiors from the period. The screen keeps less privileged spectators on the edge of this most important of church spaces, the choir with its high altar.

altar. Some churches retain a sense of this visual complexity today, such as St Martin at Halle, near Brussels, St Leonard at Zoutleeuw, near Liège, or St Lorenz in Nuremberg [**103, 149**].[9] The van Eycks' altarpiece would have been viewed in a similarly rich visual context that we can only evoke today.

The destruction witnessed by van Vaernewijck in Ghent in 1566 was not the first or last wave of image breaking in northern Europe: from Tallinn to Prague, Edinburgh to Montpellier, images were removed, mocked, damaged or destroyed from 1520 up until the mid-seventeenth century in recurring bouts of reformist fervour. As in Ghent, the sheer scale of the destruction is astounding: in Zurich in 1524 Ulrich Zwingli (1484–1531), on the more fanatical side of the reformers' teachings, swayed the authorities

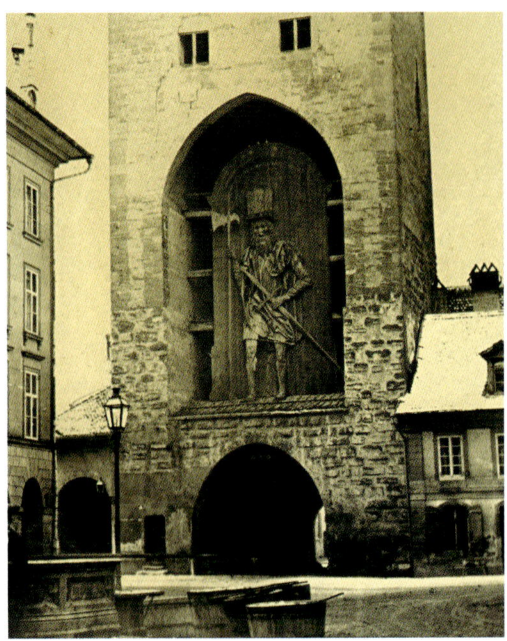

7
Photograph of the city gate of Berne, *c.*1864, showing **8** intact and *in situ.*

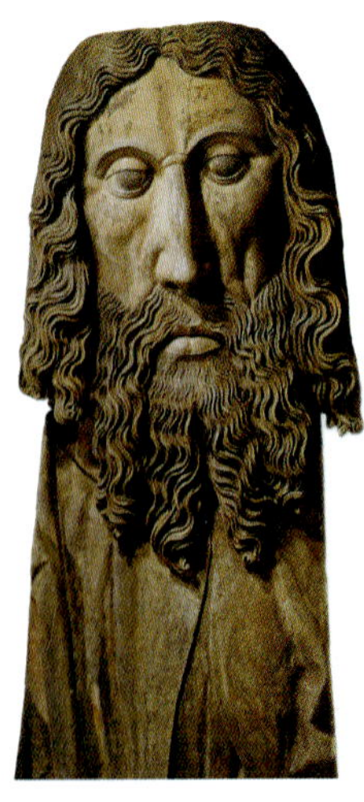

8 Albrecht of Nuremberg (?)
Fragment of a colossal St Christopher, limewood, 1496–8.
Monumental works like this vast St Christopher were more subject to destruction by iconoclasts than smaller objects, which has led to the mistaken impression that northern art of this period was mostly small in scale.

into removing all the works of art from every church in the town, destroying them and whitewashing the walls. Indeed, Switzerland was so badly hit that today it is almost impossible to get a sense of its artistic output during this period. In England, the destruction wrought following Henry VIII's split from Rome has left us with a situation almost as bad. The Counter-Reformation, too, had an effect as the need to instigate new types of images and new liturgical practices meant out with the old: many altarpieces which had survived the iconoclasts were dismantled or destroyed at this point.[10] Works that did survive the religious wars did so often through dispersal—in the 1550s large numbers of English alabaster altarpieces were on the market in Paris following the dissolution of the monasteries by Henry VIII[11]—or through disguise: the 10-metre-tall wooden statue of St Christopher which once stood on the town gate in Berne survived the iconoclasts by being transformed into a Goliath [**7**]; despite this inventive ploy, when the town gate was torn down in 1865 the statue was cut up and all but the head used as firewood [**8**].[12]

Wars which raged between France and Spain in the seventeenth century, fought mostly in the Netherlands, also took their toll: in 1695 Brussels, one of the central towns of the southern Netherlands from a political and artistic point of view, was bombarded, the most tragic loss being in the town hall, where a work which was as famous and significant as the Ghent Altarpiece, the monumental scenes of the *Justice of Trajan and Herkinbald* by Rogier van der Weyden, perished in the fire.[13] The loss of these works is perhaps the single most destructive blow to our understanding of early Netherlandish painting, since if they had survived our view of the most influential and inventive painter of this period would have been very different: art historians trying to reconstruct the artistic personality of Rogier in the nineteenth and early twentieth centuries would have had a signed,

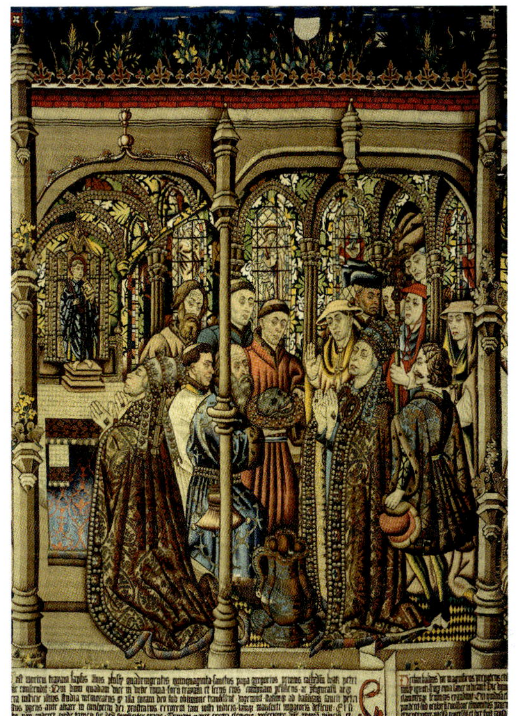

9 Brussels tapestry workshop, after Rogier van der Weyden

Justice of Trajan and Herkinbald, wool, before 1461.

Rogier's vast panels which decorated the 'Golden Chamber' in the town hall in Brussels are known only through this tapestry copy. The paintings were extraordinarily famous, being admired by a similar set of people as the Ghent Altarpiece, including Albrecht Dürer; our earliest description of them is from 1453, when the German cardinal, Nicolas of Cusa, referred to them as 'the very precious painting which is in the council room, of the very great painter Roger in Brussels'.

undisputed, accessible work by him. In addition, these panels would have provided rare examples of monumental, narrative panel paintings of secular subjects, set *in situ*. Today we can only get a shadow of their impact from a tapestry copy made in the mid-fifteenth century [**9**]; the closest surviving parallels in scale and nature are the *Justice* scenes by Dieric Bouts (**111**, Part IV).

A century after van der Weyden's works and many others in Brussels were burnt, a huge number of tombs, portraits and other commemorative images, anything with royal or noble connotations, were defaced or destroyed in the aftermath of the French Revolution, which affected large areas of Europe including the southern Netherlands and Germany: churches were looted, convents and monasteries disbanded, their contents dispersed or destroyed. Tombs were particular targets, and our only record of many of the most important monuments of the period is through the drawings made by antiquarians like Roger de Gaignières or Jacques-Philippe Gilquin in the eighteenth century [**10**]. Probably the biggest casualty for us in this context is a Burgundian monument: the Chartreuse de Champmol in Dijon [**11**], built for Philip the Bold, Duke of Burgundy (1342–1404) between 1375 and 1410, which was razed almost entirely to the ground and most of its paintings and sculptures destroyed in the years between 1798 and 1815.[14] The making of this monastery and its decoration will feature heavily in this survey despite the destruction since the few elements from it that remain are both well documented and extraordinarily inventive [**12, 133, 146–8**]. Its decoration involved large teams of the very best artists of the day, recruited from the Netherlands (such as the sculptors Claus Sluter, Claus de Haine, and Jan van Prindale) and beyond (for

10 Jacques-Philippe Gilquin

Tomb of Philip the Bold, Duke of Burgundy, pen and wash, 1736.

This drawing shows the ducal tomb from the Chartreuse de Champmol, made by Claus Sluter and Claus de Werve, before its dismantling and partial destruction in the Revolution. It provides vital evidence concerning the effigy of the duke (the present figure, seen in **133**, is nineteenth-century), its polychromy, and the order of the pleurants surrounding the base of the tomb.

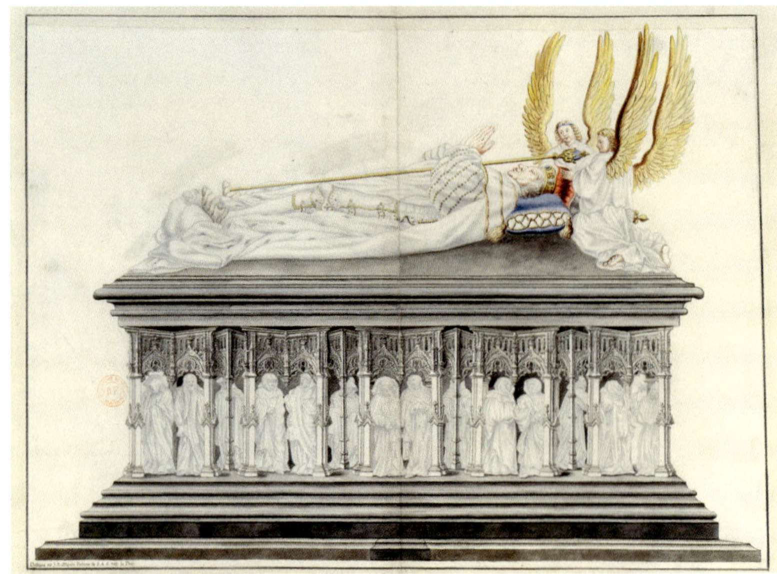

11 Aimé Piron

View of the Chartreuse de Champmol, Dijon, 1686.

This seventeenth-century drawing shows the church (lower right) where the tombs of Philip the Bold [**10, 133**] and John the Fearless were placed; this was attached to a large cloister around which the monks had their cells, in the centre of which sat the Great Cross (the 'Well of Moses') [**146–148**], hidden here by a later building designed to protect it from the elements. All that remains of the complex on site today are the base of the Great Cross, the portal of the church and some architectural ruins.

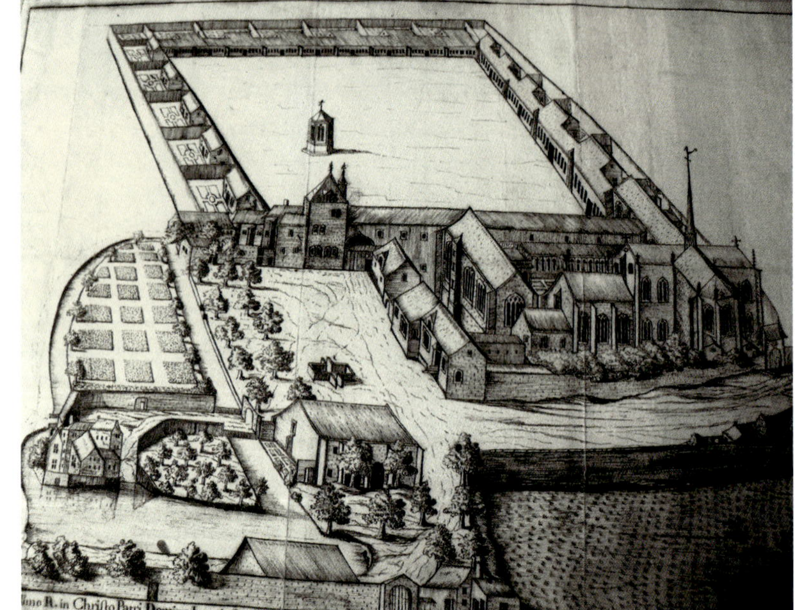

example, the tile maker Jehan de Gironna, a Spanish ceramicist capable of making the new and much-coveted blue and white glazed tiles). It will never be possible to envisage the full splendour of the church in which the ducal tombs [**133**] and an array of sculpted and painted altarpieces sat, but more frustratingly, with its destruction we lost the main, and sometimes the sole, documented works of many of the most highly respected and sought-after artists of the day, such as the woodcarver Jean de Liège (*fl.* 1381–1403); the painter Jean Malouel (d. 1415, uncle to the painters Pol, Jean and Herman de Limbourg, all d. 1416); Jean de Marville (*fl.* 1366–89), the head sculptor prior to

Claus Sluter; and Sluter's best-paid assistant, Jan van Prindale (d. after 1424), the most important member of a family of Brussels sculptors, who went on to work at the cathedral in Geneva and for Amedée VIII, Count of Savoy.[15] If the Chartreuse de Champmol had remained relatively intact, our view of this whole period of production would surely be rather different since we would have an array of artistic identities to place alongside Sluter, André Beauneveu (*c.*1335–*c.*1401/3, see **17, 78**), the painter Melchior Broederlam (*c.*1355–*c.*1411, see **12**) and the de Limbourg brothers (see **74–6**), who tend to appear, deceptively, as isolated giants.

The French Revolution was not the last of the events to impact on works of art from our period: a century later came two world wars. These were fought, again, mostly in northern France and Belgium. This time the symbolic or strategic value of many churches made them natural targets: their towers were potential lookout points, and cathedrals were potent symbols of nationhood. In turn, the Allied bombings devastated German heritage, with what were probably the two most important artistic centres in the region at our period, Cologne and Nuremberg, particularly badly hit: in Nuremberg only one in ten of its buildings escaped unharmed and every single one of its churches was damaged; in Cologne almost all the churches are post-war reconstructions, sometimes controversial in themselves.

It is not just the level and range of the destruction outlined above that is important for us in our study of the art of this period. Its pattern is also crucial since it concerns, firstly, the type of object most affected: works in some media were hit harder than others. Wooden sculpture, for example, was a most rewarding target for iconoclasts [**5**], being overtly life-like, relatively light, and flammable: there are many reports from across Europe in the sixteenth century of wooden figures of saints being dragged round the streets by a noose (often by crowds of children), or thrown into rivers to see if they would drown, or tied to a stake and burnt. Moreover, northern sculpture had become, by the eighteenth century, even more unfashionable and unappreciated than northern panel paintings, its rich polychromy and extensive gilding, vividly seen in **12**, being most obviously at odds with the (Italian) High Renaissance ideal of pure white stone which formed the taste of subsequent centuries. Consequently, the surviving record is particularly unbalanced in respect to sculpted works, and does not reflect the dominant role this media played in the north at this period: sculpture, as we will see in Chapters 15 and 16, was often the most prominent, monumental, and interactive of imagery in religious settings, and by far the majority of altarpieces throughout northern Europe had sculpted not painted centres. Many of the painted panels in art galleries today were merely adjuncts to these richly gilded sculptures, but now their status as fragments of larger, multimedia entities is not usually apparent.

Another pattern of significance for us today is the geography of the destruction outlined above. Italy was relatively unscathed and Italian art never fell out of favour, which has resulted in a much higher survival rate of its objects that in turn has helped create and sustain a false impression of its artistic dominance at this period. Moreover, the devastation of iconoclasm and successive wars was most extensive and continuous in exactly the areas that were the most active and important for artistic production the period: the southern Netherlands and northern France, central and southern

12 Jacques de Baerze (sculpture) and Melchior Broederlam (painted wings and polychromy)

Crucifixion Altarpiece, polychromed and gilded wood, oil and tempera on panel, 1391–9.

This altarpiece was commissioned by Philip the Bold in Flanders for the Chartreuse de Champmol in Dijon. It is the earliest carved wooden retable surviving from the Netherlands; while its shape is unusual, probably dictated by the need to hinge the wings securely in what may have been an experimental form, the extensively gilded, sculpted interior was to remain a standard feature for the next hundred years [**55**]. The exterior presents us with the most important surviving example of Netherlandish panel painting before 1400, but it can only be properly understood with reference to its sculpted interior.

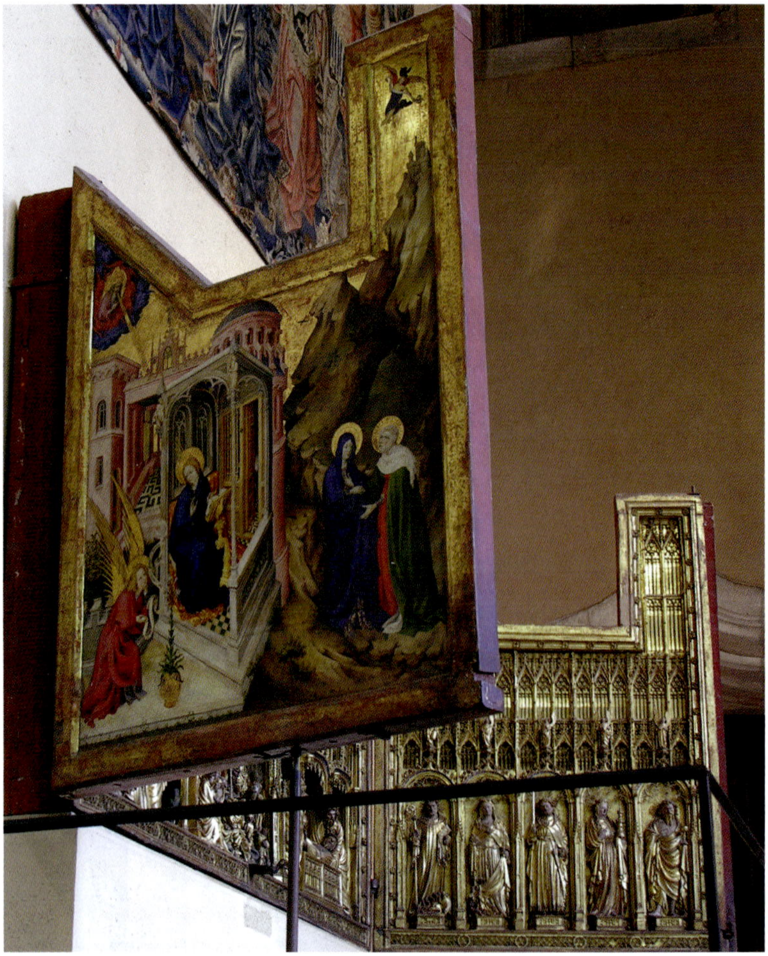

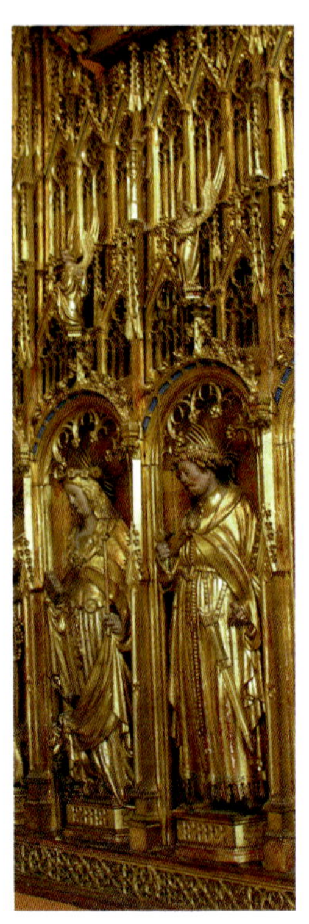

Germany. Consequently, our knowledge of much northern painting has had to be constructed in large part from works that left the Netherlands early in their history, usually for Italian or Spanish destinations, and thus escaped the events outlined above. So, for example, not one major work by Rogier van der Weyden remains in Brussels, the town in which he worked for thirty years: his three most important works were all in Spain in the sixteenth century (notably **20** and **33**). There is nothing (legible) by Robert Campin (*c*.1375/9–1444) in Tournai, and he was that town's leading painter for over thirty years. There is nothing by the Ghent painter Hugo van der Goes (*c*.1440–1482) left in Ghent: his most important surviving works are in Florence [**66, 67**], Edinburgh, and (via Spain) Berlin. Indeed, for each of these painters there are only one or two major works anywhere in Belgium. By comparison, the large numbers of works made in Florence in the fifteenth century remain in Florence (which is especially true of artists like Fra Angelico, Botticelli, or Ghirlandaio); this has naturally made their study easier, and their impact and appreciation more immediate.

For works in other media the situation is just as extreme: of the 350 or so carved wooden retables (altarpieces) that represent the surviving production

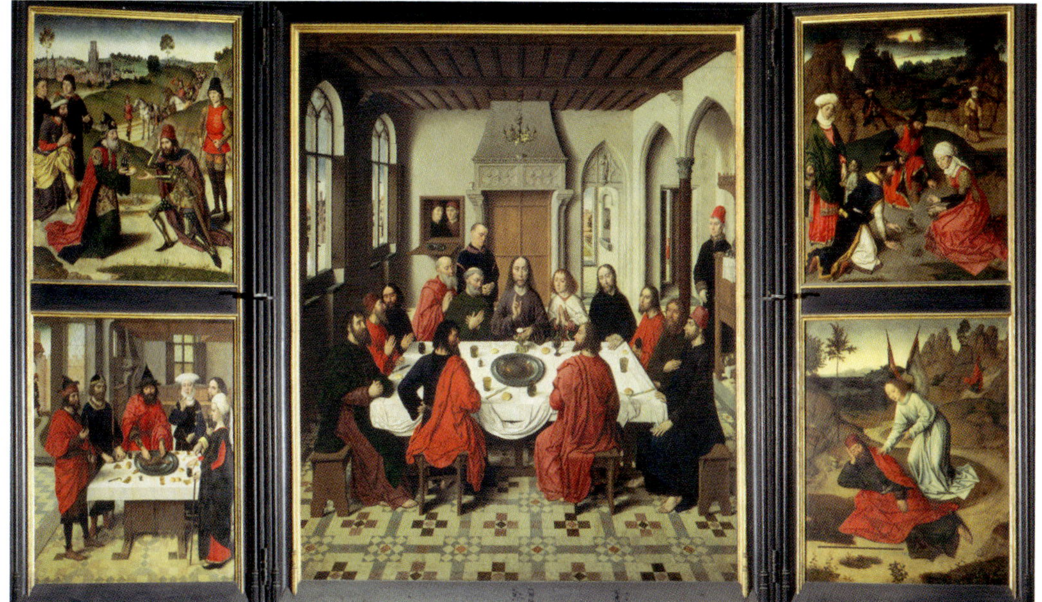

13 Dieric Bouts

Altarpiece of the Holy Sacrament, oil on Baltic oak, 1464–8.

This work was painted for the confraternity of the Holy Sacrament in Leuven, devoted to the worship of the Eucharist. Two theologians were to advise Bouts on the subject matter: the institution of the Eucharist at the Last Supper in the centre, and its Old Testament prefigurations in the wings. The standing figures in contemporary dress are the four members of the confraternity who signed the contract with Bouts: they appear not as donors in prayer, but as witnesses and attendants at the event which their confraternity was dedicated to commemorating and celebrating.

of the southern Netherlands from the period *c.*1380–1550, it has been estimated that only 25 per cent are now in that region, and many of these only returned there in the nineteenth century, like the de Villa Altarpiece made for the Italian family of that name and destined for a church in Chieri [**56**]. We see a similar pattern for tapestries: three of the most important surviving monumental productions from the fifteenth-century Netherlands are now in Spain (Zamora, **53**, and Zaragoza) and Italy (Doria Pamphilj collection), having been exported there early in their history. Many of the most important pieces of metalwork made in Paris *c.*1400 are now in treasuries which are decidedly off the beaten track, such as Altötting (southern Germany, **24**), Montalto (northern Italy), and Burgos (northern Spain).[16] While this is testament to the international demand for such works at the period, the effect that such a scattered corpus has had on the study of Netherlandish art in particular should not be underestimated: art historians like van Mander in the early seventeenth century, Jean-Baptiste Descamps in the eighteenth century, and Eugène Fromentin in the nineteenth century composed their histories from works they had seen in their travels in the Netherlands and rarely beyond; they thus had relatively little left to build their writings upon.[17]

Just as important to the study of northern art as the destruction and dispersal of its objects has been the destruction of documentation about these objects. The burning of the town halls of Brussels in 1695 and of Paris in 1871, and the bombing of Tournai and Ypres in the world wars of the twentieth century, are just the most obvious instances where vast archives were destroyed. Even when documentation in a city does survive well, there is often a complete mismatch between these written records and the surviving works: in Cologne, for example, we have around 300 painters documented in the town records over the period 1300–1500, and a fairly large body of surviving works, but not one painting can be tied to any one of these documented names.[18] The dispersal of works from their original settings has exacerbated this problem, as has the different nature of record keeping in many northern towns, as opposed, most notably, to Italy, where the tendency to have agreements witnessed by notaries has meant that probably more written records were made in the first place, as well as more being preserved. In addition, the nature of much northern art production simply did not generate written records, since a large proportion was made speculatively for the open market, or was of a type where contracts would not have been necessary: they were rarely if ever made for the production of an illuminated manuscript or for small devotional objects, for example, even if these were highly personalized works. The extent of the difference is clear when we consider that for central Italy in the period 1350–1500 there are dozens of painted altarpieces for which both the object and the contract survives, while there is not one single example from Bruges, Brussels, Ghent, or Antwerp before 1500. Although we have documentation of other types like inventories and payment accounts to provide (limited) evidence of authorship, the fact remains that only one extant panel painting from the whole of the southern Netherlands at this period can be matched to a surviving contract: the triptych by Dieric Bouts (*c.*1415–1475) for the confraternity of the Holy Sacrament in Leuven [**13**].[19] There is a slightly better situation with German carved retables, but only slightly so.

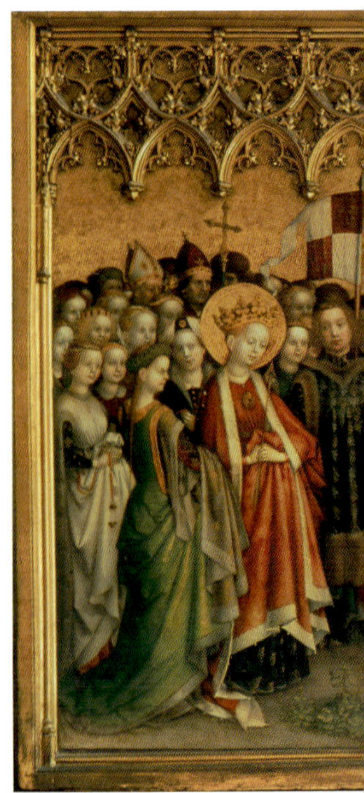

The consequences of this problem of documentation for the north are far reaching: more so than in Italy, much of the study of Netherlandish, German, and French painting and manuscript illumination in particular has necessarily concerned itself with the basic questions of who produced what, and when, and much of what cannot be firmly attributed remains less studied. In many cases we are left with artists of the highest talent who are given pseudonyms, 'Notnames' as the Germans term them, an emergency name, such as the Vienna Master of Mary of Burgundy (after a particular prayer book made for one of this artist's patrons, **199**, **200**) or the Master of the Embroidered Foliage (named after a distinctive way this artist had of painting grass and trees).[20] Artists to whom we cannot attach a real name, and thus a real documented history and even a personality, do not present the same potential for investigation, or the same appeal to a wider public, as named artists.

In addition, the identities which have been established for major artists in the north often hang on remarkably thin threads: for the Ghent painter Hugo van der Goes, for example, the only document which ties a painting to his name is the testimony of Vasari in 1550 that the large triptych then in the church of S. Egidio in the hospital of Santa Maria Nuova in Florence [**66**, **67**] was the work of 'ugo d'anversa' (Hugo of Antwerp). Despite the fact that Hugo van der Goes had no known relationship with Antwerp (and because

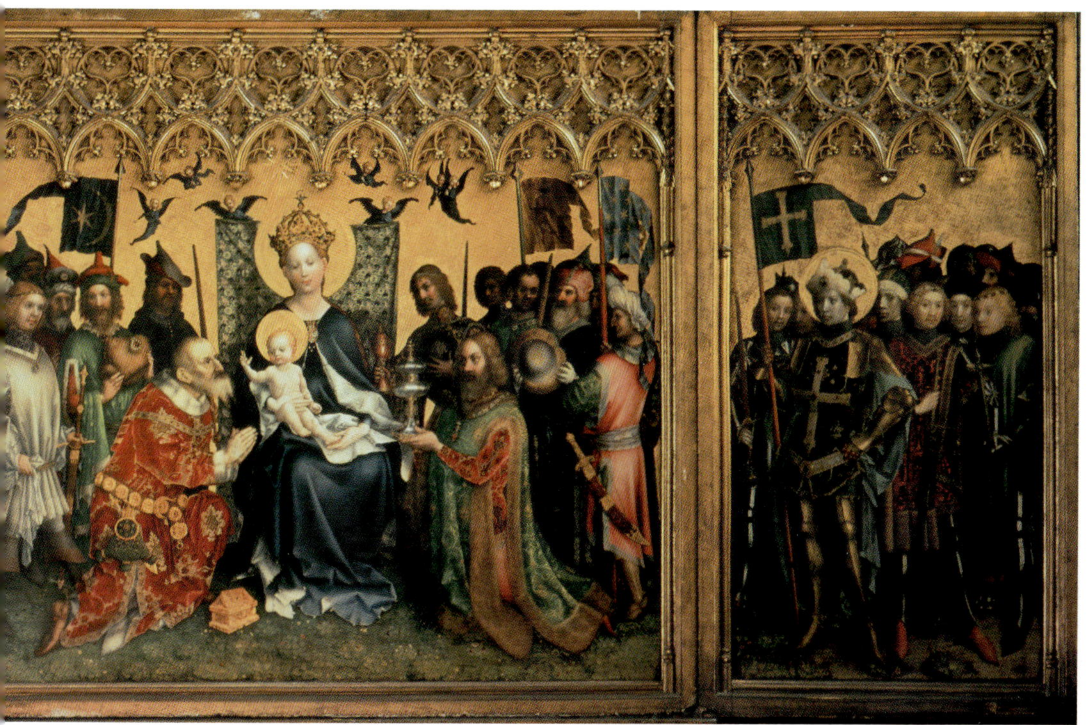

14 Stefan Lochner
The Dombild Altarpiece, oil on panel, *c.*1445, 469 cm wide when open.
This large altarpiece is the only work by a fifteenth-century Cologne painter to which a name may be attached, but even this is now disputed. Made for the newly built chapel of the municipal council in Cologne, the subject combines a Virgin Enthroned with Saints with an Adoration of the Magi—the Magi being particularly venerated in Cologne since that city held their relics. To achieve its richly decorated surface the painter deployed a range of gilding methods, brilliantly executed, making it a tour de force technically as well as in terms of its visual invention.

we can explain Vasari's assumption in terms of the importance of this town by the time he was writing), we accept that this is Hugo van der Goes of Ghent and therefore use the Portinari Altarpiece as a starting point for the creation of his oeuvre, basing all attributions on their similarity to this work.[21] While there is general agreement in the case of Hugo concerning this match of works to a name, for the Cologne artist Stefan Lochner (*fl. c.*1440–51) increasingly close scrutiny of the documentation and the works themselves, has recently caused consensus to collapse.[22] The construction of Lochner's oeuvre centres around the only document to tie any Cologne painter to any work at this period, an entry in the diary of Albrecht Dürer written on his journey to the Netherlands: during a stopover in Cologne in 1520 he recorded how he gave '2 silver pfenning to have the altarpiece opened that Master Stefan has made'. This was universally presumed to be the monumental work made for the chapel of the municipal council [**14**], but Dürer's text is not specific about its location so the identification has been questioned. However, circumstantial evidence still points strongly to this having been the painting Dürer paid a fairly substantial amount to see: it is certainly a likely candidate for Dürer's attention, being both monumental and skilfully painted, and clearly well known—it was a highly influential work in Cologne and beyond.

There are also artists who figure significantly in our histories of this period, such the Tournai painter Robert Campin, or the painter-illuminator Simon Marmion (*c.*1425–89), called 'the prince of illuminators' by Jean Lemaire de Belges in 1505, yet for whom today we have, arguably, not one documented work to their name, not even from sources distant in time and place like

Vasari; indeed, for both these artists the possibility remains that what we think they painted may not be by them at all.[23]

Destruction, however, does not account for perhaps the most challenging lacunae in the documentary records of the north: the absence of theoretical writings about art or descriptive passages which would give us a sense of what contemporary northerners valued in their images, or a framework for a discussion of their qualities in fifteenth-century terms. In Italy, and in Florence in particular, at the same period we are relatively rich in such sources, with artists like Ghiberti, Alberti, and Leonardo da Vinci writing whole books about art. By contrast, in northern Europe, we have to wait for Dürer's various theoretical works (begun in outline in 1512) and the writings of Lucas de Heere (1565) and Karel van Mander (1604) to get an artist's perspective on his craft in this concerted manner. One result of this has been the assumption that northern artists were illiterate and unlettered. This is clearly not the case: Jan van Eyck, being sent as part of diplomatic embassies to Portugal and elsewhere, would probably have had to be able to read Latin for these roles; the extent, richness and complexity of his inscriptions on his works are also suggestive of his ability to read and write in several languages [**97, 98, 106**]. Reading and writing, in the vernacular if not Latin, was one of the things an apprentice painter in Ghent might be taught along with his craft.[24] Even an apparently humble and today totally unknown artist like Bartolomeo Avella (d. 1429), who worked in Valencia making mostly painted leather chests, owned books by Cato, a selection of notes on grammar, and a book on dialectics.[25]

In Italy, along with artists writing about art, we also have many humanist scholars and men of the church doing the same, often extensively, although usually as asides in their literary output.[26] Outside of Italy, and indeed to an extent outside Florence, it would seem that people did not write about art in this self-conscious or explicit way, perhaps because they saw little point in trying to explain or describe the stupendous visual achievements of their artists in verbal form: the first literary source which has more than a passing reference to art and artists in the north are the poems by Jean Lemaire de Belges (1473–*c.*1523), *La Plainte du Désiré* (1503–4) and *La Couronne Margaritique* (1505).[27] One of the consequences of this is that the fifteenth-century literary appreciations we do have of northern art are entirely by Italians, such as Cyriacus d'Ancona (1449), Bartolommeo Fazio (1456), Francesco Florio (1477), and Giovanni Santi (1482). Again, this is testimony to the fame of Netherlandish painters, in particular, across Europe, but it also means that our contemporary view of their achievements is primarily an Italian one, and this has had certain consequences.

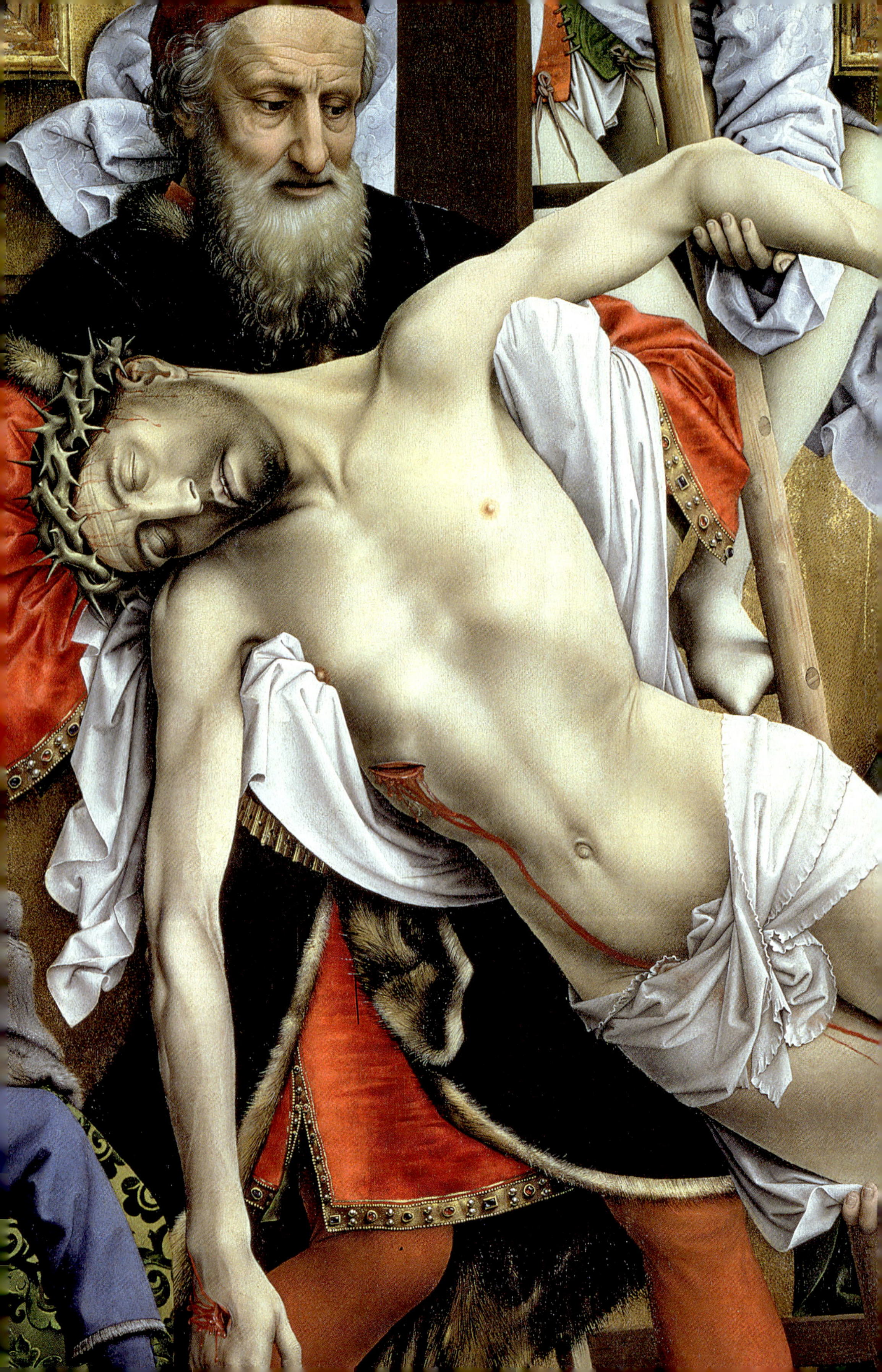

Italian Perspectives

In Flanders they paint with a view to external exactness such things as may cheer you and of which you cannot speak ill.

Michelangelo on Flemish painting, as reported by Francesco da Hollanda, *c.*1540[1]

3

Fifteenth-century Italians were generally very positive about northern art; as the Neapolitan humanist Pietro Summonte remarked in 1524: 'works from Flanders ... at the time were the only ones to be reputed fashionable'. As early as 1400 Uberto Decembrio, another Italian humanist writer, placed the court painter of Philip the Bold, Jean d'Arbois, alongside Gentile da Fabriano and Michelino de Pavia as 'pictoribus prestantissimis dici posset': painters of the first rank working at his period.[2] Ghiberti effused about the works of Master Gusmin, a mysterious northern goldsmith working for Louis of Anjou, in terms more fulsome than he used for any other artist he discussed.[3] But mostly the attention of Italian writers was drawn by Jan van Eyck and Rogier van der Weyden, who were generally considered the most important artists of their day. These artists were two of the four painters Bartolommeo Fazio (*c.*1410–57) chose to devote biographies to (the other two being Gentile da Fabriano and Pisanello) in his *De viris illustribus* ('On Famous Men') of 1456, which provides us with the most extended appreciation of northern art and artists from the period.[4] Fazio was in a good position to know something about Netherlandish painting since his patron, Alfonso of Aragon, King of Sicily (1396–1458), for whom this text was written, had, like many other rulers at the period, a particular interest in collecting such works. Several of the paintings Fazio eulogizes about were in Alfonso's possession, and others he had seen in Genoa, Ferrara, or Urbino. His accounts of them are both particularly valuable and particularly frustrating since none of those he describes survive to this day, so while we have important records of otherwise lost works, we cannot compare his words with the images.

Fazio begins by remarking on Jan's learning and technical mastery: 'He was not unlettered, particularly in geometry and such arts as contribute to the enrichment of painting, and he is thought for this reason to have discovered many things about the properties of colours recorded by the ancients and learned by him from reading Pliny and other authors.' The hint here of some new technical invention on Jan's part marks the beginnings of this tenacious myth which continues to this day (for further discussion of it, see below, pp. 30–31). Fazio goes on to effuse warmly about the verisimilitude of Jan's works: in a triptych made for the Genoese merchant Battista Lomellini he describes an Annunciation with 'an angel Gabriel of exceptional beauty and with hair surpassing reality', and on the right wing, 'Jerome like a living being in a library done with rare art for if you move away from it a little it seems that

Detail of 20

15 Follower or workshop of Jan van Eyck

St Jerome in his Study, oil on paper glued to Baltic oak, c. 1435.

The inscription on the folded paper on the saint's desk reads: 'To the most reverend father and lord in Christ, the lord Jerome, cardinal-priest of the title of the Holy Cross in Jerusalem'. Some art historians think that this small panel may have been given to Cardinal Albergati (who was the holder of that post between 1426 and 1443) by Philip the Good at the congress of Arras in 1435, and that it can be identified with a work subsequently owned by the Medici. Something like it was certainly known to Florentine painters such as Ghirlandaio, but this panel appears to have been in Mantua in the sixteenth century, so it is unlikely to be the Medici version.

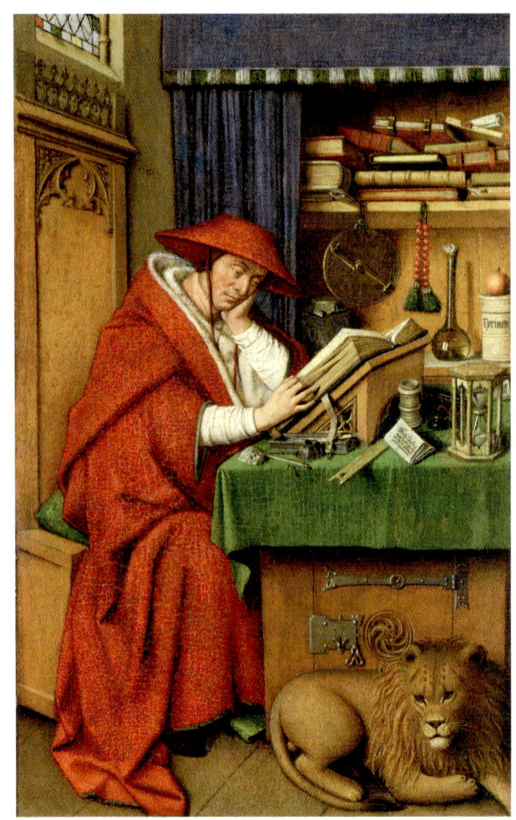

it recedes inwards and that it has complete books laid open on it, while if you go near it is evident that it is only a summary of these.' Of Lomellini's portrait which appeared on the outside of the triptych, 'you would judge he lacked only a voice,' and his wife, 'she too is portrayed exactly as she was down to the nails'.[5] The Jerome may have looked something like the small St Jerome from the workshop of van Eyck [**15**],[6] and as for the portraits we might evoke those of Joos Vijd and his wife on the exterior of the Ghent Altarpiece [**3a**]. Fazio is most taken, however, with the mirror in an image of nude women bathing: 'But almost nothing is more wonderful in this work than the mirror painted in the picture, in which you see whatever is represented as in a real mirror.'[7] One thinks immediately of the mirror in the Jan's *Portrait of Giovanni (?) Arnolfini and his Wife* [**37**]. According to Fazio, Rogier also painted nude women bathing, and he begins his biography of Rogier with a description of a picture he had seen in Genoa, which had clear erotic overtones, although it may have been a religious subject such as Susanna and the Elders (despite the mention of 'youths'): 'A woman sweating in her bath with a puppy near her and two youths on the other side secretly peering in at her through a chink, remarkable for their grins.' Fazio's description of these two paintings provides us with a sense of the wider range of subjects these artists produced, if still probably within a religious framework.

Fazio's discussion of Rogier's work focuses also on its ability to imitate reality, but here the emotive qualities of his paintings are also emphasized. In a triptych showing the Deposition he had seen in the collection of the Duke of Ferrara, he remarks on how 'grief and tears are so represented you would not think them other than real', and in a set of Passion scenes, cloth paintings acquired by Alfonso of Aragon from the manager of the Medici bank in Rome in 1455, he praises the appropriateness of the portrayals and their variety: 'in this you may easily distinguish a variety of feelings and passions in keeping with the variety of the action'.

Fazio's text is a key document in the intense appreciation of Netherlandish painting in Italy, and as such it is representative of what Italians admired in Netherlandish painting in general: a similar mode is found in Cyriacus of Ancona's (1391–*c*.1455) description of 1449 of the same triptych by Rogier in Ferrara:

> There you could see those faces come alive and breathe which he wanted to show as living, and likewise the deceased as dead, and in particular many garments, multi-coloured soldiers' cloaks, clothes prodigiously enhanced by purple and gold, blooming meadows, flowers, trees, leafy and shady hills, as well as ornate porticoes and halls, gold really resembling gold, pearls, precious stones and everything else you would think to have been produced not by the artifice of human hands but by all-bearing nature herself.[8]

However, as texts giving us insights into how northern art was valued outside the humanist court circles of Italy, or more crucially, as texts which set up criteria for the appreciation of northern art in general terms, they are not without problems. Although Fazio's and Cyriacus's response to these paintings reveals a very real appreciation of their skill and impact, their language and the *topoi* they use are the rhetoric of antique texts. Fazio in particular draws on Quintillian, Pliny, Horace, and Philostratus: the praise for variety, for appropriateness (*decorum*) in how figures are treated, and for the ability to paint in such a way as to fool the eye (Apelles' grapes), and the idea that good painters had learning, are all deeply imbedded in classical *ekphraisis*. In sum, what Fazio and Cyriacus admire in Jan and Rogier was framed by their knowledge of how the ancients praised their artists, and here we have the seeds of a real problem—that northern art should fit into, and be judged by, criteria which are those of classical authors, via the Italian Renaissance and its humanist scholars.

This is not to say these qualities are not present in Jan's and Rogier's paintings, but their images work on many other levels, which may or may not have been apparent to Fazio. An interest in distortion, pattern, line, the use of scale and form to convey meaning, and to create an illusion of a reality which in effect is very unreal (see pp. 33–6), are also key features of Netherlandish art, but ones Fazio does not have a language to describe and which do not fit with what was becoming a canon for the appreciation of good painting and sculpture.

It was not Fazio, however, but Florentine writers like Alberti and later, and most importantly, Giorgio Vasari who, in his hugely successful and widely read *Le Vite de più eccellenti pittori, scultori ed architetti* (known in English as 'Lives of the Painters, Sculptors, and Architects', 1550, second edition 1568), crystallized and made universal these classically inspired ideas about what good painting and sculpture should be. The Vasarian story of the rebirth of the visual arts through observation of nature combined with a knowledge of antique models, and the importance given to correct rendering of space and

18 Jan van Eyck

Virgin and Child with Saints Donatian and George and Canon Joris van der Paele, oil on Baltic oak, dated 1436.

This panel is Jan's largest surviving work after the Ghent Altarpiece [**3a, 3b**]. It is a virtuosic display of his ability to represent different materials, surfaces, and the effects of light on them. This extends to his treatment of the frame, where the inscription on the lower part (relating to the donor, his foundation, and the painter) appears to be in raised cast brass letters while that running round the rest of the frame (which alludes to the saints and the Virgin) is depicted as if cut into its surface. A small figure, possibly the painter, is reflected in the steel shield of St George, emphasizing the facture of this work in a similar, if less immediately evident, way to the signature on the back wall of **37**.

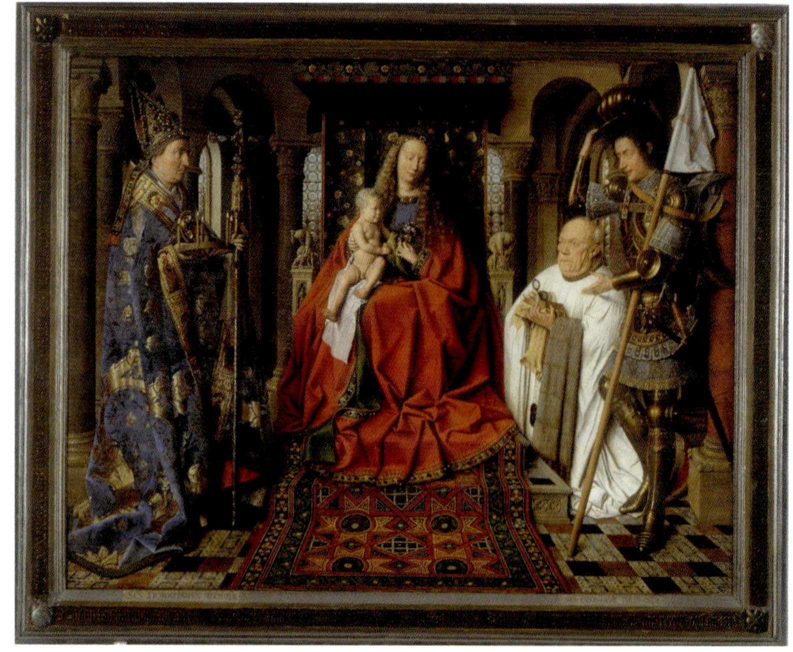

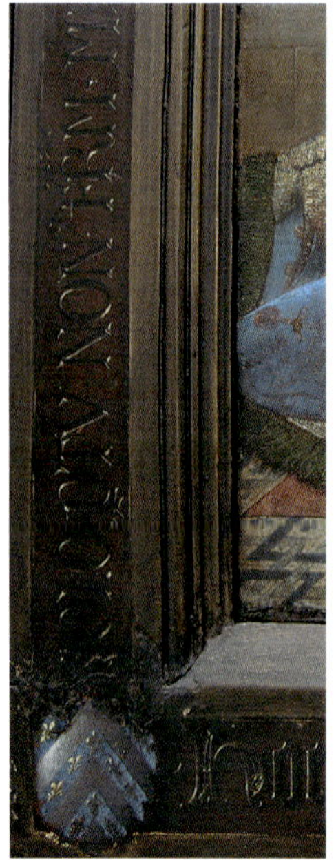

ment. If we consider the *Van der Paele Madonna* in relation to visual traditions in the north rather than the south, we can see it instead as part of a genre of works with memorializing rather than liturgical functions, such as memorial tablets and images commemorating religious foundations and donations, mostly in stone or brass but sometimes in painted form, and which would not routinely have been placed on an altar. In these, the Virgin and Child with saints and the donor kneeling before them, with a text recording the date of death or the date of a foundation, is common, almost standard [**19**]. Viewing the *Van der Paele Madonna* in the context of works from its own environment leads us, then, to a different possible conclusion about its original function, and opens up more fruitful ways of interpreting the image; we can see it now in relation to sculptural traditions and a mode of commemorative patronage particularly favoured by canons,[14] and we should be wary of reading its imagery primarily in relationship to its position on an altar and the liturgical rites which would have been celebrated there.

Most significantly of all, applying Florentine Renaissance criteria to works made in other regions does not allow for or encompass the interests and achievements of so much of northern production. A work like Rogier van der Weyden's *Descent from the Cross* [**20**], made for the crossbowman's guild of Leuven around 1435, is a good example of where the devices employed by the artist for expressive effect do not conform to a fifteenth-century Albertian view or a sixteenth-century Vasarian perception of 'advanced' painting, despite the fact that many of them are not foreign to Italian artists. In Rogier's work the figures are deliberately distorted and correct anatomy is second to expressive effect; space is severely restricted and geometric forms, line, colour, and pattern are among the powerful tools marshalled by the artist.[15]

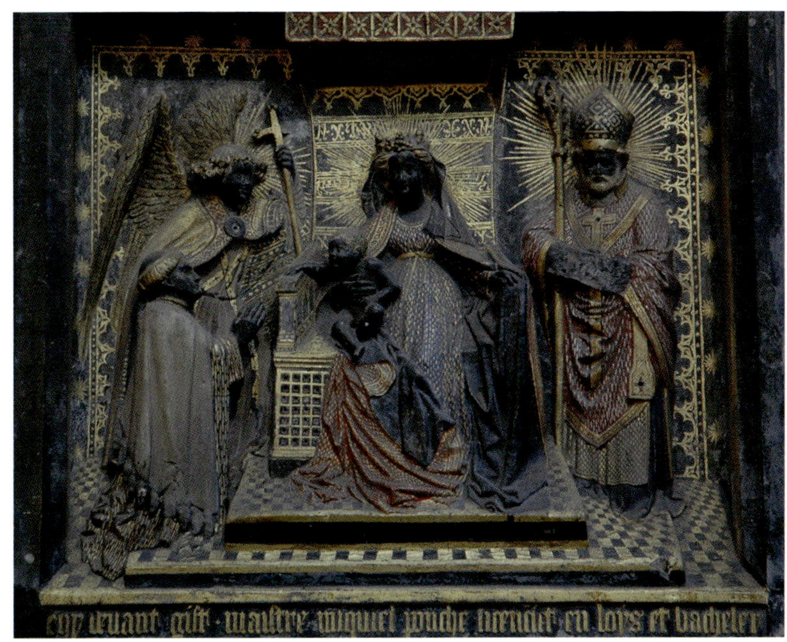

19 Anonymous Netherlandish sculptor (Jean Delemer?)

Epitaph (memorial tablet) of Michel Ponche, Tournai limestone with nineteenth-century polychromy, 1431–6.

Canons like Michel Ponche and Joris van der Paele [**18**] were an important class of patron across northern Europe at this period; they were well educated, though often not of noble or legitimate birth, but their office allowed them to amass considerable wealth; they were at pains to have themselves commemorated properly, not least because they did not have (legitimate) children to leave property to, or who might pray for their souls. Many commissioned stone memorial tablets such as this with that end in mind.

This mismatch of expectations and achievements, and the tendency to apply later values to our view of the works of the fifteenth century, is perhaps most evident for tapestry and sculpture. Northern works in these media were very popular in Italy (see Chapters 7 and 8), but they would not match either Fazio's or Alberti's ideas about 'good' art. The dominant aesthetic of tapestry is not the creation of space but its denial. Scale and recession are eschewed (see **52** and **53**), which is an essential aspect of its character because the weave is always visible and the work itself would hang in a manner which was undulating and malleable [**21**]; in much tapestry design the impact of a given work cannot be dependent on all parts being seen at once, since its portability, and its deployment in settings of varying size and shape, might entail some sections being folded back or rolled up (as is done at Jean de Berry's banquet in **75**). In northern sculpted altarpieces, the dominant visual effect is of extensive gilding [**12**]. Indeed, gold, contrary to what is often assumed, does not go out of fashion at our period. It continued to be widely demanded by patrons and used routinely by most painters well into the sixteenth century, both in the polychromy of sculpture and in the production of panel paintings: van der Weyden [**20**], Bouts, Hugo van der Goes and Gerard David all, for example, employed it in various types of works and for various effects; these are, however, far from most Florentine sculptural or pictorial concerns at the period.

Of all the ways in which we might view northern production through Italian eyes, the most insidious and tenacious today is the idea that Netherlandish painting, in particular, reproduces reality, merely imitating, observing, and describing rather than inventing. We can trace the beginnings of this to Fazio's positive remarks discussed above, but the more negative version of this view of northern painters, and ultimately the more influential, is to be found in a famous statement purportedly by Michelangelo to Vittoria Colonna, recorded by the painter Franceso de Holanda (1517–1584). This was written in the 1540s

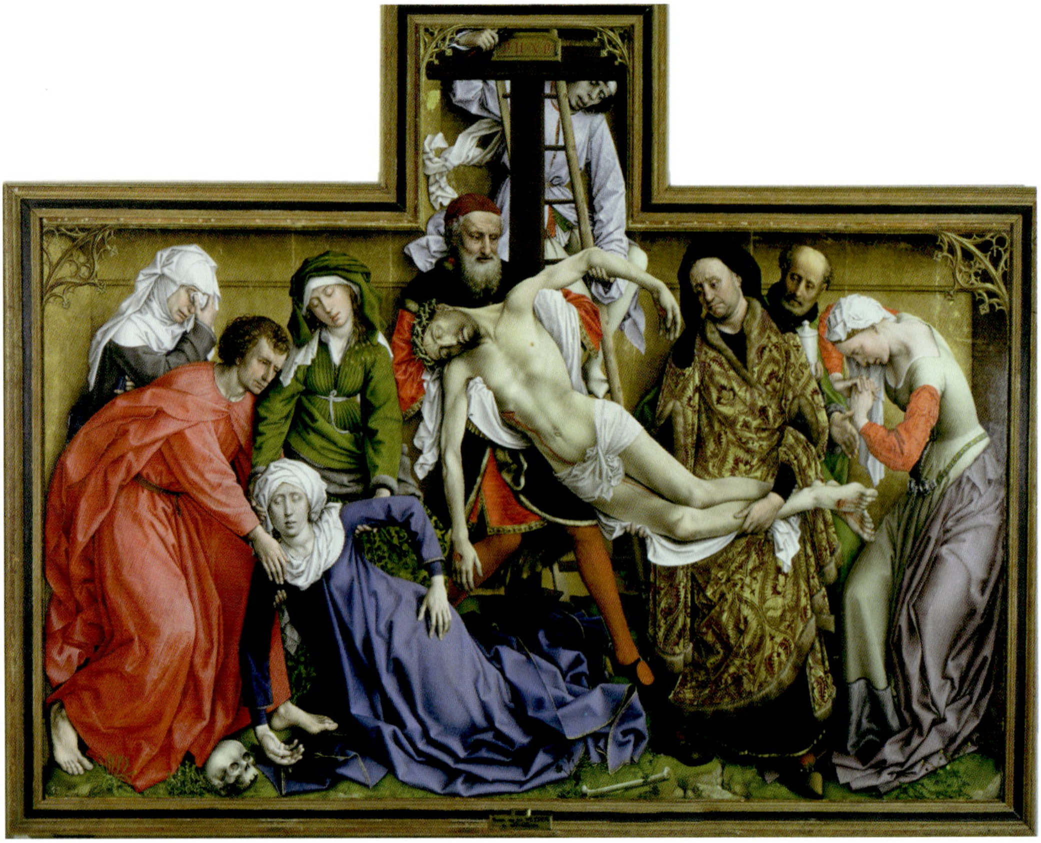

20 Rogier van der Weyden

Descent from the Cross, oil on Baltic oak, before 1443.

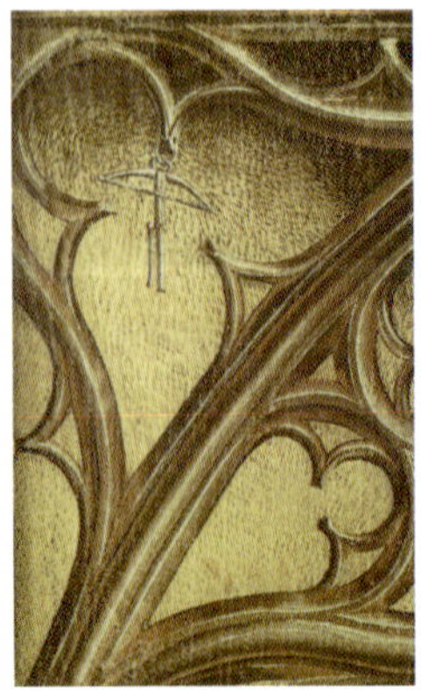

In this altarpiece made for the chapel of the crossbowmen's guild of Leuven, Rogier creates a powerful liturgical and devotional image through a range of visual devices, none of which are about constructing 'real' space or historical narrative. These include setting the figures in a gold box, which allows no distracting extraneous detail; this may make reference to sculpted altarpieces like **12**, **55**, **56**, but those rely mostly on small-scale figures, heavily gilded, in dense narratives; it is more comparable to life-size stone entombment groups like **181**. Rogier, like van Eyck in **18** and **174**, may be consciously promoting his medium and its potential: the central part of the image, the area around Christ's chest, is a tour de force of pure painting—at this point we find flesh, blood, fur, hair, veins, velvet, jewels, wrinkles, and cast shadows, all created in paint in a manner which defies what polychromed stone or wood could achieve. Rogier also deploys the poses of his figures to create dramatic impact and convey meaning: they are unstable in their footing, dishevelled in some manner in their clothing, and their grips on the figures of the dead Christ and the swooning Virgin are deliberately lax; Rogier intensified this effect in the process of painting by loosening their grips further. The Virgin's pose, in echoing Christ's, underlines her co-passion—she was believed to have suffered the same pain as he did at the Crucifixion; but his pose, and hers, are also brilliantly designed to refer to the patrons of this work, since both evoke the shape of a crossbow. Thus while the actual crossbows in the image are tiny, hanging from the tracery in the corners, the poses of Christ and the Virgin stamp the guild's identity on this work in an unmissable way. The originality of these figures, and the beauty of their shapes, were so powerful that artists repeated them throughout Europe for a hundred years: this is arguably the most influential painting of the fifteenth century.

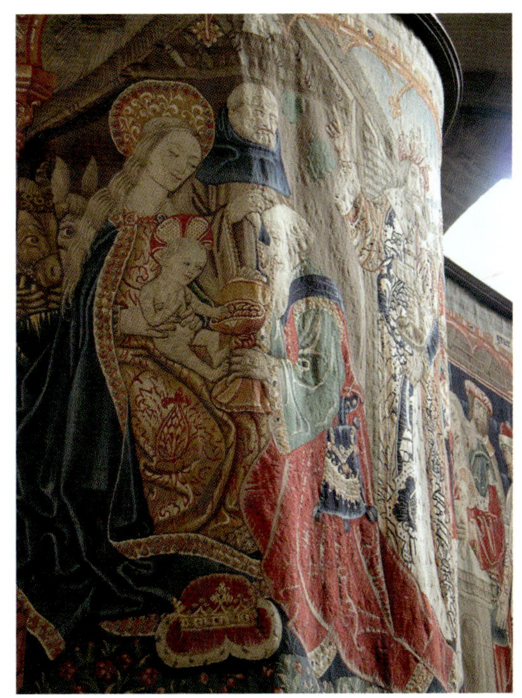

21 Southern Netherlandish weavers, probably after a cartoon by Pierre Spicre

Scenes from the Life of the Virgin, tapestries around the choir of the collegiate church of Notre Dame, Beaune, wool, designed 1474, woven 1500. See also [**179**].

Tapestries were not designed to be hung completely flat; they often had to go around corners and over oddly shaped architectural features; good tapestry design exploits this, acknowledging their woven texture. Later taste, informed by the ideals of the High Renaissance, favoured clearly organized space and clarity of composition, neither of which is part of tapestries' visual language. This has hampered our ability to appreciate the cleverness of their design and invention.

at a point, it must be said, when Netherlandish art was less universally admired but was still in demand, and pouring into Italy in some quantities, much of which was probably not of very high quality. The text is worth quoting in full:

> Flemish painting will, generally speaking, please the devout better than any painting of Italy, which will never cause him to shed a tear, whereas that of Flanders will cause him to shed many; and that not through the vigour and goodness of the painting, but owing to the goodness of the devout person. It will appeal to women, especially the very old and the very young, and also to monks and nuns and to certain noblemen who have no sense of true harmony. In Flanders they paint with a view to external exactness such things as may cheer you and of which you cannot speak ill, as for example saints and prophets. They paint stuffs and masonry, the green grass of the fields, the shadow of the trees, and rivers and bridges which they call landscapes, with many figures on this side and many figures on that. All this, though it pleases some persons, is done without reason or art, without symmetry or proportion, without skilful choice of boldness and finally without substance or vigour. Nevertheless, there are countries where they paint worse than Flanders.[16]

While the remarks about its appeal and lack of reason, art, symmetry, or proportion can be easily dismissed, especially in the light of what has been already said above, the claim that 'In Flanders they paint with a view to external exactness' leads directly to some of the most widespread, and wrong, assumptions about what Netherlandish paintings do. Because artists like Jan van Eyck and Rogier van der Weyden painted the effects of light, the surfaces of stone, skin, materials, jewels, and metal with such supreme skill, we can be seduced into the belief that what they paint is simply observation. So the room in which the Arnolfini stand must be a real room, and the moment represented a real event [**37**], or the landscape behind the Virgin and Child in the *Rolin Madonna* [**207**] must be a real town (Maastricht, Lyon, Dijon, Bruges, Liège,

22 Simon Marmion

The Last Judgement, miniature from the Hours of Charlotte de Bourbon-Montpensier, parchment, after 1474 and before March 1478.

Marmion painted some of the most inventive images of the period. Imagining both heavenly and natural light sources, and using paint and fine lines of liquid gold, he creates dramatic effects (the de Limbourgs could do this brilliantly too, see **74**). This manner of visualizing heaven and hell was one of his 'signature' subjects: it is repeated, revised, in several other luxury manuscripts. Excluding the decorative borders commonly set around miniatures maximizes the space available for this panoramic image, making it visually more akin to a small panel, an effect which was to become very popular in later manuscripts by this artist and his associates [**206**].

and Prague have all been put forward as candidates), or the settings for the Virgin in works like **137** must be a 'real bourgeois interior'. Of course, they are in fact contrivances, inventions based on observations of some real elements but not a reality in itself, put together instead to convey specific meanings or effects, and to solve particular visual problems. It is in their unreality that we find their meaning.[17]

Assuming their skill is simply reproductive plays down the inventive powers of these painters, and suggests something less intellectual, more mechanical, is at work. When we do come to a northern view of what the great artists of the time can do, we see in fact that it is this invention, combined with the powers of observation and technical skill, which is heralded as their greatest achievement. The terms 'artificeux ouvriers' (workers of artifice) and 'dengigneux mestiers' (ingenious trades or crafts) are applied to the famous craftsmen in Paris listed by Gillebert de Metz around 1435, which include the de Limbourgs; the term 'engin', which implied imagination and memory, was likewise evoked as a crucial quality for the best (legendary) artists in a set of manuscripts lauding famous women which were illuminated and read in court circles in Paris *c*.1400 (see image heading Chapter 14).[18] Our first comment by a northern artist on a northern work of art is Dürer's on the Ghent Altarpiece, and it is invention he remarks on: 'a most precious painting, full of thought'.[19] Jean Molinet (1435–1507) in his epitaph of 1489 to the illuminator Simon Marmion claimed this artist had 'tout painct et tout ymagine': painted everything and imagined everything, something which seems particularly borne out by the visualizations of heaven and hell in various manuscripts attributed to his hand [**22**].[20] And when Jean Lemaire de Belges, Molinet's godson, described in his poem *La Plainte du Désiré* a personification of Painting, she had all the equipment and materials needed to produce fine works, but what she had in most abundance, her last and most important asset, was invention:

Invention I have by the basket-full,
I have what I have; I have more than I need.[21]

The ability to invent is something we should never underestimate in the best northern artists of the period.

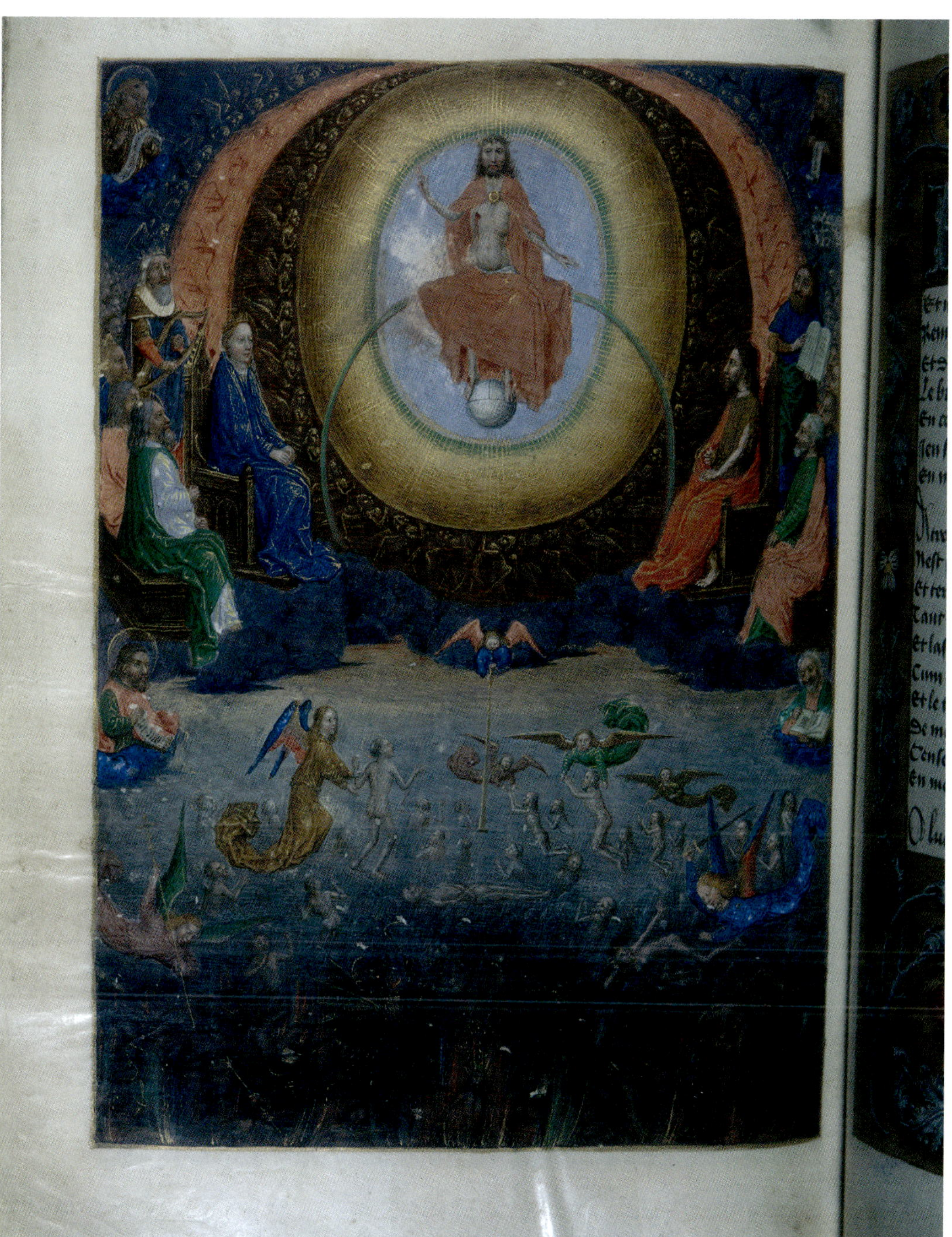

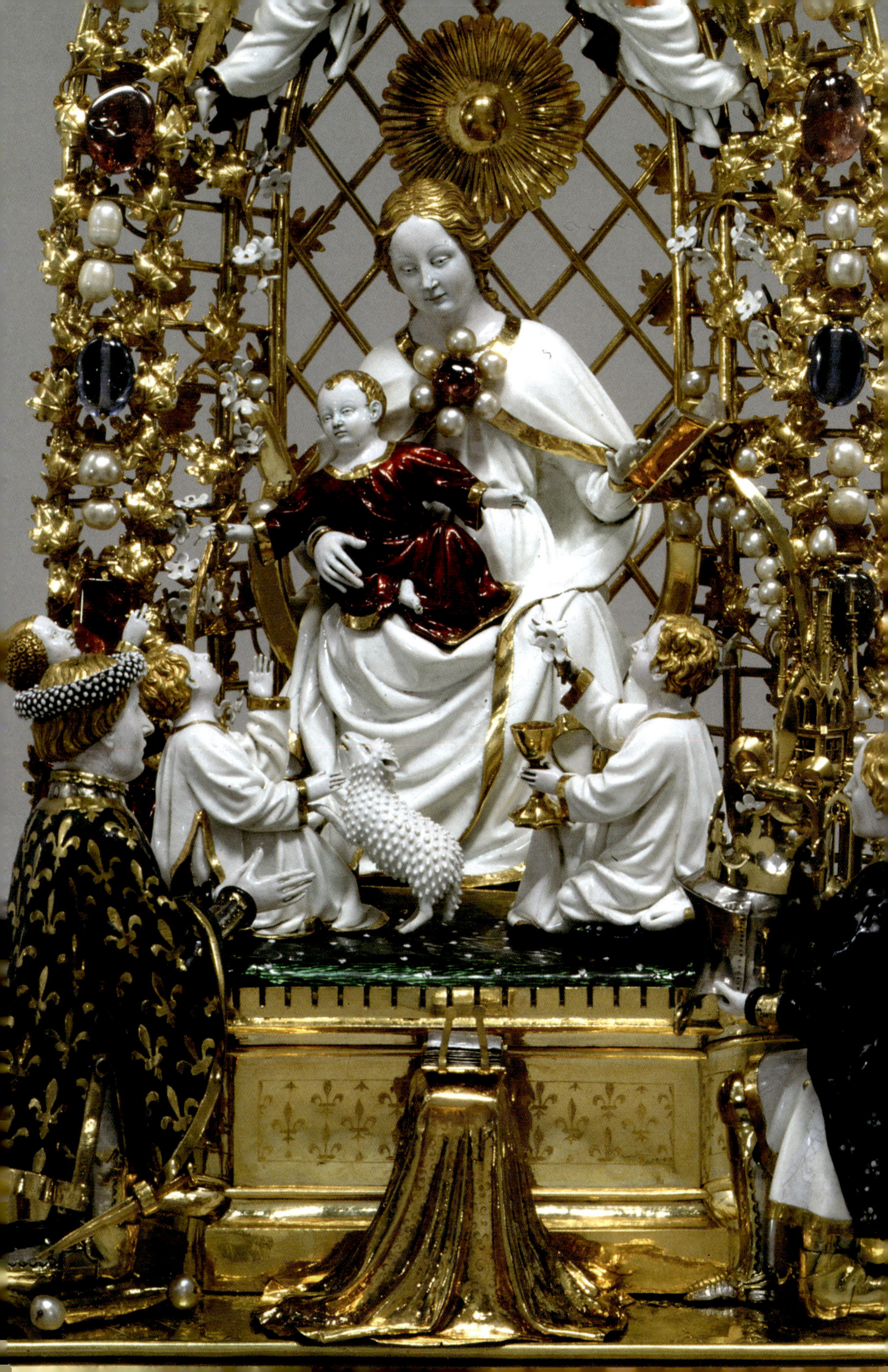

Sources and Documents

... the said inventory should be made in triplicate, one of which will remain close to the King in his coffers and locked with a key which he will keep on his person; the second will be put in a chest locked with two keys, in the chamber of accounts, and these keys will be guarded by two such persons as pleases the King to command, and the third will be split between the places where the said *joyaux* are kept.

Instructions in the inventory of Charles V, made in 1379[1]

4

We may not have an abundance of literary texts dedicated in whole or even in part to verbalizing about visual imagery in northern Europe at this period, but we do have other types of written evidence about artistic production and consumption, which include inventories, wills, payment accounts, contracts, and guild regulations. Although appreciation and response are implicit rather than explicit in these texts, we can garner from them some sense of what was valued and how. They are important in establishing our perspective on the production of this period since they indicate, vividly, the relative importance of different media, and emphasize how materials, quality, and skill mattered. Moreover, since these sources often record lost works in vast numbers, without them we would have an extremely limited view of artistic output and ownership. They will be used extensively throughout this study so it is worth considering the nature, context, potential, and limitations of at least some of these different types of documents here. Many of these sources are also new and distinctive to our period, since they were produced as a result of developments in civic, religious, or royal administration and organization at this time or as a response to changing economic, social, or political situations.

Inventories

Most notable among these administrative developments was the establishment of the *Chambre des Comptes* of the Valois kings and their dukes who in the late fourteenth century evolved accounting procedures that meant, among other things, that inventories of their belongings were made, and kept. From the 1360s onwards we have surviving documents of this sort for all the key players on the political and artistic stage in France, England, and the Burgundian Netherlands, where the most expensive and elaborate luxury goods were being made and acquired: Charles V (1363, as Dauphin, and 1379–80),[2] his three brothers Jean de Berry (1401, 1406–8, 1416),[3] Louis of Anjou (1379),[4] and Philip the Bold (1388, 1404);[5] Charles's son Charles VI (several from 1391 to 1422);[6] Philip the Bold's wife Margaret of Flanders (1405),[7] their

Detail of 24

son John the Fearless (1412), grandson Philip the Good (1420, *c.*1430), and great-grandson Charles the Bold (1467–9);[8] the widowed and powerful Jeanne d'Evreux, aunt to Charles V (1373);[9] Louis of Orléans (1407) and his wife Valentina Visconti (1408).[10] We also have examples for Richard II of England (1400)[11] and for the regent of France, John, Duke of Bedford (*c.*1447–9).[12] This practice continued to be important throughout the period, and there are major examples relating to Margaret of Austria (1523), Isabella of Castile (1504), and Henry VIII (1547).[13]

These inventories were first and foremost important official documents made to provide a record of ownership, track its location, and to account its value: as such they were highly valued in themselves and carefully guarded. Charles V's inventory of 1379, begun during the last year of his reign, was made in triplicate, carefully guarded (see quote heading this chapter), and copies made by later generations [**23**]. This inventory, representative of many, enumerated over three thousand items, ranging from metalwork, textiles (chapel hangings, bed hangings, cushions), tapestries, manuscripts, jewellery, relics, cameos, small-scale sculpture in wood, metal, and ivory, tableaux (for these see Part V), to mirrors, chess boards, prayer beads, hats, purses, belts, and even dog collars. It was made by a team of Charles's counsellors including a goldsmith who was vital for purposes of evaluation and description. The team went from residence to residence—beginning at the king's palace in Melun and moving on to those of Vincennes, then to the Louvre and other Paris residences such as the Hôtels Saint-Germain and Saint-Pol. The process of making an inventory involved detailing where objects were kept, with what, and to an extent how, so we can get an idea of what was kept in the chapel or in the study, for example (see p. 237). The entries tend to begin with the metalwork, and within each section with the best, most elaborate, and valuable item: in Charles's case, item no. 1 is the 'very large, very beautiful and best crown of the King', moving down through the less great and beautiful crowns to the gold images and reliquaries, pieces of gold plate, and eventually to the silver plate. Then follow the textiles, his chapel and chamber hangings, beginning again with his most precious mitre, the 'great mitre' decorated with rubies, emeralds, diamonds, and pearls, and so on. These two media—textiles and metalwork—dominate royal and ducal collections of the period: well over half of charles V's items were metalwork or jewelled objects and around a quarter were textiles. These were indispensable symbols of magnificence, seen deployed as such in **75**.

Frequently entries in these inventories are frustratingly brief or uninformative, but on occasion they can be remarkably loquacious: Louis of Anjou (1339–84), who in 1379 himself dictated all of the 3,602 entries enumerating his collection, has one entry for his most important gold cross that runs over 13 pages and is around 7,000 words long, and while it is mostly concerned with describing the number of jewels, their quality, size, and placement, we also occasionally get some sense of what Louis appreciated in the figurative elements of such a work. In narrative scenes he might enumerate how many figures are depicted, and remark on how they were represented: thus the gilded and painted figure of Saint John below his aforementioned gold cross is described as having 'his hands together with his fingers interlaced in a gesture of real discomfort'; in an image of the Annunciation on the base of his most elaborate tabernacle he notes how the Virgin 'is shown as if

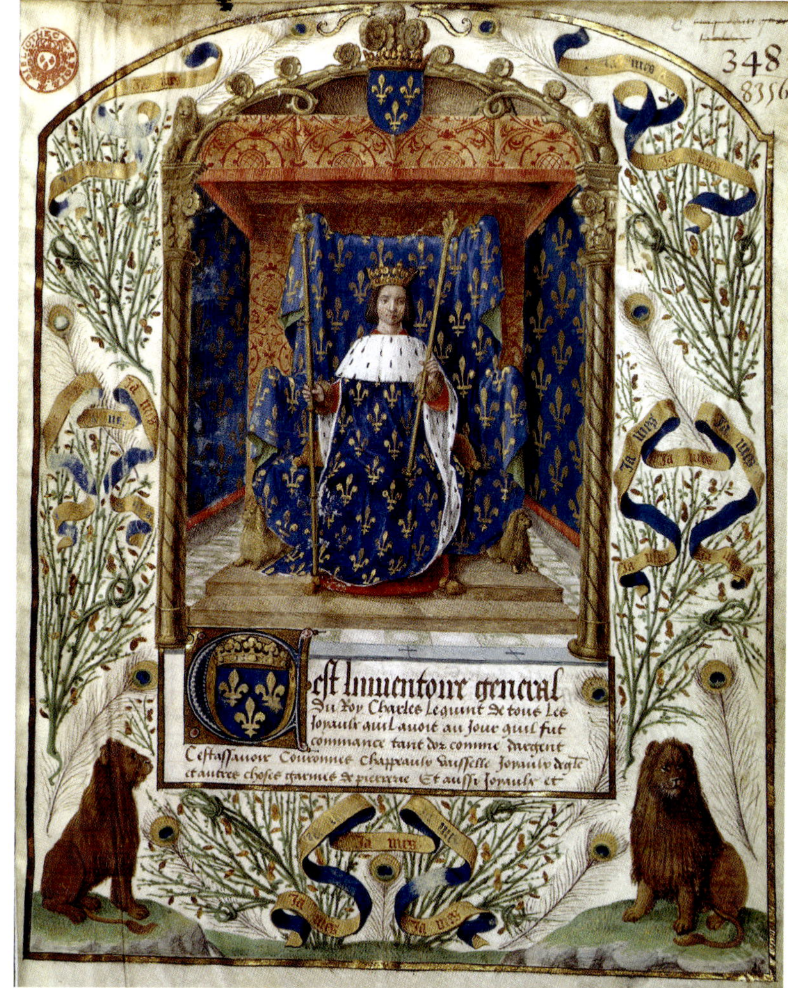

23 Jean Perréal

Charles VI Enthroned, frontispiece to a late fifteenth-century copy of the inventory of Charles V.

This copy of the inventory of Charles V was made more than a hundred years after the compilation of the original document, at a point where many of the items listed in it were no longer in French possession, having been melted down or acquired by the English after the death of Charles VI in 1421. As such it is a record of past glories. Perhaps, because of this, the king depicted is not Charles V or Charles VIII but Charles VI: his device, the broomcod, and his motto, 'ja mes', decorate the border.

listening to the angel's greeting'. Similar attention to narrative moments is found in contracts of the period (see below). Sometimes the remarks extend to assessments of old and new, especially in regards to how figures are dressed: the Virgin and Child from what was probably an Italo-Byzantine painting from *c*.1300 are described as 'dressed in a very ancient fashion' ('vestu bien anciennement').[14] Dress was certainly one of the aspects which most caught Louis's eye as he surveyed and described the imagery of his large collection: in a cup on which there were images of Louis himself, his wife, and his children, the description of their figures concentrates entirely on the style, colour, and length of their robes, and their headdresses. This hints at one way in which images were read, or what was thought important in visual depiction; it is something confirmed by again other texts of the period (see below).

Because monetary values were often assigned to the objects described, especially in post mortem inventories, we can also use them to consider their relative worth. For example, a painted, hinged quadriptych (now lost) owned by Jean de Berry in 1416, with portraits of his brother, Charles V, his father, John II, the Holy Roman Emperor Charles IV (for whom see pp. 255–8 below), and

Edward III of England, was valued at 26 livres, while a psalter with images by André Beauneveu [**78**] was 100 livres, but the extraordinary *Grandes Heures*, his largest prayer book by far, in which each page measures 40 × 30 centimetres, was valued at 4,000 livres tournois, more expensive than his most valuable tapestry, a 19-aulne (about 13-metre) wide piece with the seven Vices woven with gold thread, valued at 1,700 livres tournois, and not far off the bullion figure of 4,371 livres tournois attained by Berry's most elaborate large gold cross when it was sent to the mint in 1417.[15] Interpreting these documents is not without problems, however: how much of the value of the *Grandes Heures* was due to its jewelled binding? And how much of the value of the portrait was due to its provenance (it was previously owned by Charles V) and its historical value? Moreover, those compiling these texts may have had agendas in terms of the values they assigned to certain works, or may have been less expert in certain areas, or simply some items with intrinsic values like metalwork and jewels were easier to apprise than items made of paint and panel or parchment alone. It is also often impossible to know the size of many objects if they no longer survive, or, when scale is indicated, what was meant by relative terms such as large or small.

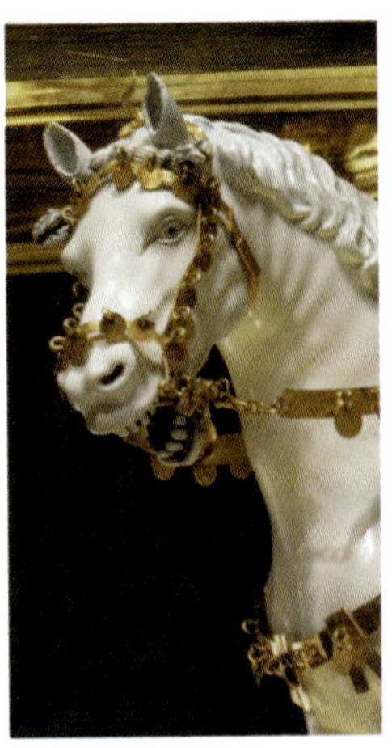

24 Anonymous Parisian goldsmith

The *Goldenes Rössl*, gold, silver gilt, enamel, pearls, rubies, and sapphires, 1405.

The technique of *émail en ronde bosse*—enamel in the round—is seen in this object at its most ambitious and virtuosic: the Virgin, at 15 cm high, is at the very extreme of what is possible in terms of size with this method. The extraordinary decision to show the three saints around her as children may have had significance for Isabeau of Bavaria, who commissioned this work for her husband Charles VI, but it also ensures a realistic scale to the figures while allowing them all to fit happily onto the terrace without obstructing the king's view of the Virgin and Child.

Looking at one of the rare instances in which we have both the object and a contemporary description of it in an inventory highlights the potential and limitations of such documents. The most ambitious, successful, and technically brilliant piece of metalwork surviving from this period, the *Goldenes Rössl*, so-called after the white horse which features in it [**24**],[16] was described in the collection of Charles VI (1368–1422) in the Tour de Coin (then known as La Tour des Joyaux) of the Bastille, in cupboard A, opposite the fireplace, in 1405:

> Item, an image of Our Lady who holds her child, sitting in a garden made in the manner of a trellis, which is enamelled. Our Lady is in white and the child of rouge cler and this image [of Our Lady] has a brooch at her neck, decorated with six pearls and a ruby, and above the head of Our Lady is a crown decorated with two small rubies and a sapphire and 16 pearls, and holding this crown are two small angels enamelled in white; the garden decorated with 5 large rubies and 5 sapphires and 32 pearls and there is a lectern where there is a book and this is decorated with 12 pearls, and in front of the image there are three images of gold, that is Saint Catherine, Saint John the Baptist, Saint John the Evangelist, and below these the image of the king, kneeling on a cushion decorated with 4 pearls, wearing the arms of France. And in front of him his book on a small bench of gold, and behind him a tiger, and in front of the king, on the other side, a squire, dressed in white and blue enamel, who holds the gold helmet of the king, and below there is a horse enamelled in white with the saddle and harness of gold, and a valet enamelled in white and blue who holds the horse by the bridle held in one hand, and in the other hand a baton. And this weighs about 18 *marcs* of gold and the base on which these things are set weighs around 30 *marcs* of silver gilt, and it was given by the Queen to the King the first day of the new year 1404 [1405 new style].[17]

Clearly a major concern here was to enumerate anything removable and valuable, such as the jewels and the pearls, and indeed some of the elements described are now lost: the horse's rein, the baton held by the valet, and some of the pearls on the lectern. So first and foremost we have a way of reconstructing the original appearance of the object. The compilers also note details of the techniques employed, especially the difficult and distinctive *rouge cler* (the method of translucent enamelling in red found on Christ's robe, which could only be done with success on gold) and the white enamel, called today *émail en ronde bosse*, used principally for the Virgin, horse, valet, and the angels, as

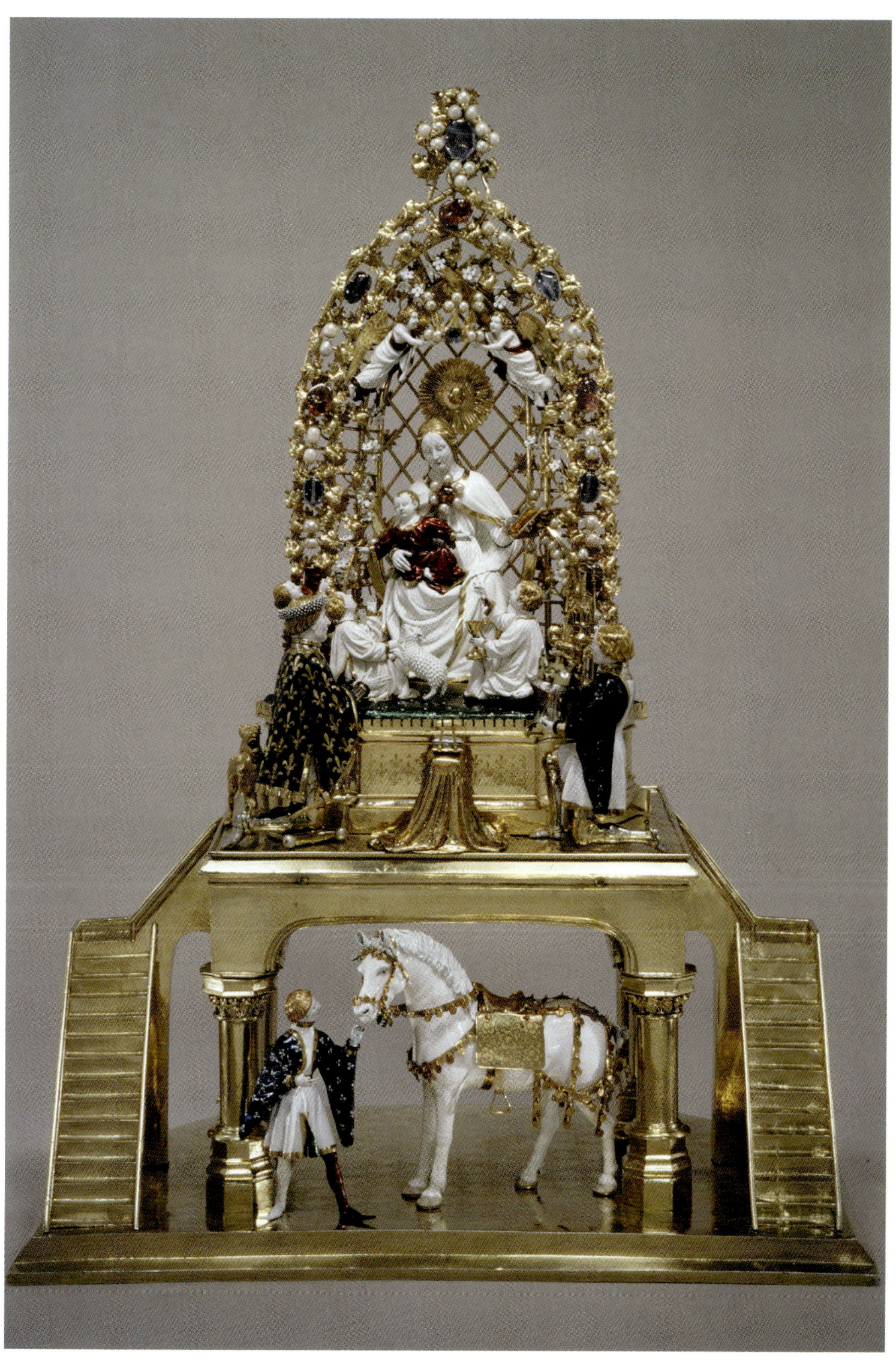

well as for faces and other details.[18] The weight listed at the end is also a mandatory, since this is how the actual bullion value of the object would be calculated: at 48 *marcs*—around 12 kilogrammes or 24 pounds—this object was not easily portable (it stands 62 centimetres high).[19] The last sentence of the entry gives us the precious information about its origin—a New Year's gift from the queen, Isabeau of Bavaria (1370/1–1435), to her husband Charles VI in 1405, part of an important ritual of gift-giving that took place in its most elaborate form at the courts of France at this period.[20]

If we look at the wider context of the entry, that is what is listed with this object, for example, we find that in the same cupboard were kept several other similarly elaborate items, some featuring images of the king and queen (all now lost) weighing similarly heavy amounts. The Bastille was not a residential palace at the period, but it was very close to the Hôtel Saint-Pol where Charles VI, who was mostly insane at this point, spent much of his time, allowing for easy access to his precious *joyaux* and plate. It is clear, however, that like most such objects the *Goldenes Rössl* was not on constant display and, if examined at all, only at distinct moments, possibly brought to the king at the Hôtel Saint-Pol, or even to be admired in the light and comfort of the fire opposite its cupboard in the tower of the Bastille. Within months of the writing of this entry, however, the *Rössl* was pawned to Charles's brother-in-law, Louis of Bavaria. All of this is a salutary reminder that although this object included the king's portrait it was neither made at his behest, or indeed used by him for very long (if at all), and its original context and function changed early in its history.

This inventory entry is also striking for what it does not say: it conveys nothing of the complexity and ambition of the design of this work, or of the brilliance of its conception and execution. It is frustratingly inexplicit about artistic quality or character, which is of the most astonishing virtuosity and invention: over two levels the image presents its devotional subject (Charles before the Virgin and Child) in a narrative form: the king is not simply shown kneeling in prayer but his arrival is implied by his horse, from which he has dismounted and, while it is held by the valet, he has climbed up the steps on the left-hand side, accompanied by his tiger-dog and his squire (who presumably mounted the steps on the right); the king then removed his helm which the squire, kneeling, takes charge of, while the king himself kneels in devotion at a prie-dieu draped with a cloth of gold (literally) in front of the Virgin and Child. The realization is all the more impressive for the vivid likeness of the king, and the equally individualized portraits of the squire and the valet, and the very convincing treatment of the horse, who seems to be tossing his head in irritation at the bit in his mouth.

Authorship, even of the most accomplished and recently made objects, was very rarely recorded in these documents: either the name of the artist was not known or not of relevance to the value or identification of the piece. In all the 3,602 items described by Louis of Anjou, not once is a maker's name mentioned; in the 3,000 or so items detailed in Charles V's collection, we have just three where the name of the artist who made it is given (a painted panel, an ivory diptych, and a painted cloth altar hanging).[21] There are more occasions in Jean de Berry's inventories, perhaps unsurprisingly given the nature of his patronage and intense interest in the making of his works (but here, still, there are only sixteen items with a clear attribution concerning their making).[22] This general lack of artistic identification is, however, indicative in another way of how much material mattered. When artists *are* named it may indicate that there is something about the object that was valued in terms of its maker rather than its medium, or that was only possible to value in terms of skill, such as paintings, rather than the materials employed. By the end of our period this changes to an extent: the collections of Margaret of Austria, Duchess of Savoy and Regent of the Netherlands (1480–1530), contain more panel paintings and they more often have names of artists recorded with them.

Payment Accounts and Contracts

As well as inventorying objects owned by the royal and ducal households, the extensive and centralized administrative system established by the French royalty and in particular by the Burgundian court at Dijon and Lille under the Dukes of Burgundy meant that a full accounting system, recording payments to artists as well as other employees, was also developed and widely employed.[23] These Burgundian ducal accounts are one of the richest sources for documentation about artists, their conditions of work, and the supply of their materials at this period, and can be supplemented by town accounts which are well preserved for some centres, such as Bruges or Amiens.[24] Payments concerning particularly important events like the Feast of the Pheasant at Lille (1454), or the marriage of Charles the Bold and Margaret of York in Bruges in 1468, can reveal the huge sums and vast teams of artists involved in pulling off such an extravaganza, which might involve stage sets, costumes, mirrors, lighting, and mechanical devices, all of which might be designed or executed by painters, sculptors, carpenters, and embroiderers.[25] On a more routine but equally illuminating level, payments to master craftsmen, such as those to the sculptors Jean de Marville and Claus Sluter at Dijon, can provide information about the number of assistants present at any one time in their workshop, what their specialized roles or skills might be, and what they were paid (see Chapter 14).

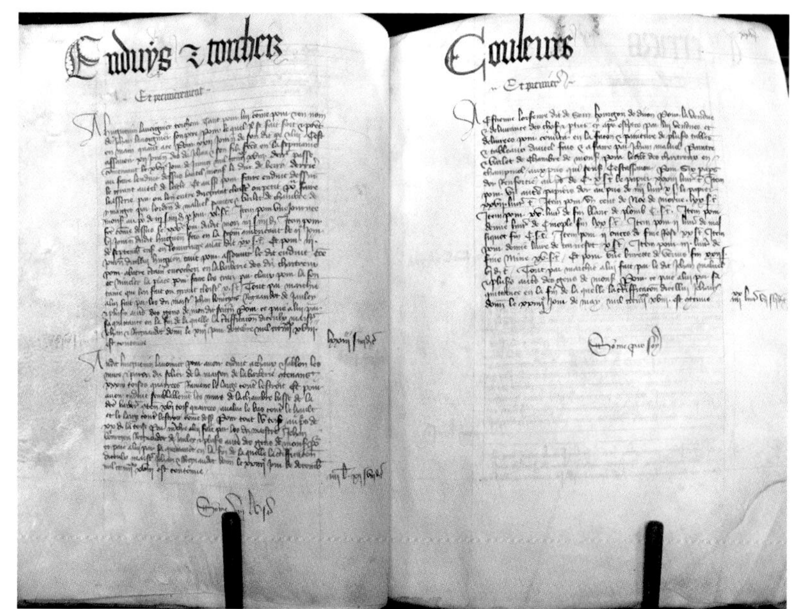

25

Accounts of Amiot Arnaut, receiver-general of Burgundy, recording yearly expenses at the Chartreuse de Champmol. Folio showing entries for lights, torches, and pigments for 1398, parchment.

These entries record payments to a father and son team for holding torches at the Chartreuse de Champmol so that the painter Jean Malouel had light to work by, and so that the designs made by Claus Sluter for the *Great Cross* [**146–8**] could be properly seen. Under 'Couleurs' are listed pigments and other materials supplied to Malouel; they include 12 'papiers' of gold leaf (books, usually containing 300 sheets), 15 pounds of lead white, 2 pounds of lead tin yellow (costing seven times as much as the lead white), and 2 ounces of fine rose—a lake pigment (costing three times as much as the lead tin yellow).

Other accounts might be devoted entirely to a single project, as were those kept for the Chartreuse de Champmol at Dijon, the most ambitious building project of Philip the Bold's reign.[26] These were kept by the receiver-general of Burgundy, who collected each year's receipts and orders for payment together and transcribed them at the end of each year into the fair and elaborate copy we have today [**25**]. They are among the most revealing of the ducal accounts because they are so full and detailed, and because they relate to objects which, in part at least, survive. They exist almost in their entirety for the period 1377–1409, that is spanning the whole of the construction and decorating history of this project. As can be seen in **25**, they are organized according to the nature of the materials and services provided, so for each year there are sections such as 'stone', 'glass', 'lead', and 'pigments'; the classification by materials is reflective of period thinking and indicates the centrality of materials in the organization of artistic production as well as ownership.

With these accounts we can follow the construction of the large-scale sculptural projects and other works for the Chartreuse with rare precision. In the case of the *Great Cross* (better known as the *Well of Moses*) made under Sluter's direction between 1395 and 1404 [**146–8**], we have payments for materials for each part of its complex structure, from iron rods for the 7-metre high cross it once supported, to metal eyeglasses for the figure of Jeremiah. We can follow the blocks of stone as they are cut from the quarries at Tonnerre and Asnières, carried to Sluter's workshop at the ducal palace in Dijon, moved around to avoid frost damage, worked on by various members of his team, and then, when complete, transported to Champmol in their specially made wooden boxes. We can see pigments, oil, and gold leaf delivered, prepared, and employed to polychrome the whole structure, and we can watch scaffolding go up, come down, go up again, and winches appear and disappear as the figures are installed and painted. We can even know how many nails (4,700), how much cloth (260 aulnes, about 175 metres), and how much wax for the cloth (70 pounds) was used to make the wooden structure put up around it not long after its completion to protect its elaborately painted and gilded surface.

The payment records for more ephemeral visual displays than seen at Champmol can often be further supplemented by the official and unofficial descriptions of the events themselves written by chroniclers or observers at the Burgundian court, which provide a more evocative sense of the splendour and exotic nature of many of these celebrations.[27] However, unlike our inventory descriptions or the Champmol accounts, where we can compare the written sources on occasion, at least, with surviving works, this genre of display has disappeared entirely, and our only visual evidence concerning it are the few depictions of joyous entries like those recording that of Joanna the Mad into Bruges in 1505;[28] more evocative, perhaps, is the famous image by Jean Fouquet of the martyrdom of St Apollonia, from the Hours of Etienne Chevalier, made around 1450. Fouquet chose to set this event not in a historical past but as contemporary theatre, and the two-tiered platform surrounding the stage with props like the maw of hell (on the right) evokes the type of ephemera that artists were employed to create for such performances [**26**].

Contracts, legal documents setting out the obligations of the artist and the patron in the production of a work, also emerge as a major source for us at this period, with the majority of extant examples dating from *c.*1400 onwards:

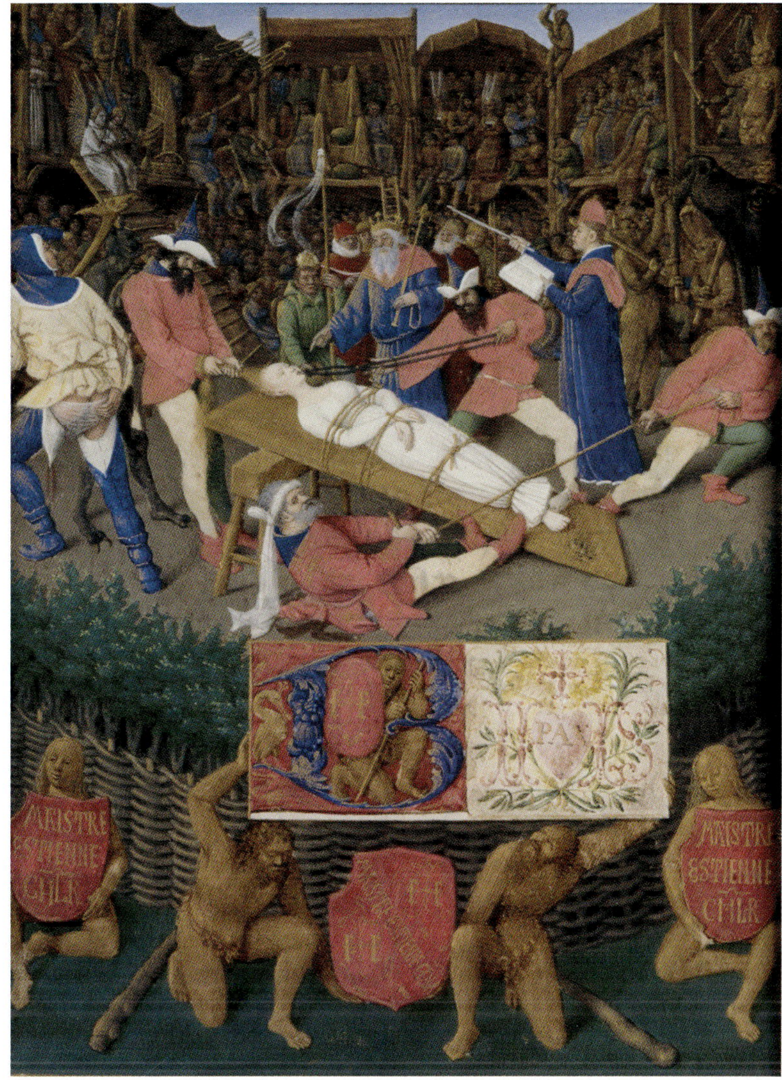

26 Jean Fouquet

Martyrdom of St Apollonia, from the Hours of Etienne Chevalier, parchment, *c.*1452–60.

The martyrdom is depicted as a contemporary mystery play, in which the action is being directed by the man in blue on the right holding a baton; the stalls around the stage contain further elements of the performance: heaven is on the left (note the angels); hell on the right. The throne at the centre is empty because its occupant is currently taking part in the drama centre stage—he is the bearded king who orders the saint's torture.

we see an equal acceleration in their making as we do for the compilation of accounts and guild regulations (see below), and possibly for related reasons, as practices of accounting, the recording and witnessing of transactions developed and became increasingly widespread. However, their ubiquity must also be in part due to the boom in patronage from confraternities, guilds, and individuals, who were increasingly building or founding chapels in the churches and cathedrals of their towns and who needed an altarpiece, stained glass, and other fixtures, often commemorative or funerary, to furnish them with. Contracts were usually made in two copies at least, one kept by the patron, the other by the artist, and sometimes a third lodged with a notary or the town administrators. In certain regions, for various historical reasons, many contracts survive, notably from Spain (Aragon, Valencia, and Catalonia), Provence, and southern Germany, while for some major centres, such as Bruges and Paris, we have relatively few.[29]

Contracts, like inventories and payment accounts, allow us to survey the field of lost works and to balance our perceptions about production at the period: we can see how ubiquitous carved retables were as the patrons' choice throughout northern Europe (although spotting that a contract is for a carved and painted work can require careful reading of the texts, since the artist orchestrating the commission was often a painter). These more constructionally complex and expensive carved works were, perhaps, more likely to engender such documentation than painted panels but we should consider the probability that most altarpieces made in the Netherlands and Germany, at least, were carved and richly gilded, 'de dorure et estouffure', and not made entirely 'de portraiture', or 'de platte peinture'—flat painting—as some contracts refer to it to distinguish it from the polychromy of sculpture.[30]

Contracts can be mined for what they can tell us about procedures and costs, but also about values and preferences of patrons, and in this respect they are a rich, and relatively unworked, seam. Concern for materials comes across very vividly, as might be expected. Particular types of wood, even the origin of trees or when they should be felled, can be mentioned (this in Spanish and German contracts in particular);[31] the type of stone, where and when it is to be quarried might be indicated; pigments and gilding are often carefully prescribed, notably the expensive blues (ultramarine and azurite) and reds (lakes in particular), and terms for its delivery are often detailed, since the potential risks of damage in transport and installation were high (see pp. 223–5). This all speaks for the concern that works would last, and be made with material integrity: in a contract for a carved altarpiece commissioned in 1448 from a sculptor called Ricquart by the Abbess of Flines near Tournai, specifications such as 'bien et proprement fait'—well and properly made—'sans fraude' and 'sans malengien'—without fraud or deception—are peppered throughout the document, repeated in various forms around fifteen times.[32] Guild regulations (see below) played a part in ensuring this was so, but sometimes a group of other artists might be brought in to judge the finished product, or the final payment to the artist was withheld for a year or more after the work was installed so that there was time to see if any defects would emerge. As part of this concern for quality, another, existing work was often cited in the contract as a model, but rarely in the sense that the cited work should be copied. They are evoked, rather, as exemplars in terms of size (a tomb commissioned by Charles de Bourbon in 1448 from the sculptor Jacques Morel had to be as high as that of Philip the Bold's at Champmol, **133**),[33] or quality and craftsmanship: the parishioners of Warchin, near Tournai, wanted their altarpiece commissioned from the painter Philippe Truffin in 1474 to be 'the same and not less, in its carving, gilding, and polychromy, likewise in its painting' as that in the church of St Catherine in Tournai.[34]

A range of these concerns are well illustrated in the contract for the *Virgin of the Councillors* commissioned from the painter Lluís Dalmau. For this work not only the contract but the *mostra* (the drawing which was part of the contract) and the work itself survive [**27, 28**].[35] Perhaps unexpectedly, the drawing does not include a depiction of the disposition of figures in the work, but instead sets out in words placed in the appropriate areas of the painting what will be depicted, indicating that the *mostra* may have been made for, rather than by, the painter. The contract is concerned, expectedly, with mate-

27 Lluís Dalmau

Virgin of the Councillors, oil on Baltic oak, 1443–5.

The iconography and format of this work are unlike most Spanish altarpieces, which tend to be multi-panelled works, but its form may reflect its intended location, a relatively small, 12-square-metre chapel in the chamber of the city councillors, as well as its commemorative function. The work has clear visual references to the Ghent Altarpiece [**4**] and the *Van der Paele Madonna* [**18**], suggesting Dalmau, who went to the Netherlands, knew these works made there in the early to mid-1430s.

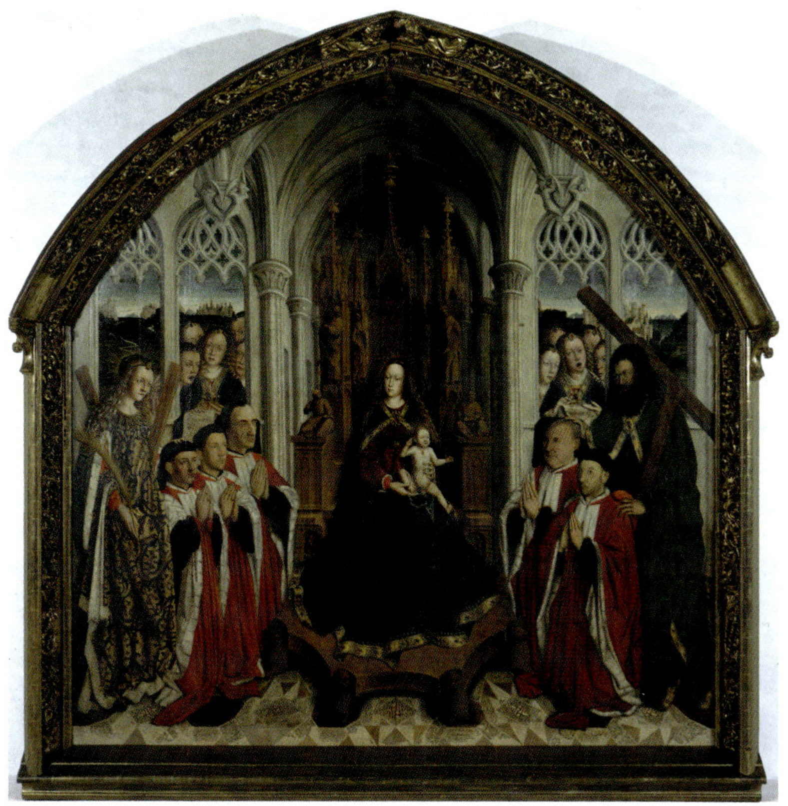

28 For or by Lluís Dalmau

Virgin of the Councillors, *mostra*, ink on parchment, 1443.

This contract drawing represents in words instead of images what should be where on Dalmau's altarpiece, the notes being placed in the spot where the subject they refer to should be shown. The positioning of the city's coat of arms at the top centre and at the lower edges of the *banco* (the lower register, now lost) receives precise attention, as does the frame, suggesting that the drawing may have as much to do with the carpentry of this work as its painting (see also **124**).

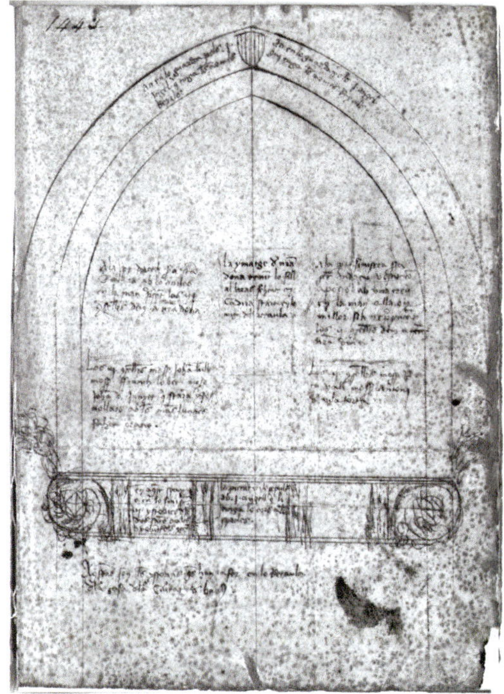

The spiralling institution of such guild regulations across Europe reflects an increasing degree of technical specialization and a growing complexity in the organization of artistic practices. For the art historian, they can reveal much about the value given to certain skills and abilities, and much more besides. We find, for example, an ubiquitous emphasis on gilding throughout the period, which relates in part to the cost of the raw material and the need to avoid any fraudulent use, but also underlines its continued importance in polychromed sculpture and in painted panels until well into the sixteenth century.[65] Masterpieces, required in many guilds, give some sense of what was expected of a fully trained artist. Again gilding features prominently, but also drawing, design and invention, and the ability to paint or carve the human form, horses, landscape, and to tell a narrative story (see pp. 183–4); a sense of decorum in terms of materials and how they should be applied, by whom, and on what, comes through very strongly too.

Guild regulations can also reveal something about how the makers of one type of image (say, woodcarvers) saw themselves in relation to other, related, co-dependent or competing trades (say, joiners, coachmakers, printmakers, or painters), since guilds defined relationships between crafts with some care and precision: in most northern centres, if you were trained as a painter you could not work as a sculptor, although in German towns the same workshop combining the two trades, usually undertaken by different craftsmen, was allowed and not uncommon – Bernt Notke (c. 1440–1509) in Lübeck or Lucas Cranach (1472–1553) in Wittenberg are good examples. Often this relationship was defined by the tools and material used in each trade, another way in which materials provide a framework for our perspective on this period (explored further in Part IV). However, because of the nature of such regulatory material, it is important to recognize that what was specified *should* happen was not necessarily what *did* happen. The rules, indeed, may have been in place and rewritten, as they frequently were, because what was forbidden was actually occurring with some frequency.

In this respect the disputes between different guilds are perhaps most revealing about actual practice, about how different craftsmen saw their areas of expertise, and about how the practitioners of, say, painting in Brussels interacted with the woodcarvers or the tapestry makers. The case of the dispute between the weavers of Brussels and the painters highlights guild concerns:[66] in 1476 the painters complained that 'various journeymen, foreign and others, have made particular patterns on paper with charcoal and chalk for some tapestry weavers'. The weavers, however, argued that they had done no wrong and that they ought to 'be able to do this kind of work, or cause it to be done, without having to take the painters into account'. The result was a victory for the painters, in some respects: weavers could no longer design works which included figurative elements, but could produce 'drapery, trees, foliage and grass', and could alter or extend designs already in their stock. Painting may not have been the most expensive or desired art form at this time, but painters held a position of key importance in artistic production with an influence beyond the realm of painting alone, due to their skill and carefully guarded role as designers (see Part IV); we are back again to the invention that the best painters have in abundance.

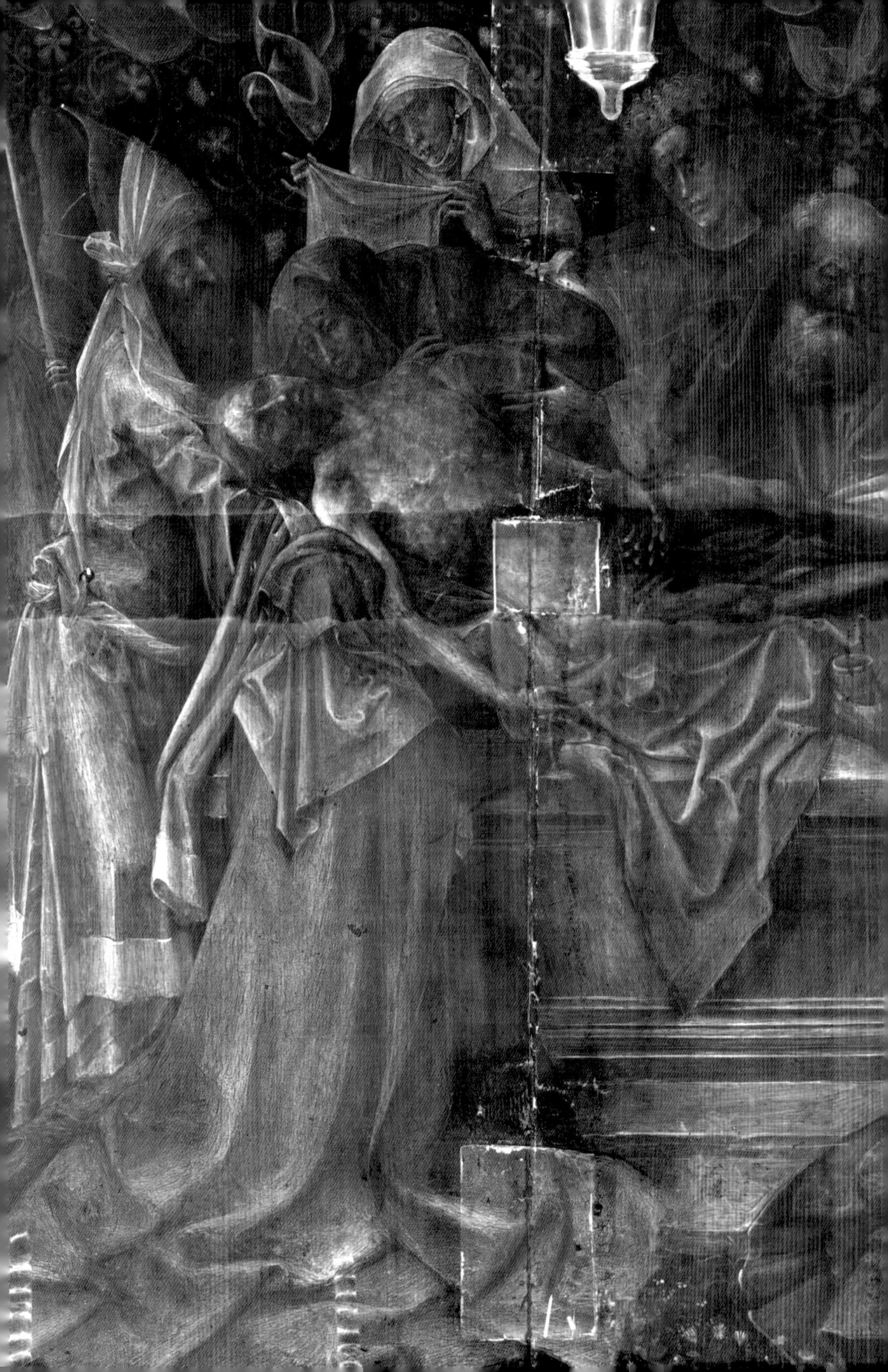

Physical Evidence and Technical Examination

Knowledge of materials and processes is part of the equipment for understanding why a painting is what it is and not otherwise

W. G. Constable, from *The Painter's Workshop*, 1954[1]

5

Another way in which we can get, more literally, under the surface of the works of this period is with technical and physical examination of the objects themselves. In the last forty years increasingly sophisticated technical methods of examination, using techniques from radiography and infrared reflectography to dendrochonology and gas-chromatography-mass-spectrometry have presented us with a vast body of new material about how, when, and where paintings, and increasingly sculpture and other art forms, were made and how they may have originally looked. Like the documents, the results of these studies are an indispensable tool used throughout this book and some introductory remarks about their methods are pertinent here, focusing on Netherlandish panel painting, since within our period this area has received the most concentrated attention from these methods of study over recent years.[2] Although technical findings may be termed scientific, they are no less open to interpretation than documentary evidence, and their limitations as well as their potential must be understood. Physical evidence, not easily divided from technical evidence, relates to the information gleaned from a close study of every facet of an object: the frame of a painting, the bottom of a sculpture, the reverse of a print or drawing, the back of a tapestry, the

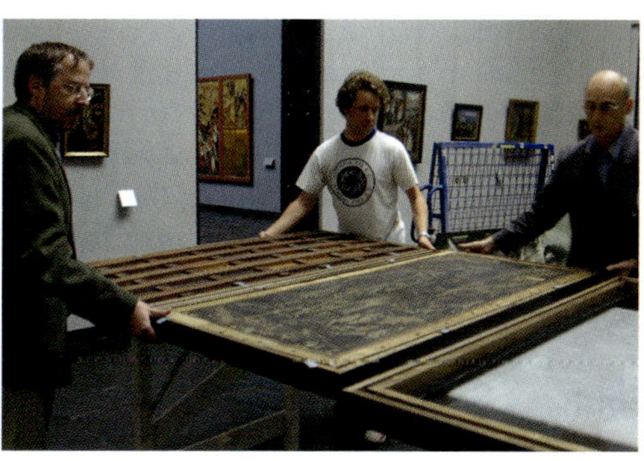

29

The Flémalle panels [**35**] being removed from the wall for reframing by curators and staff at the Städel, Frankfurt.

Detail of 32

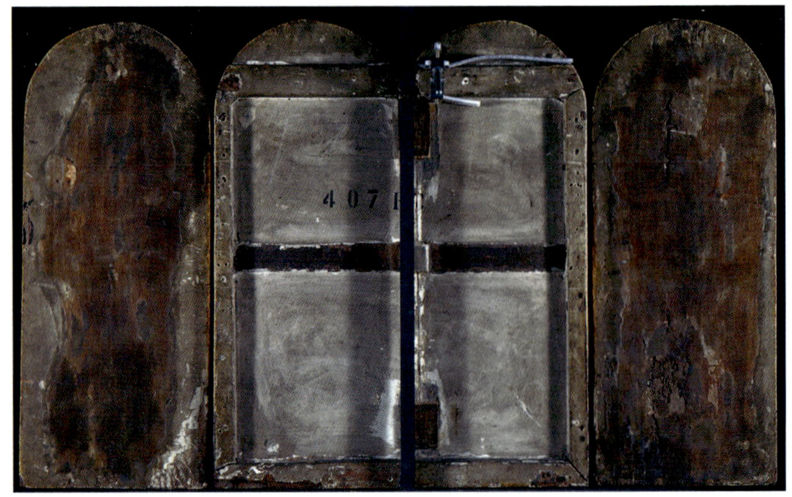

30 Circle of the Master of Flémalle (Robert Campin?)

Reverse of the Seilern Triptych with wings open [**31**].

There is no trace now of paint or ground on the exterior wings (which have been scraped down), but these would have been painted, possibly with fictive marbling and coats of arms.

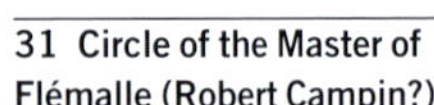

31 Circle of the Master of Flémalle (Robert Campin?)

The Entombment and Resurrection of Christ with a Kneeling Donor (the 'Seilern Triptych'), oil with some egg tempera on Baltic oak, *c.*1425.

The donor's scroll is blank. Our only clue to his identity is the purple flower set prominently against the tomb of Christ, which also reappears on either side of the donor in the wing, and may be his emblem. Although traditionally attributed to the Master of Flémalle, the paint handling and technique of this triptych are very different from the Flémalle panels [**35**] or the *Nativity* (cover).

32 Circle of the Master of Flémalle (Robert Campin?)

X-ray of **31**.

The x-ray registers the paint surface, the ground, the support, and whatever is on the reverse all at the same time. Heavy elements like lead white or metals appear white. The dense, straight, vertical grain of the wood, characteristic of Baltic oak, is made visible where the white of the chalk ground sits in the grooves of the grain. X-rays will also reveal areas of loss and restoration.

hinges of a gold triptych, the gatherings of a manuscript, can each reveal much about original appearance and use, condition, place of production, and the artist or date.

The reverse of an object is often the best place to begin any investigation [**29, 30**]; the back of a carved work can reveal whether it was intended to be seen in the round, or if and how it was attached to something, or part of a larger ensemble, as well as how it was made [**138**]. Conversely, if a panel is painted on the back, with imagery, coats of arms, or fictive marbling or jasper (a technique found in many of van Eyck's smaller panels), then we can be fairly certain that the reverse was meant to be seen, and such panels cannot have been intended for a fixed position against a wall but were designed either to be handled or to be set in a manner which allowed the back to be visible.[3]

The reverse is also often the place where evidence concerning an object's earlier history or provenance is found. The back of the Seilern Triptych, attributed to the Master of Flémalle (identified by some as Robert Campin), a work with no external evidence to locate or date it, looks initially unpromising [**30, 31, 32**]: however, the nineteenth-century inscriptions written on it give us some indication as to its provenance, since they record two Neapolitan names, suggesting the work was at some point in that region, possibly an early export as were so many Netherlandish panels. The material evidence of the traces of a wooden baton running vertically down the back, clearly a later addition, and its treatment, supports this: this baton is made of poplar, and the coating is of gesso (calcium sulphate), both of which are Italian materials (the north more commonly used chalk, calcium carbonate), indicating these additions were done in Italy; however the panel proper, as with all paintings made in the Netherlands, is made of Baltic oak (for its supply and properties see p. 20).[4] The type of wood used can thus be an important indicator in localizing an object. Baltic oak indicates a northern, usually Netherlandish place of manufacture; walnut is found mostly in France, but was also used for carving in the Netherlands; spruce is found in Germany, while pine was used in much of Spain, although both Spain and

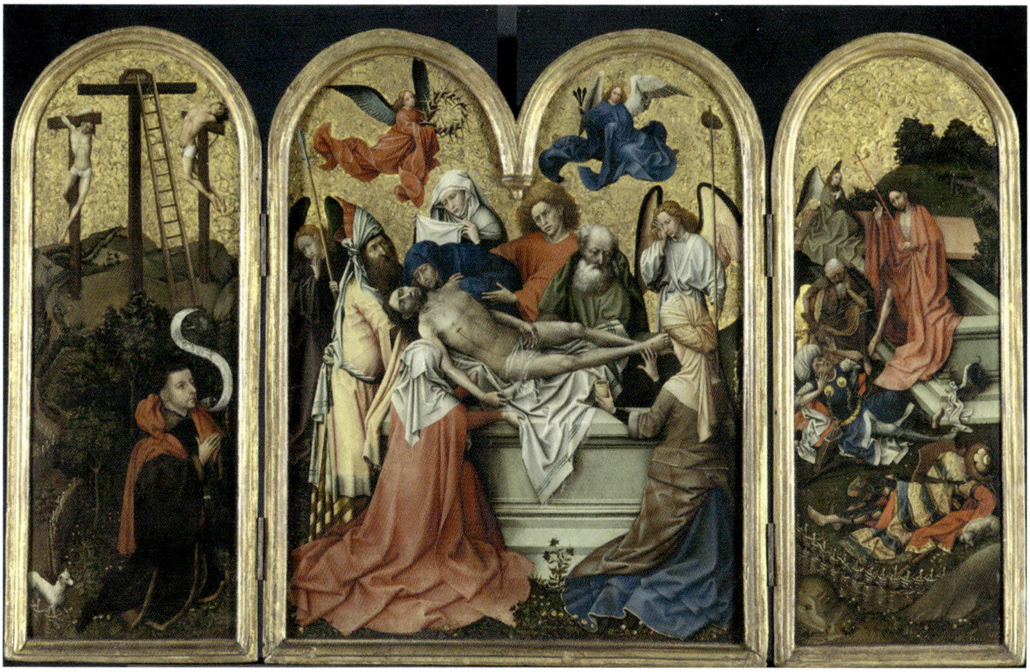

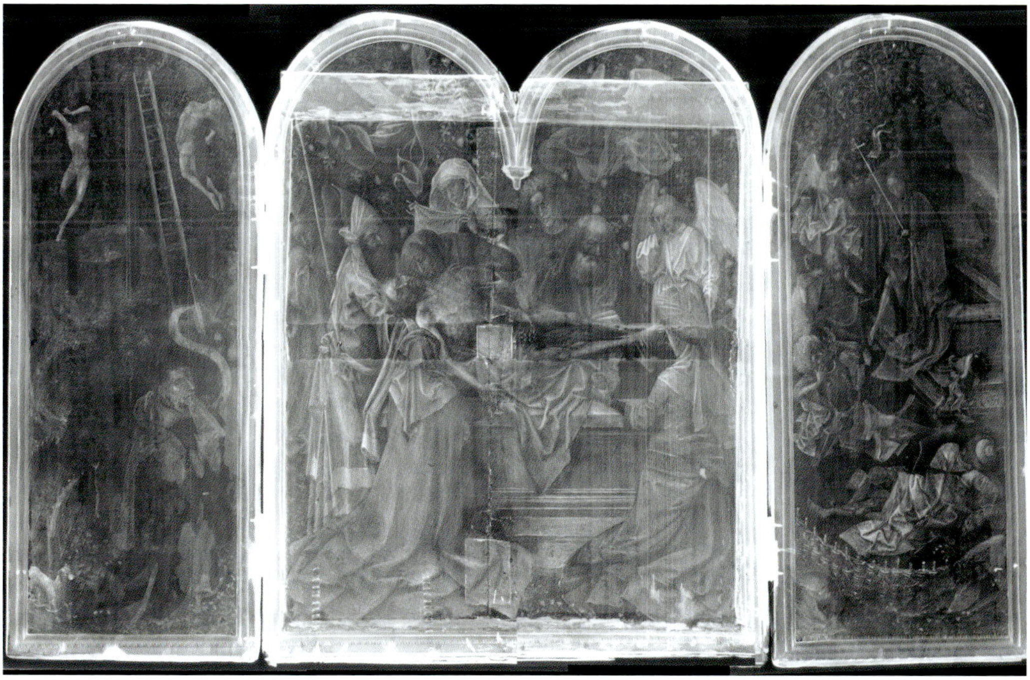

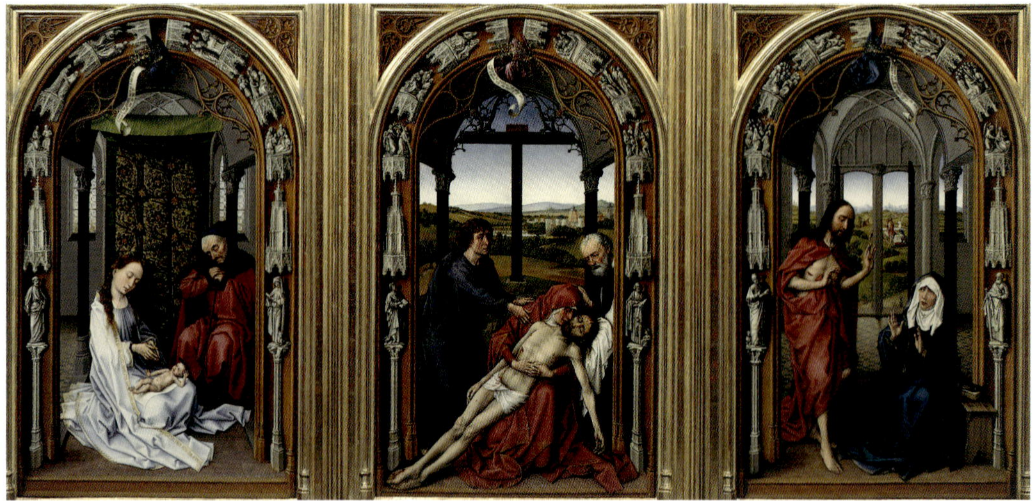

33 Rogier van der Weyden
Triptych of the Virgin (the 'Miraflores Altarpiece'), oil on Baltic oak, *c.*1442–5.
The fixed form of this triptych with three equal parts which did not fold was foreign to the Netherlands and must have been dictated by its Spanish patron. The decision to place the Virgin in red in the centre scene, which provides such a dramatic framing for the body of Christ, was the one element not followed in the copy made for Isabella of Castile [**34**], perhaps because in consequence St John the Evangelist, to whom she had a particular devotion, could not be dressed in his traditional red.

Portugal imported Baltic oak and used it on occasion for panels; in Italy, poplar was used universally for panel paintings.[5]

The huge advantage of Baltic oak for art historians is that its growth rings over a period of hundreds of years have been mapped using a body of reference material of known date to create a master chronology that can provide a sequence by which any piece (if the edge can be examined) may be compared and through statistical analysis dated by dendrochronology.[6] Allowance has to be made firstly for rings removed with the sapwood when the wood was cut into planks, usually radially, which can be anything from 9 to 36 rings for Baltic oak, with a median of 15; secondly for seasoning time, which is generally thought to be around 10–15 years for fifteenth-century paintings; and thirdly, with narrow planks, for the possibility that they have been cut from the centre of the tree, the heartwood (suggesting a misleadingly early date). Dendrochronology cannot then tell us a precise year for the creation of a work, but it can give us an absolutely reliable point before which a work cannot have been painted or carved because the tree from which it was made was still growing. This has been most useful in distinguishing works which, once thought to be contemporary versions made in the same workshop as the original, are now shown to be replicas made at an often much later date, and not even, necessarily, in the same region or country as where the original was produced. This was most dramatically demonstrated for the two almost identical versions of a triptych associated with Rogier van der Weyden, one in Berlin, long thought to be a copy produced in his workshop, and one split between Granada and New York [**33**, **34**], long thought to be the original given to the monastery of Miraflores near Burgos by Juan II of Castile, since it had a provenance to the collections of Isabella of Castile, his daughter. When the wood of these works was tree-ring dated, however, it was revealed not only that the Granada-New York one was in fact the copy, but that it was a copy made long after Rogier's death since the tree was still growing in 1473 (Rogier died in 1464). Moreover, because tree-ring dating can identify if the planks in

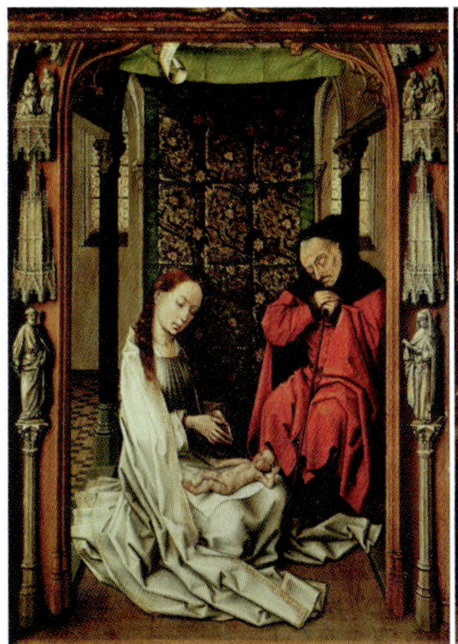
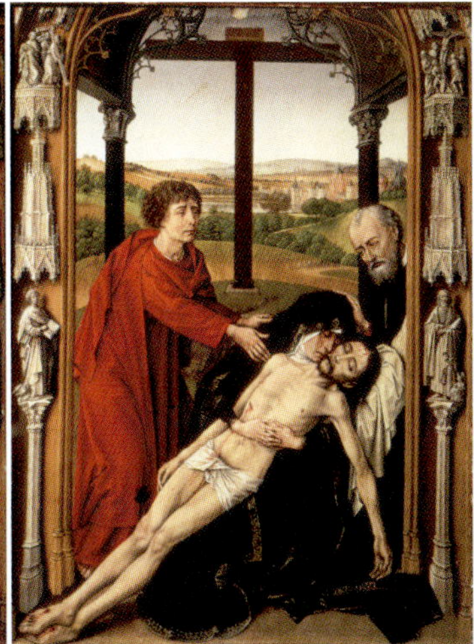
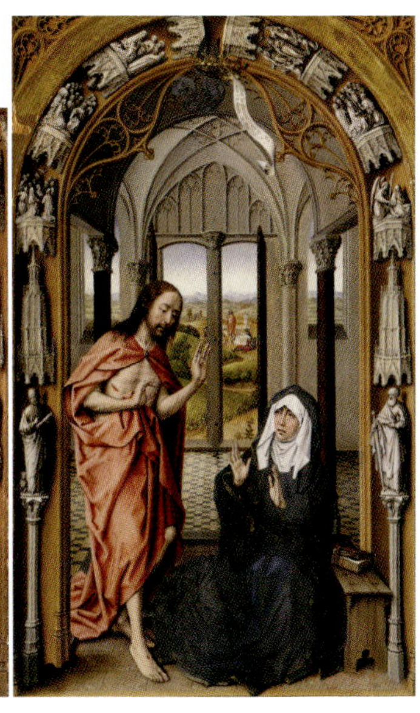

34 Spanish copy after Rogier van der Weyden (Juan de Flandes?)

Reduced copy of **33**, oil on Baltic oak, *c.*1490–1500.

one panel come from the same tree as those in another panel, it can give us fascinating evidence of origins and associations: in this case, it could also be determined that the Granada–New York copy was made in Spain, not the Netherlands (which makes sense), and that it was probably made by Juan de Flandes (*c.*1465–1519), Isabella of Castile's court painter there, since planks from the same tree were used to make another altarpiece painted by that artist for Miraflores around 1500.[7]

With both panel painting and wooden sculpture we should always look for their joins: these are often visible with the naked eye, however well constructed a work is, although for panel paintings in particular an examination of the back or an x-ray can confirm their composition, and reveal how the planks were fixed together [**32**]. It will be the areas along the joins where most restoration is likely to have taken place and so attention should be paid to them for this reason alone. Looking at panel joins in relation to the composition of the work painted on to them is also insightful: the better artists composed, wherever possible, with these points in mind, and avoided placing the faces of the key figures in their narratives over these areas, since they knew this was where the damage would occur over time as the wood expanded and contracted with varying weather conditions; in the Seilern Triptych [**31**], the joint in the centre panel is off-centre, running down between the Virgin and St John but avoiding both their faces.

The construction of panels and their frames can also be an important indicator of a work's original appearance, display, or use. Differences in construction across the same work require explanation: the three large panels of similar dimensions, showing the Trinity, the Virgin, and St Veronica, now in Frankfurt [**35**], which form the centre of the group given to the Master of Flémalle, were long thought to be part of a painted triptych. However, the methods by which each panel was constructed vary radically from one to another (see **36**), and thus demand another explanation—either the panels are from three

35 Master of Flémalle (Robert Campin?)

Virgin and Child, St Veronica, the Trinity (the 'Flemalle panels'), oil on Baltic oak, *c.*1440.

The panel of the Virgin has an unusually broad unpainted edge, indicating that it had a thicker frame than the Veronica and the Trinity, presumably because its reverse was set with sculpted reliefs which required extra support and fixings.

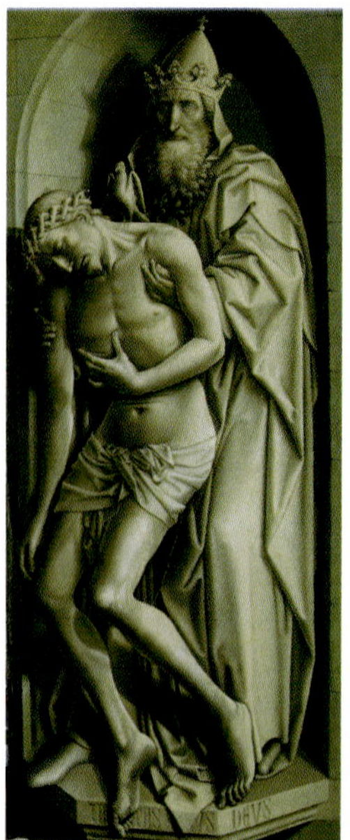

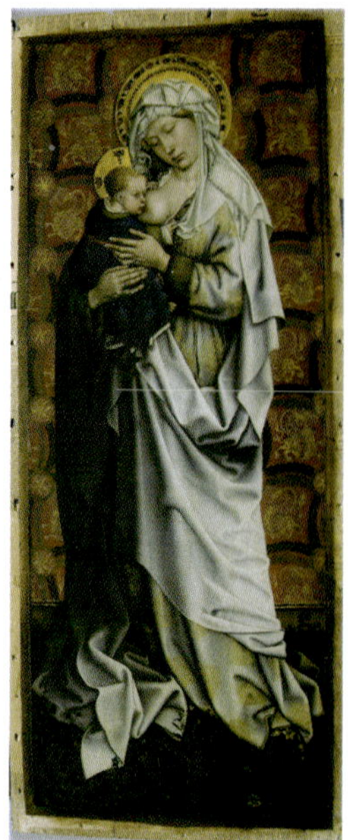

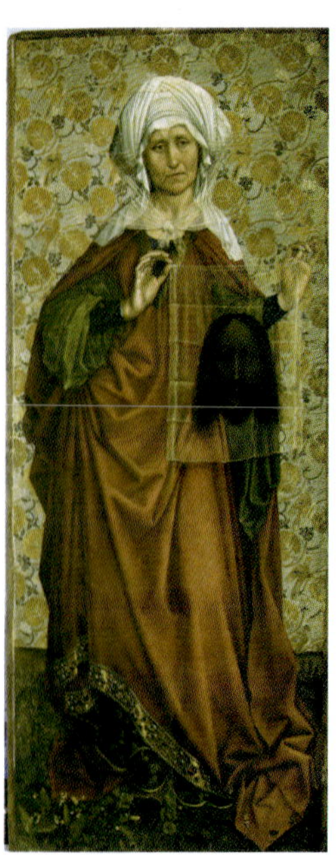

different works (which the visual evidence and that of provenance makes highly unlikely) or they formed a different type of object; the Trinity cannot be the reverse of the St Veronica, as had been assumed, but the Virgin and the St Veronica had to be visible together, given how carefully the visual plays between them have been thought out. The vital clue was in the series of dowel holes running in a horizontal line almost halfway up the Virgin and Child panel. These dowels, which do not hold the plants together, must have had a purpose, suggesting something was fixed along this point: the likely explanation is that the panels originally formed part of a double-winged folding triptych which had a sculpted interior (see **36** and **169** below). The Trinity would then be seen when the altarpiece was closed, the Virgin and Veronica would be seen together as part of the first opening, and on the reverse of the Virgin, as it, in turn, opened up to reveal the interior, would be two smaller

36

Diagram of construction of the three panels in **35** (by Joachim Sander) and hypothetical reconstruction (by Stefan Kemperdick).

This diagram of the construction of the Flémalle panels shows clearly that the Trinity cannot be the reverse of the Veronica, and that the Virgin and Child panel has a series of dowels across the centre which need to be explained. The reconstruction of these works into a double-winged, carved retable, would explain the structural differences and anomalies.

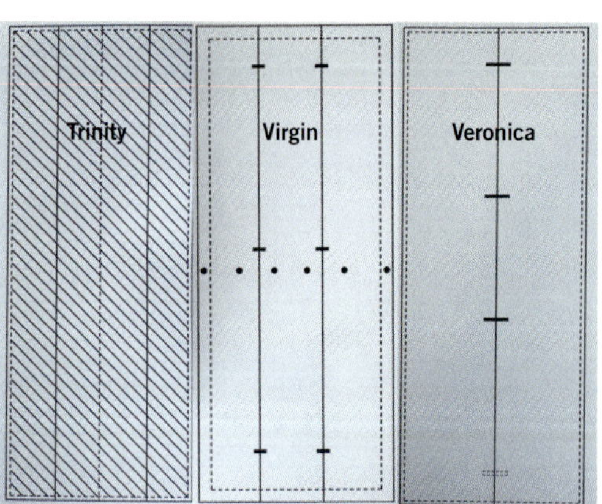

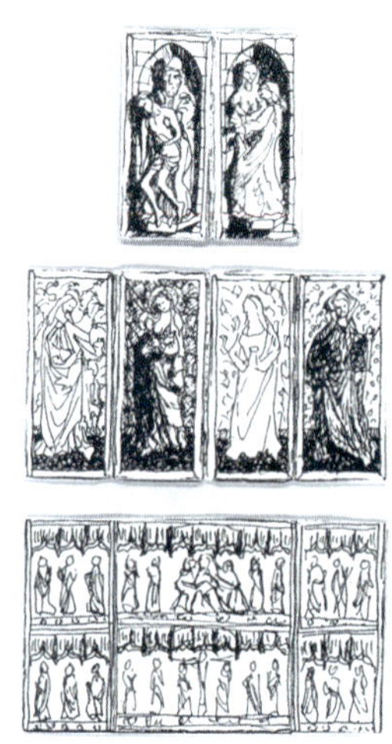

sculpted or painted scenes, the frame of which would have been held in place by the horizontal dowels.[8] This double-winged form was particularly popular in Germany (see Part V), and might suggest that these panels were painted for a location in that region.

Close attention to the construction and condition of works can also give us evidence about possible ways they were kept, handled, and viewed: evidence of wear on parts of an image might suggest it was held frequently, touched, or kissed in a particular manner (the faces and feet of Christ and the Virgin or depictions of relics are particularly likely candidates for such wear, evident in **31**). Original frames can reveal a surprising amount about display and viewing practices: Jan van Eyck's portrait of his wife, Margaret van Eyck [**98**], has a frame with a type of construction that suggests it was never intended to be hung from a chain or other form of suspension, but possibly set on a stand of some sort.[9] The way the frames of diptychs are treated can reveal which was meant to be the primary side when shut, and thus indicate which way they were meant to be opened: Hans Memling's Diptych of Maarten van Nieuwenhove [**208**] has a more fully carved, complex frame on the reverse of the panel with his praying portrait on it, suggesting that this side was the 'top', which would be opened to reveal the other panel, showing the Virgin, below;[10] Jan van Eyck's Annunciation Diptych [**174**] has reverses painted to resemble red marble, but finished to be smooth flat surfaces with no frame at all. This is an unusual form for panels painted on the reverse, chosen perhaps to enhance the illusion that, when closed, the object was a solid slab of stone.

For insights into the various possibilities for how painted works were designed and executed, two investigative methods have provided remarkably fruitful, although the images they produce are rarely straightforward to read or interpret. These methods are infrared reflectography and x-radiography, both of which reveal more than is visible to the naked eye. What an x-radiograph registers is the atomic weight of materials, so that any pigments or parts containing heavy elements, usually metals (iron hinges or nails, lead-based pigments like lead white, lead tin yellow or red lead), will show up very white on the image. They are therefore excellent tools for understanding the construction of a panel, revealing how and where planks are joined and traces of original hinges, which might indicate that a single panel originally formed part of a diptych or triptych, but also for considering the actual paint layers.[11] It is important to compare the x-radiograph to the panel itself, both its back and front faces, since x-rays pass right though the work, creating an image of the whole object simultaneously, so that back and front are superimposed, and what might appear to be on the surface in an x-radiograph may not be so at all. In the x-ray of the Seilern Triptych [**33**], the white band across the top is the added baton on the reverse, which is coated with a lead-rich white pigment or preparation, while the band across the centre which registers as darker than the rest in the x-ray is where the surface has no coating at all on the reverse, as the baton has been removed.

An x-ray will also show something of how paint was applied and manipulated: it can reveal the brushstrokes of a priming layer, and it can indicate how heavily lead white was used to model forms (which can help date a work or distinguish copy from original—painters earlier in our period tended to use lead white relatively sparingly, while by *c.*1500 it is much more heavily applied). In the Seilern Triptych the x-ray reveals how the three areas of red drapery in the central panel (that of the robe worn by the Mary seen from behind, that of the angel in red above, and that of St John) are all modelled using very different distribution and application of lead white pigment (see detail heading this chapter). The reasons why such a variety of paint handling is to be found in this work are open for speculation—it may be that several different hands were involved, but it may also have been a deliberate choice on behalf of one artist to create varying effects, thereby suggesting the differences between the fabrics represented: the angels' robes appear to be shot silk, while that of the Mary seen from behind is clearly a heavy wool.

Most importantly, perhaps, x-rays can reveal changes made at a relatively late stage in the creative process, when something already established in the paint layer has been altered by another layer of paint, revised by the artist or by a later hand. This is evident in the x-ray of the Seilern Triptych, where we can see how the painter has adjusted the area around the heads of Christ and the Virgin to make less fussy conjunctions of form and colour, extending the hair of Christ in the final paint layer to cover much of Joseph of Arimithea's sleeve. This sleeve, as can be seen in the x-ray, is painted in full underneath Christ's hair: artists would normally leave a reserve, that is an unpainted area, for the whole of a figure, and would not paint in parts of a figure which were not to be visible.[12]

To see beneath the paint layers, that is to view the underdrawing on the white prepared surface of the panel before the painting stage began, a different method is needed—using infrared radiation.[13] This does not penetrate all the layers of a painting as x-rays do, but instead the rays reflect off the white surface of the ground, while being absorbed by any carbon-based materials, as were routinely used for drawing, such as black chalk and inks. The contrast between reflecting areas and absorbing areas gives a black and white image; however, the image produced is a composite one of all the upper layers, and as such the visibility of any drawing on the ground of the panel will depend on the nature of these paint layers themselves: black and gold cannot be penetrated at all; the green pigment malachite and the blue pigment azurite absorb all but the longer wavelengths of infrared radiation, requiring equipment sensitive to these longer wavelengths to detect the signal,[14] whilst red lake absorbs little of the infrared radiation, allowing exceedingly good penetration. As a result, the number of layers and their thickness will have an effect on how much is seen, as will the nature of the drawing material used: iron gall ink does not show up at all, while silverpoint can register very faintly, which leaves some works looking as if they have very little underdrawing, like Jan van Eyck's *Self-Portrait* [**106**], when this may not be the case at all, as close examination of the surface under the stereobinocular microscope can reveal.[15]

Interpreting reflectograms, like interpreting x-rays, is not always easy. Which lines are drawings under the surface, and which are painted lines in black on the top surface of the work, can be hard to distinguish. Our expectations of these types of images can be too high: we are tempted to imagine a reflectogram is of a similar validity as a picture of the surface. Moreover, scholars have wanted to see this technique as the way forward in attributional issues, which it has, on the whole, proved not to be. The creative moment, the hand of the master, may not be this one: underdrawing could be a stage in the production process given to assistants who transferred up a model onto the panel for the master, and works documented as by the same painter may have completely different styles of underdrawing. Indeed, underdrawing may vary in style and form even within a single work: thus the exteriors of the Portinari Triptych by Hugo van der Goes [**66**] and the Dombild Altarpiece by Stefan Lochner [**14**] are underdrawn in a different manner to their interiors, less freely and with more detail, which may have several explanations: an assistant may have transferred the drawing up in this area, or the artist may have wanted a more extensive graphic plan for himself or for an assistant to follow in these areas in the paint layers.[16]

Infrared reflectograms can, however, provide dramatic insights into the creative processes of painters, which in turn, like x-rays, can have important implications for how we interpret works of art. The most rewarding example of this is probably the famous *Portrait of Giovanni (?) Arnolfini and his Wife* by Jan van Eyck, for which we have remarkably clear and informative reflectograms [**37, 38**]. These reveal how Jan's underdrawn design had no indication at all of many of the elements which are so arresting in the finished work: absent were the dog, the beads, the chair and the shoes, and possibly the chandelier; these he only developed, and apparently conceived, as he worked the picture up in paint. The reflectogram also shows how Jan altered, once he started painting, many elements of the design that he had established in the underdrawing: the mirror became smaller, the robe of Arnolfini longer, and shifts were made to the placement of hands and feet.[17] This intense development of the composition on the panel itself, with the artist making significant changes to the drawing in the paint layers, and enriching and altering the composition visually and iconographically, is characteristic of other works by Jan van Eyck.[18] It shows that there cannot have been a preconceived meaning established at the start, which every object in the picture helped to expound, which has been one deeply entrenched way of interpreting the works of Jan van Eyck and the Arnolfini painting in particular.[19] It also shows how Jan was developing his image with the visual demands of picture making in mind—in many cases the primary motivation for the inclusion or alteration of objects and the poses of the figures was to balance or improve the way the picture worked visually. So the added shoes provide a vital light area necessary to balance the white of the woman's headdress; the changes in the position of Arnolfini's raised right hand, which turn it from a more open form in the underdrawing to one seen side on in the paint layer, probably relate to the need to minimize its surface area, and thus reduce the tendency for hands to compete for attention with the face, although it also allows for an impressive piece of foreshortening; while the dog, added only in the paint stage, presents both a virtuoso passage of fur painting as well as providing a direct link with the spectator by looking straight out of the picture.

While x-rays and reflectograms can reveal something about the pigments used and the way paint was applied (because of how different pigments react under these types of radiation), to get precise information on the chemical

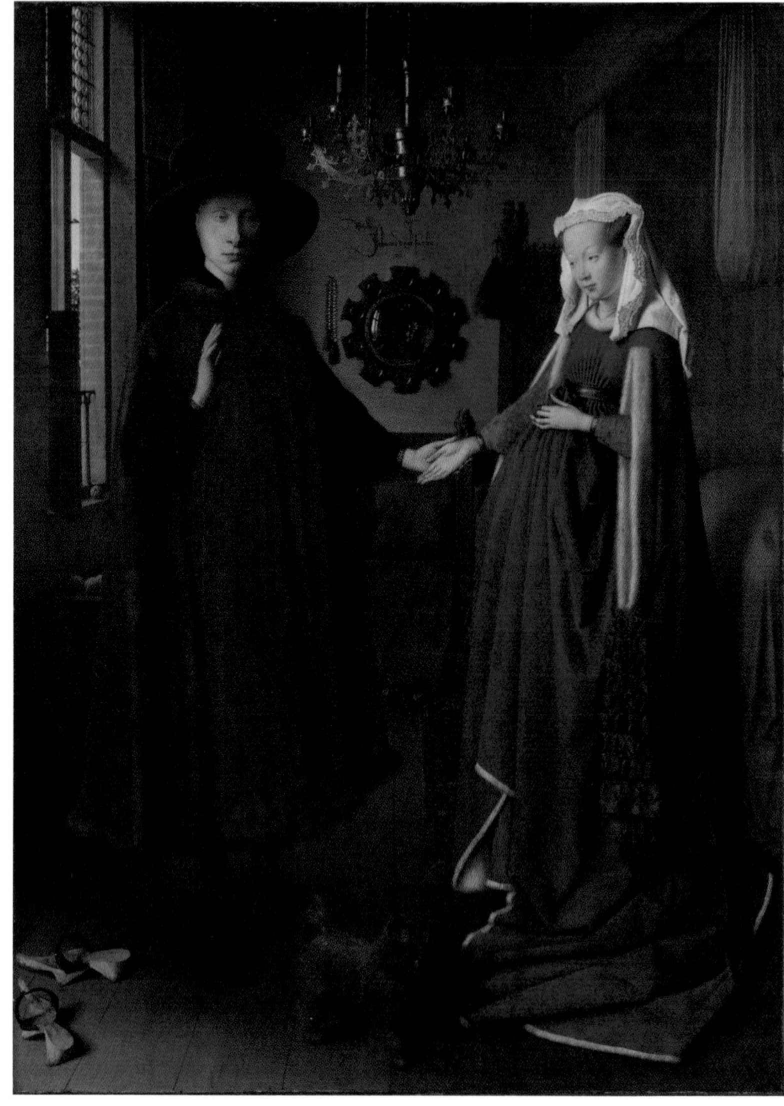

37 Jan van Eyck

Portrait of Giovanni (?) Arnolfini and his Wife, oil on Baltic oak, 1434.

The figures stand in a reception room, not a bedchamber (beds were common features in such spaces). The woman is not pregnant; her large stomach is a fashionable norm (see Eve in **3b**) exaggerated by the heavy train of her dress which she holds up in front of her. Sixteenth-century descriptions record a frame inscribed with verses from Ovid (which, if original, remain difficult to explain) and shutters. The identity of the woman, in particular, remains in doubt: her idealized features suggest van Eyck may never have seen her.

38 Jan van Eyck

Infra-red reflectogram of **37**.

Technical examination has aided in establishing that this room is an imagined rather than actual setting. Jan's underdrawing concentrated on establishing the space and the fall of light and shade. In the underdrawing stage the mirror was larger; the feet, hands, and facial features of Arnolfini were differently placed; and the dog, shoes, beads, oranges, and probably the chandelier, were not included at all.

content of the paint layers and the ground, minute samples, often mounted as cross-sections for examination using microscopy [**141**], remain vital; these can also reveal the order, number and thickness in which the layers of paint were applied, and the way paint was prepared—for example, how coarsely or finely ultramarine was ground. For analysis of organic materials, gas-chromatography-mass-spectrometry (GCMS) can be used on samples, but even with such sophisticated methods, interpretation of the evidence where the nature of the paint medium is concerned is a very highly skilled task.[20] Complex layer structures which used varying organic materials present considerable challenges for analysis, and the subsequent history of the object, including conservation treatments, must also be considered, and further samples may be investigated at a later date with different conclusions being drawn. This is particularly the case in the history of the debate over whether artists at this period painted with a mixed media of oil and egg (now thought to be very

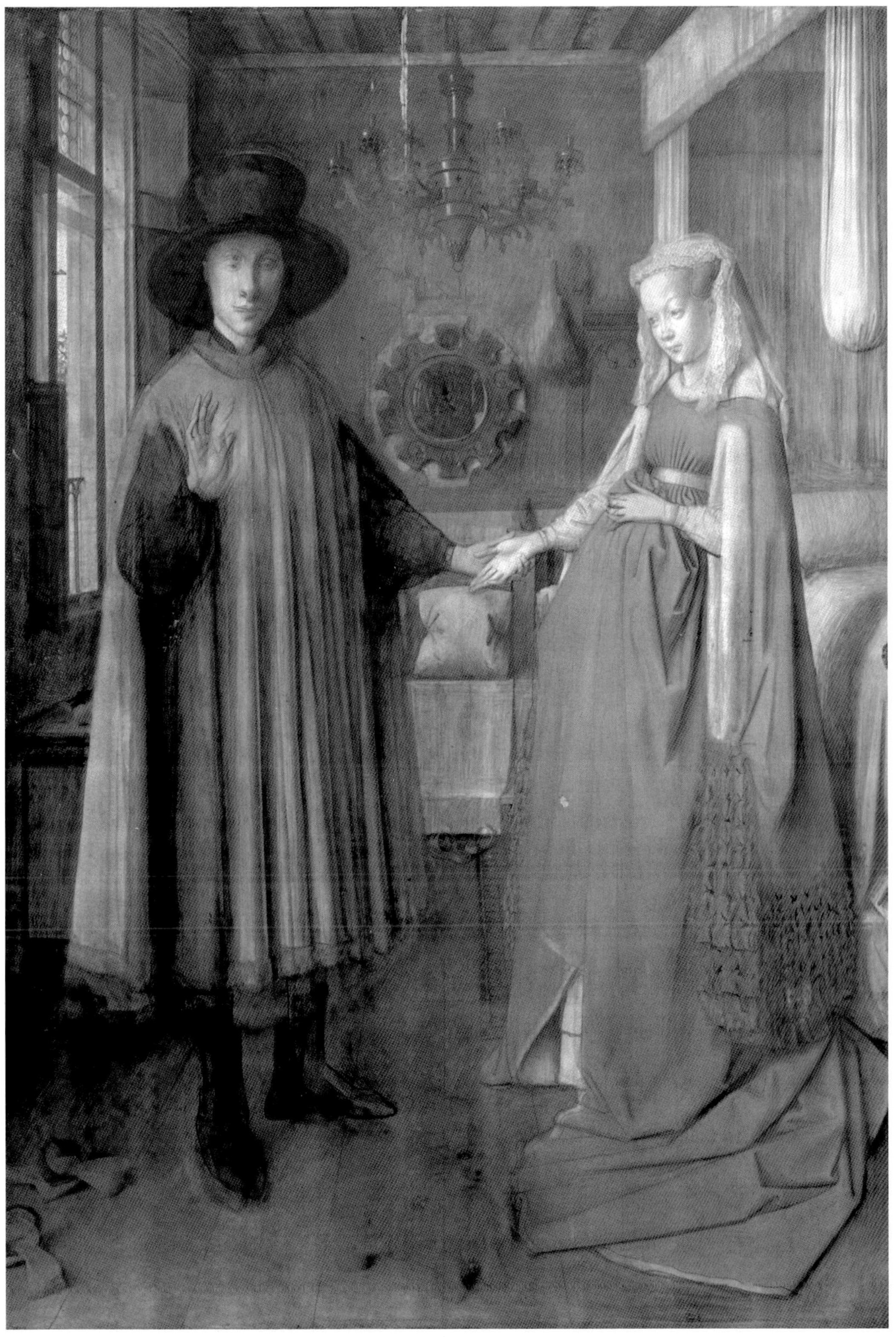

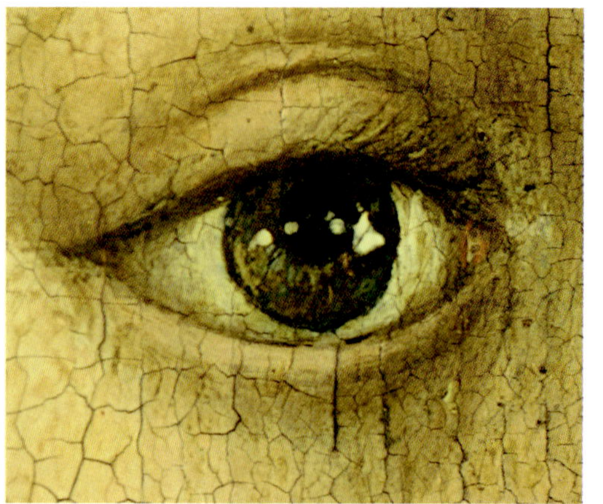

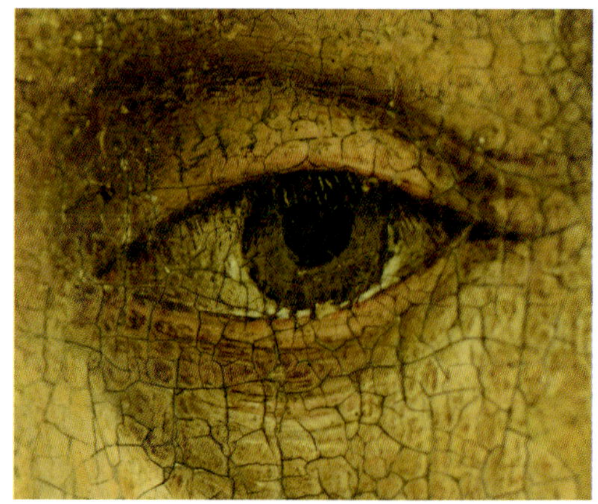

39 Master of Flémalle (Robert Campin?)

Detail of the eyes of the Christ Child and St Veronica from **35**.

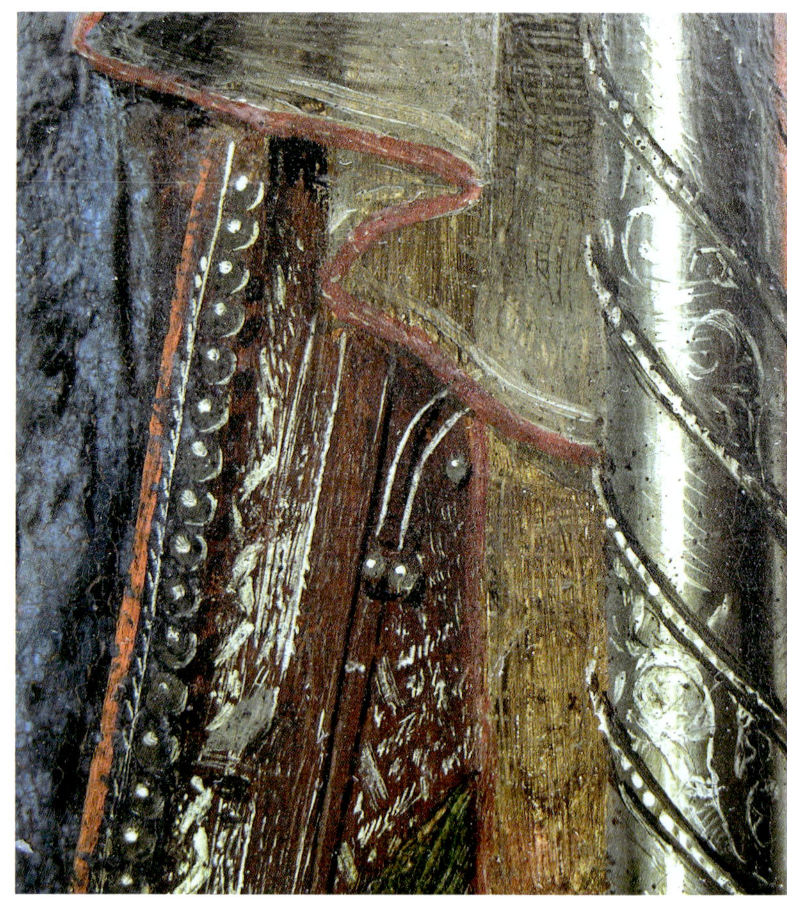

40 Jan van Eyck

Detail of the cope of St Donatian from **18**.

unlikely, although egg tempera was used as an underpaint below oil layers).[21] What GCMS and cross-sections techniques have increasingly revealed, as more and more data are collected, is the remarkably sophisticated understanding painters had of the nature and properties of their medium and the pigments they used. This is explored in Chapter 15 below.

However, it is in the examination of the paint surface itself, with the aid of magnification, and the reproduction of these magnifications in macro images, where perhaps the most enlightening perspective of all might be found: these images allow us to witness just how skilled painters and illuminators were in manipulating paint, and how that manipulation of paint might enrich effects and meaning.[22] This is very clear in macro photographs of eyes of the figures of the Christ Child and Veronica [**39**] from the Flémalle panels discussed above. Those of the Christ Child display an astoundingly precise and detailed handling of paint—the iris has flecks of blue, red, white, and yellow in its brown base, each colour being applied separately and each thus requiring the painter to pick up a different brush; the lights on the eyes were made with six different flecks of white lead, while the eyelashes are individually defined, each being created with two strokes of different colour to mimic the way the light catches them. The contrast with how Veronica's eyes are painted is striking and immensely successful: here the iris is one colour, with no catchlights, lead white used instead to suggest a rheumy effect or imminent tears, while incredibly fine lines of white among the brown eyelashes indicate age and red around the upper and lower lid suggest she has been crying. These are the eyes of an old, sorrowing woman, and the difference in handling is clearly not the result of different hands at work but a deliberate choice, deployed to enhance meaning: the brightness of youth, and a joyous moment in the life of Christ and the Virgin, are contrasted with the dullness of age and the sorrowing caused by Christ's suffering which Veronica witnessed, and which she holds a record of.

By contrast, perhaps surprisingly, when we view van Eyck's paintings at high magnification, what is most apparent is the speed and relative economy with which he achieves his equally astounding effects. He worked in a free, fluid manner, sometimes using the end of the brush to scratch away the paint (particularly evident in **40**) or manipulating the surface with his fingertips (a thumb print has been found in the area below the dog in the Arnolfini portrait), and evoking pearls, for example, with one or two strokes of the brush using lead tin yellow or lead white alone. The Master of Flémalle tended to paint the same type of object with many more individual strokes and by using several pigments, entailing several changes of the brush, a much more painstaking way of working.

The virtuosity revealed in these details is astonishing. Van Eyck's skill, in particular, was recognized by succeeding generations of painters, including Lancelot Blondeel and Jan van Scorel, who in 1550 began to 'wash' the Ghent Altarpiece (where we began), apparently undertaking their task 'with such love that they kissed that skilful work of art in many places'. Displays of extreme prowess were not just the preserve of painters, however: the technical facility of the best sculptors, metalworkers, embroiderers, weavers, and printmakers was equally astounding, if differently expressed, and was also recognized and lauded at the time. Some of their methods are explored in Parts III and IV.

Part II

Markets for Art: Centres, Products, and Patrons

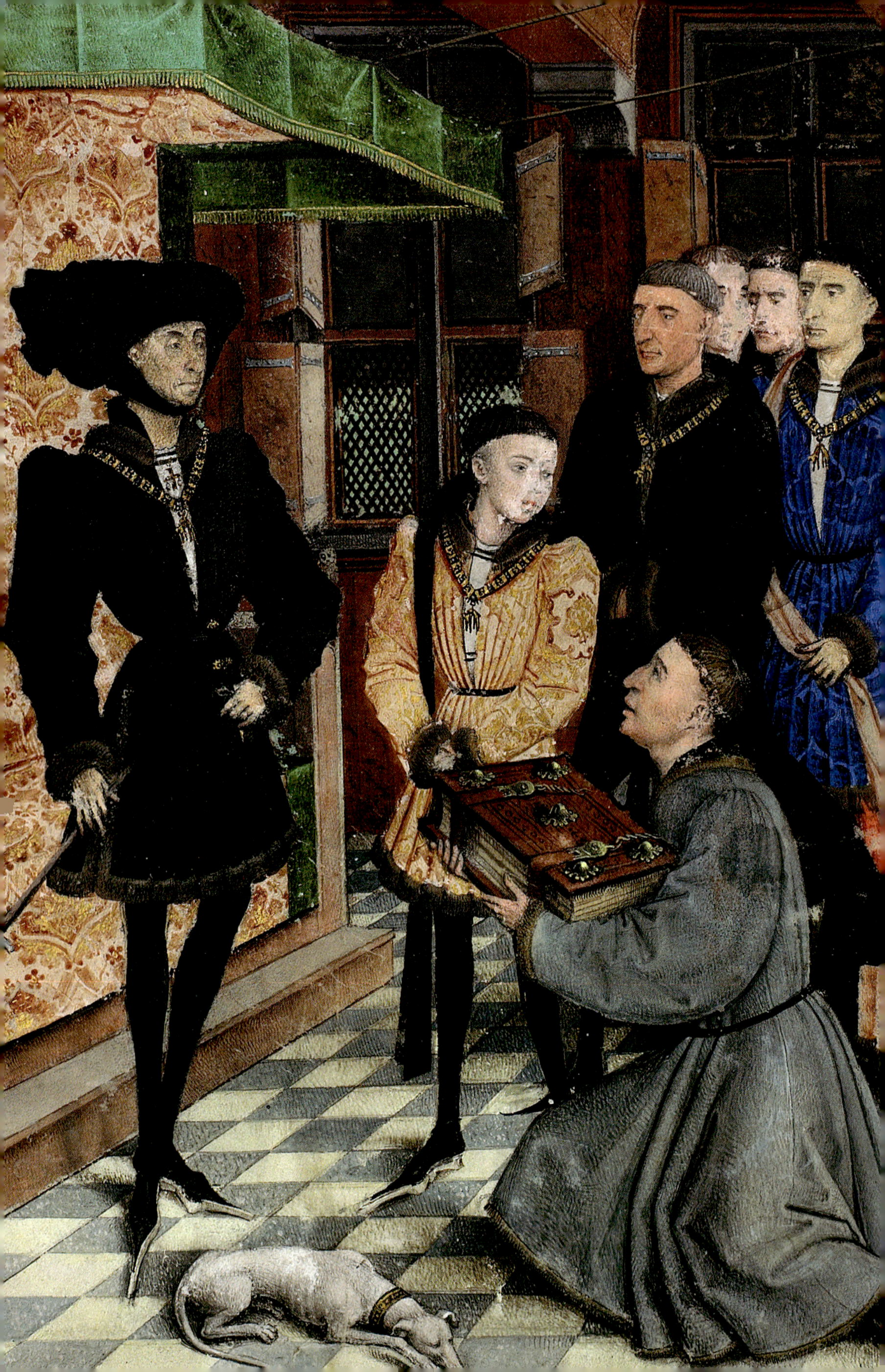

Centres

… the most renowned in all the world by dint of the merchandise that can be found there.
Philip the Good on Bruges, 1450[1]

… there is nothing which one could desire which is not found here in abundance.
Pero Tafur on Antwerp, 1438[2]

6

By the mid-fifteenth century Philip the Good, Duke of Burgundy, was the richest ruler in Europe, outstripping the Kings of France and Aragon, the Dukes of Milan, and the Venetian Republic.[3] His wealth came primarily from the towns in his northern territories, which covered present-day Holland, Belgium, Luxembourg, and large parts of northern France (see Map 2). The foundations for this Burgundian state had been laid by his grandfather Philip the Bold, who, in the late fourteenth century, had by diplomacy, marriage, duplicity and force set in place the acquisition of these extensive and very wealthy regions. The jewel in the crown was Flanders, which had been inherited through Philip the Bold's brilliant marriage to the heiress Margaret of Flanders in 1369. Her territories were densely populated and immensely rich though the trading activities of Bruges, Ypres, and Ghent. The region of Brabant, which Philip the Good acquired in 1430, also boasted the politically and economically significant towns of Antwerp, with its great port and market-places; Leuven, the ancient capital of the duchy, with its recently founded (1425) university; and Brussels, situated on the crossing of several major trade routes, and which was to become the administrative capital of the Burgundian Netherlands.

Benefiting from access to a developed infrastructure of waterways and roads, and the increasingly important sea routes to England, Scotland, the Baltic, Portugal, Spain, and Italy (see Map 1), these towns had, in varying degrees throughout the fourteenth century, moved their specializations away from cloth-making and selling to the production, purveying, and distribution of luxury goods, acting as the market-place for wares from the far points of Europe and beyond, a situation acknowledged both by the partisan Philip and the outsider Tafur in the quotes beginning this chapter. Although the extent to which Bruges' economic prosperity continued into the fifteenth century has been debated by historians (and there were certainly moments of crisis), there is no doubt that at this period it was still the most important of these centres and, indeed, the most prominent commercial city of northern Europe, with the years 1440–75 being exceptionally prosperous by any account: wages were at their highest in real terms for over 400 years, and large numbers of craftsmen were immigrating into the town, attracted by earnings which were as much as two and a half times higher than other cities. Bruges positively encouraged this immigration, by periodically lowering or suspending its

Detail of Philip the Good from 48

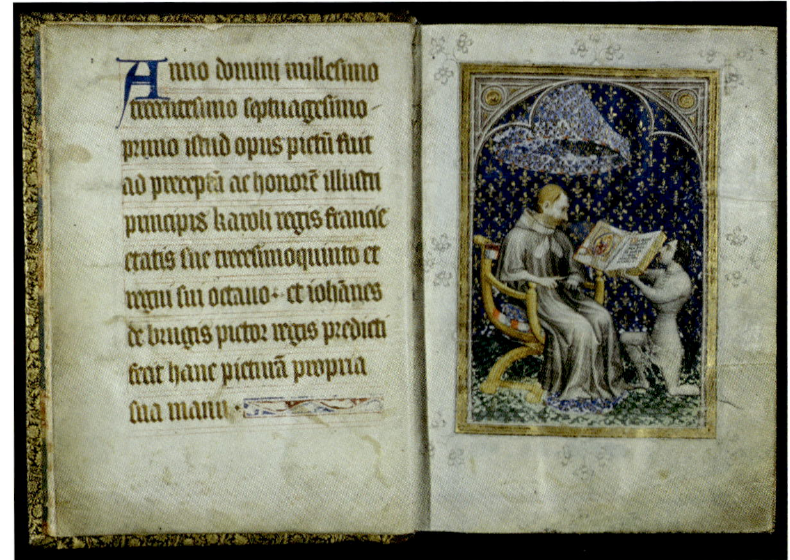

41 Jan Baudolf

Jean de Vaudetar presents his book to King Charles V.

The text, written in gold, records the artist's name and the year of its making: 'Johanes de Brugis, pictor Regis predicti, fecit hanc picturam propria sua manu' (John of Bruges, aforementioned painter of the king, made this image by his own hand). Baudolf also worked for Louis of Anjou, providing the designs for his *Apocalypse* tapestries [**143–145**].

rates for foreigners to become masters in the town, and it has been estimated that at some points around 35 per cent of new registrations in the guilds were of outsiders.[4] Indeed, it is hard to find a famous native painter in Bruges at this period: Jan van Eyck came from Maaseick near Maastricht, Petrus Christus from Baarle in Brabant, Hans Memling from Seligenstadt in Germany, Gerard David (*c.*1460–1523) from Oudewater in Holland, Michel Sittow (*c.*1468–1525/6) from Reval (now Tallinn) in Estonia, William Vrelant (*fl.* 1449–1481) from Utrecht, and Ambrosius Benson (*fl.* 1518–*c.*1550) from Lombardy.

This shift towards the production of luxury goods by these Netherlandish towns had begun in the late fourteenth century, but these centres only became such a strong magnet for artists and consumers following the misfortunes of Paris and the collapse of the demand for luxury goods there in the years around 1420. Prior to this the French capital had been by far the largest city in Europe, with 200,000 inhabitants, and for long the most important place for the acquisition of beautifully crafted objects, many made in the city itself, most notably metalwork (such as the *Goldenes Rössl*, **24** above and **155–9**), manuscripts [**41, 43, 44**], tapestries (such as several sets of the *Apocalypse* series, **143–5** below), embroidery, ivories, and painting [**161–3**], with highly specialized guild regulations, dating back to the 1260s, reflecting the well-established and organized nature of these industries there.

Paris was also, crucially, where the French kings were resident until the 1420s. During the 1360s and 1370s, Charles V, 'wise artist, learned architect' in the words of his biographer Christine de Pisan (*c.*1364–*c.*1430), undertook extensive artistic patronage and acquisition which included large numbers of richly illuminated manuscripts, with frequent depictions of himself in them, often emphasizing his learning, such as the full-page frontispiece heading a Bible Historiale painted by the 'pictor regis' Jan Baudolf (*fl.* 1368–81) [**41**].[5] He also commissioned tombs for himself and his ancestors as soon as he came to the throne [**17**], and began ambitious building projects, with all the

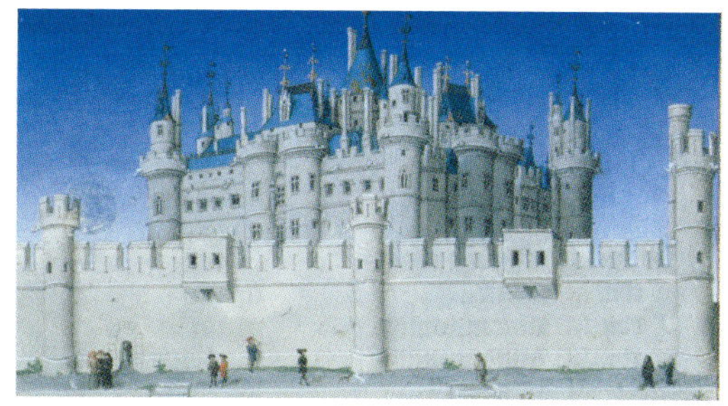

42 The October Master (Barthélemy d'Eyck?)

Detail of the October miniature from the calendar of the *Très Riches Heures*, showing the medieval Louvre palace, parchment, *c.*1440.

Charles V's remodelling of the Louvre entailed an ambitious programme of sculptural decoration, including the famous 'grande vis', a large stairwell 20 m high and 5 m wide with 83 steps set with 10 life-size stone figures of the king, the queen, their male children (the future Charles VI and Louis of Orleans), the Dukes of Berry, Burgundy, and Anjou, and at the top figures of the Virgin and St John. Only its foundations remain today.

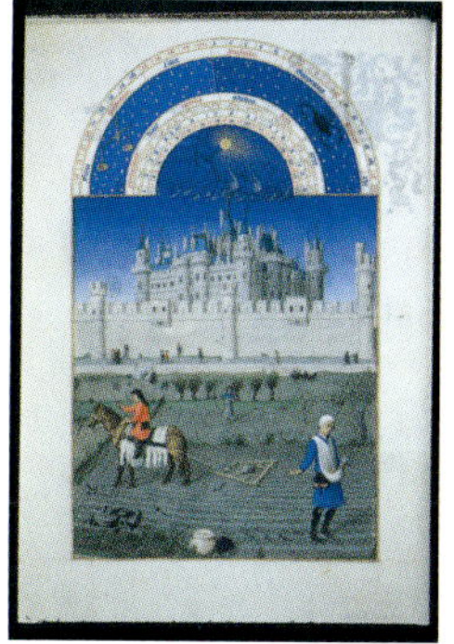

concurrent decorative work they entailed. At Vincennes he built a palace with a vast courtyard surrounded by nine towers and enclosing a Sainte-Chapelle; at the Louvre he remodelled and expanded Philip Augustus's building, adding four stories of apartments on the north and west flanks and new towers [**42**]. One of these housed his large library complete with grills on the windows to 'keep out birds and other flying creatures', and in another—the 'Grosse tour'—he placed dynastic portraits in the form of full length statues against the walls of the spiralling staircase that connected the apartments. According to Christine de Pisan, these projects were a social duty, akin to giving alms.[6]

Following Charles V's death in 1380, his son Charles VI continued his acquisition and commissioning policies, accumulating the vast collections which, on his death in 1421, were to be inherited in large part by the English duke, John of Bedford (1389–1435). Charles also spent huge sums on jewels and elaborate clothes, decorated with his devices such as the winged stag, the tiger (seen next to him in the *Goldenes Rössl*) and the broom cod plant. This was a different sort of spending on splendour to that of his father, which the epitaphs on their tombs [**17**] make clear reference to: there Charles V was called 'sage et eloquent', while his son was 'large et debonnare'. Charles VI's queen, Isabeau of Bavaria, shared his tastes in rich attire, and was an important patron of manuscripts, tapestries, and metalwork, especially during the periodic bouts of madness the king suffered from, when she took charge of the royal finances.[7] Isabeau spent large sums of money on gifts for her children and family, notably metalwork: most famously, as we have seen, the *Goldenes Rössl* [**24**]—a work which epitomizes the high level of technical skill and invention one could find in Paris around 1400—was ordered by her as a present for the king for New Year 1405. In **43** she is shown fabulously dressed in a room hung with heraldic tapestries on which the arms of herself and her husband are displayed, receiving a book from Christine de Pisan, who kneels at her feet, a gift-giving moment which took place at New Year 1414. The relative social positions of all the women in the room are made clear by the levels of expense in the fabrics of their dresses and the elaborateness of their headresses.[8]

As well as the king and queen, in the late fourteenth century the princes of the blood (Berry, Burgundy, Anjou, and Orléans), all avid consumers of luxury goods (as their extensive inventories attest), used Paris as their principal residence, and all embellished their *hôtels* here: it was from Paris that Philip the Bold ran his territories in the late fourteenth century, not from Dijon or Lille. Paris was also where the great ecclesiastics of France, the arch-

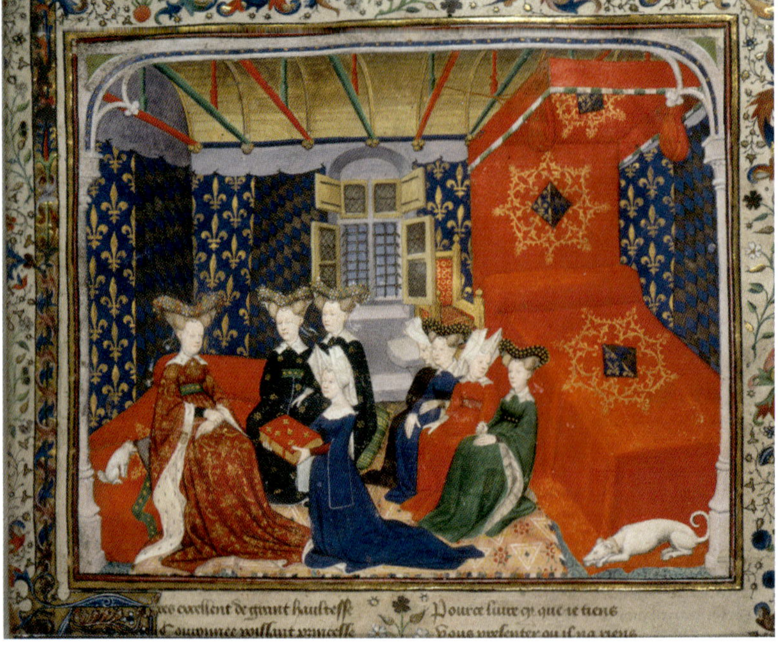

43 Cité des Dames Master
Christine de Pisan presents her book to Isabeau of Bavaria, miniature heading Christine de Pisan's *Œuvres*, parchment, 1414.

bishops of Rheims, Sens, and Rouen as well as a host of lesser bishops and many wealthy abbots such as that of Cluny, had their residences. All this, along with the most prominent university in Europe, ensured high levels of demand for visual culture, with the making of manuscripts and their illumination possibly the most widely recognized and sizeable of these trades, as the large numbers of *libraires*—bookmen who organized the production of manuscripts—recorded there attest.[9]

Representative of the very discerning and wealthy patronage available to artists in Paris is the Book of Hours commissioned by Jean II le Meingre, called Boucicaut (1365–1421).[10] Boucicaut held the post of Marshal, one of the great offices of the French crown, and was also governor of Genoa following the capture of that city by Charles VI in 1396. The manuscript he commissioned, completed around 1408, is famous for its extensive landscapes and complex and innovative architectural settings; they were to be widely reused by this artist's workshop and by later Parisian illuminators. Such elaborate vistas and settings were made possible, and perhaps encouraged, by the very ambitious aims of the patron in this book: instead of having miniatures integrated with the text, the standard form for even the more elaborate Parisian books of hours at this period, this manuscript had, in its original programme, forty-two completely full-page miniatures, set independent of, and facing, the text [**44**]. These include twenty-seven suffrages (prayers) to saints that the Marshal had particular devotion to, set at the beginning instead of at the end of the book (as was usual) and organized, again exceptionally, not according to their rank in the litany but with reference to his personal devotions and interests. The book also has portraits of Boucicaut and his wife in prayer, as well as a separate portrait of the Marshal kneeling in front of Saint Catherine [**44**], a Saint to whom he had a

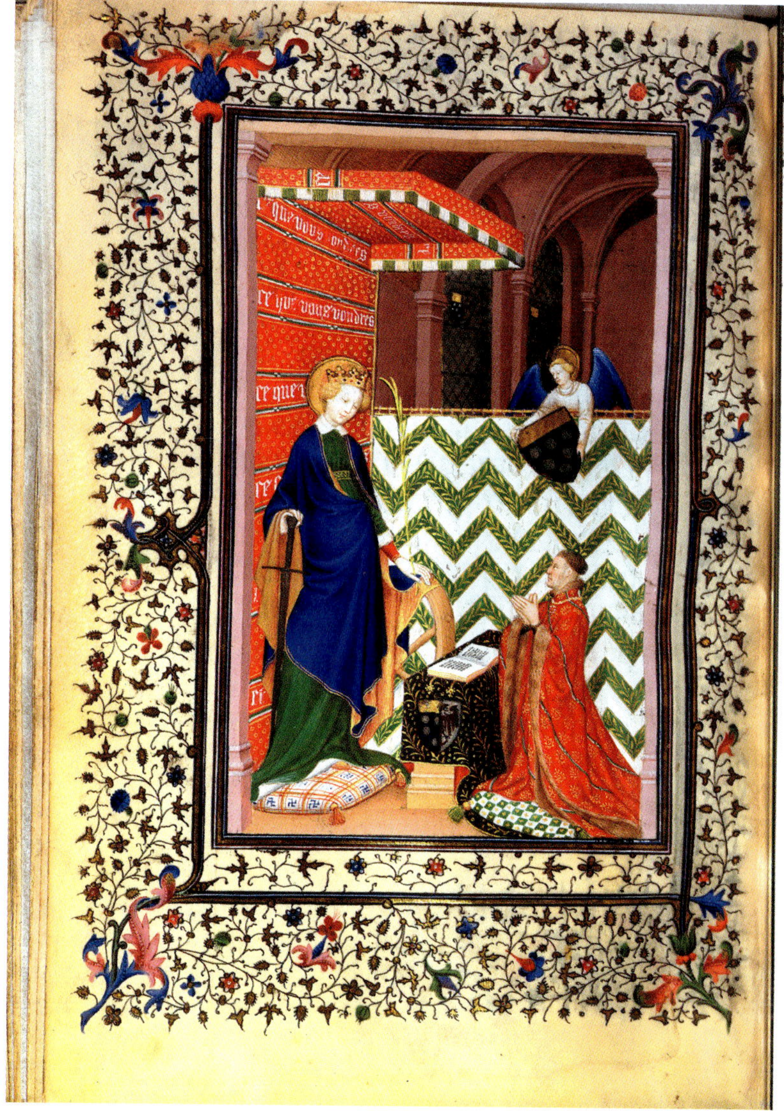

44 Boucicault Master
Marshal Jean II le Meingre de Boucicault praying before St Catherine, miniature from the Boucicault Hours, parchment, *c.*1401–8.

Throughout this manuscript the spaces the holy figures are set in, and the figures themselves, are marked out as Boucicault's, whether he is present in the scene or not. Cloths of honour, hangings, and clothes are depicted as woven with his motto and devices and made in his personal colours of green, white, and red. The coats of arms held by the angel and on the prie-dieu are those of a later owner

special devotion, having visited her tomb on Mount Sinai. The heraldic displays in this book are extraordinary, and permeate every part of its imagery: while they were usually confined to the borders of manuscripts (see **48**), here they are brought into the centre of almost every scene, and his personal colours of green, red, and white dictate the colour scheme. This extensive display of heraldry is more than a mark of ownership or a statement of status: it is a method of association, in this case between the religious figures and Boucicault, emphasized again and again as the devices, colours, and arms run through image after image as the pages are turned. This is about *his* devotion, to these saints and these stories, and about how these saints can be, literally, marshalled to his cause: as a seasoned campaigner in Prussia, Spain, and the Holy Land, against the infidel Lithuanians, Moors, and Ottomans, for Boucicault this was a very real need.

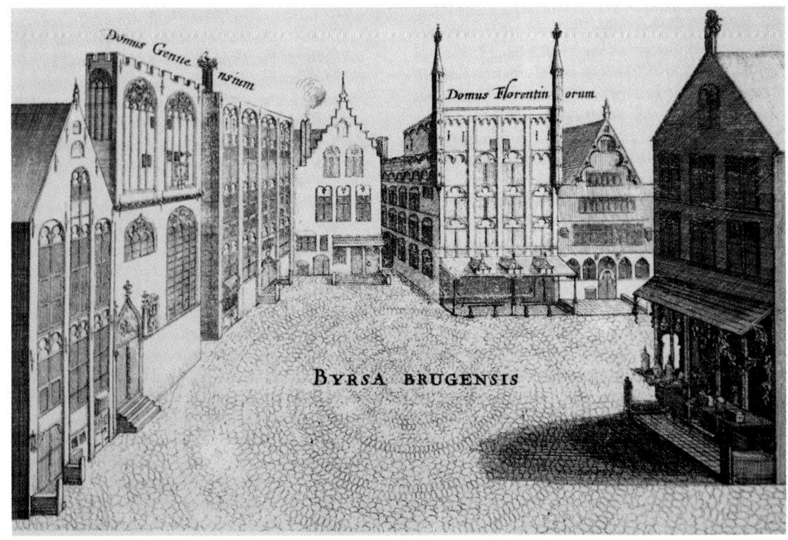

49 Antonius Sanderus
The Beursplein, Bruges, from *Flandria Illustrata*, hand-coloured engraving, 1641.
This shows the area in Bruges where the Italian nations had their lodges: visible here are, from left to right starting with the second building on the left, the Genoese lodge (inscribed 'Domus Genuensium'), the Ter Bourse inn, the Venetian lodge (facing us), and the Florentine lodge (inscribed 'Domus Florentinorum'). The house at the far right with wares displayed outside was owned by the painter Ambrosius Benson in the sixteenth century.

50 Marcus Gheeraerdts
Panoramic plan of Bruges.
This map shows the two central squares of Bruges: the Markt, the commercial centre, with the Belfry (1) and the Waterhouse (2) where boats unloaded undercover, and the Burg, the administrative centre, with the town hall (3) and St Donatian's opposite it (4) where van Eyck's painting [**18**] was displayed; works of art were initially sold in the Franciscan monastery (5), which boats could reach via the Waterhouse with the canal network; the Ter Bourse inn, with its cluster of Italian lodges (6), was close to the Poortersloge (7) and the city crane (8), one of the first major unloading points for boats. The Prisenhof, the ducal palace (9), is to the north.

Both official court artists and those without formal ties to the court saw the benefit of being near the seat of power and in centres which had such a wealthy population: it is unsurprising that Rogier van der Weyden located his workshop in Brussels on the Cantersteen, not far from the Coudenburg, as did the court illuminator Dreux Jehan, his neighbour, although Jehan spent a period in between court appointments in Bruges from 1457 to 1461. Gerard Loyet, Charles the Bold's goldsmith, settled in Bruges immediately on his appointment to the post (and owned two houses, one in the St Nikolas quarter and one in St Jacobstraat, not far from the Prisenhof); the illuminator Willem Vrelant settled in Bruges from Utrecht in 1454, where he picked up many court commissions, and Jan van Eyck moved from Lille to Bruges in 1431.

In Bruges, an extra clientele to supplement the income from a court appointment was also assured in the form of the large population of foreign merchants and bankers. In the fifteenth century Bruges was probably the most cosmopolitan town in the whole of Western Europe, having representatives of over thirty different nations within its walls: for Tafur it was 'the meeting place of all the world'. These communities included the influential Hanseatic League, who, having boycotted the city for some years, returned in 1392; the Genoese had moved their base there from England in 1397 and, with the Venetian, Florentine, and Lucchese merchants, constituted the largest of any Italian colony abroad. The Spanish, Portuguese and English communities were also important presences. All of these nations had lodges where they met and did business within a small area of Bruges, clustered on or near the Vlamingstraat, which was the main axis up from the Markt, the large market square with its belfry and extraordinary 'Waterhouse' for unloading boats undercover, and close to the Poortersloge, and the Ter Bourse inn, which had become an important place for money exchange [**49, 50**]. The foreign nations had chapels in various churches in the town (the Catalans in the Carmine, the Portuguese in the Jacobins, the Castillians and the Florentines initially in the Friars

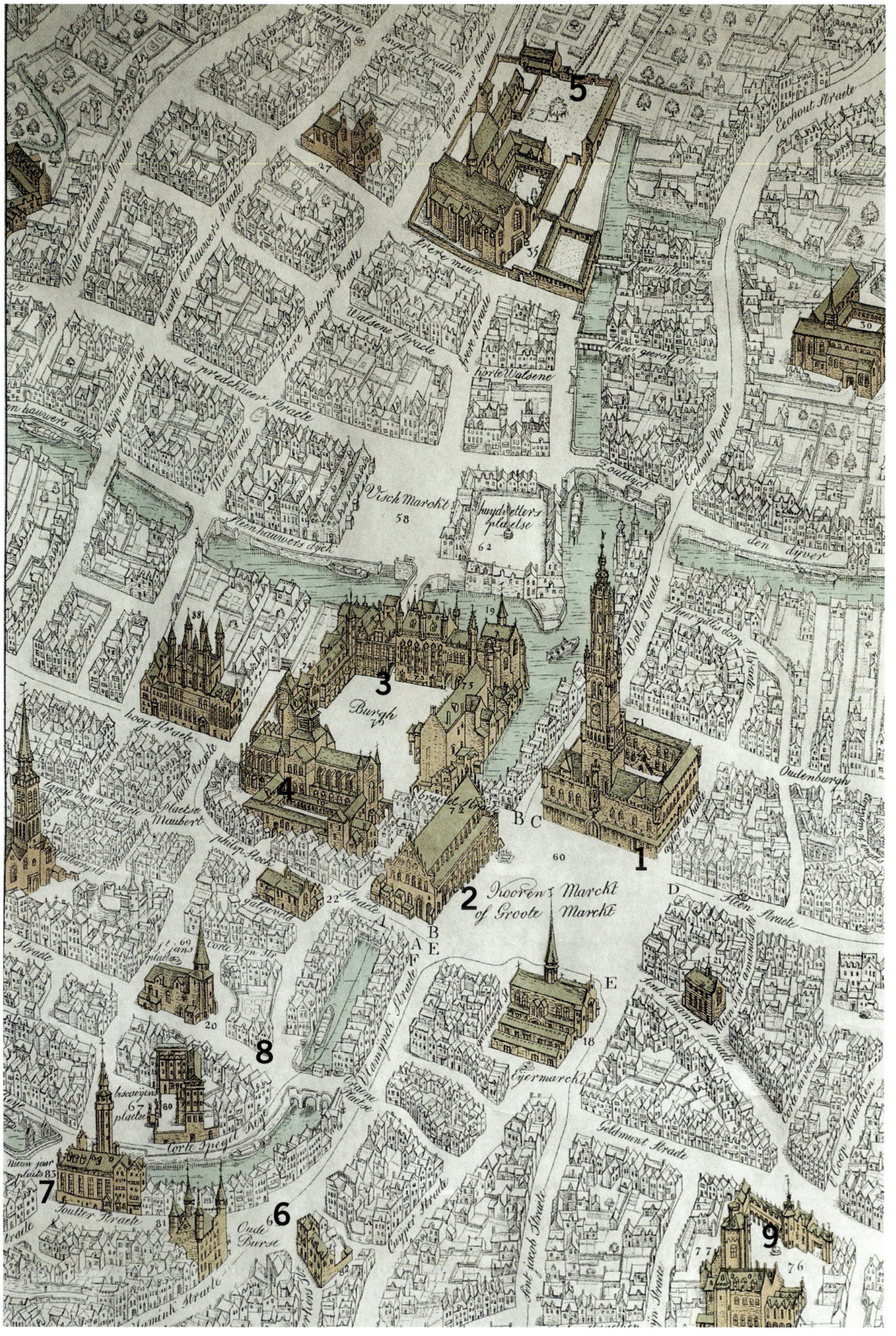

Minor, the Florentines moving in 1460 to the new observant Franciscans), for which they commissioned works of art alongside works to send back to their home towns. They also acted as agents for their countrymen who wanted to acquire the best in visual culture Europe could offer, buying at the fairs in Bruges and Antwerp or organizing the commissioning of bespoke objects from individual artists or entrepreneurs (see Chapter 8).

This market, the wider world beyond that of the residents of the city itself, was perhaps the most important of all, and it is certainly one of the distinguishing features of towns like Bruges, Antwerp, and Brussels: it was in these centres that the Kings and Queens of Castile, Aragon, and Portugal, the royalty of Hungary and Poland, England and Scotland, the Medici, Sforza, Este, and Gonzaga in Italy, and other wealthy groups or individuals from Lübeck and Västerås to Lisbon and Valencia, bought tapestries, manuscripts, metalwork, carved wooden retables, and paintings on cloth and panel. But these Netherlandish centres did not just cater to the top end of the export market: the shipping of works abroad for a wider spectrum of consumers was sometimes done in astonishing quantities. Between 1429 and 1481 alone Antwerp sent around 2,500 cloth paintings to England, a figure which probably reflects the dominance of the Antwerp markets rather than the role this town played in their production. Painting on cloth seems to have been a Bruges speciality, given that around 40 per cent of the painters registered in that town were *cleederschrivers*, cloth painters.[35] By the mid-sixteenth century, small wooden statues of the infant Christ, a Mechelen speciality, were being exported by the tonne from Antwerp to Spain (they would have been of a similar type to **177**, below).[36]

Bruges and Antwerp also had both guilds and guild regulations which acknowledged the demands of working for the export market: in Bruges a clause in the carpenters' and sculptors' guild by-laws allowed craftsmen to work at night when 'a sale or a contract has been made with a merchant (whose) ship is there ready to sail', and by the sixteenth century in Antwerp there was a guild of St Anne which specialized in the packing of items for export using large chests.[37] More importantly, these towns were host to the largest fairs for luxury goods and art works in Europe. They were active as such from the early years of the fifteenth century, although our evidence for their specialization in luxury goods and images escalates after around 1460. One of the earliest documents about the selling of works of art in Antwerp relates to a certain 'artist and master' who stopped in Delft several years before 1411 on his way to Antwerp to market his wares, which included a carved Pietà.[38] He was going there because the fairs were 'free' markets, where foreign merchants and local craftsmen could buy and sell unrestricted by the guild regulations which controlled such activity at other times of the year: normally, outside of fair times you could not trade your works in Antwerp or Bruges unless you were registered as a member of the guild there.

In Bruges, the fair was held once a year, in May, and in Antwerp twice a year, the Pentecost fair or *Sinxemarkt* beginning on the second Sunday before Pentecost and the St Bavo's fair or *Bamismarkt* starting on the second Sunday after Assumption, 15 August. These tended to run for at least six weeks although their duration gradually increased over the fifteenth century. Pero Tafur thought the Bruges fair was 'one of the greatest markets of the world', but in describing the markets of Antwerp, he was lost for words: 'As a market Antwerp is quite unmatched. Here are riches and the best entertainment, and the order which is preserved in matters of traffic is quite remarkable . . . I do not know how to describe so great a fair as this. I have seen other fairs, at Geneva in Savoy, at Frankfurt in Germany, and at Medina in Castile, but all these together are not to be compared to Antwerp.' Tafur was obviously impressed with the market's range and management, especially the specialist emporia in the town: 'Pictures [*pintura*] of all kinds are sold in the monastery of St Francis; in the church of St John they sell the cloths of Arras [*panos de Ras*—tapestries]; in a Dominican monastery all kinds of goldsmiths' work, and thus the various articles are distributed among the monasteries and churches, and the rest is sold in the streets', and he concluded that 'there is nothing which one could desire which is not found here in abundance'.[39] These emporia, known as *Panden*, set up in different venues, must have made purchasing at the fairs much more productive and easier for an outsider, since all the type of object you were looking for was available in a particular place. As well as gold and silver work available at the Dominican convent, the surviving documentation shows that paintings and sculptures were also displayed there, at stalls rented out to the painters' guilds of St Luke of Antwerp and Brussels. The convent records reveal that exhibitors came from towns throughout Brabant, Flanders, and the northern Netherlands, with Brussels painters outnumbering the locals of Antwerp. The activity of this particular *Pand* was growing so fast that it was enlarged in 1460 and again in 1479 when the Brussels painters pressurized the authorities for more space. This demand for exhibition space instigated the construction in the 1460s of a completely new, specialist market, a large galleried building enclosing a courtyard, run by the cathedral church of Our Lady and on a site just south of it. This became known as Our Lady's *Pand* and from 1484 all art sales had to be conducted there during the fairs.[40]

The markets certainly acted as points where goods could be brought on spec from early in the fifteenth century, including most notably small panels, manuscripts, books and prints, sculpture but also larger flexible items like cloth paintings and tapestries, both of which could be rolled up and transported with some ease (see below). However, for objects like large carved wooden retables, the craftsman or dealer probably brought one or two examples to the fair for display purposes, allowing the client to see the type of object you could procure, and then a deal was struck to supply something like it with whatever particular specifications were required. The advantages of these centres with their highly developed markets for purchasing luxury goods were clear: they offered ease of use, sheer concentration of ready-made works for immediate sale, opportunities to order speedily produced, high quality customized objects, the infrastructure to pack and dispatch these goods, and they were situated at the convergence of major land and sea trade routes (Map 1). All this helped ensure the distribution of Netherlandish specialities far and wide.

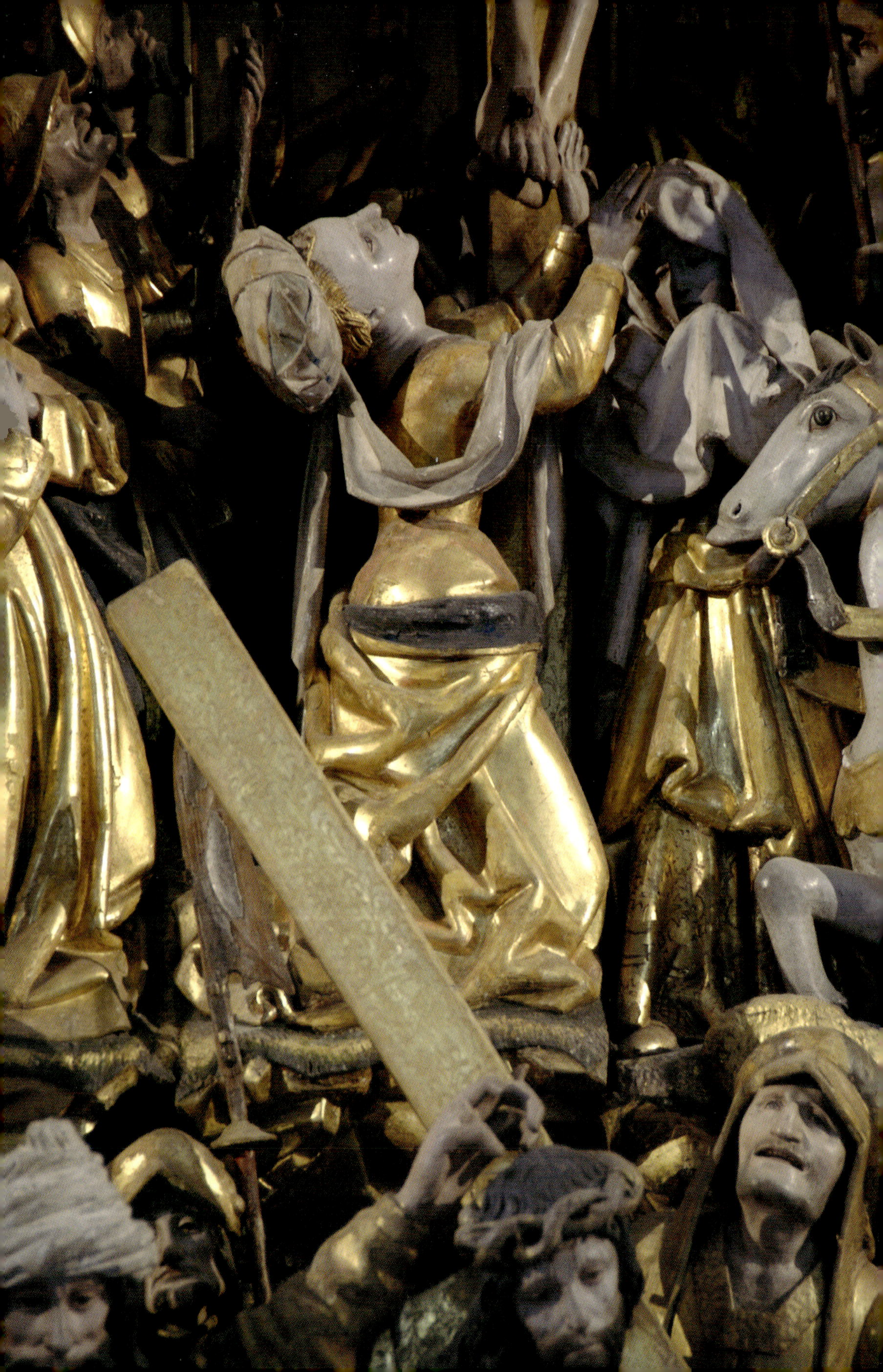

Products

In this country three things are excellent: the many fine and beautiful linens in Holland; the beautiful figured tapestries of Brabant; the third is the music, which one could say is perfect.

The Venetian ambassador Vincenzo Quirini in *Relazione di Borgogna* (1506)[1]

In this art the Flemings and the French have succeeded better than the other nations.

Giorgio Vasari on the art of stained glass (1568)[2]

7

We are becoming more accustomed to the idea of how popular Netherlandish paintings were in the fifteenth century, with recent exhibitions and studies highlighting their impact in Florence, Venice, and the Mediterranean, but a much wider range of the Burgundian Netherlands' products and specialized skills were in demand across Europe, and many of these were more highly prized and certainly more costly than paintings. Indeed, apart from the best steel armour (in which Milan was supreme), silk textiles, marquetry work, and the new invention of glazed terracotta by the della Robbias in Florence, there was almost no form of moveable visual culture or artistic medium in which the Netherlands did not lead the way, with specialist expertise and techniques of production at such a high level that no one else could compete with them in quality or in speed of execution. Part of their ability to achieve this position was down to their role as centres where raw materials were brought to trade for manufactured goods. This meant that glass, brass, tin, copper, zinc, silver, gold, jewels, cloth, silk, dyes, wool, parchment, paper, and pigments—all the materials needed for making luxury objects and images—could be had on their doorstep, in large quantities, and of high quality; indeed, in northern Europe it would seem that Antwerp and Bruges had the finest and most abundant supply of particularly precious mineral and organic pigments like ultramarine (which came only from Afghanistan) and the red lake kermes (which shipped from Genoa and other Italian ports), which were certainly not on sale universally. Dürer took the opportunity of being in the Netherlands in 1521 to acquire his ultramarine at Antwerp:[3] it was not available easily or at all in many regions of Germany, as pharmacy price lists from that area demonstrate (see pp. 198–200 below for more on this aspect of supply and production).

Tapestries

Perhaps the most sought after and distinctive of visual artefacts manufactured in the Netherlands were tapestries. They were valuable and magnificent enough, and perhaps also representative enough of 'Burgundian' production, to be deemed suitable diplomatic gifts, several being given by Philip the Good to participants in the peace treaty signed at Arras in 1435, and others being sent to Popes Martin V and Eugene IV by Philip in 1423 and 1440.[4] They could be extraordinarily large, as **51** vividly demonstrates.

Although there were sporadic attempts to set up tapestry workshops in Italy (notably in Ferrara, Mantua, Siena, Rome, and Venice), this was an

Detail of 55

51 Librado Romero, photographer

A tapestry being carried up the main staircase of the Metropolitan Museum of Art in 2002.

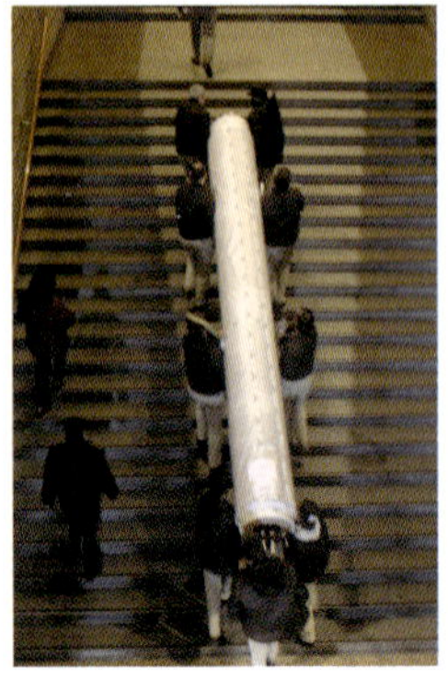

industry on which the Burgundian Netherlands, by the 1450s, had a virtual monopoly, with Arras, Lille, Bruges, and Tournai but especially and increasingly Brussels being important centres. We have already noted the size of this industry in the Brabant capital, and its reputation by the early sixteenth century was clearly well established. Indeed, in 1506, the Venetian ambassador celebrated Brabant's tapestries as among the greatest attractions of the Netherlands (see the quote heading this chapter), and it was to Brussels that Pope Julius II sent the huge cartoons by Raphael to be woven into hangings for the Sistine chapel in 1517. It was also Brussels' fame as a centre of excellence which instigated the use of a system of marking tapestries: from 1528 onwards, the BB sign 'Brussel Brabant' woven into the borders of their products guaranteed the quality of these works.

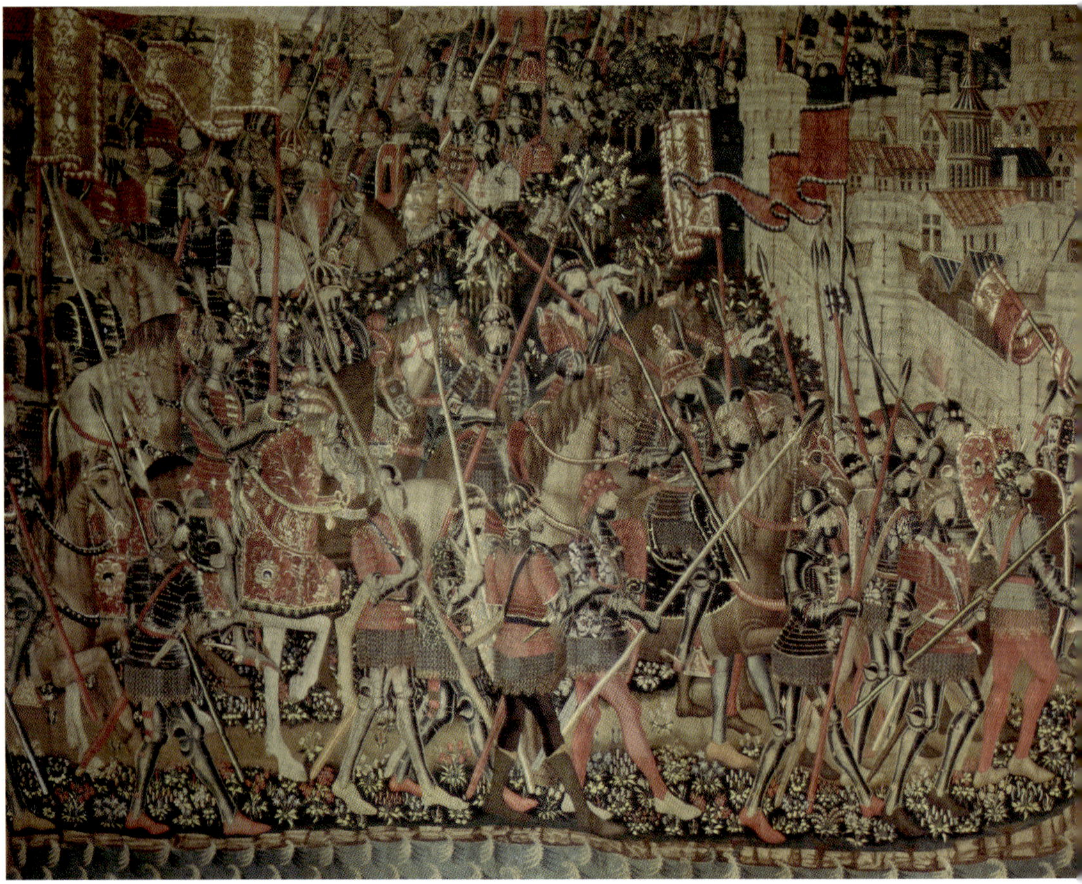

Tapestries woven in several centres in the north were in huge demand at the courts of Europe. In 1451 the agents of Alfonso of Aragon, basing themselves in Bruges, acquired more than 40 for their king, sent back to Naples via Venice; Isabella of Castile owned around 300 tapestries by her death in 1504, some acquired from the fair at Medina del Campo through her agents, some gifts made from her daughter Joanna the Mad, and commissioned from the workshop of Pieter van Aelst in Brussels. Alfonso V of Portugal (r. 1438–81) sent designs, probably made by his court painter, Nuño Gonclaves, up to Pasquier Grenier in Tournai, to weave a vast set of six pieces showing the very recent event of *The Expeditions of the Portuguese in North Africa in* 1471 (three survive, now in Pastrana, Colegiada, Guadalajara, **52**).[5] In Italy, the Este and Gonzaga courts acquired major sets of figurative and heraldic hangings sent from the Netherlands, many with the aid of Arnold de Boteram, a Brussels-trained weaver who was based in Italy; the Medici used their agents in Bruges, such as Tommaso Portinari, to accumulate a collection of around 100 'Arraz', the well-documented mechanics of which is explored in more detail in Chapter 8.

Tapestries were a reproductive medium, if a hugely expensive one: once full-scale cartoons had been made, potentially several sets could be woven from them (a process explicated in Part III below). Because of this, it was possible for every major court in Europe to own versions of the same set, which was the case with one of the most monumental and illustrious of all Netherlandish tapestries, the Trojan War series produced by the Tournai weaver and entrepreneur Pasquier Grenier. Over twenty years or so, Grenier and his sons produced as many as nine weavings of these tapestries, examples being owned by the Dukes of Burgundy, Milan, and Urbino and the Kings of Hungary, France, Scotland, and England.[6] These vast ensembles comprised eleven pieces, each one measuring 5 × 10 metres, which when (and if) hung together stretched for well over 100 metres and covered over 500 square metres of wall. Only the Netherlands had the expertise, workforce, and equipment to produce tapestries on this scale and of this quality, and at this speed.

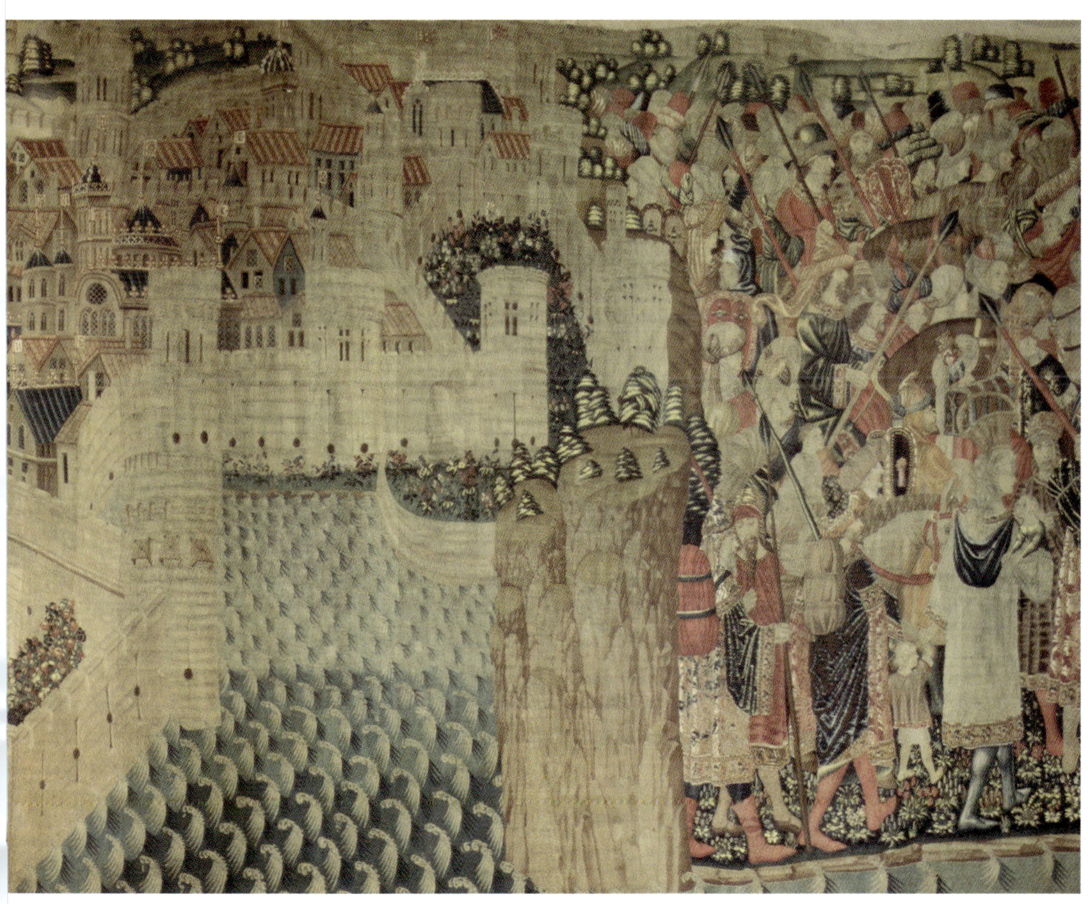

52 Netherlandish weavers organized by Pasquier Grenier (?), design by Nuño Gonclaves (?)

The Capture of Arzila and Tangier, from *The Expeditions of the Portuguese in North Africa in 1471*, wool and silk, 1470s.

Because this set recorded recent events played out far from the Netherlands—the taking of various African cities by the forces of Alfonso of Portugal—and because the style of the battle scene is rather different from that found in Netherlandish-designed pieces [**53**], it is likely the cartoons for these vast tapestries were painted in Portugal and sent up to Tournai to be woven, a practice we find documented for other foreign patrons like the Medici (see Chapter 8).

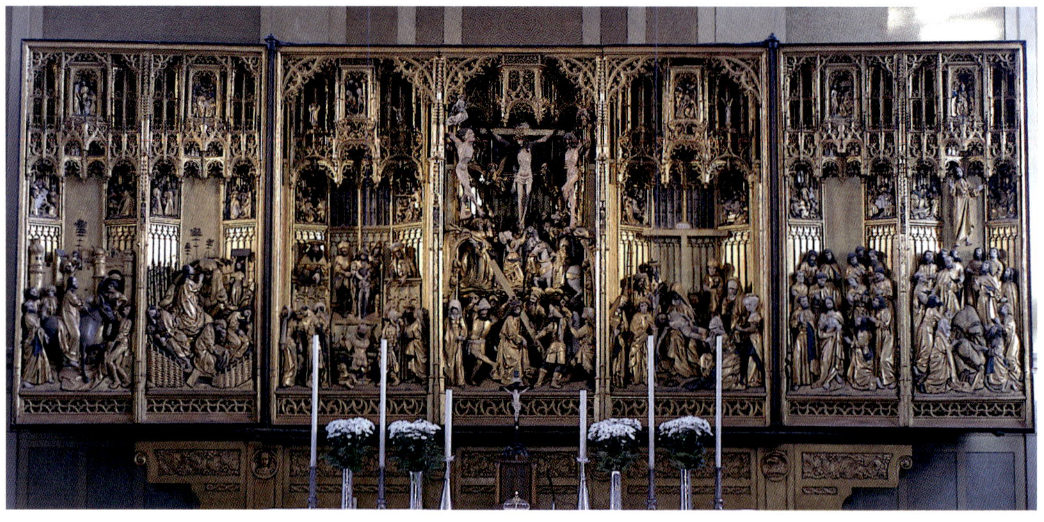

55 Brussels workshop, circle of Jan Borman

Retable for Bishop Rogge, called Strängnäs I, oak with original polychromy *c.*1490.

This is one of the largest of Netherlandish exported retables; its two sets of wings allow a dense iconographic programme, with three stages of viewing (see **169, 170**). Closed, it presents paintings of the Annunciation and Last Judgement across four panels; these open to reveal six painted panels of the infancy and ministry of Christ, which in turn open to reveal the sculpted, gilded interior (seen here) with its extensive Passion narrative. Its patron, Conrad Rogge, was educated in Perugia but turned to the Netherlands when he wanted a monumental, bespoke work such as this.

This work was designed to order and as such has some custom-made features: the ogee-arched shape (which seems to be something Italian patrons favoured); portraits of Claudio (?) de Villa and his wife included in the Crucifixion scene, their mottoes and arms carved into or set on the lower frame, and the iconography reflecting their specific interests, with a clear focus on the Magdalene and her role in the Passion, explicable by the intended destination of the retable in the de Villa burial chapel dedicated to that saint in the Dominican church in Chieri, Piedmont. Its visual language is in many respects, however, typical of a Netherlandish carved retable of the period, with the central section divided into three compartments, and a large part of the surface occupied by elaborate architectural canopies.[9] It creates its impact, as do tapestries, through a densely packed array of figures which build up vertically, recession being limited by the depth of the *caisse* in which the reliefs are set. Like tapestries too, the nature of the materials, with gold used extensively, works against any illusion of real space, and its impact is not dependent on clarity of composition. This type of carved retable impresses with the complexity of the arrangement of the figures, and above all with the richness and variety of effects in the skilfully produced gilding and press-brocade, something that was as much an expense in terms of expertise and time to produce as in terms of the material used (for more on polychromy, gilding and press-brocade, see pp 220–22).

Illuminated Manuscripts

The foreign market was also an important one for manuscript makers: for long Flemish centres like Bruges had exported fairly routinely illustrated books of hours across the channel, written for Sarum use (a textual variant used most commonly in England), and, it would seem, further afield, as the reference to 'an Hours of the Virgin, [a] work of Flanders, of parchment' in the inventory of the royal treasurer of Mallorca, Pere de Casaldàliga, made at the castle of L'Almudania in Mallorca in 1423 indicates.[10] By the late 1470s this export market had expanded to include the very highest ranks of patron, as internal court patronage began to wane following the death of Charles the Bold in

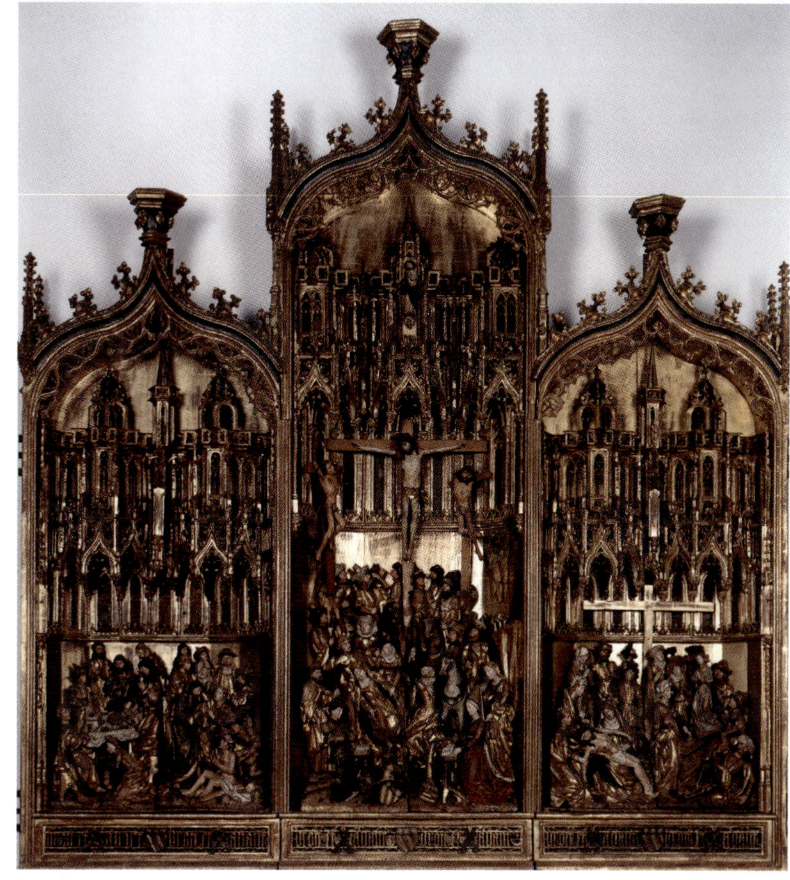

56 Brussels workshop

Passion Altarpiece of Claudio de Villa (?) and Gentina Solaro (?), oak with original polychromy, *c.*1470.

This retable would originally have had wings, probably painted rather than carved, and is missing the sculpted figures which would have sat on the pedestals on top of each of its compartments, but its polychromy is original and fairly well preserved.

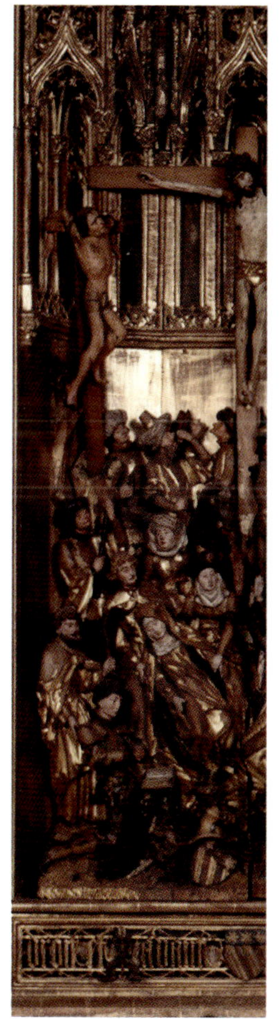

1477, and many of the most talented illuminators like Simon Marmion [**22**] and the Master of the Dresden Prayer Book (*fl. c.*1470–1520) who had worked on large historical and secular volumes for the court now adeptly turned their skills to producing the most splendidly decorated devotional books, hours and breviaries, for foreign nobility such as Englebert of Nassau, Eleanor of Portugal, and James IV of Scotland [**197, 198**]. The style of illumination developed in Bruges and Ghent at this period (generally referred to today as the Ghent-Bruges school because its focus of production was in those towns), depended for its effect on a very distinctive form of finely rendered illusionistic border decoration and script flourishes and forms [**57**]. Another stimulus to the development of such a style, designed to appeal to richer patrons, may have been the changes in the market caused by the increasing competition of printed books, an industry which was being established seriously in the towns of the Burgundian Netherlands at just this moment. Printed books could certainly not compete with such subtle, painterly, and colour-rich decoration, and the elaborate refined *bastarda* script of many of these manuscripts.

The extraordinary inventive style of illumination developed in these towns *c.*1470 found new ways to play with scale and space, and of finessing the relationship between the three main elements of a decorated manuscript page: the border, text, and miniature. The Book of Hours that Englebert of Nassau commissioned in the 1470s and early 1480s written by Nicolas Sperinc of

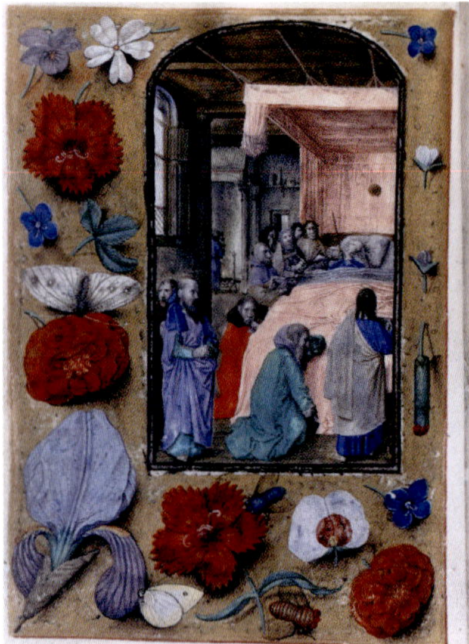
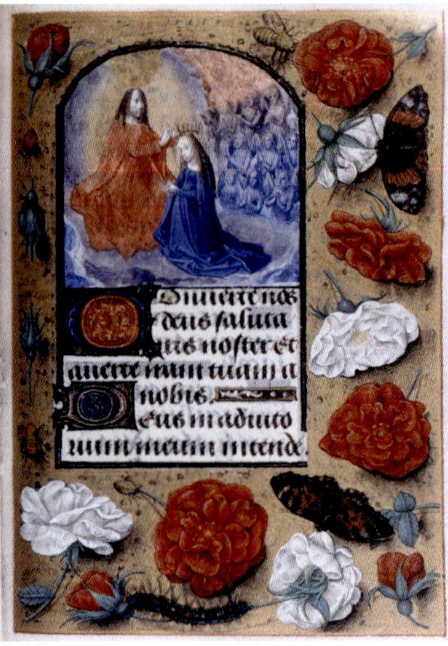

57 Vienna Master of Mary of Burgundy

Death of the Virgin and *Coronation of the Virgin*, from the Hours of Englebert of Nassau, parchment, *c*.1475.

The illusionistic treatment of the flowers and insects arranged on the flat gold ground of the borders in books such as these was a hugely popular invention, and manuscripts which featured them were in demand Europe-wide.

Ghent [**57**] is one of the earliest and highest quality examples of a work in this style, illuminated by the artist at the forefront of its development, the Vienna Master of Mary of Burgundy.[11] Its effects depend on the border occupying 'real' space, where large-scale objects or flowers appear to have been scattered on its solid, sometimes gilded surface, which then, by contrast, makes the miniature appear as if it is at some distance from the beholder, seen through the border, dissolving the page in doing so. This clever play with levels of reality and with page design was to become a hallmark of the Flemish illuminators and its inventiveness knew no bounds, ensuring a continued market for top-level illuminated manuscripts. Artists such as the Master of James IV of Scotland and the Master of the First Prayer Book of Maximilian continued to develop the ways the border, frame, miniature, and text could interact, sometimes setting the text as the primary plane, conceived as an object tethered by ropes or hanging from chains floating on top of a scene happening behind it [**58**]. How these devices fostered and responded to the needs of contemplation and imagination are explored in Chapter 18.

Glass and Brass

Two other important media which were widely exported from the Netherlands are stained glass and brass. While there were important centres of glass making in England, France, and Germany, the skill of Netherlandish glaziers was internationally renowned and desired: this was recognized by Philip the Bold when he sent his sculptor Claus Sluter to Mechelen to purchase stained glass there for the church at the Chartreuse de Champmol, by Isabella of Castile in the 1480s when she ordered her stained glass for Miraflores in the Netherlands [**59**], and by Henry VI, King of England, in 1449 when he retained a Fleming, John Utynam, to make coloured glass but also to 'give instruction in this and other arts new to England', although they could not be practised there for twenty years without his consent.[12] This tradition was continued in England with the appointment by Henry VII of the Netherlandish glazier Bernard Flower in 1496.

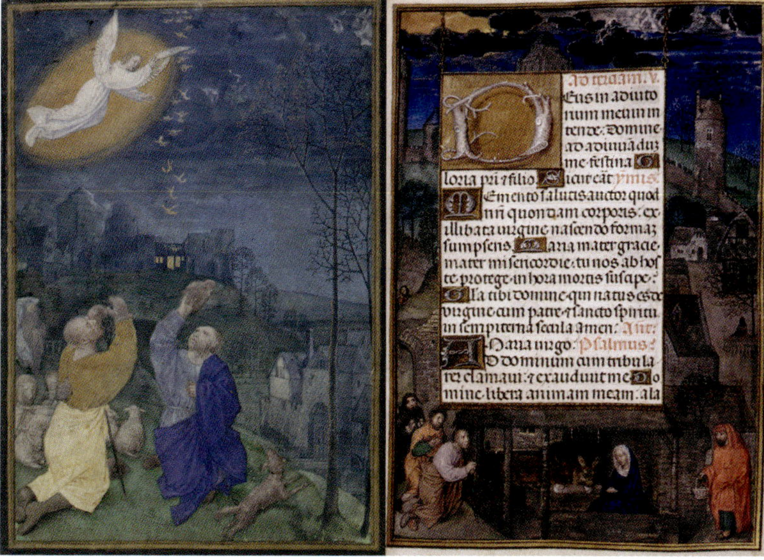

58 Master of the Houghton Miniatures and Ghent Associates (?)

Annunciation to the Shepherds and *Adoration of the Shepherds* from the Emerson-White Hours, parchment, *c.*1475–80.

This double-page opening is typical of the narratively dense and inventive compositions of illuminators working in Flanders at the end of the fifteenth century. The inspired idea of a spiral of angels lit from the shed of the Nativity in the background marks out the shepherds' destination. They arrive, the next day, on the facing page, in a setting which relates architecturally to the distant view we see of it the night before from the hillside.

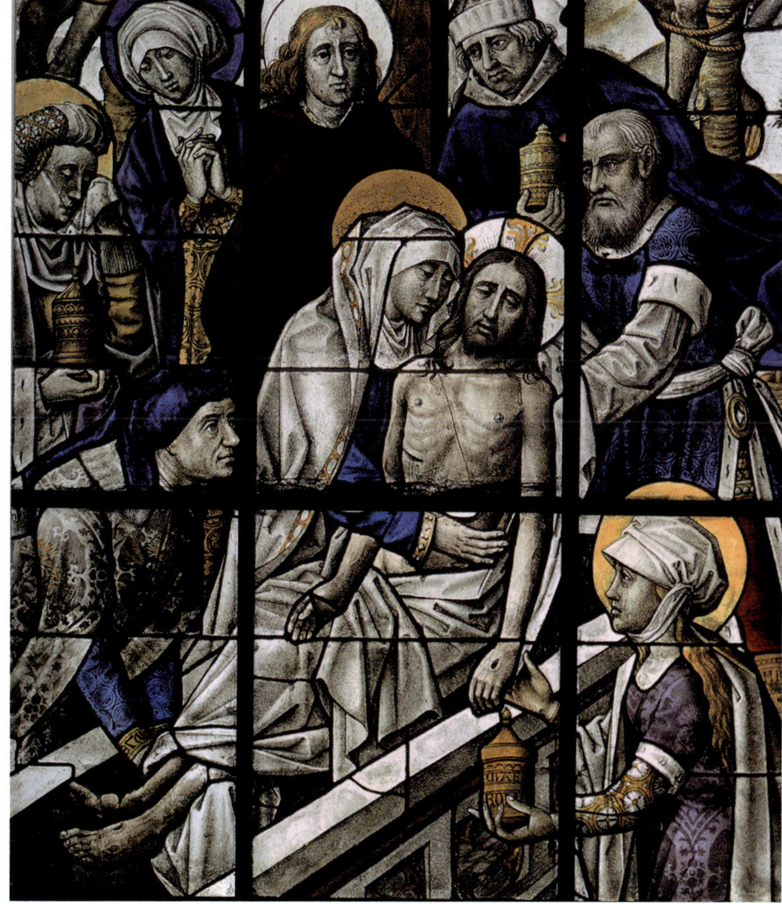

59 Niclaes Rombouts

Entombment, stained glass, 1480–84.

This is one of a series of ten large windows, five of which still survive, made by the Brussels-based glass painter Niclaes Rombouts (*c.*1450–1531) for the church of the Charterhouse of Miraflores, Burgos (see also **70, 71**). The commission was negotiated in the Netherlands for Isabella of Castile, patron of the monastery, by the Burgos merchant Martín de Soria. Rombouts, who was the official glass painter to Philip the Fair, Margaret of Austria and Charles V, signed three of the extant windows, including this one, where 'Claes Romb' is inscribed on the pot held by the Magdalene.

Indeed, skill in painting glass is one of the achievements of northern artists which Vasari, who had been taught the art by a Frenchman, unequivocally acknowledges: 'In this art the Flemings and the French have succeeded better than the other nations, seeing that they, with their cunning researches into pigments and the action on them of fire, have managed to burn in the colours that are put on the glass, so that the wind, air and rain may do them no injury.' The painterly quality of the best Netherlandish and French glass (see also **185**) was widely admired, since to achieve such subtleties required considerable skill: the images are obtained as much by the subtraction of colour by scratching away at the fired surface to achieve highlights, as by the addition of liquid glaze with a broader brush; the complexities of the effects are further enriched by the painting of layers of glaze on selected areas of the back, as well as the front, of the glass. As Vasari goes on to state, 'it cannot be said that the art is not difficult, artistic and most beautiful'.[13]

As well as importing specialist producers or bespoke glass for the furnishing of religious buildings, the Netherlandish towns were centres of a whole industry producing high-quality stained glass roundels. These were in actuality not always round (they could be square or rectangular), but they are distinguished by their size (rarely larger than 30 centimetres across, which was the largest size possible in a single pane) and their technique—they were painted in silver stain, which limited their colour range to tones of yellow, black, and white. Both limitations made for commercial success—it allowed for roundels to be single images without leads, which could then be truly painterly in effect, as is the case for the roundel showing Rebecca taking leave of her parents made after a design by Hugo van der Goes [**60**], who seems to have provided a set of drawings for stained glass painters of Old Testament themes. The distinctive colour range of these roundels, the amount of light they allowed to shine through them, and their size and shapes made them eminently useable in domestic settings with smaller windows which might only be part glazed (some *in situ* can be seen in the windows in **208**). The subjects of these roundels were often religious, as was much of the imagery in domestic settings, or heraldic. Designs for such works were an industry by itself and many major artists, including engravers such as Schongauer and Dürer, as well as painters like Hugo van der Goes, produced roundel patterns. The best examples are immensely skilful in the way the stain has been handled: in **60** the paint is applied both front and back to give a delicacy and depth to the image.[14]

Technical ability and specialization, and the presence of the right raw materials in its vicinity, ensured the Netherlands were also purveyors to a Europe-wide clientele in works made of brass.[15] Zinc ore (calamine) was needed in large quantities for the production of this metal and its richest deposits were in the area around Liège and Aachen, which fed a brass manufacturing industry that went back to the twelfth century. By the fifteenth century, the production in the Meuse valley had shifted somewhat further east, to the towns of Dinant (until its sack in 1466), Tournai, Bruges, Ghent, and Brussels, all of which were important centres. Expertise in this field was carefully guarded: in 1455 three brass workers were imprisoned in Dinant, to stop them taking their skills to England.[16] Making this material was clearly something not easily done abroad, since the Netherlands also exported large quantities of brass in ingots: the Operai di San Giovanni of Florence in 1445 had 14,623 pounds of

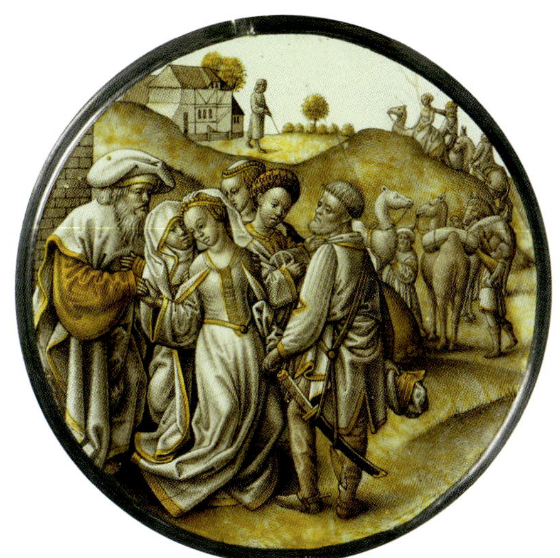

60 After a design by Hugo Van der Goes

Rebecca taking Leave of her Parents, yellow stained glass, *c.*1480–1500.

The highlights in the drapery are obtained by etching a network of short, parallel strokes into the (fired) umber base layer of paint with a stylus: to create shadows, dark paint is applied with a fine pointed brush (a pinselen, see p. 166); paint is also applied to the reverse of the roundel to give an added sense of depth. This would have been undertaken by specialist glass painters, closely allied in many towns with the painters, who seem to have routinely provided the drawn models for this type of work.

'ottone fine'—fine quality brass—at a cost of 1,135 florins, shipped from Bruges in this manner for Ghiberti to cast his second set of Baptistery doors (which technical analysis has confirmed are brass, not bronze).[17]

Much of the production of brass objects in the Netherlands was centred on making lecterns, fonts [**99**], and light fittings of various sorts, for which the home market alone was considerable: the German traveller Jerome Münzer noted with awe that in the cathedral in Antwerp in 1495 there were over 400 brass chandeliers, both large and small.[18] The domestic type of brass chandelier depicted by van Eyck in the Arnolfini portrait [**37**] was one widely desired and distinctive 'Flemish' product in this medium (possibly one reason why it, and the mirror, another Bruges speciality, are so prominently placed in this painting). The Medici had a magnificent example of such a chandelier weighing 400 pounds shipped to them by Tommaso Portinari in 1464 from Bruges, cast in several pieces each labelled for assembly on arrival. Portinari instructed Piero de' Medici to put it back together with care, since, he notes, it was the finest example of this sort he had seen for a long time; it was probably the most valuable chandelier recorded in the 1492 Medici inventory, where it is described as having '12 candle holders with many branches, figures and foliage'.[19]

More common still and more widely exported were the engraved brass tomb slabs that were a Flemish, and particularly a Bruges, speciality (not solely a Tournai one as the earlier literature asserts). From the early fourteenth century these were being shipped to Spain, Germany, England, Scandinavia, and France.[20] Some of the most impressive and inventive of these are still to be found in churches in Bruges, however. That of Kateline Daut (d. 1460) in St James's church is particularly well preserved; its effects are reliant on the yellow colour of the brass and its high polish, which is only obtained by the correct combination of copper and zinc [**61**].[21]

Some of the brass objects made for liturgical use, like baptismal fonts and paschal candelabra, could be both monumental and elaborate in their figurative elements. That at Zoutleeuw, to the east of Leuven, was ordered from the brass caster Renier van Thienen in 1482 and delivered in 1483 [**62**]. It stands almost 6 metres high and weighs around 1,800 pounds. The bold design of this

61 Anonymous Bruges brass founder

Brass of Kateine Daut, *c.*1461.

This brass is a tomb marker for the woman shown in the centre of it, Kateline Daut, who died young in 1461. The monument was originally placed in their family chapel in St James's church, Bruges. The other two figures are identified by texts on their robes as her guardian angel and her brother (who had predeceased her). The scrolls record a conversation between the three figures concerning their early death and their acceptance by Christ. The cloth of hounour held by angels behind them is a visual device common to panel paintings, see **35**.

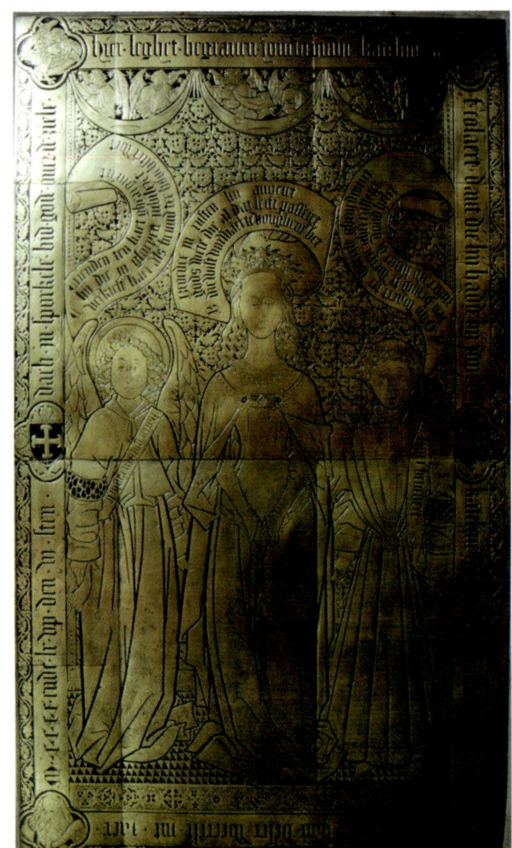

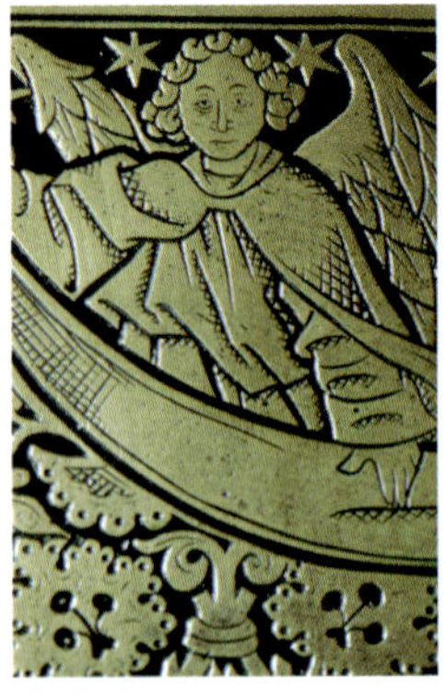

work incorporates a Crucifixion scene with the cross forming the stem for the paschal candle, while the twisted branches of its lower part unwind to form three bases for the figures of the Virgin, John, and the Magdalene, which are intended to be lit dramatically from below by six further candle holders which unwind from a lower part of the stem; this gives logical explanation to the technical necessity of its narrowing form as it rises to form the cross above.[22]

More surprising perhaps than the brass work the Netherlands made and exported so extensively is that this region was also where a foreign patron might turn for a monumental bronze equestrian group. This should not surprise us, however, as bronze was a material increasingly favoured by the Dukes of Burgundy for tombs, and thus in the late 1480s it was to 'Flanders' that the Valencian nobleman Vincent Penyarroja turned when he instructed a Catalan merchant Domenech Perandreu to commission a life-size (260 × 230 centimetres) *St Martin and the Beggar* [**63**]. This most probably in fact came from Brussels given the attribution of this work with the circle of Renier van Thienen and Pieter de Backere (d. 1527), who were based in that city (and who worked together on casting the gilt bronze tomb of Mary of Burgundy in Bruges: see **190**). Perandreu charged 356 libras and 13 sueldos for the transport and purchase of the work, which was shipped to Valencia in 1492 in several boxes; it was cast in 40 pieces and, like the Medici's chandelier and most larger objects made in this material, was reassembled on arrival. This work is almost unknown to art histori-

62 Renier van Thienen

Paschal candelabrum, brass, 1483.

The visual solution to the problem of depicting the Crucifixion on an object which had to be seen in the round was to place the Magdalene behind the cross with her arms raised up in a dynamic expression of grief, creating interest from several angles of view.

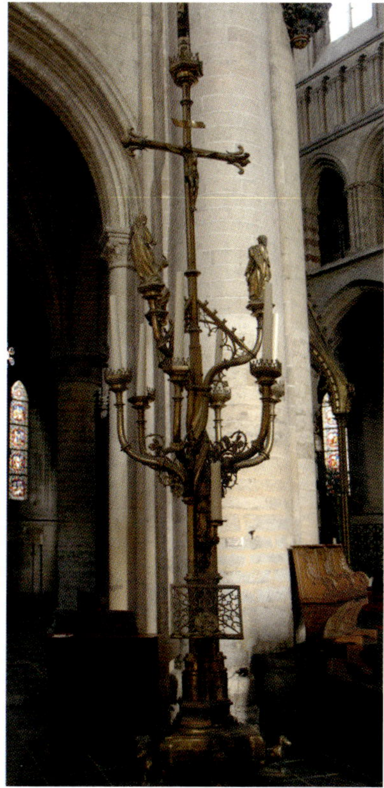

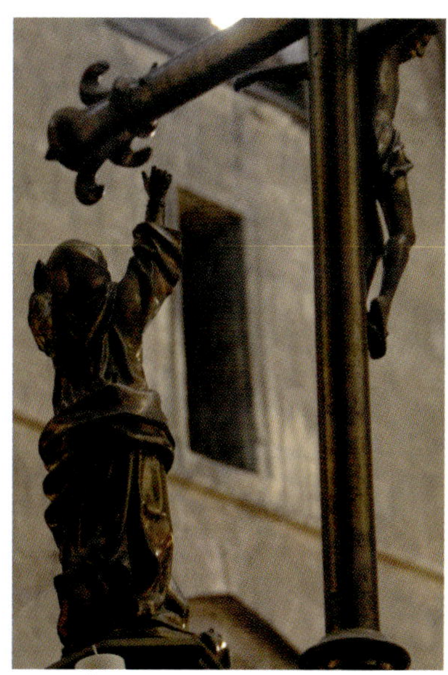

63 Circle of Renier van Thienen and Pieter de Backere

St Martin and the Beggar, bronze, 1492.

This work was originally gilded; it was placed above the main door of the church of St Martin in Valencia, but was taken down periodically to be re-gilded and processed around the town.

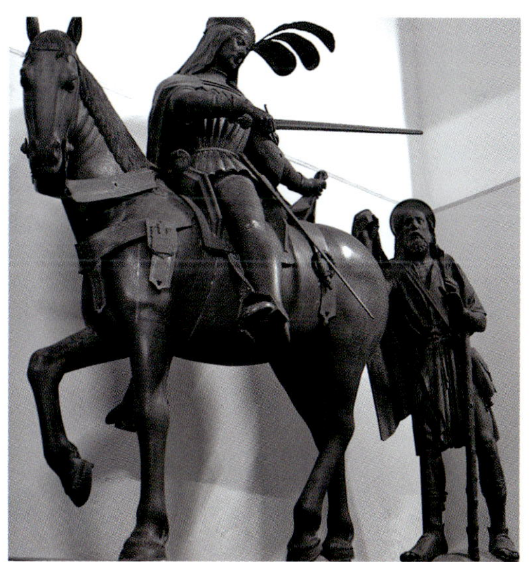

cal literature outside Valencia, yet in terms of the realization of a monumental, semi-narrative work combining two figures and a horse, it compares well with contemporary and much vaunted Italian bronze works like Verrocchio's *Christ and St Thomas* for Orsanmichele, which grappled with similar artistic challenges.[23]

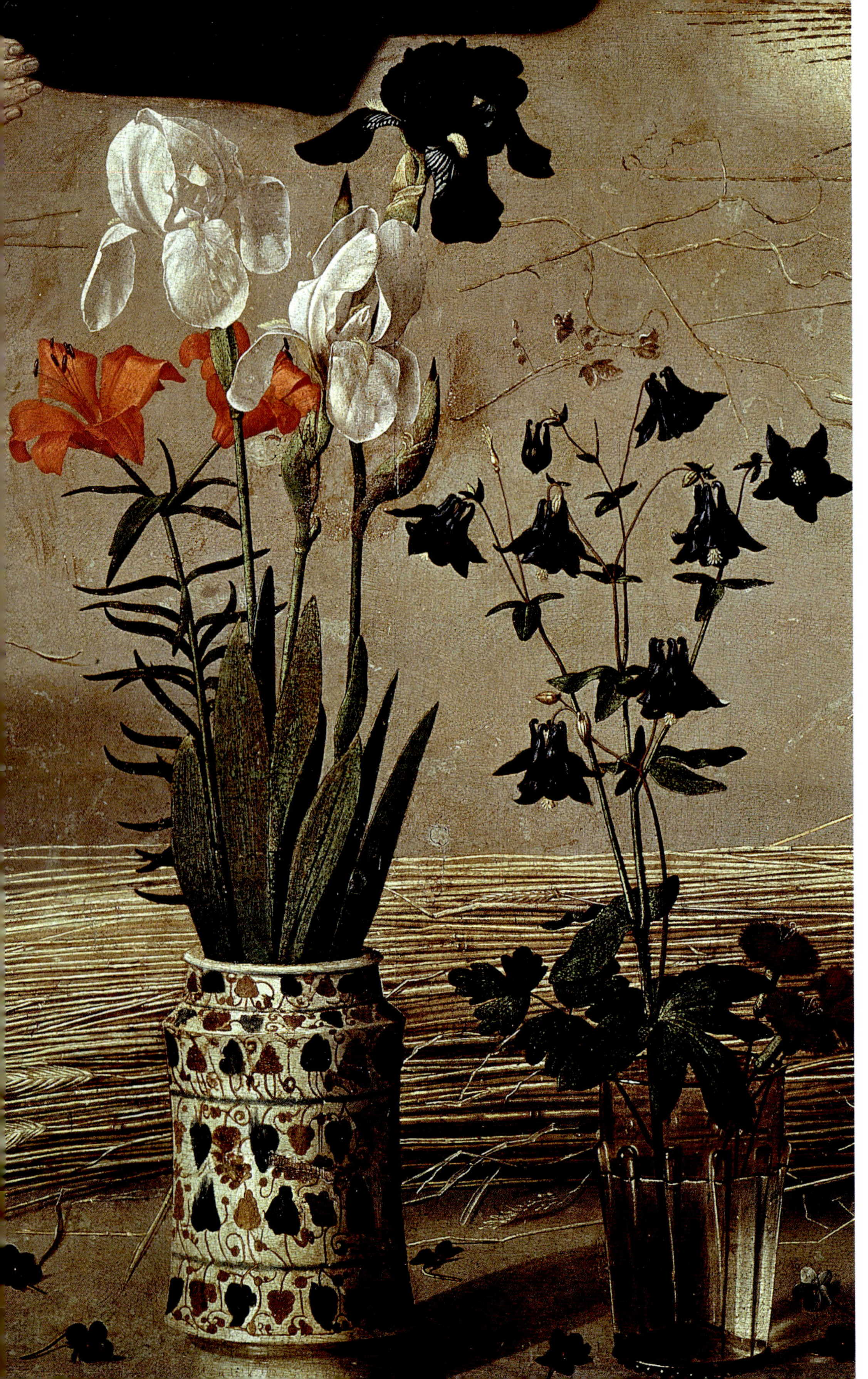

Patrons: Importing Art and Artists

... for painted cloths we must await the Antwerp fair, and then I will furnish some beautiful ones.

Tommaso Portinari to Piero de' Medici, 1466

8

The well-documented example of the Medici family and their agents in Flanders provides a useful case study of the mechanics of art acquisition and gives us some insight into what Netherlandish works offered that Italian artists could not provide. The attraction was certainly strong since, despite the access the Medici had to many now-famous artists in their native city, around a third, possibly more, of the 142 paintings they owned in 1492 were 'di fiandra', Flemish. An inventory made of their palace in Florence at that date shows that there at least 20 per cent of the pictures on display were from the Netherlands, while in their villa at Coreggi it was a huge 75 per cent.[1] Among the most treasured, and most highly valued, of all their paintings (although works of other sorts in material like agate and gold were vastly more valuable) were a small picture of St Jerome by Jan van Eyck, valued at 30 florins, and a small portrait by Petrus Christus of a young girl, valued at 40 florins. Both were kept in Piero de' Medici's study at the Medici palace in Florence. The Petrus Christus painting, described as 'a small panel painted with the head of a French lady, coloured in oil, the work of Pietro Cresci from Bruges', may well be the exquisite image of a young girl now at Berlin [**64**]. The *Saint Jerome* is probably lost, although some idea of the type of image it was can be seen in **15** above. These works seem to have been acquired rather than commissioned, the portrait being of a girl whose identity was clearly not the main criteria for its value (it was not known, or thought of as important, to the compiler of the inventory at least): what the Medici appreciated must have been, in part, the quality of their artifice, and presumably the repute of the artists who made them, since this was known, and recorded, suggesting the works were signed. Owning a work by Jan van Eyck, the Duke of Burgundy's court painter, must have been a significant factor in its acquisition. Both of these pictures were to have an impact on Florentine painters, notably Leonardo and Ghirlandaio.

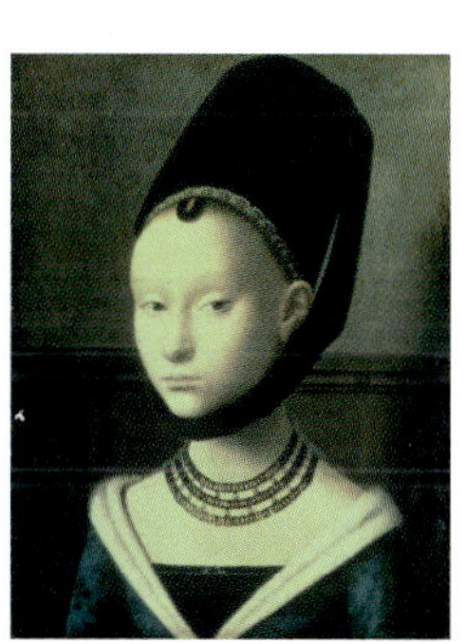

64 Petrus Christus
Portrait of a Young Woman, oil on Baltic oak, *c.*1460–70.

The majority of paintings the Medici bought from the Netherlands were, however, on cloth. None of the thirty-eight they owned survive, but their religious ones might have looked something like Dieric Bouts's *Resurrection* [**65**], which itself may have been made for an Italian, since it has a Venetian provenance.[2] Although some may have been decorative rather than figurative, the Medici's 'panni dipinti' were clearly not simply wall hangings but pictures. They showed a wide range of subjects, as many secular as religious, and often tantalizingly hard to envisage, such as an image of a man at half-length with

Detail of 67

65 Dieric Bouts

Resurrection, glue size on cloth, *c.*1470.

This is one of a set of five paintings on cloth that originally formed a larger altarpiece, in format similar to **13**. Bouts understood the potential of this medium, employing certain pigments which were effective in glue size, such as white chalk, which would not be usable in oil. Painting on a fabric support was both economical (quicker to prepare and produce, and cheaper pigments could be employed) and flexible (the form was ideal for export, since they could be rolled up and shipped in barrels).

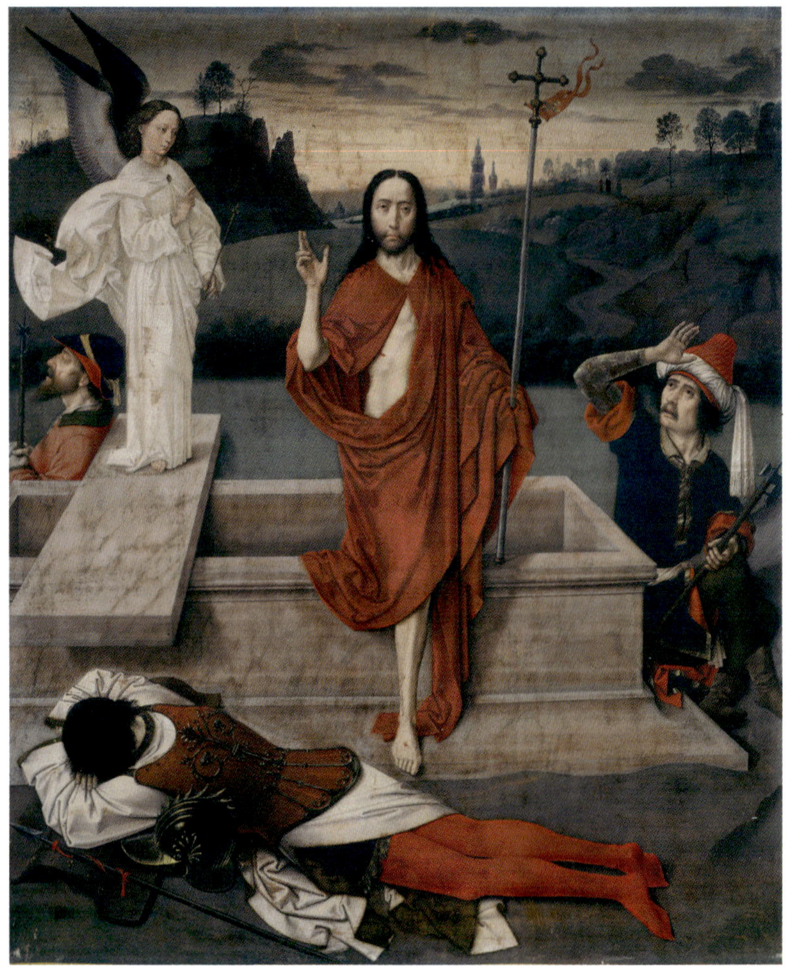

books above his head and a pike biting his finger, or that described only as showing 'arches and landscapes and figures', which at 25 florins was their most expensive cloth painting. Since paintings on cloth were mostly (although not exclusively) produced in a glue size medium and not oil, and given their technique and support could not reproduce the characteristic effects of a smooth mirror-like surface that oil on panel could attain, it is clear that it was not simply an admiration of the Netherlanders' ability to paint with veracity in oil which attracted these patrons: the subjects, and how they were treated, must also have been a primary appeal. This was certainly the case for one of the Medici's compatriots, Alessandra Strozzi, who, on being sent a group of cloth paintings from Bruges by her son Lorenzo (their subjects being an Adoration of the Magi, a peacock, and a Holy Face), decided to sell two but to keep the Holy Face because it was 'a devout and beautiful figure'.[3]

Many of these cloth paintings were acquired in the market in Antwerp described by Tafur: this was certainly where the Medici's agent in Bruges, Tommaso Portinari, recommended buying them, telling Piero de' Medici in 1466 that 'for painted cloths we must await the Antwerp fair, and then I will furnish some beautiful ones', which he eventually did do, sending four of them rolled up in a bale of wool.[4] Panel paintings were, however, often ordered directly from Netherlandish artists by the Italian community when something personalized or of a particular size or quality was required. Most famously, Tommaso Portinari commissioned the enormous triptych now in the Uffizi (**66**, **67**, over 5 metres wide when open) from the Ghent painter Hugo van der Goes and shipped it to Florence in 1483.[5] Its size was such that sixteen men were needed to haul it through the streets of the city to the church of Saint Egidio in the hospital of Santa Maria Nuova. Shipping such huge panels was both risky and expensive: an earlier, equally large triptych commissioned by Angelo Tani, Portinari's predecessor as manager of the Medici bank in Bruges, had failed to reach Florence since the ship was commandeered in the English Channel. Tani never recovered his triptych, which is still in Gdańsk in Poland where the privateers eventually took it.[6] Given this, the choice to have a work painted in the Netherlands rather than produced in your home town reveals a very particular, and potentially risky, choice, and is indicative again of the strength of the appeal of Netherlandish works.

Such an astounding object as the Portinari Altarpiece must have seemed in many ways truly foreign and exotic, even to those familiar with Netherlandish paintings, since nothing so elaborate, so bespoke, or of this scale had yet arrived in Florence. This would have been apparent in its form (a folding triptych—not an Italian format), its visual language, technical skill (the oil medium deployed with great surety to evoke an array of different materials and surfaces, from the stubble on the shepherd's chin to the figured white velvet of the Magdalene's dress), and the representation of the donors (dressed in assertively foreign, northern fashion, kneeling so prominently with their saints arrayed behind them). It did not go unnoticed by Florentine painters, although much of its invention was beyond them: Ghirlandaio quoted extensively from it in his *Adoration of the Shepherds* for the Sassetti chapel in Santa Trinita [**68**], while the placement and scale of the donor portraits there might have equally been adopted in response to the Portinari couple's self-imaging display.

While we know nothing of the negotiations which may have gone on between Portinari and van der Goes in the commissioning of this work, we are well informed of the deliberations between weaver, agent, and patron in regard to the Medici's commissioning of tapestries from the Netherlands. The correspondence between Cosimo, Piero, and Giovanni de' Medici and their agents in Bruges over a fifteen-year period is enlightening, and begins with a frustrated search by Cosimo's agent Fruosino da Panzano in 1448.[7] He has been to the fairs at Antwerp but he cannot find anything that has the right combination of size, quality, cost, and subject matter. There was one

with the story of Samson, very well executed but so large it would have been difficult to hang in your room, and in any case it did not seem to me to meet your needs; and also I will tell you that the story did not please me because it showed a great number of dead bodies, which seems to me contrary to what is called for in a bedroom, where cheerful and pleasing things are wanted, here there were only things to cause terror and fear, and it also seemed to me too expensive, for it would cost about 700 ducats

66 Hugo van der Goes

Annunciation, exterior of the Portinari Altarpiece, oil on Baltic oak, *c.*1474–8 (?), arrives in Florence in 1483.

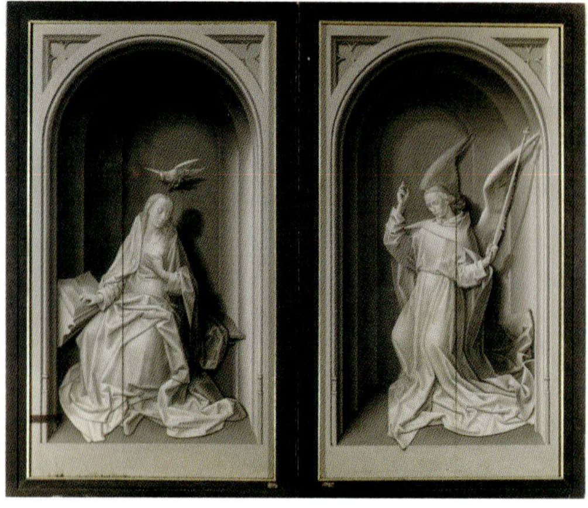

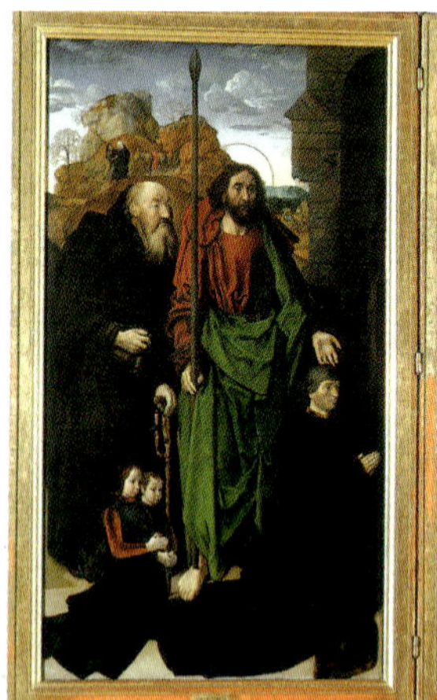

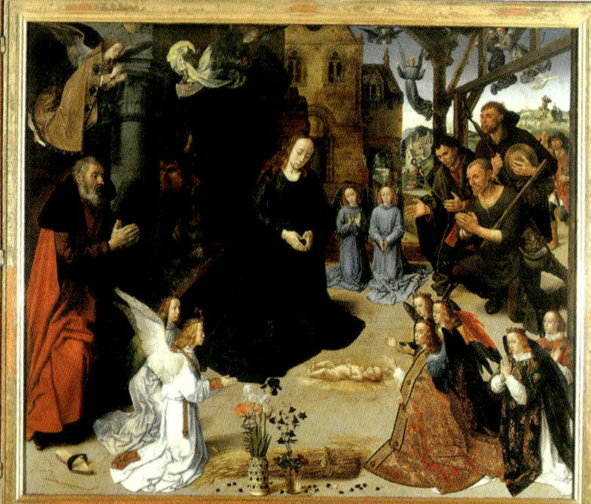

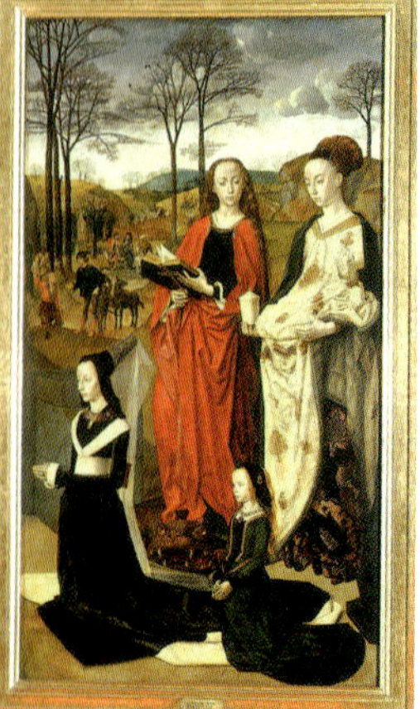

67 Hugo van der Goes

Interior of **66**.

Many aspects of the visual language of this triptych would have seemed exotic to its Florentine audience, such as the figures on its reverse [**66**] painted in imitation of stone, the angels on the interior dressed in liturgical vestments, the blatantly symbolic but brilliantly rendered flowers set in vases on the ground of the stable, and the landscape used with such invention to convey time and place and to expand the narrative content.

He had seen a cheaper tapestry of Narcissus which he thought 'would be the right size, and had it been a little more richly woven I should have taken it, which would have cost about 150 ducats'. He finishes by saying, 'there was and is nothing that would fit your needs because nearly everybody who wants work out of the ordinary has it made to order ... send me the measurements and the story you want in it and I'll have it made by the best master that can be found.'

Cosimo's sons Piero and Giovanni took this advice and set in place a series of orders placed with the Lille-based weaver Pierre de Los, described as 'the best master in these parts', initially through their agent Gierozzo de Pigli, with the aid and advice of a certain Giacetto of Arras, who Piero sent to Bruges to oversee or advise on some of these works. Designs were sent up from Florence which were then used by painters in the Netherlands to make the full-scale cartoons: these were valuable objects in themselves, those for the set of five hangings of Petrarch's *Triumph* commissioned from de Los taking alone four to six months to make. In other instances, negotiated this time by Tommaso Portinari, who had been appointed the Medici agent in Bruges in 1459, the full-scale cartoons, not just the small drawings for them,

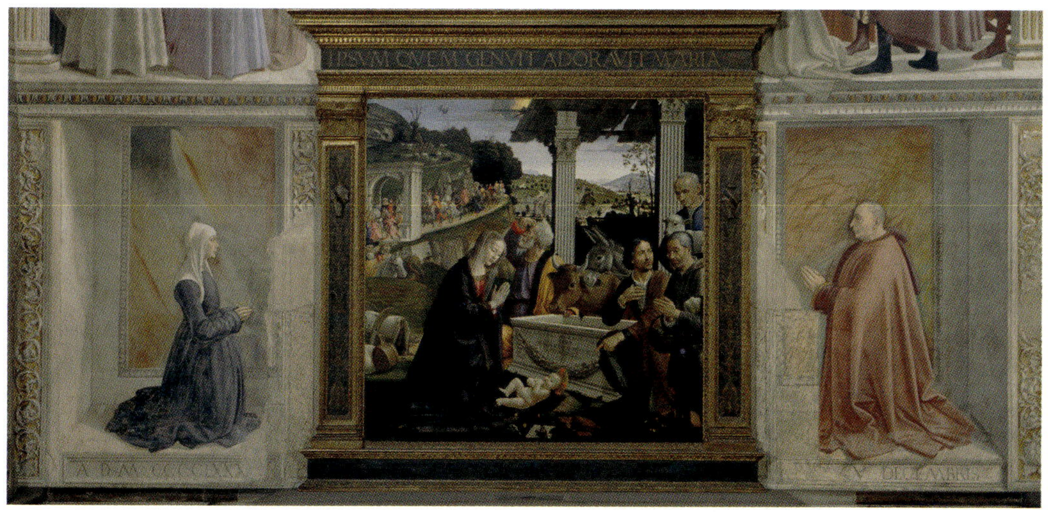

68 Domenico Ghirlandaio

Altarpiece of the Adoration of the Shepherds with portraits of Francesco Sassetti and his wife Nera Corsi, from the Sassetti chapel in Santa Trinita, Florence, panel and fresco, 1485.

Ghirlandaio's paintings respond to their northern exemplar in many ways: the shepherds and the winter landscape, the ox and ass, the wheatsheaf and the flowers in the foreground are all quotes from **66**, but the figures are idealized and lack Hugo's dramatic impact, creating a less decorative and more stable, 'rational' composition. The Sassetti were, like the Portinari, managers of the Medici bank, and must have seen their artistic commissions in relation to those of their rivals.

were made in Florence and sent up to the weavers; however, the Florentine painters were clearly inexperienced in painting on cloth in the appropriate manner for tapestry design, as Portinari advises Giovanni that next time they should be told not to apply the colours so thickly, as it was flaking off and needed to be restored if the patterns were to be used again.

In such a situation, the advantage of having an artist trained in 'foreign' techniques at hand is obvious, but only the most powerful patrons were able to bring the artists to the project, rather than commission foreign works from afar. This was a viable option for the rulers of Europe, who wanted works made with the technique, skill, and invention of Netherlandish craftsmen, but on site and thus more easily under their direction and possibly scrutiny. The presence of these foreigners at court brought with it a certain prestige and also raised the possibility of their training other, local artists in their particular skills and techniques. Thus the Duke of Urbino, according to Vespasiano da Bisticci, sent to Flanders to find a distinguished master because he was unable to find in Italy any suitable painters skilled in the oil technique;[8] the Sforza at Milan agreed to let their painter Zanetto Bugatto go to study with Rogier van der Weyden, who they thanked for 'demonstrating to him freely all the things you knew about in your special trade';[9] Alfonso of Aragon gave the painter Lluís Dalmau 100 Castilian florins to go to Flanders in 1431, perhaps to negotiate a tapestry commission, since he was accompanied by a tapestry worker, but also perhaps to learn something from the painters there (which he did, to an extent, see **28**, above).[10] Alfonso also had a weaver from Tournai working for him in Naples, something other Italian courts and cities attempted too. Most notable of the Netherlandish weavers who were lured to work in this region was Aert van der Dussen, called Boteram, who was registered as an apprentice in Brussels in 1431–2 but by 1438 was in Siena, where he was employed by the commune there to teach his art to three or four Sienese citizens each year. Subsequently he worked for the Este and the Gonzaga courts, where he set up workshops, later basing himself in Venice where he acted as an intermediary for the northern Italian courts purchasing tapestries from the Netherlands.[11]

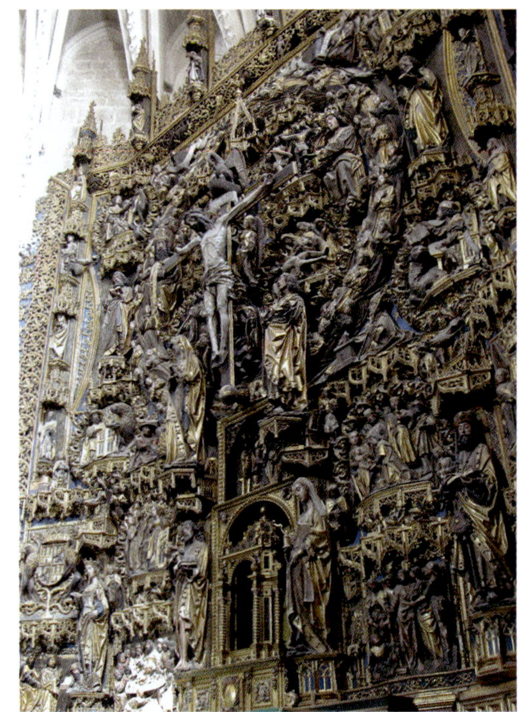

71 Gil de Siloé (sculpture) and Diego de la Cruz (polychromy)

High altarpiece for the church of the Carthusian monastery at Miraflores, polychromed wood, 1496–9.

This retable cost the enormous sum of over one million marvadis, twenty times Michel Sittow's and fifty times Juan de Flandes's annual salaries at Isabella's court.

Isabella's artists were put to extensive use on the decoration of the Carthusian monastery of Miraflores outside Burgos where Isabella's father and mother were buried. This complex is a good example of how a major project far from the Netherlands might be furnished by artists with Netherlandish skills and stylistic language in various media but creating something which was distinctively bespoke and not alien in form or effect—a result very different (and presumably deliberately so) from that achieved by Portinari when his altarpiece was unveiled in Florence. This is evident in the two great sculptural ensembles which dominate the east end of the Miraflores church: the alabaster tomb of Isabella's parents, Juan II of Castile and Isabella of Portugal [**70**], and the vast wooden retable filling the entire altar wall, both made by Gil de Siloé.[14] These works make their impact through the virtuosic handling of their materials but more emphatically by the sheer mass of figures and iconographic detail they contain, something achieved for the tomb by its extraordinary shape: Juan and Isabella lie on a chest in the form of an eight-pointed star. Whatever the symbolic associations of this Mudéjar ornamental form for the Castilian rulers, in artistic terms it allows for a hugely increased vertical surface area, and thus much greater potential for extensive figurative decoration, with sixteen faces instead of the four a standard rectangular tomb chest would present. But that in itself clearly was not sufficient: these sixteen surfaces are multiplied up to thirty-two with the insertion of buttress-like walls set between each point of the star, and increased to forty-four with the addition of square extensions on the four points facing north, east, south, and west. By exploiting every part of these surfaces Siloé has managed to create a tomb with several hundred sculpted figures and animals on it.

72 Olivier of Ghent (sculpture) and Jean d'Ypres (polychromy)

Retable of the high altar of Sé Velha de Coimbra, wood, painted and gilded, 1499–1501/2.

This vast work was commissioned by Don Jorge d'Almeida, Bishop of Coimbra, who, by attaining the services of a northern sculptor and painter, ensured that he was associated with the most up-to-date artistic mode. Recognition of Almeida's role is not left to chance: his coats of arms appear three times, aligned on the central axis, increasing in size as they go up. The smallest is placed on the bottom at the centre of the altar, directly where the priest would say mass, the second embedded into the Assumption between the apostles and the Virgin, the third, and largest, set at the foot of the Crucifixion. Their placement and increasing scale ensure their visibility to a range of audiences within the cathedral, from the priests performing mass at the foot of the altar to those who have just entered from the far west end.

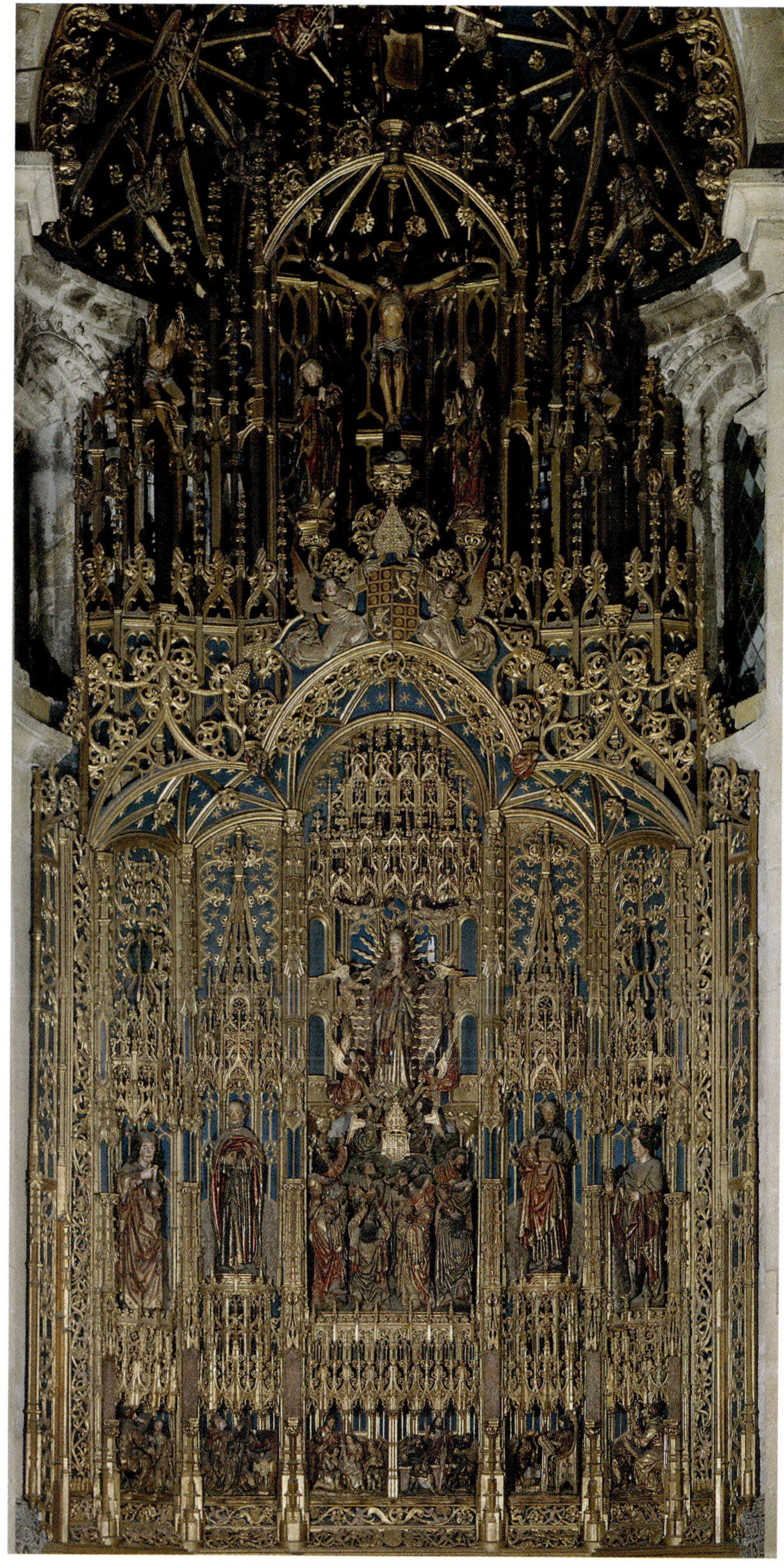

73 Anonymous Brussels workshops

The Annunciation, the Virgin and Child, and the Crucifixion (the 'Laredo Altarpiece') *c.* 1440, oak and walnut with polychromy, much of which is not original, set into a later framework.

Although made in the Netherlands this work is different in format and iconography from most Netherlandish retables of the period (compare **55** and **56**, both of which were also exported but to Italy and Sweden), which were folding works with densely packed narrative scenes of the Passion or Infancy of Christ as their primary focus, not the Virgin and Child. The small narrative scenes set around the arched frames are also found in painted form in the Miraflores Altarpiece [**33**], another export to Spain.

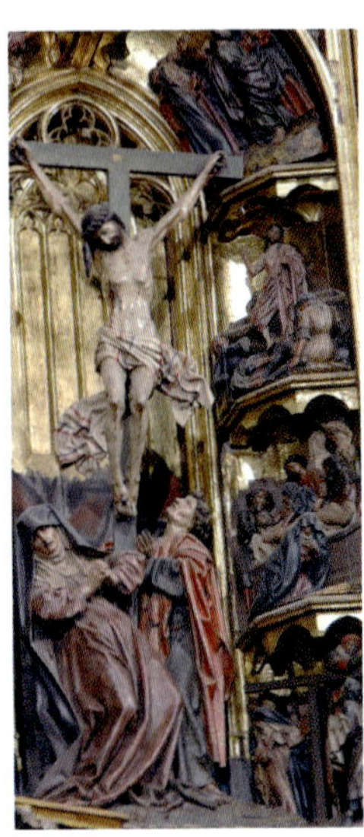

The altar wall manages a similar feat of ingenuity and iconographic complexity by using figurative forms to create a framework for the scenes contained in them [**71**]. The huge circle in front of which the Crucifixion, combined with the Trinity, seems to hover is made up of a host of angels and their wings; below this four over-life-sized figures of Saints Catherine, John the Baptist, the Magdalene, and James serve similarly architectural roles, dividing the lower section into five parts, into which are set, on the outer edges, the kneeling king and queen with their patron saints and their coats of arms above, moving in towards further narrative scenes from the Nativity and Passion of Christ. The strong plasticity of this wall, with its dramatic overlays, the gravity defying effect of the Crucifixion, and the extension of forms out into the space of the church, is only really achievable in wood. Siloé's training in the Netherlands would have given him the expertise to create this complex wooden retable (and Diego de la Cruz, the Netherlandish painter who worked on this with him, the expertise to gild and paint it), but its form—a fixed structure covering the altar wall from floor to ceiling—is decidedly Spanish. Indeed, the aesthetic for altar walls, funerary monuments, and façades covered with extraordinarily dense figurative imagery is in itself something distinctively Iberian, if produced frequently by northern-trained artists. It can be found in the huge 15-metre-high wooden retable for the cathedral of Coimbra in Portugal carved by Olivier of Ghent and polychromed by Jean d'Ypres [**72**];[15] at the Jeronimo monastery of the Kings of Portugal in Lisbon, where the French sculptor Nicolau Chanterene, who also worked in Santiago and Coimbra, was in charge by 1517, carving a portal which has strong echoes of that of Claus Sluter's at the Chartreuse de Champmol;[16] and on the façade of the Collegia San Pablo in Valladolid, probably another work by Gil de Siloé.[17]

Indeed, it would seem that on the whole the Spanish wanted Netherlandish technical mastery, style, and invention but not, usually, in Netherlandish formats of folding triptychs. When sculpted or painted works were commissioned (rather than simply acquired) in the Netherlands for Spanish destinations, they were made to fit Spanish expectations: this is the case for the Miraflores altarpiece commissioned from Rogier van der Weyden by Juan of Castile, Isabella's father (**33** above), for Isabella's retable in her chapel in Granada commissioned from Dieric Bouts,[18] for Memling's huge altar panels for the church at Nájera (see **82** and p. 128), and for the carved retable sent probably from Brussels to Laredo around 1440 [**73**], all of which were fixed works which did not have folding wings.[19] This work is deeply indebted to the inventions of Rogier van der Weyden: the Virgin and Child with its unusual pose is repeated in a drawing from his workshop (Stockholm, National museum); in the Crucifixion the fluttering loin cloth of Christ and the pose of the Virgin and St John are all derived from his inventions, while the apostles placed along its base seem to have been carved from the same drawings as used for the painted versions in the *Exhumation of St Hubert* (**6** above). Thus from an early date this most influential of painters was extending his influence across Europe via both exported paintings and sculpture.

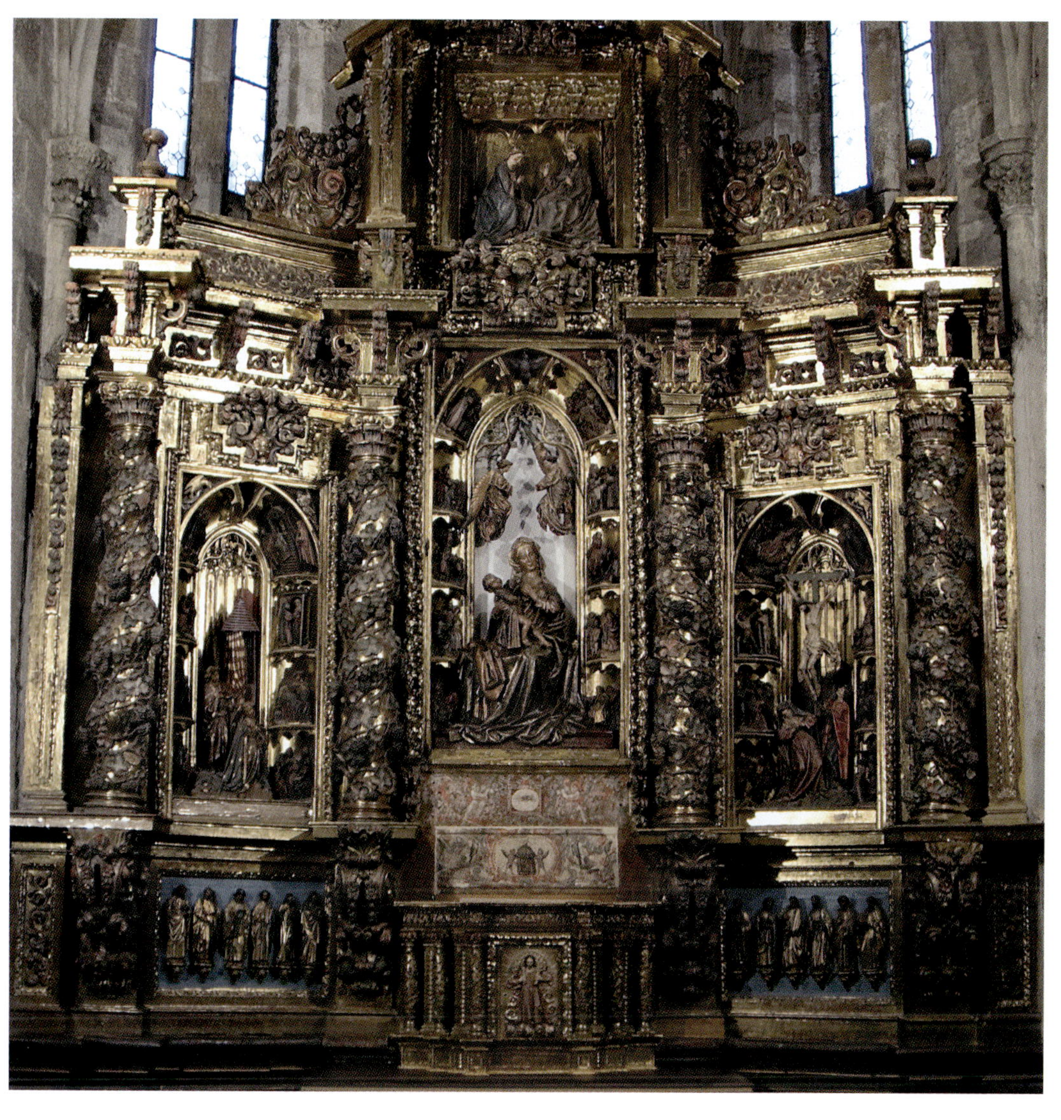

Part III

Marketing Art: Artists and the Contexts of Creation

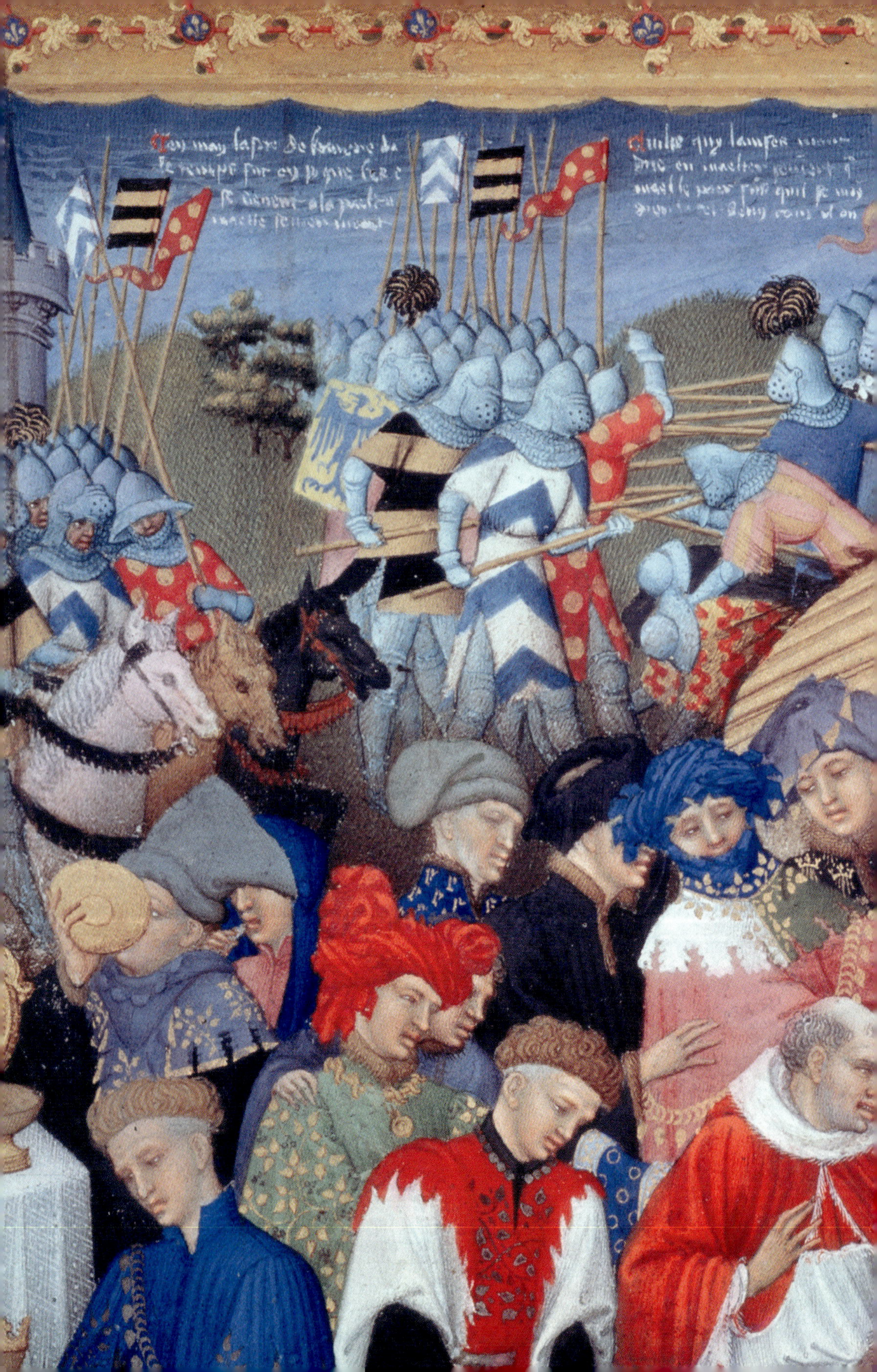

The de Limbourgs in the Service of Jean de Berry

To Pol de Limbourg, valet de chambre, in consideration of the good and welcome services he has rendered, renders each day, and it is hoped, will render in the future, and also to clothe himself and be more honourably in the Duke's service, notwithstanding other gifts given him by the Duke ...

Record of a gift of 100 écus given to Pol de Limbourg by Jean de Berry in 1413[1]

9

Many artists, like Gil de Siloé, Michel Sittow, and Juan de Flandes, travelled some distance away from their native towns for the benefit and prestige of a court appointment. What were the advantages of such a post, and might the works made in this environment differ, if at all, from a more commercial one? One of our best documented cases, although perhaps not an entirely typical one, is that of the de Limbourg brothers, who in 1404 moved from the service of Philip the Bold to that of the notoriously extravagant and acquisitive Jean de Berry. Around 1414, just after Pol received the gift recorded above, they began to paint the *Très Riches Heures* for this prince [**74, 75, 76**].[2] The parchment of this manuscript is exquisite, creamy white, extraordinarily thin and flexible; it was prepared with such care that it lies unusually flat with no undulations or wrinkles; wastage would have been high as each bifolio (relatively large at 29 × 42 centimetres each) would have had to be cut from the centre of the skin to avoid the blemishing which occurs nearer the head and leg sections of the animal. It must have been a complete joy for the brothers to work on, and much of the effect of the manuscript comes from the excessively generous margins of blank parchment that surround text and miniatures [**74**]. Working with materials of this quality must have been one of the perks of life as a court artist.

The quality of the pigments the painters were supplied with was also without parallel. Ultramarine is used almost to saturation point, and combinations of one intense blue against another are constantly exploited [**75, 76**]. In addition, the application of the paint is refined in the extreme: each figure is modelled with the most intricate strokes, fabric is highlighted with delicate flecks of liquid gold or enlivened with complex mixtures of punched and burnished metals, often finished with a translucent coloured glaze to vary the effect, Experimentation and innovation, technical and iconographic, abounds, not least in the extraordinary night scenes such as the *Ego Sum* [**74**], a rarely depicted moment where Christ displays his power over his own fate, causing the soldiers who have come to arrest him to fall to the ground.

Detail of 75

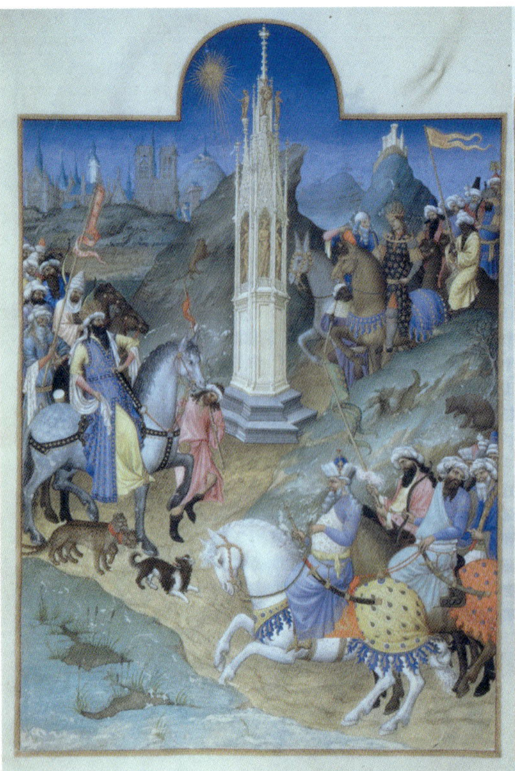
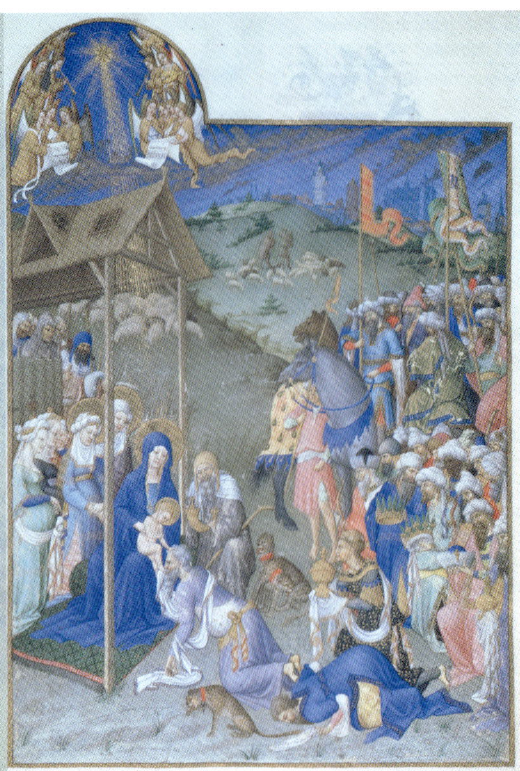

76 Pol, Jean, and Herman de Limbourg

The Meeting of the Magi and the *Adoration of the Magi* from the *Très Riches Heure*, parchment, 1411–16.

This double spread was the result of a change of plan during this manuscript's production; some of the opening sections to the Hours of the Virgin were rewritten, new sheets with full-page miniatures inserted, and here another leaf with a full-page miniature set opposite to form this expansive treatment of the Magi story. Their meeting is taking place outside Paris (note Notre Dame and the Sainte-Chapelle on the horizon).

It must have been quite extraordinary, as the tone of the description, from one of the inventories of Berry's goods, implies. That it was appreciated by the duke seems likely since it was kept with his real manuscripts as if it had been one of those precious objects: although on his death it was only valued at 50 sous (2½ livres), other real books from his inventory had similar values.[3] Nothing else like it can be found in all of the extensively documented possessions of the French royal family at this period; the painters knew their patron well enough to anticipate his delight in a cleverly crafted object, and to rely on him appreciating a sophisticated practical joke.

A sense of this relationship can also be gained from the January miniature in the *Très Riches Heures*, which shows the duke, in profile against the firescreen, feasting at New Year, in an all-male gathering [**75**]. Throughout this image visual jokes abound: the deliberate blur between the figures in the woven hangings of the story of Troy on the wall and the real figures in the room is cleverly manipulated, with the tapestry arranged to turn the wall at the precise point which allows the mounted soldiers emerging though the stone gateway in the hanging to appear to be entering the duke's hall, while the bunching up of the tapestry over the fireplace gives the illusion of the woven figures falling down over it into the hall below. Moreover, the effect of the vast firescreen behind the duke's head may well have been a deliberate reference to portrait medals—an art form that Berry collected and commissioned, buying some examples from Italian merchants in Bourges and Paris. The de Limbourgs certainly knew this part of Berry's collection well, and may even have made examples for the duke. Some would have had Berry's portrait on them; most

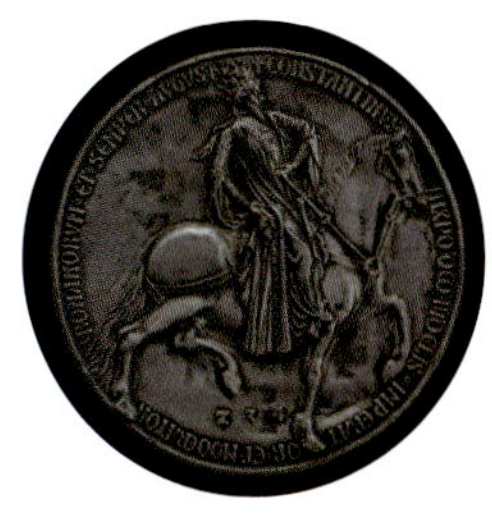

77 Artists in the circle of Jean de Berry

Constantine the Great, silver, obverse of medal made from two *repoussé* plates soldered together, *c.*1410.

These medals are copies of originals made of gold, and set on chains to be hung around the neck, but the surviving examples are either of *repoussé* silver like this (a goldsmith's technique) or cast in baser metal. The medals were certainly known by the de Limbourgs – they used this figure of Constantine on horseback as a model for the second Magi in the *Très Riches Heures* [**76**].

intriguing is a description of one from the duke's 1416 inventory which lists 'A round gold piece of jewellery, not decorated [with jewels], on which there is, on one side, an image of our lady holding her child and four small angels bearing a canopy, and on the other side a half-length image of Monseigneur [the duke] holding a golden tableau in his hand ... which Monseigneur purchased from Michelet Saulmon, his painter.'[4] Whether the de Limbourgs designed and/or made these works or not (two of them had been trained as goldsmiths so this is very possible), they quoted extensively from them in the *Très Riches Heures* and in other works for the duke [**76, 77**]. Berry was certainly keen on getting his artists to work in sometimes unexpected ways, engaging with favoured objects in his collection (such as older manuscripts by artists like Jean Pucelle which he had inherited from his father) and employing them on projects which were not their normal sphere of expertise, most notably having his sculptor, André Beauneveu, provide a series of twenty-four miniatures of matching prophets and apostles for a psalter [**78**].[5] Procuring works, engaging with the duke's collection, and working in a medium that may not be your principal training were something Berry's court artists were expected to do.

Most artists did, however, have to negotiate competitive commercial situations; they had to worry about the size, location, and cost of their premises; they had to think about attracting clients or selling their works on the open market; they had to weigh the cost of time and materials against the quality of their finished product, and navigate through the restrictions, potential penalties, and strict divisions imposed by the guilds which structured artists' lives in most of the cities of northern Europe. Their working environments, the materials they used, and how they employed them were governed very largely by the expediencies of making a living from their craft. In this, the case of Hans Memling in Bruges, who enjoyed considerable commercial success, is worth examining in some detail.

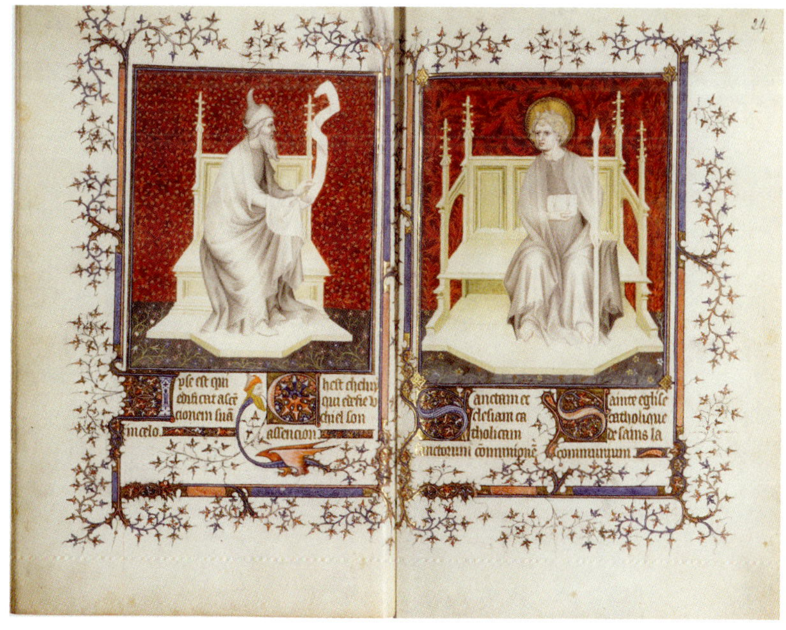

78 André Beauneveu

Amos and Matthew, miniatures from the Psalter of Jean de Berry, parchment, *c.*1390.

Beauneveu worked primarily in stone, but in Berry's service he was given a wider range of artistic challenges, such as painting these miniatures, identified as by his hand in the duke's inventory. They are on quires constructed so that each double-page opening alternates with a completely blank opening; in so doing, every miniature could be painted on the flesh side of the parchment (smoother than the hair side), leaving the reverses blank to ensure no distracting blood though from ink or pigments, providing a perfect working surface.

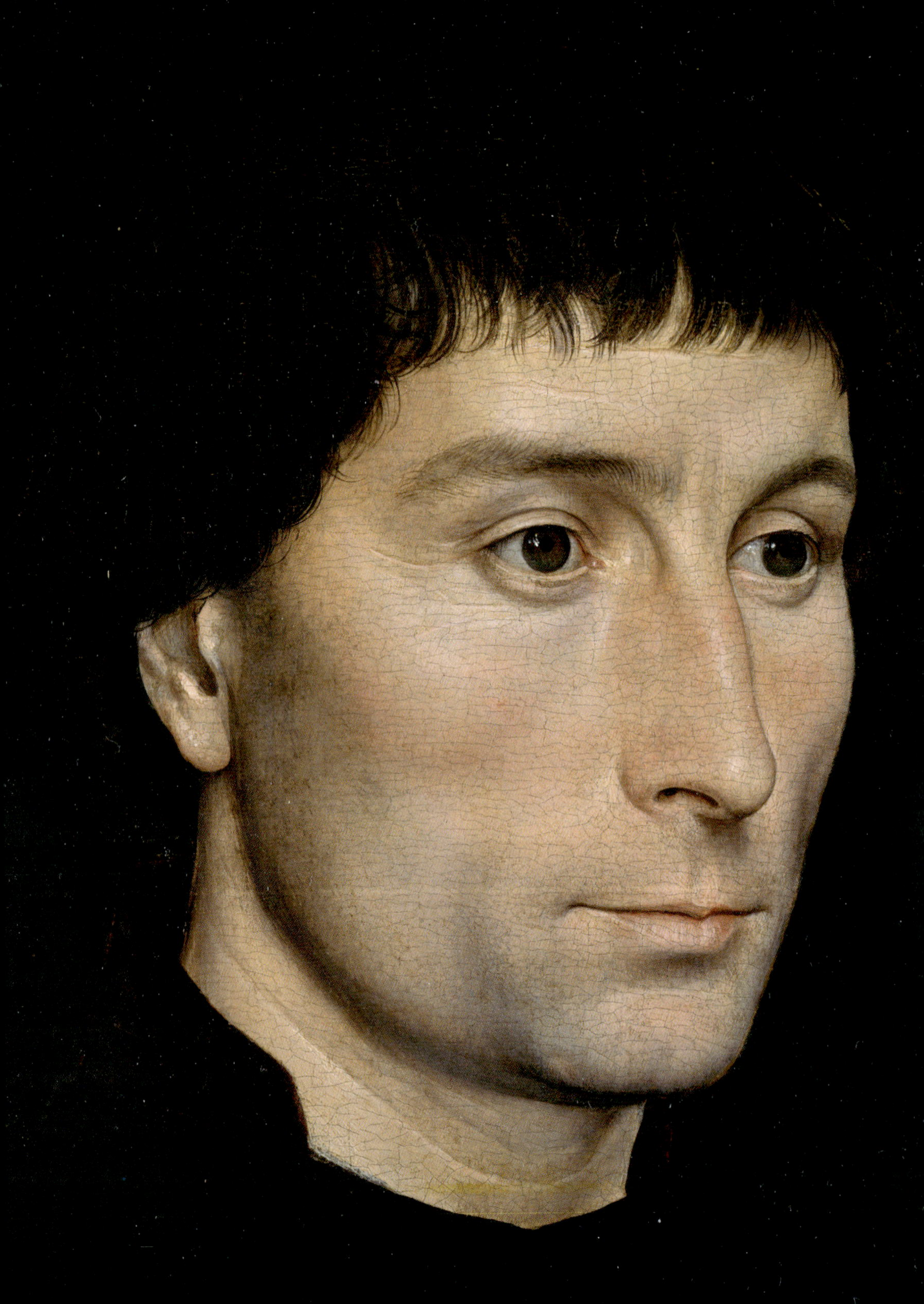

Hans Memling Painting Panels in Bruges

The greatest painter in the whole of Christendom.

Rombout de Doppere on Hans Memling, 1494

10

Few documents survive concerning Memling's life and activities, but one of the most suggestive, if perhaps overinterpreted, is his appearance in 1480–1 in a list of 875 individuals who were assessed as the richest 10 per cent of Bruges citizens.[2] This commercial success was matched by admiration which went beyond that of the local citizen Rombout de Doppere, whose epitaph for the painter is quoted above: Vasari knew of Memling,[3] and his considerable output for clients from the merchant communities ensured his paintings were sent to Spain, Germany, Italy, and the British Isles.

How did this painter, who settled in Bruges in 1465, achieve such success? It must be said that he was not alone in making a very good living from painting, and, arguably, there are other artists of our period who made more money. This could be done by various means, not always entirely though their craft alone: Dieric Bouts's wealth had come in part at least through marrying an heiress, imaginatively called Catherine 'Mettengelde' ('Catherine with the money');[4] Rogier van der Weyden and Simon Marmion both invested in stocks and property;[5] Lucas Cranach supplemented his considerable court salary by running a pharmacy and dealing in paper among his other entrepreneurial activities; Mathias Grünewald may have been in the business of manufacturing and dealing in pigments, as the inventory of his belongings on his death in 1528 indicates (see p. 200); the painter Bernt Notke was Master of the Mint in Stockholm from 1491 to 1493, and on returning to Lübeck became supervisor of the works of St Peter's church there, which entailed managing a large brickworks that exported to the whole of the Hanseatic area.

When Memling settled in Bruges he initially rented a large stone house in Sint Jorisstraat, the road which ran directly up from the Beursplein, the commercial heart of the city, where the Italian lodges were clustered [**49**] and slightly to the west of the Spanish merchants' area (see **50**); although not the most prestigious quarter of the city it was a strategic point for the custom of both these clients who were to provide him with such an important part of his trade, being close to the Augustinian abbey favoured by foreign merchants

Detail of 83

from Spain, Italy, and Nuremberg. By 1480 he had bought this rented house and in subsequent years acquired two other adjoining properties and added an extension at the rear.[6]

Memling's expansion was necessary for the many monumental works he was increasingly commissioned to undertake from the late 1470s onwards: these included the Two St Johns Altarpiece (dated 1479), 388 × 193 centimetres when open [**79**]; the Moreel Triptych (dated 1484, Bruges, Memlingmuseum) 348 × 141 centimetres when open; the double-winged Lübeck Passion Altarpiece (late 1480s, Lübeck, St Annenmuseum), 333 × 202 centimetres when open; and the Nájera Altarpiece (late 1480s), whose three surviving panels measure together 7½ metres wide [**82**].[7] Being able to handle such large panels in terms of time and space was part of the key to his financial success: Memling must also have had a highly competent and well-managed team. We know little about them apart from references to two apprentices: a Jan Verhanneman and a Passchier vander Mersch, neither of whom went on to become masters in Bruges.[8] Visual evidence of workshop participation in Memling's works is remarkably slim, but that does not mean they were produced single-handedly by him: more likely, his skill at training and managing his team meant that such intervention is not easy to find from the surface of his works alone.

Memling's success was of course dependent in large part on the fact that he was a very good painter indeed. But his output also suggests he was a canny professional who saw the potential of a market and played to it. This is evident early on in his decision to move to Bruges in 1465: this was the year after the death of Rogier van der Weyden in Brussels with whom, all the visual evidence suggests, Memling trained or at least spent time in his workshop.[9] By deciding to settle in Bruges rather than to remain in Brussels (where Rogier's son, Pieter, presumably looked set to take over his father's clientele), Memling perhaps saw the potential of supplying the wealthy foreigners there, a market that Jan van Eyck and then Petrus Christus had already tapped into. He certainly succeeded: of his surviving works for whom the patron has been identified (amounting to 28.7 per cent of his oeuvre), 20.2 per cent were made for Italians, 7.4 per cent were for Spaniards, and 4.3 per cent were for other foreign nationals; but if measured instead by painted surface area, 22.1 per cent were painted for Spaniards, 17 per cent for Italians, and 17.7 per cent for other foreign nationals.[10] It would also appear that Memling managed to specialize entirely in panel paintings, and seems not to have been required to undertake polychromy of sculpture, or more decorative work for the city or court; he also did not seem to have needed to diversify into paintings on cloth.

Although Memling was clearly armed with pattern book drawings made while in Rogier's workshop, in Bruges he adopted elements of painting from the Eyckian tradition which were to prove very appealing to both his native Bruges clients and his foreign patrons. This is most evident in a painting like the Altarpiece of the Two St Johns for the hospital of that name in Bruges, one of Memling's largest and most arresting works [**79**]. The central panel adapts many elements of van Eyck's most famous painting on public display in Bruges—the *Madonna of Canon van der Paele*, then in Saint Donatian's [**18**]. These include the semi-circular architectural setting of rich marble columns with figuratively carved capitals, the distinctive Anatolian carpet, the

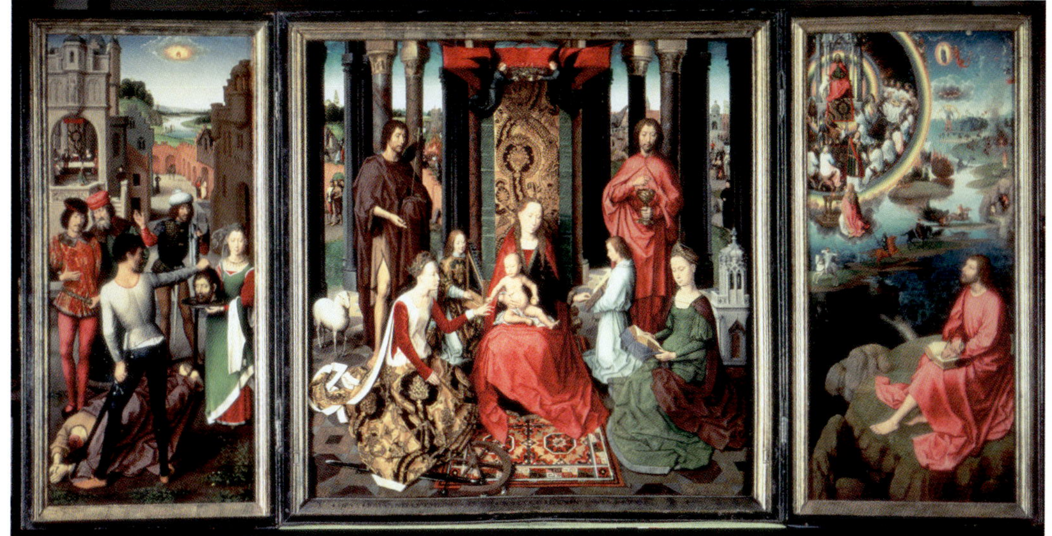

79 Hans Memling

Two St Johns Altarpiece, oil on Baltic Oak, 1479.

Memling's composition is in many ways a direct quotation of van Eyck's *Van der Paele Madonna* [**18**], but he has opened out the enclosed architecture of van Eyck's setting to provide glimpses of landscape and townscape beyond. He uses these areas to set narrative scenes which expand on the iconography of the foreground, a device which was to become one of the most inventive aspects of his work.

brocade cloth of honour and canopy behind the Virgin, and the Virgin robed in red.

Memling's paintings also refer to the Eyckian tradition in their overt inclusion of reflective surfaces, something which Rogier van der Weyden showed comparatively little interest in, using different devices to assert his skill. Some of Memling's most impressive depictions of reflections include the convex mirror in his Diptych of Maarten van Nieuwenhove (**208**, discussed in Part V below) and in the water in the seas of the apocalyptic vision in the Two St Johns Altarpiece [**79**]. His reflections are often complex and clever, although what they reflect is always part of the scene itself, its setting and occasionally its continuation outside the painting, but never the painter, in contrast to how van Eyck used the mirror in the *Arnolfini Portrait* and the armour in the St George in the *Van der Paele Madonna,* both of which reflect a figure set outside of the picture space (**18** and detail heading Chapter 12). Memling was, it seems, less interested in making a point concerning his facture of these works and their artificiality as created image, and more interested in a clever expansion and explication of his invented space and the figures in it, using them to suggest the continuation of his images beyond the painted surface.

Memling's paintings also continued the epigraphic tradition of van Eyck and Petrus Christus in both spirit and form with the inscriptions, dates, and signatures he frequently includes within his pictures and on their frames. Like van Eyck, they are sometimes represented as if of relief metal or as carved into stone; like van Eyck, Memling often paints the back of his smaller, portable, panels which were intended to be handled, not hung, in imitation of brown-red marble or porphyry; and, again, like van Eyck, the frames of several of his works are painted to imitate stone, down to the fictive breaks in the blocks from which it is supposedly constructed [**80**].[11] In many ways, then, the view of Memling as a pupil of Rogier has distracted us from the more emphatic and deliberate resonances of van Eyck in his works, which should be seen as a response to the tradition of painting in Bruges rather than the result of

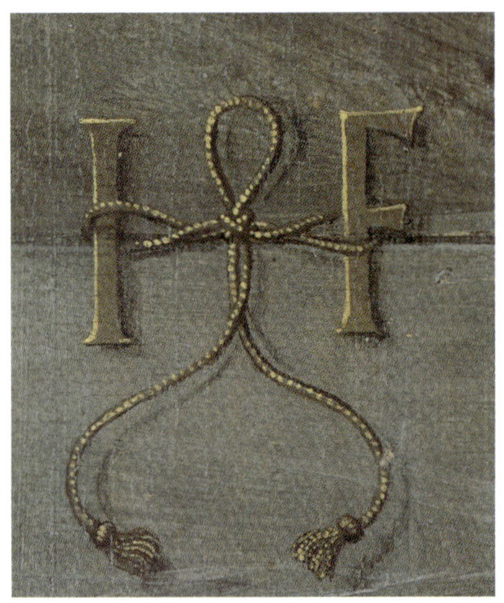

80 Hans Memling

Detail of the painted frame on the exterior wings of the Triptych of Jan Floreins, oil on Baltic oak, 1479.

The exterior frame of this well-preserved triptych (it has its original base, lock, and hinges) shows the subtlety with which Memling treated this element of his works, following the example of Jan van Eyck. Here he imitates in paint a variety of marble and porphyry blocks, the breaks in the masonry joined by the initials of the donor I and F, painted in imitation of metal relief, tied together by a painted cord that hangs loose from the fictive marble on which it casts a fictive shadow.

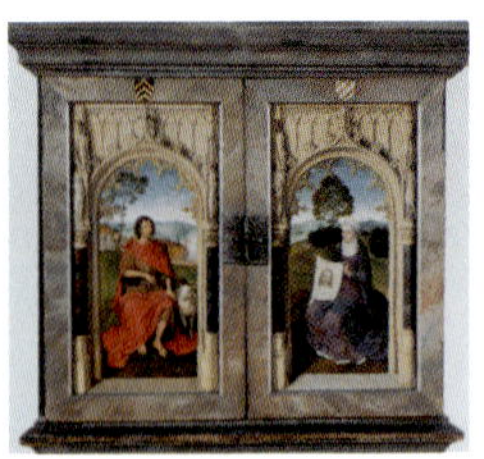

a master–pupil relationship or 'influence'. This Eyckian tradition was continued in a similar manner in Bruges by Gerard David and his workshop, who catered for the continuing taste for works in this style, and who worked for a similarly international clientele, sending monumental altarpieces to Genoa and Mallorca.

Memling not only understood how to make paintings that had a distinctive brand, he knew how to make them both beautifully and fast, by means of both economic invention and economic execution. In terms of invention, his works reuse ideas, once developed, several times. Most popular, and adaptable, of these was the Virgin and Child with saints, seen in its grandest form in the Two St Johns Altarpiece [**79**]. Variations on this theme are found in works for the English courtier and diplomat Sir John Donne [**81**],[12] for a member of the Flemish Floreins family, but which may have been destined for Spain (Paris, Louvre); for the Dominican friar Benedetto Pagagnotti [**2**], and for various other unidentified clients.[13] The repetition here may have been patron-driven, with clients wanting something similar to an impressive work they had recently seen on display in a church or chapel (such reference being a standard form in many contracts of the period, see above, p. 48) or they may have been seduced by a work of this sort that Memling had in his workshop for just this purpose—to demonstrate the possible options and the level of quality to prospective buyers. Whatever the motivating factors and their origin—and they were probably a mixture of these—Memling makes clever and inventive reuse of existing patterns. He never simply repeats; every figure is varied in some manner, or their arrangement is revised, the settings altered, or backgrounds changed. This can be seen even in the settings and props, like the cloths of honour behind his Virgins: they look similar, and may sometimes be rendered from the same bolt of cloth, but they are never the same pattern in the same area of its repeat.

The economic execution evident in Memling's work is achieved in several ways, the first of which is the limited number of relatively thin paint layers he uses to achieve his effects. This is confirmed and explicated though tech-

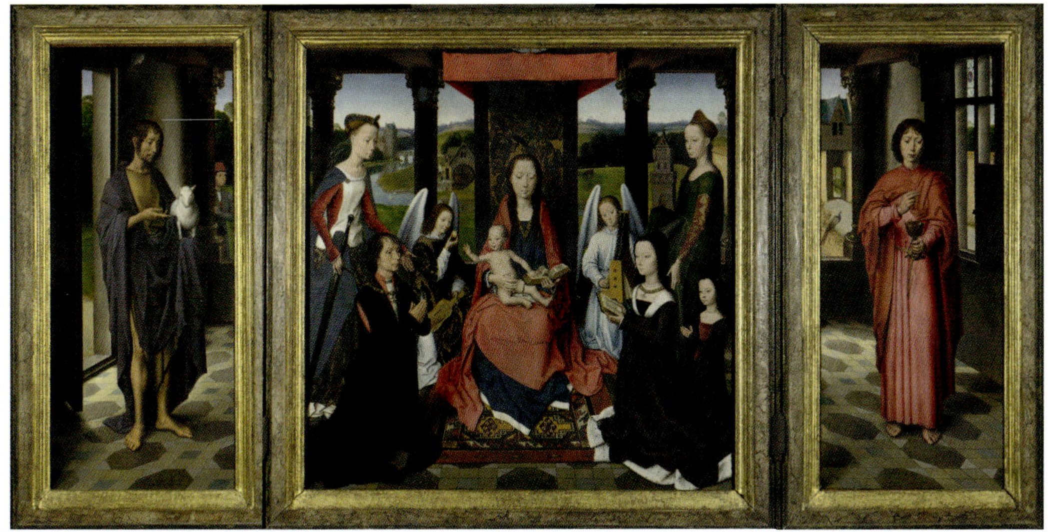

81 Hans Memling
The Virgin and Child with Saints and Donors (the 'Donne Triptych'), oil on Baltic oak, 1478.
This triptych has been rightly described as one of Memling's most successful variations on a successful theme [see **2, 79**]. Its patron, Sir John Donne, was frequently in the Netherlands on diplomatic missions for the English King, Edward IV; his wife Elizabeth Hastings, kneeling with her daughter on the right, was depicted in the first paint layers in a more idealized fashion, and was repainted to be sharper featured, thinner lipped, and presumably more like Lady Donne herself either when Memling met her or when an image of her was made available to him.

nical examination but also visible today to the naked eye: often his flesh tones are applied sparingly enough that with increased translucency over time the underdrawing shows clearly through. Fabrics and materials are described in a minimalist manner, evident in how he has painted (impressively) the red velvet of St Catherine's robe in **79** or the white fur edging of Maria Portinari's dress [**83**]. Throughout, he manages to achieve depth of colour with speed. In his red draperies, which required particularly slow-drying red lake glazes, Memling often adopts a system whereby a single layer of cross-hatched strokes creates depth of colour and shadow over the opaque vermilion base, rather than several layers of translucent glaze, each of which would have taken several days to dry. Whereas Jan van Eyck and Rogier van der Weyden built up their paint surfaces at the point of their deepest hue with as many as five or six layers, Memling used fewer, sometimes just two. Yet such economy would be counterproductive if the finished effect was not up to standard. Memling's skill is in retaining an effect of depth and richness with such an amazingly light touch.[14]

Memling was also clearly able and happy to alter his formats and his imagery, to an extent, to foreign tastes. No client going to the trouble of acquiring a Memling would want it to not be recognizably so, or at least recognizably a product of Bruges, but working to the foreign market did often require that he produce paintings in different formats or with different iconography than would have been required by more local patrons. The double wings of the triptych made for the chapel of the Hanseatic merchant Heinrich Greverade and his brother in the cathedral of Lübeck, would have been demanded by the patron as necessary for the liturgical practices in use there, where two sets of wings were routine (see pp. 241–2). The triptych made for Benedetto Pagagnotti [**2**] is distinctly Netherlandish in format as most paintings for Italian patrons seem to have been, but its imagery of garlands held by naked putti and the choice of Lawrence as one of the saints depicted on the wings must have been included because of its Italian patron and his tastes.[15]

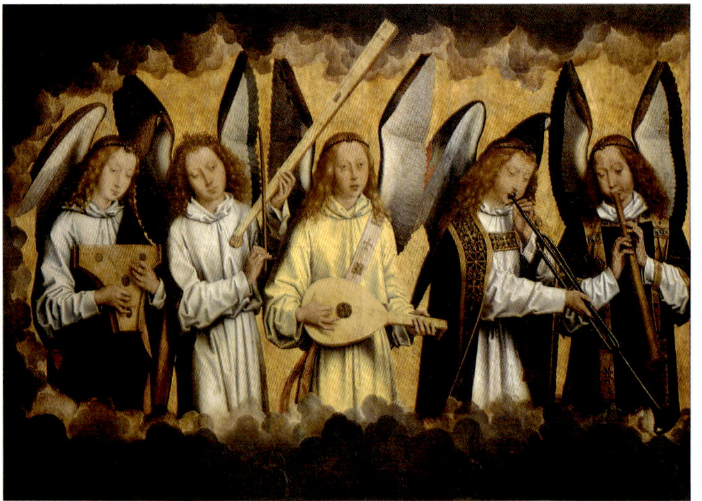

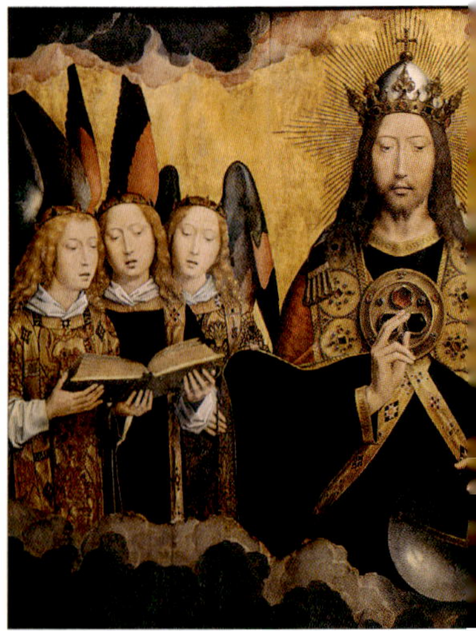

82 Hans Memling

Christ as Salvator Mundi with Music-Making Angels, panels from an altarpiece made for the Benedictine church in Nájera, northern Spain, *c.*1487–90.

These panels form the top of a vast altarpiece, which originally was an ensemble of at least nine fixed panels, with a large image of the Assumption and Coronation of the Virgin forming its centre. This required Memling to produce a whole range of iconography outside his normal repertoire, since these subjects were not common in Netherlandish panel paintings; the panels are customized in their details, too, with the arms of Castile and León on the robes of the angels.

The work in which Memling had to stretch himself most extensively professionally as well as artistically, perhaps, was the Nájera Altarpiece [**82**]. This was a truly major commission, a set of panels that was to fill the whole altar wall of the Benedictine monastery church of Santa Maria la Real in Nájera, in Navarre in northern Spain, and which required him to plan and paint a vast, non-folding polyptych with unusual iconography and large areas of gilding. The scale of this project may possibly have entailed moving the workshop or members of it to Spain for a period, at least to see the setting before work began or to install the panels properly when they were complete.

It is, however, in the realm of portraiture that Memling shone most brightly and led the field by a very long way indeed.[16] More than a third of his large surviving output is made up of portraits, which indicates the level of demand he catered to and the extent of his specialization in this field. The Italians, in particular, wanted to be painted by Memling, and his portraits for Italian sitters show why. That of Tommaso Portinari and his wife [**83**], originally the wings of a devotional triptych, reveals the sheer skill of paint handling and mastery of texture: the sheen of the skin with its subtle changes of tone around the cheeks and nose, the liquidity of the eyes, and the softness of the hair are all impressively evoked. The ability to observe and render the smallest of surface details is also remarkable: the tiny pimples on Portinari's cheek are described, as is the scar on his chin where no stubble grows, the reddening of the whites of the eyes, and the eyebrows and eyelashes are, almost to a hair, individually drawn (see detail facing this chapter). But this is combined with an ability to marry likeness with a rendition which softened and subtly flattered, as can be seen from comparing the portrait of Maria with the image of her by Hugo van der Goes on the Portinari Triptych [**67**]. Memling smooths out the planes of the face, and chooses the most flattering of angles to represent his sitters from, preferring for example a seven-eighths view rather than a true three-quarters view, which ensures that more of the far side eye is visible, and that the nose does not break the outline of the far cheek, both of

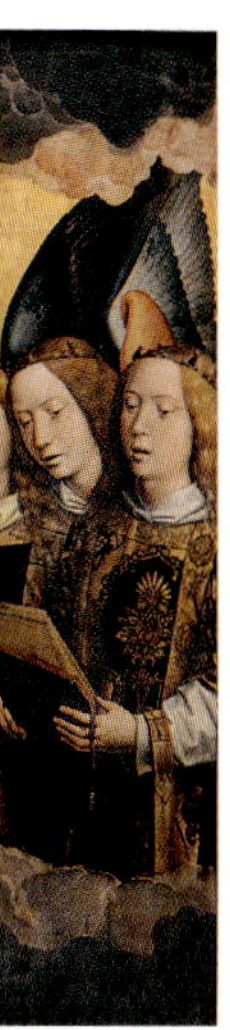

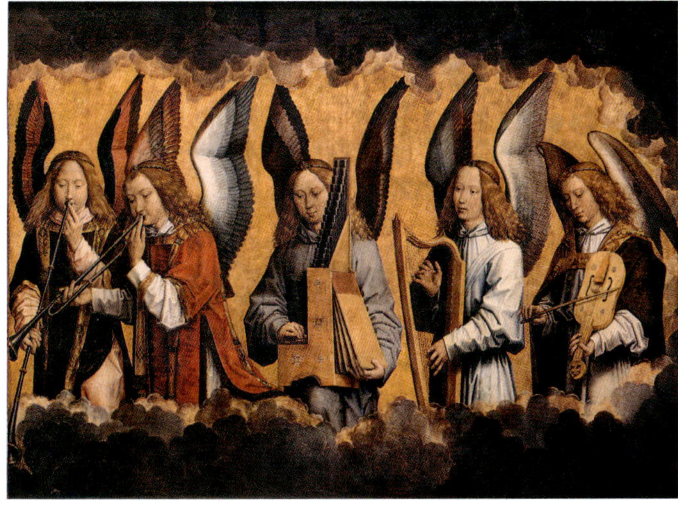

83 Hans Memling

Portraits of Tommaso and Maria Portinari, oil on Baltic oak, *c.*1470.

An inventory of the Portinari palace in Florence taken in 1501 on Tommaso's death records this work as 'a small valuable panel with an image of our lady in the middle, and on the sides painted Tommaso and mona Maria his wife'. The central panel is now lost.

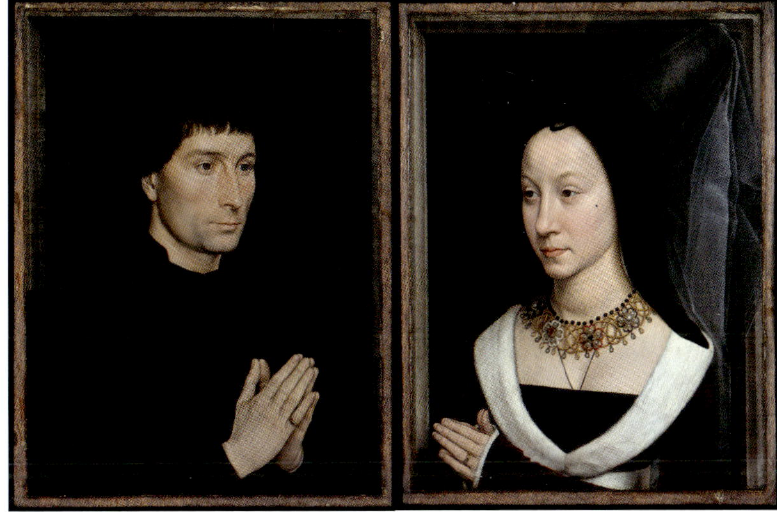

which make for the appearance of more regularity. He also tends to give luminosity to the eyes and sense of motion to the face with eyes that sometimes look in slightly different directions, and he sets the irises of his sitters' eyes in such a manner so that they float clear of the lower lid. In Memling's portraits his power to depict an illusion of life and likeness is blatantly in evidence: he was also an innovative constructor of narrative devotional works, which are examined in Chapter 18.

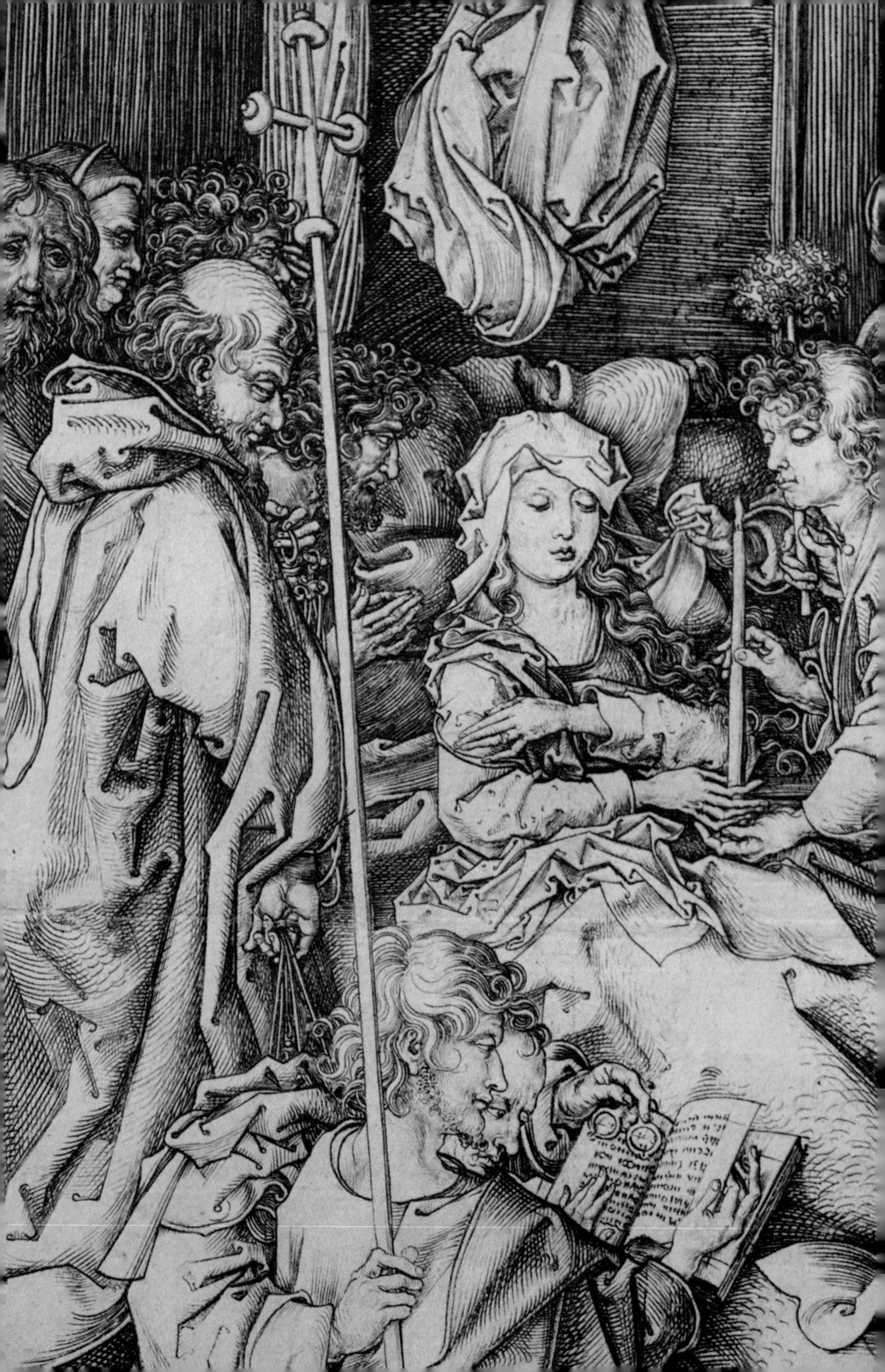

Printmakers in the Rhine Valley Inventing, Marketing, and Distributing Images

This image was judged in my youth to be the finest work to have come out of Germany, therefore I pasted it into my Bible ...

The embroiderer Hans Plock, 1550, on Martin Schongauer's *Death of the Virgin* [**91**][1]

11

There were other ways of making money and extending one's artistic inventions across Europe than through high-quality panel paintings for the merchant communities. More effective in certain respects was the new medium of prints, since although small in scale, they allowed the production of true multiple copies, enabling the same image to be seen at different places across Europe by different people at the very same time. Moreover, while an artist in the employ of a court patron (like the de Limbourgs) or one working for various local and international patrons (like Memling) might have the form and appearance of their works specified to greater or lesser extents to them, the printmaker worked in most instances speculatively, creating his images without patronal intervention, but instead with an eye to what would sell. He could, potentially, shape as well as respond to the demands of the market. Most successful in this respect were probably the engravers based on the Rhine like the Master of the Berlin Passion (*fl.* late fifteenth century), Master ES (*fl.* *c.*1450–67), Israhel van Meckenem (*fl c.*1457–1503), and Martin Schongauer (*fl.* 1471–91), although twenty years later Dürer was to completely redefine the enterprise of printmaking and its economic and visual potential.[2] Dürer's activity falls in the most part outside the scope of this study, but his written testimony concerning how he sold, bartered, and gave away his graphic works is indispensable. The output and the strategies these engravers employed to make their prints desirable, useful, and collectable will be the focus of this section.

Detail of 91

Engraving emerged in the Rhine valley and southern Germany around 1440.[3] Primarily this type of print was made by those with a training or background in metalwork (like Israhel van Meckenem, who signs himself 'goldsmith', or Master ES, who used goldsmith's punches on many of his prints) or painting (like the Housebook Master (*fl. c.* 1470–1500), who also painted manuscripts, or Dürer, who also made woodcuts), or both, like Schongauer (whose father and brothers were goldsmiths, but who was trained as a painter). Setting up as an engraver was an appealing option for metalworkers since the outlay and equipment needed were less expensive than those needed to be a goldsmith: the raw materials were cheaper (copper plates, paper and ink, as opposed to more precious metals), and the equipment was much less elaborate and bulky (printmakers did not need a furnace, and they did not necessarily have to own a printing press). Indeed, printmaking also presented similar advantages over the painter's craft, since it did not require expensive pigments, laborious preparation of panels, grinding of pigments or gilding.

For printmakers to be successful, however, they needed a good distribution network: the fact that so many of the most productive engravers were active on the Rhine where the river ensured easy traffic in their goods is no accident (we return to the issue of distribution below). Centres on rivers such as the Rhine, Main, and Schussen were also important in the manufacture and distribution of the key raw material for printmaking—paper. A good supply of paper was a vital, although not the only, ingredient in the development of this medium at the period. Paper seems to have become more widely available in the north, and less expensive, from the late fourteenth century: previously Italy and Spain had been the main centres for its production (and continued to be important for northern markets) but competing mills had been set up in Troyes, in France, in the 1330s, followed by other centres in the Auvergne and Champagne regions, with the first mill in Germany established outside Nuremberg in 1391 by Ulmer Stromer. Prices for paper rose again at the end of the fifteenth century, but they remained a small fraction in relation to the finished article: it has been estimated, for example, that three or four impressions of one of Dürer's ambitious whole sheet engravings like the *St Jerome in his Study* could be exchanged for a 500-sheet ream of good-quality printing paper [**84**].[4]

One appeal of prints to their maker, and to those marketing them, was how widely and easily they could be sold and distributed, sometimes in extremely large numbers. In 1440 in Padua a local skin-dyer had agreed to sell 3,500 woodcuts (origin unknown) for a Flemish trader,[5] while the scale in which Dürer distributed his prints to artists (painters, goldsmiths, sculptors, glass painters, their apprentices and journeymen), dignitaries, and collectors in the Netherlands on his journey there in 1521 is further testimony to how they might be widely dispersed: during his year-long stay he offloaded at least 108 of his 'Large Books' (the woodcut *Apocalypse*, *Life of the Virgin*, and *Great Passion*), 24 sets of his *Engraved Passion*, 22 sets of his *Small Woodcut Passion*, dozens of his single-sheet engravings that were not parts of sets (such as 14 *St Jeromes* [**84**]), 21 unspecified 'whole-sheet' engravings, 34 'half-sheets', 71 'quarter-sheets', many others just estimated by value (for example, 12 ducats' worth of prints traded for 1 ounce of ultramarine), and no fewer than 8 complete sets of his prints (one, for example, to Margaret of Austria, another to an Italian artist 'to send to Rome').[6] Dürer

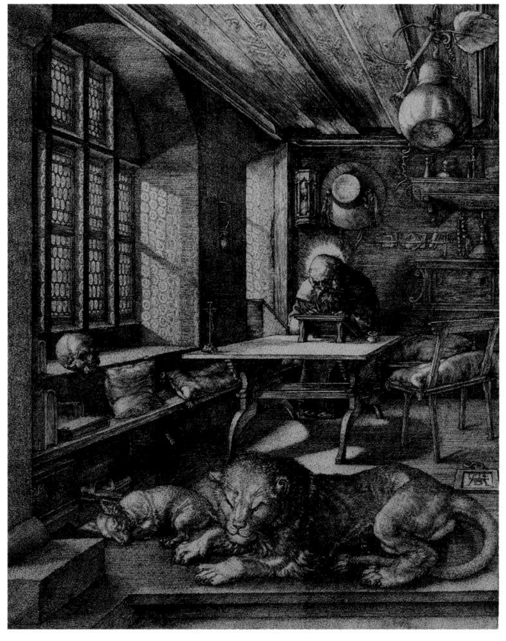

84 Albrecht Dürer
St Jerome in his Study, engraving on paper, 1514.
This was the print Dürer distributed most extensively on his journey to the Netherlands, and it is the most ambitious of his works in terms of the description of light, textures, and interior space.

also famously engaged his wife and mother in selling his prints in centres like Cologne, some distance from his home in Nuremberg. For Dürer, clearly, the speed at which his prints could spread an idea or invention across Europe provided a particular appeal, and this may have been recognized by his predecessors too. Schongauer's works reached almost as large an audience as Dürer's (they were used by artists as divergent geographically and artistically as Bosch, Michelangelo, and Veit Stoss). Like Dürer, he travelled as a mature artist, and may, also like Dürer, have engaged his family members in the distribution of his works: at one time or another Schongauer had strategically placed brothers, who were either goldsmiths or painters, in the major trading centres of Ulm, Leipzig, Augsburg, Basel and Strasbourg (see Map 1).

In the many instances where we cannot trace with documentary evidence the travels of prints, printmakers, their family members, or agents across Europe, we can instead follow their passage with the visual evidence of the wide and often very speedy adoption of their inventions by other artists. This allows us to track the movement and trade in prints from, for example, the Netherlands to Paris, Florence, Burgos and Palma, and from the Rhine to Nuremberg, Bruges, Venice, Milan, Florence, Poland, Zaragoza, Pamploma, Salamanca and Seville.[7] The development by engravers of marks indicating their authorship must relate in part to this likely, intended, and realized wide distribution network: you could not rely on local knowledge to inform any interested parties about the name of their maker, as you might for an altarpiece or other major public work.

For an artist making engravings the commercial success of their venture also lay in large part in how many good quality impressions they could pull from their plates, which, because of the relative softness of copper (the material most widely used in the north), eventually wore out. It has been estimated from a range of evidence that the most a copper plate might yield was around 200 fine impressions, 600 good ones, and another 1,200 to 1,500 poor if usable

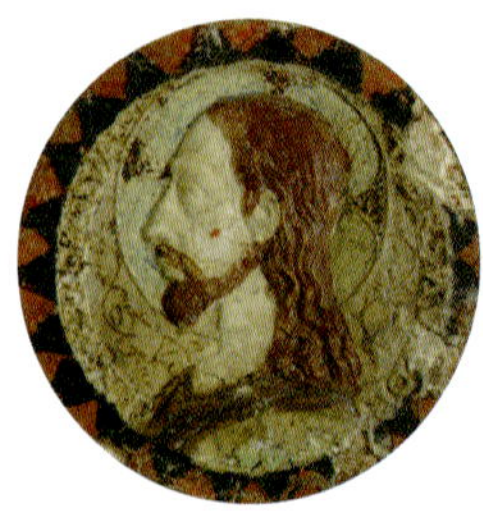

85 German, found at the convent of Wienhausen, near Celle

Head of Christ, papier-mâché roundel, *c.*1500.

This object reproduces a famous and revered profile image of Christ based on a letter describing his features known as the 'Lentulus Letter'. Papier-mâché reliefs were made with moulds and then hand coloured, one of the cheapest ways of mass producing a three-dimensional image. They were particularly ephemeral images and few survive, but a cache of them were found under the floorboards of the convent at Wienhausen.

ones, with the plate exhausted.[8] Just how many, however, depended on how the plate was made (hammering the metal increased its density and thus longevity under the press), how it was cut (deeper burin cuts would print more good images), and how it was printed (the evenness or strength of the pressure used in the printing process would affect how many good prints could be achieved before the finer lines were obscured). These elements were experimented with and improved by the most skilled and canny of engravers like Master ES and Schongauer. That we have over 30 complete sets of Schongauer's *Passion* series in existence today, and over 70 impressions of some individual prints from this cycle, is testament to how many good quality impressions he could pull before the plate was exhausted, as well as an indication of how popular and successful these particular works were.[9] The success of these artists was not based solely on their ability to saturate the market: perhaps more importantly, these engravers developed ways of using a burin to create immensely subtle and varied lines capable of mimicking materials and the fall of light in black on white, and thus producing images refined enough in their visual language to rival the illusionistic, painterly, or decorative achievements of competing media like painting, illumination, and metalwork. With a work like Dürer's *St Jerome in his Study* [**84**], these painterly qualities reach their apogee.

Simple woodcuts were on the whole easier to make and print from than engravings: the blocks still wore out, but not as fast, allowing a larger number of reproductions to be made fairly quickly and relatively cheaply by anyone who could purchase or have a block cut, and who had access to ink and paper. In 1466, for example, the Abbess Jacoba van Loon at the convent of Bethanie at Mechelen had in her rooms on her death 'an instrument for printing words and images' and 'nine blocks of wood and 14 blocks of stone for printing images'.[10] The large number of woodcuts owned by the Dominican nuns of St Catherine's convent at Nuremberg in the fifteenth century, which included a 'picture panel' (*Bild-tafel*), an assemblage of 85 painted woodcut prints incorporated into a wooden triptych, has led to the suggestion that the

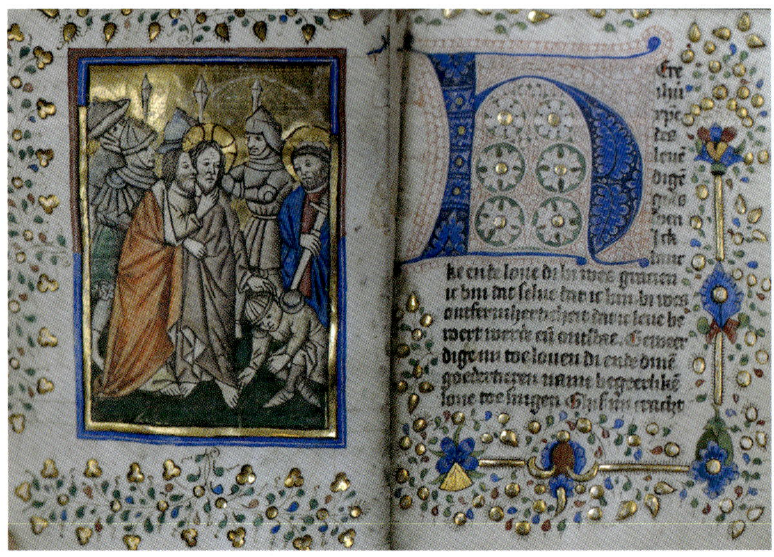

86 Master of the St Erasmus scenes

Arrest of Christ, copperplate engraving on paper stuck onto parchment, gilded, and painted, *c.*1470.

Despite its careful incorporation into a manuscript, the nature of this image as a print has not been entirely disguised, since the thin colour wash allows the strong lines of the engraving to remain: perhaps this was to avoid the need to recreate these lines again in the paint surface.

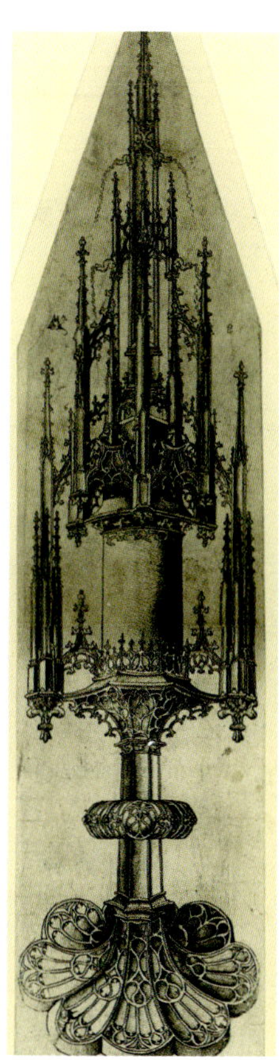

87 Master W with the Key (Willem vanden Cruce?)

Design for a Monstrance, copperplate engraving on paper.

The market for designs which could be used by other artists, working in a wide range of media, was relatively large. This large engraving of a monstrance was printed over two sheets to enable it to be of a sufficient size to function as a model for a goldsmith; such images were also used by painters who needed to portray similar objects within their works.

nuns here, too, printed woodcuts themselves in the convent.[11] Many convents certainly bought them in large numbers and spent time embellishing them, as is indicated by the cache of items that were relatively recently discovered under the floorboards of the convent of Wienhausen near Celle in Germany. They include painted papier-mâché reliefs [**85**], tin reliefs and woodcuts, and also brushes, shells with traces of paint in them, and other tools used to decorate these works.[12] The addition of text, paint, and even embroidery to printed images was an activity which, while creating functional objects, fulfilled the needs of the nuns' religious activities. Decorating images of Christ was one way in which they expressed their devotion to Him.[13]

Some engravers, like the Master of the Berlin Passion and his associates, targeted this monastic market with some success, producing images in a format and iconography which could readily be incorporated into manuscript texts. They issued extensive Passion cycles of as many as 45 or more images printed 8 to a sheet which could be cut and pasted or bound into manuscripts, or even, if printed in a certain sequence and position on the sheet, folded into booklets. The images themselves were consistently around 7–8 × 5–6 centimetres, a size comparable to small miniatures, and often had similar decorative frames incorporated into their design. These works could thus be used as a base from which a more richly decorated, coloured work could be created, alleviating the need to invent, and draw, the subject required, and thus saving time and money. A good example of such substitution at work is a manuscript made around 1460–75 in Arnhem [**86**]; here instead of miniatures drawn onto the parchment, prints have been stencil cut (that is, cut out around the main outlines of the figures) and then stuck onto the parchment leaves, the backgrounds and borders around them extensively gilded and sometimes also tooled.[14]

Prints could thus serve as actual, physical bases for the creation of more elaborate works, and were apparently marketed by their makers as such. Many engravers also saw the potential their medium presented for fulfilling the considerable demand for design ideas and patterns by professional artists. Indeed, one of the most important, and possibly underestimated, markets for printmakers was other craftsmen, and it could be claimed that engraving was initially developed by artists for other artists. The major part of the output of the Bruges artist Master W with the Key (*fl.* 1465–85), for example, consisted of designs for metalwork or carved stone or wood: patterns for decorative carved leaf motifs, for chalices, censors, crosiers, water stoops, and monstrances, some with cross-sections showing how an object might be constructed, or printed over two sheets to provide a large design to scale [**87**]. He also produced a series of elaborate, empty architectural 'stage sets' [**88**], possibly patterns or ideas for the *caisses* of carved retables, metalwork shrines, or even *tableaux vivants*.[15] Master ES, Israhel van Meckenem, and Martin Schongauer all produced similar designs, sometimes also with cross-sections and sometimes also printed over more than one large sheet to allow a full-scale model, although some seem to be more about artistic and technical display than about a practical pattern to follow. Master ES, notably, seems to have produced works which were directed towards this market: it is not just that his engravings were used extensively by a very wide range of artisans, from goldsmiths to glass painters, but the form and format in which he issued

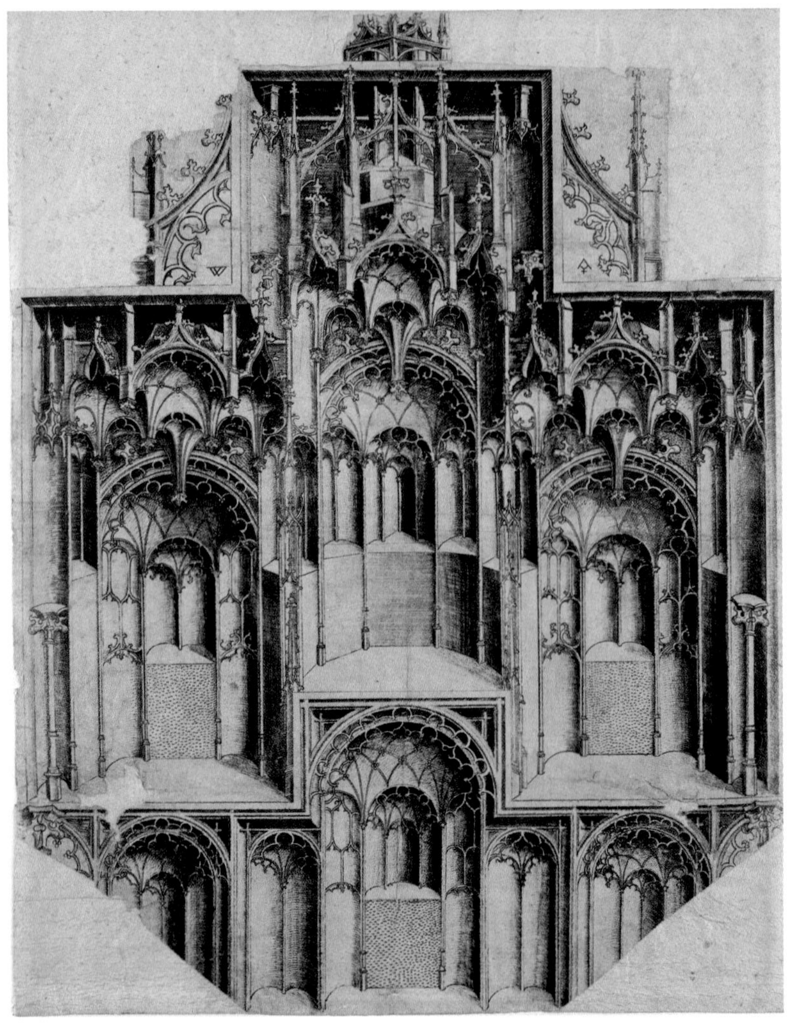

88 Master W with the Key (Willem vanden Cruce?)

Design for an Altarpiece with Eight Niches, engraving on paper.

This is another large-scale print at 31 × 25 cm, and can only have been intended as a model or a display of invention; in either case its intended audience and buyers were other artists. The print has been cut down at its lower corners.

many of his prints show that he created them specifically with such a buyer in mind. His favoured small roundel format (with diameters of around 8–11 centimetres) was exactly the right shape and scale for mother-of-pearl carvers (who mostly produced small round plaques) or for metalwork decoration, and the round form of many other engravings may relate to the huge market for stained glass roundels.[16]

Master ES was also one of the first to recognize the potential of issuing his engravings in sets, something Schongauer, van Meckenem, and particularly Dürer later exploited to great success. Dürer distributed his various *Passion* and *Life of the Virgin* series as complete sets on his Netherlandish journey, which indicates that he certainly expected them to be viewed and acquired this way. Moreover, he distributed his sets most widely to the painters, sculptors, metalworkers, and glass painters he met there, and to their journeymen and apprentices, which provides further indication that he envisaged other artists as a major target audience for his prints. The appeal is obvious: subjects like

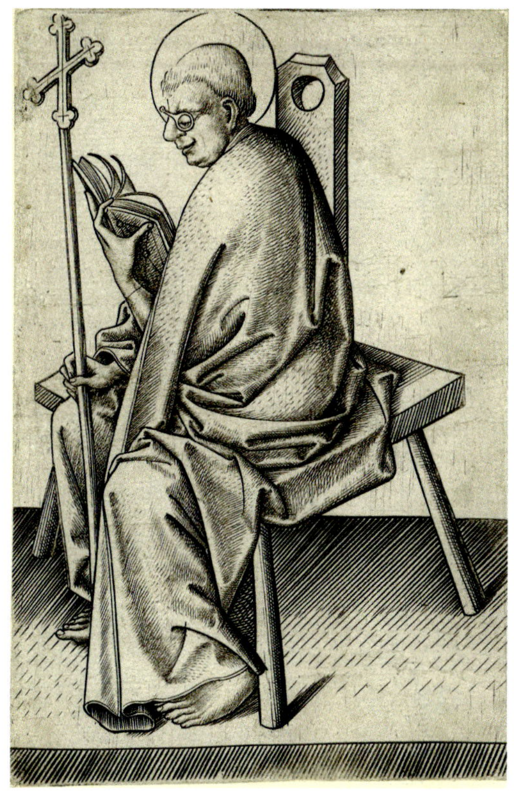

89 Master ES
St Philip Seated, copperplate engraving on paper.

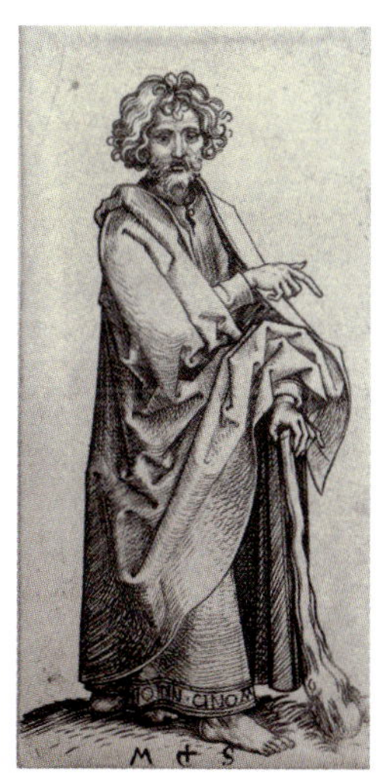

90 Martin Schongauer
St Judas Thaddeus, copperplate engraving on paper.

the twelve apostles, the four evangelists, the Passion, or the life of the Virgin presented craftsmen with a complete 'package' of their most often-used subjects (see below, p. 168, for the artist Bernadino Simondi, who in his will left among his patterns sets of engravings of the twelve apostles and a Passion series). Sets also allowed for buyers of any sort to purchase in smaller or larger numbers, whetting an appetite to collect the whole run.

Master ES issued four different sets of apostles, clearly designed to appeal to different needs: a small set (9.3 × 6.3 centimetres) with the saints standing and each holding part of the text of the apostles' creed (to get the whole text you needed the whole set); a large set with the saints standing, without scrolls (14.7 × 9.7 centimetres), a third with them seated in a slightly wider format (15.2 × 9.7 centimetres [**89**]) which, it has been posited, was targeted specifically at sculptors, and a fourth small but visually complex set (9.5 × 6.5 centimetres) where the apostles are paired in architectural niches. In addition, he produced two sets of seated evangelists (one square, one round). The apostle sets are a master class in variation within a potentially repetitive theme: the seated saints are particularly inventive, with unusual and complex viewpoints [**89**]. Many of the apostles are shown with their backs almost entirely to the viewer, or in strong profile, or from a high viewpoint. They are seated on different benches and chairs, and with varied physical types and poses. It was Schongauer [**90**], however, whose sets of apostles and Passion series were most widely used by other artists, and they

91 **Martin Schongauer**
Death of the Virgin, copperplate engraving on paper.

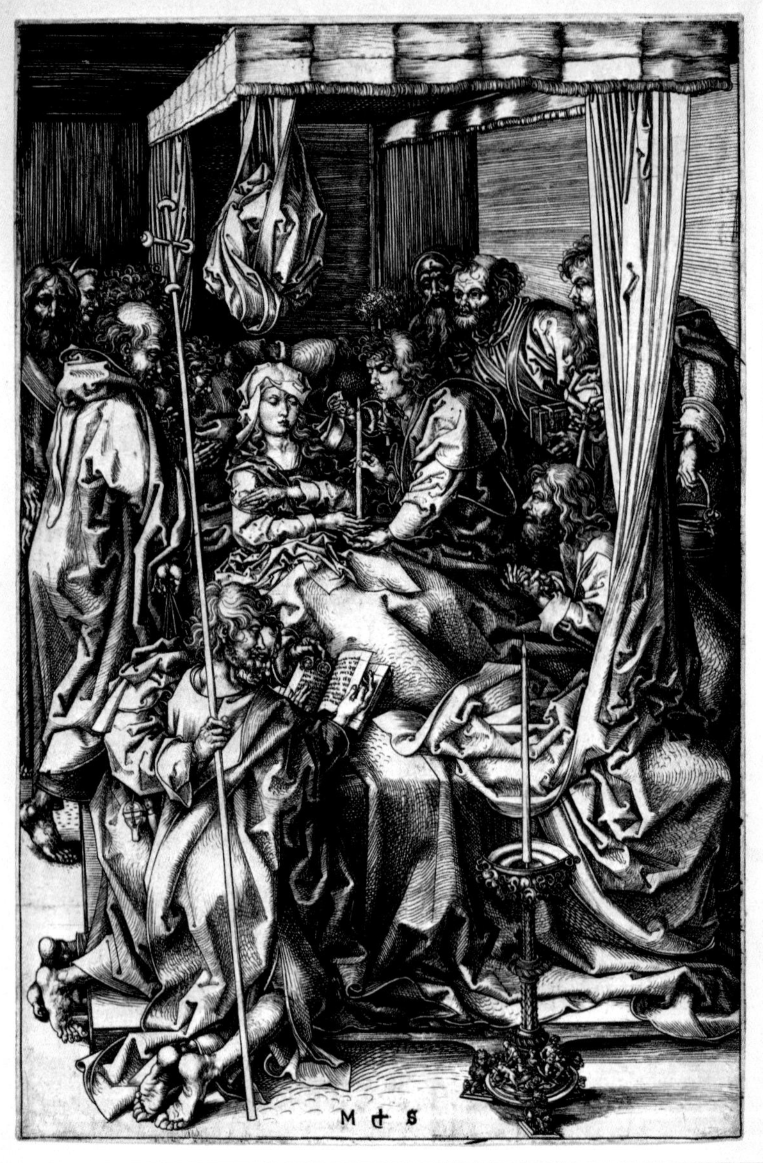

must have been present in very many sculptors' and painters' workshops of the period. They served, for example, as the basis for entire carved choir stalls or altarpieces; they were distributed as models to the assistants of Veit Stoss and Tilman Riemenscheider and were copied by artists from Poland to Spain, and Italy to the Netherlands, the plates being recarved and the series reissued by Ishrahel van Meckenem and other engravers.[17] His *Death of the Virgin* [**91**], so admired by Hans Plock (see quote and detail at head of this chapter) was one of his most influential inventions, and is a brilliant set piece which references other traditions and media, with the eyeglasses held over the text and altering the words below being a quote from van Eyck's

Van der Paele Madonna [**18**]; the elaborate candlestick set right at the front of the image is like a design for metalwork incorporated into this narrative scene, and the range of decorative patterns created by the bed curtains and covers are like a master-class in depicting drapery and its expressive possibilities.

The materiality of prints allowed them to be used for multiple purposes: the potential of engravings to cater to a different market—that for small, relatively cheap (though not always so), lightweight devotional images, which also had something of the richness and detail achieved in more expensive media—was recognized by early engravers. It was also recognized by those who commissioned prints, which, if not a common practice, certainly occurred. Master ES, for example, produced three engravings for the Benedictine monastery of Einsiedeln, near Lake Constance in modern Switzerland (designated today as *Large*, *Small*, and *Smallest Virgins of Einsiedeln*, **92**, **93**, **94**). These were designed as souvenirs to be bought by the thousands of pilgrims who were expected to visit the monastery in 1466 for the 500-year anniversary of the institution of a papal bull recognizing a miracle involving the dedication of the chapel of the Virgin there. Here the engraver was clearly working on commission rather than on his own initiative, since the monastery had a monopoly on the sale of images relating to the site (he could not have produced and sold such works without its instigation). The potential market for these engravings was huge: during the fourteen-day celebration of the anniversary it is recorded that the monastery sold over 130,000 souvenir images (of all sorts), which would easily take up the largest of possible print runs from the Master's three plates.[18]

The production by the Master ES of three different versions, at three different sizes and with three different levels of elaboration in their imagery, allows us to see how both artists and patrons understood that prints of this sort were targeted at purchasers with different budgets or needs. The differences between the versions are telling. All three include the building (the miracle after all involved its dedication, so this element was key) and all three show the Virgin and Child with an angel and St Benedict (it is a Benedictine monastery, and the angel was a key player in the miraculous event, having performed the dedication ceremony). But here the similarities end. These are not simply the same print made in three different scales: the differences are in iconographic richness (there are 24 figures in the *Large* version, which has a host of 14 angels, and 5 pilgrims in supplication, as opposed to 6 figures in the *Small* and 4 in the *Smallest* version), in complexity of forms, in narrative realism, and moreover in skill and refinement of technique.

While the Master ES and Schongauer seem to have designed and printed all their own engravings, Israhel van Meckenem, a goldsmith from Bocholt who may have been the son of the Master of the Berlin Passion, worked in quite another way, exploiting very quickly a potential distinctive to this medium—that the copper plates used to make prints could be recut. This allowed a whole series of similar but not identical works to be produced with little actual invention or design and far less time and effort on the part of the artist. Van Meckenem acquired no fewer than 41 of the Master ES's plates (suggesting he was working in that Master's shop at his death), as well as

92 Master ES

Large Virgin of Einsiedeln, copperplate engraving on paper, 20.6 × 12.3 cm.

Prints were ideal pilgrimage souvenirs and could be targeted, like these three, at different markets and purses. The large version is distinguished by its visual complexity but also by its technical refinement and observation of detail: the date and the initial E on the archway are described as if chiselled into the stonework; the stones used to make the archway are marked with mason's marks, and the method by which the stones of the altar are joined with a metal rod is carefully imagined.

93 Master ES

Small Virgin of Einsiedeln, hand-coloured copperplate engraving on paper, 13.3 × 8.7 cm.

94 Master ES

Smallest Virgin of Einsiedeln, copperplate engraving on paper, 9.7 × 6.5 cm.

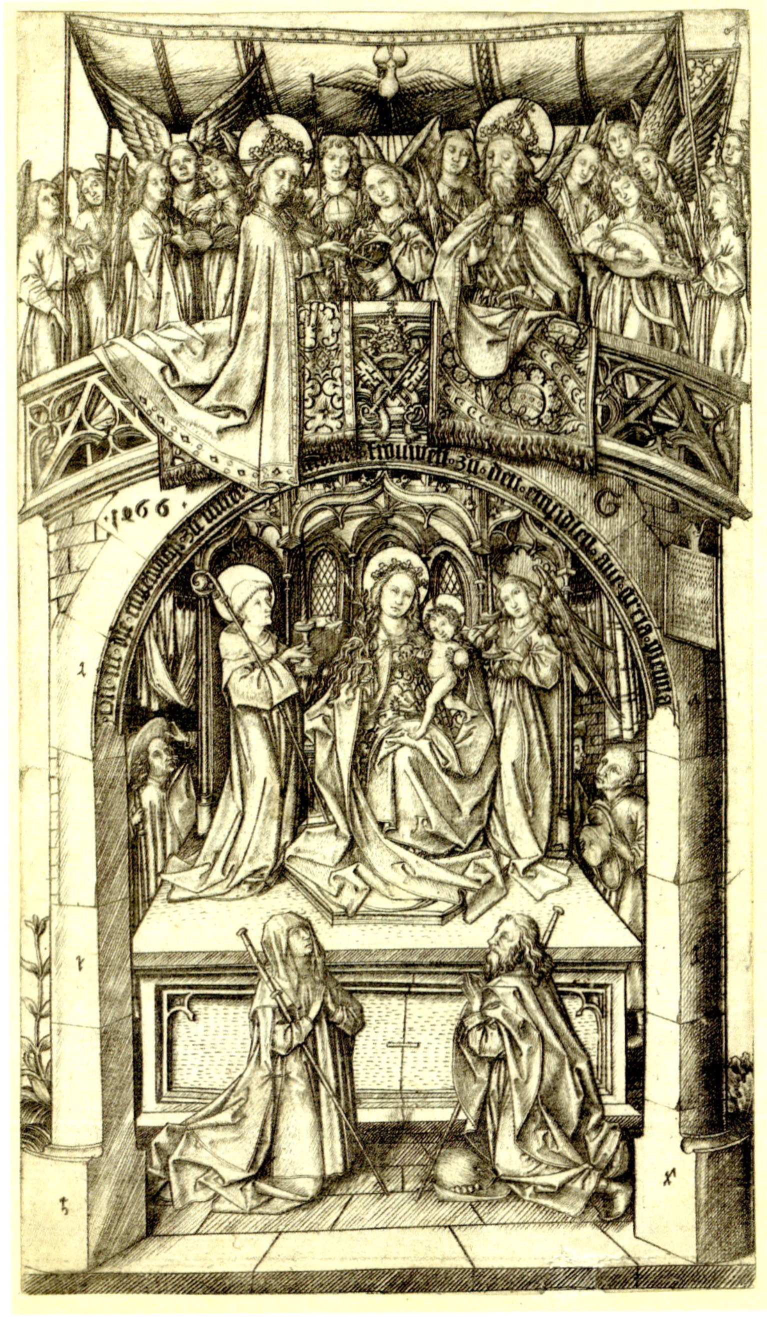

several by the Netherlandish engravers Master FVB and Master W with the Key. He then recut them, adding his own initials, thus claiming the prints pulled from them as his own inventions. It has been estimated that 90 per cent of his engravings were copied from other artists, either by reworking their plates or by other means. These methods account for the size of his

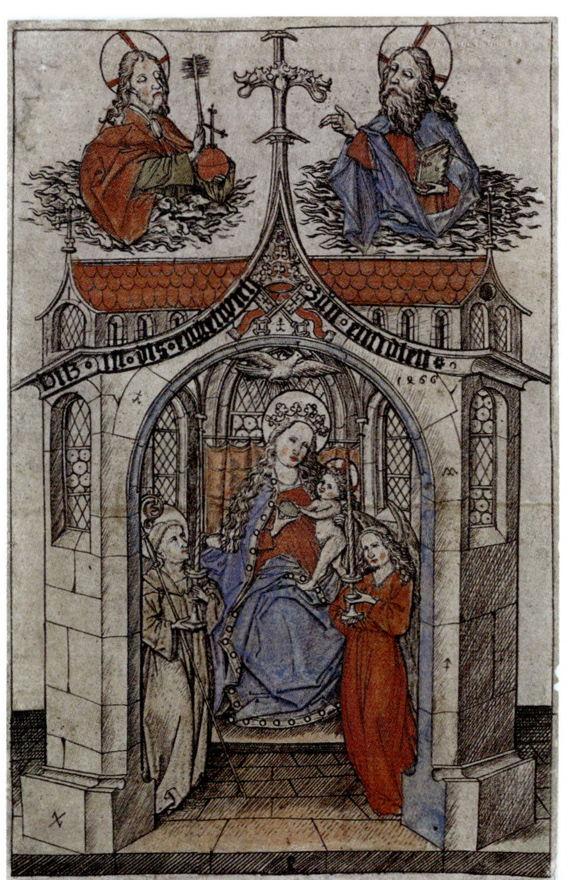

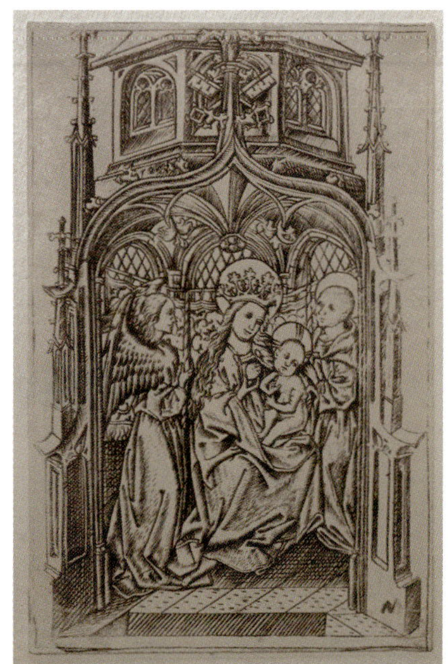

output—over 620 different engravings are attributed to him, as opposed to 116 by Schongauer.[19]

One of the sets of engravings made by Israhel van Meckenem which appears not to have been copied from other engravers is his series of *Couples* [**95**]. Here we see another market niche engraving both filled and expanded—the demand for secular imagery, albeit often with a moral overtone. This set of twelve couples places some in abstract backgrounds and others in detailed interiors, which are the most inventive of his works. Like so many other engravings, these had a wide and fast influence: the *Dissimilar Couple* was copied in Salamanca in a blockbook produced there in 1497.[20] The decision to include blank banderoles in some of the engravings in this series suggests an invitation to the purchaser to become involved in the game—to make up their own dialogue or titles. This was yet another inventive marketing strategy developed by this most commercial of fifteenth-century printmakers.

Engravers could, however, target the very top end of the market: Dürer did in a highly successful manner but in this he was preceded by Martin Schongauer, whose work he admired: Dürer had tried to visit him in Colmar in 1492 but arrived too late—the master had died the year before. It must have

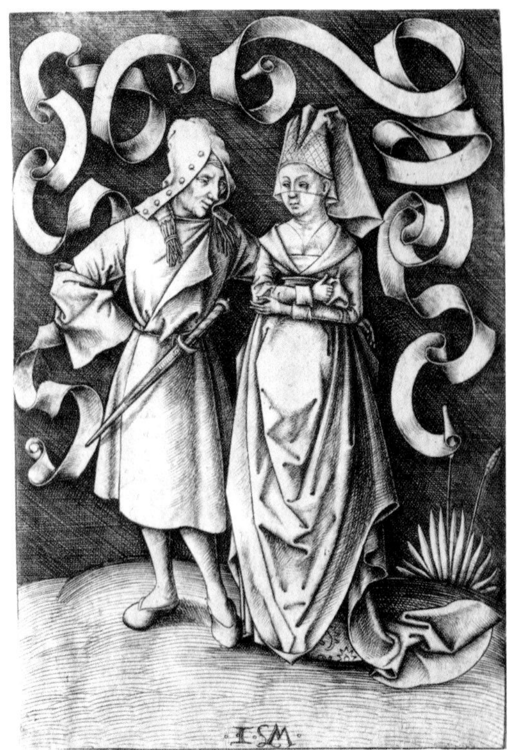

95 Israhel van Meckenem

The *Dissimilar Couple*, copperplate engraving on paper, *c.*1495–1503.

In 1505, the German chronicler and humanist Jacob Wimpheling placed Israhel van Meckenem alongside Schongauer and Dürer as a founder of the printmaker's art, claiming his works were sought after by painters across Europe; this engraving was copied by Spanish artists shortly after it was made.

been the virtuosic large prints by Martin Schongauer, such as the *Death of the Virgin* [**91**] and the even more ambitious *Way to Calvary* [**96**], which would have most impressed Dürer. Schongauer's *Way to Calvary*, which has been called 'the most influential print made in northern Europe',[21] is not an image whose only or even primary purpose was as a devotional tool. Rather, it seems to have been created in large part to exhibit the technical mastery and rich artistic invention of its maker. Its scale, form, and format suggest that it was intended to be admired, displayed, and collected. At 28.4 × 48.6 centimetres, it is the largest plate made in Germany to that date. Cutting such a large surface without making any mistakes, and then inking and printing from it evenly, would have been especially difficult. The inclusion of a number of long, straight lines, some set very close together, is also technically challenging, as is the use of such faint lines against such a large expanse of white sheet in the area on the far right where the sky dissolves. The print is also extraordinarily dense in its invention: it displays elaborate armour, complex clothing, and exotic headgear; dramatic poses and variety of facial types, as well as virtuosic drawing seen in the foreshortened horses and the overall sense of movement and action. This is all overlaid with the patterns created by the sharp, straight lines of the pikes, spears, ropes, and cross.

It is easy to see why, in the mid-sixteenth century, Schongauer continued to be admired, and why he was almost as influential in the fifteenth century as Dürer was in the sixteenth. He created inventive compositions, he marketed them well, but he also produced engravings made with the most virtuosic skill, and he consistently signed his plates, claiming his inventions and assuring his reputation.

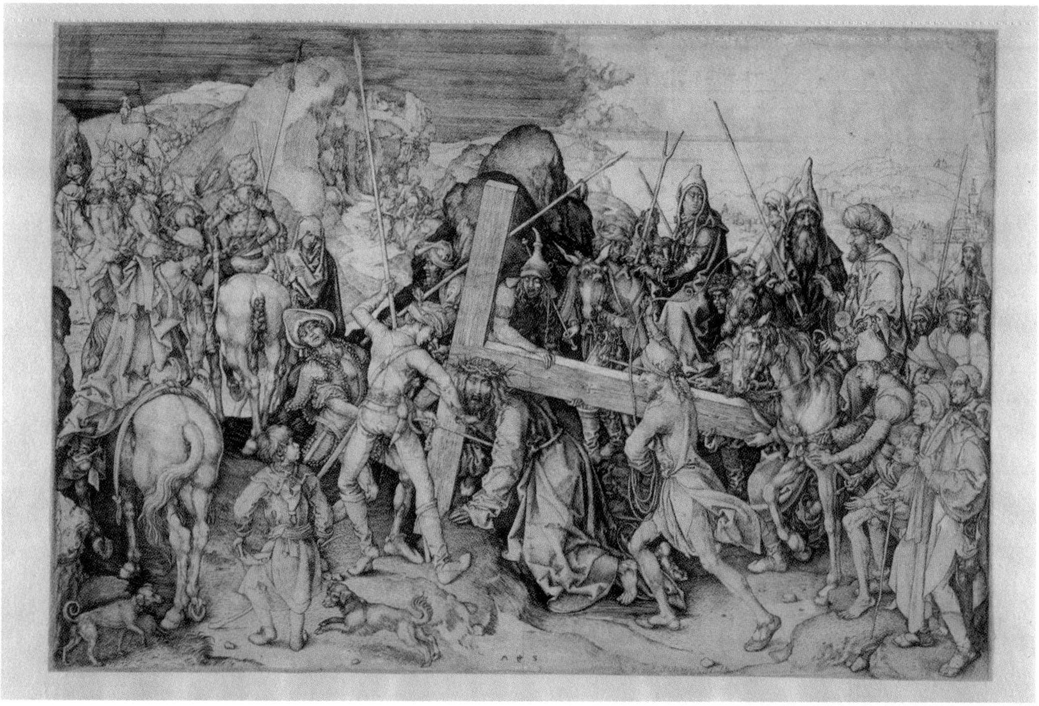

96 Martin Schongauer

The Way to Calvary, copperplate engraving on paper, *c.*1480–5.

The range of marks employed by Schongauer in this large print and their deployment to aid the narrative are particularly impressive: he uses dense hatching to create a dramatic build-up of dark tone behind the head of Christ, and in the sky leading to the scene of his Crucifixion; distance is suggested by varying the depths and density of lines, so the background figures are defined with thinner, less distinct outlines.

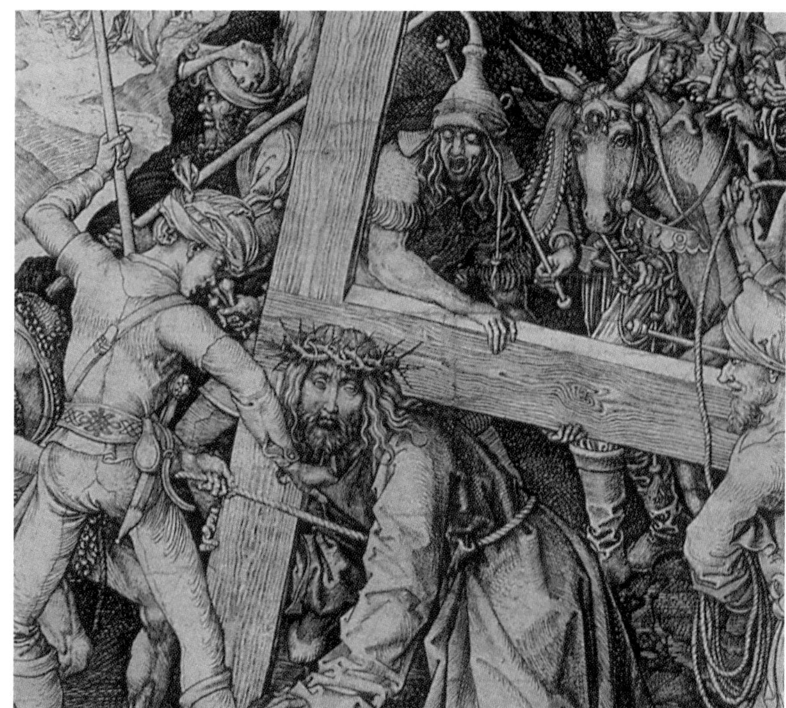

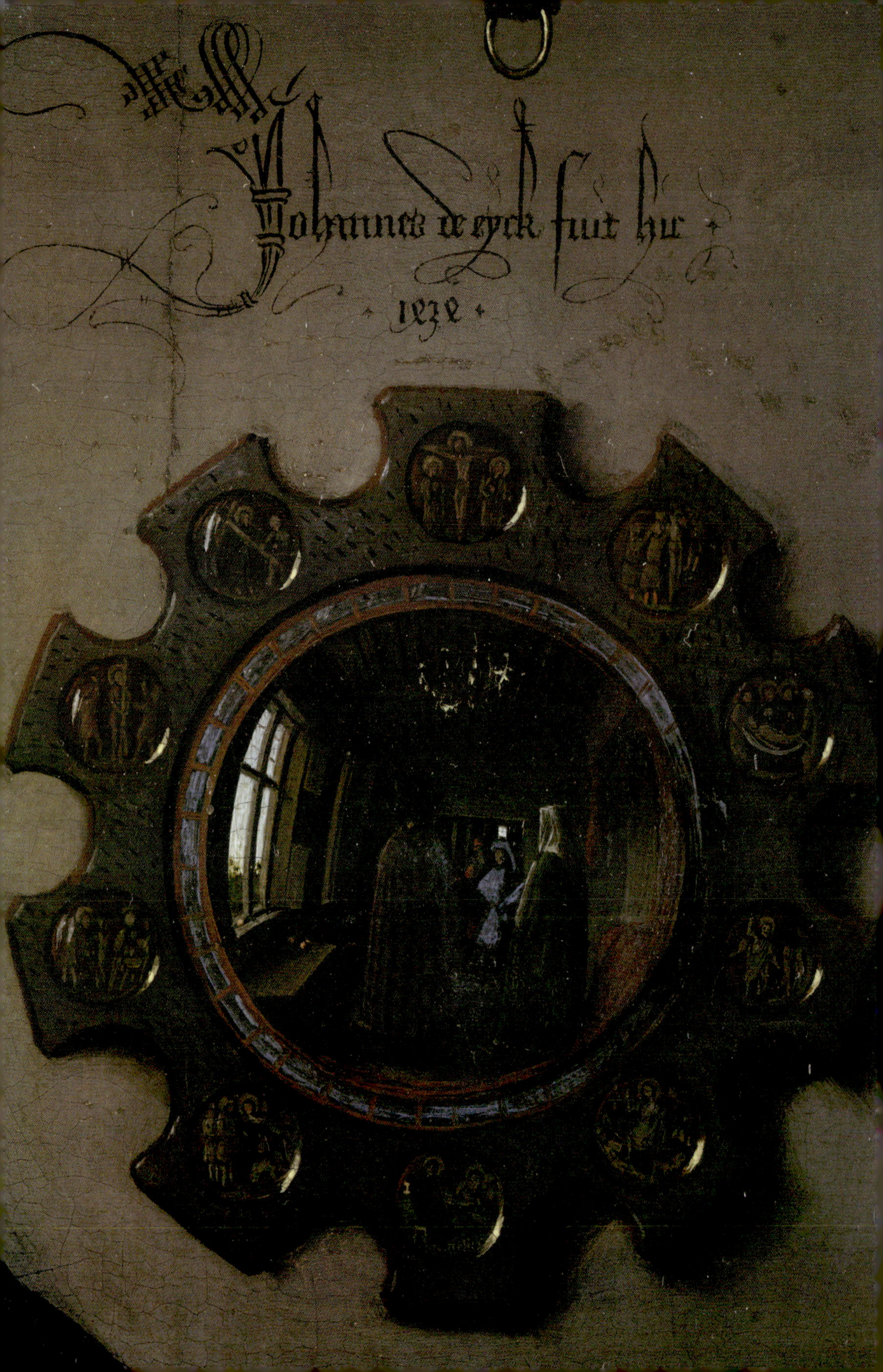
Johannes de eyck fuit hic
1434

Declaring Authorship and Expertise: Signatures and Self-Portraits

Johannes de eyck fuit hic / .1434.

Painted in black calligraphic script on the back wall above the mirror in the *Portrait of Giovanni (?) Arnolfini and his Wife*, London, National Gallery

12

Engravers like Schongauer were not the only northern artists to sign their works. Painters, metalworkers, sculptors, glass painters [**59**] and other craftsmen claimed authorship of their images in various ways, and more frequently than might be supposed. Most famously, Jan van Eyck's general practice was to inscribe his name on his works, frequently but not exclusively on their frames.[1] He put great care and thought into the variety, placement, and facture of these inscriptions. They thus hold meaning in their form and phrasing, some of which as yet may elude us. On the *Arnolfini Portrait* (**37**, and facing detail) the calligraphic flourish across the back wall in the centre of the picture between the two figures and above the mirror in which the artist himself is reflected demands explanation, stating, without a specific day or month, that 'Johannes de eyck fuit hic' ('Jan van Eyck was here'). Not that he made the work but that he was present, the implications of which have led to many interpretations but the most plausible is that only Jan van Eyck had, in his imagination, been there, creating this fictive space and moment, allowing his signature to emphasize, as do the figures seen in the mirror, his facture, the work as creation of his hand and his mind.[2] His apparently unfinished *Saint Barbara* [**97**] is also given meaning by the inscription and its form: the frame is fully painted in an illusion of red marble and on it as if carved into the stone is written 'IOHES DE EYCK ME FECIT .1437.' ('Jan van Eyck made me, 1437'). This makes the status of this work particularly intriguing, since from it one might deduce that the work was finished, yet on the prepared chalk ground is only a drawing, done with great refinement mainly with a stylus, brush, and black paint. In other such inscriptions he sometimes includes the word 'complevit' (completed). Does its absence on the *Saint Barbara* have meaning?[3] Did van Eyck always intend this image to remain in its drawn stage, and has he thus created a work which was meant to be a puzzle, or a display of his skill in design as well as paint (the tower and the blue wash of the sky behind it are comparable to architects' drawings of the period). Or is it about materials and trickery, in the way the de Limbourgs' fake book was (pp.117–18)? Framing a 'drawing'—an

Detail of 37

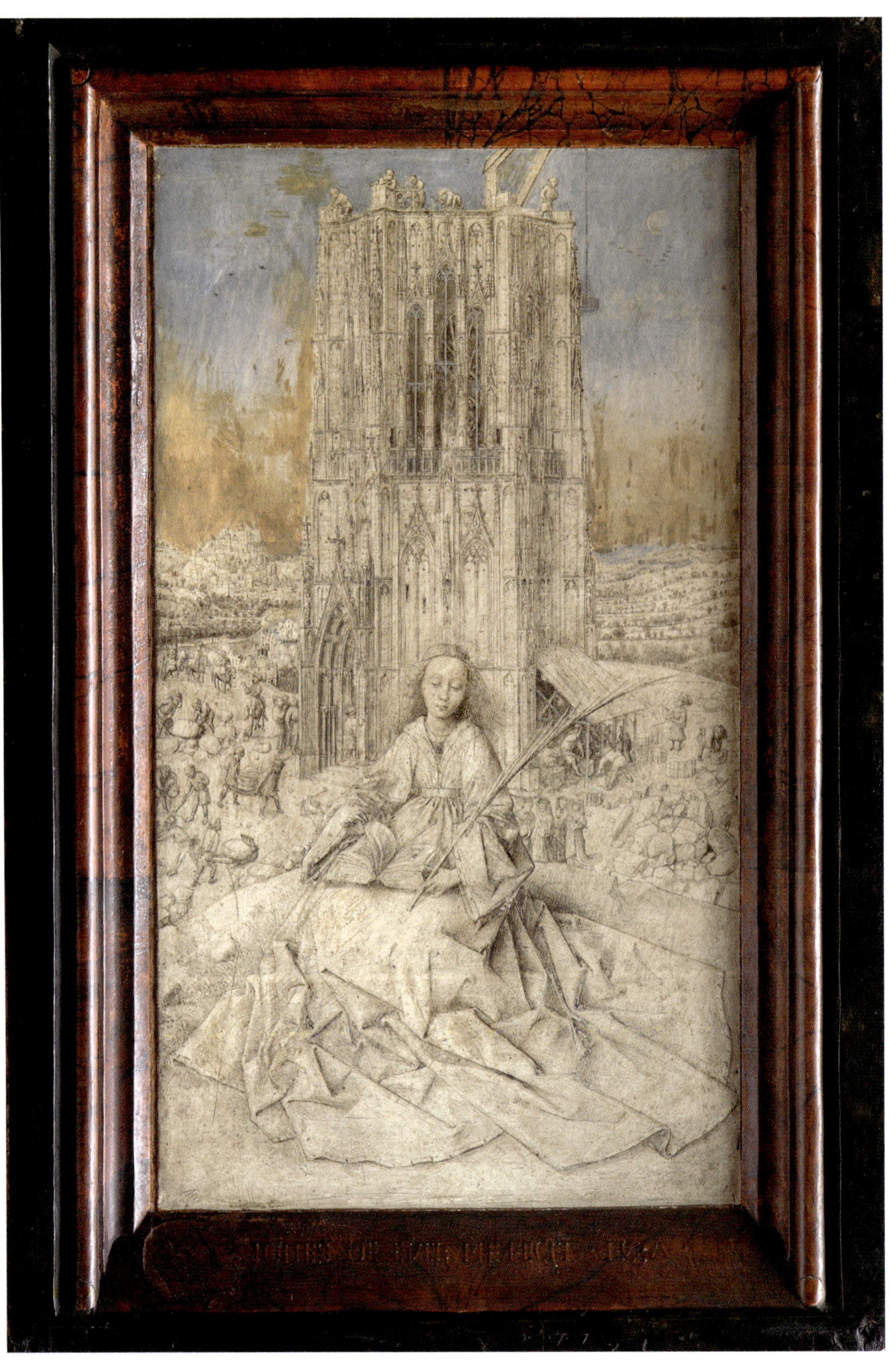

illusion of parchment—in (fictive) solid red marble is suggestive of such a game. Or is the unfinished nature of this work part of its meaning? The tower behind the saint, her attribute, is unfinished too, as the construction in progress on it indicates. Van Eyck was capable of, and adept at, such clever interplays between materials, form, and message (see also pp. 245–6).

In portraits of himself, his wife, and the goldsmith Jan de Leeuw (Vienna, Kunsthistorisches Museum), possibly his friend as well as his colleague, Jan van Eyck makes all the sitters turn to look directly out at the viewer and, significantly perhaps, the inscriptions make the images speak: in the portrait of his wife, along the top of the frame, are the words, 'My husband Johannes completed me in the year 1439, June 17', and along the bottom of the frame, 'My age is 33 years. Als ich can' (as I can, Jan's personal motto) **[98]**. By contrast, in a more public, formal work, the *Van der Paele Madonna* **[18]**, a religious memorial not an intimate portrait, van Eyck instead records authorship from the patron's point of view: along the lower edge of the frame we find the following: 'Master Joris van der Paele, canon of this church, had this work made by the painter Jan van Eyck, and he founded here two chaplaincies to be served by the clergy of the choir, in the year of Our Lord 1434, although the work was com-

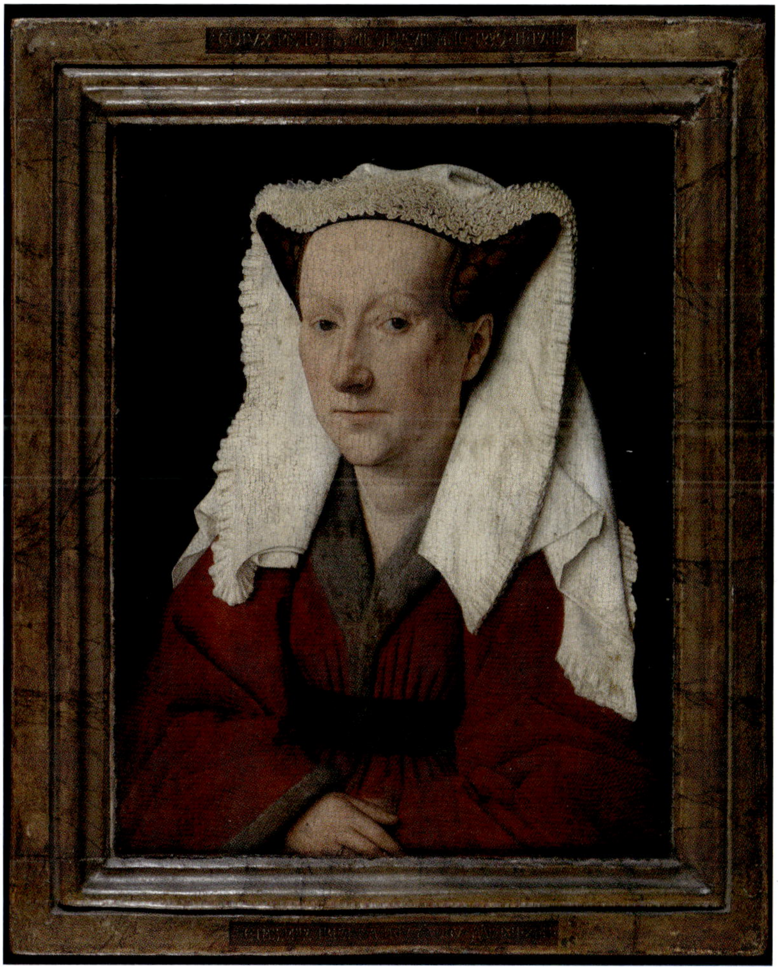

97 Jan van Eyck

Saint Barbara, brush with ink, silverpoint, and pigment on oak, oil on oak, 1438.

The inscription on the frame is painted as if carved into the stone, in roman capitals, of an archaic form typical of the late twelfth century. The punctus used at the beginning and end strengthens the connection to real inscriptions on stone monuments. It is debated whether the ultramarine blue and yellow paint are original.

98 Jan van Eyck

Portrait of Margaret van Eyck, 1439.

The texts here are painted to appear incised into a plate fitted into the (fictive) stone of the frame. The construction of the frame itself indicates that the work was designed to be stood or set on something. The back is painted with fictive marbling, so was clearly intended to be seen.

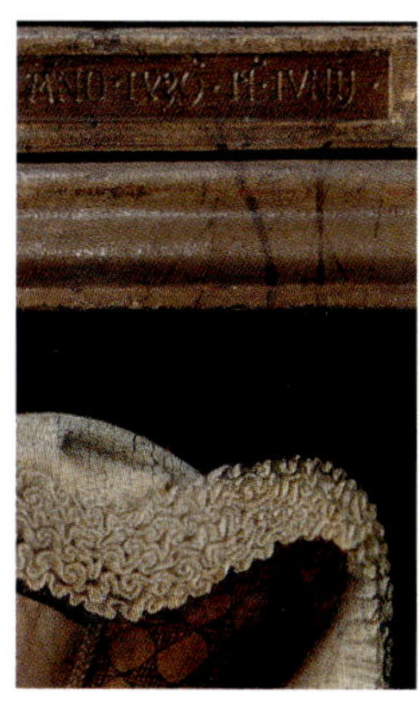

101 Jörg Syrlin the Elder
Choir stalls in Ulm Minster, oak, 1469–74.

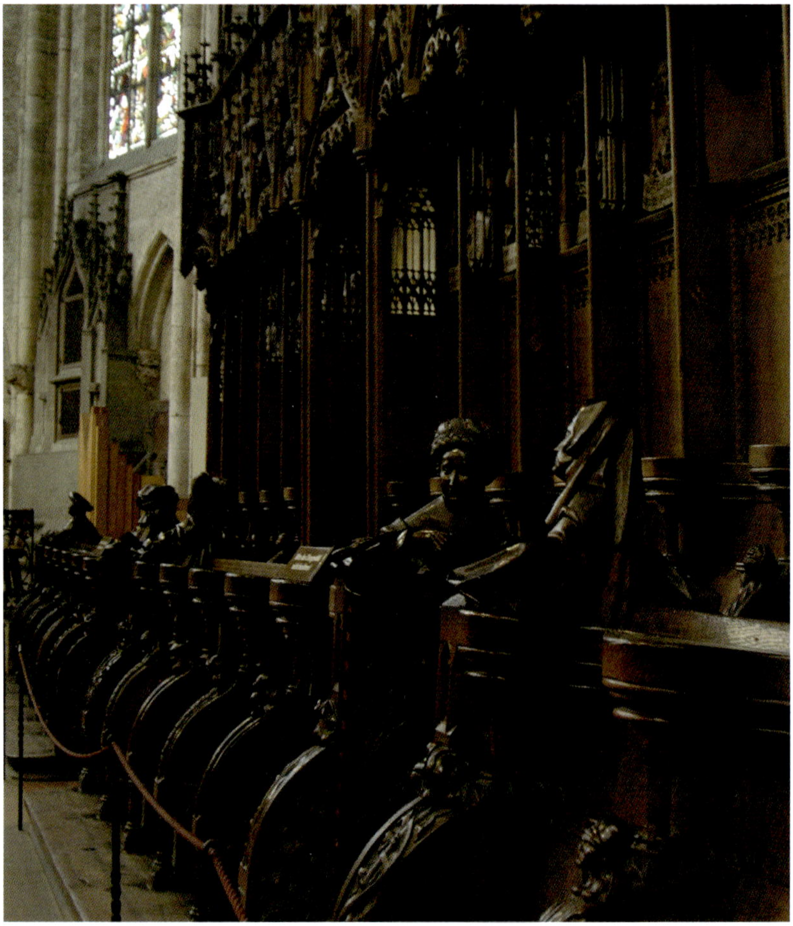

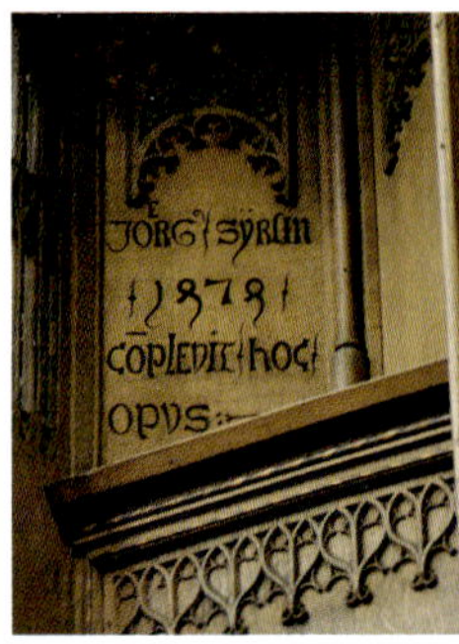

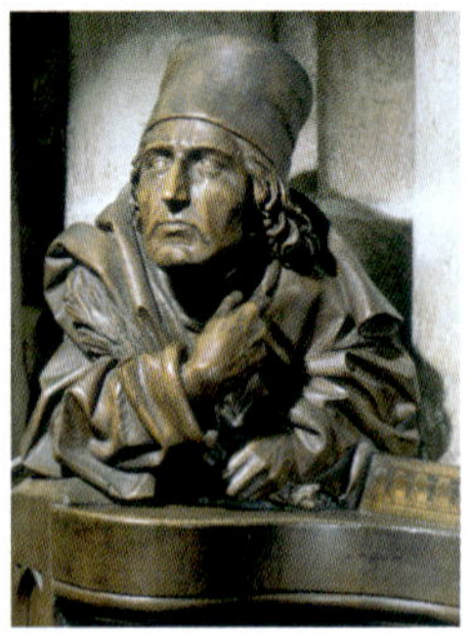

102 Jörg Syrlin the Elder
Details of **101** showing the inscription giving Syrlin's name and marking the completion of the work, and bust of Virgil, possibly a self-portrait.

highly visible; they tend to adorn, mostly, larger liturgical furnishings, works in public spaces; they are often written in the vernacular rather than Latin, and, most significantly, the town in which the caster or carver was active is a mandatory element—any potential client would know where to go to get something similar, and the reputation of the town as a centre for production of such works was also spread.

Wooden choir stalls, one of the most expensive and elaborate of church furnishings, were also very frequently signed (as are those at Amiens, Aoste, Lausanne, and Saint-Claude),[8] and often by the craftsman in overall charge of the project (usually a carpenter and carver of decorative elements) rather than by the collaborating sculptor working on the figurative elements: Jörg Syrlin the Elder, active in Ulm from 1449 onwards, was a joiner who ran a workshop employing sculptors who made the figurative elements of his larger scale works.[9] He asserted his authorship most prominently on the choir stalls he carved for the town church of Ulm [**101, 102**], which are signed and dated three times: these works are among the most elaborate of the period, adorned with sixteen large busts carved in the round, of scholars from antiquity and sibyls, and with apostles, saints, prophets, and Old Testament women in low relief set behind and above each seat. At the first stall on the north side, furthest from the high altar, we have the record of Syrlin beginning the task: 'Georgi Syrlin 1469 incepit hoc opus'; on the last stall on the south side, nearest the high altar, the completion of the work is recorded: 'Jeorgi Syrlin 1474 complevit hoc opus'.[10] Possibly the time span of five years was part of the point of this inscription—as with the brass founders, it acts as an advertisement to other patrons, indicating the dedication and care taken by his workshop. Placing your name, or even more so your image as Vischer did, so close to the liturgical centre of a church may also have provided the same type of potential spiritual benefits that a donor portrait might be hoped to elicit: your name was set in conjunction with powerful images, in the case of the Ulm choir stalls next to the monumental high altar (see **124**), which would have been almost adjacent to Syrlin's name.

Positioning is also key to the interpretation of the self-portrait of the Nuremberg sculptor Adam Kraft (*c.*1440–1507) on the sacrament tower (used to reserve the consecrated host) for St Lorenz, Nuremberg, commissioned by the patrician Hans Imhoff in 1493 [**103**].[11] The contract for this work is particularly informative about the levels of finish and detail required on the different parts of the tower, stating that most care should be taken on the areas most visible, like the gallery around the sacrament house proper: this was to be carved 'with great subtlety and excellent craftsmanship, and whatever part of the base rises above the gallery shall also be done with great craftsmanship since it will be clearly visible', while the parts highest up needed less care because they are 'not so clearly visible to the beholder'; but the base itself, around which the portrait figures are set, is to be carved 'solidly, but not expensively, since not much can be seen under the gallery'.[12] Imhoff's coats of arms and those of his two wives are placed in this most important, most visible area—on the gallery providing access to the door to where the consecrated hosts were kept. However, visually more prominent is the figure of Adam Kraft himself, who kneels under the base of the tower, on a scale close to life-size and thus larger than the religious figures represented, on its most important and visible westward face, directly below the doors giving access to the host, and thus also in direct vertical alignment with Christ at the Last Supper, with the supplicant Magdalene at the foot of the cross, with Christ's crucified form on the cross, and with his resurrected form at the very top of the monument [**104**]. Moreover, the heads of Kraft (and his assistant, portrayed on the right-hand side of the monument) could be interpreted as coming into the area of 'whatever part of the base rises above the gallery' and thus those regarded as requiring most care and attention because they are most visible and important (as indeed is evident). Kraft, his figure very carefully worked indeed, holds a mallet and a chisel and is dressed in the clothes of his trade. Although not mentioned in the contract, Imhoff must have agreed to the inclusion of these figures. Perhaps here the patron gains as much from the presence of the sculptor's image in his work as the sculptor does: the self-portrait emphasizes the process of creation, made possible only by the generosity of the patron who employed the sculptor, choosing someone with the skill and devotion to execute the task with such sucesss.

The potential act of piety on the part of the artist in making such an image, and the power of placing your name, if not an image of yourself, in proximity to those of Christ and the saints, must lie behind the types of signatures we

103 Adam Kraft

Sacrament House in St Lorenz, Nuremberg, sandstone, partially polychromed, 1493–6.

Adam Kraft was primarily a stone sculptor, but he also advised on architectural projects, an expertise evident in this 20-metre high tower. It is set, as was required for sacrament houses, in the choir to the left of the high altar. Regulations also governed the materials which could be used for such structures: they had to be made of inflammable materials such as stone or brass, which ensured the reserved hosts they contained were protected from fire. Visible here, too, is Veit Stoss's *Annunciation of the Rosary*, which hangs in the centre of the choir; see **149**.

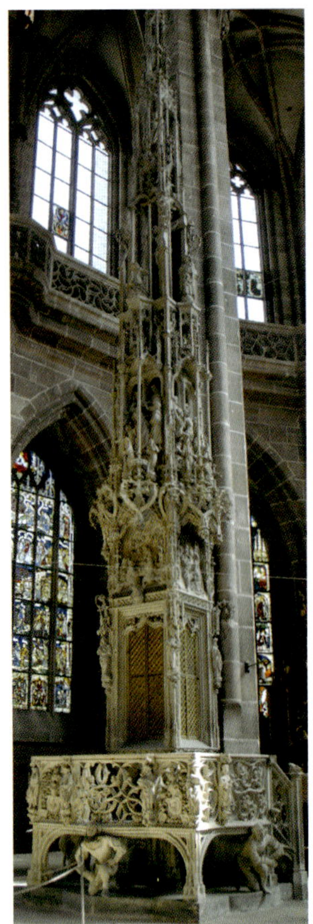

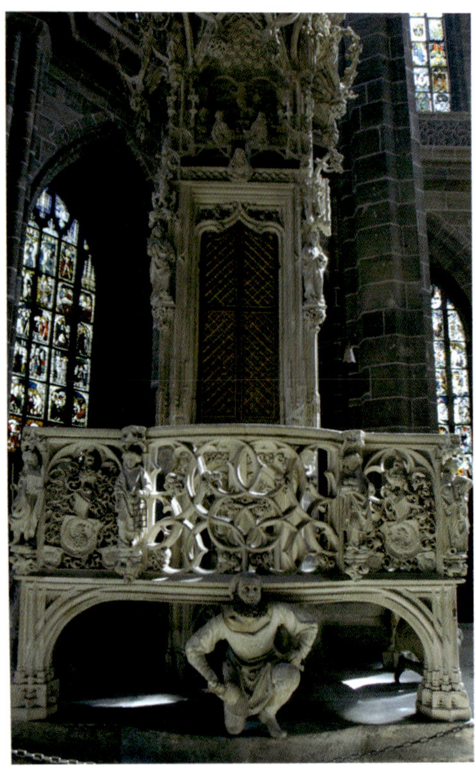

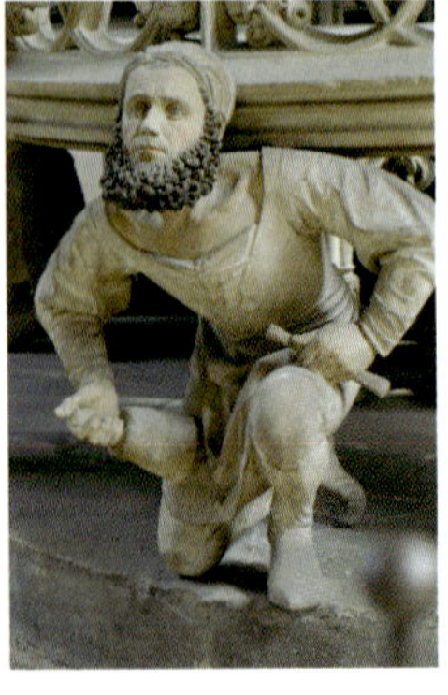

104 Adam Kraft

Self-portrait of the sculptor in **103**.

The sculptor, holding his mallet and chisel, plays a literally supporting role here, bearing the weight of the elaborate stone tower above. His figure retains more visible polychromy than any other part of the monument.

find in places which were adamantly not meant to be seen. Most remarkable of these are those found during the conservation of the early 1970s (in process in **110**, below) inside the monumental carved wooden figures of Christ, the Magdalene, and St John on the rood screen made by Bernt Notke for Lübeck cathedral [**151**]. Inside the Magdalene, in black chalk directly on the board used to close the back of the hollowed out figure, is written:

> The master, Berent Notke, the journeymen, Hegert the carver, Lukas the Bereiter [preparer, applier of grounds, see p. 189], Hertyg the young one ... [illegible line] in the year MCCCC LXXI made this work. God give them all eternal life.

Inside the St John, on a long strip of irregular, roughly cut parchment *c.*31 × 7 centimetres, stuck onto the board which closed that figure, is the following:

> Anno Domini in the 1472nd year Bernt Notke made this piece of work with the help of his journeymen, whose names are firstly Eggert Stuarte the woodcarver; Lucas Meer the Bereiter; Bernt Scharpeselle the Bereiter; Ilges the Bereiter; Hartich Stender, a painter. Pray to God for their souls so that God be merciful to them.

And in the hollowed out figure of Christ:

> Berent n[otk]e me fe[cit] [Bernt Notke made me].[13]

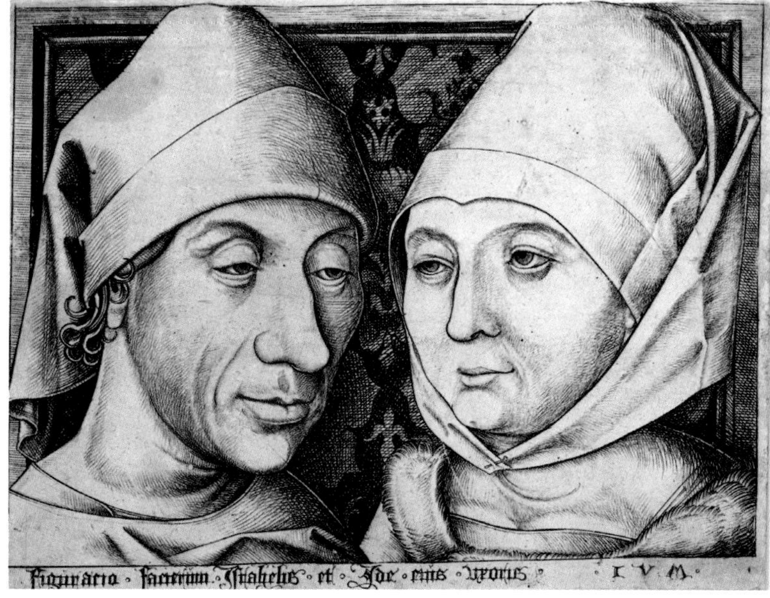

105 Israhel van Meckenem
Self-portrait with his Wife, copperplate engraving on paper, 1490.

These inscriptions are set inside figures placed several metres high on the rood and it is clear that the backs were not designed to be removed at any point—doing so would have damaged the layers of ground and paint set over them to disguise them. Their purpose was in their presence rather than their visibility: their existence was potentially powerful, a plea for salvation, as is evident from their supplicatory nature. Placing the name of Notke alone and a more traditional statement of facture 'me fecit' in the figure of Christ, whilst the supplicatory inscriptions and the names of the workshop team are in the Magdalene and John, suggests a decided meaning behind their form and placement. Christ cannot be Notke's work alone—he would have needed the same team of carvers and preparers since he did not perform all these skills himself—but this figure was of course the most important and powerful, and it also contained relics, set in a hollow in Christ's head and in a (removable, now lost) gold, jewelled cross attached to his chest.[14] As we will see in Part V, proximity of names and words to relics was something that was understood as having important power and protective benefits.

In the light of these inscriptions, we might view the presence of a sculptor's mallet found, during the restoration of 1978, inside the body of the monumental St George in Stockholm [**127**] as more significant than just an oversight on behalf of Notke or one of his workers. The wooden mallet was one of the defining tools of the sculptor, often appearing as one of their attributes and in self-portraits (it is held by Adam Kraft, along with a chisel, in his self-portrait above, **104**), and it was chosen for the mark certifying carved retables made in Brussels (**54** above). Perhaps the mallet was a different way of Notke signing, or leaving his presence on, or rather in, the St George.

Self-portraits which stand alone, free from a larger work and thus not part of the mark of authorship, clearly do not have these supplicatory or devotional functions. They were mostly produced by painters at our period, although Israhel van Meckenem engraved an extraordinary one of his wife

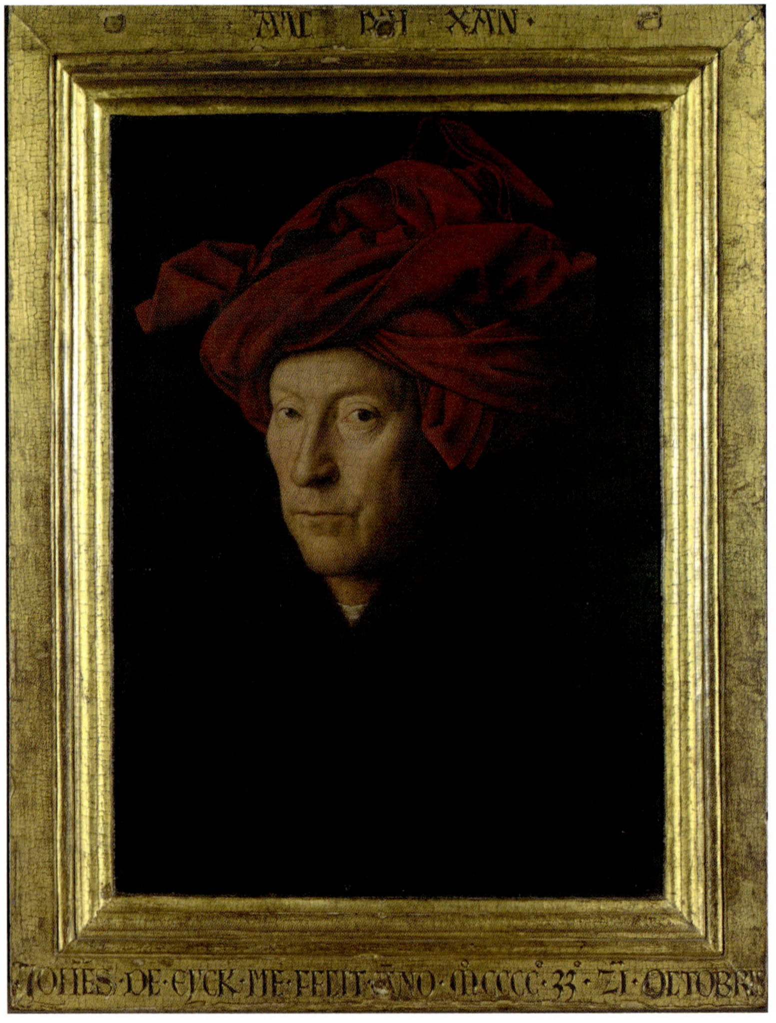

106 Jan van Eyck

Portrait of a Man (self-portrait?), oil on Baltic oak, 1433.

This is the only frame in van Eyck's surviving oeuvre that is gilded rather than painted (see **97, 98**). The reason why may be related to its subject—a presumed self-portrait—but exactly how or why remains unclear.

and himself, presumably, given his acutely honed business sense, made with an eye to expanding his reputation and his market: it is signed in a different, more extensive and flamboyant way than any of his other works: 'Figuratio facierum Israhelis et Ide eius uxoris' [**105**], in a script not dissimilar to that used by van Eyck in the *Arnolfini Portrait*. Possibly this work is a demonstration of the power of engraving to achieve a remarkably impressive illusion of surfaces, if differently from oil paint, but able to compete with it: brocade, fur, and flesh are all described here by the engraver's burin most effectively.

Two painted self-portraits which seem to be most emphatically about the skill of the artist are those by Jan van Eyck and Albrecht Dürer [**106, 107**].[15] The inscription within Dürer's painting, set (significantly) at the level of the artist's eyes, asserts its nature without any doubt: 'I, Albrecht Dürer of Nuremberg painted myself thus, with undying colour, at the age of twenty-eight years.' By contrast, van Eyck's *Portrait of a Man* suggests its subject more subtly. The painter's motto, 'Als Ich Can' (as I can, possibly a pun on his surname: 'as I/Eyck can'), in Greek capitals is placed in isolation on the upper

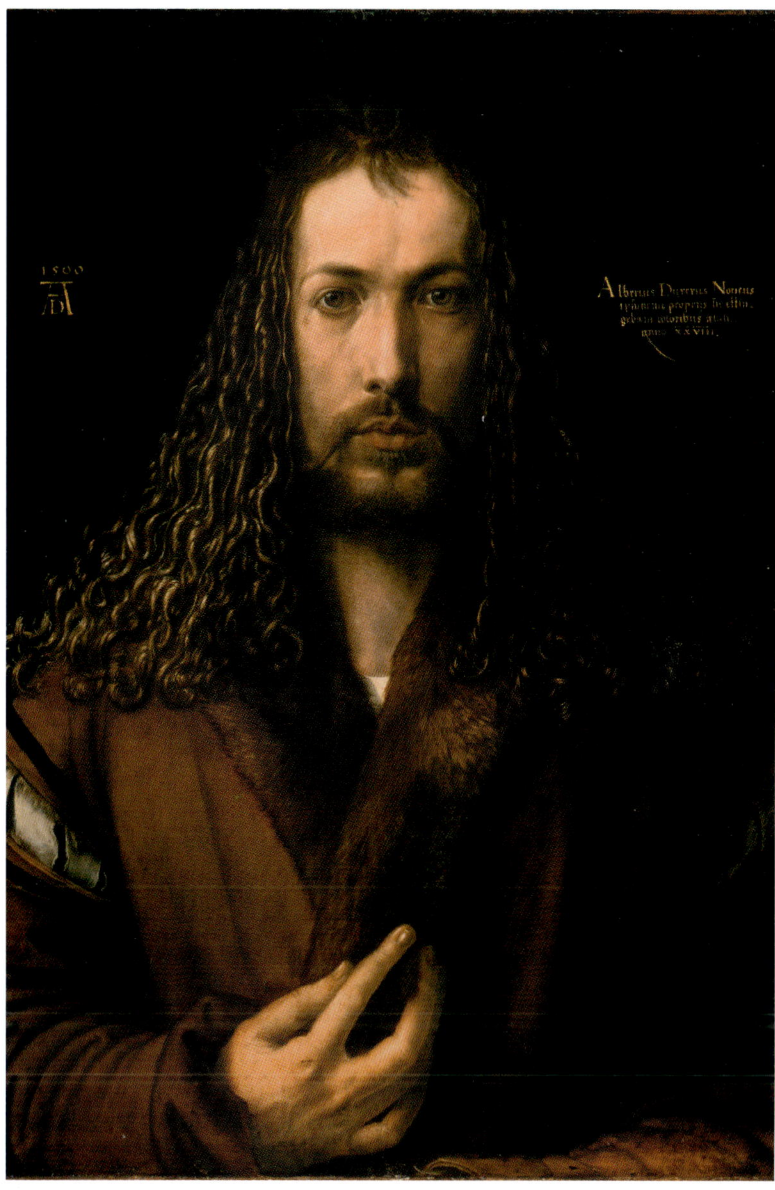

107 Albrecht Dürer

Self-portrait of 1500, oil on panel, 1500.

horizontal of the frame, the place van Eyck normally inscribed the sitter's name. It is also larger and far more prominent than in any of his other works. This, along with the direct gaze, is strong evidence for it being a self-portrait, but it also perhaps gives us a clue to at least one possible purpose of such an image: Jan paints it because he can and because there would be no better way of showing how life-like you could make a portrait than by having an image of yourself for prospective clients to compare to the reality. Dürer clearly understood this potential too. His self-portrait (the illusionistic skill of which apparently fooled his dog into licking it) is overt in the virtuosic nature with which fur, flesh, and hair are painted, and it should be seen in a similar spirit. In the van Eyck, it is possible that a subtle allusion is drawn between the painter and Christ: along the bottom of the frame is written 'Johannes van Eyck made me on 21 October 1433', and the 33 is distinguished from the rest of the year by being written in arabic, not roman numerals: 33 was the age at which Christ died.[16] That such an allusion might be an intention of van Eyck's is supported by the undeniable visual presentation of Dürer as Christ in his self-portrait: it is evident in his frontal pose, the position of his hand, and the treatment of his hair and face. The reference in both cases is perhaps to God-given skill, something painters were certainly thought to have: in the contract made with Dieric Bouts for the Holy Sacrament altar [**13**], he is asked to 'do his utmost to demonstrate in it the art which God has bestowed on him'.[17]

The painter's skill is certainly evoked in these images: van Eyck's portrait emphasizes the eyes, with their direct, slightly bloodshot gaze, while Dürer's makes his right hand, with which he painted, equally part of the visual focus: neither holds a brush. Although in the van Eyck, some indication of his profession may be intended by the form of the *chaperon* headdress with its long *cornette* wrapped up around it to create the turban-like effect—this would keep it out the way while painting—Dürer wears very rich fur robes which were unlikely to have been practical for any such activity (Dürer was constantly concerned about his status and would never want to suggest anything other than that he was of the upper ranks of society). In both images the process of painting, the artist's profession, is thus implied in less overt ways, emphasizing the skills of eye and hand needed rather than the tools of their trade, in contrast to the prominence of such attributes in the self-portraits of Kraft and Vischer. Despite these painters' apparent desire to direct us away from such practicalities, to understand the extraordinary achievements of their hands and eyes we must focus on just these things, on the technical aspects of image making at this period: artists' tools and materials, their processes, their workforce, and their working environment. This is the subject of Part IV.

Part IV

Making Images: Equipment, Materials, Methods

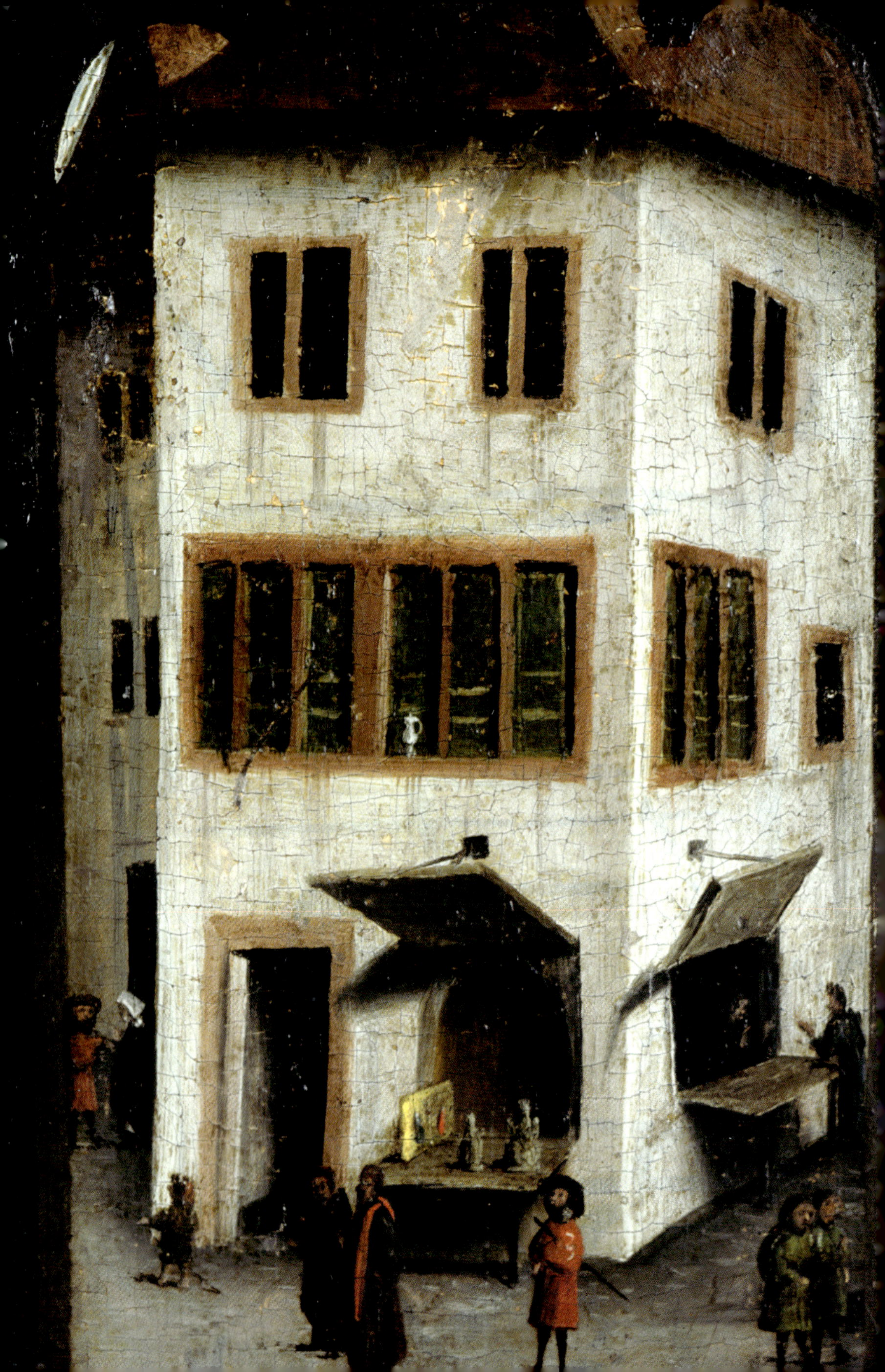

Workspace and Equipment

Their studio is completely full of panels / Some painted, some to be painted, and many noble tools. / There are charcoals, crayons, pens, fine brushes / Bristle brushes, piles of shells / Silverpoint, which makes many subtle marks / Polished marbles, as brilliant as Beryl

Jean Lemaire de Belges, *La Couronne Margaritique*, 1504–5[1]

13

The equipment, materials and working space that artists used, the organization of their studios and assistants and how they acquired their materials and employed them to solve artistic problems are the main concerns of this part. Our evidence is drawn from the works themselves, through technical examination, but we are also heavily reliant on documentary material: the accounts, contracts, and guild regulations introduced in Part I, as well as inventories and wills listing artists' belongings. These are supplemented further with images of artists at work. We have many of painters from the period but we must approach these with caution. They usually show Saint Luke or legendary practitioners such as Thamar (detail heading chapter 14) and cannot be considered straightforward historical documents. The image of Saint Luke by Rogier van der Weyden [**108**], for example, shows the artist in a grand room with a barrel-vaulted ceiling, stained glass windows, and an inlaid tiled floor; it has an open loggia situated improbably on a bridge across a river or at the bay of a harbour. It is as far from what and where an artist's workshop might be as is possible; indeed, it is an unlikely architectural space for the Netherlands in general, and anyway the source for much of this is another famous image—the *Rolin Madonna* by Jan van Eyck [**207**]—which further distances it from any real setting: it serves Rogier's artistic purposes but is not a historical reality.[2] However, some depictions tally more closely with the documentary sources, and can help us evoke the artist's working space, equipment, and the workforce they drew on.

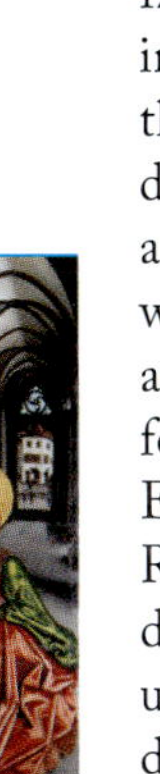

Conrad Witz, detail from *St Catherine and St Mary Magdalene*, oil on panel, *c.* 1440

'A High Spacious Building': The Artists' Workshop

The depiction in the background of a painting by Conrad Witz (detail heading this chapter) has all the features necessary for a successful artist's business, and is a good example of a visual depiction which matches documented reality. It is a substantial structure set over three floors with a large stone entrance, not dissimilar to the house Albrecht Dürer owned in Nuremberg [**109**];[3] it is well located, on the corner of a busy street, to catch passing trade. It has an area to display and sell works, and a well-lit working area, clearly on the first floor judging by the large and extensive windows; the top floor is noticeably less well-lit and would have been where the artist, his family, and his apprentices and journeymen would have lived.

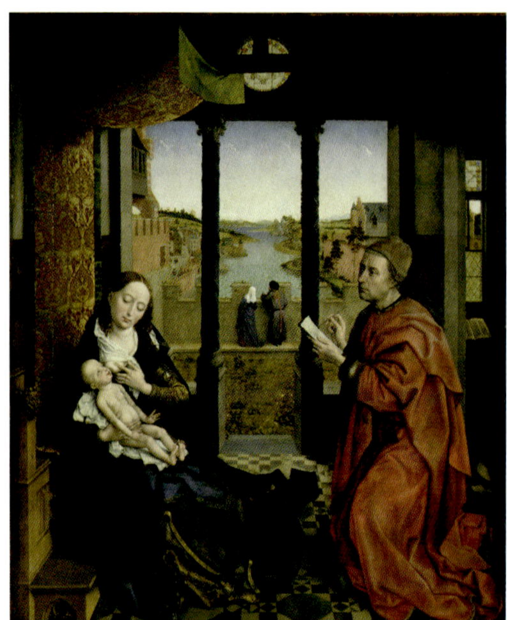

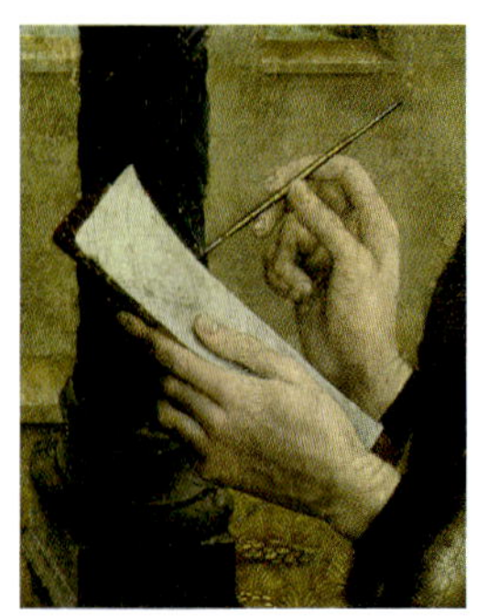

108 Rogier van der Weyden
St Luke drawing the Virgin, oil on Baltic oak, *c.*1440.
This large panel may have been made for the painters' guild chapel in Brussels (see **169, 170** for another example of a work for such a location). Its invention lies in part in showing the saint making a silverpoint drawing of the Virgin, and thus in the preparatory stage of making his image rather than the painting stage (compare **112, 114**). This choice, however, allowed the painter to dispense with the easel, his seat, and other paraphernalia which would clutter the composition and provide a barrier between saint and Virgin.

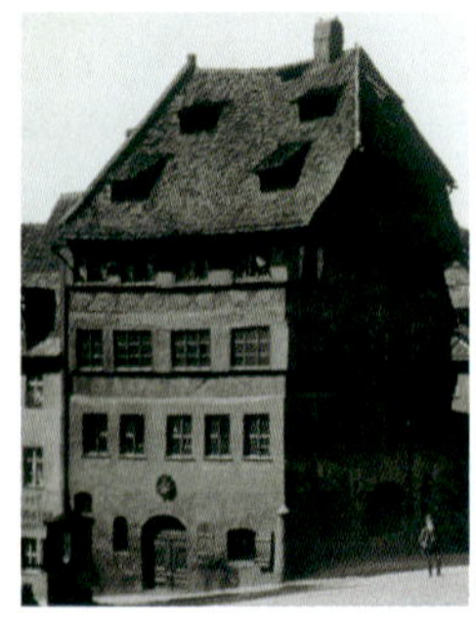

109
Dürer's house in the former Zisselgasse, Nuremberg, photographed before the Second World War.
Dürer's house was an imposing four-storey stone and brick edifice built around 1420; it had previously belonged to the astronomer-mathematician Bernhard Walther, who had an observatory installed there. Dürer acquired it in 1509 for the considerable sum of 274 guelden and it served as his working and living space until his death in 1528.

These features of size, light, and selling space were crucial. The most successful artists owned large houses which enabled increased productivity, commercial expansion, or diversification. Those in which the painter and printmaker Lucas Cranach lived and worked in Wittenburg were very large indeed: the first, acquired in 1510, was in fact two adjoining properties in a prime site on the market square and on which Cranach immediately undertook major building work, presumably to create a large studio area. This proved to be insufficient for his growing business, and in 1518 he purchased a larger property on the corner of the square, No. 1 Schloßstraße, now known as the Cranachhof; it had four floors, a gated side entrance, and six outhouses disposed around a central courtyard. The outhouses allowed discrete spaces for workshops for carving, printmaking, and panel preparation, which needed to be undertaken in separate areas given that wood dust would ruin oil paintings. Although it is not certain where in this array of buildings Cranach's painting studio was located, it has been plausibly suggested that it was in the two- and three-storey sections on the east and south wing, which boasted a large ground-floor entrance and a room two stories high, 25 metres long and 7 metres wide, and a south-facing wall set with as many as ten windows.[4]

Such size was important since the ability to successfully produce large-scale images in any quantity was dependent on having the space to do so. The figures Bernt Notke made for the rood screen of the cathedral in Lübeck [**110**] were carved out of complete tree trunks around 3 metres tall: the photograph of these huge works in conservation gives some sense of their scale, which is impossible to appreciate when they are viewed *in situ* [**151**].[5] Sculptors, particularly those specializing in stone, also had to have considerable space to store unworked blocks, blocks in progress, and finished works awaiting delivery and installation: this is vividly indicated by the inventory of Jean de Liège, a Paris-based stone sculptor, who worked for Charles V and

110
Photograph of figures by Bernt Notke and workshop from the *Triumphal Cross* in conservation *c.*1971 (see **151**).

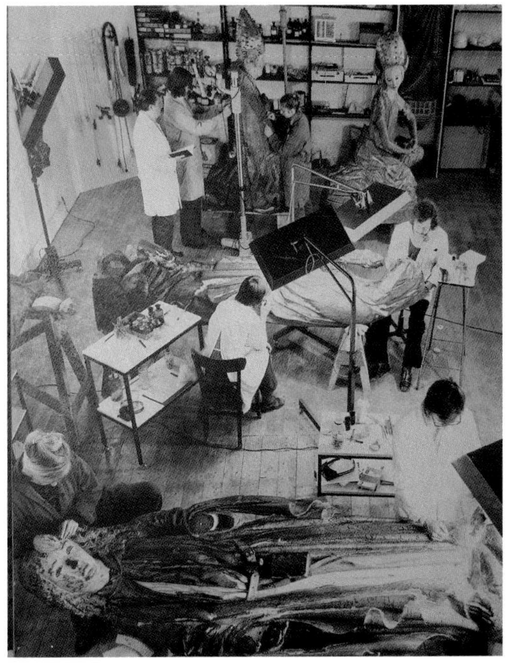

other royal and noble patrons in France in the 1360s and 1370s. In his workshop on his death he had no fewer than twenty-four large and twenty-three smaller blocks of alabaster and marble, other smaller uncounted pieces of marble and stone, two completed tombs, an altarpiece, and life-sized figures of the Virgin, St John the Baptist, Charles V and his wife Jeanne de Bourbon, among other pieces.[6] For painters, works on the scale of the *Justice of Otto* painted by Dieric Bouts for Leuven town hall, each panel measuring 3.24 × 1.82 metres [**111**], were not uncommon. Part of an intended series of four such panels, these were constructed (presumably to ensure they fitted correctly) in the town hall but not painted there—they were kept there until needed by Bouts, when they were then delivered, one at a time, to his workshop (the first between November and January 1471), then transported back, when complete, and swapped for an unpainted one (in June 1473); the panels were so large that they had to be taken in and out through the first-floor windows of the town hall with the aid of a pulley system.[7] A similar commission for four, even larger panels (possibly as large as 4 × 4.5 metres), showing scenes of the *Justice of Trajan and Herkinbald* for Brussels town hall (see **9**, above), which Rogier van der Weyden was working on in the early 1440s, may have precipitated his move to two adjacent properties on the Cantersteen in 1443–4.[8] These were substantial houses previously owned by aldermen of the city, and one was described as having a 'groete poirte', a large doorway, clearly an added attraction for the needs of a painter, vital for getting such large works in and out again.

Buying adjoining properties seems to have been a common solution to the need for a large working area and commercial expansion (Hans Memling in Bruges, Stefan Lochner in Cologne, Jean de Liège in Paris and Simon Marmion in Valenciennes, for example, all did so), and was not a solution

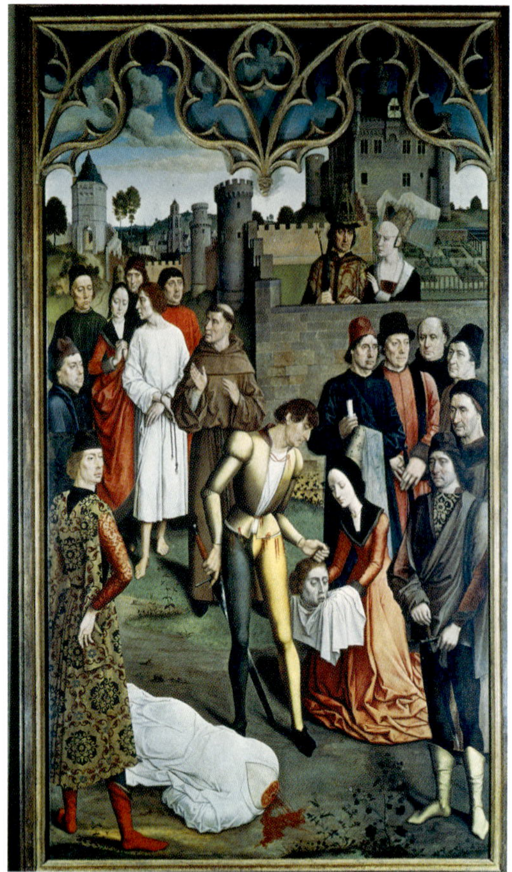

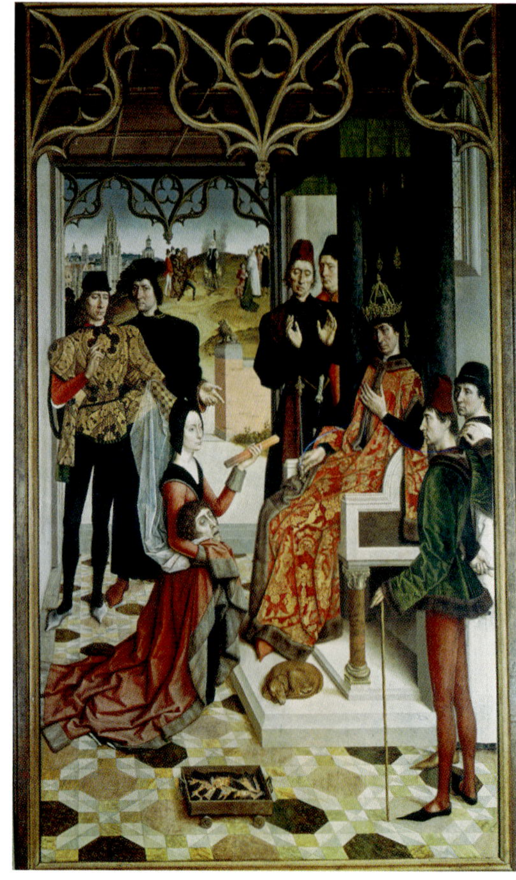

111 Dieric Bouts

The *Justice of Emperor Otto III*: the *Beheading of the Innocent Count* (left) and the *Ordeal by Fire* (right), oil on Baltic oak, 1468–82.

just for those working on a large scale: the successful Parisian illuminator and *libraire* (bookseller) Andry le Musnier (d. 1475) acquired three adjoining houses, Nos 12, 13, and 14 on the rue Neuve Notre-Dame in Paris, in the 1460s. His properties gave him a corner block of considerable size on the entrance to the street from the west, which was the main thoroughfare for pilgrims and other visitors to the cathedral.[9] This trebled the size of his shop and, crucially, its display footage onto the street. This type of expansion could be perceived by the guilds, who regulated such matters, as commercially threatening: when Bernt Notke, whose workshop produced the huge sculptures in **110**, tried to extend his studio in Lübeck by buying an adjoining property, he was banned by the town council from doing so, and in 1506 had to pull down an extension he had built; presumably this was seen as unfair competition.[10]

Space was important for selling as well as making works: in Strasbourg in 1466 the painter Hans Ernst had a house in the rue de Hallebardes with a façade over 4 metres long, a canopy projecting into the street over a metre and a half long, and below it a stall 2 metres long and a meter wide, on which 'doer sin helgen uffstelt' (he displayed images); see a similar structure in the detail heading this chapter.[11] That the size of Ernst's display area was carefully measured is indicative of how this privilege was coveted and regulated by the guilds and town authorities, since shop windows were the primary means by which painters sold their works. In the town of Mons, for instance, a painter paid a higher fee to the guild if his workshop had a window leading on to the street, while in Bruges, a town notorious for the power and vigilance of its painters' guild, a favourite solution to the problem of whether certain (lesser) crafts could undertake work seen as the painters' domain (and thus potential competition) was to forbid them to display such works for sale in the windows of their shops.[12] Thus, in 1458, the *cleederscrivers* (cloth painters) of Bruges were allowed to carry out the polychroming of wood and stone, and the painting of panels, but not, crucially, to show these works in the windows of their shops, or to use oil.[13] Clearly, without these privileges, it was deemed that the competition was not very serious.

After size and location, perhaps the most important factor in any artist's working space would be good light. Theophilus, a twelfth-century German monk and practising metalworker, in describing the construction of a goldsmith's workshop, emphasizes light as much as height and size, and is very precise regarding the size and arrangement of windows:

> Build a high spacious building whose length extends to the east. In the south wall put as many windows as you wish and are able to, provided that there is a space of five feet between any two windows ... The windows should not be more than a foot above ground level and they should be three feet high and two feet wide.[14]

He also prescribes that workbenches should be set at right angles to the window, ensuring the best position in respect to the fall of natural light (although not for glass painters, who would have required the panes to be set so that the light was behind them). Images of artists at work usually show them positioned in the manner suggested by Theophilus. Looking at Jan van Eyck's portraits it is possible to surmise that his studio was set up so that he sat with the windows on his left-hand side, observing his subjects with the light falling on their right [**98, 106**]. A left-handed artist, as it seems the Master of Flémalle was (judging from the left to right direction of the hatching in the brocades of his paintings such as the Nativity, cover image, and the Flémalle panels, **35**), would have had to reverse this set-up to achieve the best effects, and avoid casting shadows across his work with his hand; although the direction of observed light in a painting might be conditioned by its intended location, it is noticeable that in the core group of works attributed to the Master of Flémalle, the fall of light is from right to left, the reverse of van Eyck's preference.

Light had financial repercussions, since its absence potentially limited the length of the working day: this is a point made by Dürer in 1508 in giving his excuses for the slow progress on a work for one of his patrons, Jacob Heller. The artist writes, 'I am only sorry that the winter will so soon come upon us. The days grow so short one cannot do much.'[15] Because candles were expensive, working at night was only practical for court artists like Cranach and Malouel, both of whom were supplied by their patrons with candles for this purpose.[16] It was certainly undertaken when time was short: in 1420, in order to prepare the huge number of painted flags and coats of arms needed for a visit to Troyes made by Philip the Good to meet Charles VI of France, the duke had his court painter Hue de Boulogne and his six assistants work 'day and night, because of the necessity for great haste, for twenty days and twenty nights, without a break'.[17] However, in general, working by candlelight ran the risk of producing shoddy work, and many guilds, including the Brussels tapestry makers, the Bruges carpenters and wood-

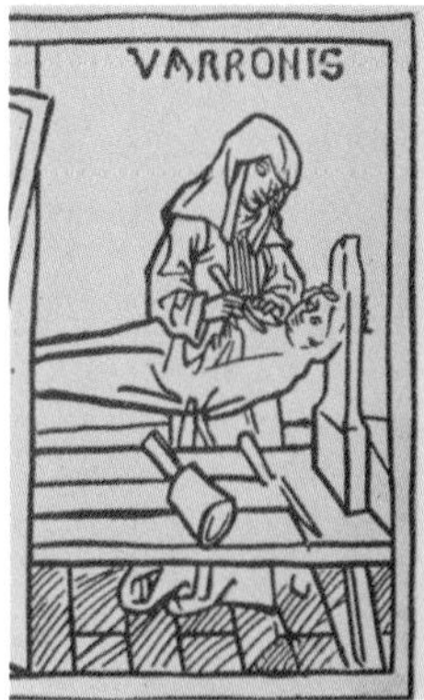

113 German *c*.1480

Marcia Varronis carving an Image, woodcut, *c*.1480.

Traces of the vices used by sculptors to fix their figures on workbenches, the like of which is shown in use here by the legendary painter-sculptor Marcia Varronis, can often be found on sculpted (mostly wooden) images, in holes made by the fixings at the top and the bottom of the blocks. Sometimes in the base of a carving there are several slots, which reveal how the work was repositioned, turned around its axis on the vice.

each to be set up and in use at the same time. By contrast, sculptors routinely worked standing up, with their objects lying horizontally rather than vertically, as the two woodworkers are doing in **115** and Varronis is doing in **113**, which meant they literally saw their objects differently. This arrangement was necessary to exert the required pressure with the chisel; stability was vital, and to this end some of these tables would be fitted with vices or metal hooks to keep the lighter wood blocks, in particular, rigid during carving; sculptors also used special benches with vices which held the figure free and allowed it to be turned, as seen in **113**. Many elements of the painters' craft also required a flat surface rather than an easel: gilding a panel or sculpture was often done with the work lying flat as the burnishing of gold leaf required pressure best exerted on a horizontal surface, although sometimes gilding (and painting) was done *in situ*, as Jean Malouel did on Sluter's Great Cross (see below). Paintings on fabric using a medium liable to run such as ink, as seen in the technically flawless *Parement de Narbonne* [**194**], must have also been done with the work lying flat, since there is no evidence of even the slightest of drips.

A strong table or bench (like those listed in van der Stockt's inventory) was also needed in painters' workshops for grinding pigments: this is what the assistants standing at the tables in **112** and **114** are doing, and it required one of the more valuable tools of the painters' trade, a large stone slab on which to mix prepared pigment into whatever medium was required to make paint. In **114** the medium seems to be oil, because the painter is using a mahlstick, only necessary if your worked surface remained sticky and did not dry quickly, as with oil, but it could be egg, water, or glue, depending on whether you were painting on panel, parchment, paper or cloth. The grinding stone had to be made from a hard, dense, and non-porous material, the best being porphyry: these may be the 'polished marbles, as brilliant as Beryl' from Lemaire's verse cited above. In Jan van der Stockt's inventory there are four such slabs, although their precise material is not specified. The Valencian painter Bartolomeo Avella had three, as well as eight cone-shaped mullers, the instrument used to grind the pigment onto the stone (seen in use in **112**, **114**, and the detail heading Chapter 14).[26] The numbers suggest that more than one may have been in use at any time, as seen in **128**, an arrangement which would speed up paint production.

Once the colours were ground they were placed into shells or small pots, ready to be used by the painter. An array of shells serving this purpose are laid out on the table in the foreground of **112** and **114**. These 'piles of shells', as described by Jean Lemaire de Belges above, were often mussels although oyster shells were also used.[27] In **112** the mussel shells sit in a bowl, apparently under water: this method was employed to keep the oil paint from drying out.[28] In several of these images little pots sit alongside the shells. These and other small containers must have been used interchangeably with shells for holding paint, but were a more durable and somewhat more valuable item of the painter's equipment. Jean Malouel took delivery in Dijon in 1398 of 100 clay pots 'to put in the colours with which the painter does his work'.[29] Jan van der Stockt had many different sorts of pots and jars, the Valencian painter Avella had 'six little pots for keeping colours' and another 'two dozen little dishes for keeping colours'.[30] The wording of the documents makes it difficult to know which of these were to store pigments, or made-up paint, or both.

114 Niklaus Manuel Deutsch

St Luke painting the Virgin, oil on panel, 1515.

On the bench in the foreground are the two different types of brushes used by painters: the *brosses*, made with pig bristles and string, and the *pinceaux*, made with finer hairs of squirrel or fox tails, set in quills which gave a tighter form of construction and made a more flexible tool than the relatively rigid wood-only construction of the bristle brush.

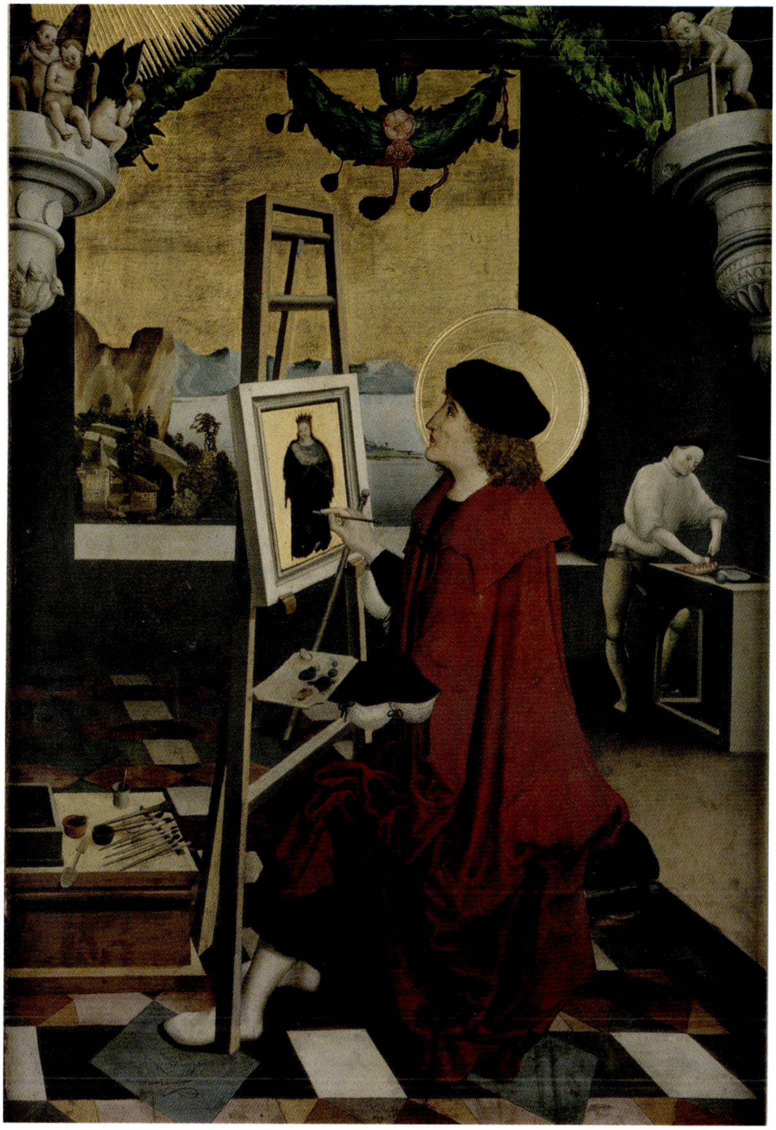

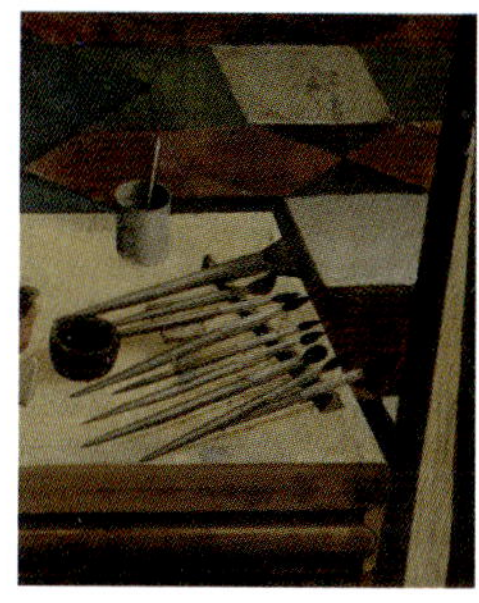

The item of equipment singled out most frequently in guild regulations and disputes as the identifying tool of the painters' craft was, unsurprisingly, the brush: this is the first and only tool specified in the long list of items—mainly materials, and mostly pigments—listed as the preserve of the properly trained painter in the Tournai regulations of 1480.[31] The use (or not) of the brush was also, as we have seen, a key argument marshalled in disputes as to who should pay fees to the painters' guild by scribes, textile printers and printmakers in Ghent, Bruges and Antwerp.[32]

The quality of your brushes was vital, and they could be bought ready-made: Dürer records that in Antwerp in 1521 he bought '13 bristle brushes for 6 stivers, and 6 bristle brushes for 3 stivers, then another 3 stivers for another 3 bristle brushes'.[33] However, many artists would have made them themselves, perhaps preferring to do so; it must have been an important skill apprentices had to acquire. There were two types used by painters, one made with pig or hog bristles (Dürer was buying this type in Antwerp), the other with fine hairs from squirrel or fox tails. They are carefully distinguished in the documentary sources—Jean Lemaire de Belges's poem describes *pinceaux* (fine or small brushes) and *brosses à tas* (bristle brushes); Lucas Cranach's accounts refer to *porspensel* (bristle brushes) and *harbensel* (hair brushes); Jan van der Stockt's inventory lists *pinselen* (fine brushes) and *borstelen* (bristle brushes), and the Tournai painters' regulations of 1480 distinguish between *pinceaux* and *brosses*.[34] These two types of brushes were also constructed differently, as is made clear in the payments for supplies to Jean Malouel at the Chartreuse de Champmol where, in 1399, he received pig bristles, wax, and string to make *brosses* and 100 swans' quills to make *pinceaux*.[35] The two types are depicted sitting next to each other on St Luke's table in **114**.

Painters must have owned literally hundreds of brushes: Jean Lemaire, in *La Plainte du Désiré* (1503–4), makes his artist exclaim, perhaps with some exaggeration, that 'I have thousands of *pinceaux* and *brosses* and tools'.[36] That Dürer brought 22 fairly casually in Antwerp, and that Malouel received equipment to make 100 of the fine sort alone, indicate just how many a busy painter's shop would need: they must have had a limited working life, but it was also because a wide range of different sizes and shapes were needed: X-rays of paintings by Lucas Cranach have revealed that he used a large blunt-bristle brush around 30 millimetres wide for painting the imprimatura, or priming layer, and a range of smaller sizes of bristle brush varying between 5 and 15 millimetres wide for blocking in areas of colours and their subsequent modelling.[37] For the finer details, and areas like faces, the *pinselen*, again in a range of sizes, would be used. The eyelashes of St Veronica in the Flémalle panels [**39**], for example, could only have been achieved with a brush made to have a very fine point indeed.

In the same way as the brush defined the painters' craft, the wooden mallet and the chisel defined the sculptors' (as we have seen regarding Bernt Notke, p. 151 above). For woodcarving, the mallet normally had a round head, and the chisels were skew-bladed, that is they had an edge which was oblique, and sometimes slightly curved (see the tools lying on the bench in **115**); for stonecarving, wood mallets, flat and claw-bladed chisels, and drills were required.[38] Chisels, like brushes, would have been needed in large numbers for a sculptors' workshop of any size, and they required constant sharpening, something that in large enterprises was outsourced to iron workers: in 1398 over 1,370 chisels, hammers, and punches were repaired and sharpened by the smith Jehan Perenin for the stoneworkers in Sluter's shop alone.[39] Mallets would have been used for driving the chisel when areas were being roughed out, although for woodcarving an axe would be used on the first blocking out of large sculptures. The final stage would be undertaken with the chisels held in the hands alone, as the two woodcarvers represented in **115** are doing.[40] One is at work on a large figure carved in the round, while the other works on a flat, small piece of wood, presumably intended as a relief panel. Both are holding skew-bladed chisels. The representation of the tools, the placing of the objects, and the handling of the tools is all very convincing—the chisels had to be held in two hands, with one hand applying pressure through the

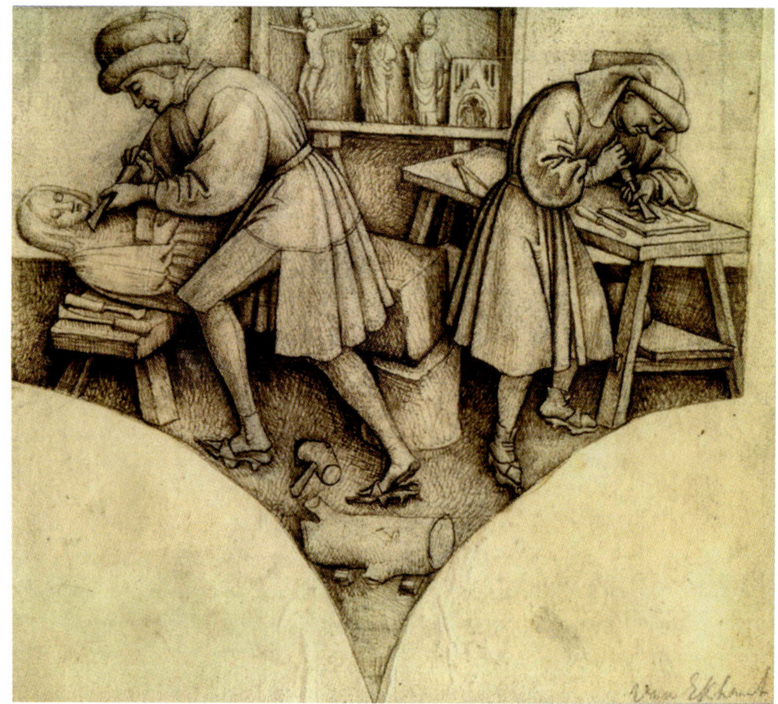

115 Vranke van der Stockt (?)

Two sculptors at work, pen and brown ink over black chalk on paper, *c.*1445.

This drawing, possibly a design for a carved architectural relief, shows two woodcarvers, their material indicated by the log on the floor in the foreground. The shape of this drawing suggests it was itself a design for sculpture, possibly a relief in the spandrel of an arch. On the shelf in the background are some finished or part-finished pieces: a crucified Christ (yet to be affixed to its cross), two small standing saints, and a piece of architectural canopy waiting to be incorporated into a larger work.

handle while the other restrained and guided the blade, sometimes threading it through the fingers. This representation is remarkably close to the way woodcarvers hold their tools today.

'All the Patterns, Papers, and Portraits Belonging to Me': Drawings and Patterns

Perhaps the most valuable items of equipment owned by artists were their collections of drawings and models, referred to collectively in the documents as *patrons* or *pourtraicts* (French), *patroonen* (Flemish), or *Entwerfen* (German), best translated as 'patterns' or 'designs'. Such collections often represented years of work or careful acquisition, some having been inherited, bought, hired, or even stolen; they would be difficult if not impossible to replace, and they played a fundamental role in creating images of all sorts. It is unsurprising then that they were much coveted, and we have records of disputes over their ownership and allegations of theft concerning them (see below).

Painters' wills present further evidence of the value of patterns, since they are often the only items of equipment singled out for special mention. A typical example is that of the Tournai painter Pierart Machelier made in 1461: he left to another Tournai painter, Haquinet de Haulterue, 'so that he will pray to God for me, all my tools used for my trade, with all the patterns, papers, and portraits [*patrons, papiers et pourtraitures*] belonging to me'.[41] Haulterue had not been Machlier's apprentice (he had registered for his apprenticeship with another Tournai painter eight years before), but he may have been his journeyman or colleague. Indeed, the distribution of patterns after your death could be both widespread and precise, determined by a variety of professional contacts, and need not be a simple line of descent: this is evident in the 1498 will of Bernardino Simondi, a Piedmontese painter active in Provence. His drawings and patterns were carefully divided between a range of artists with whom he had collaborated during his career: his engravings of the Passion and the twelve apostles (Master ES and Martin Schongauer, among others, had issued sets of both these subjects, see above, **89**, **90**) were to go to his compatriot and journeyman, Bartolomeo Dabanis; Claux Roux, his apprentice, was allowed to choose any twelve other drawings from his collection of models and patterns (*poncifs*); Josse Liefernixe, an established painter with whom Simondi had worked on several large altarpieces, was to have a *pertracturarum*, perhaps a sketchbook or modelbook; finally, Antoine Regis and Honorat Labe, two more journeymen, were to have his jointed wooden mannequin that came with its own clothes.[42]

The dispute in 1519–20 between Ambrosius Benson, a painter from Lombardy working in Bruges, and Gerard David, who by that date had been established as a master painter in Bruges for over thirty years, gives us further insight into the potential make up of an artist's collection of workshop drawings, and how such works might circulate. Benson, recently registered as a master in the Bruges guild, claimed to have left two chests in David's studio, where he had been previously working as a journeyman. These contained mostly drawings, described as various projects or patterns for the painters' and the illuminators' craft (an interesting distinction), a small book full of studies of heads and nude figures, various patterns belonging to Benson but which came from Adrien Ysenbrandt (another Bruges painter), and more patterns, this time hired from yet another Bruges painter, Aelbrecht Cornelius, at the cost of 2 florins phillipus, a fairly high sum. In response, David claimed that he had looked in the trunks and found that some of the drawings were unfinished studies which belonged to him, and anyway Benson owed David money, which Benson in turn had promised to pay off by working in David's studio. Eventually David ended up in prison for not returning the chests to Benson, perhaps an indication of how keen he was to hold onto this precious stock of patterns.[43] Somewhere in all this the idea of intellectual property may well be lurking: a trunk of brushes would not, one suspects, have elicited such a passionate response from both parties.

Surviving drawings provide further evidence of the range of media and form such patterns could take. They might be designs on paper, parchment (more durable), wood (even more durable), or if required to be very large, cloth. By the latter part of our period they must often have included engravings, like Simondi's; in Spain by the sixteenth century, inventories of artists' belongings can list hundreds of prints.[44] Some must have been coloured, wholly or in part (see **116**). It is also implicit from much of the above that these collections of patterns were mostly (but not solely) composed of loose-leaved sheets, routinely kept in some form of box or chest: as we have seen, Ambrosius Benson's were split between two coffers, and the Valencian artist Bartolomeo Avella kept his, described as 'a great number of diverse painted and outlined patterns in diverse paper sheets', in a decorated pine wood box.[45] Loose leaves would, anyway, have been the most practical format, allowing them to be shared around the workshop, traced from, pounced, hired out, or sold.

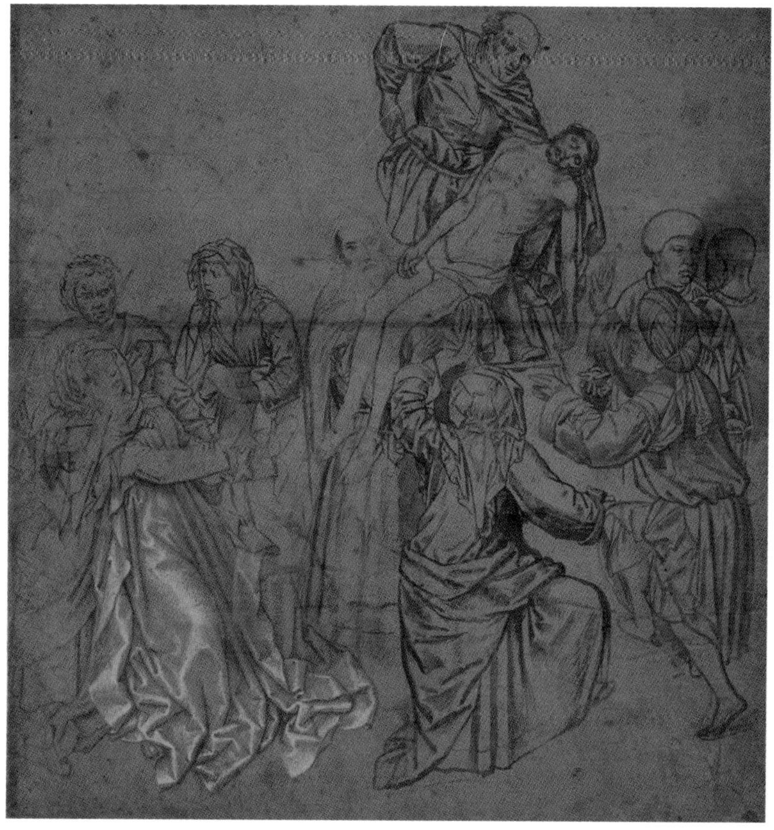

116 After the Master of Flémalle

Descent from the Cross, brush drawing in ink with white body colour and red chalk on paper, late fifteenth century.

Many drawings would have been produced by copying finished works, either your own or those by other artists. A drawing on paper from the late fifteenth century of the *Descent from the Cross* [**116**] is a good example of an artist making a careful study of one section of a finished painting, rather than inventing and working though a composition from scratch: indeed the work it copies was a now-lost panel of this subject by the Master of Flémalle.[46] Here the figures are what have interested the artist, and they are drawn without any real sense of their relationship to a background or to the props such as the ladder that would have been needed to support them, and which would have had to have been indicated more fully on the drawing if the artist was inventing rather than recording.

As well as focusing on groups or figures from certain works, drawings might record a complete composition in all its details, as is the case for **117**, made after Rogier van der Weyden's *Exhumation of Saint Hubert*. This drawing includes around twenty notations in French and Flemish indicating the colours, and also the textures or material nature of objects. This suggests that the drawing was made in front of the original and with an eye to producing a painted version of it at some point; the notations also minimized the detail needed in parts of the drawing, making the task of recording faster: thus on the robe of the bishop to the right is written *velour bleu* ('blue velvet'), on his mitre *perle*, and on the antependium *vert damast* ('green damask').

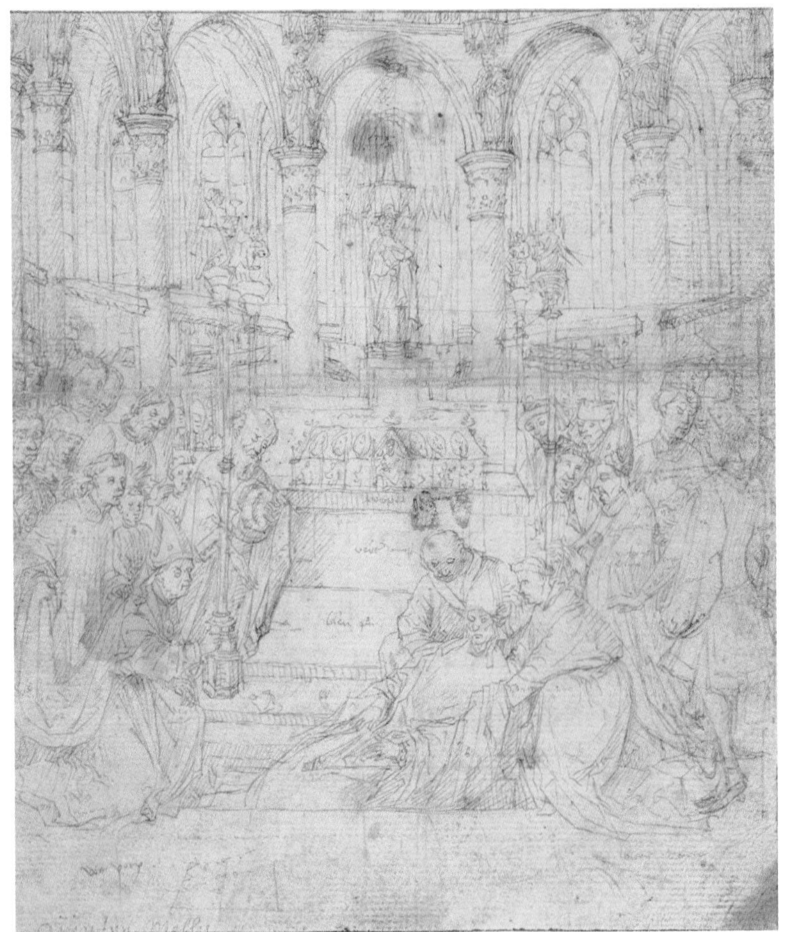

117 Netherlandish artist (after Rogier van der Weyden)

The *Exhumation of St Hubert*, pen and brown ink on paper, *c.*1480–1500.

The painting by Rogier van der Weyden from which this drawing was made [**6**] was clearly accessible to artists in the Church of St Gudule in Brussels: the apparent speed at which this copy of it was made and the colour notations suggest it was done in front of the work itself, rather than from a drawing after or for it, and as such is a quick impression of an image worth recording for its invention and form.

Other drawings would have focused on single figures, or on heads or hands: the very fine drawing in pen and ink on prepared green paper by a close associate of Hugo van der Goes of a seated female saint [**118**] was eminently versatile: she wears royal dress so could be reused as an Ursula, a Barbara, or a Catherine, all very popular saints. Indeed, the pattern or one very close to it was reused for a wide variety of different female saints in numerous illuminated manuscripts made in Bruges and Ghent in the late fifteenth and early sixteenth centuries.[47] These types of drawings may in part have been a learning exercise, but it was also a key method of building up a resource of different ideas, figures, poses and faces, which could then be reworked, or copied directly into your own productions.

When we look at paintings created in a busy commercial workshop like that of Rogier van der Weyden or Hans Memling, it is evident how such drawings would have been employed. Certain figures or faces are repeated, revised, and developed across a series of works, although exact reproduction is eschewed: the figure of the man wearing a red and gold brocade robe and seen from the back on the far right of Rogier's *Exhumation of St Hubert* [**6**] is a version of a similar figure found in his *Justice* scenes for Brussels town hall (**9** above) and is reworked again in works like the Seven Sacraments Altarpiece

118 Associate of Hugo van der Goes

Seated royal female saint, brush and ink with white bodycolour on green prepared paper, *c.*1475.

By contrast with **117** this is a finely drawn, carefully made study which records in some detail a particular figure, made probably after another drawing or a painting in the workshop of Hugo van der Goes. That it is by a copyist, not the first invention of the master, is indicated by the positioning of the hands, which suggests they are playing with a ring (as St Catherine might hold in an image of the mystic marriage with the Christ Child), but the ring has not been drawn in.

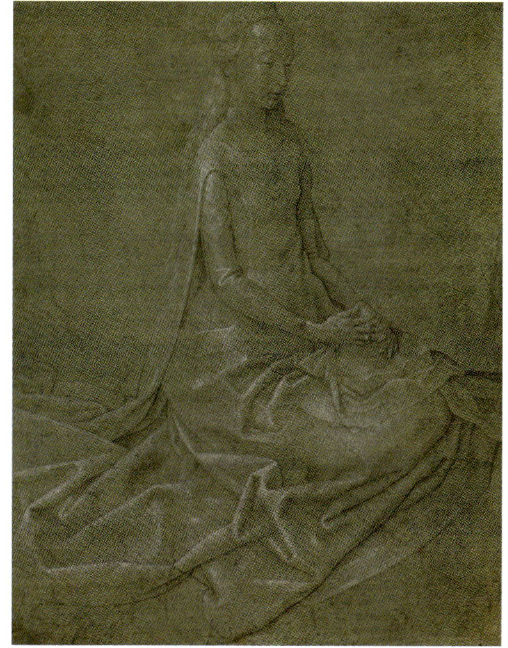

(Antwerp) and the Columba Altarpiece (Munich).[48] A comparison of versions of St John the Baptist by Hans Memling in his Altarpiece of the Two St Johns [**79**] and his Donne Triptych [**81**] shows a similar adaptation of a workshop pattern across different commissions.

While single loose sheets were practical in many respects for such drawings, in some instances a bound collection may have been more useful: it would solve the problem of losing track of leaves if you were an itinerant artist, or might be a better way of preserving and presenting drawings primarily intended as display items that a customer could view to see the 'house style' or select a composition or figure type. This might have been the purpose of a group of fourteen small square maplewood panels, each with four compartments on to which a total of fifty-four drawings on paper of heads of figures and animals, including a skull and a spider seen from above, are pasted [**119**]. These panels are bound together in a manner which allows them to be folded up, leporello-fashion, into an object measuring

119 Bohemian *c.*1400

Modelbook drawings of heads of figures and animals

Silverpoint, pen and brush on green-tinted paper, mounted on maplewood tablets held together by strips of parchment, with tooled-leather storage box.

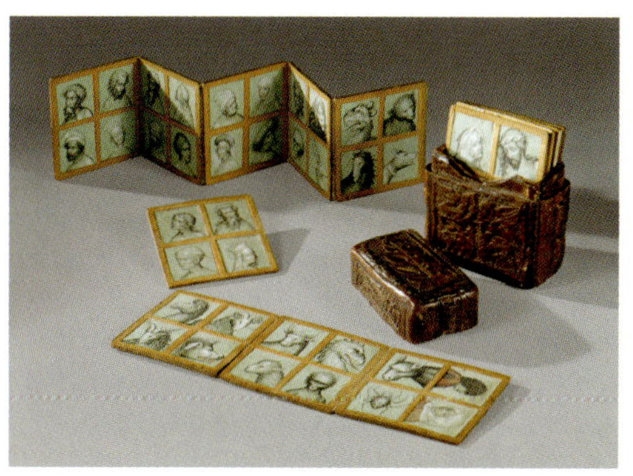

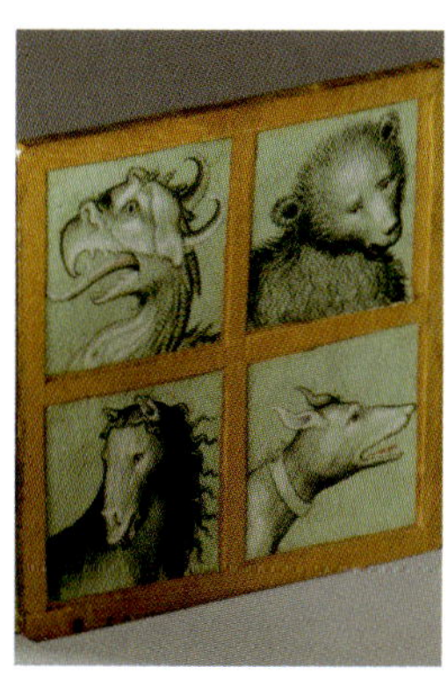

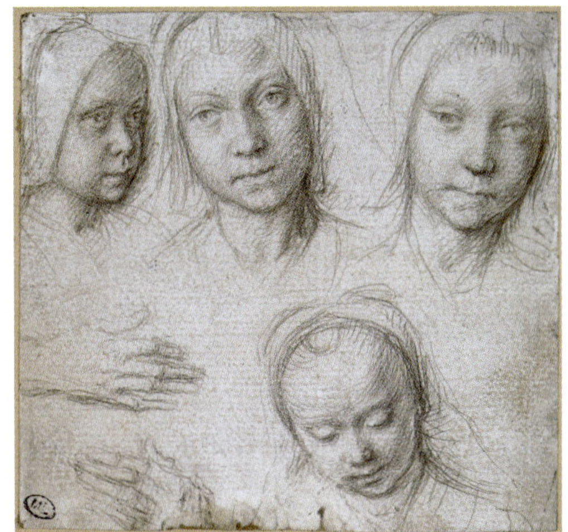

120 Gerard David

Four girls' heads and two hands, silverpoint over black chalk on prepared paper, *c.*1500–5.

This small sheet, probably once part of a sketchbook, contains studies of the heads of two different girls, one clearly younger than the other; such studies were enlisted by David for both donor portraits of children and for his young female saints. The hands are observed from, and for, another figure entirely. These heads and hands were drawn first with black chalk that was erased almost entirely when David went over the initial sketch with silverpoint, fixing and refining the image.

just 10 centimetres square; a contemporary, tooled leather case also survives in which they were kept. The form and materials used here suggest permanence—this is a set of designs and, as such, collectable, as indicated by the presence of something very similar in the possession of René of Anjou and of Margaret of Austria.[49]

The 'sketchbooks' referred to in the dispute between Benson and David and in the will of the Piedmontese artist Simondi suggest a different type of object: we hear that Benson's contained 'studies of heads and nudes'. Some drawings clearly by David which may have made up such a sketchbook survive [**120**]. What distinguishes them in large part from the other drawings discussed here is the quality of observation, the sense that they are studies from life, taken with some speed, as explorations of poses, faces, and hands.[50] Although we have little direct evidence concerning the activity of drawing from life, it must have been well established in artists' workshops since both the practice of portraiture, and the creation of highly individualised heads like that of St Veronica in the Flémalle panels (**35, 39** above), demanded such a method of observing and recording.

Life drawing is in a sense represented in Rogier van der Weyden's depiction of *Saint Luke drawing the Virgin* [**108**]. In Rogier's image we see the artist making a study of the Virgin's face with silverpoint (shown as a metal stylus into which, at each end, a point of silver is set) on prepared paper. Silverpoint was another tool expressly mentioned by Jean Lemaire de Belges; it allowed fine, controlled lines and a subtle exploration of shadows and tones, perfect for producing refined, detailed studies of heads, whether they were portraits or more idealized inventions. It was neither forgiving nor dynamic, encouraging precision rather than expansive sketching. Jan van Eyck used this medium to make his life drawing of Cardinal Albergati [**121**]. Across the top of the drawing and down the left-hand side van Eyck wrote detailed colour notes concerning the hair, eyes, skin, nose, chin and lips of the sitter, recording their subtle variations and appearance, allowing him to use the drawing alone as an aide when he came to paint the portrait.[51] Portrait drawings (and others in instances where exactness was required) were sometimes

121 Jan van Eyck

Cardinal Niccolò Albergati (?), silverpoint on prepared paper, *c.*1435.

This is one of the few drawings from our period that can be attributed with certainty to a named artist, and it is one of the few which, like **120**, is clearly preparatory rather than made after a work to record an existing invention. The working method revealed in it—of writing colour notes down the side as an aide-memoire—may not be typical of van Eyck's practice, but rather a response to a situation in which he knew he was unlikely to have another sitting with his subject at the painting stage.

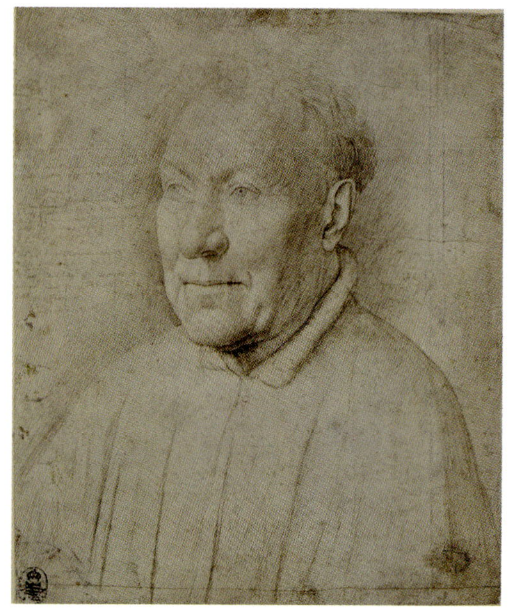

transferred up to the panel by mechanical means of pouncing or tracing, evidence for the use of which can be found either on surviving pounced drawings or in infrared reflectograms of the panel itself, visible in the nature of the line made by such a method in the underdrawing; indeed, from technical evidence where painted portraits have been produced on another support and then stuck onto panels in larger compositions (for example, the head of Tommaso in the Portinari Altarpiece, **67**) it would appear that painting, not just drawing, from life was sometimes insisted on.[52]

There is little evidence to suggest that sculptors amassed the collections of elaborate and refined preparatory or study drawings so precious to the painter: inventories of sculptors' belongings make no mention of such items, and in terms of surviving material there is little one could claim was definitely produced by a sculptor (who was not also a painter, like Veit Stoss), rather than being made as a drawing after a sculpted object, or by a painter for a sculptor [**122, 124**]. Sculptors, however, certainly used graphic works as sources for their images, as the widespread employment of engravings by Schongauer, van Meckenem, and the Master ES in their workshops attests (see Part II). It could be argued that sculptors simply needed to make drawings less, or that they were fairly simple affairs, because of the nature of their craft: as carvers today make clear, drawings would not be the main way in which you would work though the demands and form of a piece of sculpture in its preparatory stages. A few guidelines directly on the wood or stone were probably more practical: in proceeding with a block any drawing loses its validity as the sculptor begins to see in the round. The difficulties of making a flat design for a three-dimensional object are well illustrated by the drawing for one of the capitals of Brussels town hall made around 1444 in the workshop of Rogier van der Weyden.[53] This large drawing ingeniously provides a method of showing all sides of the three-dimensional relief for

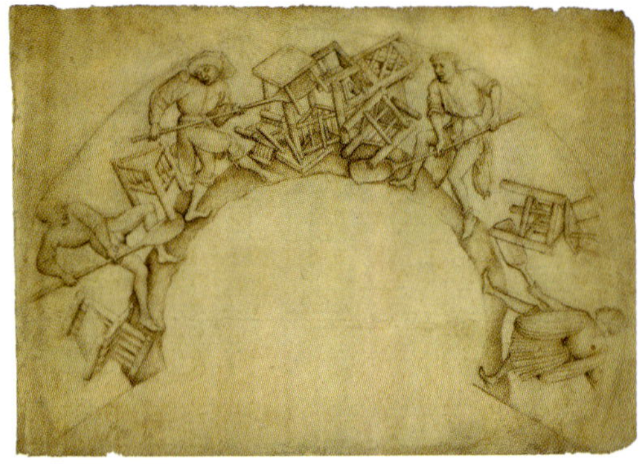

122 Workshop of Rogier van der Weyden

Drawing for a capital on Brussels town hall (the 'Scupstoel'), pen and grey-brown ink on paper, *c.*1440.

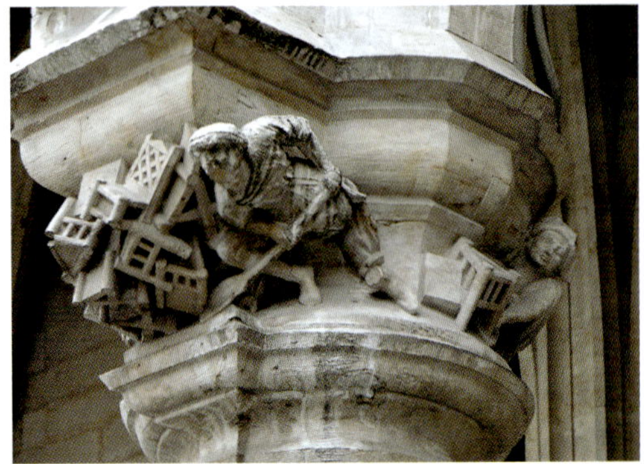

123

Modern copy of carved capital of *c.*1440 from Brussels town hall, carved after the damaged original and the drawing in **122**.

the awkwardly shaped capital on one sheet, as can be seen by comparing it to the recarved version *in situ* [**122, 123**].

Sculptors were certainly provided with drawings, usually by painters, as the *scupstoel* attests, and it was a particularly widespread practice for large complicated works like tombs and carved altarpieces: the sculptor Michel Colombe was given drawn models by the painter-illuminators Jean Fouquet and Jean Pérreal for the tombs, respectively, of Louis XI in 1474 and Philibert of Savoy in 1511 (neither, in the end, executed by Colombe). In the latter case, Colombe had the drawings reinterpreted by two members of his own workshop, his nephews the illuminator François Colombe (who redrew the *gisant*) and his mason Bastyen François (who redrew the ground plan and elevation), presumably to make them more practical as patterns for the sculpted monument. Providing designs for sculpture, metalwork, tapestry and stained glass was an important part of a painter's trade, and one which they often went to some lengths to protect, through disputes with artisans in other crafts who were undertaking this design process themselves rather than contracting to painters for it. However, sometimes the models made by an artist trained in one craft could prove impractical for translation into another medium with its particular limitations. This was clearly the case with a pattern provided to the bronze founder Henri Costerel in Troyes in 1494 for a large cross showing the Magdalene at its foot and nine prophets around its base; Costerel complained that he could not make the figures in bronze following the wooden models provided by the Flemish sculptor Nicolas Halins because their form would endanger the stability and strength of the work.[54]

124 Hans Schuchlin (?), for the use of Jörg Syrlin the Elder and Michael Erhart

Viserung for the high altarpiece of Ulm Minster, ink on parchment.

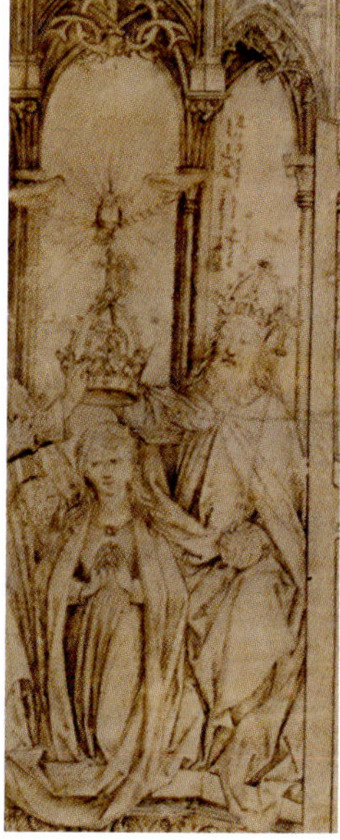

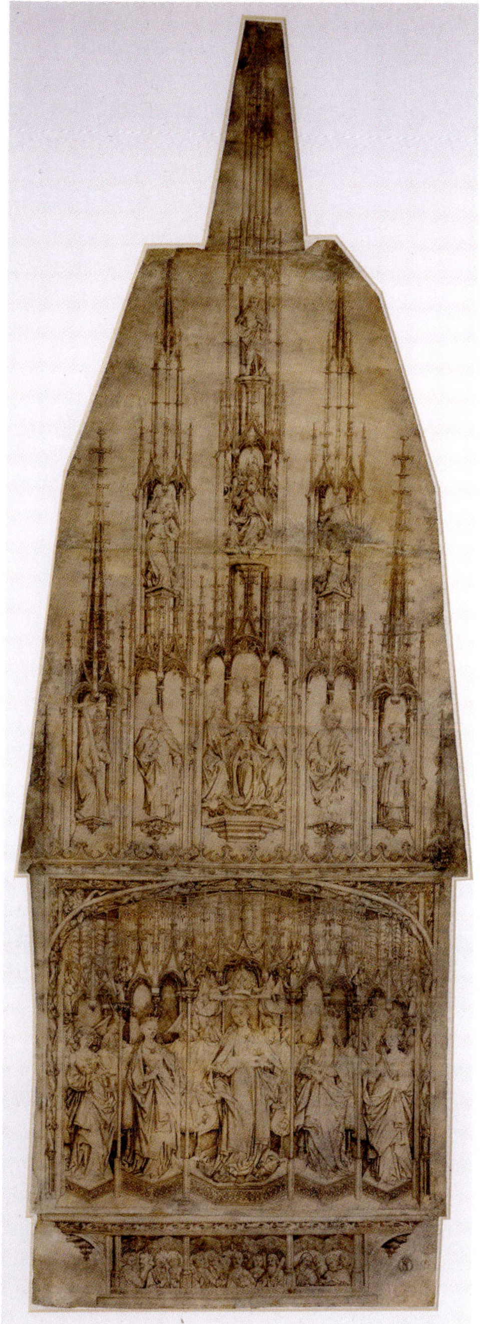

A similar division between sculptors and painters with regard to providing patterns for large-scale works can be seen in the production of carved wooden retables in Germany, where the *viserung* (contract drawings) which were routinely made for them survive in relatively large numbers.[55] These drawings were themselves often very large indeed: that for the high altarpiece of the Ulm Minster is 2.31 metres tall, in ink on five parchment sheets of different sizes joined together [**124**]. This drawing was given to the carpenter-carver Jörg Syrlin (who had also carved the choir stalls for the same church, see **101, 102**), and whose name is inscribed in a contemporary hand on the back of this sheet. According to the contract for this work, which survives, Syrlin was commissioned to carve the architectural framework 'in the shape of a design presented to him', presumably this one, indicating that he did not produce the drawing himself. The sculptor Michael Erhart was commissioned to undertake the figurative elements of the Ulm altarpiece, but stylistic analysis suggests that he did not do the drawing either, and it has most recently been attributed to the local painter Hans Schuchlin.[56] The scale of the design suggests that what was required were the details of the subject and form in a legible format for the commissioners to approve. Once they had seen it, they made some changes: inscribed next to the figures of the Coronation group in the upper register is a note phrased in the terms of a written contract: 'Item, the subject should be a crucifix with Mary and St John.'[57] Apart from this addendum there are no traces of paint or other indications that it was used in a workshop.

For sculptors a three-dimensional model was far more helpful, and it is probable that this was the main way a carver would realize his initial ideas and from which his assistants could work. We have already seen that wooden models were provided for the bronze founder Henri Costerel. This was a common practice for large-scale cast metalwork (such as the tomb of Mary of Burgundy, see **190**) but also for stone and alabaster, documented in instances such as the alabaster altarpiece at Zaragoza (see **134**). Sculptors' models might also be in terracotta or stone: Michel Colombe produced two three-dimensional models for the tomb of Philibert of Savoy, a terracotta one made 'with my own hand, without anyone else touching it', and another small one in stone, carved by his assistants, following the terracotta.[58] This carved model served both for Margaret to approve (it was coloured to mimic the effects of the black and white marble and sent to her 'so that Madame will be able to see the whole tomb') and also as practice for the sculptors before carving the final work. We have no examples of the first type of model Colombe made surviving from northern Europe at the period, although we do have an example of the second type: a small-scale limestone relief, for another tomb project, intended to be in marble, made by the Ulm sculptor Hans Multscher for Ludwig of Bavaria in 1430 [**125**].[59] Such models in cheaper materials allowed mistakes to be made and changes to be requested without any expensive marble or alabaster wasted. The imagery in this case is also unusual and complex for a tomb monument at this date: Ludwig is shown kneeling (the artist was allowed to choose whether it was to be on one or two knees, 'whichever is better'), holding a banner which is given heavenly support by the angel above. Ludwig's prayer, in the form of a scroll, links him to the angels and the Trinity above, while his emblems, the crowned sun-disks and ravens, are 'scattered', as specified in his will, across the background, the whole surrounded by another of his emblems, chestnut leaves. The patron must have wanted to approve the design in carved, not just drawn, form before the sculptor began on the huge block of red marble 414 × 188 × 48 centimetres which Ludwig supplied. These models were thus as important in the commissioning process for the patron as they were in the creative process for the sculptor.

125 Hans Multscher

Model for the tomb of Ludwig of Bavaria, limestone, 1430.

This is a small-scale model for the tomb of Ludwig of Bavaria, brother-in-law to Charles VI of France, which was to be erected in the church of Our Lady in Ingolstadt and was to be carved from a huge block of red marble; it was, however, never executed.

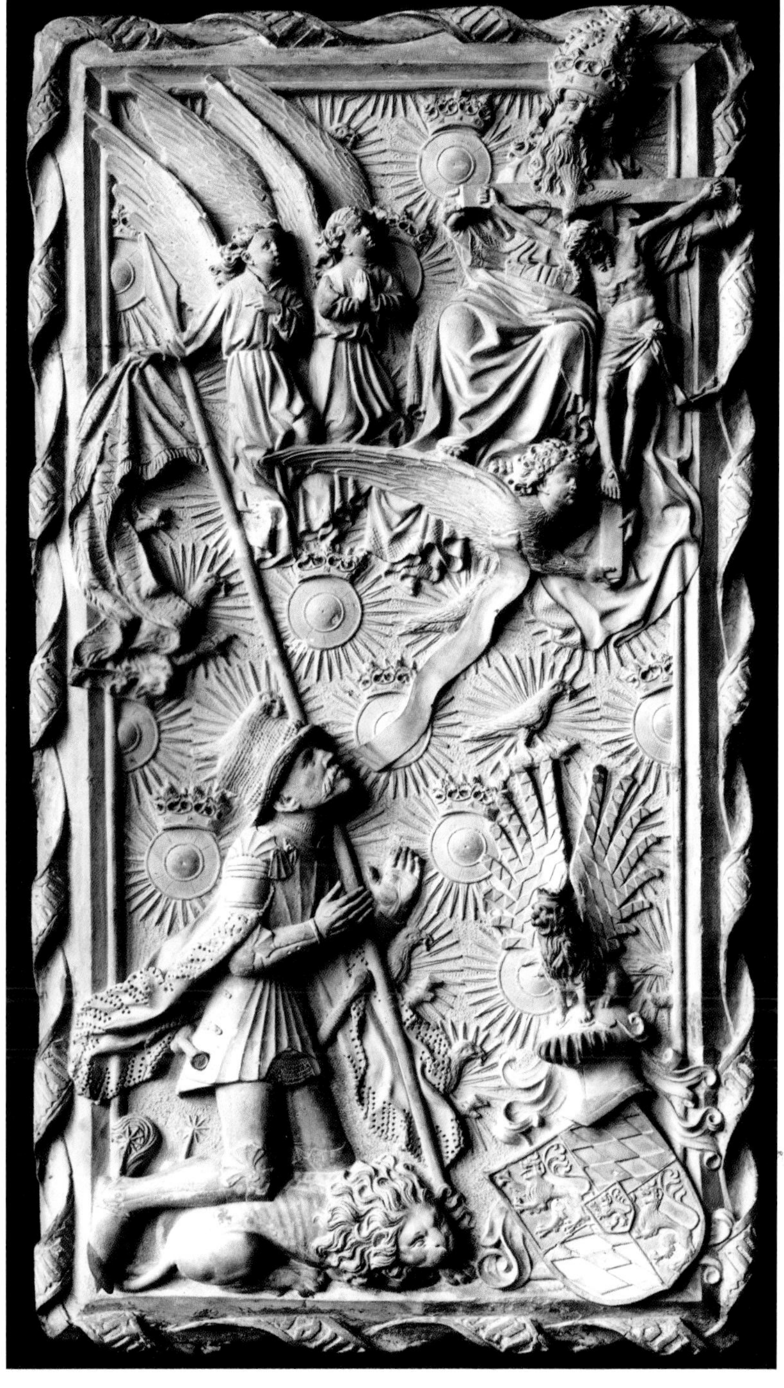

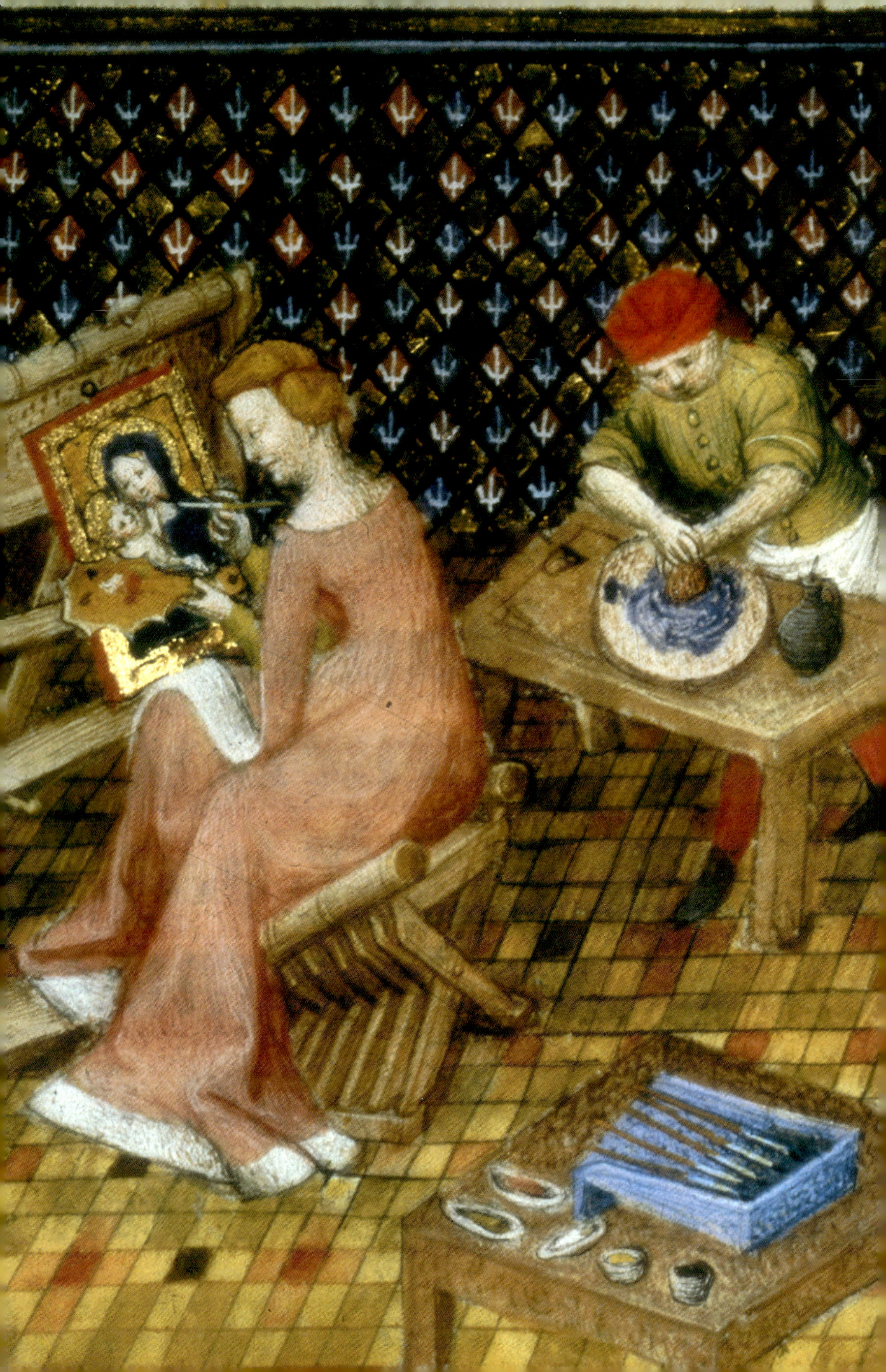

The Workforce

Every trade that is done has to be learnt, and also, when it is necessary, one should be able to employ assistants to satisfy the customer.

The *libraires* and illuminators of Bruges, 1457[1]

He can do nothing alone and without help.

Philip the Bold on Jean de Marville, his court sculptor, in 1381, concerning the commencement of work on the duke's tomb[2]

14

Parisian illuminator *c.* 1400, *Thamar Painting*, from Boccaccio's *Des cleres at nobles femmes*, illuminated manuscript, 1403.

The assistant grinds the blue pigment into oil on a stone slab, using a muller; this needed to have a large flat area at the bottom with either a handle or a tapering point at the top. Considerable skill, as well as strength, was needed for this task.

Size, Training, Experience, and Expertise

These two comments, one concerning the frequently large-scale enterprise of stonecarving, the other regarding the production of much smaller works, illuminated manuscripts, indicate how at each end of this spectrum, collaboration and the employment of assistants was a routine, essential practice, even if it was only a family affair involving your children and wife. Larger enterprises might, however, encompass as many as ten or fifteen fully trained assistants working together, as are recorded in the sculpture studio of Jean de Marville in Dijon in 1387, or in the painter's shop of Lucas Cranach in Wittenburg in 1513.[3] In general, these teams would involve three main categories of workers: apprentices, who were learning the trade; journeymen, variously referred to as *cnapen* (Flemish), *gesellen*, *knechts* (German), *valets*, *compagnons*, *ouvriers*, and *serviteurs* (French), terms which are not necessarily interchangeable, but seem to have denoted different levels of experience—they were trained in the craft but for financial or other reasons had not yet set up as independent masters; and hired hands (*ouvrier de bras*, *lohnknaben*). These journeymen and helpers made up a pool of available, variously skilled workers who might move from town to town or shop to shop with some freedom.

We begin, however, with the more tightly controlled category of apprentices. These, vital to the continuation of the craft and its standards, were an important but limited part of the workforce. In many centres their numbers were strictly controlled: painters in Amiens, Bruges, and Brussels and painters and sculptors in Ulm could only have one apprentice at any one time, although in Brussels and Ulm a second was allowed when the first was in his last year; in Munich and Krakow painters were allowed two at any one time, and in Brussels tapestry weavers were also allowed two at any one time, as long as one was their own child, while for painters and sculptors in Paris (after 1391), in Lyon, Rouen, and Tournai, there were no restrictions on their number.[4] Most apprentices were young (although not necessarily) and should not be seen as the main source of assistance for an artist: for much of their first year, at least, they may have been a drain rather than a resource within the workshop and were not expected to do as much as a paid assistant: Lucas Cranach made occasional special payments to his apprentices when they had 'done as much work as a journeyman', clearly not a level of help which was routine.[5]

Perhaps because of this, some artists never had apprentices: it has been estimated that 60 per cent of the woodcarvers in Antwerp between 1453 and 1479 took on no apprentices at all.[6] In addition, attracting them may not always have been easy and training them was an investment of both time and money, from each side. Apprentices had to commit to the master and pay a fee, while the master had to feed, house, and clothe them, promising also to train them for a set period regulated by the guilds, which varied from town to town and from craft to craft, lowered or raised as economic conditions or the agenda of the guild altered and, in some places, made shorter if an extra payment was forthcoming. Paris, prior to 1391, had some of the longest apprenticeships, with twelve years for paternoster (prayer bead) makers working in coral or mother of pearl, ten years for weavers, and eight (if an extra payment was made) to ten (if it was not) for sculptors; apprenticeships were six years for painters, glaziers, and woodcarvers in Cologne in 1449, raised from four years in previous regulations; five for painters and sculptors in Rouen in 1507; four for painters in Antwerp in 1470 and Tournai in 1480; four to six years for painters and sculptors in Ulm, Augsberg, and in most Spanish towns; three years for painters in Leuven and Amiens and for tapestry weavers in Brussels; two for illuminators in Tournai in 1480 and only two for painters in Bruges (except between 1479 and 1497 when it was four).[7] In Brussels, painters, gold beaters, glass makers, and goldsmiths were among the very few crafts that dictated four years' apprenticeship—less taxing to learn, it would seem, was the work of the embroiderer (three years), the illuminator (two years) or the joiner (one year).

That apprentices were seen as an investment is indicated by the fines imposed by many guilds for those who did not complete their agreed term, and for masters who lured away apprentices 'with words or works' from another master.[8] Their literal monetary value is vividly illustrated by a dispute between the Parisian illuminator and *libraire* Andry le Musnier (who we have met renting houses on the rue Neuve Notre-Dame in Paris) and his brother-in-law, who worked in the same trade. On the death of Andry's father Guyot, also an illuminator-*libraire*, the control of his apprentices had fallen to his wife. She, however, loaned both of them, sometime before 1456, to her son-in-law to help complete work on a commission for the duchess of Brittany Françoise d'Amboise. Andry complained about this, saying they 'were mine, by virtue of the division we made, my mother and I, of the other apprentices'. In the end, Andry sold his interest in them to his brother-in-law for the not inconsiderable sum of 16 écus.[9]

The pattern of apprentice enrolment for one Tournai artist, the painter Philippe Truffin (d. 1506), who trained with Rogier van der Weyden's nephew Louis le Duc and became a master in 1461, is probably not untypical: over the forty years of his very busy and successful activity, as one of the leading artists in the town, he took on fourteen apprentices. Some of these were relatives of his, or sons of his colleagues in Tournai, but several came from further afield: from Ghent, Haarlem, Bruges, and even Spain. Only twice, in the early part of his career, does Truffin have more than one at a time, despite there being no limit to this in Tournai, and in both cases they were taken on close together in time. Patterns of enrolment for other artists in Tournai indicate that enrolling apprentices at a similar date was a common practice, and must have made teaching them easier, since they would progress at similar rates. It would seem, however, that having a workshop full of apprentices was not always necessary, possible, or desirable.[10]

How artists were taught is something about which we have lamentably little evidence. However, some sense of the progression through the four years of apprenticeship needed to become a painter in Tournai can be had from the regulations of the guild there, which allowed that it was possible to learn to draw in one or two years or to illuminate in two. This suggests that training began with learning to draw—as the small boys are doing in the workshop in **128**. Drawing was something that could be learnt independently of painting in Tournai and elsewhere, and was widely envisaged as a skill which artists from other crafts might spend time with a painter to learn. The technically more complex and challenging painting of panels and sculpture (using oil) took two years longer than learning to draw or to paint on parchment, which was routinely done with other media, egg or glue size.

This extra two years must in part have been taken up with learning the properties of pigments, how to prepare them in oil as well as how to apply them. Grinding pigments (that is, mixing their powdered form into the required medium) was a skilled task, requiring an understanding of the characteristics of different colours, their behaviour over time or with different types of oil or other binding agents, and the effects of combining them. The importance of grinding and paint preparation is verbalized in the complaints of the painters of Seville in 1480, who claimed that regulations were necessary since some painters in the city 'don't even know how to classify colours as they ought, or to process them for painting, and because of this what they paint is badly and thoughtlessly painted and the colours are lost and fall off'.[11] Similarly, the Córdoba guild regulations of 1490 state, following a list of allowable pigments, that 'all these colours should be well ground because they will be more stable and more pleasing to see'.

Judgement was needed at every stage in preparing colours: to grind the pigment to the appropriate degree before mixing with the paint medium, to ensure the correct ratio of medium to pigment, and then to assess how long to grind them together to ensure the pigment was suitably absorbed into the medium, without ruining its colour strength. This varied from pigment to pigment: red lake, for example, has an almost infinite ability to take up oil, so the longer it was ground the better the quality of the paint. Similarly, the final colour obtained from vermillion corresponds directly to the amount of grinding it undergoes: the more finely it is ground, the more vivid red its hue. By contrast, if azurite (a blue) or malachite (a green) are ground too much the intensity of the colour they produce is diminished. In addition, the proportion of oil to pigment had to be varied according to the thickness of paint required and the nature and properties of the oil itself (which might vary from batch to batch, depending on its preparation), as well as the characteristics of each pigment—the blue pigments tended to need more oil to make them workable than the reds. Given the responsibility, skill, and physical demands of the job of grinding, it seems this was not, as is often thought, a role for the young apprentice: they would be learning this skill but it would not be their primary task, since it needed a worker with considerable experience and physical strength and was therefore more likely undertaken by a journeyman or other fully trained assistant. When Jean de Beaumetz, the head of the painters' workshop at the Chartreuse de Champmol in Dijon, needed help in this aspect of his craft, an independent painter from Dijon, Jehan Gentilz, was brought in for the job, to work for five months 'continually with Beaumetz, grinding colours to make into certain works of painting.'[12] In **128** the two men grinding pigments are certainly not young apprentices.

Gilding was used extensively for panel paintings and on sculpture, and must have been one of the tasks which justified the extra two years of training indicated in the Tournai guild regulations. Many guild regulations are loquacious about gilding and its proper application and use, and while the cost of materials and the potential for fraud partly explain this, it was also one of the most technically challenging and time consuming aspects of the painters' craft. For gilding to be successful, the chalk ground laid on the panel or sculpture had to be carefully prepared and perfectly smooth, free of bubbles or wrinkles and of sufficient depth to withstand the pressure of burnishing (guild regulations constantly advise on the importance of the preparation of surfaces). Handling the thin gold leaves requires dexterity, judgement, and the right conditions: any hint of a breeze, even a sigh, makes the task impossible, and the moist layer used to affix the gold to the ground is only at the right stickiness for a very short period, which has to be judged with care. Applying gold leaf evenly without a wrinkle to a flat surface was tricky; applying it to the three-dimensional surfaces of carved figures was even more so. Burnishing and working the gold, punching without breaking its surface, and adding moulded tin-relief decoration for brocades required the acquisition of yet another level of mastery. The potential for mistakes was high, and irretrievable in material terms: getting it wrong was literally throwing money away.[13]

We can also get some sense of what painters and sculptors were meant to be capable of by the end of their apprenticeship through the stipulations in many guild regulations concerning masterpieces. These had to be submitted in Paris, Tournai, Amiens, Rouen, Lyon, Krakow, Munich, Vienna, Strasbourg, Luneburg, Prague, Hamburg, Lübeck, Constance, Mallorca and Córdoba, but were not something reserved for painters and sculptors: they are common in tapestry makers' regulations, for example, and are also found in non-image-based crafts like clothmaking, dyeing and parchment-making. Again, gilding is emphasized as a key skill, since it was often specifically (and sometimes uniquely) required to be displayed in painters' masterpieces. In Tournai in 1480 a piece of painted sculpture had to show competence in the application of a chalk ground, display both matte and burnished gilding, and show a command of *draps d'or* (brocades) and other decorative techniques; in Constance in *c.*1495 the painting of a panel had to display skill in burnished gilding and incised or raised decoration (possibly pastiglia work as seen in the Seilern Triptych, **31**), and in Munich in 1448 and 1461 the painter's masterpiece had to be of a Virgin and Child panel that had a burnished gold background with punchwork decoration.[14]

Polychromy is revealed here and in other masterpiece requirements as another of the key skills of a painter. Indeed, in Tournai and Constance, it was possible to submit just the polychromy of a statue as evidence of mastery in painting, which, at least in Tournai, did not then limit them to practise only this aspect of their craft. Van Eyck, Campin, and van der Weyden all polychromed sculpture, and the fact that Memling and other later fifteenth-century painters in Bruges did not, as far as we can tell, marks them out as the exception, not the rule, in the wider northern European context. Clearly, painting and gilding sculpture was emphatically not a task left to less talented artists or seen as having less status in the painters' craft: the need to work extensively with gold, and the technical difficulty of gilding a three-dimensional surface, ensured that this could not be the case.

Polychromy must have been the major, even the principal, activity for many painters, given the high proportion of altarpieces produced at the period with sculpted parts which required such work. Although some sculptors, especially in the earlier part of our period, undertook the polychromy of their works themselves, this task was increasingly the preserve of painters alone as refinements in guild regulations in most Netherlandish and German towns ensured the division between the two crafts.[15] As we have seen, most altarpieces at this period had sculpted centres, and the vast majority of painting work required by most municipal authorities would have been the painting, and repainting, of sculpture, especially exterior works. The importance of polychromy in a painter's output is also underlined by looking at the contents of the workshop of Philippe Truffin (who we have already met, above, taking on apprentices in Tournai), whose stock consisted of a number of polychromed sculptures as well as paintings on panel, cloth, and parchment.[16] It was also a relatively highly paid task: painters often received more for polychroming carved retables than sculptors did for carving them, even accounting for the cost of pigments and gold involved with the painters' part of the job.[17] This would seem to reflect the degree of expertise and the amount of time that the preparation, application, and working of the gilded surfaces required. It was not that painters were more highly valued than sculptors, necessarily: polychromy simply took a long time as well as a great deal of skill.

Working figures on a large scale and the ability to design were also areas in which a trained painter was required to display ability: when the size of a masterpiece was specified it was substantial (5½ feet in Lyon for single carved figures, for example). Skill as a draftsman was something emphasized in several masterpiece specifications. Those for Córdoba of 1490 are perhaps the most precise on this, requiring both drawn and painted submissions because 'the examiners shall judge from a drawing of his whether he is a draftsman and capable of arranging whichever subjects he might be asked to represent. Likewise they will judge from a piece of *imagineria* worked in colours, whether he is a master for such work.'[18] A similar stipulation is found in the Amiens regulations of 1491, where the painter applying to be a master (but not a candidate in sculpture or embroidery) had to submit the design of his work as well as the finished painted version.[19] These were relatively unusual specifications, however, and the ability to draw or design well, to compose groups, to convey action and drama was assessed elsewhere either by setting a challenging subject for the masterpiece or by specifying the elements it must include. Thus in Constance in *c.*1495 panel painters had to include depictions of a building, a landscape, and both clothed and nude figures; other guilds required a Virgin and Child and/or a Crucifixion (Munich, Hamburg, Krakow, and Luneburg, for example), while in Mallorca it was a Virgin and St

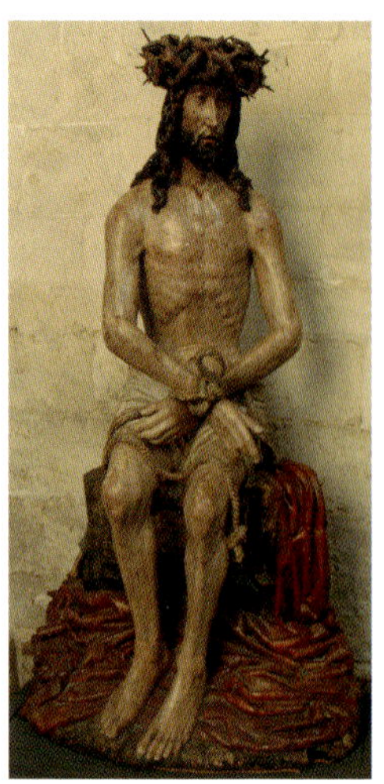

126 Anonymous Brussels sculptor

Christ on the Cold Stone, polychromed wood, *c*.1500.

The image of Christ sitting awaiting the Crucifixion became intensely popular around 1500; a convincing depiction of the suffering, naked Christ at life-size was clearly a challenge for sculptors.

127 Bernt Notke

St George and the Dragon, wood, parchment, paint, metal, hair, bone, string, and polychromy, completed 1489.

The virtuosic potential in depicting St George is apparent in this monumental (around 3.5 metres high) version by Notke, who plays all his dramatic cards at once: the horse rears, the knight is about to deliver the killing blow, the dragon has broken off the lance, which has gone through his neck, with his claw, but the horse will die, too, his belly ripped out by the dragon's other claw. Notke defied the limitations of wood sculpture by using other materials to create his forms, such as antlers (for the dragon's wings), parchment, leather, real hair, string, and metal, including coins.

Joseph with the nursing Christ Child (which would show babies, beautiful young women, and old men all at once).[20] The most extensive of all the specifications for masterpieces, and those which reveal these concerns about skill in representation most clearly, are those for potential master sculptors in Lyon in 1496, who could produce one of the following:

> a Jesus Christ of stone [see **126**], all nude, showing his wounds, a small cloth covering him, having wounds in his hands, side and feet, with a crown of thorns on his head, done with good countenance and piteous as it should appear in this image, this image will be of five foot and a half high and of appropriate width to the height, and all as if real [*après le naturel*]; or an image of Our Lady holding her child in her arms, of the same height as the above, with good countenance, a well decorated cloak, good drapery, good painting, and all as if real; or other images of the same height, like Saint Margaret or Saint Barbara or Saint Catherine; or a history of two foot and a half high and three foot wide, with eight people well made and carved in the round, and this history will be of the Arrest of Jesus Christ, or the Carrying of the Cross, or of a building which is the house of Caphias, or another story of the Passion, or when he was baptized in the river Jordan by John the Baptist, full of angels holding his robes, and all done with good countenance and piteous, and all made like the above; or a Nativity of Christ, as given above.[21]

The subject that may have been regarded as a classic masterpiece demonstration, since it is specified by several different guilds (Krakow, Hamburg, Lyon, Luneburg, and Prague, for example), was the figure of St George. Its challenges were obvious: no other subject demanded, all together, a horse, a dragon, an armoured figure, motion, drama, action, shiny surfaces, weapons, landscape, buildings, and a young princess. It is unsurprising that the major printmakers of the fifteenth century issued engravings of St George, which allowed such a display of invention. Just how dramatic works of this subject could be is demonstrated by the monumental version by Bernt Notke made for the City Church in Stockholm in the late 1480s [**127**]. Originally set right in the middle of the nave of the church, possibly directly under the chancel arch, it functioned as an altar and tomb for its patron, Sten Sture, ruler of Sweden and as a container for relics (these were set in a pendant around St George's neck). Some of the challenges of the subject were precisely specified in the loquacious guild regulations of Lyon of 1496:

> Item, another masterpiece, a Saint George on a horse, five foot and a half high, for him and for the horse, a girl on a rock near him, a serpent near the girl looking as if it is going to devour her, the image of Saint George also made of good countenance, looking as if he will destroy the serpent either with a lance or a sword, all done as above.[22]

In **128**, an engraving made in the late sixteenth century, the master painter in the centre of the studio, meant to represent Jan van Eyck, is working on an image of St George. A painting of St George by van Eyck, now lost, relatively large in scale (4 × 3 palms, around 84 × 63 centimetres, similar in size to the *Arnolfini Portrait*) and very highly priced (at 2,000 Valencian sous reyals, roughly 128 Venetian ducats), was among the most famous of the artist's works, having been acquired by agents of Alfonso of Aragon in 1444 and sent, via Barcelona, to Naples, carefully packed in wool.[23] This was possibly the painting that Vasari later said 'became very dear to that King both for the beauty of the figures and for the novel invention shown in the colouring'.[24] It was described by the Neapolitan humanist Pietro Summonte in 1524 as:

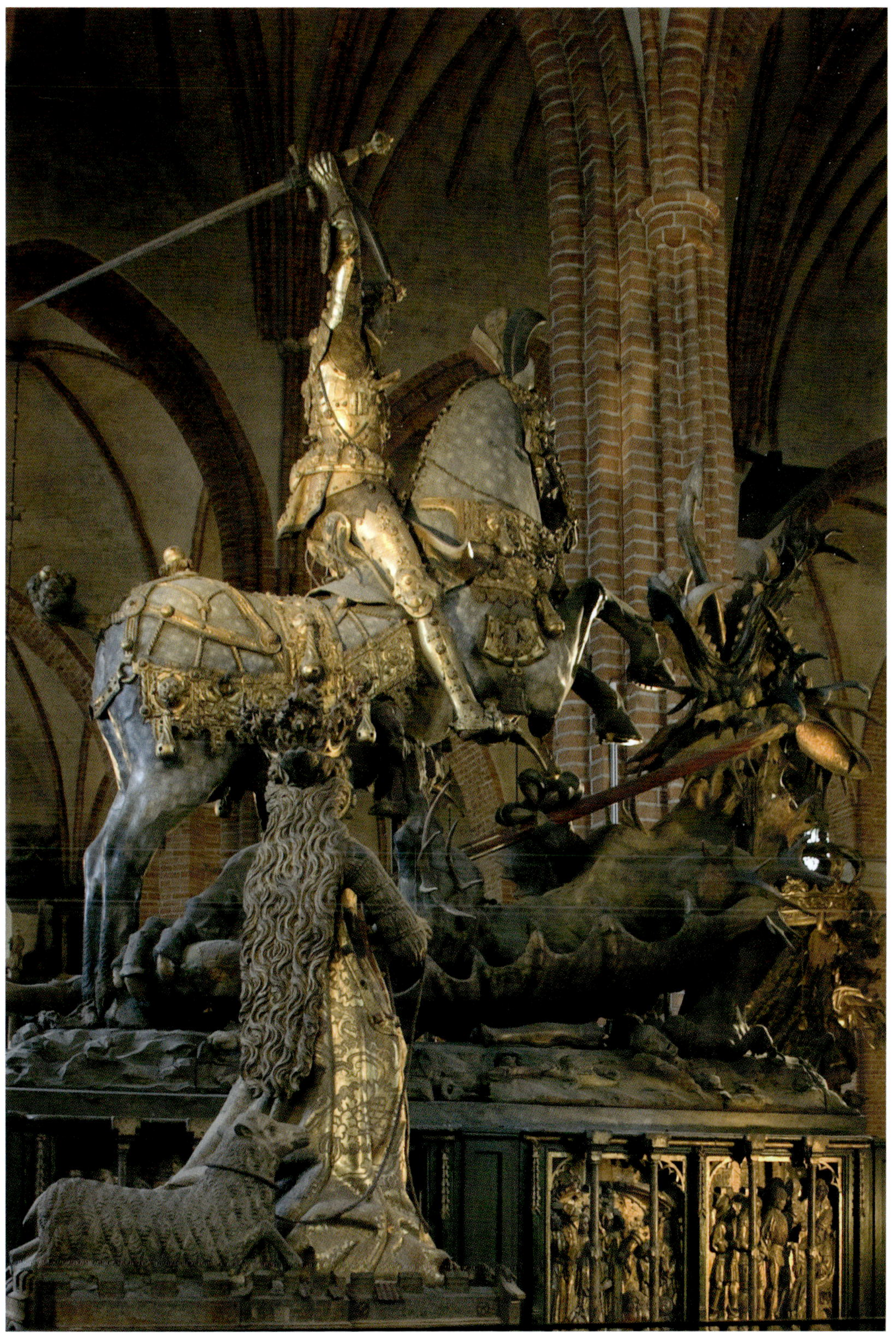

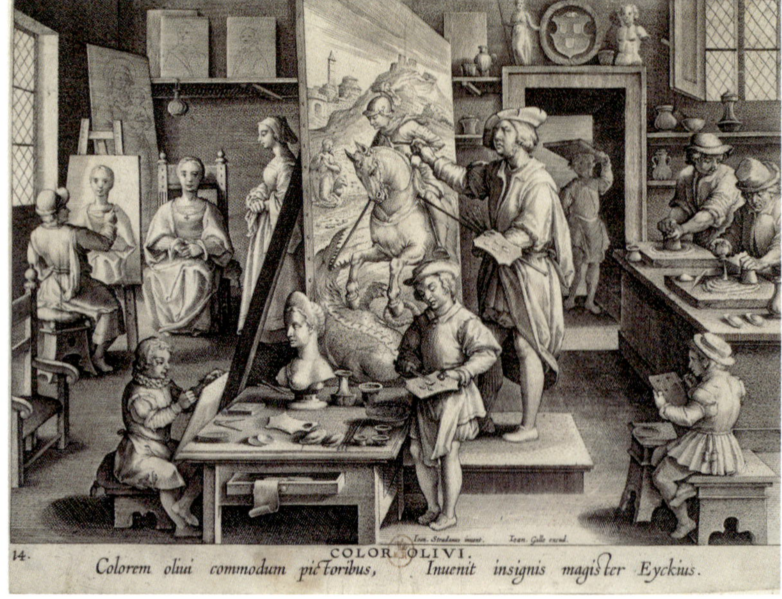

128 Johannes Stradanus (Jan van der Straet), engraved and published by Philips Galle

Color Olivi (Oil Colour), engraving from *Nova Reperta* (Modern Inventions), designed in the 1580s, published 1600.

The Latin inscription states: 'Oil colours, suitable for painters, discovered by the master van Eyck'. The myth of van Eyck's invention of oil painting, established in the sixteenth century, persists today.

a renowned work, where one could see the knight leaning and throwing the spear into the mouth of the dragon, piercing through so deep that the skin on the other side was already swollen and stretched outwards. And the fine knight was so bent forward and so strained against the dragon that his leg was seen losing the stirrup and he himself almost unseated. The reflection of the dragon was visible on the left leg of the shiny armour as if in a mirror and the rust on the tree of the saddle stood out against all that metallic splendour.[25]

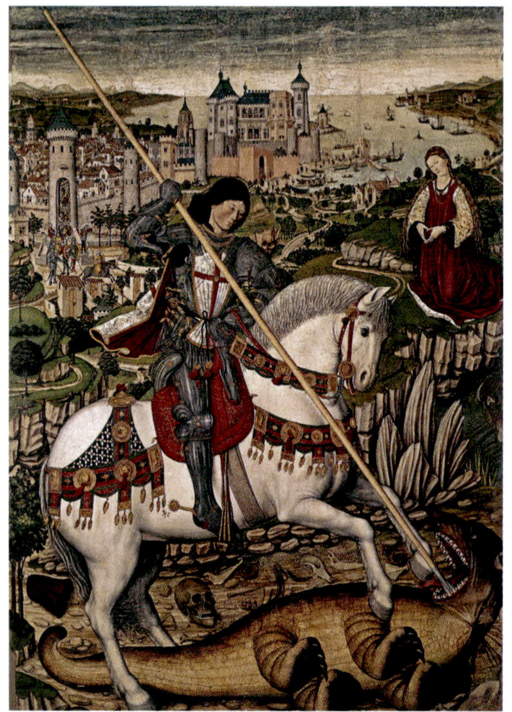

129 Pedro Nisart

St George and the Dragon, oil on wood, 1468.

Although the description of the lost St George by van Eyck suggests that this version by Nisart was not an exact copy of it, it still seems to have been inspired by an Eyckian image, especially evident in the extensive landscape, river, and city view.

Here we see, from a different viewpoint, the potential of this subject and the opportunities it presented for dramatic invention and illusionistic description: some reflection of this lost work might be found in the large central panel of an altarpiece painted by the Mallorcan Pedro Nisart in 1468 [**129**].[26]

To acquire these skills and a mastery of all the elements of the craft, it would seem that copying panels in progress or producing replicas of pictures in the workshop stock must have been an essential method. A glimpse of this practice in van Eyck's workshop, where parts at least of finished panels were certainly traced for future use by his assistants and followers, might possibly be had by the two versions of the same image of *St Francis receiving the Stigmata* that could conceivably have been produced as part of such a task [**130, 131**].[27] The primary version of these two surviving works (there were several in international circulation at the period) is that in Turin, which shows typical Eyckian underdrawing and some shifts in the composition from drawn layer to paint surface, indicating its likely status as the original, and it is painted in the expected manner in oil on panel [**130**]. The version in Philadelphia [**131**] is painted by a different hand from that in Turin (to judge from a close examination of the details of its handling), is exactly a third of the size (and as far as we can tell exact painted copies tended to be the same or reduced size), and is painted on parchment, stuck onto a wooden panel made up (bizarrely given its tiny dimensions) of three even smaller pieces of wood. This must have been constructed as a rather odd, perhaps makeshift support within van Eyck's studio itself since dendrochronology shows that the wood used comes from the same plank as that used for the portraits of Baudouin de Lannoy and Giovanni Arnolfini (both Berlin, Gemäldegalerie), both painted by Jan van Eyck. Quite why small pieces of this wood were lying around in the workshop is not clear, although Dürer describes in one of his letters how he dismantled the frame of the Heller Altarpiece because it was not well made, so perhaps these were discarded elements of this sort. The possible genesis of the St Francis panel as a practice piece might explain this strange technical choice, but it is obviously an accomplished copy, preserved and valued in its own right since it mimicked the style of the master and convincingly attained some of the effects so admired in his works.

Being able to copy works and adapt your style to that of your master was an important requisite for trainee artists, who would often spend some years working as assistants in other masters' workshops before becoming masters themselves. Some would travel long distances to do this, which might even be a guild requirement, as in Krakow, where a period journeying, a *wanderjahre*, to 'practise and improve his skills before he marries', was specified in the regulations. These trained painters—journeymen—who sought experience, work, and money (and possibly a wife, as some regulations stated masters had to be married) in the hope of eventually setting up their own shop, were the largest and most flexible group within a workshop, the regulations for whom, in general, were nowhere near as extensive or restrictive as for apprentices: they did not need to be, since there was no issue of proper training and its concomitant investment at stake. Nevertheless, flexibility could cause problems, and there were occasional attempts to regulate journeymen's terms of employment, from both sides: they had to pay a fee to the guild to work in some towns, often after only a few days, perhaps to ensure that, once the fee was paid, they would remain to make the investment worthwhile; in Basel in 1463 they could

130 Workshop of Jan van Eyck

St Francis receiving the Stigmata, oil on Baltic oak, *c.*1440.

This is the version now in Turin, which measures 29.2 × 33.4 centimetres.

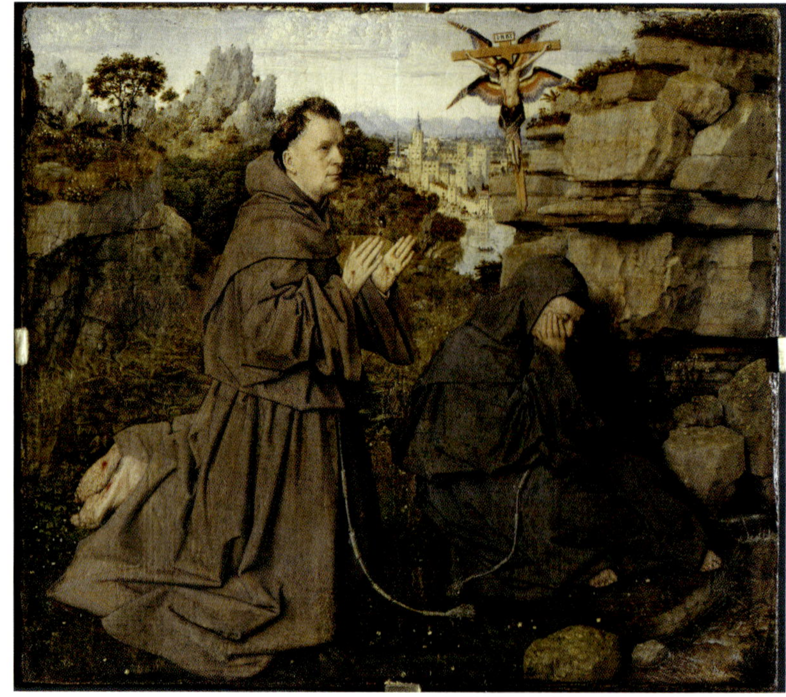

131 Workshop of Jan van Eyck

St Francis receiving the Stigmata, reduced copy of **130**, oil on parchment stuck onto Baltic oak, *c.*1440.

This version now in Philadelphia measures less than half the size of the Turin version at 12.4 × 14.6 centimetres.

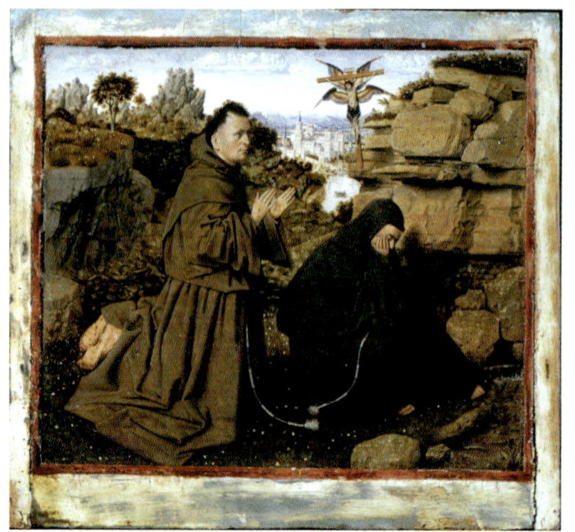

be employed by either the week, month, or year; in Prague in 1490, a master had to give two weeks' notice to any journeyman he no longer needed. Assistants absconding just when you needed them most may have been a regular problem: Gerard David claimed that his journeyman, Ambrosius Benson, had left without having worked the days he had been paid for; in Krakow, the guild tried to control such behaviour by stipulating that journeymen painters could not leave work without the master's permission, nor arrive late for work, or else the master was allowed to keep a week's salary. One imagines such behaviour was fairly common and a practical nightmare for master painters when large projects were on the go, and a reliable team was essential.[28]

In many towns there was no limit put on the number of journeymen you could employ: in Ulm, the painters' and sculptors' regulations stated that 'a master may engage as many as he wants'.[29] Mostly, what would limit numbers were the financial resources to pay wages and the space available. Sometimes the type of journeyman was regulated, especially in Germany and eastern Europe where the combination of painting and sculpture in the same workshop was a possibility (in the Netherlands, the two trades were much more strictly separated): in Munich in 1473, painters were allowed a journeyman sculptor, and vice versa, a new regulation which enabled the production of polychrome sculpture within the one workshop, a set-up that was common in other towns like Lübeck.[30] In Prague, the regulations of 1490 allowed for a master to have in his workshop one painter, one woodcarver, and one *zubereiter*. 'Zubereiters', perhaps translatable as 'preparers', were specialists in making panels and sculptures ready for painting by laying on the layers of chalk ground, smoothing them down, and also often applying gilding—the two skills being interrelated since good gilding, as we have seen, relied on the quality of the ground.[31] From the inscriptions hidden inside the monumental figures of the rood screen in Lübeck Cathedral by Bernt Notke and his team in 1471 and 1472 (**151** and see p. 150–51 above) we learn that he had working with him on this project a woodcarver, an apprentice, and three *zubereiters*: clearly, preparing the ground was such a large task in this instance that these specialists made up the bulk of Notke's team. *Zubereiters* could work independently: in Antwerp it was possible for a 'zubhereiter' to become a master craftsman within the painters' guild, and in 1507 in Nuremberg Dürer records how he had given the panel he was working on for Jacob Heller 'to the preparer [*zubereiter*] who has whitened it and painted it and will put on the gilding next week'.[32] The time it took to produce paintings or polychrome sculpture could be considerably reduced by employing specialists within the workshop or by outsourcing this element of the making of an image.

Along with apprentices and fully trained journeymen who may or may not be specialists in certain fields, many artists also relied heavily on their wives or other female family members in the running of a workshop; they might be trained as painters themselves, but if not they could handle other aspects of the business of making, selling, or delivering art. In 1459 Rogier van der Weyden's wife, along with several of his journeymen, accompanied a large altarpiece to Cambrai for delivery to the abbot of Saint-Aubert there,[33] while Dürer's wife and his mother were employed by him selling and marketing his prints, something common in Nuremberg and other German towns.[34] Wives might also take over the running of a workshop completely on the death of their husband: such an event is catered for in the Lyon regulations of 1496, which specify that 'all women widowed by the death of their husband in one of the aforesaid metiers of painting, sculpture, or glass painting may and should continue to hold shop in the manner of their husband when he was alive … and may have the same rights and privileges'.[35] Other regulations, such as those of Krakow, specify that if a master dies the apprentice must continue with the widow so that her financial hardship is alleviated. It is likely that for a few years after Jan van Eyck's death his widow Margaret [**98**] continued the business of his workshop, ensuring the completion of commissions or selling off part-completed works.

'Mature, Solid, Wise, Reliable, Self-Assured, Experienced, Well-Behaved People': Recruitment, Collaboration, and Specialization

This quote comes from a letter written by the aged court sculptor Michel Colombe to his patron Margaret of Austria.[36] Their correspondence gives us some of the most illuminating and precise evidence we have concerning the possible collaborations and specializations within a workshop at the period. In his letter, Colombe sets out how he will proceed with a tomb for Margaret's late husband, Philibert of Savoy (d. 1504), the models for which we have discussed above. Because Colombe had been informed that Margaret was concerned about the qualities of her workforce, he was at pains to clarify their respective skills and roles. The tomb was not, in the end, executed by Colombe, but a project by him of similar scale and form is that for François II of Brittany and Marguerite de Foix in Nantes [**132**]. From the letter we learn exactly how the work on such a project would be divided up, and are told about the different roles and skills of Colombe's assistants, their relationship with

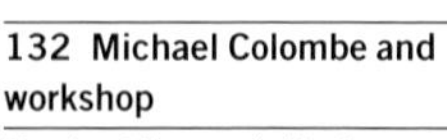

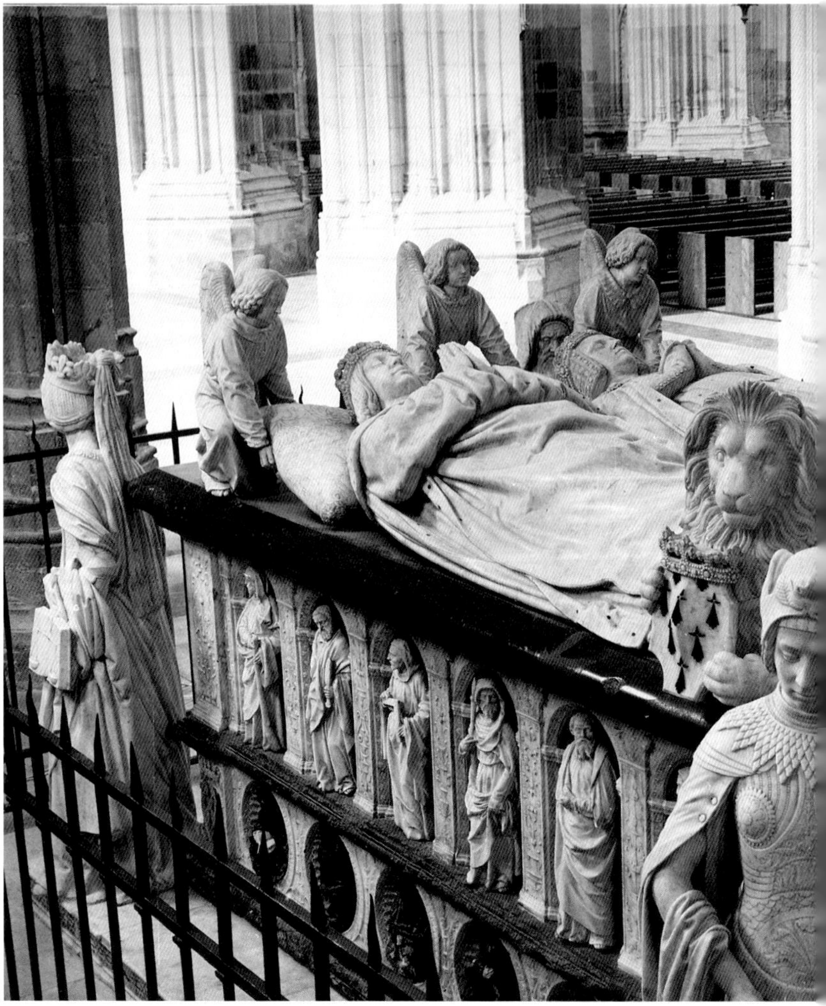

132 Michael Colombe and workshop

Tomb of François II of Brittany and Marguerite de Foix, white and red Italian marble, black Dinant marble, begun 1499, completed 1507.

White marble for this tomb was imported from Genoa and coloured marbles acquired from Florence; the sculptor also had two Italian marble workers with him on this project, and the architectural decoration reflects this. The design's most original feature, however, is the four life-size standing figures representing the cardinal virtues. A sketch of this tomb was sent by Colombe to Margaret of Austria to demonstrate the type and quality of his work when he was negotiating another tomb commission with her.

him, and how long they have been employed. The mainstays of Colombe's team were his three nephews, respectively a sculptor, a mason, and an illuminator. The sculptor, Guillaume Regnault, had been with him for over forty years and clearly undertook most of the actual carving in the workshop, as Colombe states he is:

able and experienced enough to execute in large scale the carving of the figures used in said tomb, following my models; for he has served and aided me in such matters for forty years of so, in all large, small and medium-sized undertakings which by the grace of God I have had in hand up to now.

The mason, Bastyen François, undertook the architectural elements of projects like this tomb; as Colombe states:

as to said Basteyn François, son-in-law of that nephew of mine, I can vouchsafe that he is capable of utilizing and executing on large scale the models of said tomb, with regards to masonry and architecture. These models will be made in small size by his own hand.

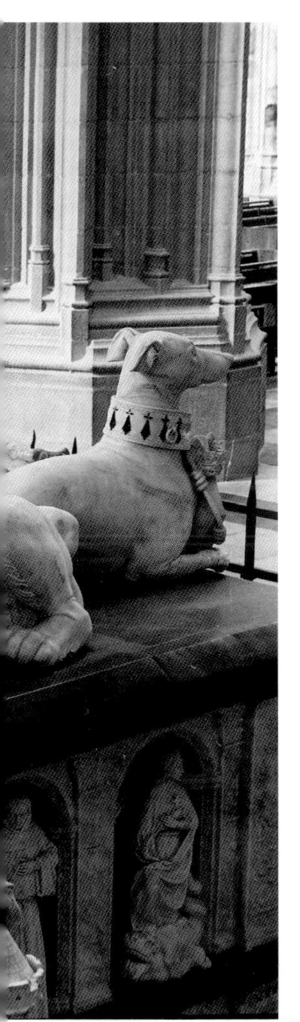

The role of the third nephew, François Colombe the illuminator, was in making drawings and then painting the small-scale model which would be produced by Guillaume and Basteyn, so as to emulate the rich materials to be used in the full-scale version—black and white marble, gilt-bronze inscriptions and 'borders', coats of arms, and flesh tints on the faces. When it came to installing Philibert's tomb in Brou, its intended destination, Colombe states that he will employ further assistants: one Jehan de Chartres, who he calls 'my pupil and assistant, who has served me for eighteen to twenty years' but who is now working for the Duchess of Bourbon, 'as well as other assistants of mine for whose artistic skill and probity I shall stand responsible and by whom I am sure I will not suffer shame or disadvantage'. Clearly, as well as the long-term members of his shop, Colombe had a network of other artists, some of whom he had trained, whom he could call upon to aid him in the more labour-intensive stages of such a project.

The ways such networks might function, and the fluctuating number and variety of personnel in artists' workshops, can be examined from another rich documentary source from the beginning, rather than the end, of our period: the records of payments to the artists employed under Jean de Marville and then Claus Sluter at the ducal sculpture workshop in Dijon.[37] This outfit was well financed by the Duke of Burgundy, Philip the Bold, who required, at various points, swift progress on the works. It was housed within the ducal palace in Dijon itself, and produced several major projects between 1385 and 1406, including the tomb of Philip the Bold [**133**] and the Great Cross, better known as the *Well of Moses* (**146–8** and below).[38]

In 1384–5, when the records begin, Marville was head of the team and in that year he employed ten different workers, most for periods of between twenty-two and fifty-two weeks, paid by the week or sometimes by the day. These were all fully trained workers, not apprentices learning their craft. Of this ten, there was one father and son, and two pairs of brothers. Such family teams, as we have seen with Colombe and his nephews, were common at the period—the de Limbourg brothers and their uncle Jean Malouel being another famous example from the French courts. Guild regulations encouraged sons to train in their father's trade: they paid less to become an appren-

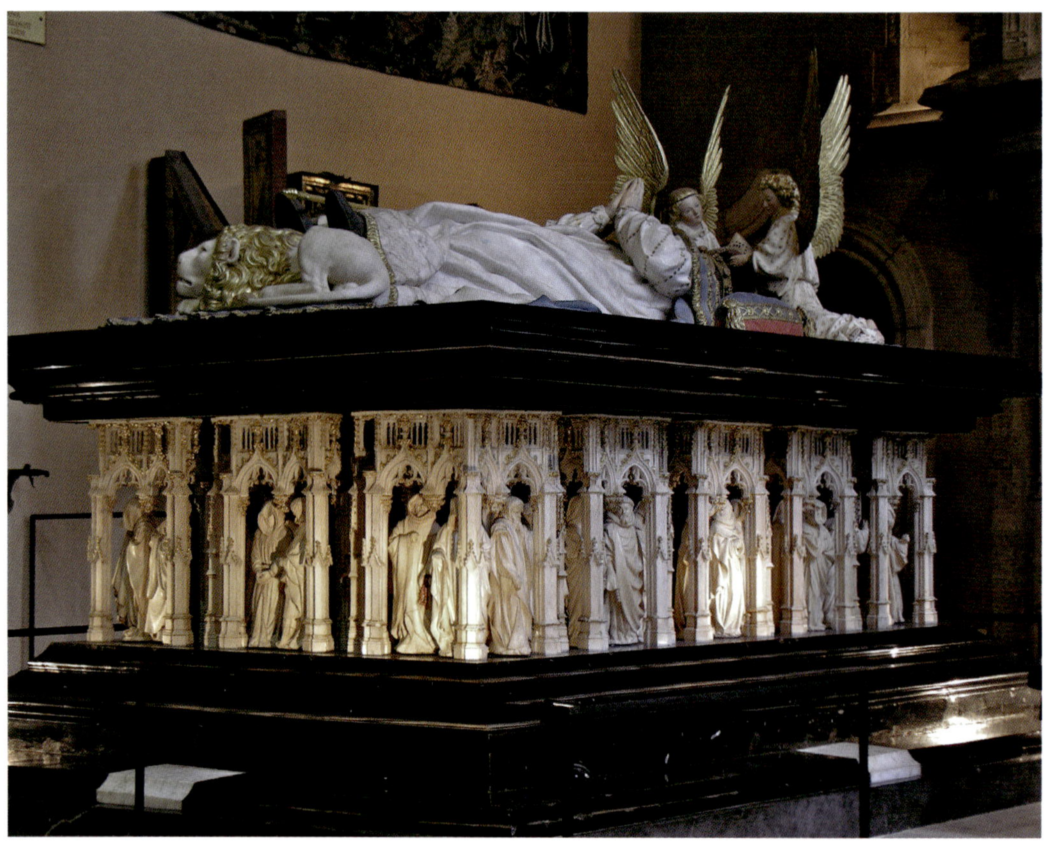

133 Jean de Marville, Claus Sluter, Claus de Werve, and workshop

Tomb of Philip the Bold, Italian marble, Dinant marble, alabaster, and polychromy, 1384–1411.

Only the hands of the effigy, the lion at its feet, and the angels at its head are original, the rest having been destroyed in the French Revolution [**10**]. The procession of mourners, which begins at the duke's head, is carved in the round and moves through the open arcade, an inventive and influential device which appears to have been developed when Sluter was head of the workshop; most of the pleurants, however, were carved after the duke's death in 1404 and probably after Sluter's death in 1406 under the direction of his nephew Claus de Werve.

tice and to register as a master. Moreover, family and professional ties were important ways of gaining employment, and patrons would rely on such contacts to help build up a known, expert, honest, and reliable workforce. As we have seen, such concerns were paramount for Margaret of Austria, and presumably also for Philip the Bold. Sluter would, like Colombe, have had to vouch for his assistants; he attracted several compatriots such as Jan van Prindale from Brussels, where he had previously worked, to Dijon and his own nephew, Claus de Werve, would take over the workshop after his death.

By 1386–8 there were between thirteen and fifteen workers on the payroll of Marville's workshop each year, many of whom worked for the full fifty-two weeks. The team included two specialist polishers from Paris (one of whom was a woman), brought in by Marville to work on the marble of Philip the Bold's tomb, the artistic impact of which relies heavily on the effects of the highly polished and reflective surfaces [**133**]. In the 1390s, with Sluter at its head, the workshop generally had a smaller workforce of between five and nine people on the books in any one year.

The varying titles and rates of pay given to the members of the ducal stone workshop indicate the nature of their contributions and activity: the most highly paid assistants like Jan van Prindale and Claus de Werve were *tailleur d'ymages*, *ymagiers*, or *ouvriers d'ymages*, figurative sculptors who are almost always paid for 'working continually with the said Claux [Sluter]'. This is the

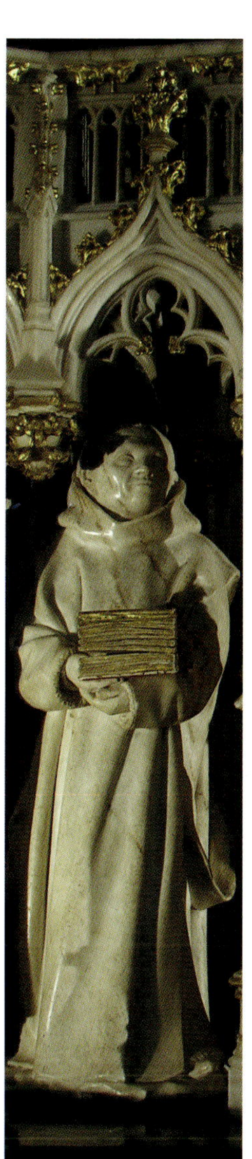

phrase used for Claus de Werve's contribution to the angels and Prindale's to the Magdalene of the Great Cross [**147, 148**]. Sluter also employed *tailleurs de pierre*—cutters or carvers of stone, who worked on larger, non-figurative elements. Some of these were marble specialists (*ouvrier de/tailleur de pierre/ de marbre*), brought to work the huge slabs of the base of the ducal tomb, and there were also several masons who supplied stone, cutting it from the quarry, overseeing its delivery, and blocking it out in the workshop ready for more detailed carving by the *ymagiers* or *taillers de pierre* in the team. These masons, the *tailleurs de pierre* and the lowlier *ouvriers de bras*, are usually paid for 'working in the shop of said Claux', but not specifically with him, indicating a less involved relationship, and a looser collaboration, than the *ymagiers*. Their rates of pay reflect this too: Marville and Sluter, as workshop heads, received 4 francs a week; Jan van Prindale and Philipe Vanerum 2 francs; other, presumably less experienced *ymagiers* like Claus de Werve were paid 1 or 1½ francs; the masons and cutters of stone got around one franc; and the *ouvriers de bras* around half a franc. Some work might be contracted out of the shop entirely: in 1389 Philippe Vaneram, who had been a member of the workshop in 1385 but now seemed to be working independently, was paid by the piece for 'carving, finishing and delivering' the hanging capitals of the tomb to Sluter, at the rate of 3 francs per capital. Given that his salary when he was in the workshop was 2 francs a week, it is plausible that it took a week and a half to carve each one.

That sculptors (and painters) within a workshop could also have produced works entirely by their own hand from start to finish which would then be sold as products of the shop is a possibility documented for us in the case of the painter-sculptor Wilhelm Klover, working in Lübeck at the end of the fifteenth century. In his will of 1504, when the stock in his shop and its intended recipients are listed, several works are identified by the names of the craftsmen who made them. To his daughter Brigitte and her husband 'the painter' Claus Heyne, Klover left all the wooden carvings: the 'big cross and Our Lady and Saint John' which was unfinished, and four Virgins, one of which was also unfinished, and one of which was by the hand of a Hans Nyckels. The panel paintings he left to religious institutions: one painted by a Pavel Grove was given to the House of the Grey Sisters and another, by a certain Wolter, was given to the 'Pockenhaus', the smallpox house.[39] Clearly Klover's journeymen produced identifiably independent works, which were also part of the workshop output. That experienced journeymen within a painter's workshop made their own works is also implied in the dispute between the master, Gerard David, and the one-time journeyman, Ambrosius Benson, in Bruges in 1519: in the disputed coffers, along with the drawings and pigments, were several panel paintings, some finished some not, which Benson clearly views as his property, presumably because he had made them himself and not in collaboration with David.

We have little documentary evidence concerning how panel painters divided up the tasks of producing their products between workshop members, although contracts for paintings sometimes specify, as they do in Italy, that the hands and faces of the figures must be by the master: thus, by implication, the rest of the work might be by assistants. Practice would certainly vary across and within workshops, according to pressures of time or financial considerations. To glimpse the varied possibilities for collaboration in making panels we have to scrutinize the evidence of the works themselves; and while it is possible to distinguish, on the surface of some paintings, differences in paint handling which seem to suggest different hands were involved, any artist overseeing a project like a painted retable in which the whole was visible in one, two, or at most three stages (closed, first opening, and second opening of a double-winged altarpiece), would aim to ensure that any teamwork it might entail was as seamless as possible. This aim, and its desirability for patrons, is made very clear in relation to the craft of printing by the blockcutter Jost de Negker, who, writing to Maximilian I in 1512, promises that despite employing two other cutters to undertake a certain work for the emperor, he will 'take care to arrange and prepare everything ... and finally complete and add the finishing touches in my own hand so that the entire work and all the individual blocks will in the end have similar carving and appear to have been made by one cutter, without anyone being able to distinguish more than one workman'.[40] Such a process of the lead artist intervening at either end of the process, in the design and then unifying the surface at the end, may have been common in the production of paintings, too. It is unsurprising, then, that it is in this 'middle ground', beneath the surface of paintings, revealed to us in infrared reflectograms, where evidence of collaboration in their making, albeit often hard to interpret, can best be found.

Reflectograms reveal that the drawing of the composition onto the panel was not always undertaken by the master, or by the master unaided, and in workshops under commercial pressure may routinely have been left to assistants working from detailed preparatory drawings like those discussed above (p. 167–73). Indeed, this is certainly the case for some of the large-scale works by Rogier van der Weyden, such as the *Exhumation of Saint Hubert* **[6]**, where the underdrawing reveals a complex collaborative procedure, with different workshop members transferring up the patterns for each of the three main figure groups in this design.[41] This painting was apparently produced with some speed and at a point, the late 1430s, when Rogier's workshop was exceptionally busy but also fairly newly established in Brussels; his assistants may have been inexperienced in working with him, and because of this we can here trace their participation on the paint surface as well, which shows clear variations in how jewels are depicted, brocade painted, or eyes defined. However, the allocation of parts of the underdrawing to a range of assistants is a feature found in other works by Rogier, such as the large altarpiece made in the early 1450s for Chancellor Rolin and now in Beaune, and would seem to be reflective of Rogier's workshop practice in general: he clearly prepared his designs sufficiently for his assistants to transfer them up to the panel as necessary, and follow them though into the paint layers as required. It would appear that after the design was transferred the master might intervene with adjustments, specific rethinks possible once the composition could be seen full scale on the panel; this, too, might be the point at which a patron might view the work and request changes, as seems to have happened with the inclusion and alterations to several of the bystanders in the *Exhumation of St Hubert*.[42]

In contrast, the working practice of van Eyck was rather different: judging from the consistency of the style and form of his underdrawings, he seems to have routinely undertaken this stage (and indeed the painting) by himself, without assistants. As a highly valued court painter to the Duke of Burgundy, he presumably did not need to take on commissions for purely commercial reasons. Although he is documented as having 'varlets', who Philip the Good tipped on a visit to the painter's workshop in Bruges, we may assume that van Eyck worked essentially unaided when he wished since he was not under financial pressure. His underdrawings, best seen in the *Arnolfini Portrait* [**37**], focus on establishing the tonal layout of a work rather than all its iconographical details, which the artist tended to add in the paint layers, with often no indication of what appear to be vital elements in the initial drawing at all (see pp. 63–5).

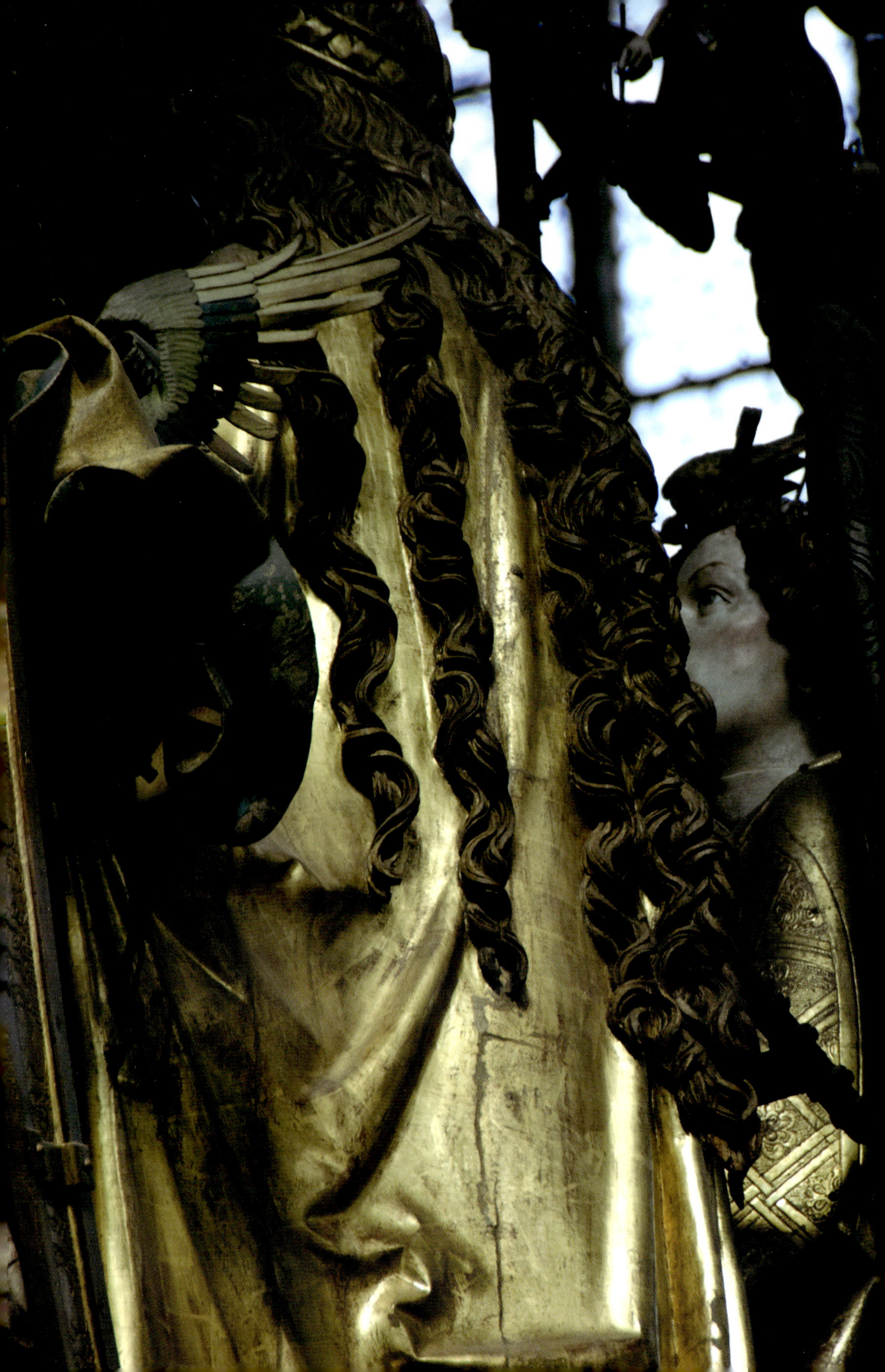

Materials, Methods, and Technical Virtuosity

No one in the said craft of carving images should provide a work in stone from the quarry of Pont-Remy in place of stone of Longue, nor stone of Longue for stone of Braumetz, because there is a difference in quality between these said stones, one is better than the other.

Regulations of the painters, sculptors, illuminators and glasspainters of Abbeville, 1508[1]

15

Acquiring Materials: Availability, Cost, Expertise, and Decorum

To produce images of the best quality required the right materials, as well as the right equipment and well-trained, skilled assistants. Sourcing these materials could take considerable time and be as complex as the working of them: this is particularly the case for large sculptural projects, where the quality of the stone or wood was of particular importance, and could turn into something of a quest. The Spanish sculptor Pere Johan (d. after 1447) travelled over 1,000 kilometres around Spain at the cost of a whole year's salary in the mid-1430s to find the best alabaster for the high altarpiece of the cathedral of Zaragoza [**134**]. Clearly he was looking for something specific, presumably a very white, unveined stone, since he began with a 350-kilometre journey south to the quarries at Cuenca, but the alabaster there was not of the quality he desired; returning to Zaragoza he tried a more local quarry at Gelsa, 50 kilometres to the south; this satisfied him at first, and 110 cartloads of alabaster were transported by river to Zaragoza over a period of 4 months. But something was not right with the material this quarry was supplying and so the search was resumed, with Johan eventually travelling another 460 kilometres to a quarry he had used earlier in his career, at Besalu, north of Girona. The material there was again initially acceptable as 46 cartloads were extracted and transported the long distance to Zaragoza, although another unsuccessful voyage to Gelsa suggests he still was not entirely happy and did not yet have the quantity of alabaster at the right quality he needed. As funds, unsurprisingly, were running low, it appears that the sculptor and the chapter of the cathedral compromised at this point, and, rather than producing parts of the retable in lower grade alabaster, made do with sections carved in wood, presumably incorporating the wooden models that would have been made before the reliefs were carved out in stone. Thirty years later, in the 1470s, these wooden parts were replaced with alabaster ones at a point when the funds and the right, or acceptable, alabaster was found.[2] A comparable quest for wood is docu-

Detail of reverse of 149

134 Pere Johan and Hans de Suabia

High retable of La Seo Cathedral, Zaragoza, 1435–44 and later fifteenth century.

The German humanist Jerome Münzer, travelling through Spain in 1495, was particularly taken by the quality of the materials in this work. He admired the 'very white alabaster' and noted that the carvings had been 'magnificently gilded'. He concluded that 'there is not a more precious alabaster retable in the whole of Spain'.

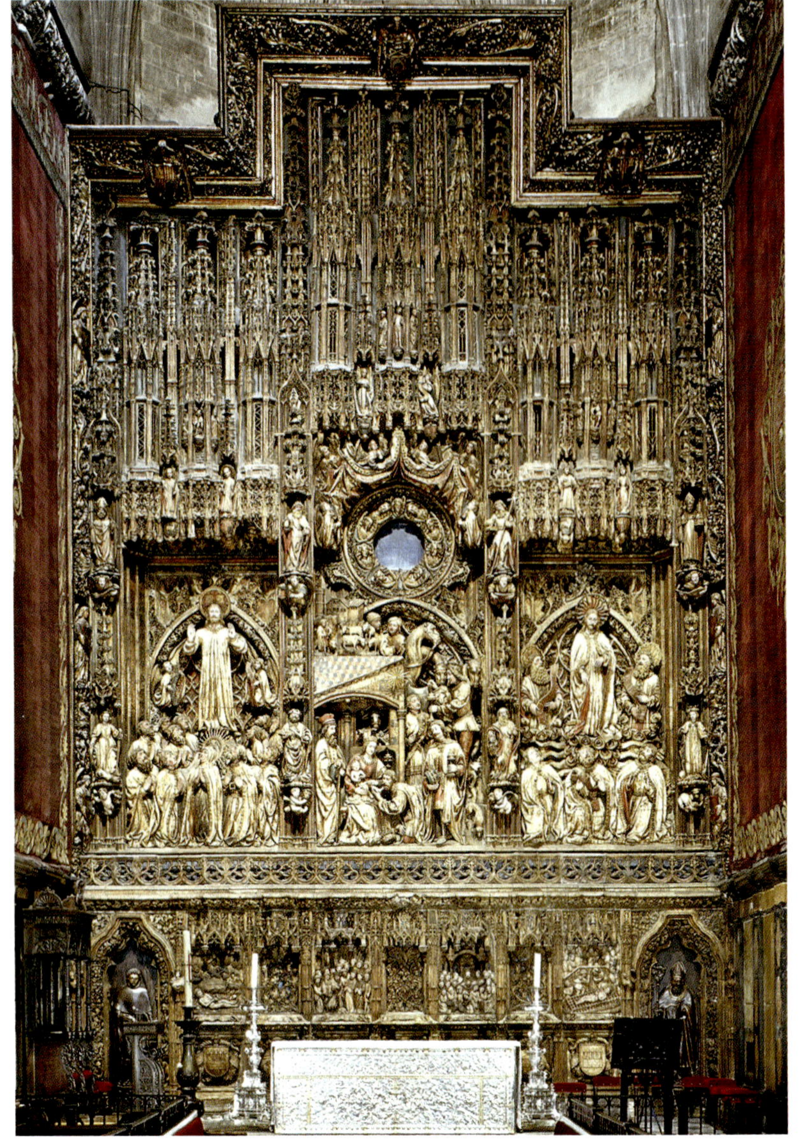

mented in the case of an altarpiece commissioned by the Brotherhood of Our Lady at the church of St Nicolas in Kalkar, who in 1488/9 made three attempts to find wood of the right quality for their altarpiece.[3]

The supply of more portable artists' materials like pigments was dependent instead on the networks of merchants and trade routes across Europe, as we have seen in Part II. Unsurprisingly the best and most abundant supplies were clearly to be had in the largest and more cosmopolitan cities like Paris, Bruges, Antwerp, and London.[4] Many of the more exotic pigments came to northern Europe via land or sea from Venice (particularly ultramarine from Afghanistan) and other Italian ports like Genoa (who shipped red lakes and alum, vital as a substrate in many pigments). These arrived ready prepared or at least partly so—artists did not routinely manufacture them themselves, despite the complex recipes to do so which were circulating at this period. They would instead purchase them in a powdered form from merchants, apothecaries, or, in the later part of our period in Germany, from pharmacies.[5] In Dijon, the painters working at the Chartreuse de Champmol were regularly supplied with pigments and metal leaf (gold, silver, and tin) by a merchant called Perenot Barbisey, but some supplies came from local painters; various specialist spice merchants were also drawn on, often for the more expensive blue pigments, while goldsmiths tended to supply much, but not all, of the gold leaf. A similar range of sources of supply is found in the Burgundian court accounts for 1420.[6] However, when something of a particular quality was required, the acquisition was more complex and often involved the artists or their assistants travelling to obtain them from more specialist suppliers or producers, rather than the patrons simply providing them. Jean Malouel in 1403 sent an assistant to Paris with written instructions to give to a goldbeater there (a specialist in producing and supplying gold leaf), who was to supply five *papiers* (books of gold leaf, containing 300 leaves per book) of fine gold. The assistant was to wait while the goldbeater produced the leaf 'in the manner specified by Malouel'. Paris was the source for many other materials used at the Chartreuse, from Baltic oak to Italian marble for the *gisant* (recumbent effigy) of Philip the Bold's tomb [**10**], which Sluter himself went to Paris to purchase from a Genoese merchant there in 1392.[7]

Bruges and Antwerp must have been similar repositories of high-quality artists' materials and pigments given their status as international trading centres: it was in Bruges that Jean d'Arbois, painter to Philip the Bold, bought *asur* from a spice merchant in 1375; Philip the Good's court painter Hue de Boulogne travelled backwards and forwards from Arras and Hesdin to Bruges in 1420 to get the pigments and materials he needed for the extensive (and last minute) works for the commemorative services for the recently deceased John the Fearless.[8] By the sixteenth century Antwerp was only rivalled by Venice as a purveyor of pigments in the whole of Europe. Local production could influence availability, of course: Germany had good supplies of azurite, for example, since a high proportion of this pigment used in Europe was mined there (one mine alone produced 5,285 pounds of the mineral in 1511). Possibly because such abundant supplies were at hand there, the more expensive ultramarine was almost unheard of in this region: it could not be bought in German pharmacies supplying pigments and it is rarely found on German panel paintings, with the exception of those from Cologne, judging from the current state of knowledge.[9]

The relative expense of different pigments can be gauged from a variety of sources, although comparisons are made difficult since ultramarine, azurite, and other pigments were processed and sold in three different qualities: generally the larger the particles the better the grade, and the deeper and more intense the colour it could produce. However, the constant references to blues in contracts and the specifications concerning their use indicate that these, as is well known, were among the most costly pigments. A single ounce of ultramarine cost 4 francs in the accounts of the Chartreuse de Champmol in Dijon in 1389, which would have paid for a week's wages for the head of the ducal sculpture workshop, Claus Sluter. In the same year 4 francs would also have bought 600 sheets of part gold (a lesser quality mixed-metal leaf, selling for 2 francs per book of 300 sheets) or almost 300 sheets of fine gold (at 4½ francs a book of 300 leaves), or 8 pounds of vermillion, or 16 pounds of lead white; put another way, to buy 16 pounds of fine blue would have cost 1,280 francs, as opposed to 4 francs for the equivalent amount of lead white. At the other end of our period in Antwerp it cost Dürer 12 ducats for 1 ounce of ultramarine in 1521, while in Munich at that date he could have bought ten times the quantity of the best quality azurite for that price. Similar relative values for these pigments can be found in the prices paid for them at the Burgundian court later in the fifteenth century.

Almost as costly as the blues could be scale insects, usually kermes beetles, from which the most intense red lakes were made—in Germany this was the most expensive pigment you could buy, costing more per ounce than the very best available azurite blue; thus again it is unsurprising that most German, and Netherlandish, paintings use the far cheaper madder root, or madder mixed with kermes, as their main red lake pigment.[10] In Munich in 1505 it was forty-five times cheaper per gram than kermes, although the insects would have made a more intense colour which might have gone further (though presumably not forty-five times further). The high value of blues and certain reds, and their special treatment and handling in the painters' repertoire, are also indicated in other sources: Jean Lemaire de Belges declared, 'Keep apart sinoper (vermillion), and azur of Acre (ultramarine)/Lake, verdigris, all high colours/Guard them well, for some sacred image.'[11] It is also the expensive reds and blues that the Brussels painter Vranke van der Stockt set apart in his will of 1489; they were given to his wife to sell, while all the others were left to his son, another painter.[12]

Of course the cost of pigments, and thus the hierarchy of their employment, might vary from region to region and from year to year: for example, the yellow mineral pigment orpiment (rated as one of the lower status pigments in the guild regulations of Tournai) was fairly expensive in Germany, judging from pharmacy price lists: to buy an ounce in Munich in 1488 would cost you four times as much as buying an ounce of lead tin yellow; seventeen years later in 1505 the price had fallen, but it was still double that of its rival yellow, costing as much as a medium grade azurite. Unsurprisingly, given its expense, orpiment was little used by German artists around 1500, although Cranach, who owned a pharmacy, did employ it, and large quantities are listed in the Frankfurt workshop of Mathias Grünewald in 1528; Grünewald may have been in the business of manufacturing and dealing in pigments.[13]

As well as cost and availability, there were other factors that dictated the use of materials: guilds might, as we have seen, establish certain limits, allowing the use of some pigments and not others, depending on the type of work. As a rule painters of panels, who were working in oil, were allowed to use the full range of pigments available, so long as they did not pass off one material for another of lesser quality or cost, a universal concern for all the crafts, not just those making images. Thus in Tournai in 1481 the makers of playing cards 'may not employ gold, nor silver, nor azur nor any other fine colour', although

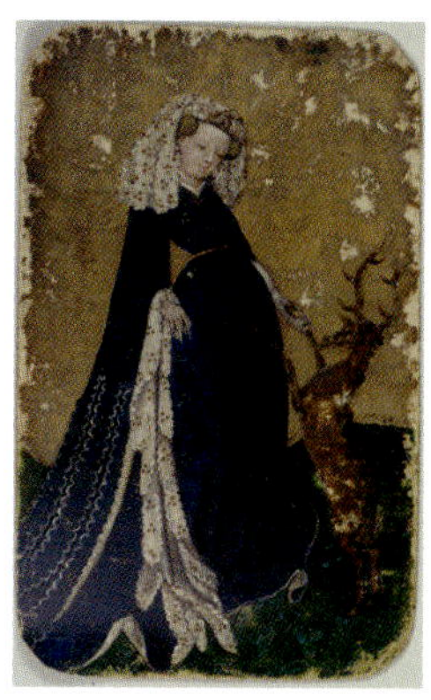

135 Lucas Moser (?)

Playing card of the *Lady in Waiting of Stags*, paint and gilding on cardboard, *c.*1420.

Technical examination of these cards have shown they are painted on cardboard made up of six layers of paper glued together, the paper having been made at the Ravensburg mill between 1427 and 1431; the pigments identified are the more expensive range: azurite, vermillion, red lake, and lead tin yellow, while the gilding techniques are particularly complex and varied, ranging from twist gold (silver and gold mixed together), mordant gilding with gold leaf, to mosaic gold (mostly an illuminators' material).

sets produced elsewhere such as **135** were certainly made with the best pigments and finely gilded.[14] Perhaps rather unwisely given its highly poisonous nature (it is an arsenic-based mineral), in Tournai orpiment, along with the even more toxic vermillion, were among a limited range of pigments allowed for use by painters of children's toys, wooden horses, and parrot perches.

Behind these limits lay a general desire to avoid shoddy work, which would bring the trade into disrepute: certain pigments did not last as well as others, or handle as well, or were not suitable for use in a glue- or water-based medium. In addition, by limiting the range of pigments and other materials like metals that painters working on cloth, parchment and paper could use, and who appear to have had lesser standing (their training was shorter and they paid lower dues), the regulations were limiting competition between different types of object: a painting on cloth would not be able to compete directly with one on panel if cloth painters could not use the same range of expensive pigments and gold that a panel painter could. Running through all this was also a concern for the appropriateness of materials for each type of object, from a panel painting in a church to a parrot perch. Various guild regulations specify, for example, that certain liturgical items should be made with particular care or with the best quality gold: these tend to be monstrances, which would hold the consecrated host, altarpieces, or more generally works 'for the church'.[15] This sense of decorum in terms of the matter from which an object is made is one of the defining characteristics of the period.

As well as benefiting from access to high-quality pigments, Netherlandish towns also had, through their pole position in relation to the northern sea routes, abundant supplies of Baltic oak, cut from Polish forests and exported by the merchants of the Hanseatic League in increasing amounts from the mid-fourteenth century, primarily from Gdańsk in Poland.[16] Baltic oak was exceptionally good as both a support for panel paintings and a material for carving, since it was slow growing with dense, straight grain, which made it less subject to warping, providing a superior surface on which to gild and paint, in contrast with the softer woods such as poplar or pine that were used extensively in Italy and Spain. It was also superior to other types of oak, like English oak, because it grew in dense forests, which meant that the trees were tall and straight with few branches low down—all of which meant a better wood for making straight flat panels, as the trunks could be split into flat planks, something nearly impossible with English oak. The perceived superiority of Baltic oak, and that its use was associated with Netherlandish products, is indicated by the contract for one of the most expensive and deliberately Netherlandish retables commissioned in Spain in the early fifteenth century: the *Virgin of the Councillors* by Lluís Dalmau [**28**]. The town councillors were concerned that their image was painted by 'the best and most able painter to be found', and among other things to ensure its quality the contract specified that 'Flemish' oak ('bonua fusta de roure de Flandres') was to be used (see p. 48–50), the term reflecting how the support, in fact not Flemish at all, had come to be identified with its products.

Painters did not produce their own panels or the frames around them. This job was undertaken by specialists: after the wood was imported by the Hanseatic merchants who dealt in Baltic oak, cutters (*scieurs*) would cut the

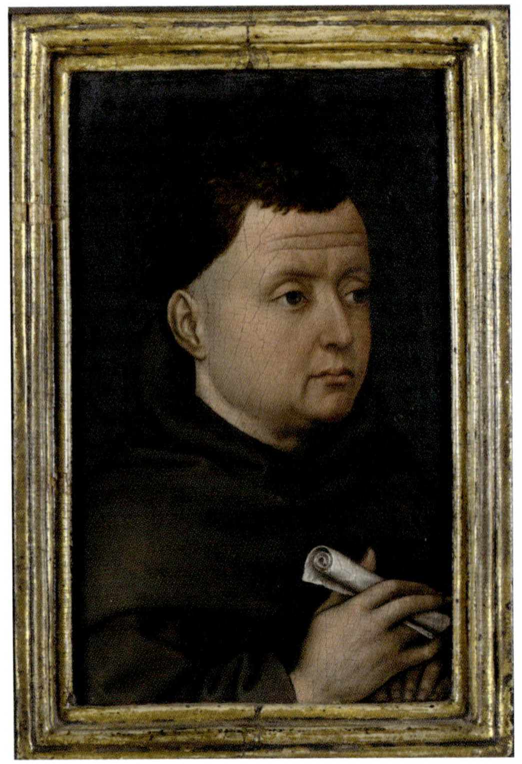

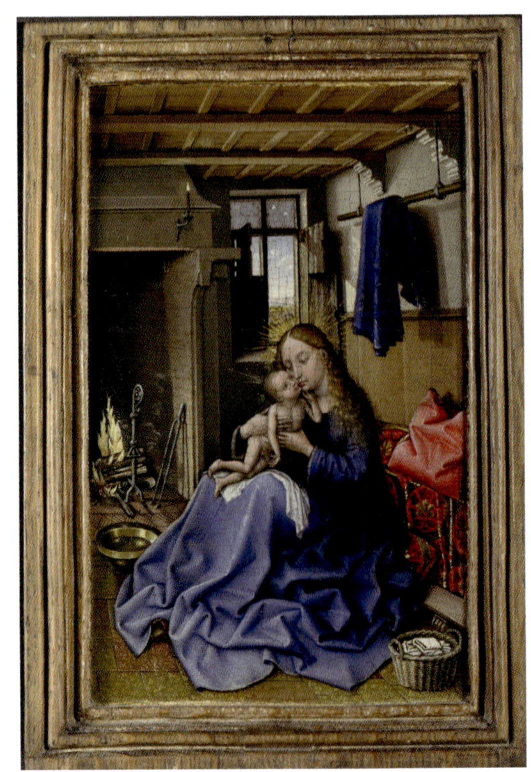

136 Workshop of the Master of Flémalle

Portrait of a Franciscan (?) Monk, oil on Baltic oak, *c.*1430.

137 Workshop of the Master of Flémalle (Jacques Daret?)

Virgin and Child in an Interior, oil on Baltic oak, *c.*1430.

planks to size, and the joiners or carpenters (there were two distinct crafts, the joiner being the more skilled and more frequently involved with making altarpiece frames and panels, but carpenters could do this job too) would then construct the panels and carve and attach frames. This was often done to order, as for example with the large-scale paintings commissioned for Leuven town hall from Dieric Bouts [**111**]; in this case, a joiner, Renier Cocx, was sent from Leuven to Antwerp in 1467 to buy the wood at the fair. He sent back the forty-five large planks, each 12 feet of Riga long (the maximum length available at this time in the Netherlands), by boat to Leuven. Cocx then constructed fourteen of these into the two large panels we see today, and several more, cut in half, into a triptych on which Bouts painted the Last Judgement. Another specialist, an ironworker, was then paid to provide four hinges and a lock: the making of a painted triptych or polyptych thus required three specialists (the cutter, the joiner, and the metalworker) before it even reached the painter's workshop.[17]

Painters might also acquire their panels in ready made, set sizes: two small paintings made from wood from the same tree, identical in size and with integral frames carved in the same manner, remarkably can be seen hanging together in the National Gallery in London [**136, 137**]. These were presumably acquired by one workshop or two neighbouring painters in Tournai around 1430, since their style relates to that of Jacques Daret and the Master of Flémalle: while related stylistically, these are clearly two independent works by different artists. Presumably several small panels of the same format were acquired for a variety of different projects—one

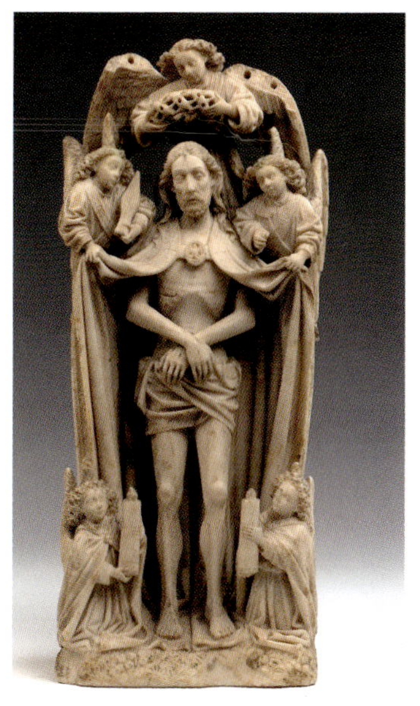

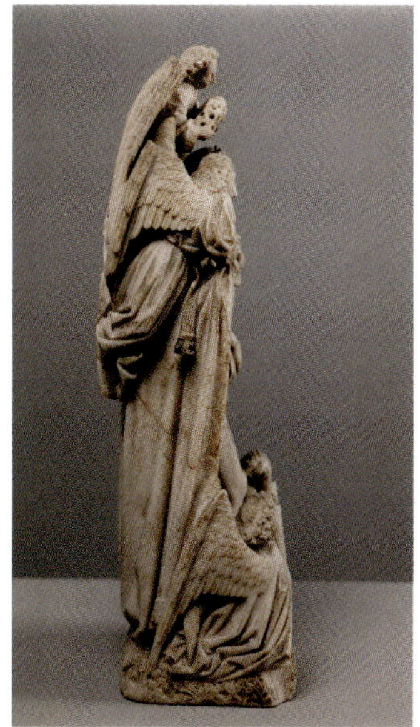

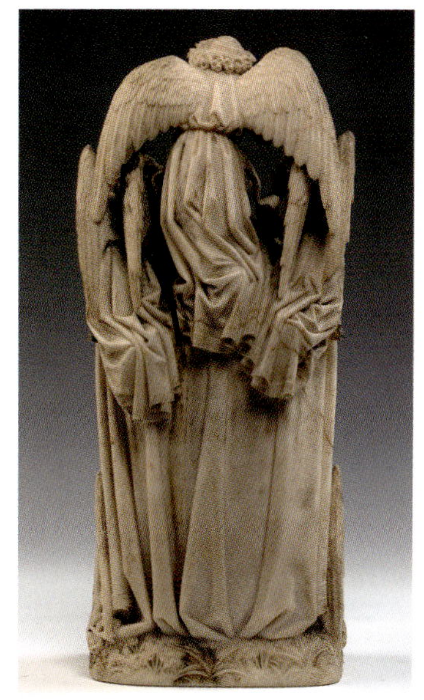

138 South Netherlandish sculptor

Man of Sorrows with Angels, alabaster, *c.*1470.

This compact group, carved with great technical skill from a thin piece of alabaster, has many of the features of earlier ivories. The five angels inventively enrich the iconography: two hold open Christ's cloak to reveal his body while grasping instruments of the Passion, the lance and nails (now broken); one holds the crown of thorns above his head, while two kneel and hold candles. These are not part of the standard iconography of this scene, suggesting rather its function as a devotional object which would have actual candles set in front of it.

panel for a commission (the *Portrait of a Franciscan (?) Monk*, **136**), while the other a work designed, presumably, to be sold on spec (the *Virgin and Child*, **137**).[18]

Concern for the quality of the wood in painted and carved retables, and the construction of these 'supporting' elements, is evident in many contracts. Often more words are spent on detailing the age of wood, its quality, how long it should be seasoned for, that no sap or green wood be used, and how it is to be constructed, even when it was to be felled, than on detailing the subjects to be painted or the other materials to be used.[19] Guild regulations for sculptors, in particular, reveal similar concerns: the Antwerp regulations specify that wood should only be oak or walnut, that it should be dry, and that no sapwood was used;[20] the Paris regulations demand that wood is not too green (because if it is 'la peinture s'ecailleroit et ne dureroit point', the paint will fall off and not last), that it is dried in the oven in the artist's shop, that all the faults are filled properly with wood and good glue, and that it is inspected before it is painted.[21] Works needed to withstand the changes in humidity, temperature, and (with winged retables) frequent opening and closing: patrons wanted their expensive carved altarpiece to last.

While the increased availability of oak for painters in the southern Netherlands, or of limewood for carvers in southern Germany, might help explain patterns of production in these regions, similarly lack of supply can help explain why some types of objects almost cease to be made: around 1400 it seems that supplies of elephant ivory, the source of which had always been India rather than Africa, became extremely scarce, and in turn the production of ivory carvers, so abundant in the previous two centuries, decreases considerably.[22] Of course other factors, concerning shifts in taste, and the disruption of Paris and its luxury trades, must have come into play, but the availability of materials here may have been a major factor in this particular pattern of production and consumption. What takes its place are either lesser quality substitutes, bone or horn, which could not produce such a luminous effect, or alabaster, which certainly could approximate the effects of ivory, and many small devotional works made in this material in the fifteenth century follow formats and iconographies established and popularized in ivory carving at an earlier period. A small alabaster relief of the *Man of Sorrows* probably made in the Netherlands around 1470 is a good example of this, appearing to mimic ivory in the compactness of its form and shape [**138**].

'For Clearness and Durability's Sake': Painting Panels in Oil

The importance of durability and technical excellence in the making of images, and the time and skill involved in the process of painting a panel, are well expressed by Albrecht Dürer in his correspondence with Jacob Heller in 1508 concerning progress on his altarpiece for that patron. He declares that:

> The wings have been painted in stone colours on the outside, but they are not yet varnished; inside the whole of the ground has been laid so that it is ready to paint on. The middle panel I have outlined with the greatest care and at cost of much time; it is also laid over with two very good colours upon which I can begin to paint the ground. For I intend ... to paint the ground some four, five or six times over, for clearness and durability's sake, using the very best ultramarine for the purpose that I can get.[23]

The emphasis on laying a good ground should not surprise us: this is something we find across many documentary sources for both panels and polychromed sculptures, as we have seen, and without good preparation no panel painting, polychromy, or indeed manuscript illumination would last well.[24] Dürer's comments also make reference to the coloured layers applied over the ground of the panel before painting proper began; these were probably an imprimatura, and cross-sections of Netherlandish and German paintings have revealed that it was standard practice to apply a layer of this type over the whole of the panel after the underdrawing had been completed: this was mainly to ensure that the absorbent chalk ground bound in animal glue did not soak up the subsequent paint layers, and was usually in an oil-based medium. Often it was very light in colour, sometimes almost white, but a greyish, pinkish, or yellowish tone seems to have been favoured by most painters. It would subdue the brilliance of the ground, and allow for easier coverage of the black underdrawing in the paint layers. Rogier van der Weyden's priming layer in the *Exhumation* [**6**] has small quantities of black pigment, which would have produced a very light grey layer;[25] in his *Descent from the Cross* [**20**], the priming layer seems to have been tinged with red and black to create a very light, pinkish-grey layer, similar to that St Luke has applied to his panel in **139**.[26] Sometimes it contributed to the surface appearance of the painting: in the Seilern Triptych [**31**], the priming layer is a dark greyish tone which forms the base for the flesh of the figures, modelled unusually from dark to light.[27]

Once the priming had dried, the painter and/or his assistants were ready to start building up the first layers of colour. Because of the nature of the medium, painters working in oil created their images to some extent vertically, moving towards the final finish across the whole surface in layers (these are the four, five, or six applications Dürer refers to for his altarpiece in the extract above), rather than working on one section at a time, as fresco painting and (to an extent) tempera painting demanded. However, in general the

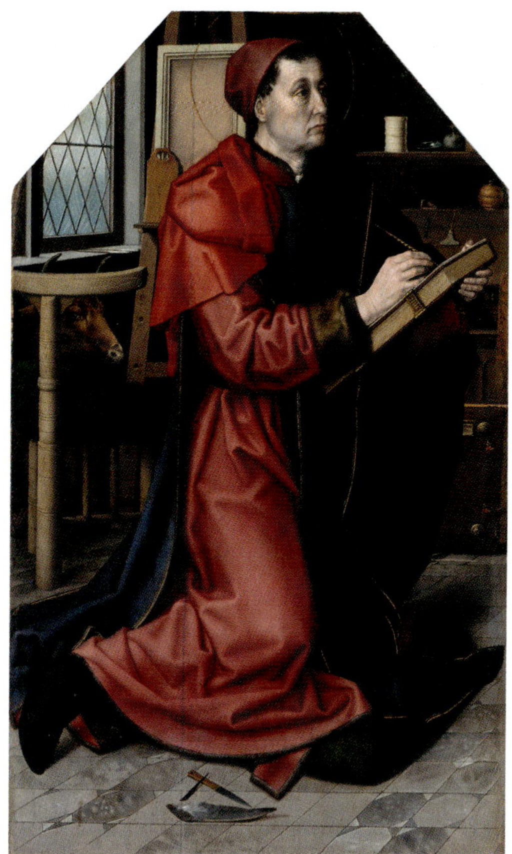

139 Hugo van der Goes or follower

St Luke drawing the Virgin, oil on panel, *c.*1480.

St Luke is shown using a metalpoint (seen also in **108**; Jan van Eyck would have used a similar tool to make **121**), drawing on a sheet of paper which has been folded into quarters. His easel is set at right angles to the window, with the light falling from the left, the best arrangement for a right-handed artist. His primed, framed panel is propped against his easel and on the windowsill are two *pinceaux*, brushes made using birds' quills; a wing from a bird and a knife are shown on the floor in front of the saint, suggesting he has just finished making these brushes.

drapery and the background were worked up first, followed by the faces and hands: these were crucial areas, and establishing them at an early stage ran the risk of their detail being spoiled by a few drips from a brush. St Luke, who tends to be shown painting the face of the Virgin, is always doing so after the other elements in the painting have been completed [**112, 114**].

The layer structures used by Netherlandish painters as revealed to us in cross-sections [**141**] show an intense understanding of the characteristics of their binding media and their pigments, their handling properties, and their potential optical effects, an understanding based on the experience of generations, since painting in oil was a centuries old and thoroughly established technique by the early fifteenth century. Their expertise is evident in their choice and treatment of oils and in their occasional, judicious use of egg tempera. The latter was sometimes employed as an underlayer between the priming and the oil layers; here egg was exploited for its quick drying properties and the good coverage it provided (colours in egg tend to be more opaque than in oil). It was used as such by Rogier van der Weyden, the Master of Flémalle, and Dieric Bouts.[28] It may also have been employed on occasion for its optical effects—there is some evidence it was used for areas of cooler, lighter colour in Gerard David's paintings, for example, and the interpretation of samples from the Ghent Altarpiece and Jan van Eyck's *Annunciation* (Washington National Gallery), appear to suggest that the top layers of

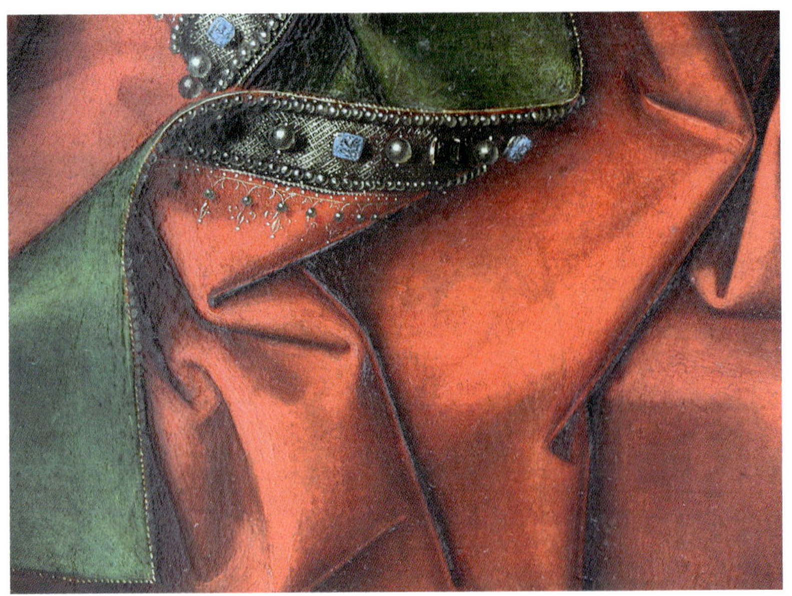

140 Jan van Eyck

Detail of red robe of the Virgin in the *Van der Paele Madonna* [**18**] taken in raking light – and the cope of St Donatian.

The technical superiority of red pigments in oil may account for the frequent use of this colour as the central focus in northern paintings (see, for example, **2**, **3**, **4**, **6**), as artists chose visual effects over material cost as a way of marking out the central figures in their works. It also conveyed connotations regarding royalty or the Passion (see its use in **33**), and perhaps an added potential allusion to an important product of Flanders—dyed red woollen cloth of the best quality.

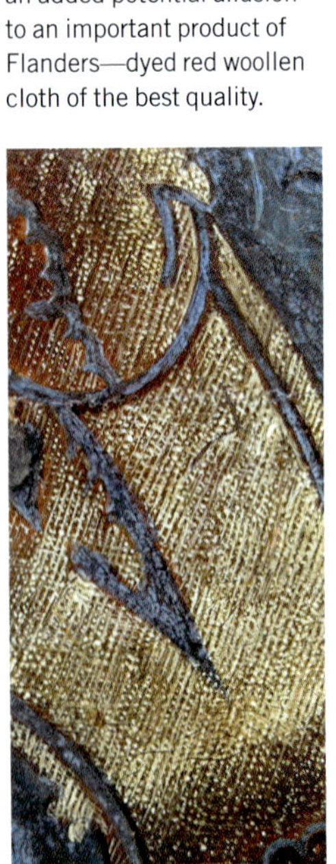

ultramarine—a pigment which tends to look dark in oil—were here bound in egg, which would result in their colour appearing strong and bright.[29] Its use in this manner is sporadic, however, if existent at all, and in general most painters working on panel mixed the upper layers of their colours in oil alone. This was usually linseed oil, but other types might be deployed depending on the effects required: for example, within the same painting the artist might switch to walnut oil for certain areas or pigments, perhaps because it was less prone to yellowing, since it is often chosen for white areas, presumably to ensure, again, their tone remained bright (walnut oil was used for some of the white areas in paintings in the National Gallery, London, by Gerard David, Joos van Wassenhove, Jan Gossart, and the German Master of the Life of the Virgin).[30]

Another choice the painter made concerning his medium related to the treatment of the oil itself: heating it, directly or by standing it in the sun (where the term stand-oil comes from), to create pre-polymerized oil, had an important effect on the results achieved. This heat-bodied oil was thicker, and made a more viscous paint, which would shrink less when dry; used with red lakes and copper greens it ensured that the smoothest of translucent glazes, free from brush strokes with intensely saturated colours, could be achieved. However, it was more difficult to grind with pigments, and was slower to apply. Heat-bodied oil is used by Jan van Eyck and by Rogier van der Weyden, and by many other artists working in the Netherlands and Germany (notably the Dombild Master/Stefan Lochner), but it seems to have been used less often in the paintings of Memling, perhaps because of its slower working properties.[31]

Oil painting also required an understanding of the different properties of pigments as well as the media they were mixed with: some pigments would be translucent in oil (like red lakes, copper greens, and to a lesser extent ultramarine), while others would be opaque (like vermillion, lead white, lead tin

141

Cross-sections taken from Rogier van der Weyden, *The Exhumation of St Hubert* [**6**]. Blue sample from the cope of St Abelard (the bishop in blue on the right of the picture), photographed at a magnification of 480×; red from the robe of St Hubert, in an area of half-shadow, photographed at 400×.

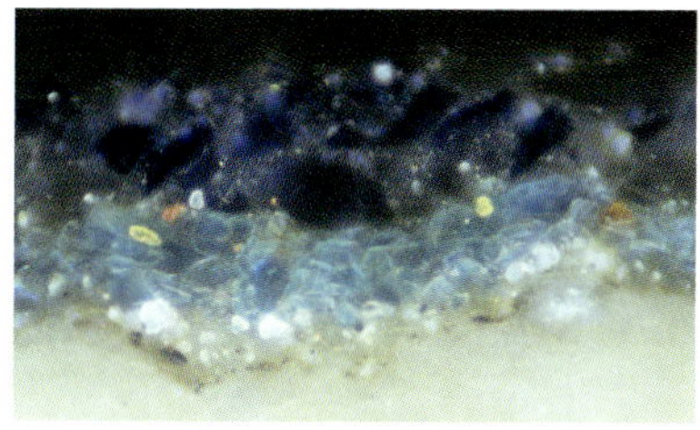

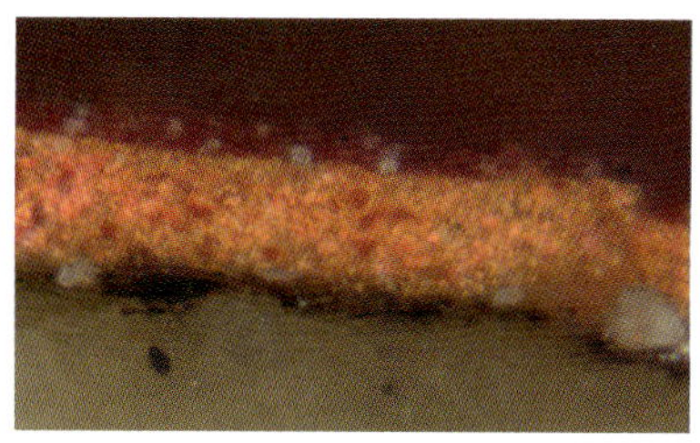

Working from the bottom upwards, the red sample shows the chalk ground, then a layer of underdrawing (the black particles); over this is a thin priming layer followed by two paint layers: the lower, thicker, more orange-red layer is the opaque red underpainting done with vermilion into which a little red lake is added; over this is a thinner pink layer, which is the glaze containing red lake and a little lead white. The blue sample also has a chalk ground layer, then some traces of underdrawing and a white priming layer, followed by two paint layers: an underpaint of azurite, which is the paler, less intense blue, and an upper layer containing ultramarine, which has a large particle size and is an intense, dark colour. In both layers the blue pigment is mixed with a little lead white, which would lighten the blue and increase its opacity, but would, importantly, improve its handling qualities and preserve the intensity of its colour.

yellow, or azurite). The translucent pigments were eminently suited for use as glazes over another paint layer, either to enhance and deepen the colour below (as with red lake applied over vermillion, see below) or to produce another colour (as with red lake applied over azurite to produce purple). Northern painters show a sophisticated understanding and exploitation of these properties and the relative advantages and potential of different pigments. This is perhaps most evident in the employment of blues: ultramarine and indeed a good quality azurite were very costly, as we have seen; consequently their employment had to be thought about carefully. In general, Netherlandish painters built up their blue areas using azurite for the lower paint layers, with ultramarine reserved for the final glazes: this is the system we see employed in Rogier's *Exhumation* [**6**] and van Eyk's *Arnolfini Portrait* [**37**], which thus achieved an ultramarine effect with minimum pigment. But cost was not the only issue to consider: azurite in oil tended to darken over time, and ultramarine could appear very dark because its refractive index is very close to that of oil. To maintain a really brilliant blue, the pigment used to make the paint could not be finely ground, but needed to retain its large particles (as we see in the cross-section in **141**); however, a coarsely ground blue meant the handling qualities of the paint were compromised. It would be thicker and more difficult to apply, often coming away from the ground or the layers of paint below, and it was hard to achieve a smooth, wrinkle-free surface. Van Eyck traded off intensity of colour for handling qualities in the *Arnolfini Portrait*, where the blue of the sleeve of the Arnolfini's wife is created with a paint in which the ultramarine is of a lower grade with a smaller particle size. Rogier in the *Exhumation* uses an ultramarine of a higher grade, with larger particles, which creates a stronger blue but which was thicker and harder to apply: presumably the effect of the intensity of colour here was more important.

Rogier and Jan both mixed a little lead white into their blue pigments; this was a standard practice and necessary to improve their handling qualities and retain a strong colour. In the *Exhumation*, even the deepest shadows in the blue areas include lead white.[32]

The red lakes in some ways had all the opposite qualities to the blues when mixed in oil: they are translucent, not gritty at all, can be ground extensively without losing their colour, and are a pure joy to handle and manipulate. They are the most successful, malleable, and effective of all pigments in oil, which is not insignificant for an understanding of colour choices in early Netherlandish painting. By using lakes mixed with heat-bodied oil, and by adding a touch of pine resin to the medium, their translucency and surface quality could be further enhanced. The only negative property of red lake was that it dried particularly slowly, a feature which could be alleviated by the addition of a sicative: in the *Arnolfini Portrait* the red glazes on the bed are mixed with ground glass, which would have increased its drying properties. Glazes of red and green might also be blotted, with a cloth or hand, to take off the thickness of the glaze and speed up its drying time; van Eyck blotted the green paint of the robe of Arnolfini's wife with his fingers. He also used his fingertips to blend paint; prints from them have been found beneath the dog in the *Arnolfini Portrait* and in other works by him. The ability of oil to be manipulated in this manner—to be blended, blotted, and worked wet-in-wet—distinguishes it from egg tempera, which by contrast dries fast and cannot be blended, and in which pigments are generally less translucent. In oil, artists could achieve a range of illusionistic effects which were not possible in other media.[33]

A detail of the robe of the Virgin from van Eyck's *Van der Paele Madonna* [**140**] and a cross-section from Rogier van der Weyden's *Exhumation of St Hubert* [**141**] show how the effect of rich, heavy red drapery was created in oil paint by a standard system whereby a layer of vermillion (a red which was more orange in tone than the pinker lakes, and opaque in oil) was applied first. Once this was dry, the modelling of the forms was established by applying successive translucent glazes of red lake. Where deep shadow was desired, more layers of glaze were applied, intensifying the colour, and less, or none at all, in the areas of highlight. The detail in **140** was taken in raking light to show this accumulation of layers in the darkest areas; a cross-section of a similar area of red drapery in Rogier's *Exhumation* [**141**] explicates this technique. Van Eyck further intensified the depth of the shadows in his reds with the addition of a touch of ultramarine, a method seen in **140** and in the *Arnolfini Portrait*.[34]

While the brilliant depiction of red fabric in Netherlandish panels relied on the translucency of lakes in oil, the imitation of gold brocade—another distinctive feature of the Netherlandish painter's repertoire in particular—relied on the opaque qualities of lead tin yellow. Because this pigment was manufactured rather than of mineral or plant origin, its particle size was tiny, making it workable with just a small amount of medium, and producing a paint which was densely opaque in oil and held its shape and body, allowing for impasto effects. These qualities are seen exploited in what is possibly the most impressive piece of paint handling from our period—the brocade robe of St Donatian in Jan van Eyck's *Van der Paele Madonna* [**18, 140**]. Here van Eyck stroked, hatched and dotted lead tin yellow using a very fine-tipped hair brush, the marks varying in size and form to evoke the threads of gold in the fabric as they catch the light; the properties of this pigment, and lead white, which has similar qualities, were also enlisted by Netherlandish painters for the depiction of jewels and pearls, and seen deployed here by Jan van Eyck with particular economy but to extraordinary effect.

Designing and Weaving Tapestries

Tapestry design and production required an understanding of materials and their manipulation in a different way. Unlike panel painting, their making involved two distinct stages often undertaken by two different groups of diversely trained artists: the design stage might even be geographically and chronologically distant from the weaving process, since cartoons could be reused many years after they were made and in a different town or even country (see pp. 104–5). Like much metalwork, stained glass, embroidery and larger scale sculptural projects, tapestry designs were mostly provided by painters (although not without exception or without challenge, see p. 52), passed on to weavers, and the whole process coordinated and financed by an entrepreneur who may have trained initially as a painter (as did Pasquier Grenier in Tournai) or a weaver (as did Nicolas Bataille in Paris), but who was now, essentially, a merchant-producer.[35]

The first step in making a tapestry required the production of the initial design (called the *petit patron* in French documents; *klein patroon* in Flemish), which was a drawing on paper or parchment of the whole design. A rare surviving example, in pen and wash on ten pieces of paper (the largest measuring 31 × 57.5 centimetres), gives an idea of the nature and level of detail such a design might entail [**142**].[36] Once this was approved by the client or the entrepreneur organizing the project, the large cartoon (called the *grand patron*, *groot patroon*) could be made (although changes could still occur at this stage: Isabeau of Bavaria rejected designs made by her painter Colart de Laon on seeing the *grand patron*, and this may have been just as crucial a point, when the full impact and success, or otherwise, of the design could be appreciated).[37] Because the cartoons had to be to scale, they had to be made on a material which could be large, light, and flexible. This meant cloth: in a commission of a tapestry made for the church of the Magdalene in Troyes in 1425–30, bed sheets, sewn together, were employed,[38] but paper was also used, increasingly so by the early sixteenth century. Flexibility was vital because these *grand patrons* would function as the guide for the weavers, who would cut them into strips and pin them against the warp threads of their loom to trace the outlines of the design onto these uncoloured threads; then the strips would be placed, usually (and most efficiently) underneath the loom as they worked, the weavers parting their warp threads to see the details of the design below. The consequence of this working method was that the cartoon was reversed in the tapestry as the weavers worked from the back of the textile, a consideration which had to be taken into account in their design. As each section was completed by the weaver, it would be wound onto the lower roller of the loom along with the cartoon, which would be crushed against the face of the tapestry. Cartoons thus had a limited working life, and were often repaired or entirely reworked to enable more sets to be produced from them; it is unsurprising that no examples of these full-scale cartoons survive from our period.

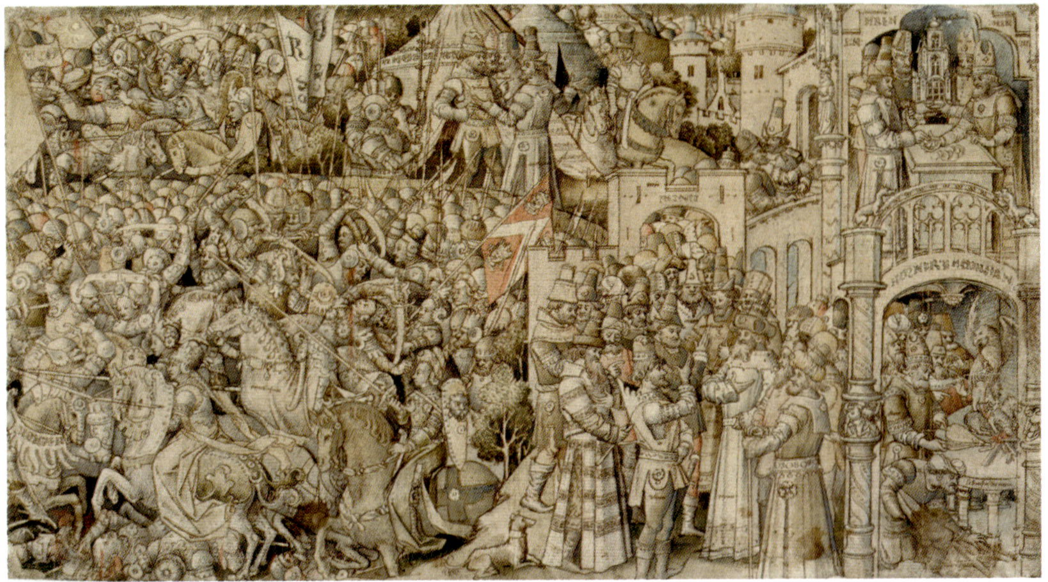

142 Attributed to the Coëtivy Master

The Sack of Troy, *petit patron* for tapestry 11 of the *Trojan War* series, pen and wash on paper, *c.*1475.

This coloured drawing is the *petit patron* or small design stage for one of the large Troy tapestries as seen in **53**. A great deal of decorative elaboration, particularly in relation to the dress and fabrics worn by the figures, occurred between this and the weaving stage.

The design procedure involved in making a large-scale tapestry is seen in action in the best documented, and largest, of surviving works in this media, the Angers *Apocalypse* [**143, 144, 145**]. Produced between 1377 and 1381 for Louis of Anjou, the brother of Charles V of France, this was a truly monumental project: it consisted of six pieces each around 5.5 metres high by 25 metres long, making the entire work when hung together around 150 metres in length.[39] To undertake its design, Louis borrowed the king's painter, Jan Baudolf (who also painted **41**), as well as one of the king's manuscripts, an illuminated *Apocalypse*, for him to follow as a guide, a process made known to us by a marginal note in the inventory of the manuscripts of Charles V. There it is recorded that an illuminated *Apocalypse* 'in French, fully historiated' (meaning with miniatures) had been 'lent to Monsieur d'Anjou, to make his beautiful tapestry'.[40] Such a model was vital since the concept of telling the Apocalypse narrative in tapestry form was both ambitious and, it would seem, new; on the other hand, a formula for illustrating this text

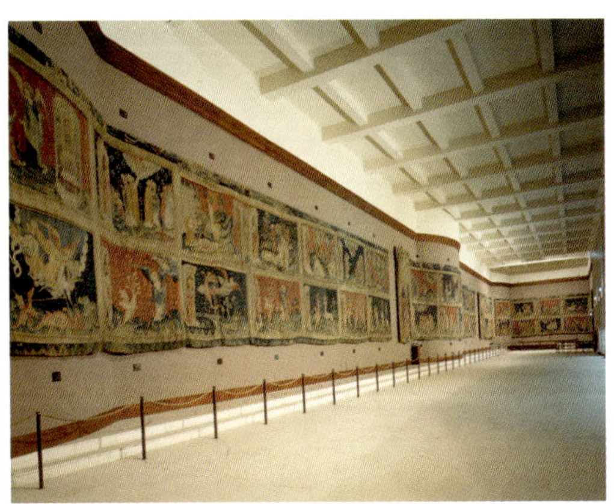

143 Designed by Jan Baudolf, partly woven by Robert Poinçon, coordinated by Nicolas Bataille

General view of the full set of six Angers *Apocalypse* tapestries, wool, 1377–81.

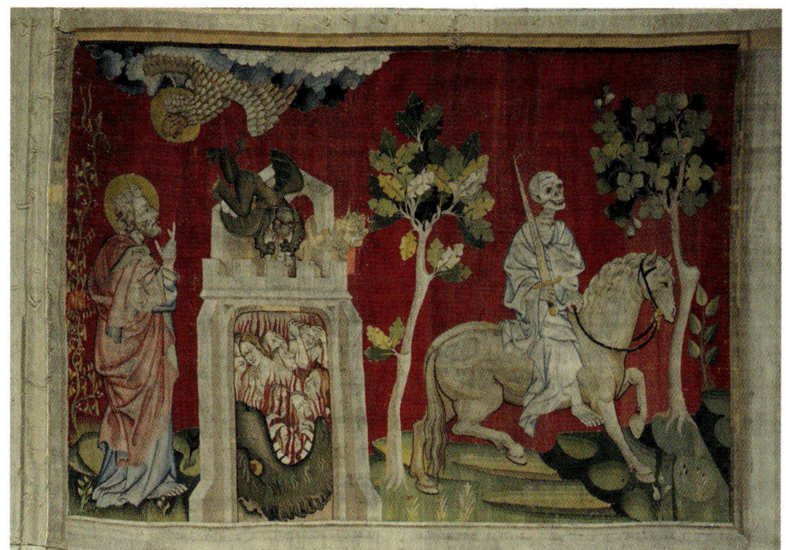

144 Designed by Jan Baudolf

Detail of **143**: scene from the first piece, showing the *Pale Horse of Death*.

This image shows the tapestry's back face (reversed in this image to read in the same direction as it would from the front). Here, protected from the light, the colours have remained true and virtually unfaded. The tapestry is legible from the back because it was woven with extraordinary care, with few (visible) loose, tied off or crossed over threads.

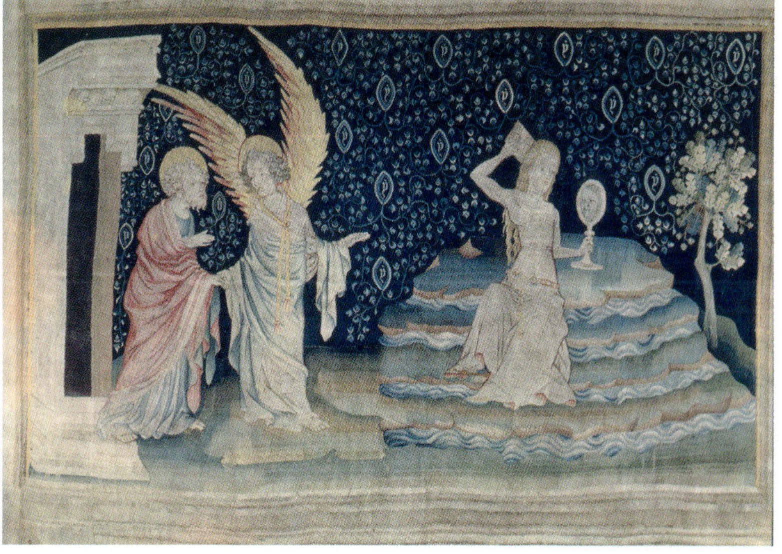

145 Designed by Jan Baudolf

Detail of **143**: scene from the fifth piece, showing the *Whore of Babylon*.

Some dyes used in weaving were more stable than others: the yellow dye weld was particularly light-sensitive; consequently this colour has virtually disappeared from the front of the tapestry, while colours which were made using weld also have altered more dramatically than others: oranges have faded to red and greens to blue, reducing their visual impact and their narrative drama (compare this with **144**).

in an expansive number of individual scenes had been developed since the thirteenth century in illuminated manuscripts.

Written rather than visual directions seem to have been provided with relative frequency in the process of tapestry making, probably since the narratives demanded were not always well known, or they needed to be more expansively told than was common. This was certainly the case with many choir tapestries (designed to be hung, facing inwards, above the choir stalls of a church, see **179**), which often depicted narratives of locally venerated saints, such as Eleuthère and Piat (for the cathedral of Tournai) or Urbain and Cecilia (for the papal college of St Urbain in Troyes). The former tapestry survives, the latter does not, but we have highly detailed written instructions (no fewer than thirty-six pages) for its production which specify everything from the attitudes and actions of the figures, how they should be dressed, to the coats of arms and the texts set next to them or issuing from their mouths.[41]

For the Angers tapestries, the pre-existence of a visual model in this case made everyone's life easier. That the model was a manuscript was to impact on their narrative organization and appearance, notably in the decision to tell the story though a series of alternating red and blue 'cartoon-like' spaces with only one narrative moment in each rectangular field. This is not, in fact, an obvious choice for tapestry design, which, indeed, throughout the fifteenth century eschewed this formula for a very different, surface-rich mode that instead often presented many different narrative moments in one visual field, or divided narrative scenes up in less emphatic ways (as seen in **52**, **53** and **179**).

Jan Baudolf was paid initially 50 francs for his designs, the 'pourtraitures et patrons par lui faiz'. This was only a fraction of the cost of the weaving of the set, which was around 1,000 francs per piece. Another payment to Baudolf of 120 francs 'for certain designs' made between 1379 and 1381 might also relate to the *Apocalypse* series, but it is not clear from any of the accounts if he was being paid for just the large or only the small cartoons: 170 francs equates to around 42 weeks' work if we calculate a rate of 4 francs a week, which was what the higher paid master craftsmen like Sluter and Malouel were receiving in Dijon at a similar period. It seems plausible then that Baudolf made the full-scale designs too. Painters were often responsible for these large cartoons, but not always the same painter as had made the small cartoon—so the distance between conception and production was potentially increased further, with a possible scenario where the initial designs were made by one artist in one region, the large cartoons by another elsewhere, who might be a specialist painter of *patrons*, as was Baudouin de Bailleul (who Philip the Good had specified as the desired painter for the cartoons of his *Gideon* series),[42] and then translated into woven form in a third location by another group of artists, with yet another set of specialist skills.

Weavers, too, could produce designs: Baudolf's patterns were augmented by the weavers in ways that made the surface more decorative and visually rich, perhaps in a desire to fill in areas which appeared too empty (this would have been done onto the cartoon, not simply invented in the course of weaving). This can be seen in the scenes showing the *Pale Horse of Death* [**144**], where the trees and foliage are in two distinct styles: the two trees flanking the horse are an intended part of the painter's plan, as they are integral with the landscape and are painterly in form. By contrast, the decorative tendril-like plant snaking up beside John on the far left of the scene would appear to be an addition to the cartoon by the weavers. Such embellishments are seen throughout the first two tapestries, whose figures silhouetted boldly against the alternating plain expanses of blue or red must have been visually unsatisfactory, since after the weaving of these first two pieces there was a change in design and the last four of the set have a different visual language with flowers, heraldic letters, or patterns filling the blue and red backgrounds [**145**]. A similar development of decorative detail is seen in the transition between the design and its woven form in the *Troy* tapestry [**53** and **142**]. Enriching the design in this manner entailed increased costs, since more detail would have taken longer to weave (the last four pieces of the Angers tapestry cost 1,000 francs a piece as opposed to 500 francs a piece for the first two). The weaving in this case was organized by the merchant Nicolas Bataille (called a *tapissier* in the documents), who contracted the project to a weaver Robert Poinçon: Poinçon had shops in Arras and Lille but was at this point resident in Paris, so it is not clear in which centre the works were woven.[43] Bataille was primarily an entrepreneur who had enough money to underwrite large commissions of this sort: tapestry production involved big investments in equipment, material, and personnel. The richly dyed threads were expensive (the reds were achieved with madder, a lake, the blues with woad, both of which were costly),[44] and decisions about materials had huge implications for the cost and appearance of the finished product: according to the levy charged for different grades of tapestry imported to England in the sixteenth century, tapestry woven with silk could cost four times as much as that woven with coarse wool, while that including metal-wrapped threads could cost twenty times that of coarse wool alone.[45] Unsurprisingly we find patrons being specific about these elements: in 1449 when Philip the Good wrote in confirmation of a very expensive eight-piece set of the *History of Gideon and the Golden Fleece* worth 8,960 écus, he requested that 'whatever is in yellow on the patterns is in the best gold thread of Venice in the tapestry, and whatever is shown in white is of silver thread of Venice, except for the flesh and the faces of the people'. In addition, the rest of the tapestry was to be woven in well dyed silk and the best quality wool.[46] Patrons could specify in another direction for the sake of economy: Piero de' Medici stipulated in a tapestry commission of 1454 that there should be no gold, silver or silk thread used, which his agent obviously thought unwise, pleading, 'I wish that you had agreed that there should be silk, because it is needed in many things, if one wants good work.'[47]

Weaving also cost in labour and equipment, and premises had to be substantial to incorporate the looms, which had to be as wide as the tapestry you were weaving was tall (you could not successfully join a tapestry horizontally): the loom for the Angers set would have been around 6 metres wide. To make a monumental tapestry in anything like the few years involved for the *Apocalypse* required a considerable team of well-trained weavers: it has been estimated, for example, that a single weaver could produce around 50–70 square centimetres of fine woven tapestry a month; the production of a set of six tapestries measuring 5 by 8 metres (similar to the Zamora *Troy* set, [**53**], but a third of the size of the Angers *Apocalypse* set) would take thirty weavers between eight and sixteen months, excluding the time taken to set up the looms. This estimate of working time would vary according to how close together the warp threads were (the threads which are held tight and horizontal in the loom, and around which the weft is woven): the closer together, the longer the weaving took, and thus the more costly the tapestry would be. The materials used would also affect time as well as cost—silk and metal-wrapped threads took longer to weave since they generally required a denser warp. Thus measurements of how many warp threads there are per centimetre in tapestries is a useful guide to their cost and level of fineness: a high-quality tapestry in wool alone tends to have 5–6 threads per centimetre; add silk and it rises to around 6–8 per centimetre; those with metal-wrapped threads and silk, the most costly, have as high as 9 or 10 warps per centimetre. The Angers tapestries, made almost entirely of wool, have 5 and 6 warp threads per centimetre;[48] the Zamora *Troy*

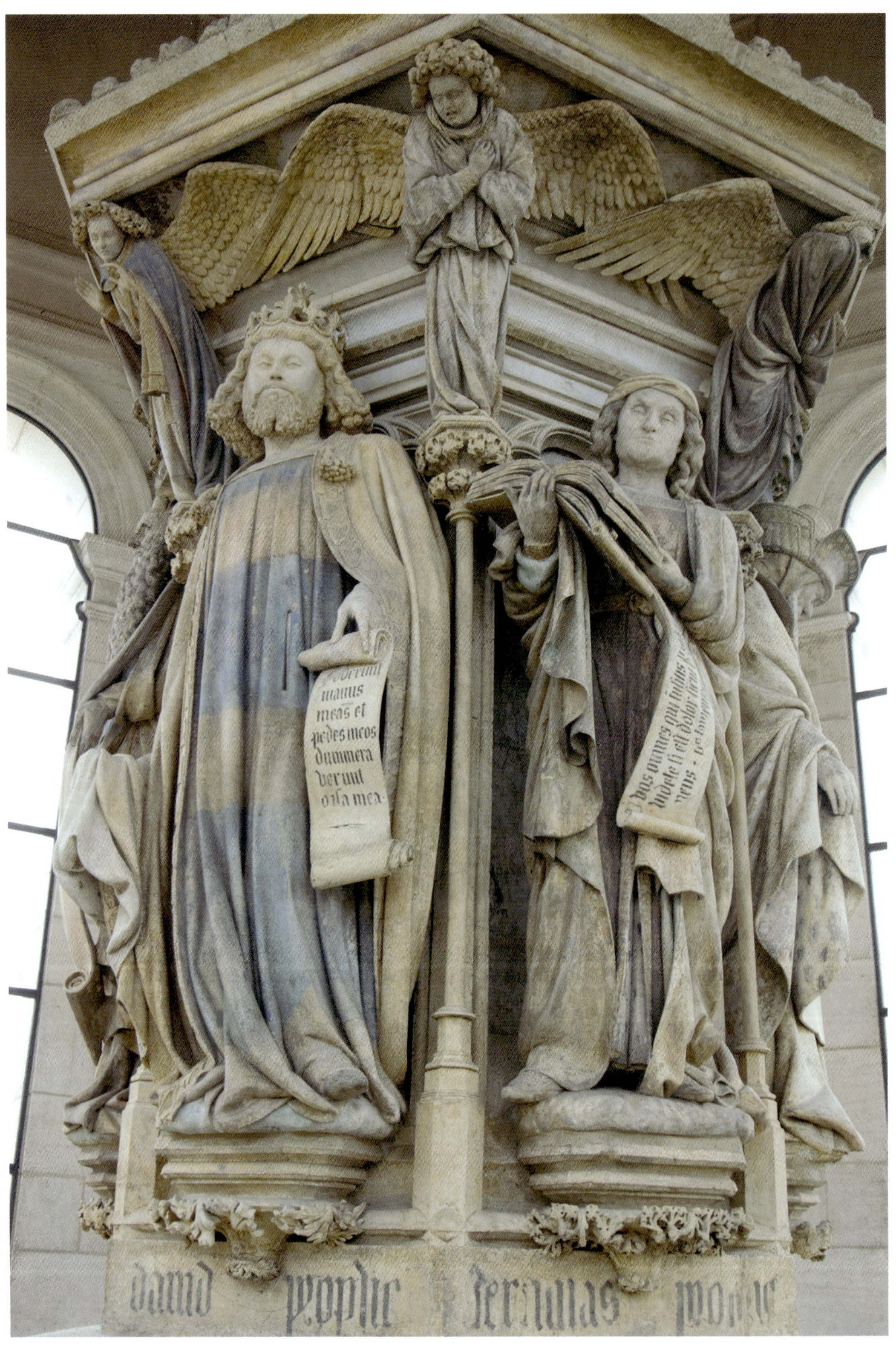
manus
meas et
pedes meos
dinumera
verunt
ossa mea
david
Jeremias

146 Claus Sluter, Claus de Werve, and workshop

The Great Cross (the *Well of Moses*), with figures of prophets and angels, Asnières stone, traces of original polychromy and gilding, 1395–1404.

set [**53**] have 6–7; the Vatican *Life of St Peter* set designed by Raphael have 7; Bernard van Orley's *Passion* set for Cardinal Wolsey or Henry VIII made *c.* 1525–8 has 10–12 per centimetre.[49] In general, warp density rises in the later fifteenth and early sixteenth centuries in the highest level of production as weavers sought ever increasingly subtle effects of tonal transition and illusion.

The Angers tapestry may not have the densest possible weave, but it is technically extraordinary in another way: it is woven so that the back is as refined as the front. No weft threads cross over from one area of colour to another, and none were left hanging, but were hidden instead inside the weave of the tapestry. The result is that the tapestries could, in theory, be viewed from both sides, at least in terms of visual effect (the narrative and the text elements would not, of course, work from the reverse). Was this important for their original viewing and intended use, or was it simply the weavers working at an extreme of technical refinement? Whatever, such a procedure could only have been achieved by a highly skilled team and it would have slowed down the process considerably; that these tapestries were produced in as little as three, and no more than four, years is then all the more remarkable.

'So High a Point of Subtle Skill that They Astonish the World': Manipulating Wood and Stone

The deep understanding of the behaviour, limitations, and possibilities of your given media is perhaps most vividly seen in the production of large-scale stone and wood sculpture. Two artists from either end of our period, the stonecarver Claus Sluter and the woodcarver-painter Veit Stoss, illustrate the technical challenges such works presented and demonstrate the sophistication and mastery with which they were met.

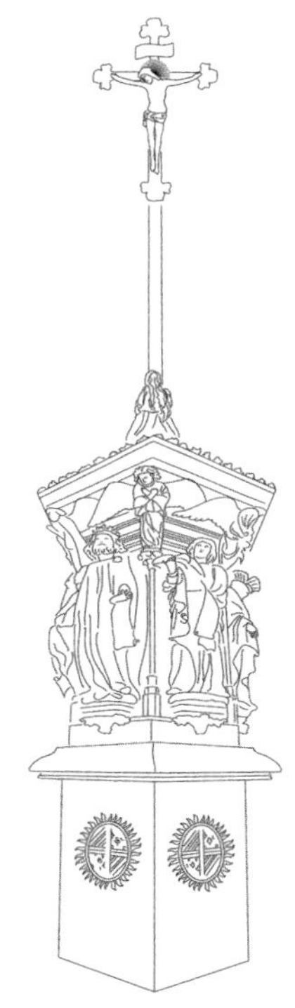

147

Author's reconstruction of the original appearance of the Great Cross [**146**].

The production of the *Well of Moses* (properly termed the Great Cross) occupied Claus Sluter and his team in Dijon for almost a decade from 1395 to 1404 [**146, 147, 148**], and was a feat of engineering as well as artifice and invention.[50] Originally topped by a huge crucifix, set with the figure of the Magdalene alone at the foot of the cross (the Virgin and St John, contrary to earlier belief, never existed), what remains is just its hexagonal base with its six angels and six life-size prophets, the cross having collapsed in the eighteenth century. The challenge for Sluter in planning and executing this work was to produce in stone a monumental crucifix, with complex figurative elements which would enrich the meaning of the work, and which would be suitably visible and visually interesting from 360 degrees in the large 100 metres square cloister for which it was intended (see drawing of this complex, **11**). It had to withstand the nature of the site (Champmol literally means marshy field) and the full blast of the elements (a protective structure was not part of the original plan). The solution he came up with allowed him to construct a visually astounding object, which defied the constraints of his materials and which stood around 11 metres high above the ground, with a base sunk around 4 metres into the earth, creating a well around it. The well has always been viewed as a fundamental iconographical feature of the piece, but it may have been conceived initially as a solution to the technical problem presented by the wet ground—indeed a sump—even if the symbolism of the water it created around it was then recognized and exploited.

We are remarkably well informed as to how Sluter achieved this feat of engineering and about his careful choice of materials and method. Concerns for structural integrity run through every part of this work: the top section of the two-part base around which the prophets are set was constructed from seventeen pieces of precision-cut stone set in eight horizontal layers, each made up of two or three stones cut and set at different angles, like a three-dimensional jigsaw, to ensure their stability.[51] This base supported a terrace, from which rose the cross in two sections, a column with the cross proper sitting on top of it, together around 7 metres tall, made possible by an iron rod running all the way through both elements and sunk deep into the base of the monument [**147**]. Sluter sealed this rod into the sections of the cross with a large quantity of lead to prevent the iron rusting and weakening the stone. He chose the stone for these various elements with great care: the figures of the prophets, angels, and the kneeling Magdalene on the terrace were carved out of a local stone from Asnières, which was good for figurative work, but for the cross and the figure of Christ on it he arranged several exceptional trips to a relatively distant quarry at Tonnerre, where stone of a denser and stronger nature, but still retaining its carving qualities, could be found. Fragments of the cross and column indicate that it was a remarkably slim: 15 to 17.5 centimetres in diameter. The terrace on which the Magdalene knelt was also designed and its material chosen with its function in mind: it was the most exposed part of the monument, effectively protecting the carved figures of the angels and prophets below, presenting a horizontal area where water could potentially collect. Sluter used a particularly waterproof stone for this, from the local quarry at Ys, and designed it so that it had a slightly sloping surface carved with rainwater channels to encourage drainage.

Sluter choreographed the carving and installation of the various figurative elements of this work with equal aplomb. Records show that deliveries of stone were timed to arrive in his workshop at the ducal palace for one element when the finished figures for another were ready to leave, packed in specially made

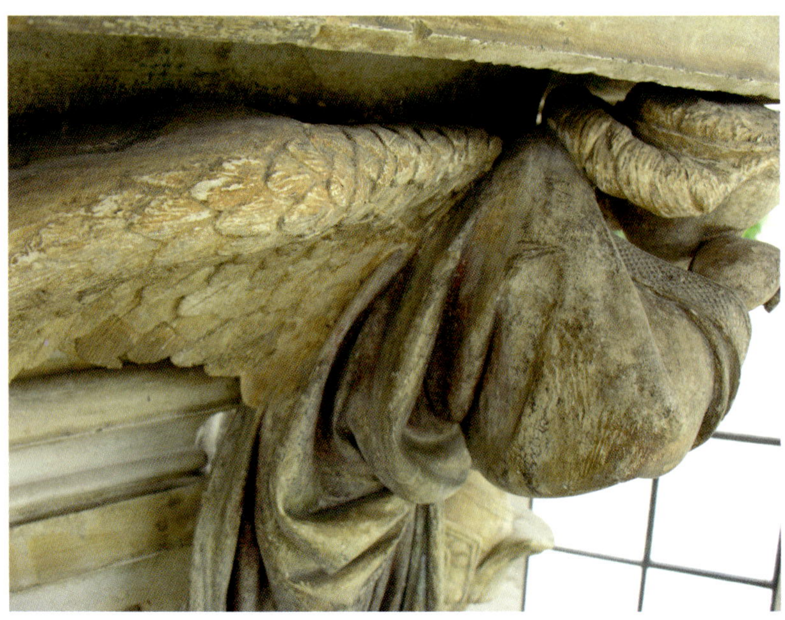

148 Claus Sluter and Claus de Werve

Detail of angel between Jeremiah and Zachariah, from the base of the Great Cross.

This photo, taken from up a ladder well above normal viewing level, shows how the angels' wings were carved *in situ* from the stone slabs of the top layer of the base, while their bodies were carved separately and fixed to the monument with metal rods. Neither the plaster disguising the joints, nor the true thickness of their carving, is visible from below (see **146**).

149 Veit Stoss

Annunciation of the Rosary, limewood, original polychromy, 1517–18.

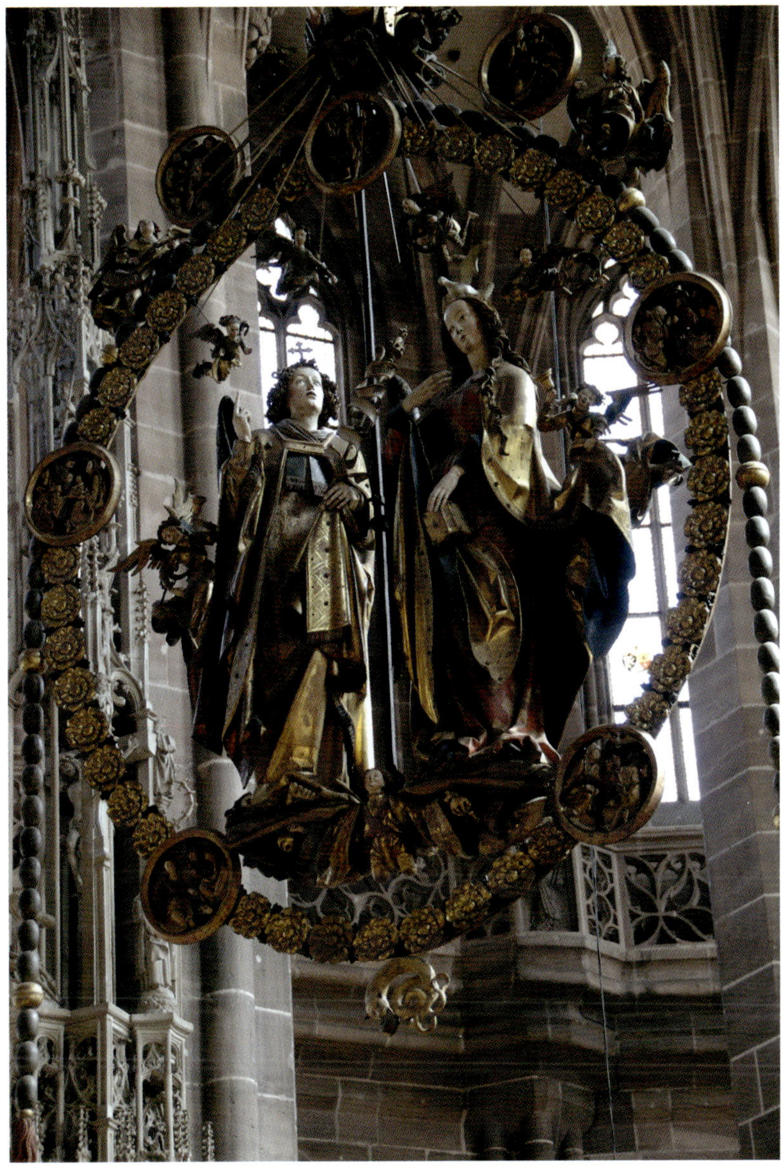

boxes, for installation on the monument at Champmol, ensuring there was enough working space for the next stage. He also organized the work so that it was possible to proceed with the figurative elements from top to bottom to limit any potential damage to areas lower down when the upper parts were being installed. First to be carved and set in place were Christ and the Magdalene, then the angels; last of all the prophets, in two batches of three: David, Jeremiah, and Moses in 1402, then in 1403–4 Daniel, Isaiah, and Zachariah.

It is in the angels where we see most clearly the nature of Sluter's genius for defying the limitations of his medium, and for understanding the distortions of viewpoint and exploiting their possibilities. From below it appears as if their wings are paper thin, but as an image of them taken head on shows, this is all an illusion [**148**]; it is impossible to make out the nature of their

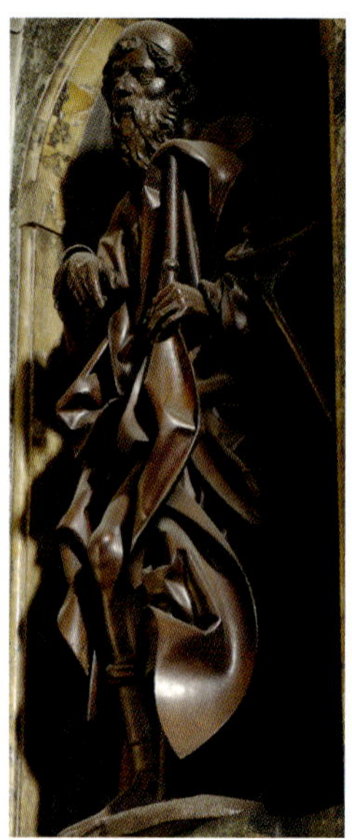

150 Veit Stoss
St Roche, limewood, unpainted, *c.*1510–20.

151 Bernt Notke
Triumphal Cross in the cathedral of Lübeck, oak, polychromy, and other materials, consecrated 1477.

This cross beam with its vast figures was made for Albert Krummedick, Bishop of Lübeck; its placement marked both his grave and the high altar, which he moved to have set directly below it. Krummedick's donation is recorded in the inscription along the beam in Latin (on the front) and German (at the back), set so that his name comes directly below the cross and above his coats of arms set at its base. This vertical alignment of grave, altar, arms, inscription, and crucifix (which contained relics) was a deliberate and meaningful one (see a similar alignment in **72**).

facture from below, however. Sluter must have had a three-dimensional model with which he established the various viewpoints since, while having one primary view—that over which Christ was orientated, between David and Jeremiah [**146**]—the cross still needed to work fully in the round.[52]

Veit Stoss was, like Sluter, capable of working with success on a truly monumental scale, although the material he manipulated was limewood, not stone. The *Annunciation of the Rosary* [**149**], made in 1517–18 to hang in the choir of the church of St Lorenz in Nuremberg, measures no less than 5.12 metres high, with the figures of the Virgin and Gabriel over life-size at 2.18 and 2.15 metres respectively. A very large limewood tree (a wood which was softer than oak, more tractable in the carving process, and widely used in southern Germany) was required for such big figures; this was provided directly by the patron, Anton Tucher II. His account book records that he ordered the tree to be felled for Stoss in the St Sebald forest on 12 March 1517; by 17 June 1518, just fifteen months later, the Annunciation group was installed in the choir.[53] The speed at which this ensemble was produced meant that Stoss worked with the wood unseasoned, a choice which allowed him to create the deeply undercut forms of his drapery and such virtuosic effects as the corkscrew curls of the Virgin's hair more easily.

Stoss's technical mastery was recognized by Vasari, who, not knowing the identity of the artist, wrote the following about Stoss's monumental figure of St Roche which had been commissioned by a German merchant in Florence for the church of the Annunziata there [**150**]:

> Though foreigners do not have the perfect *disegno* Italians show in their things, yet they have worked and still do in such a manner as to bring things to so high a point of subtle skill that they astonish the world, as one can see in a work or rather a miracle of wood from the hand of Janni the Frenchman ... with such subtle carving, so soft and hollowed, and as if it were paper-like, and with such fine movement in the arrangement of the folds, that nothing more wonderful is to be seen.[54]

Wood, unlike stone, allowed for the carving of thin edges and extended forms if undertaken with skill; with stone, the support of every element which extended from the body of the block has to be carefully considered, and cutting away areas to produce effects like the scrolls of the prophets in the *Well of Moses* [**146**], ran the risk of elements breaking off and the figure potentially being ruined. However, the tractability of wood meant that it was also less stable and homogeneous than stone; wood like limewood contains a high proportion of water, but in differing amounts: there is much more moisture in the sapwood, the youngest wood (on the outside of the trunk), and almost none in the heartwood, the oldest wood (on the inside of the trunk). This meant that when the wood dried, it shrank more dramatically in one part than the other, and the result is a tendency for it to split, radially, across the trunk.[55]

Limewood sculptors like Stoss minimized this risk by hollowing out the figures, removing the heartwood; in the Annunciation group this is taken to a radical level and the Virgin and Gabriel are mere shells, a process which also alleviated the weight of the work: it was to be suspended by a chain 8 metres above the choir of the church, and hoisted up and down presumably at various points in the liturgical year, so it had to be as light as possible. To further minimize the tension in the wood, parts could be cut off during carving and

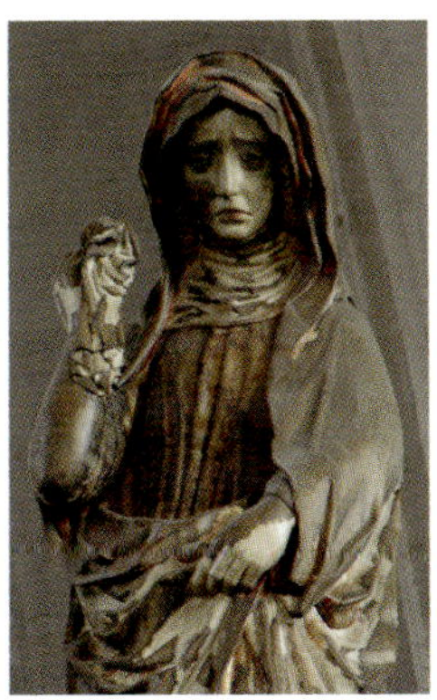

reattached later: this was done for the head of Gabriel, which is solid, and which was reattached when the figure had been completely hollowed out. If figures were to be seen in the round, like Stoss's, the back was sealed up with a plank which was carved to follow the form of the figure and the joins disguised with the polychromy over it. With the St Roche, which was unpainted, such joins were undesirable, and here the figure is carved from one piece of wood, with only a single small attached piece at the rear.

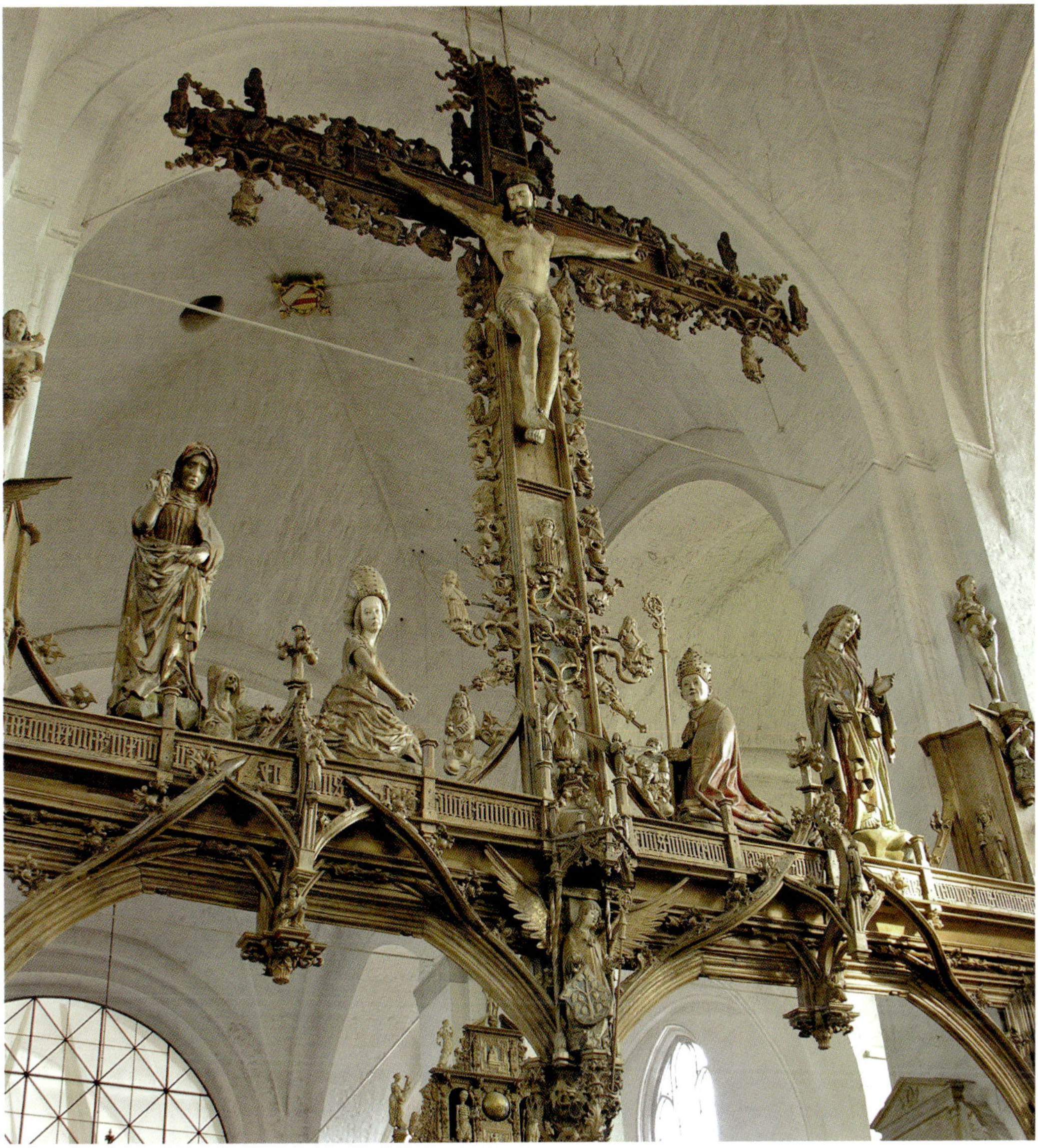

Using young wood, carved unseasoned, was also a solution adopted by Bernt Notke for the even larger figures of his *Triumphal Cross* for the cathedral of Lübeck (**151**, well over life-size, the figure of Christ is 338 centimeres tall). These were made from Baltic oak felled locally, while the architectural structure of the screen was made from oak imported from Poland; the local wood may have been chosen because the sculptor wanted it young and unseasoned, since carving oak, like limewood, is much easier in fresh wood than in dried wood.[56] To make these figures as large as was possible from the trees available, Notkte carved into the sapwood of the trunks, and in some cases even the bark remains, allowing a precise dendrochonologial date for their felling: this shows that the tree used for the figure of St John was felled in the winter of 1470–1; from the inscriptions inside the figures (see p. 150–51) we know that this was carved at least to a certain stage by 1472.[57] To solve the problem of drying the new wood, and perhaps to prevent parasites and mould from damaging it, Notke and his shop singed the figures, evident from the soot inside them and in the cracks of their carved surface; a similar process was used for the limewood figures produced under the coordination of Friedrich Herlin for the Rothenburg altar discussed below. Notke's figures, like Stoss's, are also radically hollowed out, to the extent that in parts the surface was broken into, creating holes through it.[58]

Whereas stone could in theory be cut from the quarry in whatever shape of block was required, with wood the form of the figure was limited by the size and shape of a tree: vertical, round, and fairly contained. The shape of the *Annunciation of the Rosary* posed a particular challenge in this regard since the form of the work required figures which filled its circular space—that is, wide and flat, but still in three dimensions. Luckily, adding sections to a wooden figure was much more possible than it was in stone, and Stoss solved this compositional problem by introducing two flying angels that hold up the robes of the figures of the Virgin and Gabriel, allowing them to fill the area of the circle formed by the rosary [**152**]; he carved the angels and these extended parts of the figures' robes from separate pieces of wood which were then joined on. Indeed, to achieve the effects of weightlessness, movement, and lightness seen in this work, a host of other elements were carved separately from the main trunk of the limewood tree and then attached: these include Gabriel's wings, his sceptre, and the medium-defying scroll which wraps around it, the book of the Virgin and the dove on her head, the angels holding the cloaks, and the ground the figures stand on. Bernt Notke also resorted to attachments for his figures on the rood at Lübeck: the left hand and shoulder of St John, the right arm of the Virgin, the base and turban of the Magdalene as well as her protruding knee and foot are all carved separately; the figure of the donor, Bishop Krummedick, is made of three parts, the larger parts glued together, the smaller one nailed. In stone, to achieve really thin elements or projections free from the bulk of the figure required additions in a different material, such as metal: the sceptre and crowns of many stone Virgins were often done in this manner; Sluter, for the *Well of Moses*, resorted to metal additions for the Magdalene's halo and the eyeglasses of Jeremiah, ordered from a Dijon goldsmith but no longer extant.

The polychromy of works like Sluter's, Stoss's, and Notke's was often vital to their effect, and one of the most expensive and time-consuming parts of their making. We are well informed about the process for the *Well of Moses*, which was undertaken under the direction of the painter Jean Malouel. He subcontracted the gilding of the cross and the figure of Christ to another painter, but the majority of the rest of the work was done by him during the summer of 1402, when most of the sculpture was installed on the monument. Preliminary priming coats were applied to the entire figures before they were put in place on the pillar, but otherwise most of the painting was done *in situ*, with scaffolding and a tent to protect Malouel, the gold, and pigments from the wind and the rain. The restoration and technical examination have further revealed the brilliance and complexity of this polychromy: the wings of the angels, the hair of many of the figures, and most of their outer robes were gilded, often with red glazes over them; the lining of David and Zachariah's robes were painted to resemble ermine; the blue areas were built up with underlayers of azurite followed by a top layer of the more expensive ultramarine, a combination normally found only on panel paintings. The polychromy also added important decorative and iconographic elements: sunbursts, one of Philip's emblems, were set behind the angels in raised tin-relief and painted onto David's robe; the angels' wings were given rainbow colours or speckles [**148**]; faces were shaded, modelled, and lines accentuated in the paint layer.

The polychromy of Stoss's *Annunciation of the Rosary* is relatively well preserved despite some restorations, most notably following its dramatic fall to the floor of the church in 1817 when it smashed to pieces. It displays a range of techniques characteristic of the way wood sculpture was painted and gilded at this period, done very skilfully: gold dominates, being used for almost the entire piece, alternating with blue (azurite) and reds for the lining of the figures' robes. Press brocade (a way of creating the impression of decorative textiles with reliefs made of tin in moulds and then stuck onto the surface of the figure before being painted) adorns the robes of Gabriel and the Virgin, and is used for areas like the spine of the Virgin's book; patterns are engraved into the ground before being gilded; glazes are used over gold especially on the angels' wings; burnished gold areas are set against matt gold areas for increased variety and effect, notably the Virgin's hair and crown. The

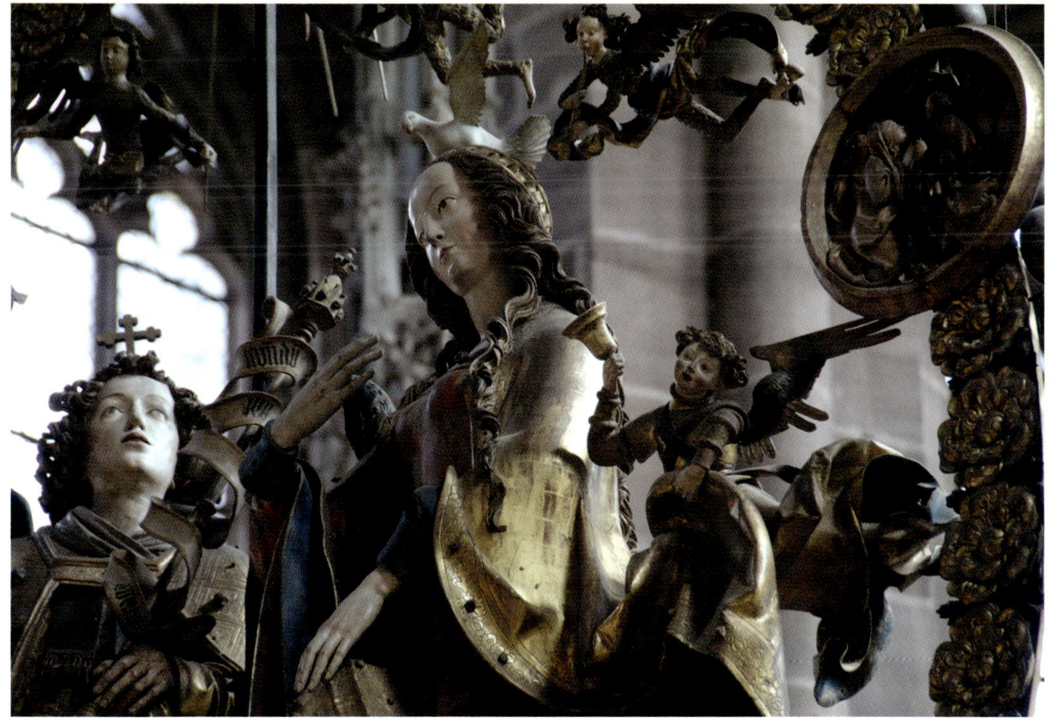

152 Veit Stoss
Detail of head of the Virgin in *Annunciation of the Rosary* [**149**].

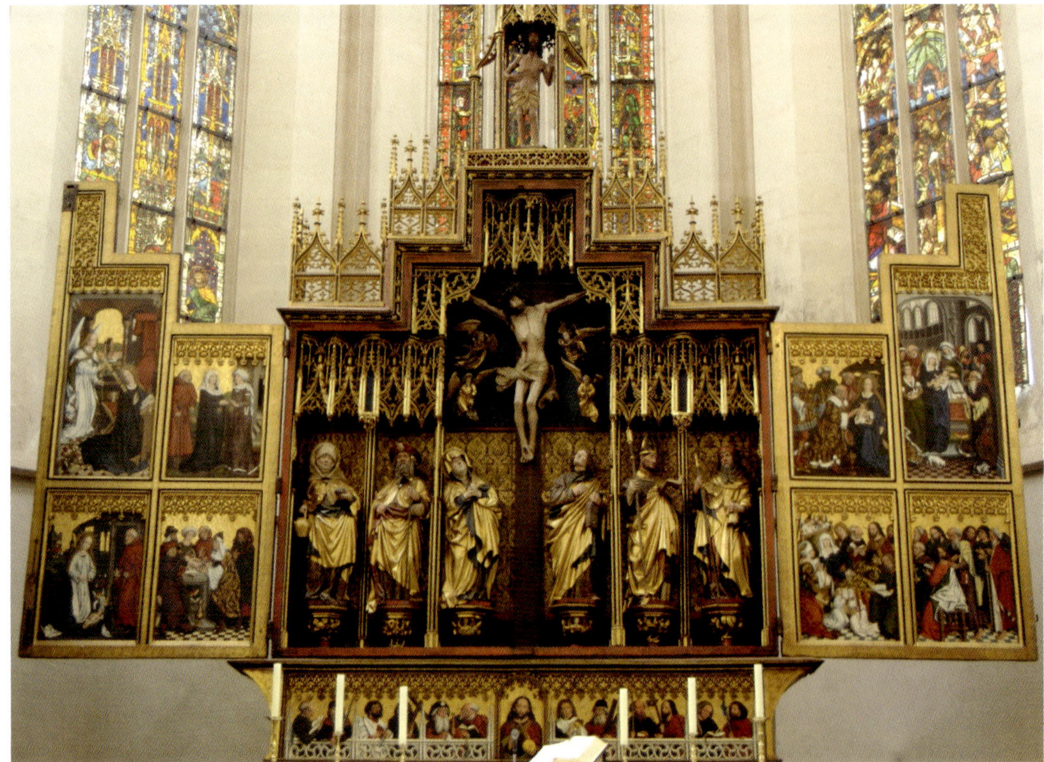

153 Friedrich Herlin, shrine and *caisse* by Hans Waidenlich

High altarpiece for the parish church of St Jacob, Rothenburg ob der Tauber, *caisse*, shrine, and painted panels oak; figures limewood, original gilding and polychromy, dated 1466.

The work is signed by Herlin with an invocation similar to those found hidden on the inside of Bernt Notke's figures in **151** (see p. 150), but here placed to be read by all, across the middle frame of the painted exterior wings: 'This work was made by Friedrich Herlin, painter, mcccclxvi, Saint James pray to God for him.' From 1545 the altar, in response to the Reformation, was kept permanently closed; as a consequence its original gilding and polychromy are extraordinarily well preserved.

painting of the flesh is particularly impressive and nuanced: Gabriel's face was delicately drawn and shaded while the paint was still wet, as were the hands; the contrast between the carved hair and face is softened by painted hairs, and the pupils of Gabriel and Mary have reflections of windows painted in white; both have painted eyelashes [**152**].

Bernt Notke, by contrast, used the polychromy of his works to create much of the detail which would normally be done in wood itself, perhaps a reflection of his training as a painter; whether he carved his works himself at all has recently been shown to be highly unlikely.[59] Notke used the chalk ground to create detail on the surface of his figures: the hair of the Magdalene in his *Triumphal Cross* is carved and moulded with the chalk ground, not in the wood surface, and other materials are also incorporated, sometimes under the paint layer, sometimes as substitutes for carved forms, like string, parchment, metal, hair, or bone, which were then painted to create the effects he desired. This is most extensively done in his *St George* [**127**], where the horse's tail is real hair; parchment is used for the dead bodies on the ground around the dragon, whose spikes are made from elk antlers, while the reins of the horse and parts of George's armour are of metal.

In Germany, painting and carving wood was occasionally undertaken by the same artist (as with Stoss), or within a workshop where painters and sculptors were practising their craft together (as with Notke). In many cases a painter, such as Friedrich Herlin (*fl.* 1459, d. 1500), ran shops which coordinated the production of large carved retables, contracting out the carpentry (the building of the *caisse* and the architectural structure), the sculpture, and even some of the polychromy, but taking charge of the overall organization of the production and installation of the work. The latter was an important part of the producer's task, at least where commissioned works were concerned. We should consider, finally, some aspects of this part of the artist's work—delivery and installation.

How an artist might plan his work with the demands of installation and delivery in mind is well explicated though the technical evidence of the large retable made for St Jacob's church in Rothenburg, commissioned from Friedrich Herlin, a painter based in nearby Nordlingen [**153**]. To set against this, we can consider the same issue from the point of view of the documentation concerning the delivery and installation of another monumental carved retable, the altarpiece made for the church of St Wolfgang, upper Austria, by the painter-sculptor from Bruneck in the South Tyrol, Michael Pacher (*fl.* 1467, d. 1498), installed in 1481 [**154**].[60]

The altarpiece for St Jacob's in Rothenburg is 7.31 metres wide when open, and 8.54 metres tall [**153**]. Herlin had the huge *caisse* and architectural framework made in several pieces small enough to be easily transported, manoeuvred through the doors of the church, and set up without extra lifting equipment. The *caisse* was made in two parts, each *c.*180 centimetres wide by 50 centimetres deep, which were then joined with a vertical metal bar *in situ*, the join being hidden by the wood of the cross in its centre. He also planned the work so that as much of the polychromy as possible was undertaken in his workshop, or, in the case of the crucified Christ and floating angels, in another shop he subcontracted them to. When the altarpiece was set up, gaps between sections were filled with paper and painted over, and iron fixings were used to stabilize the whole against the wall and to support the wings when they were open. The wings clearly presented some problems since they did not initially open properly, because the space between them and the base of the work below was not large enough: this was adjusted rather hastily, with a piece of wood inserted between the two areas and then painted red.

Michael Pacher had a more difficult challenge in some ways from that of Friedrich Herlin: his altarpiece, even larger at 10.88 × 6.60 metres when open including the carved *gesprung*, had much further to travel, from Bruneck in the Tyrol to St Wolfgang near Salzburg, through the Brenner pass. In the detailed contract it is specified that he is to bring the altarpiece part of the way himself at his own cost, part of the way at the cost of the patrons, and the last part of the journey it would be shipped up the River Inn at the patrons' arrangement and expense [**154**]. He was, however, to accompany it the whole way, and to be liable for any damage done to the work during the journey. The master or at least a workshop member would often be expected to accompany large commissions of this sort to oversee their installation and to ensure no damage occurred during transport, which was obviously a risk to delicate gilding, polychromy, or fragile stone. Sluter packed his statues in specially made boxes even for the short journey from his workshop in Dijon to the Chartreuse just outside the town; we have seen that Rogier van der Weyden's wife and several of his assistants accompanied one of his altarpieces to Cambrai, and it seems likely some of his assistants would also have gone to Ferrarra with a (now lost) triptych of the Descent from the Cross he sent to Lionello d'Este. Melchior Broederlam went from Ypres to Dijon with the altarpiece he had painted and polychromed for

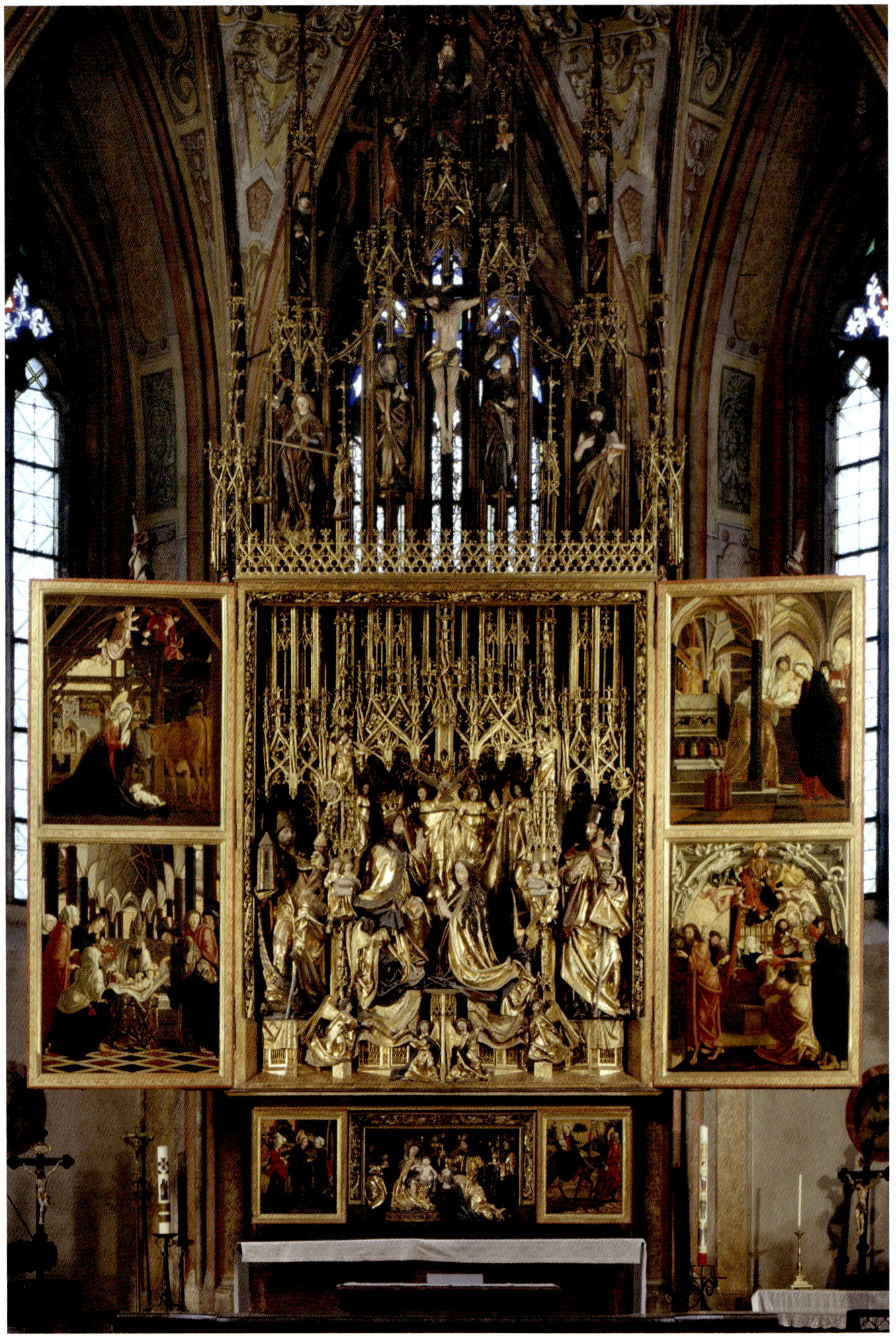

154 Michael Pacher

High altarpiece for the parish and pilgrimage church of St Wolfgang, Salzkammergut, upper Austria, stone pine (*caisse*, shrine, and sculptures), spruce (wing frames and panels), gilding, polychromy, and painting, completed 1481.

Pacher's painting style is particularly original: strongly lit and complex architectural settings are populated by elongated figures, often seen from the back, and dramatically lit or foreshortened; his palette, with its wide range of reds, oranges, and yellows contrasted with strong white which is often placed centrally in his compositions, is one of its most striking features.

the Chartreuse de Champmol there [**12**], and then accompanied it back to his workshop in Ypres, presumably because there were some major changes to be made.[61] Not all large-scale altarpieces would have been accompanied on their journeys by the artists or a workshop member of the team, but if possible some buyers at least tried to make this a stipulation. In many contracts for Spanish altarpieces installation was a major concern which exercised the patron, since these large retables had complex structures and were usually set into or against the wall of a church, rather than simply sitting on an altar.[62] The large carved and painted German retables like Herlin's and Pacher's, with heavy wings and tall architectural elements set above them, were equally a challenge to install. In the case of Pacher, the church commissioners at St Wolfgang foresaw some time spent in the process, allowing that 'at St Wolfgang, when he completes and sets up the altar, we shall provide him with meals and drinks'; they were also to provide the metalwork needed to secure the work and any help in lifting parts of the retable. Unlike Herlin, Pacher seems to have transported the *caisse* in one large piece, with the work mostly ready constructed; when it was installed, as with the Herlin altarpiece, things did not go entirely to plan and adjustments had to be made on site—the *gesprung* was around 60 centimetres too high for the church and had to be cut off at the top.

Once these huge retables with their movable wings, rich gilding and architectural forms were installed in their settings, in fully working opening and closing order, how might they have been used and viewed? These questions of use, audience and meaning, concerning objects large and small, will be the subject of our last part.

Part V

Using and Viewing

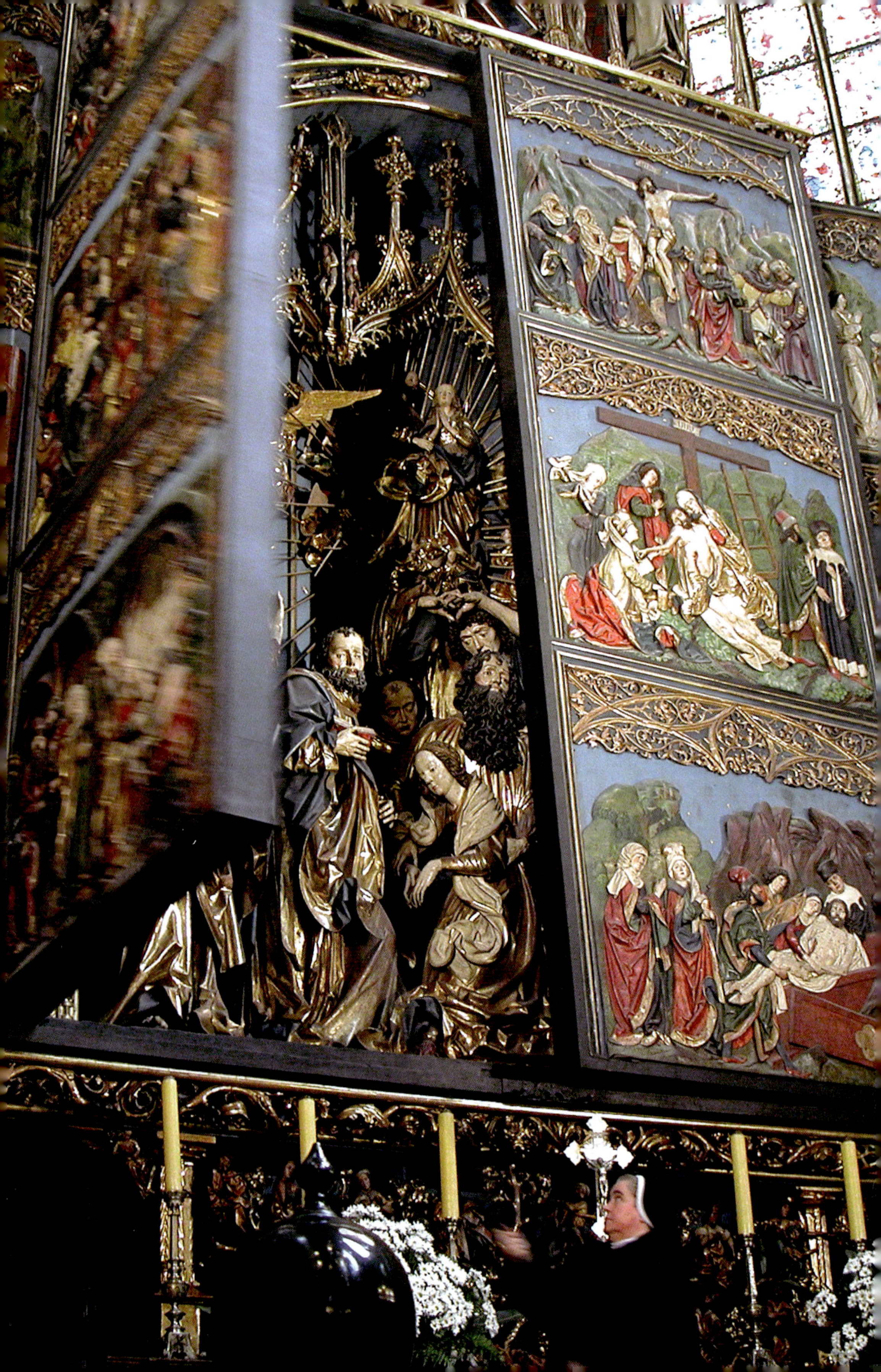

Moving Images

Note: the altarpiece is to be opened only on the festivals of the Nativity, Easter, Pentecost, and the two days following, Ascension, Trinity, All Saints, Epiphany, Corpus Christi, the Dedication of the Convent's Church, and all festivals of the Blessed Virgin Mary. On the day of a festival it is to be closed straight after second Vespers. Twice every year it is to be cleaned. And there are not to be large lights on the altar, on account of the smoke: two small wall candles are enough and any others should be placed away from the altar.

Instructions by Andreas Stoss, son of the sculptor Veit Stoss and Prior of the Carmelite house in Nuremberg, on how his father's work was to be displayed[1]

16

A high proportion of the works of art made in northern Europe at this period were designed to move, in one way or another. Their static presentation today, fixed to walls in galleries or in cases in museums, often obscures this fundamental aspect of their nature, and takes us far from the drama and meaning inherent in the process of their manipulation, whether it was opening and closing the wings of a triptych, hoisting a figure of the ascending Christ into the roof of a church, or revealing an image by removing it from its bag or box and turning it around to examine both its faces. Revelation, concealment, materiality, physical contact, and its potential power were all vital aspects of the way the images we are concerned with in this book were used and viewed.

Tableaux: Manipulation, Contemplation, Protection

We begin our exploration of moving objects with a category of mostly small-scale and intricate works termed 'tableaux' which became fashionable at the courts of France in the second half of the fourteenth century. These tableaux are found in large numbers in the inventories of the French kings and dukes—Charles V owned around 110; Jean de Berry had around 80. They came in a wide range of media: gold, silver, enamel, ivory, amber, parchment, panel, mother of pearl, embroidery, or combinations of these materials, often incorporating jewels, pearls and even cameos, their unifying characteristic being their relatively flat form. They were usually, but not always, rectangular in shape, and most were either double-sided or had multiple wings, anything from two to as many as thirteen (an object owned by Charles V),[2] which could open, close, or fold in various ways. Some had hinges, others pins or plaques: one, owned by Louis of Anjou, is described as having 'six small square parts that are held together with hinges, which fold and assemble all together one on top of the other in the form of a square book'.[3] Often they were extremely compact, designated as 'very small' and designed to be carried on the person (specified in the inventories as 'a porter sur soy' or similar); some were hung

Velt Stoss, Altarplece of the Death of the Virgin, in process of being opened.

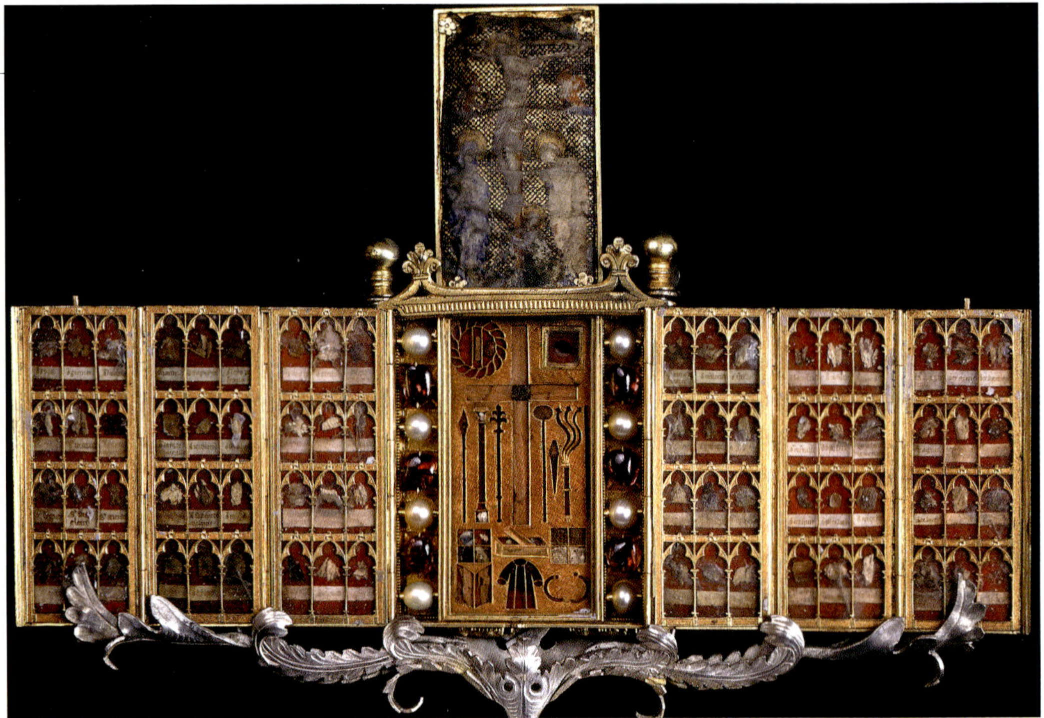

155 Parisian goldsmith c.1380

Reliquary called the *Libretto*, gold, enamel, pearls, rubies, and parchment, *c*.1380.

The silver stand is not original, and it presents the object in a fixed position, and open; originally it was designed to be kept folded shut, in a case, and carried on one's person.

156 Parisian goldsmith c.1380

Reverse of **155**.

The inscription on the reverse, in French, states that Charles V had given this reliquary and these relics, which it lists, to Louis of Anjou, his eldest brother; they include some of the most prestigious available—the blood of Christ, fragments of the crown of thorns, the true cross, the nails and lance of the Crucifixion.

above beds where they provided protection while the owner slept. This taste for small folding objects was not in itself new in the late fourteenth century: small-scale ivory, metalwork and painted diptychs and triptychs go back to antiquity and were popular in Byzantium and trecento Italy, but none of these predecessors developed the complexity of form, combinations of media, and compactness seen in the objects made in Paris *c*.1400.

The *Libretto* of Louis of Anjou, now in the Museo dell'Opera del Duomo, Florence [**155, 156**], is perhaps the most elaborate of these small-scale folding objects to have survived, and the one with the best evidence concerning its use.[4] Made of gold, its brilliant design allows for the incorporation of precious stones, enamel, painted parchment and fragments of no fewer than eighty Passion and other relics, all in a remarkably compact form. When closed, it measures just 7.5 × 6.3 centimetres, the wings opening up, concertina-fashion, into a series of seven panels with a total length of 24.4 centimetres. On the reverse an inscription describes the object as a gift from Charles V of France to his brother Louis of Anjou, and names the most important of the relics it contains.

Opening the wings is only the first stage in the manipulation of this tableau. The next step involves sliding the central section, with an image of the Crucifixion made of parchment stuck onto gold, upwards, revealing the most important of the relics, pieces of the cross, spear, nails, and crown of thorns (the last owned in its entirety by the French kings and a potent symbol of their God-given power), all set in enamelled compartments in the shape of the objects from which they come. On the reverse of the Crucifixion is another image, also on parchment, showing two figures—presumably Louis and his wife—kneeling in prayer before the Trinity. Combining paintings with metalwork like this allowed for more imagery and in a wider colour range or at a larger scale than was possible in enamel, without added weight, and was not exceptional for this type of object: Charles V owned a (large) gold tableau, probably a diptych, painted inside with illuminations of the Crucifixion on one side and the Virgin, St John, and St Andrew on the other, which was given to him by Jean de Berry,[5] while in 1377 Philip the Bold paid the king's goldsmith Jean du Vivier (who may indeed have been the maker of the *Libretto* and its other versions) 330 francs for the gold, jewels, and facture of a gold tableau, to which, for 20 francs, the king's painter Jean d'Orléans added several unspecified 'histories' (images).[6]

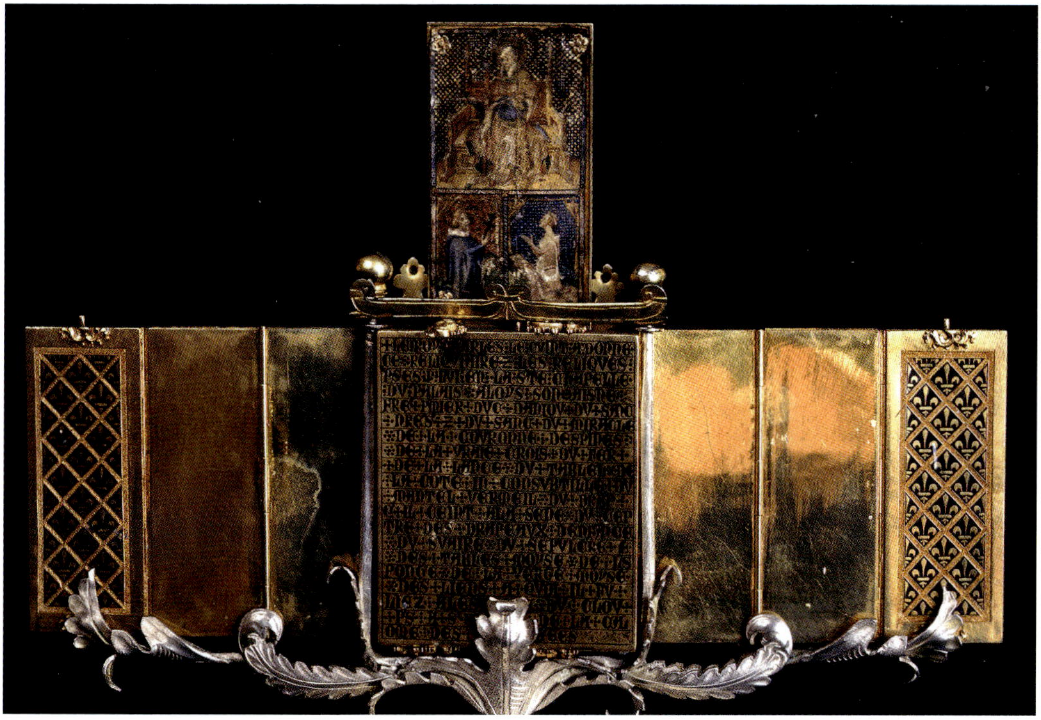

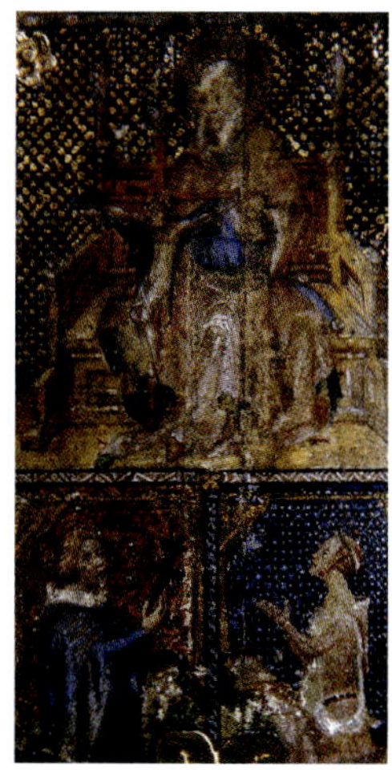

In the *Libretto* the portraits of Louis and his wife are only visible when the parchment plaque is raised, and then only from the back of the object, juxtaposed with the donatory inscription below, which in turn is set on the reverse of the gold panel in which the Passion relics it refers to are set. The placement of text, image, and relics was thus carefully considered and a determining factor in its design. When the parchment plaque with the portraits is closed, the praying figures are physically set against the most precious of the relics in the central panel, again a far from arbitrary juxtaposition: an image of yourself in literal contact with these powerful objects provided protection through that proximity.

For maximum effect, the object itself was also designed to be kept close to its owner. This can be deduced from its size and form, but its precise talismanic function is made clear from the evidence concerning two other lost but identical or near-identical objects made at the same time, also at the request of Charles V, for other members of his family. Their story can only be told by jumping forward to Charles V's great-great-grandson, Charles VIII, and

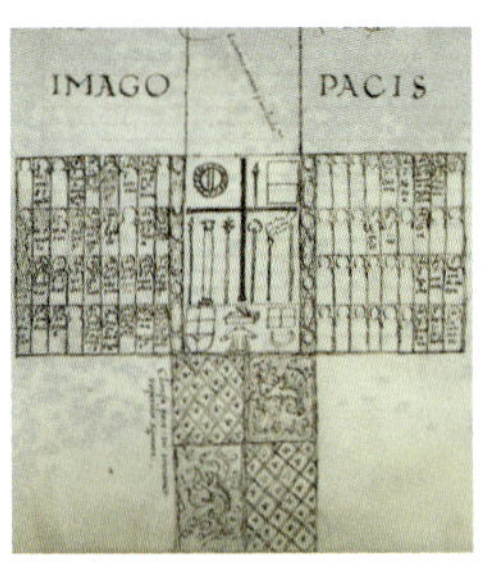

157 Anonymous Italian

Drawing of *Libretto* made for Charles V and lost by Charles VIII at Fornoue in 1495, pen and ink. Drawn below the object shown open are the enamelled exterior wings, shown closed.

his capture in battle by Milanese forces on 5 July 1495 at Fornoue. There he lost his version of the *Libretto*, later recorded in a sixteenth-century drawing [**157**], and described as a precious small folding gold tableau, containing relics. According to his page, the king 'always carried it with him, and when he fought it kept him safe'.[7] Yet another matching object is recorded in the possession of the Burgundian dukes: this too had been made at the request of Charles V. The similarity of these objects to each other, and their association with the king, must have enhanced their power and meaning. The Burgundian version, which Charles V had given to his youngest brother, Philip the Bold, was so important that it is singularly mentioned in his will, where we are told that it contained 'all the relics of the Sainte Chapelle of the Palace, and the relics of the church of *monseigneur* Saint Denis', and it is stated that it must continue down the Burgundian line and never be broken up or separated from the duke's person. They must 'hold it and keep it all together, *sans en rien oster*, nor dividing it'.[8] It was possibly the tableau for which a leather box was made in 1420–1 for Philip the Bold's grandson, Philip the Good, described as 'for putting the tableau which my lord carries with him always'.[9] It is certainly recorded in the collection of *his* son, Charles the Bold, but was lost by him also, not insignificantly, in battle, this time at Grandson where it was captured along with other treasures (see **46**) by the Swiss.[10] We have no record of a fourth object for the fourth brother—Jean de Berry—but it seems likely that one once existed. The *Libretto* and its siblings were powerful objects, containing the full complement of relics from the royal foundations of Sainte-Chapelle and Saint-Denis, but in micro-form, designed to be worn, passed down through the blood line, and evidently (if mistakenly) considered efficacious for protection in battle.

The combination of Passion imagery and portraits in the *Libretto* expands its potential function beyond that of a talisman to an aid to devotion and contemplation. Its use required physical interaction through manipulation of its elements, its imagery never entirely visible at once or from any one side. Its form makes apparent the importance of stages of viewing, of revealing and concealing, while its materials, too, are appropriate to its function. Only gold was suitable to encase such relics and the materials get progressively richer towards the last revealed view, the central section, for which the

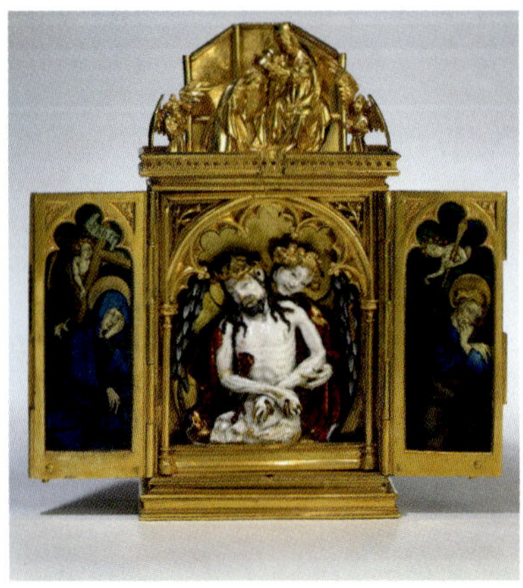

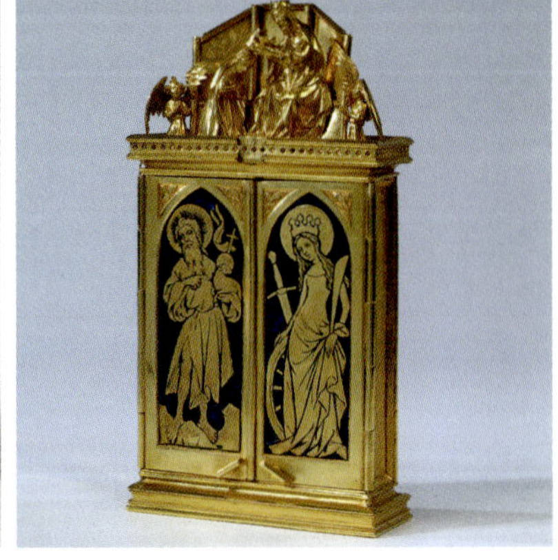

158 Parisian goldsmith c.1390–1400

Man of Sorrows with the Virgin and St John the Evangelist; above, the *Coronation of the Virgin*, gold, *baisse-taille* enamel, and *émail en ronde bosse*, *c.*1400.

The clever design and folding form of this triptych allowed for an immensely rich, intricate, and devotionally fulfilling iconography, depicting in one object just 12 cm high the Man of Sorrows, the relics of the Passion (cross, crown of thorns, lance, nails), Saints Catherine and John the Baptist, the mourning Virgin and St John the Evangelist, the Assumption and Coronation of the Virgin, the Holy Face, and no fewer than eleven angels.

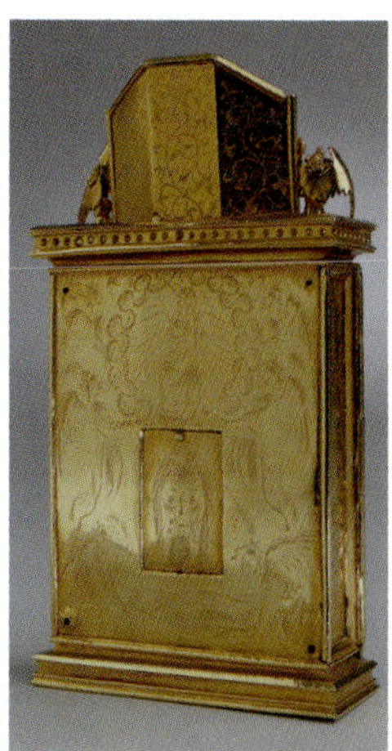

159 Parisian goldsmith ***c*.1390–1400**

Reverse of **158**, with the Assumption of the Virgin and the Holy Face in *pointillé* decoration on gold.

pearls, jewels, and enamel were reserved. These visual and material contrasts between an object closed, then opened, then turned around, are well illustrated in another small folding work made in Paris around 1400 [**158, 159**].[11] This too contained relics and is of diminutive size (12.7 × 12.5 centimetres when open) but was designed to be stood, not worn, although its use also involved physical manipulation and movement. Its quality and iconography suggest that originally it was also made for a royal French patron. It is entirely of gold, but its various visual fields are distinguished by different ways of working the metal. Closed it shows Saints Catherine and John the Baptist (favourite saints of French royalty), in a monochrome blue-grey enamel, with the Coronation of the Virgin in unenamelled gold above; as it opens [**158**], we move to full colour *basse taille* (literally 'low worked') enamelled plaques on the interior wings, with, in the centre, a deep relief image in *émail en ronde bosse* (enamel in the round) of the Dead Christ as the Man of Sorrows, wearing his crown of thorns, supported by an angel. These figures are worked with the two most distinctive elements of that method, the translucent *rouge clair* enamel on the angel's robe, setting off the opaque white enamel on Christ's body. The flat reverse [**159**] has a plaque which opens to view the (now lost) relic kept inside: this and the surface around it are decorated with some of the most elaborate and refined *pointillé* (fine punchwork decoration) work of the period, depicting both the iconic image of the Holy Face (on the plaque) and, around it, the Assumption of the Virgin with angels carrying her body upwards to a waiting figure of Christ enthroned. Only by moving the object in the light do the images created in this most subtle of techniques reveal themselves properly.

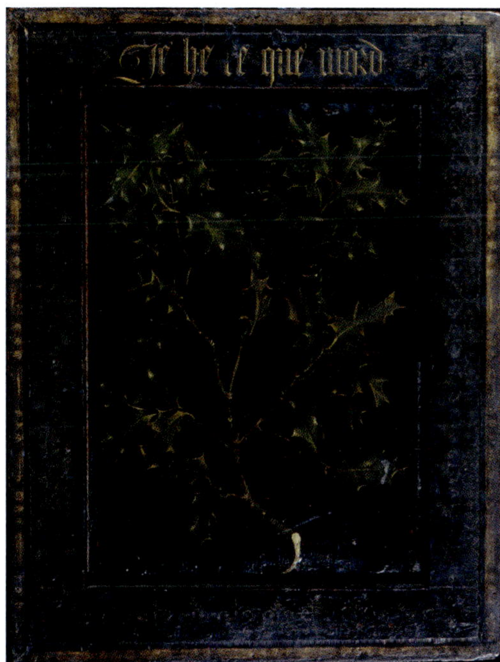

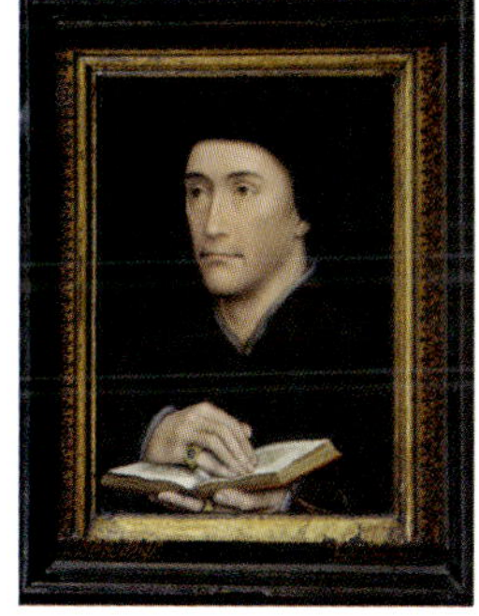

160 Circle of Rogier van der Weyden

Portrait of Guillaume Fillastre (?), front and back, reverse showing holly and motto, oil on Baltic oak.

The juxtaposition of the holly with Fillastre's motto, 'I hate that which bites', possibly refers to the holly's wish not to be eaten, and by allusion to the ability of the sitter to survive and ward off attack, as does the holly.

161 Parisian painter *c.*1400

The *Small Round Pietà*, paint and gilding on walnut, *c.*1400.

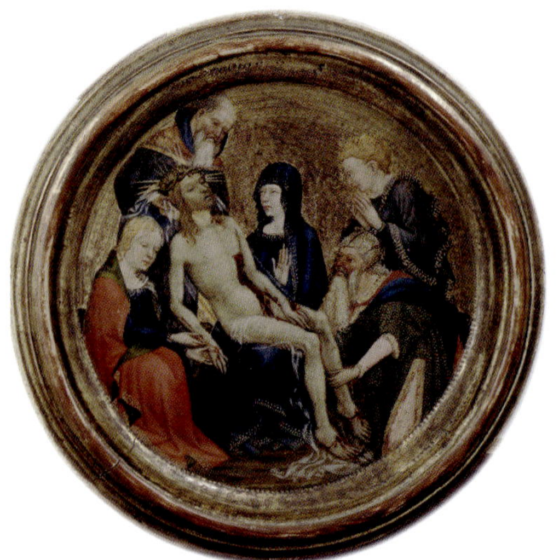

In images that did not fold, the working of both sides, front and back, was also very common; like folding objects, these were designed to be handled and manipulated, if in a different way. We find fictive marbling, coats of arms, or emblems on the reverse of many independent panel paintings, both portraits and devotional works. The reverse of a portrait possibly showing Guillaume Fillastre, advisor to the Dukes of Burgundy and later Bishop of Tournai [**160**], has an illusionistic depiction of holly, clearly a pun on the sitter's motto, 'Je he ce que mord', inscribed on the top of the frame on the reverse and on the bottom of the frame on the front, translatable as 'I hate that which bites.'[12] The idea of handling something which at first glance appears uncomfortably sharp was possibly an intended effect—it certainly seems to have been behind the dramatic treatment of the back of the *Small Round Pietà* [**161, 162**], a painting of around 1400 and again, from its imagery and form, likely to have been made for the ambit of the French kings or dukes, probably in Paris.[13] The front of this panel is beautifully worked and richly gilded with a stamped gold background. On the reverse, however, the visual effect is very different and momentarily disconcerting, since on turning it over one is faced with a blood-red object on which the crown of thorns and the three nails of Christ's Crucifixion are illusionistically painted. There is no frame on this side of the panel to hold it by, so the impression of touching the actual crown with its dangerously sharp thorns, or an object on which it sits, is vividly conveyed: this work marries form and imagery beautifully—a rectangular panel could not achieve the same effect.

Round paintings survive in relatively large numbers from Paris *c.*1400, and are also well represented in inventories of the period: three of Philip the Bold's thirteen painted panels, and three of Charles V's twenty-three painted panels, were in this format. There was no apparent functional reason to shape panels in this manner—unlike in Italy where the tondo form was used, for example, for ceremonial trays presented on the birth of a child. Moreover, the circular form was popular for works in all sorts of media, including gold, mother of pearl, and ivory [**163**], and was also used for diptychs as well as

162 Parisian painter *c*.1400

Reverse of **161**.

Crown of thorns and nails.

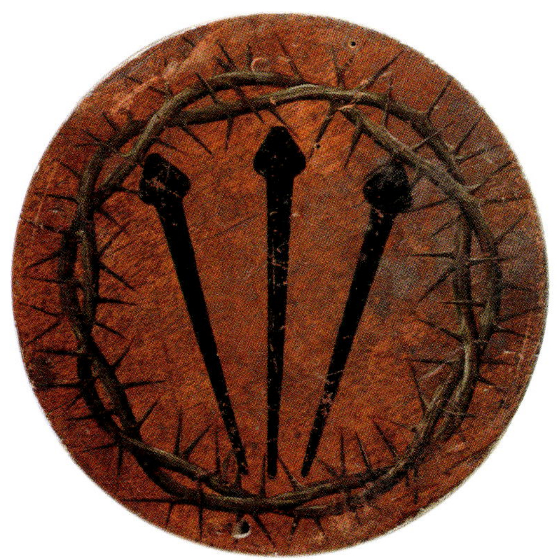

single panels. In the inventory of Jean de Berry, for example, listed amongst 'diverse tableaux' at his chateau of Mehun-sur-Yèvre, we find 'another round tableau of ivory, in two pieces, decorated with silver at the edges, with on one side a *pitie* of Our Lord [a Man of Sorrows] with two angels holding a lance and a cross, and on the other Our Lady in tears, with St John and St Catherine on either side' (**163** is an object of a similar type), which comes directly after a panel painting with a very similar form, described as a 'round *tableaux* of wood, in two pieces, in one of these is an image of Our Lady suckling her child and two angels on each side; in the other is St John the Evangelist writing on a scroll'.[14] Some of these round objects were mirrored on one side, but not always or necessarily, and this function does not explain the popularity of this form. Rather, it seems probable that handling (and wearing) objects shaped in this manner, the potential for a different sort of manipulation that they provided, which required turning the object around, along with the visual plays and challenges of fitting imagery into this form, appealed greatly to both artists and patrons. We should not, however, be tempted to see panels simply as cheap substitutes, which merely imitated the form of works in other media—these patrons did not need to watch their spending, and the relative values ascribed to paintings and small gold tableaux in the inventories are often surprisingly close. Instead the choice of paint over gold must be related to what could be achieved in each medium—panels could be larger, lighter objects for a start (enamelling could only be done to a relatively small scale, and ivory and mother of pearl, unless pieces were joined, could only be as large as their organic source). Panels could also produce illusionistic effects that would aid their impact as a devotional tool, as we have seen fully exploited on the reverse of the *Small Round Pietà*.

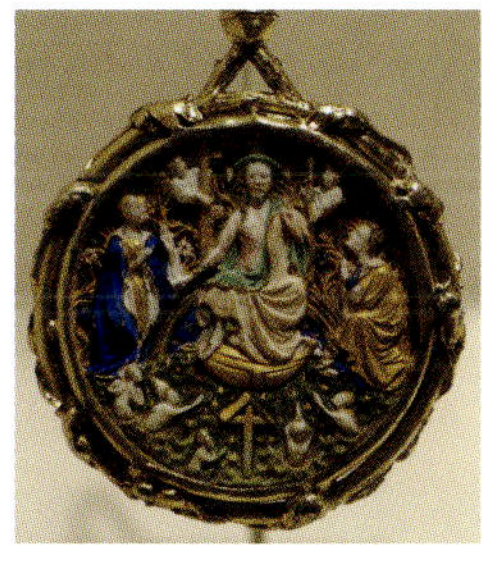

163 Parisian *c*.1400

Last Judgement, polychromed ivory set into silver gilt, *c*.1400.

There seems to have been a fashion for extensively painted, small ivory roundels showing richly crowded scenes around 1400; this coincided with a fashion for painted round panels like **161**.

Works like the *Libretto*, the Chocques Triptych, and the *Small Round Pietà* were not on constant display, but were brought out to be examined at appropriate moments of private meditation, in one's bedchamber, study, or private chapel. Such practices are alluded to in documentary sources and in images of men and women at prayer [**191**]: Philip the Bold had a panel painting

164 Juan de Flandes

Christ appearing to the Virgin with the Redeemed of the Old Testament, oil on oak, *c.*1500, part of the *Retablo* of Isabella of Castile.

This and **165** are from an original set of forty-seven panels, of which twenty-seven survive. Some have traces of painted gold frames around their edges, visible here, suggesting they were intended to be kept loose, without frames, brought out from their cupboard to be used in a variety of potential combinations, providing great flexibility in how the narratives of Christ's life and Passion might be juxtaposed.

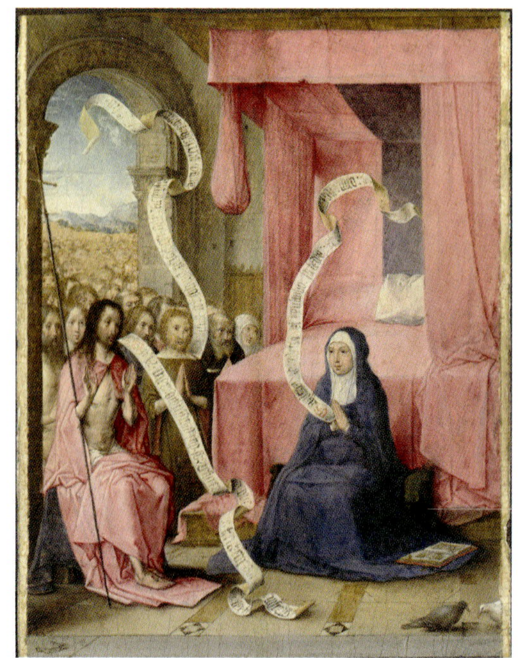

165 Michel Sittow

Assumption of the Virgin, oil on oak, *c.*1500, part of the *Retablo* of Isabella of Castile.

On Isabella's death in 1503, the forty-seven panels were dispersed; thirty-two were acquired by Margaret of Austria, in whose collection Dürer saw them in 1520, and recorded in his diary that 'the like of which for precision and excellence I have never beheld'. Margaret had this panel made into a diptych with another from the series showing the Ascension, apparently because both were 'by the hand of Michel Sittow' (possibly identified as such by Sittow himself who was at that point in Margaret's service).

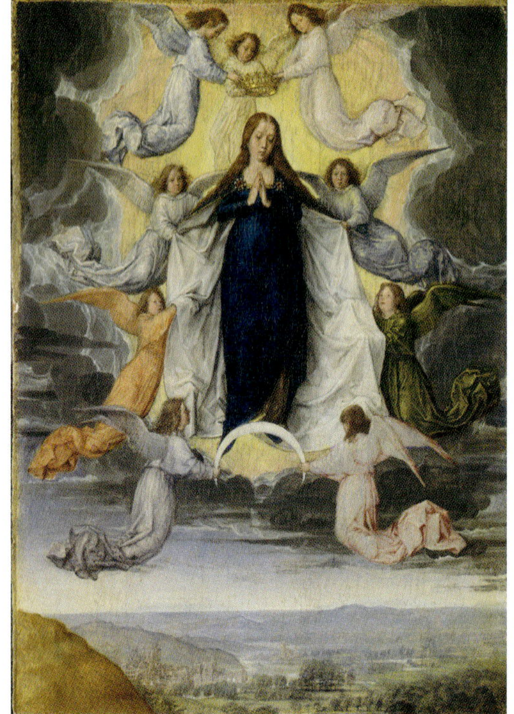

showing the apostles and St Anthony made by Jean Malouel in 1398–9 which was 'put every day in front of him in his oratory', a phrase which might imply movement from storage to place of worship.[15] Equally, items stored might be visited where they were kept, to be examined, admired, and contemplated: we are told how Charles V, after his afternoon rest, retired to his private rooms to 'peruse *joyaux* and other treasures'; in his study at Vincennes, one such location, Charles had over 500 items available to him, which included religuaries, jewels, cameos, boxes, mirrors, prayer beads, an astrolabe, and many tableaux.[16]

Storage tended to involve specially made containers or covers which were both protective and often beautifully decorated with heraldry or other imagery. Charles V's tableaux and other small precious objects were mostly in bags or boxes, kept in turn within larger trunks in his studies, chambers, and oratories in his palaces at Melun, the Louvre, and Vincennes. One of these trunks, made of cypress wood, contained around 130 of his most precious or intimate *joyaux*, and was described as being 'kept continually with him, and of which he carries the key'.[17] These bags and boxes might be of leather, felt, velvet [**167**], embroidery, metal, or wood: Charles VI's version of the *Libretto* was kept in a case embroidered with fleurs-de-lis, with a metal locking device and a gold chain from which it could hang;[18] one of Philip the Bold's paintings, a round diptych of the Man of Sorrows made by Jean d'Orléans, was in a felt bag decorated with the ducal arms.[19] Three of Jean de Berry's paintings, all single-panel images of the Virgin and, it would seem, of a large scale, had curtains in front of them, apparently attached as integral to the objects, providing a more practical solution to the need to protect an image which could not fit in a box or bag and which did not have wings.[20] This practice of keeping paintings and other images in containers or covered in some manner, rather than hanging them on walls on constant display, continued throughout our period, at least for smaller scale devotional works: a series of forty-seven small panel paintings made by Juan de Flandes and Michel Sittow for Isabella of Castile were kept by her in a cupboard, and presumably brought out in various combinations for contemplation and prayer. Their imagery extends the standard Passion cycle considerably, including several highly unusual scenes such as *Christ appearing to the Virgin with the Redeemed of the Old Testament* [**164**]. When Margaret of Austria acquired thirty-two of them after Isabella's death in 1504 she kept them in a specially made wooden box in a cupboard in her bedroom for eleven years, but two, by Michel Sittow with related iconography of the Ascension of Christ and the Assumption of the Virgin [**165**], she had made into a diptych, demonstrating an appreciation and recognition both of a particular artist's hand and the way in which religious scenes could be juxtaposed to expand and enrich their meaning.[21]

Few of these containers have survived, though we do have some original moulded leather boxes, often decorated with the arms and devices of the owner, which were made for more awkwardly shaped objects or those which required more rigid protection such as metalwork, including plate, and sculpture. What might be the original red velvet bag in which a portrait

166 Nicolas Froment

Diptych of Jean de Matheron. Interior: portraits of René of Anjou and Jeanne de Laval. Exterior: mottos and devices of Jean de Matheron, oil on poplar, c. 1480.

This small diptych was probably a gift from René of Anjou to Jean de Matheron; the artist, Nicolas Froment, worked on other projects for that king; but it is Matheron's device, a jewelled crown set over a stalk of lilies, which is set on the reverse of both panels, used to denote ownership rather than to indicate the identity of the sitters.

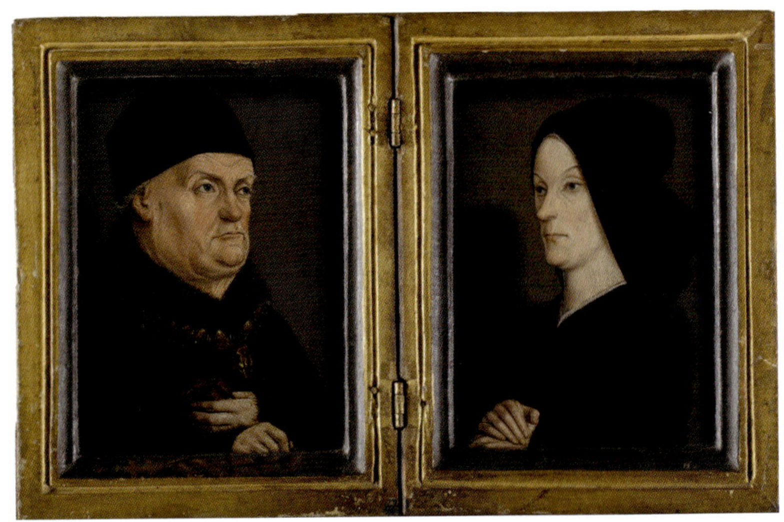

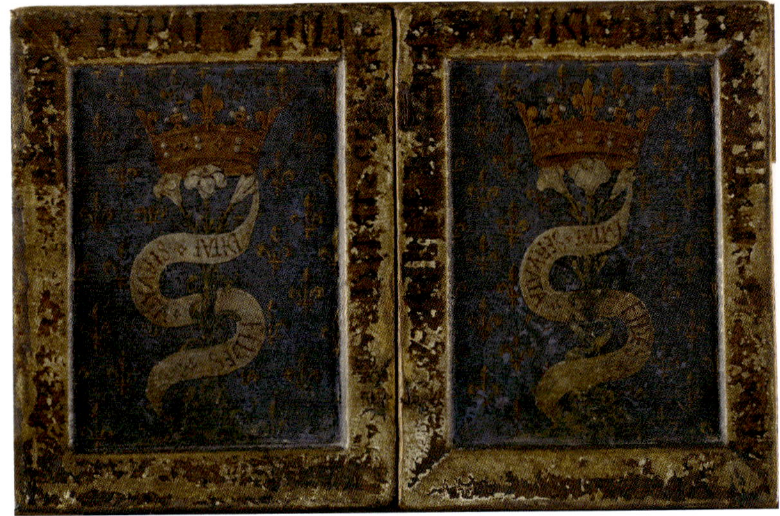

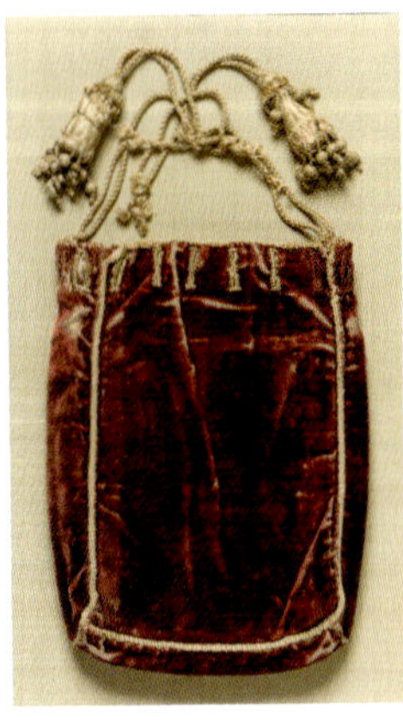

167

Velvet bag in which **166** was kept.

diptych of René of Anjou and his wife [**166**] was kept can be seen in **167**; this diptych was made for a French diplomat at René's court, Jean de Matheron (d. 1495).[22] These boxes and bags could provide a method of denoting ownership, whilst serving as a very practical way of protecting the work, especially if it was to travel with its owner. They also remind us that viewing and using objects of this type involved rituals of revealing and concealing, opening and closing, even when the object itself contained no moving parts.

Winged Altarpieces: Revelation and Concealment

The curtains, boxes, and bags made for objects like Matheron's diptych had a primarily protective function. Indeed, the need to protect images and the materials they are made of may be one of the reasons why folding forms became and remained so popular across northern Europe throughout our period, from small devotional images like the *Libretto* to monumental carved and painted high altarpieces like the 13-metre tall example by Veit Stoss in Krakow (see image heading this chapter). Having wings to close around your altarpiece, in particular, was an effective way to ensure its interior, with its delicate gilding and expensive pigments, remained undamaged and protected from the effects of light and candle smoke. This is clearly the aim of the instructions from Andreas Stoss, Prior of the Carmelite house in Nuremberg, and son of the sculptor-painter Veit Stoss, concerning how the triptych his father made for the Carmelite church at Nuremberg was to be displayed, quoted at the head of this chapter. The relatively well-preserved interiors (and comparably damaged exteriors) of many triptychs suggest that most were routinely kept shut, and that the wings' protective role worked exceedingly well.

The choice of the winged format for altarpieces was of course not just about protection: these often highly elaborate and most central of church fittings had to do many different jobs. They had to mark the dedication of the altar by including an image of that saint and to serve as a focus for the celebration of mass and other rituals. They might also play a devotional role, contemplated at less formal moments than mass by those who could approach them outside those times; some were more accessible and visible than others, depending on their placement in the church, behind or in front of the rood screen, in a chapel with locked gates or open access. They may also have had to commemorate the founders of the altar—be they a group like a guild or confraternity [**13, 169, 170**] or an individual [**56**], who may have been buried in proximity to it (as was Tommaso Portinari, **66, 67**). The winged format proved remarkably successful in catering to these varied needs, since it presented such a multiplicity of visual fields: the wings, outside or inside, were ideal for donor portraits [**67**], allowing for an appropriate division between earthly and sacred figures. Moreover, the addition of wings tripled the area available for imagery in comparison with a single panel, providing space for introductory iconography, like the Annunciation [**171**] or standing saints, often on the exterior, sometimes combined with extensive narrative scenes (particularly in altarpieces with two sets of wings, **169**), and leading to iconic or Eucharistic imagery on the interior [**172, 173**]. However, perhaps most of all, an altarpiece with movable parts presented the opportunity for intense dramatic display, as the wings were opened and the inner, most precious area was revealed [**169, 170**].

Precisely when this might occur was dictated, as far as we can tell (and as Andreas Stoss indicates), by the liturgical calendar and the celebration of particular feast days. Altarpieces would have been routinely closed throughout Lent, a period when many sculpted images, most notably crucifixes, were covered, either with plain white cloths or by blocking off the whole of the choir with a vast textile hanging, as was often the practice in Austria, Switzerland, and some areas of Germany.[23] During the rest of the year, the frequency with which altarpieces were opened might depend on the type of altar (whether it was a high altar, in the centre of the choir, or side altar against the rood screen, a pillar, or in a side chapel, see **168**), and on local practices and venerations, although they might have been opened for other reasons, such as for display to visiting dignitaries. Dürer on his journey round the Netherlands and lower Rhine paid to have some of the most notable examples, like the Ghent Altarpiece and the Dombild in Cologne, opened [**3, 14**].[24] A sense of the likely rhythm of revelation of the interiors of these works can be gleaned from surviving sexton's handbooks (*Mesnerpflichtbuchs*), which exist, for example,

168 Anonymous Utrecht painter

Apparition of the Virgin to the Dominicans of Utrecht, oil on panel, *c.*1520.

All seven retables depicted in this richly appointed Dominican church are folding triptychs with sculpted interiors; this is evident even for the two with their wings closed because of the depths of their *caisses*. The closed retable on the left has an unpainted exterior, but that on the right has Dominican saints on its closed wings. The 'Salve Regina' is being sung by the friars during an important feast of the Virgin, made clear by the number of altarpieces that are open.

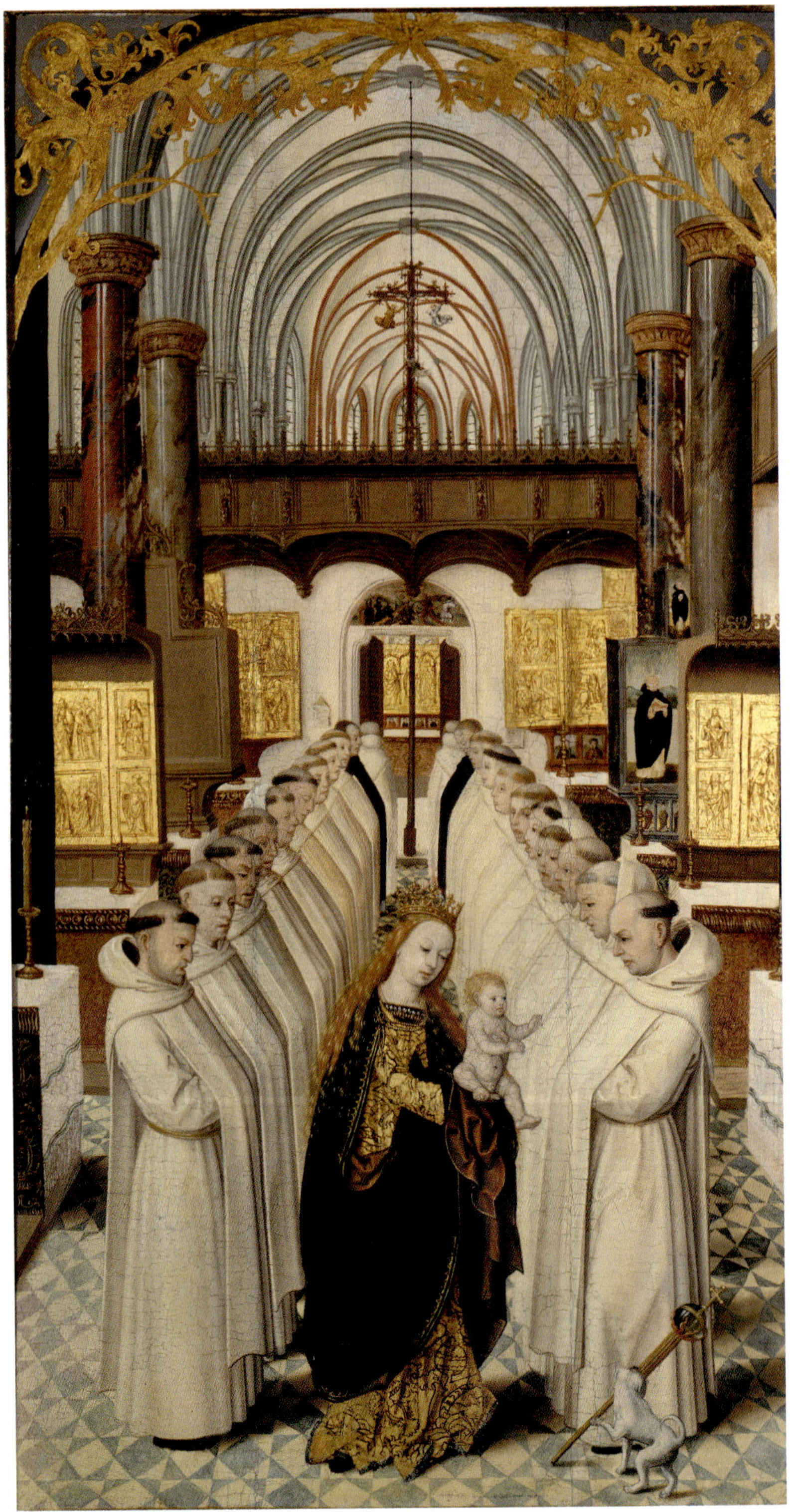

for the Oude Kerk in Delft, the cathedral in Freising, and the churches of St Sebaldus and St Lorenz in Nuremberg.[25] That for St Lorenz, home to Veit Stoss's *Annunciation of the Rosary* (**149**, itself intended to be hidden most of the time by a specially made cloth cover) and Adam Kraft's Sacrament House [**103, 104**], is particularly informative: it gives directions for how and when altars were to be dressed with textiles, lamps and candles, reliquary and other statues, and which altarpieces were to be opened on which feasts, usually those relating to the dedication of the altar or the relics it contained, although their opening, as far as we can tell, was not undertaken during mass, but was done by the sexton at the beginning of the day of the appropriate feast.[26] The St Lorenz altarpieces, and others in Germany and the Netherlands, often had two possible openings because they had double sets of wings and separate wings for the predella, which might be opened on their own.[27] In general, the first opening was used for the lesser feasts (which is probably what is meant by half-open in the Delft instructions), and the second, inner opening (fully open) for the more important ones.

That Andreas Stoss found it necessary to indicate so fiercely exactly when his father's altarpiece should be opened and closed might suggest that the procedures were not strictly adhered to everywhere. However, it seems likely that most altarpieces were only opened to their final, innermost view relatively rarely, and certainly they cannot have been opened every time mass was said before them, or every Sunday. The Marian altar in St Lorenz, now lost but set, probably, to the south of the high altar in the choir, was opened on only eleven days of the year, and other altars in that church had a similarly restrained schedule. However, because the church had at least fourteen altarpieces, there was no long period when all of them were closed, except during Lent. In a larger institution, like the collegiate church at Antwerp which had over fifty altarpieces, the potential for seeing something open every day must have been high. Nevertheless, it was only on two, exceptional, days in the year that every altar in St Lorenz was open at once—the feast of Corpus Christi (the Thursday following Trinity Sunday) and the eve of the festival of the display of the imperial relics (the second Friday after Easter). The contrast then with the normal viewing experience of one, two, or possibly three altars open at the same time would have been breathtaking, as a blaze of gold and a multiplicity of imagery was revealed around the whole church, an effect visible in a Northern Netherlandish painting showing *The Apparition of the Virgin* in a Dominican church [**168**] where all but two of the altarpieces, which are set against the choir screen, the pillars of the church, and in the choir beyond, are open.

Large-scale altarpieces with folding wings were made with an eye to the decorum of materials, as well as with the aim of maximizing the visual contrast between interior and exterior [**169, 170**]. Generally, materials become progressively richer, and scale or narrative complexity increases, as the wings open. There is a strict adherence to this hierarchy of material and visual sumptuousness, moving from subdued, flat, often painted exteriors to rich, three-dimensional interiors, carved in the round and extensively gilded. In Hermen Rode's St Luke Altarpiece in Lübeck, which has like many German retables two sets of wings hinged to one another, we can see the system in action.[28] The work moves through three stages and two openings with increasing splen-

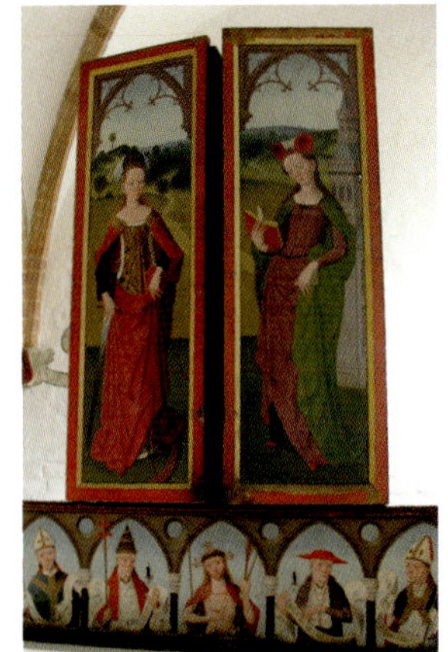

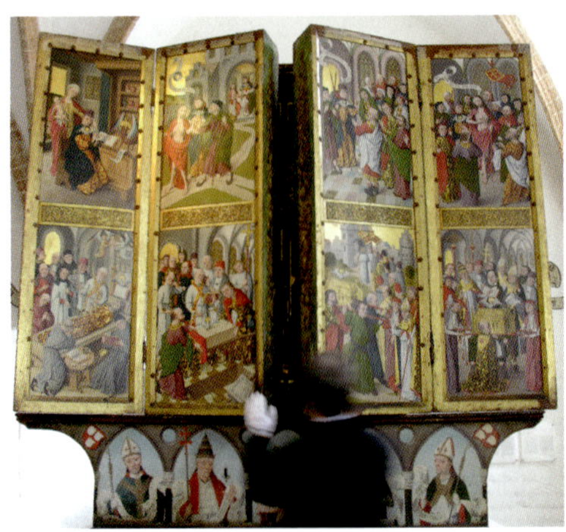

169 Hermen Rode

St Luke Altarpiece, painted panels, gilded and polychromed wood, dated 1484.

This work is signed by the Lübeck painter Hermen Rode (*fl.* 1468–*c.*1504) around the neck of the robe of a (painted) figure (a self-portrait?) helping to carry the relics of St Luke in one of the narratives of the first opening; the work has a date of 1484 on the slab of the saint's tomb in the same panel. Rode painted this retable for the recently-founded chapel of the painters' guild of St Luke in the Katharinenkirche in Lübeck.

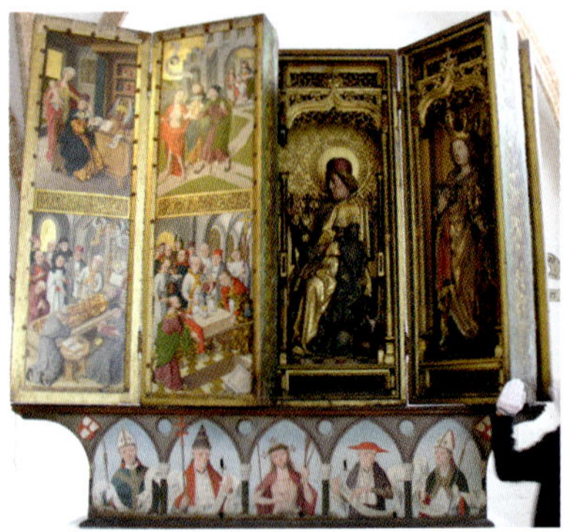

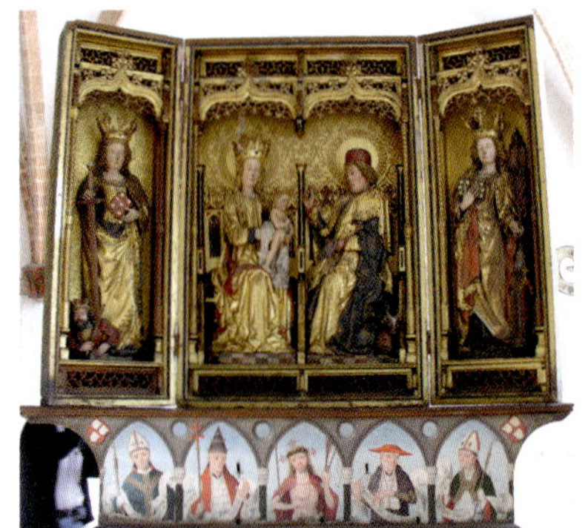

170 Hermen Rode

St Luke Altarpiece [**169**] in the process of opening the second set of wings to reveal the interior.
The interior has large carved and gilded figures of St Luke painting the Virgin, St Catherine (to whom the church in which the altar was placed was dedicated), and St Barbara. However, while the saint holds a palette and raises his hand to paint, there is no panel or easel, and there never was: the implication is that he is painting the sculpted image of the Virgin and Child represented here—a depiction which is extraordinary (compare more standard examples, **112**, **114**, **139**) but also an apt way of conflating the sculpted nature of the object with contemporary practice of polychroming sculpture and St Luke's famous painterly activity.

dour and (actual) depth as we travel from exterior to interior. Thus the altarpiece closed presents two standing saints entirely painted, in full colours but without any gilding [**169**]. The first opening displays another set of painted panels, but this time with lavish gilding behind eight scenes: we have moved up in terms of material richness as well as iconographic complexity, from two standing saints to eight busy narrative images. As this set of wings is opened (**170** shows this in action) the full splendour of the interior proper is revealed, with relief sculpture, part gilded, on the wings and three-dimensional, almost entirely gilded forms of the Virgin and St Luke in the interior *caisse*.

Of course, the move through from painted panels to low relief sculpture, to sculpture in the round or high relief that we see here and in many other retables was an artistic solution that made constructional sense: the wings had to be thinner and lighter than the *caisse* which had to support them on hinges, to make them easier to manoeuvre and less liable to sag or come away from their fixings over time. When works were as large as Veit Stoss's high altar for St Mary's church in Krakow (see the image facing the opening of this chapter), this was a serious consideration. Indeed, the development of this folding format for large-scale altarpieces may have been partly dependent on, and probably not unconnected to, the growing sophistication in carpentry and locksmithery at this period. However, we see a similar material hierarchy in

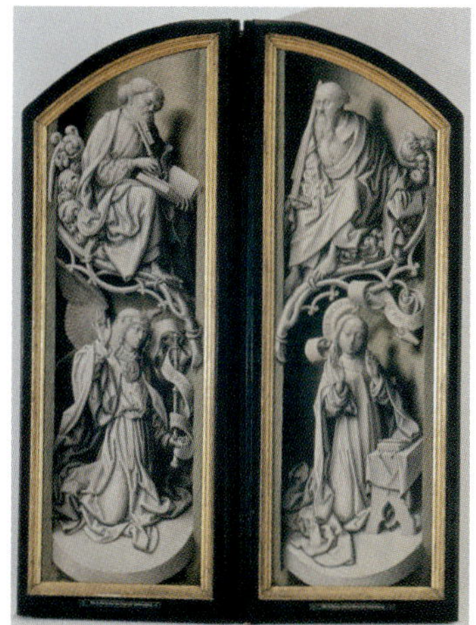

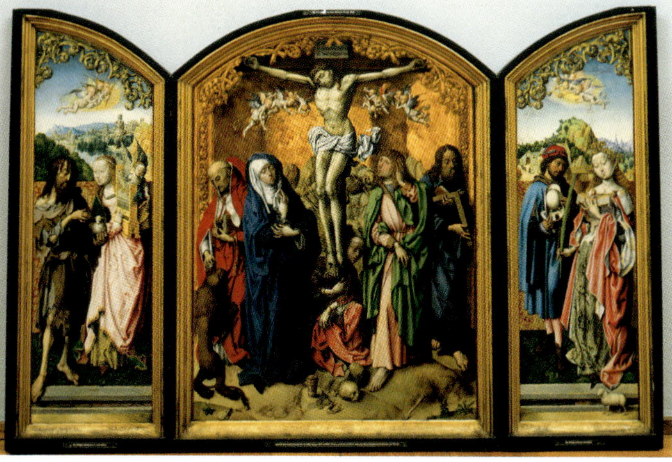

171 Master of the Altarpiece of St Bartholomew

The Annunciation with Saints Peter and Paul, exterior of the Holy Cross Altarpiece, oil on panel, 1490s/1500.

172 Master of the Altarpiece of St Bartholomew

The *Crucifixion with Saints*, interior of **171**.

The Bartholomew Master was the most inventive painter in Germany at the end of the fifteenth century. He made this altarpiece for the Cologne lawyer Peter Rink as a donation to the Cologne Carthusians. The fictive gold box in which the crucifixion is set is a device borrowed from Rogier van der Weyden [**20**], whose works this artist clearly knew: the Bartholomew Master plays with space in a similar way, the top of the cross being caught in the fictive tracery of the foremost plane of the box, while its base is set impossibly far back into the restricted landscape of the central scene.

altarpieces that were entirely painted with no sculptural interior, and where the solidity of the central panel and the lightness of the wings was less of an issue. Although the visual solutions to how interior and exterior are distinguished in these painted panels are somewhat different, they are equally successful in satisfying the dramatic, liturgical, and practical needs of such works.

In the Netherlands, and also in France and Germany under the influence of Netherlandish examples, the exterior panels of altarpieces were often painted in a manner referred to as grisaille, meaning painting in grey or limited colours, but this is not a contemporary term (having been coined in the seventeenth century by André Félibien to describe stained glass) and does not really adequately describe what is more precisely, in these instances, the imitation of stone sculpture [**171**]. This visual strategy of depicting unpainted stone sculpture on the exterior of an altarpiece worked on many different levels: it provided dramatic contrast with the sumptuously coloured interior [**171, 172**], while presenting a suitably less materially-rich image for Lent and ordinary feast days, and a more durable protective covering, easier to repaint and with no colours to fade, for the more important imagery of the interior. Moreover, it also enabled artists to develop ways of distinguishing different levels of reality—and thus presence—on the different visual fields of the work: when closed, what we see in a panel like that by the anonymous Cologne artist known as the Master of the St Bartholomew Altarpiece [**171**] is the representation in paint of a carved image, an earthly object that is made by human hands out of stone. The image on the interior, in contrast, is clearly a representation not of another image but of the sacred figures themselves [**172**].[29] Only the representation of unpainted stone could have such a clear effect in this respect. Stone sculpture was fairly frequently left unpolychromed (see the stone apostles around the choir in **6**), so the representation of it as such was neither extraordinary nor, in itself, defiantly not 'real'; however, if wood sculpture had been depicted in its almost ubiquitous polychromed state, the message that this is an image of an image, rather than a representation of a sacred figure, might have been less clear.

It was perhaps in this context—the desire to emphasize the man-made nature of images, at a period when reforming ideas about the problematic

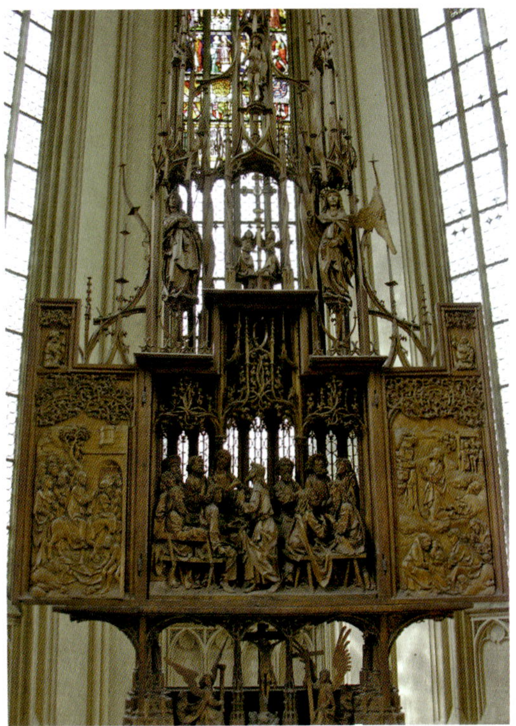

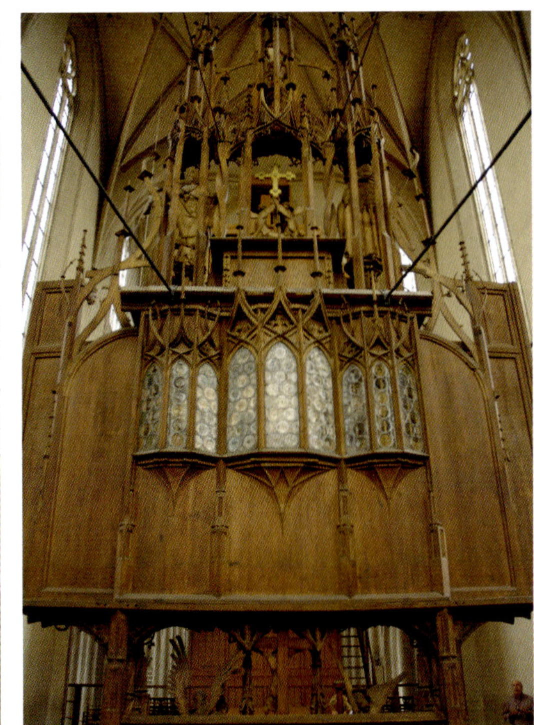

173 Tilman Riemenschneider

Altarpiece of the Holy Blood, fir (*caisse* and superstructure) and limewood (figurative work), 1499–1505.

This altarpiece was in a specially built upper chapel in St Jacob's, Rothenburg, designed to accommodate pilgrims, attracted by the indulgences attached to the relic of the Holy Blood it contained. Access must have been envisaged around the altarpiece since the reverse is finely worked with chapel-like windows; these provided dramatic and changing lighting effects for the central scene of the Last Supper, allowing the figures to stand out without polychromy. This *caisse* was not produced by Riemenschneider, however, and probably not designed by him, being contracted for separately from a cabinet maker who received a similar fee to that of the sculptor.

nature of (materially rich) images were being kindled—that the taste for unpainted carved retables developed in late fifteenth- and early sixteenth-century Germany, a mode practised and popularized by the Würzburg sculptor Tilman Riemenschneider. His Holy Blood Altarpiece (contracted for in 1499–1501) in the church of St Jacob in Rothenburg (where Friedrich Herlin had installed the high altar, **153**) was never intended to be painted, but was treated by the artist with a brown pigmented glaze to protect the wood and heighten the modelling of the surface, with touches of colour given to the lips, eyes, and drops of blood [**173**].[30] Perhaps here the focus on the relics, set originally in a (now missing) gold reliquary in the predella and in the (extant) gold cross on the top of the *caisse*, above the Last Supper, would have been made visually more emphatic by the startling sobriety of the central altarpiece itself.

In painted triptychs, the depiction of stone sculpture on the exterior wings of altarpieces also inverted the well-established hierarchy of media—a contemporary viewer would be used to seeing sculpture on the inside not the outside of wings, as in **170** (altarpieces without central carved elements, it should be remembered, remained a relatively unusual choice in most of the Netherlands and in German-speaking regions before 1500). Placing an illusion of sculpture on the exterior also demonstrated the ability of painting to defy the practical, material considerations of other media: stone sculpture could never, of course, be set on the exterior wings of altarpieces since it was simply impossible: no carpentry or hinges could support the weight of it on these moving extremities. Painting, therefore, made possible the impossible, and painters developed and complicated the idea further by representing

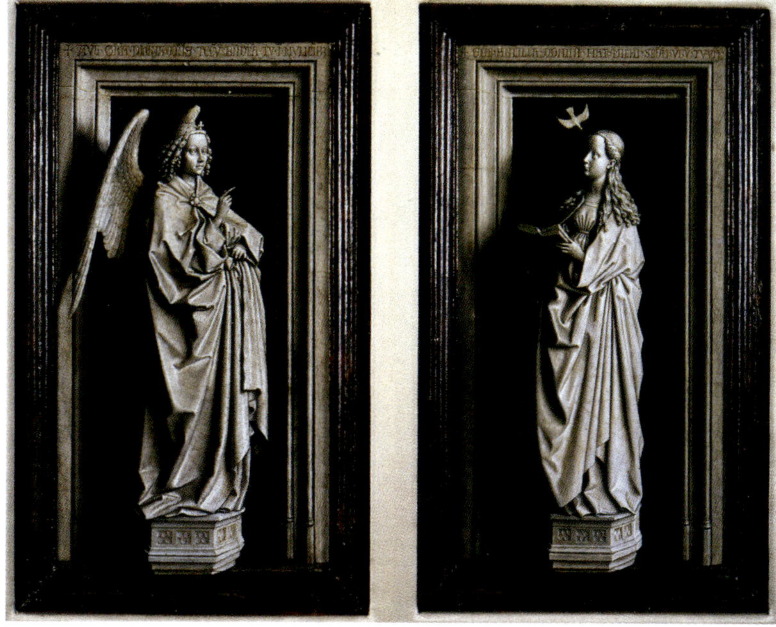

174 Jan van Eyck
Annunciation (the 'Thyssen Diptych'), oil on Baltic oak, *c.*1435.

sculpture that would have been near-impossible to carve, or in which there is ambiguity about whether what is represented is a sculpted or living form.

It is in this context which we should view the visual strategies of an image like the Thyssen Diptych by Jan van Eyck [**174**], which, typically for van Eyck, turns our expectations on their head.[31] This relatively small work (38.8 × 46.7 centimetres) creates an effective illusion of four different types of stone: the outer frame is painted to suggest red marble, the inner frame is a warm unpolished stone, probably a type of limestone, while the sheen on the figures of the Virgin and the Angel and their yellowish tone suggest they are carved from alabaster. Finally, they are set against highly polished, black Tournai stone, which reflects their forms just as the same material does on the tomb of Philip the Bold [**133**]. The illusion of stone might suggest that this work should be the exterior of a triptych, which would then open up to reveal a 'painted' interior. However, as the remnants of hinges on the inner edges of the panels indicate, the fictive sculpture is on the interior of the work. Moreover, the exterior was painted to resemble stone, and is absolutely flat, without any frame, an unusual treatment which would heighten the suggestion that this is a solid slab of marble. The impossible is thus made possible here: a diptych made of richly polished black stone, against which two figures, also of stone, are carved fully in the round, despite there being insufficient depth for them to be set there, with a stone frame, and all set into a marble block, would be impossible to close, hold, or even lift with ease. Van Eyck may, or may not, be deliberately competing with sculpture here; his acute awareness of other media and their visual language runs through many of his works [**18**, **97**]. He certainly produces here an image that displays the virtuosity of his technique and his sheer ability to create in paint an illusion of something else; the apparent totality of the illusion may be why this work, unusually for van Eyck, is not signed. But to get a sense of this play and how

175 Workshop of Hans Multscher

Christ on a Donkey, wood, polychromy, *c.*1430.

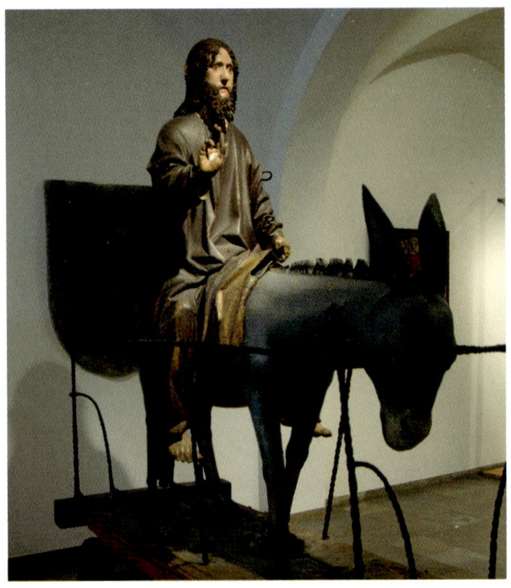

it manifested itself we need, again, to hold the object and manipulate it: it is its weight which would have seemed so incongruous, and its feel, making its nature as painted illusion absolutely clear, whether it had the painter's name displayed on it or not.

Liturgy, Ritual, and Experience

Although winged altarpieces and small devotional objects demanded handling to open and close or turn them over and round, the use of life-size sculpture in liturgical rituals and processions at this period took the physical manipulation of the image and the potential drama of its form to an entirely different level. Many wooden polychromed figures bear physical evidence of their use in this manner: they may be fitted with wheels to move them, hooks to hoist them upwards, have flexible, jointed arms and legs, removable parts, even cavities for (imitation) blood, and may show wear and tear from handling and kissing. Textual sources such as *ordinarium* (books detailing liturgical practice) and historical accounts reveal in some detail how sculpted figures were used in religious drama, which often involved music, sound, and lighting effects, while members of the clergy dressed up to play supporting roles in the performance which involved the manipulation of these images in various ways.

Most of these rituals involved re-enactments of events in the life of Christ, focused mainly on the feasts around Easter, and seem to have been most widely practised in Germany, where many of the surviving examples of sculptures used in this manner come from. The dramas began with the Palm Sunday procession, four weeks before Easter, in which a life-size carved representation of Christ on a donkey [**175**], blessing, was wheeled around the town while people threw palm leaves at its feet in re-enactment of his entry into Jerusalem; the wheels or carts which many of these carved groups still retain allow no doubt as to their having been used in this manner. Detachable figures of Christ with jointed arms, removable nails, and crown of thorns played a starring role in the Good Friday rites: Christ was taken

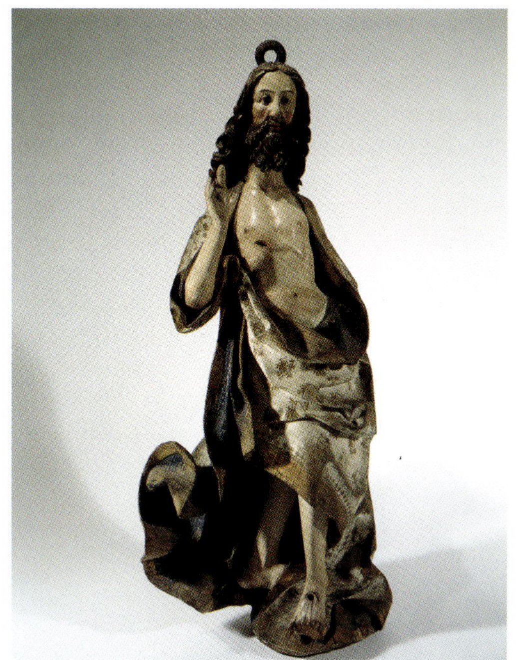

176 Martin Gramp

Christ Ascending, limewood, polychromy, 1503.

This figure retains its original metal hook by which it was hoisted up into the roof of the church, and damage to the prominently presented right foot suggests this area was frequently touched and kissed.

down from the cross, the nails and crown of thorns removed (sometimes held by two clergy dressed as angels), his wounds kissed, his body wrapped in the shroud (with his face left visible) and carried (on a stretcher) to be deposited in a tomb, often specially made for this purpose, or on the altar, which stood symbolically for the sepulchre where he remained until resurrected on Easter Day.

The resurrection drama required, however, a different figure from that put in the tomb, since it needed to present a different visual aspect, with Christ's suffering gone and His right hand raised in blessing [**176**]. On Easter morning, this life-size figure was placed on the altar, where it would remain for forty days until the feast of the Ascension at which point it was used to act out perhaps the most dramatic and mechanically complicated ceremony of all, which could involve an additional cast of sculpted figures such as angels, the Virgin and the apostles. A *liber ordinarius* written in 1532 for Cardinal Albrecht of Brandenburg (1490–1545) is precise in its details about the Ascension day liturgy as practised at Halle in Germany, where Albrecht had himself donated the figures to be used in the service (which in this case were, unusually, of silver).[32] The text prescribes how a procession carrying the figures of Christ, the Virgin, and the apostles should enter the church and stop in the nave under the 'Himmelsloch', a hole in the roof created specially for this purpose. There the figure of Christ was placed on a red velvet stool and on a table near him the Virgin and twelve apostles were set out in a semi-circle. Hymns were sung and, to the words of the rite for the feast of the Ascension, the figure of Christ was lifted up while a choir, hidden inside the roof of the church, answered with further sung liturgy. Three angels holding candles then descended from the ceiling to collect the figure of Christ, the wound on whose right foot was kissed by all the officiating clergy as ropes were attached to the statue. With the figure facing east, it was hoisted up though the Himmelsloch, a golden carpet held up under the figure until it disappeared safely (a wise precaution, as one of these figures fell and killed the provost at the Augustine convent in Bernried in 1433). Down through the hole as Christ disappeared hosts might be thrown, or in some places flowers, while a drum simulated the sound of thunder. In other even more dramatic versions a burning figure of the devil could be thrown back down from the Himmelsloch. More singing followed, and finally all the candles in the church were extinguished.[33]

The figure of Christ from the Cathedral of St Nicolas at Fribourg [**176**], dated 1503, was clearly used as part of such a dramatic staging: it has a metal ring set in its head to allow it to be hoisted skywards and it is carved fully in the round. The function of this figure has clearly had an impact on its form: it was cleverly designed to double for the rituals of both Resurrection and Ascension, combining a pose suitable for the risen Christ with a dynamic sense of movement achieved by billowing drapery, especially effective as the figure was hoisted skywards during the Ascension. Christ's right foot is set very prominently forwards, perfectly placed to facilitate its kissing as part of the ritual described above.

The importance of sculpture in the visual culture and liturgical practices of the time becomes clear when we consider its flexibility and adaptability: this is most emphatically conveyed by the practices recorded at St Lorenz in Nuremberg where a generic carved female saint was brought out at various feasts during which she was altered by the addition of appropriate props to convert her into the figure required for the day: on 19 November she became St Elizabeth of Hungary, with the addition of a veil, a crown, and a loaf of bread; on 21 January 'one puts a crown on the image and gives it a little lamb in its hand', turning her into St Agnes; an arrow made her St Ursula on 21 October.[34] The number of generic carved saints surviving from this period and region suggest that this was not an isolated practice, and the production of deliberately non-specific saints may have been an important part of a sculptor's workshop output. Such alteration was neither possible nor practical with a panel painting.

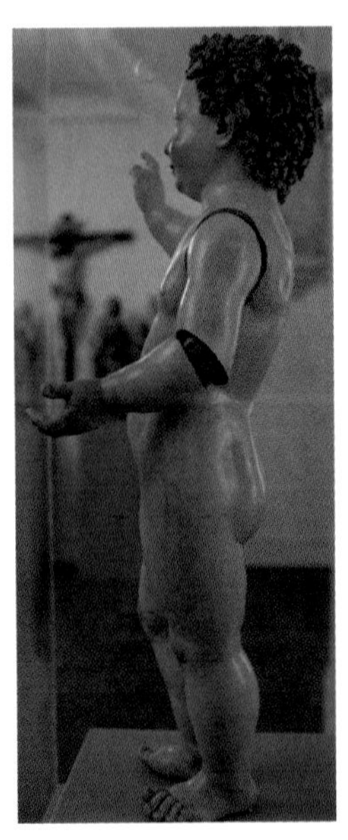

177 Michael Erhart
Blessing Christ Child with jointed arms, polychromed wood, *c.*1480.

The ability to dress sculpture and adapt it in various ways was also key to the popularity of life-size carved and painted Christ Child figures, which might have jointed arms [**177**] and their own set of clothes, some of which survive today. These figures could be used for more intimate devotional activities. Textual sources from female convent communities concern the part played by these and similar figures of the Christ Child with its crib in contemplative and richly imaginative activities, during which the nun was encouraged to pick up the child, suckle it, and so on.[35]

Sculpture could also play vital roles in civic processions: a rare surviving example is the recently rediscovered 'pareerkersse' or banner carried in the elaborate procession of the Holy Blood in Bruges, an annual event which still takes place today.[36] This object would have been fixed to a pole, carried with three other identical items by the four youngest members of the Holy Blood confraternity, and is carved ingeniously to be lightweight and to work from the front and the reverse; it still retains the metal hooks around the edge from which the heraldic shields of the confraternity members would have been attached [**178**].

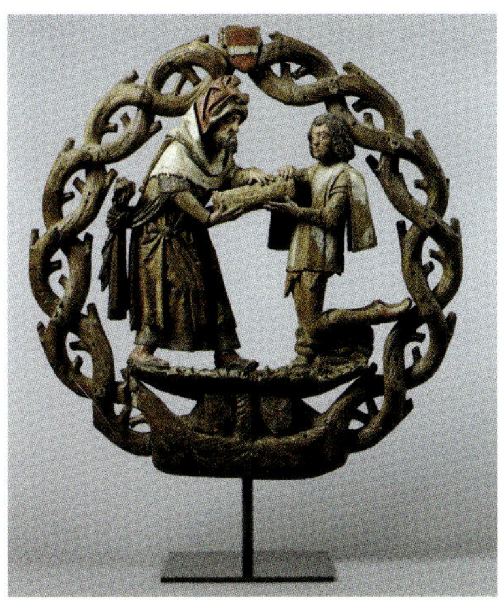
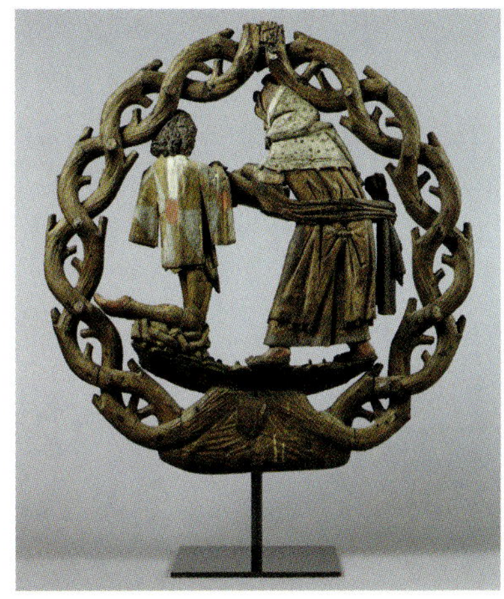

178 Bruges (?) sculptor

'Pareerkersse' (banner) of the confraternity of the Holy Blood, oak, with remains of gilding and polychromy, *c.*1480.

The banner represents an event from *c.*1150 when Baudouin III presented the relic of the Holy Blood to Thierry of Alsace, Count of Flanders. Originally a pelican feeding her chicks with her blood was set between the figures, but only their feet remain; the entwined branches in a circle represent the crown of thorns, speckled with drops of red representing the blood of Christ. This carving is designed to be lightweight and visible from front and back, being worked and polychromed on both sides.

Unlike the extensive gilding found on sculpture in the interior of altarpieces, the wooden images intended to be used in these civic and liturgical dramas and devotional activities were usually painted to be as life-like as possible, sometimes remarkably so, and it is unsurprising that in the Reformation they were a main target for the iconoclasts. The Bishop of Rochester's 'famous movable crucifix' which could nod his head, roll his eyes, shake his beard, and buckle his legs was publicly dismembered and burnt in 1538.[37] In 1533, in Augsburg, the rope hoisting the figure which Anton Fugger had newly (and secretly) had made of the ascending Christ was cut by iconoclasts during the service, and the figure, falling onto the hard stone floor of the church, was destroyed.[38]

Many of these sculptures, like the interior of altarpieces, gained part of their dramatic power from being visible only for certain periods of the year, and through the processes of revealing and concealing, bringing out and putting away, which their use entailed. Other types of imagery at this period in churches and chapels gained similar dramatic presence from being on display only at certain feasts or points in the liturgical year, or by being seen only by a restricted audience or in a particular way. This was the case, for example, with reliquaries containing the bones of saints, which would normally be kept locked away in the sacristy and only visible on the altar (as is that of St Hubert in **6**) or carried in procession on the saints' feasts or related days. It was also the case with sets of tapestries designed to be hung around the liturgical choir, where the high altar was located and in which the clergy and canons had their stalls. These hangings were often donated by bishops or canons, who specified in their donations that the works were only to be hung on certain high feasts, a practice underlined in church necrologies. That for Le Mans, whose choir tapestries were given in 1509 by the canon, Martin Guerande, states that 'the said tapestry should be unrolled, hung, and displayed in the stalls of the choir, behind the canons, all in their seats, on certain holy days'.[39] Such gifts were frequently recorded in both inscriptions and donor portraits within the tapestry as seen in those still hung around the choir of Notre Dame, Beaune [**179**]. The act of unrolling and hanging them must have been a ritual in itself. Their presence enhanced the splendour of the most important feasts; moreover, access to the choir, the most important part of the church, was often

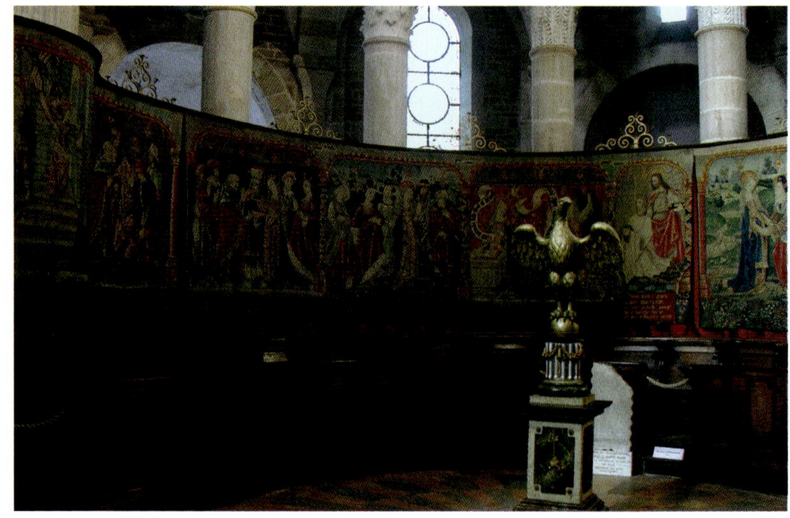

179 Southern Netherlandish weavers, probably after a cartoon by Pierre Spicre

Scenes from the Life of the Virgin, wool tapestries around the choir of the collegiate church of Notre Dame, Beaune, designed 1474, woven 1500.

Donor portraits could appear in tapestries as well as paintings, stained glass, and manuscripts; here Canon Hugues le Coq, who paid for the weaving of these tapestries (the designs had been commissioned by Cardinal Jean Rolin some twenty years earlier), was depicted twice, once in prayer to the Annunciation, presented by St John the Baptist (seen here), and again to the Coronation of the Virgin presented by St Hugues; the main audience for choir tapestries such as these was the clergy who sat in the space enclosed by them during special feasts.

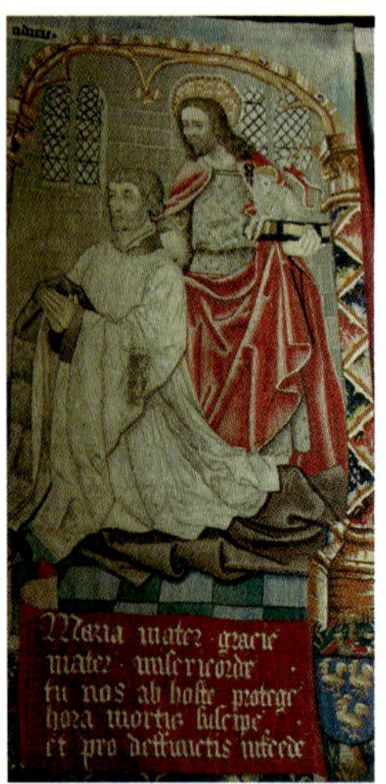

limited to the clergy, or to the highest ranking laymen and women (see **191, 197–9**, where the choice of the choir of a large cathedral or collegiate church as a setting for the devotions of the King and Queen of Scotland and the Duchess of Burgundy was not without resonance).

The act of viewing an image, of gaining access to its often restricted presence, moving towards and around it, and saying prayers before it, all appear to have been important aspects of the way certain monumental works of art were intended to be experienced, and their appearance was thus determined by this dramatic aspect of their use. This is most evidently the case for life-size stone Entombment groups, another type of work distinctive to our period, only emerging in the late fourteenth century in this particular form and reaching the height of its popularity in the second half of the fifteenth century: surviving examples are numerous in the Netherlands, France, Germany, and Spain, as well as Italy, but the largest number are in France. One of the most impressive and well preserved of these, which is also remarkably well documented, is that made in 1453–4 for the hospital foundation of Notre-Dame de Fontenilles at Tonnerre, about 70 kilometres north of Dijon [**180, 181**], by a partnership of two stone sculptors, Jean Michel and Georges de la Sonnette, who are otherwise unknown to us.[40]

This monument, like many similar examples, was not connected to an altar and played no discernible or documented part in liturgical dramas. Most frequently paid for by individuals and not by church bodies or civic groups like confraternities, they were often designed to have a funerary role, with the donor and his family buried in front of them or nearby. Some at least were expected to become objects of renown that would draw visitors and pilgrims, through which the church in which they were set would benefit financially, and the donor spiritually. Some, such as those at Langres and Neufchatel in France, had indulgences attached to them granting remission from sins for those who visited them on certain feast days (usually a lent of 40 days, but sometimes up to 100).[41] The foundation document for the Tonnerre example, which was paid for by a merchant, Lancelot de Buronfosse, makes the financial hopes of the hospital in which the monument was situated very explicit, and much more besides. It states that:

> [Lancelot de Buronfosse] has had newly made with his own money in honour of God and for the increase, great benefit, utility and profit of our church and hospital, now and for the future, a very rich, notable and godly sanctuary, that is to say a Holy Sepulchre, which is placed and set in a chapel of our said church ... which Holy Sepulchre is and will be for the time to come a thing of very great profit and great revenue for our said church and which has cost a great sum of money to the said Lancelot.

That this work, and others like it, are referred to in contemporary documents as holy sepulchres, not as entombments, indicates that it is not simply a scene from Christ's Passion which is being recreated here but an idea of the actual place, the tomb of Christ in the Holy Land. And the sense of visiting a place is created in the form and setting of this work, which carefully considered the manner in which the whole was to be experienced. Thus, it is not placed in open view in the hospital church, but is accessed by going to the far east end of that huge structure, where a small, locked door in the furthermost corner of the wall must be opened to allow the visitor to descend nine steps into a narrow vaulted room that was specially made to house it [**180, 181**].

The movement downwards, into a darker (although not unlit) space, deliberately enclosed, would have evoked the idea of the holy sepulchre itself, if not its historical form. That such considerations were important, and that their effect on the devotional experience provided by such works was actively considered, are spelled out in a document concerning another, now lost, Holy Sepulchre to be erected in the church of St Peter in Douai (northern France), according to the terms of a foundation by a citizen of that town, Giles de Buissy, in memory of himself and his wife Margaret. Giles set out how one should enter the chapel (one way, through an iron gate) and exit (another way, via a different gate) and that, most revealingly, 'this place must not be large and light, but small and dark, for devotion'.[42] Such an effect is taken to extremes at the Adornes chapel in Bruges, begun by Pieter and Jacob Adornes and finished by Pieter's son Anselm, as the family's funerary chapel and as a complete recreation of the church of the Holy Sepulchre in Jerusalem, which Anselm had visited on pilgrimage to the Holy Land in 1470–1 (before which he had bequeathed the two van Eyck paintings to his daughters, see **130**, **131**, and p. 284–5 below).[43] Here, at the back of the chapel, a small opening, only two or three feet high, allows the devotee to clamber though, on their knees, to a dark, confined space, to witness a life-size stone figure of the body of Christ.

At Tonnerre the scene acted out by the stone figures in the chapel is revealed to the visitor in stages: when the door is opened all that is visible are the feet of Christ and the figure of Nicodemus; as one descends the steps the rest of the group comes into view but Christ's head remains obscured by the back of Joseph of Arimathea. Only when one has fully entered the chapel and moved into the middle and far end of the space is the whole of Christ's body revealed [**181**]. As the viewer approaches, the inscription on Nicodemus' robe, split across the sleeves of both arms, becomes visible, in the proper sequence (first the right arm, then the left). It reads 'Adorate eum' (Worship him) on the right arm, and 'O vos vide(te)' (O you who see) on the left.

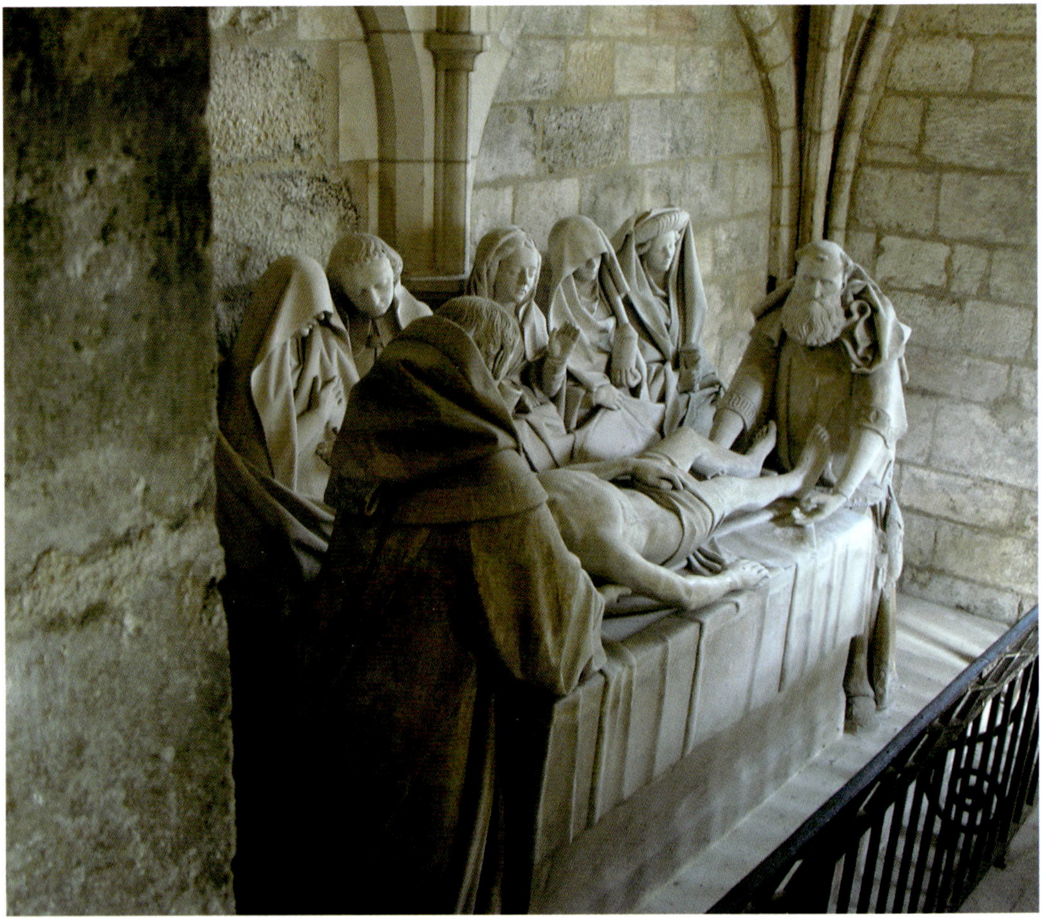

180 Jean Michel and Georges de la Sonnette

Entombment, stone 1453–4. As approached from the entrance to the chapel.

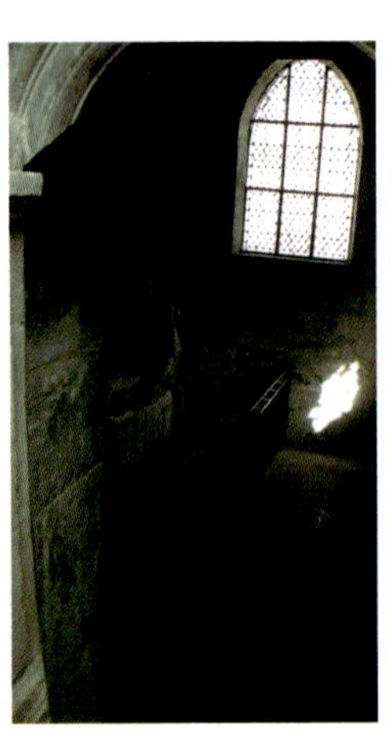

The intense immediacy of this work and the sense of being witness to an actual moment in the drama is enhanced by the scale of the figures (slightly over life-size), their powerful characterization, and the confined nature of the narrow space which forces the viewer into close proximity to them. The effect is further heightened by the showing of a very particular moment of action: Christ's body has only just made contact with the tomb slab, and has not yet been fully laid to rest on it; Nicodemus has just set down Christ's right foot and removed his hand from it, while his right hand holds the calf of Christ's left leg and is putting that gently in place; Joseph of Arimathea still supports Christ's shoulders, but as he lays them down Christ's head has fallen dramatically backwards. As in so many of the best works from our period, the technical virtuosity of the piece is vital to its impact and effect: the sense of movement and arrested drama is achieved by the sculptor's ability to carve Christ's body almost free of the slab. Most other stone groups of this sort have Christ already laid fully on the tomb or wrapped in the shroud.

In contrast to the works discussed above which relied, in part, on revelation for their effect, other images were distinguished by being permanently visible, to provide both protection and salvation. The large, folding, carved retables of Germany and Austria we have already considered were also

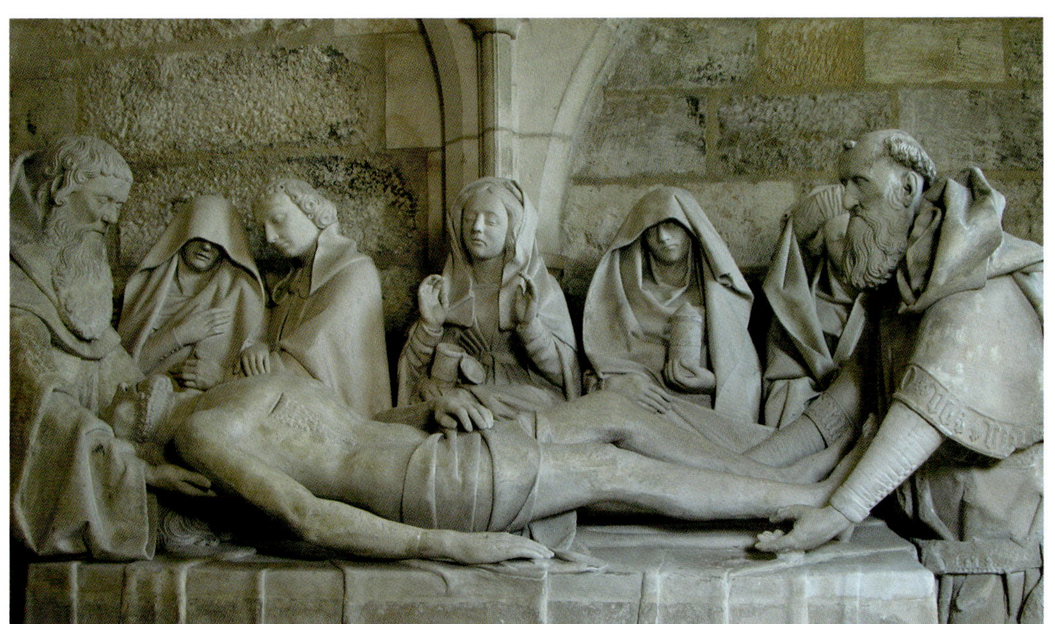

181 Jean Michel and Georges de la Sonnette

Entombment [**180**] viewed from inside the chapel.

designed so that, even when closed, an image of Christ's body, either crucified or as the Man of Sorrows, was constantly visible, since it was usually set high up in the *gesprung* (superstructure), which had no closing elements and whose height ensured it could be seen from far away [**153, 154, 173**]. Images on rood screens, often a giant crucifix and related figures [**151**] were even more visually dominant and available to anyone entering the church. Easy visual access was also a fundamental principle in the form of images of St Christopher, usually wall paintings in churches set near or opposite the door, so that they were easily visible on entering; the giant carved wooden St Christopher from Berne (**7**, **8**, discussed in Part I) was set over the town gate, providing a similarly constantly accessible situation. These settings allowed people to catch a glimpse of St Christopher on their everyday business, vital since the act of saying a prayer before an image of this saint was believed to protect one from sudden death (without last rites), which was particularly feared. Such images were in a sense public property, available to all.

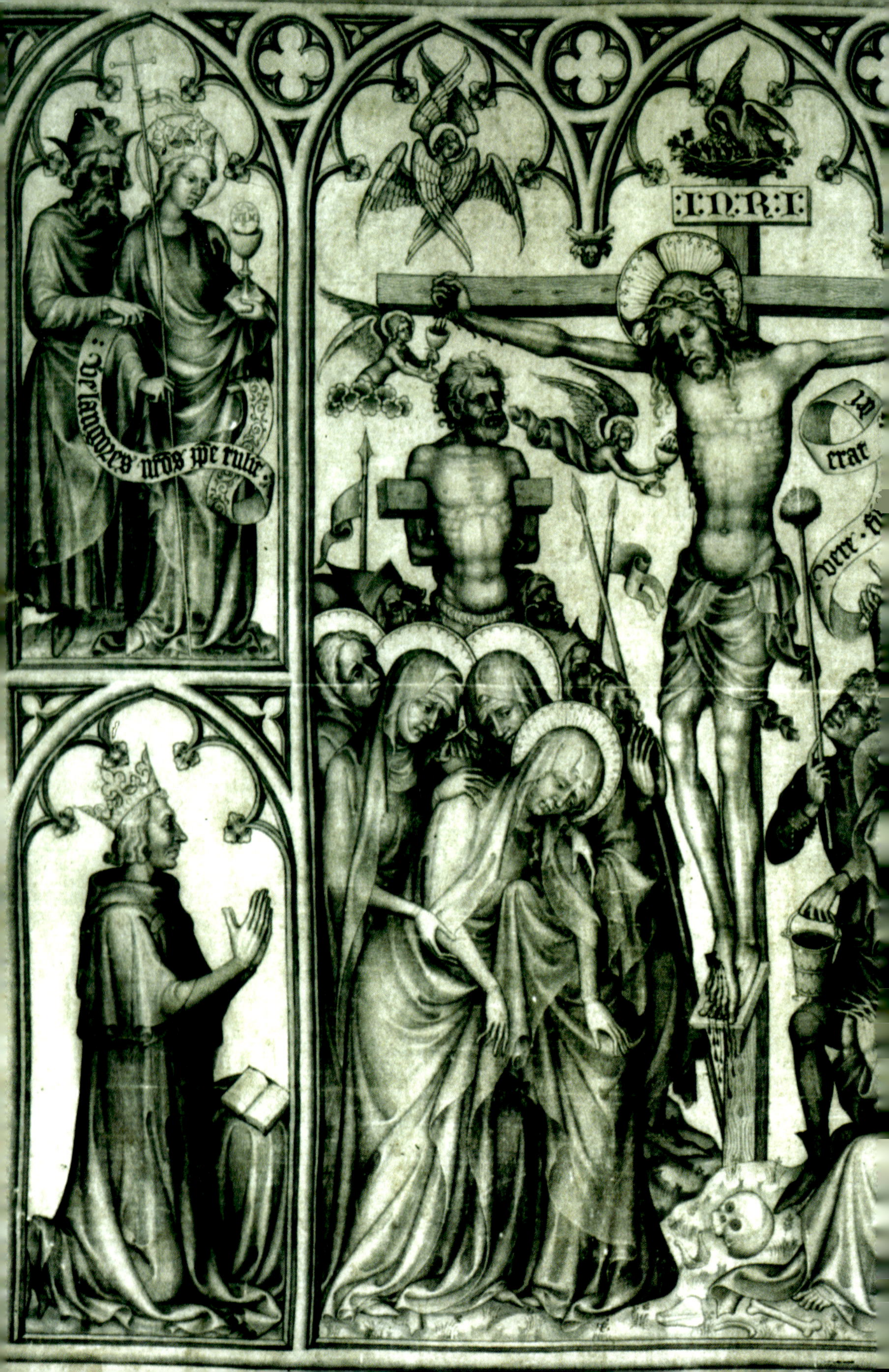

I.N.R.I.

Settings, Vistas, and Accoutrements for Mass and Prayer

... to inflame or embrace contemplation requires things of the senses: that is to say natural places, which are good for this, like the mountains of Sion, or Mount Sinai, or the Mont Saint Michel, or others and also temples, and other edifices, images, paintings, hangings, vestments, relics, smells, lights, good words, beautiful singing, lovely sounds from musical instruments ...

Nicolas Oresme (d. 1382), in his commentary on the *Politique* of Aristotle, which he translated for Charles V[1]

17

Chapels and Oratories

Mountains and natural places may have been ideal locations for contemplation and devotion, but they were not the only ones, as Oresme's text acknowledges, and they were certainly not the most accessible or convenient. In Christine de Pisan's biography of Charles V of France, we have some indication of where and when a figure such as the king might actually practise prayer. According to Christine, Charles began his day with morning prayers in his private chamber, followed by high mass at matins (around 8 am) in a 'public' arena, his domestic Grande Chapelle (which could be a fairly large space). Charles then retired to his oratory to hear mass again, more privately, later in the day.[2] These different spaces—the bedchamber, the domestic chapel (which required papal authorization for the celebration of mass), and the private oratory which was often attached in some manner to the larger palace chapel or to a public church—might be decorated and furnished in different ways and provided with a range of imagery and accoutrements for mass and prayer, the diversity and richness of which we can deduce from surviving examples, documentary sources, and visual evidence in images of people at prayer, such as **191**, **197**, and **198**.

Perhaps the best preserved, but also the most lavish and exceptional of all private chapels is that of the Holy Cross (originally called the chapel of the Passion) built by the Holy Roman Emperor Charles IV of Bohemia (1316–78) between 1348 and 1365 as part of his castle at Karlštejn, 'called after our name, in lasting commemoration of ourselves'.[3] Although Charles was not often at Karlštejn after 1365, this castle was the only one of the many he built in which he actually resided, and its foundation charter, which has many precise and detailed specifications (no contact with women allowed in the chapel tower, for example, even spouses), indicates how important its chapels were to him; indeed, in 1357 he founded a college of twelve canons, bound to reside in the castle, to undertake liturgical duties there.

Charles V in prayer to the crucifixion, detail of 194

182 Bohemian architect and builders

Karlštejn Castle, 30 km south-west of Prague, exterior, 1348–*c*.1365.

The chapel of the Holy Cross, the most sacred room in the castle, was on the second floor of the three-storey Great Tower (the tall, dominant tower on the left), reached by a staircase on the south wall; it was built with exceptionally massive masonry and its own fortification wall.

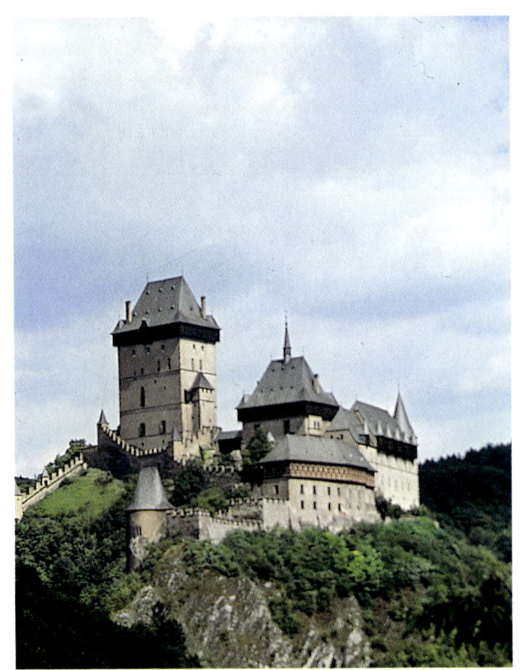

The chapel of the Holy Cross was of special significance since it housed the most precious of Charles's Passion relics, as well as the imperial relics he guarded in his role as Holy Roman Emperor; a contemporary report on its consecration stated that 'in all the world no castle or chapel is so precious and meritorious a work, for there he [Charles IV] has deposited the imperial insignia and the treasure of all his kingdom'. Indeed, relics are displayed or buried literally everywhere in this chapel: bricked up in the wall above the entrance door and under the plaster in the walls of the room (one of them a crocodile's head—perhaps meant to be part of St George's dragon), set into the altar, placed behind the grille above the altar and below the imported Italian triptych on the altar (the imperial relics), and most visibly set into a cavity in the lower frame of most of the 129 panel paintings of saints lining the walls, executed by Master Theoderic, the court painter (*fl.* third quarter of fourteenth century) [**182, 183**].

The Holy Cross chapel was thus a *libretto* on a large scale, a reliquary that one could walk into and around. To visit it was, and is, a dramatic experience: the chapel is situated on the second floor of the larger of Karlštejn's two towers, the Great Tower, and is accessed only by a long, winding, narrow staircase painted with narrative murals of the lives of Wenceslas and Ludmilla, both important Bohemian saints. The chapel walls are several feet thick and the door barring its entrance is vast and heavy, with several locks. Once these have been undone and the door opened, the contrast between dark passageway and glorious, gilded interior is overwhelming, even if the original windows in the chapel, which were set with semi-precious stones, would have provided a very diffuse, subdued light. It is as if one has stepped inside a gilded retable, not simply opened its wings: here in a large, double vaulted space, every part

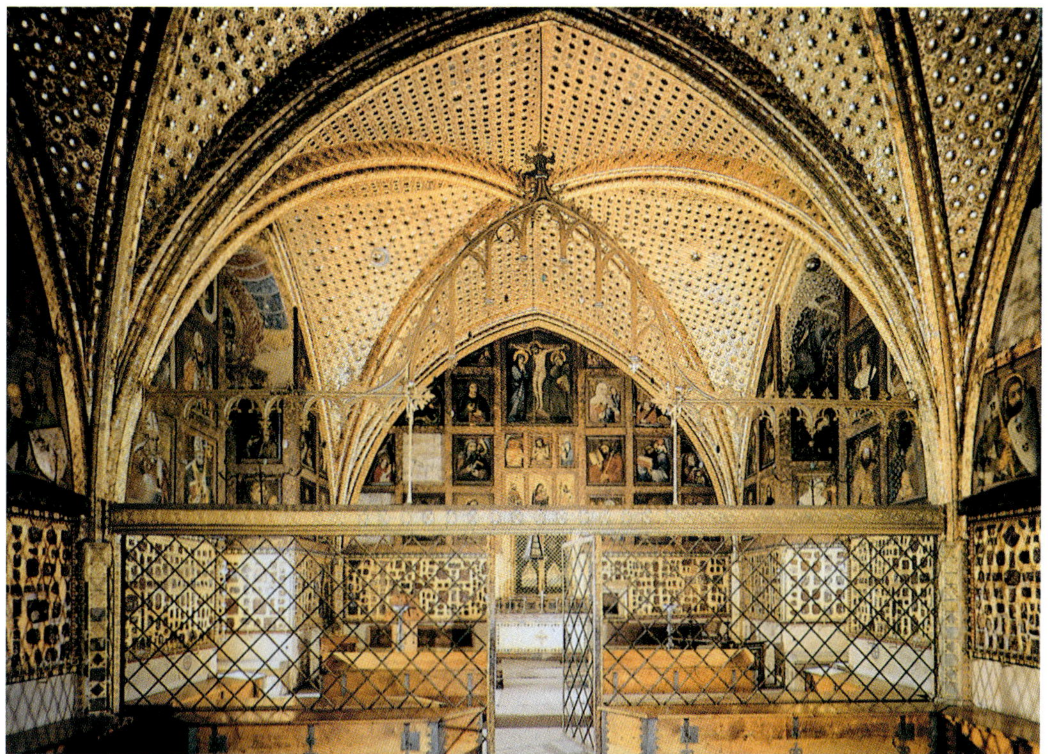

183 Master Theoderic

Interior of the Holy Cross chapel, Karlštejn Castle, view of south wall, walls set with painted panels, hard stones, and murals, vaults gold leaf and gilded glass, 1365–7.

The decoration of this large and extraordinary chapel lined with 129 panel paintings of bust-length saints is the only documented work by Charles IV's court painter Master Theoderic, for which he received a grant of land in Morina. Charles IV also incorporated an imported, earlier work into this scheme, a triptych by the Italian painter Tomaso da Modena, which was set in pride of place covering the space behind the high altar where the imperial relics and insignia were kept.

of every wall is either gilded, encrusted with jasper, or covered with wall and panel paintings, their surfaces rich in raised tin-relief decoration, while the ceiling is studded with crystal balls. Its form and painted decoration presage the Second Coming (scenes from Revelation appear in the window embrasures) while the gilding and jasper evoke the heavenly Jerusalem, described in Revelation (21:9–22) as a city of gold with walls of precious stones. The range and breadth of reference and allusion in this chapel with its extensive figurative decoration are indicated by the spiked metal railing around the entire wall of the chapel. Once thought to be a method of holding candles, it is now believed to represent the crown of thorns, part of which Charles IV had acquired in 1356 from John II of France (1319–64), father of Charles V, and which had particular meaning and power as the primary relic of the French monarchy, bound up with ideas of God-given kingship.

We do not know exactly how Charles IV used the chapel of the Holy Cross. Its deliberate inaccessibility—it was in a separate tower to the emperor's apartments and could only be reached by the steep, narrow stair—suggests that it was more a safe and suitably splendid repository for the relics than an everyday chapel: there were four other, more intimate or accessible chapels in the castle where Charles might hear mass when he was in residence. Some idea of how he may have behaved in the chapel and towards its contents can be gleaned, however, from the vivid description by Christine de Pisan of how the emperor acted before similar relics at the Sainte-Chapelle in Paris when he visited that church as part of his sojourn in the French capital in 1378. The

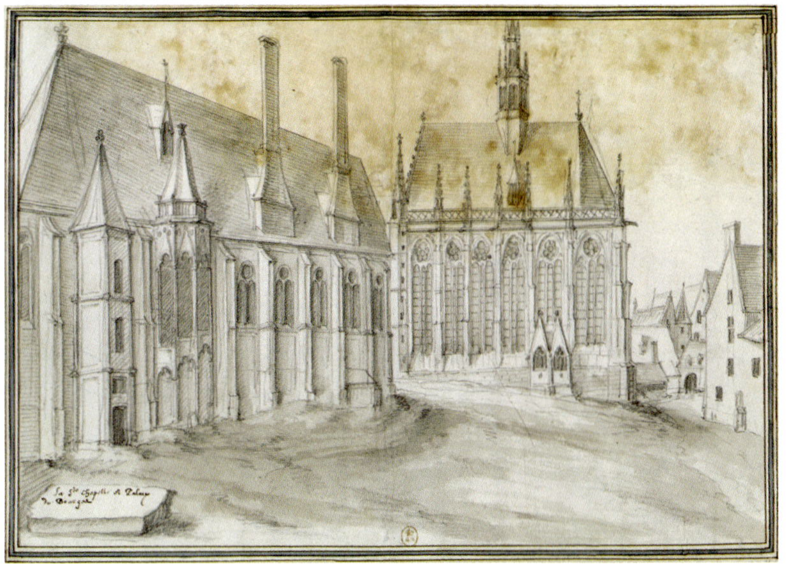

184 Etienne Martellange

View of Jean de Berry's Sainte-Chapelle at Bourges, drawing of *c.*1615.

Visible on this drawing are the private oratories built into the wall of the building, which were described in 1461 by a Florentine ambassador on a visit to Bourges. He noted that they each had their own fireplace and altar, and were cleverly designed so that the person within them was hidden from view.

day was, importantly, the feast of the Epiphany (the three kings). Christine records that the emperor 'ardently desired to see the relics' and when the *châsse* (reliquary) which held them was opened he removed his hat, and, with hands joined, prayed for a long time, fervently and in tears; he kissed the relics, asked for his chair to be placed so that they might be 'always in front of his eyes', and refused to go into the fabric oratory (see below) that had been prepared for him lest he lose sight of them.[4]

The idea of a chapel designed around the relics it contained derived, of course, from this very Sainte-Chapelle in Paris that Charles IV visited, built by St Louis in the late thirteenth century to house the crown of thorns. In the fourteenth century, the French princes of the blood, who were given thorns from this crown, established their own Sainte-Chapelles attached to their residences: most notably Jean de Berry at Bourges and Riom. For the building of a Sainte-Chapelle three criteria had to be met: it had to contain a Passion relic, to follow the form of the Paris Sainte-Chapelle, and to be a collegiate foundation. Deliberately following the architectural model of the Paris exemplar, these buildings thus had a very different effect from Charles IV's relic chapel at Karlštejn, relying instead on height, delicacy and expanses of stained glass for their visual impact. The Sainte-Chapelle at Bourges (destroyed in the late eighteenth century, but recorded in drawings such as **184**) was probably the most splendid.[5] Francesco di Neri Cecci, a member of a Florentine embassy that visited Bourges in 1461, called it, for its wealth of relics and the objects in its treasury, 'the most admirable in the world', noting in particular its vast brass chandelier and the very fine tomb of the duke set below it in the choir.[6] Some of the glass from its extensive windows survives, very possibly designed by the sculptor André Beauneveu [**185**]; it depicted prophets and apostles, themes dear to Jean de Berry, set into fictive architectural niches.[7] The same Florentine ambassador was particularly taken by the effects this produced, noting that 'the luminous colours are so strong that the

185 Designed by André Beauneveu (?)

Apostle and Prophet, stained glass from the Sainte-Chapelle, Bourges.

Glass could play a vital role in the iconographic programme of any chapel: Jean de Berry extended his interest in the theme of prophets and apostles (see **78**) through the glass in his Sainte-Chapelle, of which only fragments remain. Their design is possibly by Beauneveu, Berry's 'master of works of carving and painting', who the chronicler Jean Froissart claimed had 'no equal in any land'. The play between the figures and their architectural settings is particularly inventive; see, however, a similar effect in stone in **133**, designed at a contemporary moment.

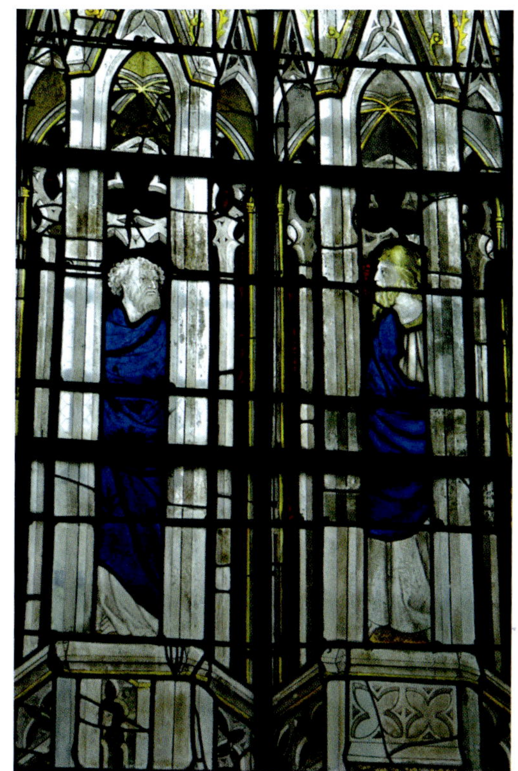

sun cannot go through them'. This chapel also had an additional purpose to the Paris Sainte-Chapelle or the Holy Cross chapel at Karlštejn: it was to be Jean de Berry's burial place, an extraordinary privilege for which he would have had to get papal permission: burial within a household chapel, which essentially this was, was not normally allowed. With this in mind, Berry not only gave many of his most precious objects to the foundation, but had at least two sets of life-size figures of himself and his wife at prayer made in stone and set, probably, inside and outside the building. In contrast, there were no images of Charles IV in his chapel at Karlštejn, although one of the Magi in a wall painting there bears his features. Berry's chapel, and its decoration, was thus as much about memory and perpetual prayer for his soul as a place to keep and venerate relics.

Domestic chapels in castles or chateaux, having begun as the preserve of the princes of the blood, were at our period increasingly being constructed in the larger *hôtels* of the rich, upper nobility. These did not rival the size and splendour of royal and ducal chapels, but they followed some of their forms on a smaller scale. One of the best examples of this (if heavily restored) is that built by the famous financier of Charles VII, Jacques Coeur (*c.*1400–56), who spent vast amounts on a large and splendid *hôtel* in Bourges constructed between 1443 and 1451.[8] This chapel is punctuated by two alcoves on either side of the altar which functioned as private oratories, forms found in both the Paris and Bourges Sainte-Chapelles, though notably not at Karlštejn. Jacques's oratory is on the right of the altar and that of his wife, Macée de

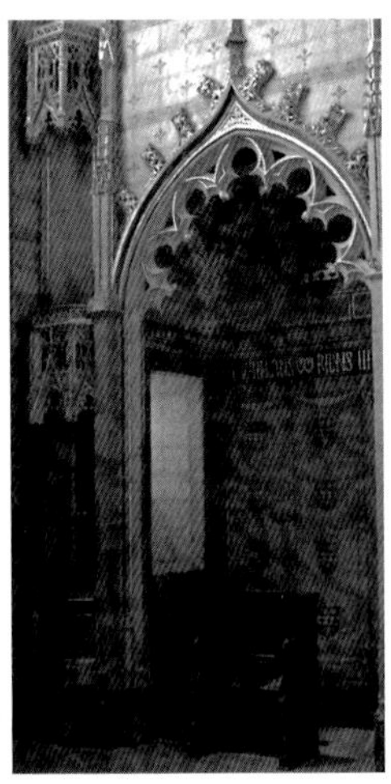

186

Chapel of the Hôtel of Jacques Coeur, Bourges, 1448–50. View showing the oratory of Jacques Coeur, nineteenth-century polychromy.

This oratory was set to the right of the altar. Its design allows the light from the hidden window to illuminate any devotional text Jacques was using in this space very effectively. The chapel would have provided a range of imagery for Jacques to contemplate: the empty niches seen on the left would have had statues of saints, and, according to Francesco di Neri Cecci, a member of the Florentine embassy that visited this chapel in 1461, it also contained portraits of Jacques Coeur, King Charles VII, René of Anjou, and an altarpiece 'painted by a great master', all now lost.

Léodepart, on the left [**186**]. These oratories are indicated with some humour on the exterior of the building by sculpted figures of a man (on Jacques' side) and a woman (on Macée's side) who appear to look out of the (fictive) window of their respective spaces (the actual window lighting the oratories is above their heads), but behave in exactly the opposite manner to what would be expected from the figures praying on the inside [**187**]: they are in casual, not devotional attitudes, interested in the view of the street and its distractions, and are turned away from the now-missing equestrian statue of Charles VII, which was in the niche above the palace's entrance, backing directly onto the altar wall of the chapel.

Oratories like Jacques Coeur's were supplied with fireplaces, prie-dieux (small prayer desks, sometimes permanent fixtures of stone), separate lighting provision, and curtains to provide privacy, and were often extensively personalized with painted or carved coats of arms and emblems. They allowed for a duality of devotional focus: the mass said on the altar of the chapel could be witnessed and followed while in the comfort and seclusion of the oratory with a range of more intimate devotional apparatus at hand. A similar desire for comfort and privacy led to the building of chapels or oratories connecting private apartments or residences to public churches, allowing access to services without having to leave the house. At the royal palace of Saint-Pol in Paris, the queen's apartments were connected to the parish church by a gallery decorated with angels holding coats of arms and playing music. At a later date, Margaret of Austria had a passageway that led directly from her apartments in the monastery at Brou, into the church and across the chancel arch to a chapel above the choir.[9] These connecting structures were not just the preserve of royal women: the remarkably preserved oratory in the house of the influential Burgundian advisor and nobleman Louis of Gruuthuse (1422–92) in Bruges was designed to provide similar access [**188**].[10] Here a corridor was built to span the street between Gruuthuse's *hôtel* and the church of Our Lady, opening into a wood-panelled oratory set into the ambulatory of the church, its large window overlooking the high altar. Access to this chapel could also be had from the ambulatory itself, via a structure built at ground level in the church and made visually prominent with the arms and devices of Gruuthuse set on and over its door, and images of Louis and his wife shown in prayer to the Trinity directly above where they would have sat in the chapel proper [**189**]. Entering the wood-panelled space of this oratory (originally more richly painted and gilded than today) from the interior of the Gruuthuse palace and kneeling at the specially designed sill in front of the window provide a vivid sense of privileged fifteenth-century devotional practice, where visual experience of the mass was highly important. As we have seen, a clear unobstructed view was greatly desired, and the particular, encompassing view of the altar given by this oratory would not have been possible from anywhere within the church proper.

Those who had enough money and influence might also build private chapels or oratories into the fabric of monastic churches, overlooking the high altar and the monks' choir, providing visual access to elements of a service otherwise inaccessible to laymen and women (since the choir of such

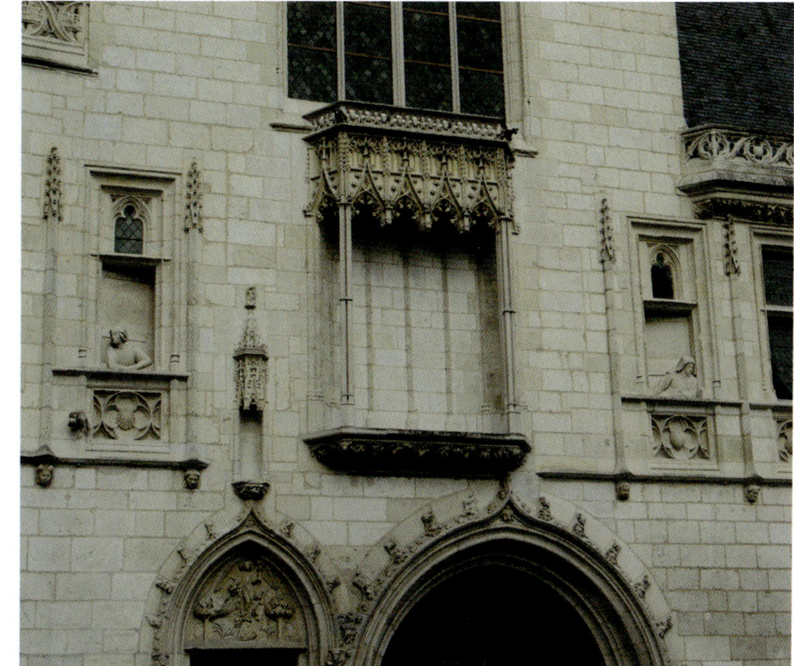

187

Eastern façade of the Hôtel of Jacques Coeur, showing exterior of chapel.

The two fictive windows with portraits of Jacques and his wife mark the spaces where, inside, they would have knelt at prayer in their oratories; the shell (the symbol of St Jacques) and the heart (*coeur*), carved in the balconies and throughout this palace, are emblematic of his name, Jacques Coeur.

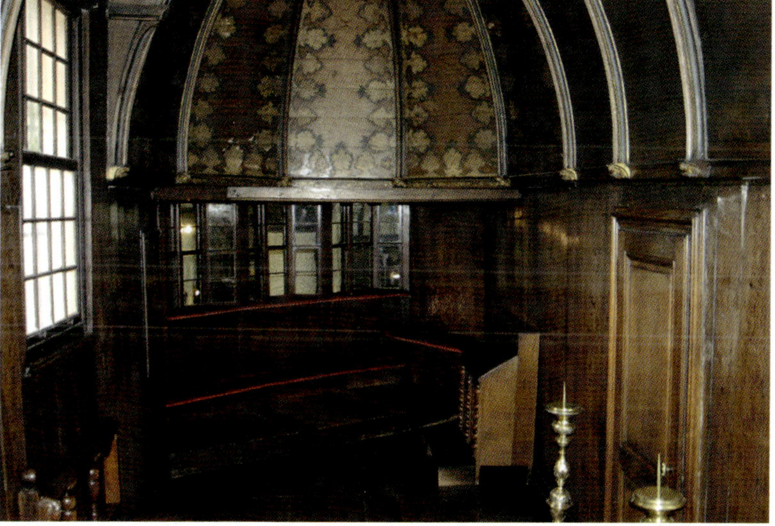

188

Interior of the oratory of Louis of Gruuthuse, spanning his palace and the church of Our Lady, Bruges, stone, painted wood panel, constructed 1472.

In 1472 Louis of Gruuthuse contracted with the chapter of Our Lady in Bruges to construct this oratory between his palace and the choir of the church. From it he had a view of the high altar of the church as well as of the splendid funerary monuments in alabaster, brass, and polished stone that he planned in his will of 1474, and which included two statues of his father and mother set on piers on either side of the choir.

churches was reserved for the monastic community). At the Carthusian monastery of Champmol in Dijon, Philip the Bold included a two-storey oratory of this sort on the north side of the monks' choir (see **11**); this comprised a lower and upper chapel for the duke and duchess, connected by spiral staircase, which could be accessed from outside the church (which was important, as women were not meant to enter any part of Carthusian foundations, let alone the monks' choir). The ducal oratory also featured fireplaces (the remnants of which still survive), glazed floor tiles, rich painted and sculpted decoration, stained glass with the duke and duchess's emblems and initials and images of the Virgin and various saints, and their own altar with an altarpiece, but with openings that gave views over the choir of the church to the high altar.[11]

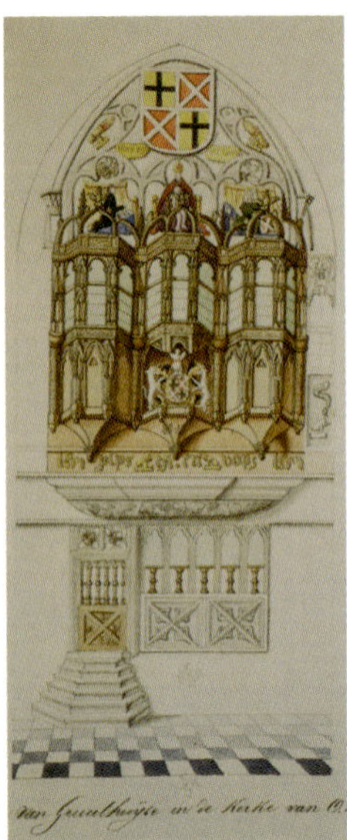

189 Jean Jacques Gaillard (d. 1867)

Oratory of Louis of Gruuthuse, coloured drawing on paper from the *Album met Brugse grafmonumentem*, *c.*1850.

This view of the chapel from the inside of the church drawn in the mid-nineteenth century shows how it was composed of two floors, the lower being accessible via steps (no longer extant) from the church itself; in its form, placement, and aspects of its decoration it seems to have emulated that built for Philip the Bold and Margaret of Flanders at the Chartreuse de Champmol, which included, like this, an image of the Trinity on its exterior.

Tombs

The vistas from Philip's oratory at Champmol, from Berry's at the Sainte-Chapelle, from Margaret of Austria's at Brou and from Louis of Gruuthuse's at Our Lady in Bruges would all have encompassed tombs as well as altars, seen mostly from high above and thus with an excellent view of the effigy of the deceased. At Champmol, Philip's own tomb [**133**] was to be set up in the monks' choir in front of the high altar, not completed within his lifetime but intended to be visible to his descendants praying in his oratory after him; Berry's was intended for a similar location at his Sainte-Chapelle. In Bruges, Louis of Gruuthuse's oratory would have overlooked his tomb and those of his family as well as, from the 1490s, that of Mary of Burgundy [**190**], also in front of the high altar which, as this pattern indicates, was one of the most privileged of possible locations for your tomb. Indeed, the placement of such important monuments, marking the burial place of the figures represented (the actual bodies were buried in the crypts below), was of great importance, both in terms of the site within the church and its proximity to either the high altar or to the tombs of saints, and in terms of the type and location of the church or chapel chosen. This is seen clearly in the process of settling on a location by the indecisive Jean de Berry: initially he had wanted to be buried in the Carthusian monastery of Vauvert outside Paris, and then at Poitiers, but he changed his mind and tried to assure himself a place in the cathedral of Bourges, in front of the high altar in the choir; when this request, granted by the pope, was denied by the cathedral chapter, he settled on his own foundation, more easily controlled, of his Sainte-Chapelle in Bourges [**184**], with its own college of canons to ensure services were continually said for his soul. Philip the Bold chose the Chartreuse de Champmol for a similar reason: around his tomb, day and night, the Carthusian monks of his foundation would pray for the salvation of his soul.

Like many rulers, and indeed lesser citizens, Philip and Jean set the preparations for their monuments in train during their lifetimes, although neither tomb was completed at their deaths. In Dijon, the ducal workshop was actively engaged on Philip's tomb for over twenty-five years (see above, **131**). Although his titles and status were marked out in brass letters (now lost) set around the top of the bier, this tomb, and its imagery, was not about marking and recording ancestry or the right to rule. The choice of an anonymous procession of mourners indicates that the purpose of this monument was primarily about salvation, about the rituals which would ensure Philip's soul entered heaven.

Other decisions about tomb locations might be more politically motivated, as is often underscored by their imagery and their materials, on which much time and effort was frequently expended. Charles V, as a king, could choose three locations for his tomb since he had the privilege of burying

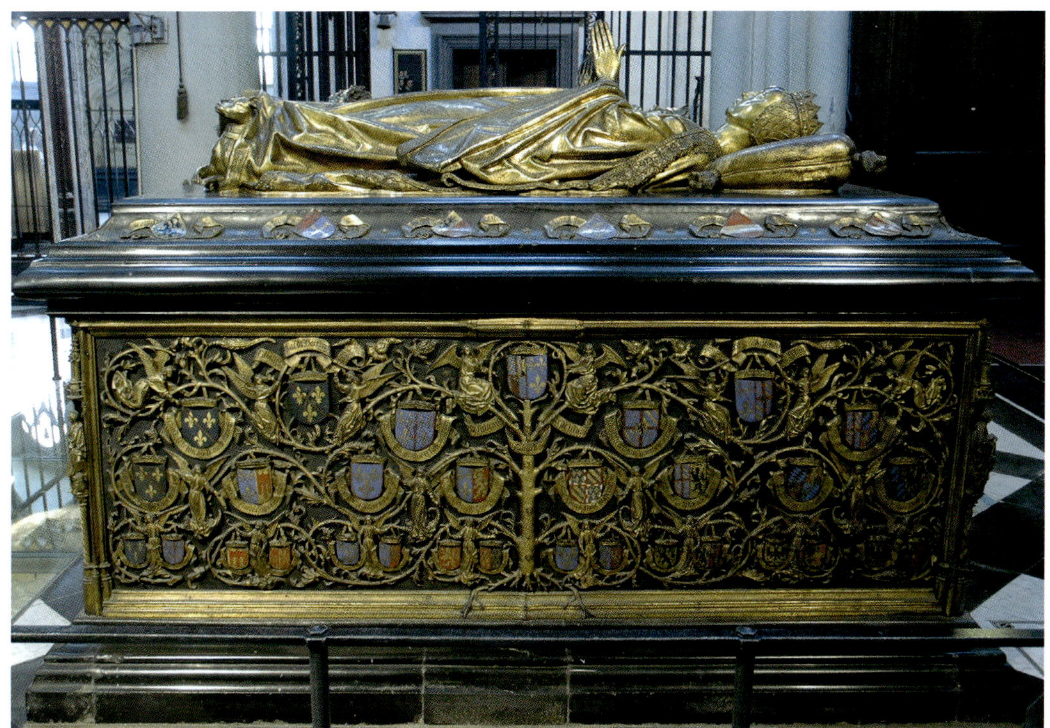

190 Jan Borman (wooden model), Renier van Thienen (casting), Pieter de Backere (gilding), Hubert Nonon (stonework and polishing), Jacques and Lieven van Lathem (heraldry)

Tomb of Mary of Burgundy, gilt bronze, enamel, and black Dinant marble, 1488–96.

Tombs had to be made in materials which would last, which were suitably rich, and which would allow elements like coats of arms to be durable and legible. Materials could also have meaning by their association: metalcasting was a technique in which Mary's territories of the Netherlands specialized, exporting works in this material across Europe (see pp. 96–9); it was also the material used for the tombs of her mother in Antwerp Cathedral, and her ancestor Louis of Mâle at Lille.

his heart, entrails, and body separately, thus spreading the influence of his physical presence more widely. He chose wisely, and made the plans almost immediately on becoming king—there was no time to waste and this was an important political statement. His body [**17**] was buried at the royal abbey and mausoleum, St Denis, in a tomb whose materials (white marble against black polished Tournai stone) and form deliberately evoked earlier tombs from the Capetian royal dynasty, a visual statement of continuity confirming the validity of his own Valois line, which had been a subject of debate prior to Charles's accession. His heart he placed in the cathedral of Rouen, capital of Normandy, of which Charles had once been duke, and whose loyalty, which had been under threat, he needed and valued. His entrails he sent to Maubuisson; this was an important royal abbey, but here, perhaps, family affections and affiliations of a different sort were the guiding force, as his will specifies Maubuisson as his mother's burial place.[12]

The tomb of Mary of Burgundy used different forms to impress on the viewer the nature of her lineage, her right to rule, and her associations with the territory in which she chose to be buried.[13] This work was not made at her direction but that of her husband Maximilian of Austria after her unexpected death in a hunting accident in 1482. It was a major project involving the woodcarver Jan Borman, the brass founder Renier Thienen (who seems to have been in charge of the whole project), painters, and goldsmiths. The tomb consists of a stone bier, but the effigy and the decoration of its faces are in bronze, richly worked, gilded, or enamelled. Mary had specified Bruges, and the church of Our Lady, as the desired place for her tomb, citing the Virgin as her 'special protectress' several times in her will. It was also a politically astute move on behalf of her husband, since Bruges was a city which had rebelled at various points against Burgundian and particuarly Habsburg rule (Bruges had actually held Maximilian captive in 1488). In a highly inventive manner which breaks from established tomb iconography (as represented in **10, 133**), the design of this tomb clearly delineates Mary's pedigree over five generations, the maternal line on her left hand, the paternal on the right, proclaiming her ties to the Valois house and her right to rule (and thus Maximilian's right to rule as regent for their son). This is done with the device of a tree (reminiscent of the biblical Tree of Jesse), whose roots extend over the edge of the tomb, and from whose branches hang escutcheons representing Mary's ancestors presented by angels, while Mary's territories are set out with further coats of arms placed around the upper edge of the monument.

Textiles

Among the most dramatic visual experiences in settings like the Sainte-Chapelle or churches like Our Lady in Bruges would have been the coming to rest of the bodies of these royal and ducal rulers following the (often long) funerary processions carrying them to their place of burial. At Bourges, Berry's Sainte-Chapelle was draped entirely in black fabric, and hundreds of candles and newly painted coats of arms were set in place for the 148 masses which were to be said while the duke lay in state in the choir of the church.[14] Textiles were just as important for instant splendour on other important feasts, and the peripatetic nature of court life meant that their portability was a great benefit. In a miniature heading a treatise on the Lord's Prayer, Philip the Good is shown attending mass [**191**]. The setting appears to be the screened-off choir of a chapel, possibly even the duke's Sainte-Chapelle in Dijon, or the choir of a church, made more personal to the duke and his household, and more private, by the rich textiles hung around the columns and the heraldic carpet set in front of the altar. Within this constructed fabric space, the duke is given additional privacy by another textile enclosure, the prayer tent in which he kneels, made of a rich blue cloth woven in gold with ducal emblems of the flint and briquette, the curtain of which is held open by the attending page. These tents were expensive objects, reserved for the very highest rank of society: usually only kings and princes are depicted with them as part of their devotional apparatus [**191, 197**]. In some respects they are a transferral of the canopy of state [**48**] to the religious sphere.

The hugely important role of textiles in creating suitable environments for prayer and mass (and indeed for other secular purposes, see **43**) is supported by the evidence of royal and ducal inventories in which textiles for the chapel are dominant and immensely valuable items. Entire fabric *chapelles*, which were not actually portable rooms, but sets of matching textiles which could fully equip a bare chapel and splendidly dress the necessary officiating clergy, appear in some numbers in royal inventories. A *chapelle complète* or *chapelle entière*, as they were called, might consist of as many as fifteen or twenty items: three copes, a chasuble, a dalmatic and tunic, orphreys, albs, amices, stoles and lappets for mitres (all items of liturgical apparel),[15] a dossal and a frontal (which hung above and below the altar, see **194** and below), an altar cloth (literally the cloth

191 Jean le Tavernier
Philip the Good at Mass, miniature from a treatise on the Lord's Prayer, parchment, 1454.

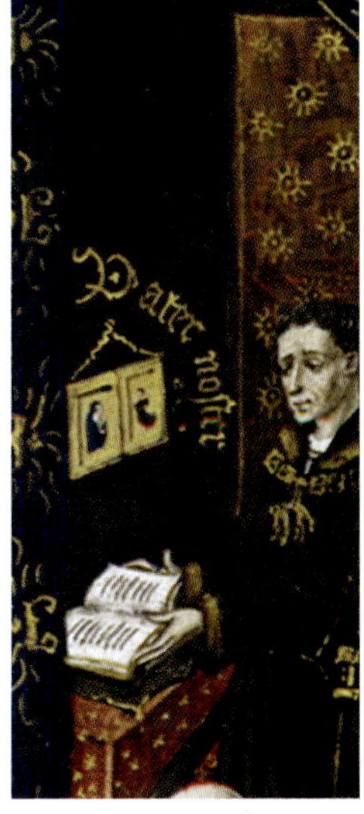

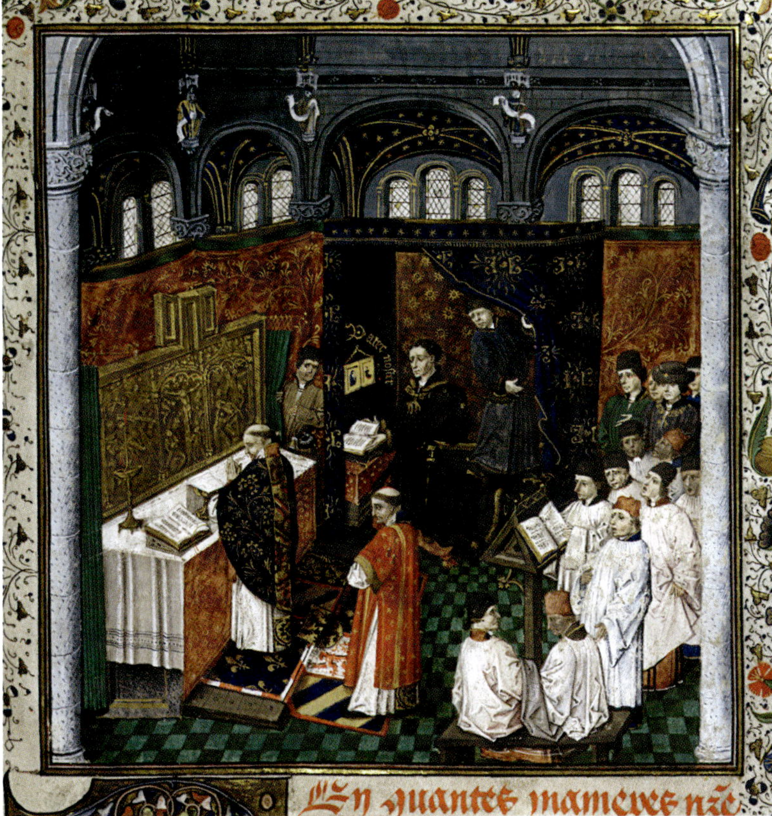

which went over the altar), and sometimes *custodes* (the curtains which hung on the rails at either side of the altar, as in **191**). Charles V owned fifty-seven *chapelles* (not all full ones); Philip the Bold's inventory of 1404 lists seventeen, while Jean de Berry has nineteen listed in his 1402–4 inventory. They were also considered necessary elements of a noblewoman's trousseau, featuring in those of Isabelle of France (who married Richard II in 1396) and Marie of Burgundy (who married Adoph of Cleves in 1405).[16] Most were made of silk, providing a dazzling array of colours and effects: cloth of gold, satin, velvet, and samite (a type of silk) were much favoured, and many were richly embroidered in coloured silks and *or de cippre* (silver-gilt thread), sometimes with pearls, enamels, and precious stones. Their value was staggering: when Charles VI's liturgical textiles were appraised at the Louvre in 1423–4 they were estimated at 11,142 livres, 2 sous parisis.[17] None of these textiles survive, but a set made for Philip the Good to serve at meetings of the Order of the Golden Fleece does [**192**], and is probably as materially and visually rich as was possible. Made between *c.*1430 and 1445 by the duke's embroiderer Thierry du Chastel, at a cost of over 10,000 livres, and designed by a painter who drew on the inventions of Jan van Eyck and the Master of Flémalle, they are worked with gold and silver threads in the *or nué* ('shaded gold') technique recently developed in Paris and the Netherlands. In this method, gold threads were laid in parallel lines onto the cloth surface and the design drawn on them to be created with silk stitch-

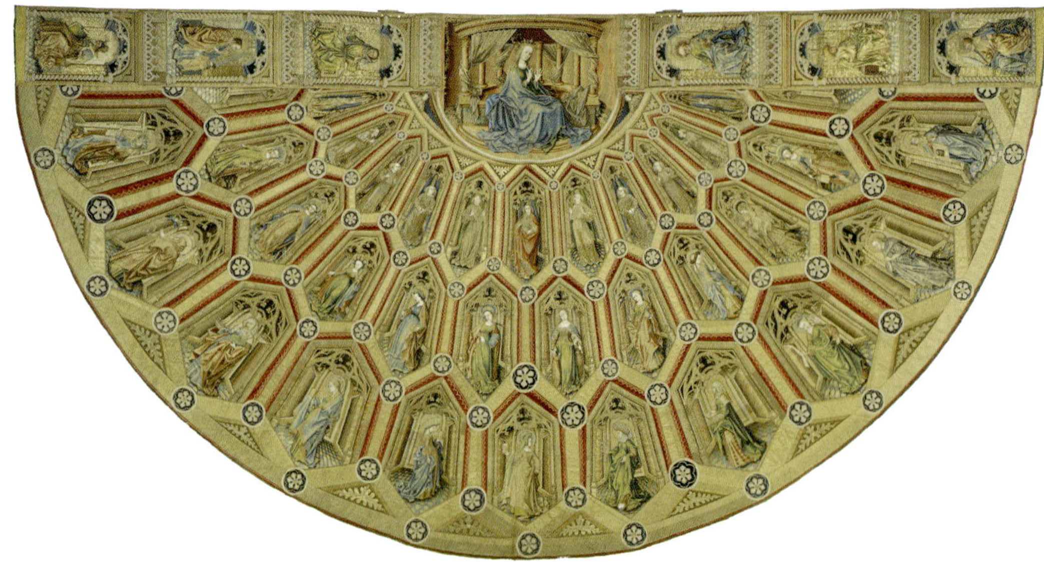

192 Thierry du Chastel, after designs by Jan van Eyck or an artist in his circle

Cope of the Virgin, embroidered gold and silk threads, pearls, *c.*1430–45.

This cope was worn during the celebrations for the order, and was intended to be seen primarily from the back; the hexagonal panels with saints decrease in scale towards the neck, where there is less material, drawing the eye to the large seated figure of the Virgin on the hood. This spectacular set comprised two other, similar copes which would be worn at the same time by other members of the clergy, one with Christ on its hood, the other with St John the Baptist. To line up correctly, the priest wearing this one would stand at the far left of the other two, forming a Deesis group, as in the top row of the Ghent Altarpiece **[3b]**, which was clearly a source for their design (compare also **193** with detail facing Chapter 2).

ing, the embroiderer placing the threads close to each other to represent the shaded parts and further apart to represent the lighter zones, allowing the gold ground to shine through. The work was then decorated with pearls and coloured glass **[193]**.[18]

The colour and material of these *chapelles* were dictated to some extent by their intended use: Charles V's were organized and inventoried by colour, beginning with white and gold, which were generally the most valuable; of his fifty-seven *chapelles*, sixteen were white, fourteen red, ten blue, five black, two green, three violet, two of white painted with black, one ash-coloured and two uncoloured. Three of the last five of these *chapelles* were specified as 'every-day *chapelles* for use during Lent'. A painting in ink on silk, the *Parement de Narbonne* **[194]**, appears to be a surviving element of a Lenten *chapelle*, made for Charles V, although probably not one of those recorded in his inventory. The hanging relies for its effect on the subtlety and skill of its painting, not its materials. The technique was difficult—mistakes could not be easily corrected; moreover, conveying the Passion narrative and creating decorative interest without the use of colour required immense skill.

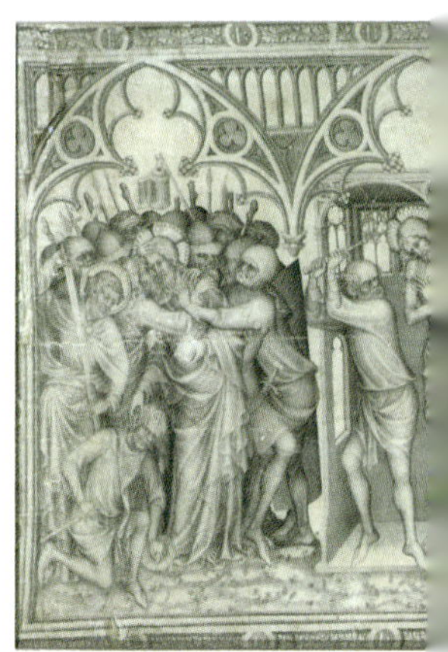

While the monochrome tone of the *Parement* was evidently chosen because of its liturgical function, the visual appreciation of painting in limited colours was deeply rooted in the taste of the courts at this period, and continued throughout the fifteenth century: many prayer books **[195]**, secular manuscripts, stained glass, panels, and even wall paintings **[196]** employed limited colour without any Lenten connection. The Book of Hours made for Philip the Good with over 150 miniatures in grisaille by the illuminator Jean le Tavernier (*fl. c.*1434–60), an artist who seems to

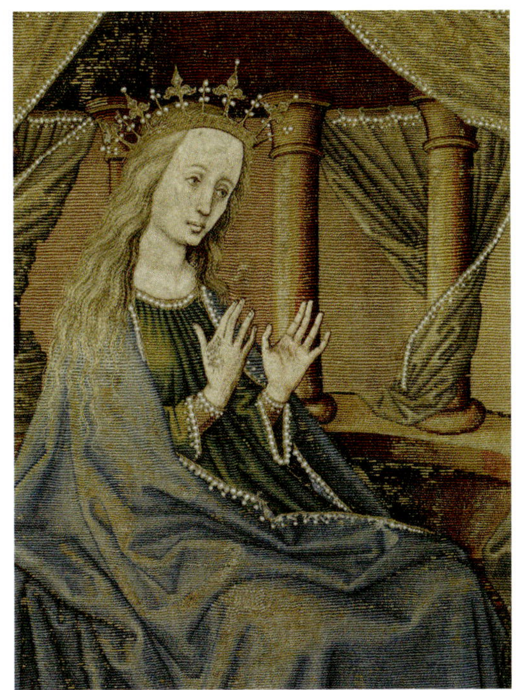

193 Thierry du Chastel, after designs by Jan van Eyck or an artist in his circle

Detail of **192**.

In 1501 the Italian ambassador Niccolò Frigio witnessed these liturgical vestments in action at a meeting of the Order of the Golden Fleece in Brussels. Astounded by their splendour, he described how they were 'all embroidered with gold and silk minutely worked in so inestimable a manner that it seemed that the lives of six men would not have been sufficient to make them; nevertheless, they all seem to have been done by one hand'.

194 Parisian painter (Girard d'Orleans?)

The *Parement de Narbonne*, ink on silk, *c*.1370.

This work was hung above and behind the altar during Lent, probably part of a larger set including another hanging of the same dimensions set below and in front of the altar. The Ks around the edge of the work are for 'Karlous', Charles V, who is shown kneeling with his wife to the central Crucifixion scene. The application of ink on silk is achieved here with great mastery, suggesting that it was an established method, but only one other piece survives in this technique, a mitre in the Musée du Cluny, Paris.

have specialized in this technique, displays the taste in this mode again at the highest level of patronage. The effect here is not to suggest sculpted forms, but to create a beautiful and restrained page, emphasized by the lack of borders (which were routinely found in devotional books). Here richness and decoration are achieved by the elaborate pen initials and the thick painted frames for the miniatures.[19]

The murals which line the nave in the chapel at Eton College built by Henry VI and completed by the executers of his will in the 1480s are perhaps the finest monumental example of the employment of grisaille for narrative scenes. They are painted in oil in a limited palette of greys and browns, with occasional accents, often for dramatic impact, of reds and greens, and were

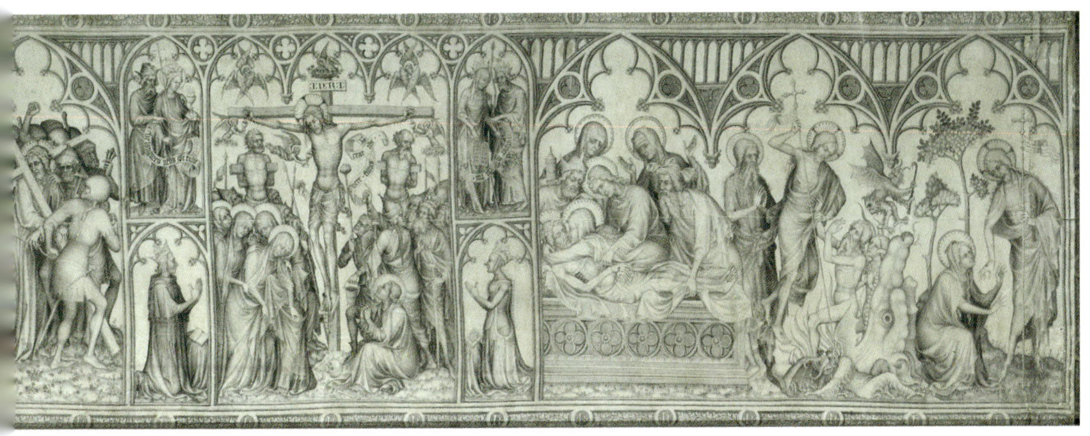

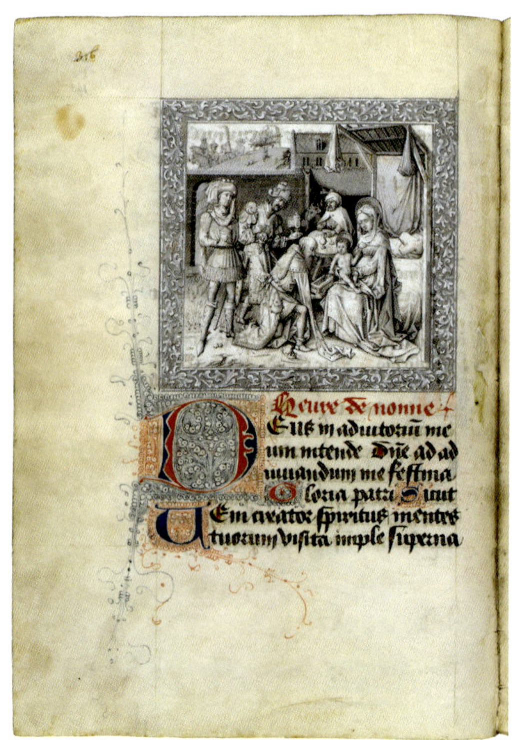

195 Jean le Tavernier

Adoration of the Magi, miniature from the Hours of Philip the Good, parchment, *c.*1450.

Tavernier seems to have been well acquainted with the paintings of the Master of Flémalle and Rogier van der Weyden. He worked extensively for Philip the Good, specializing in grisaille miniatures, called 'histories en blanc et noir' in the accounts, many of which illustrated secular volumes. This prayer book shows him employing this technique with its greatest refinement: the restricted palette still ranges widely through grey to shades of brown and blue, and the cream of the parchment is allowed to show through to further vary the effect.

probably undertaken by Netherlandish artists given the closeness of their style to the works of Hugo van der Goes and Dieric Bouts.[20] They depict a series of miracles of the Virgin, and the reason why this technique was chosen is not clear. It may have to do with contemporary taste for Netherlandish manuscripts like **195** which were popular with the English court; or it may be related to the choice of subject matter: these are not biblical narratives but legendary events (drawn from texts like the *Golden Legend*) depicting miracles worked primarily by images of the Virgin, and therefore making their nature as images evident—and restricting their material richness—may have been a concern. Or it may be that a heightened contrast was required between the chapel bare (painted) and the chapel hung with tapestries, which may have been a blaze of colour by comparison. Since the effect achieved is of a series of fictive sculpted reliefs punctuated by stone statues in niches, this might have been part of the appeal of the technique, as paintings suggesting sculpture would have been cheaper and quicker to produce than stone carvings telling such a narrative.

Returning to the image of Philip the Good in prayer in **191**, we see that, while Philip's chapel is furnished with a carved and gilded retable on the altar, the Duke also has an image at closer range, attached to the fabric of his oratory. This image shows the duke himself in prayer before an image of the Virgin and Child. The duke's prayer book, likely to be a book of hours similar to the one we have just considered [**195**], would have contained elements of the liturgical service and provided extra prayers to be said at certain moments during mass, but also included many other para-liturgical texts, some highly personalized, and themselves containing many images heading the various

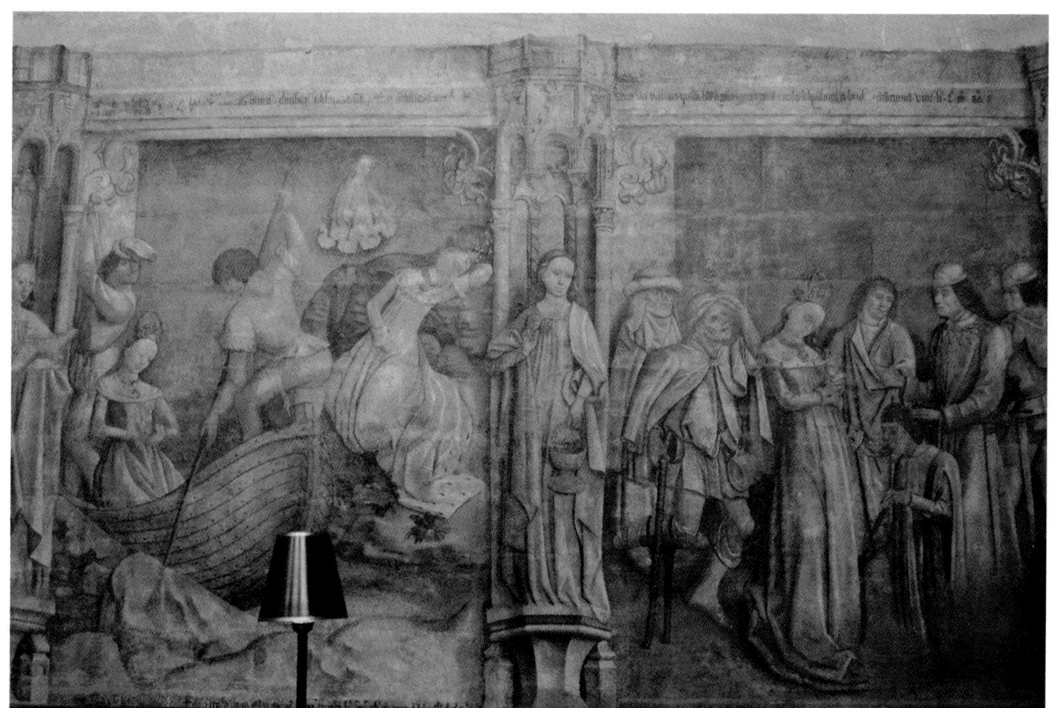

196 Anonymous Netherlandish (?) artists
Miracles of the Virgin, wall painting in Eton College chapel, 1480s.

offices and prayers (see also **44, 57, 58, 74–6**). Philip's experience is thus visually complex and rich, involving viewing a range of imagery in a variety of media: the book as he turned its pages; the small diptych set in front of him; the high altar and the larger chapel decoration, its stained glass and sculpture (note the statues of the apostles set above the columns). This multiplicity is an important element of devotional experience at our period and is similar to what a less privileged fifteenth-century spectator might experience in a larger, more public religious context [**6, 197**].

The aims of Philip's contemplation of an image in **191**, notably one of himself in the presence of the Virgin and Child, can be more fully understood both with reference to texts that explicate the purpose of the image in private meditation at this period, and by considering certain images that explicitly illustrate the goals of meditation. This is the subject of the next chapter, where we focus more closely on the particular visual features of devotional images, and how they were potentially viewed and used.

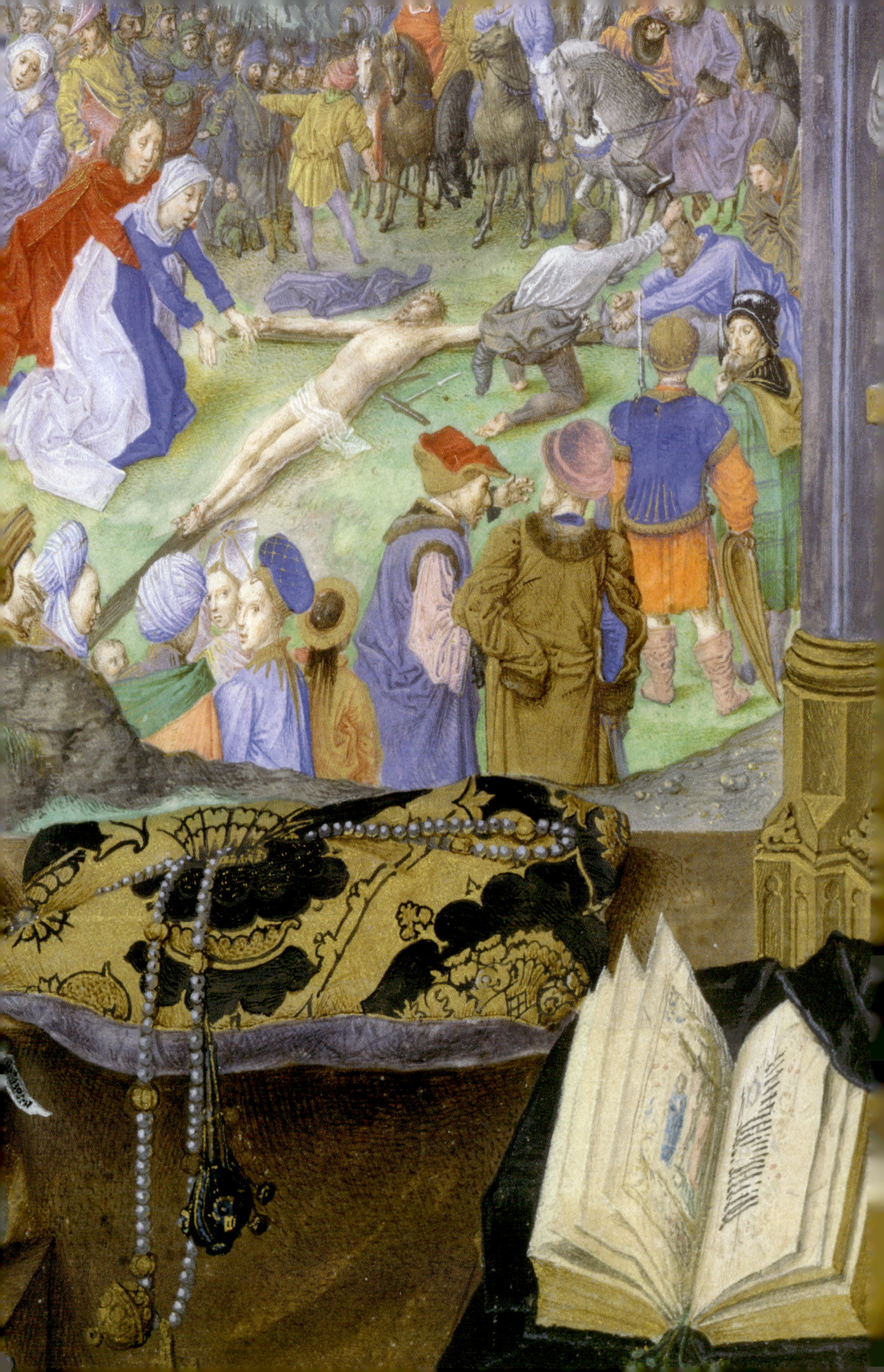

18 Meditation and Imagination

And we ought thus to learn to transcend with our minds from these visible things to the invisible, from the corporeal to the spiritual. For this is the purpose of the image.
Jean Gerson, *Opera omnia*, II, *c.*1400

The view of the extremely influential and well-connected theologian Jean Gerson (1363–1429), quoted above, justified images as a necessary starting point in devotional meditation, and was widely held by other theologians and writers of this period like the German Heinrich Suso (*c.*1295–1366) and the Netherlandish founder of the Brethren of the Common Life, Geert de Groote (1340–84). The process they advocated saw images as a first step, which would then enable the viewer to move (preferably quickly) to a mental image evoked by the physical one, and ultimately to the abstract, imageless contemplation of the divinity. This three-step ideal had been developed many years before by St Bernard of Clairvaux (1090–1153) in respect to mystical contemplation, which advocated the move from meditation to speculation and then to contemplation, but without reference to the use of actual images to achieve it; Bernard in turn had based his stages ultimately on St Augustine's three stages of vision, which began with corporeal vision (the sight of our eyes), moving to spiritual vision (imagination and recollection), and then achieving intellectual vision (the contemplation of abstract entities).[1]

The process of moving from meditation on a physical image to the visualization of a mental one is implicit in many images of the period, in different ways. It is made explicit, however, in two miniatures from a book of hours probably made in Ghent in *c.*1502–3 for James IV of Scotland (1473–1513) and his wife Margaret Tudor [**197, 198**].[2] The first miniature (and it comes, perhaps significantly, very early in the book on the verso of folio 24) of James shows him in prayer before a man-made image of the Salvator Mundi set upon an altar. That his devotions are at an early stage is indicated by the prayer book, which, although its clasps are undone, is not yet open. That James is meditating, not yet speculating, is made clearer by the contrast with the image of Margaret in prayer (which appears much later in the book on the verso of folio 243). She has opened her book and no longer sees the corporeal image on her altar (a sculpted image of the Annunciation), but instead views a non-corporeal, mental image of the Virgin and Child, its nature made clear by the aura around it. This is not Margaret receiving an actual vision of the Virgin—she was not known as a visionary and indeed was not even particularly devout, if her contemporary reputation is true: she famously requested, on her sickbed, to contemplate a parade of her best dresses instead of the crucifix. Although Margaret and James are represented in similar settings with matching accoutrements of prayer, in Margaret's image there are subtle

Detail of 200

197 Master of James IV of Scotland

James IV of Scotland presented by St James, in Prayer to an Altarpiece of the Salvator Mundi, from the Hours of James IV of Scotland, parchment, *c.*1502–3.

James IV of Scotland kneels, like Philip the Good in **191**, in well-appointed surroundings on a rich cushion at a fabric-covered prie-dieu and with a prayer tent set behind him. The chapel here, however, is set within a public space, but marked out as his by the coat of arms embroidered on the frontal and the imagery of the altarpiece, which includes St Andrew, the patron of Scotland.

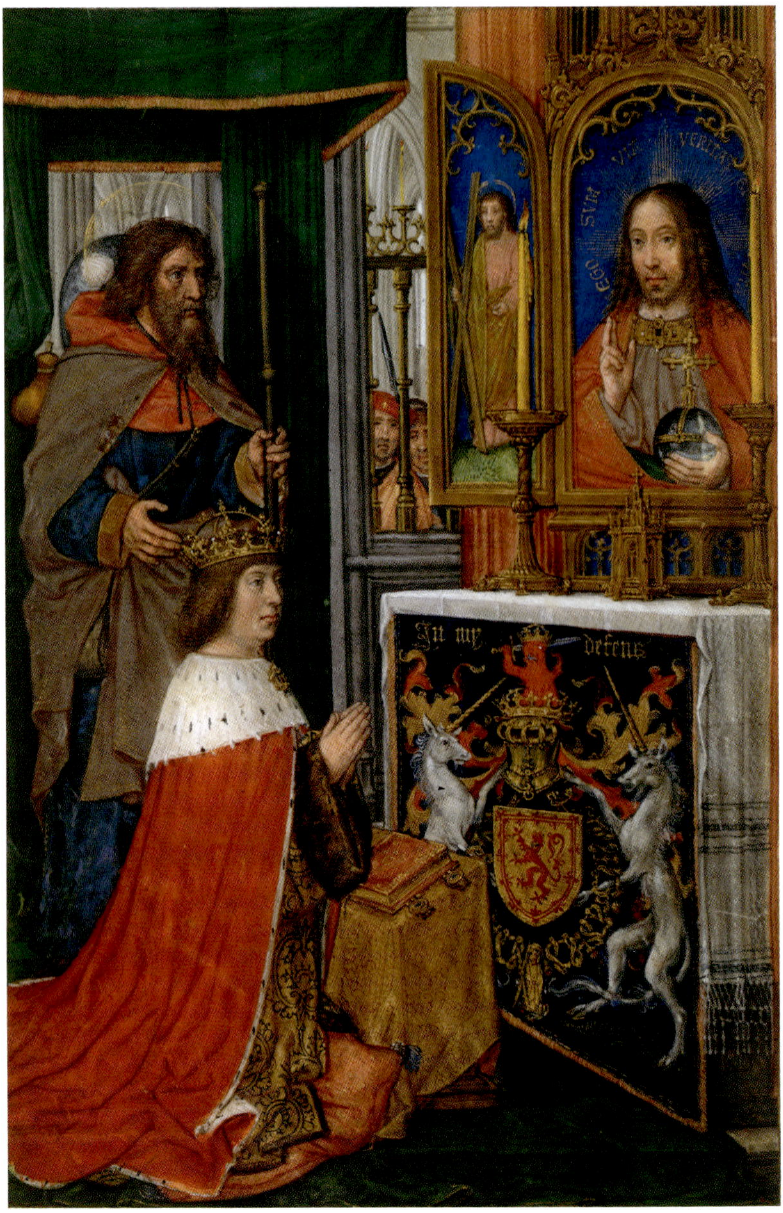

shifts to indicate the different nature of the moment. Her figure, the altar, the prie-dieu, and the prayer tent have been moved into closer proximity to the viewer; the carpet now continues to the edge of the image and the tent now forms a framing device through which we see the event, while the choir or chapel screen through which people crowd to watch is pushed much further back, and the watching crowds, though still present, are much less clearly defined. The move from corporeal meditation to imaginative speculation, from something public and removed to something more intimate and intense, is thus cleverly expressed in the wider elements of the visual language of the two depictions.

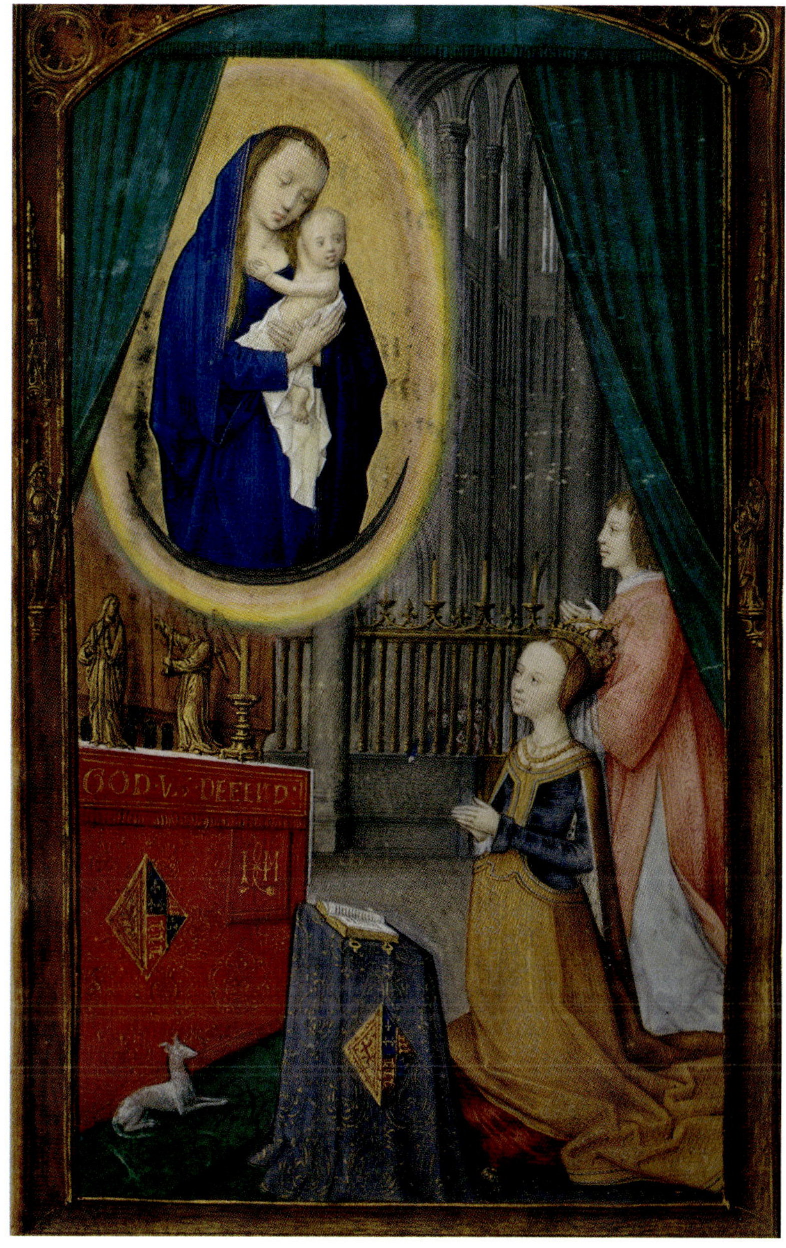

198 Master of James IV of Scotland (?)

Margaret Tudor in Prayer to an Image of the Virgin and Child, from the Hours of James IV of Scotland, parchment, *c*.1502–3.

Although attributed to a different hand than **197**, the softer, more delicate technique of this miniature might be explained by the need to represent a different devotional moment to that experienced by her husband James IV. Margaret gave this book at some point to her sister Mary Tudor, inscribing it on folio 188v: 'Madame I pray your grace/Remember on me when ye loke upon thys boke/Your lofing sister/ Margaret'. Like **209**, this book of hours was thus seen as serving a wider, commemorative function.

Two extraordinary miniatures in a book of hours made around 1475 probably for Mary, Duchess of Burgundy (1457–82) explicate the processes of meditation and imagination further, and can give us some sense of how images and texts such as that used by Philip in **191** might be used and viewed.[3] The first, appearing right at the beginning of the book on the verso of folio 14, straight after the calendar and facing the prologue to a prayer of the Seven Joys of the Virgin, shows the owner of the book, Mary of Burgundy, reading from a prayer book similar to that in which this image appears [**199**]. Behind her, through an open window, we see the choir of a large church: in front of the high altar is the

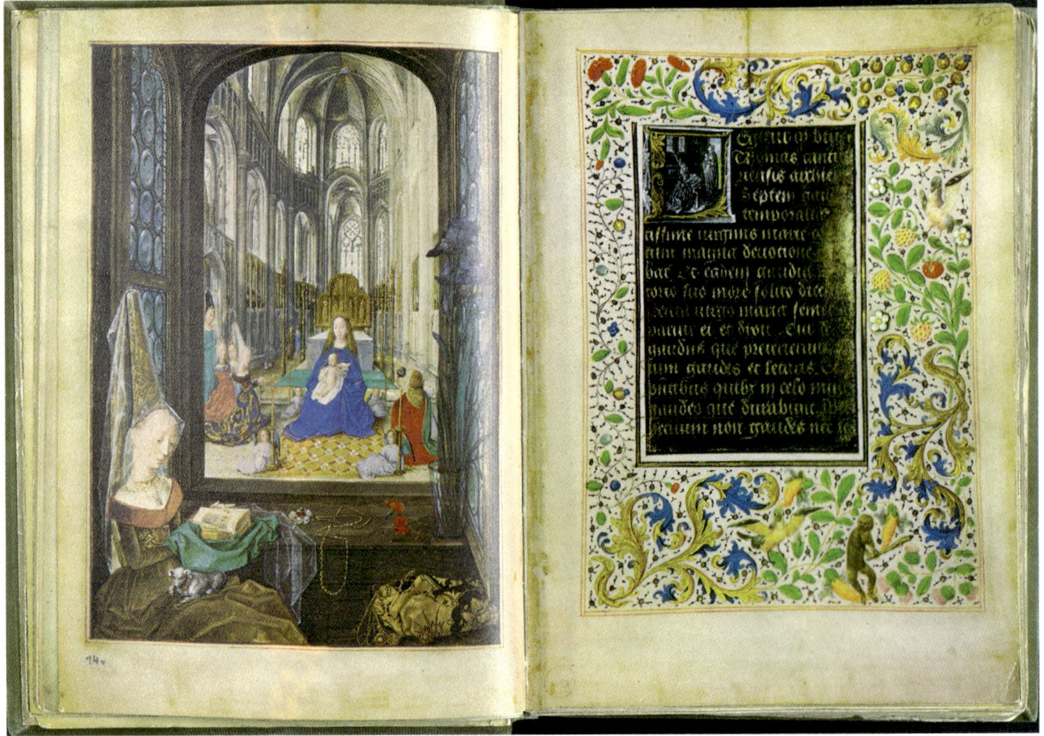

199 Vienna Master of Mary of Burgundy
Mary of Burgundy (?) in Prayer at a Window, from the Vienna Hours of Mary of Burgundy, parchment, *c.*1475.

Virgin with the naked Christ Child on her lap, approached by a group of figures who kneel in devotion; despite her different apparel, the foremost of these is presumably the same woman as sits in the foreground: Mary of Burgundy.[4] What we see here is Mary's meditation on a prayer to the Virgin, indicated by the letter 'O' in the depicted book of hours she holds (and presumably standing for the Marian prayers *O intemerata* or *Obsecro te*, standard elements in any book of hours), through which the Virgin is then revealed to her.

This is not, however, a private revelation: the kneeling Mary is accompanied by three ladies of the court, while a male figure on the right swings a censer, and two others watch on from behind the high altar; moreover, beyond the choir, crowds of further figures can be seen pressing against the screen to glimpse this event. What is depicted here then should not be taken for a vision—it is rather a visualization, or even a visitation of Mary of Burgundy to the Virgin, not the Virgin to her, in the same way that the duchess frequently visited the powerful cult images of the Virgin at Boulogne or Halle. This is after all the choir of a large cathedral or collegiate church with a tall vaulted ambulatory; it is not a private chapel, and while it is a restricted 'audience' with the Virgin it is not a private revelation, as the watching crowds make clear.

Here, then, what we see is more likely a division between public and private devotional activity: the private practice as shown in the foreground and the public one in the view through the window. This is a distinction we have found in relation to the recorded practices of Charles V, seen depicted in the miniature of Philip the Good, and expressed in the architectural structures used for prayer examined above. What we must also remember here is that the primary user of the image was Mary herself, who would be sitting, hold-

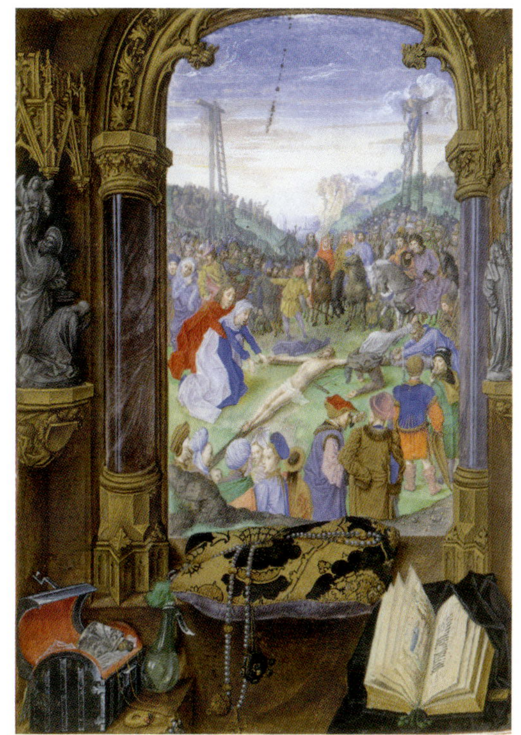

200 Vienna Master of Mary of Burgundy

Christ Nailed to the Cross, from the Vienna Hours of Mary of Burgundy, parchment, *c.*1475.

Around the image seen though the window are an open box containing various *joyaux* and a prayer book, whose black chemise binding is used to keep the page open to a folio with an image of the Crucifixion. The objects shown here may be actual ones owned by the duchess: similar prayer beads are held by the young Margaret of Austria, Mary's daughter, in a portrait of her in New York; possibly they were passed down the Burgundian line.

ing this prayer book, looking at herself holding a prayer book, and at herself in prayer in a more public context. The self-imaging aspect of these depictions is all the more important when we come to the other famous image in Mary's book, the extraordinary *Nailing to the Cross*, which comes later, on the verso of folio 43, set opposite the opening of the Hours of the Cross [**200**].

Here again the image is seen through a framing structure—this time a more elaborate carved stone window, on which rests a brocade cushion with a set of prayer beads and other objects used in devotional practice, which are clearly in use, although their owner is missing: Mary, looking at her prayer book, would see on this page a depiction of the accoutrements of prayer she might also be currently using in reality, set around the real prayer book in which they are depicted. Through the window, what unfolds, then, is the result of Mary's practice of prayer, her visualization of part of the Passion narrative, the nailing of Christ to the cross, which she sees set in a vast panorama with a cast of thousands created by the illuminator's skill at suggesting depth, recession, scale, and the fading of forms into the distance. Mary's visualization, called up though the process of contemplating a simpler, iconic image of the Crucifixion, was an ideal of contemporary devotional practice, set out in texts like the thirteenth-century *Meditations on the Life of Christ* by Pseudo-Bonaventura, or the fourteenth-century *Vita Christi* by the Carthusian Ludolph of Saxony, where the devotee was encouraged to imagine that they were actually present at the various stages of the Passion, witnessing the event, and envisaging how they would feel every step of the way. A fifteenth century 'Privity of the Passion', an English adaptation of the *Meditations on the Life of Christ*, explains the process and purpose of such meditations very well:

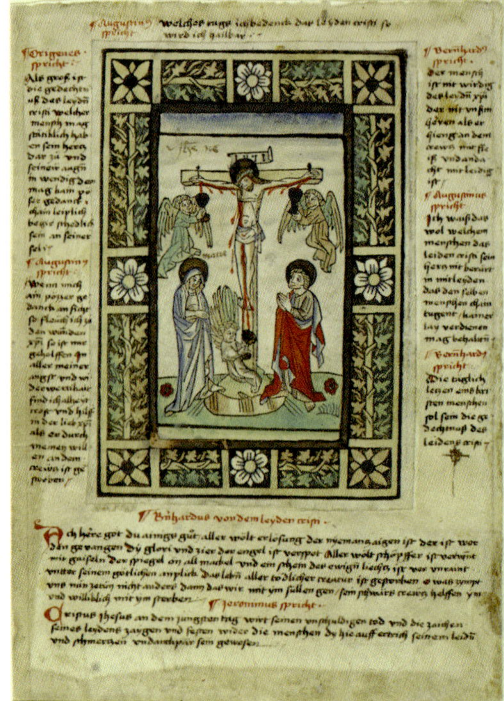

201 Southern German
***c.*1450**

The *Crucifixion*, coloured woodcut with frame printed from separate block, *c.*1450.

The flexibility of prints, in both their manufacture and ongoing use, made them ideal devotional images. This one was originally (or at least early in its history) pasted into the front of a manuscript which contained texts concerning the Passion and the Eucharist. The texts around the print personalize the image, as does the added colour: Christ's blood, which drips from his arms and runs down his legs, and which is so visually dominant, was not part of the print itself but was all applied by hand in a water-based paint.

> Whoever desires to find comfort and spiritual joy in the passion and in the cross of our Lord Jesus needs to concentrate on them and to forget and set at naught all other business ... he who examines it continuously with deep thought and with all his heart shall find very many things stirring him to new compassion ... to achieve this state I speak of ... a man needs to concentrate the acuity of his mind and open wide the inner eye of his soul to behold this blessed passion; he needs to forget and cast behind him for the time all other occupations and business. He must make himself present in his thought as if he saw with his bodily eye all the things that happened around the cross regarding the glorious passion of our Lord Jesus, not briefly and fleetingly, but lovingly, fully, continually ...[5]

The image in Mary's prayer book takes the idea of imagination and identification one step further, as a closer look reveals: here the crosses for the thieves stand on two small mounds, but there is no third, larger mound for Christ's cross, which should be set between them. Where is Golgotha? We need to readjust our viewpoint: Christ will not be crucified in the centre of the view we are looking at but on the very spot where we are standing. The rocky ground directly below the window sill is in fact Golgotha, and the viewer (that is, Mary of Burgundy) is standing on the hill where the cross is to be erected. If Mary of Burgundy, in her visualization, is actually on Golgotha, is she taking part in the drama in a more direct way than has been supposed? Possibly, since one of the most important figures in the Passion drama at this point—the Magdalene—is missing from the scene depicted. Now it is clear why there is no praying figure of Mary of Burgundy at the window: she has imagined herself into the actual event, playing the role of the Magdalene, her namesake, and the beloved of Christ. Identification with this saint has a long, varied, and rich tradition, for both laymen and women, as well as those in holy orders, because of her special relationship with Christ, her role as redeemed

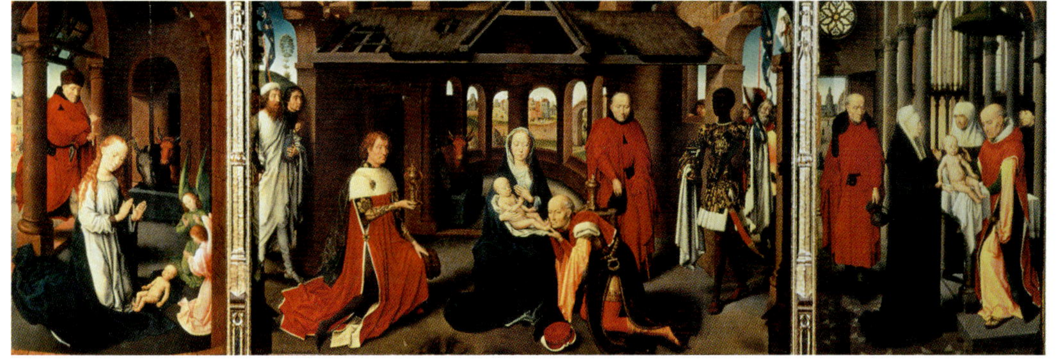

202 Hans Memling
Epiphany Triptych, oil on Baltic oak.

sinner and as a contemplative (having spent thirty years in the desert) and she was particularly venerated by the Burgundian rulers.[6]

Visualizations like those represented in the prayer books of James IV and Mary of Burgundy were not an end in themselves; the act of contemplating Christ's Passion was an important route to salvation, and its contemplation and mental re-enactment was one of the central goals of the worshipper at this period. This is made explicit in a much more ordinary object than Mary of Burgundy's lavish prayer book, and one more representative of the type of devotional tools used by less wealthy members of society: a woodcut made around 1450 in southern Germany [**201**].[7] Here, the Crucifixion, printed from two woodblocks—one for the image, one for the border (creating a frame not unlike that found in manuscripts)—was hand-coloured and then stuck onto a larger sheet (measuring 29.1 × 21 centimetres) so that texts could be carefully written around it. This speaks of active engagement with the image, as the texts recount the benefits of contemplating the Passion: one of them written across the top like a title reads 'every day that I think of Christ's suffering I will be saved' (a saying attributed to St Augustine); another (attributed to St Bernard of Clairvaux) states that reflection on Christ's Passion protects against temptations and evil thoughts and evokes compassion. These are not prayers to be said in front of the image, but reminders of why contemplating the Passion, represented here by the print, was so efficacious and necessary.

Many images created at our period seem designed to incite empathy, or encourage contemplation and imagination. Deploying a range of visual strategies, artists could heighten the impression of witnessing or participating in an event from Christ's life, and not just His Passion. Hans Memling's paintings have settings that are so carefully and logically constructed that viewers can picture themselves in relationship to the images with some precision, and even mentally enter the scene, imagining themselves walking around or through the buildings represented. This is evident in an image like the Epiphany Triptych, now in the Prado, the original patron and location of which are unknown, but which was in Spain by 1500 where it was kept in the oratory of the Holy Roman Emperor, Charles V, in Toledo [**202**].[8] Here, the first scene on the left, the Nativity, is viewed from over a brick wall, just visible at the lower edge of the panel, while Joseph enters the stable though the archway supported by the column on the left, and the ox and ass survey the scene from

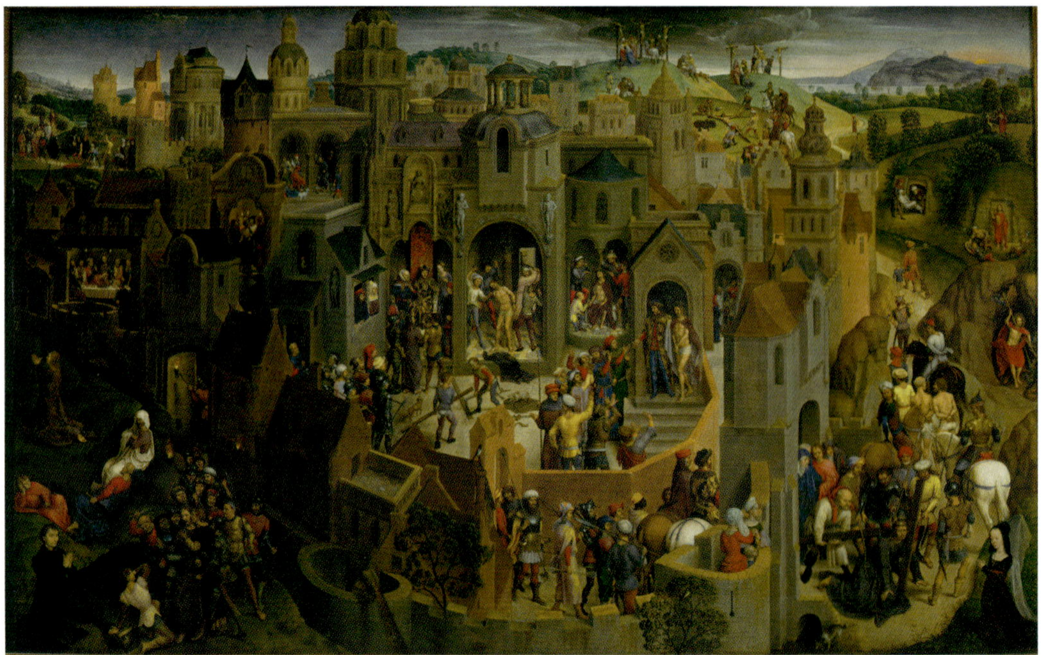

203 Hans Memling

The *Passion of Christ*, oil on Baltic oak, *c.*1470.

Tommaso Portinari and his wife are shown kneeling in prayer in the lower corners of this panoramic work; it does not seem to have been an altarpiece, but may have hung on a wall in a chapel. It was not among Portinari's possessions in Florence when he died in 1501; the first record of it is in Florence in 1550, in the collection of Cosimo I. It was known to painters in Bruges around 1510 and in Florence in the 1520s, which suggests it left the Netherlands at some point between these dates.

under an arched opening in the wall of the structure behind. In the central scene of the Adoration of the Magi Memling has depicted the same building but from a different, more distant, viewpoint, as befits the more formal nature of the scene of the three kings paying homage to the Christ Child. The viewers' standpoint when viewing the Nativity in the first panel is thus made explicit in the view of the stable in the second, the Adoration: we were behind the wall which is now at the back of the stable, peering though one of the arched openings in it (probably the one second from the left opposite the ox and ass). For the Adoration, the Virgin has come out of the inner part of the structure, and sits in front of the same column that we see obliquely, in front of Joseph, in the Nativity. Every architectural element matches exactly, and to achieve such consistency Memling must have had a mind which could envisage such things with ease.

Witnessing the events of Christ's life and Passion in the fullest way, imagining every small detail, as devotional literature encouraged the pious to do, may account for the increasing narrative richness and complexity of many images as the century progresses, seen at its most successful in a group of works by Memling, who developed a formula for mid-sized single panelled works packed with extensive simultaneous narrative, without a clear centrally dominant scene. His *Passion of Christ* in Turin [**203**], made for Tommaso Portinari, may have been intended for that patron's chapel in the church of St Jacob's in Bruges.[9] Here Memling combines, in one visual field, twenty-three events from Christ's Passion starting with the Entry into Jerusalem on the far top left, winding though the various architectural structures, out through the city gates for the Agony in the Garden, back in though the city gates, and out again at the other side as the procession wends up the road to Calvary. Not only does Memling manage to make the whole narrative read fairly consist-

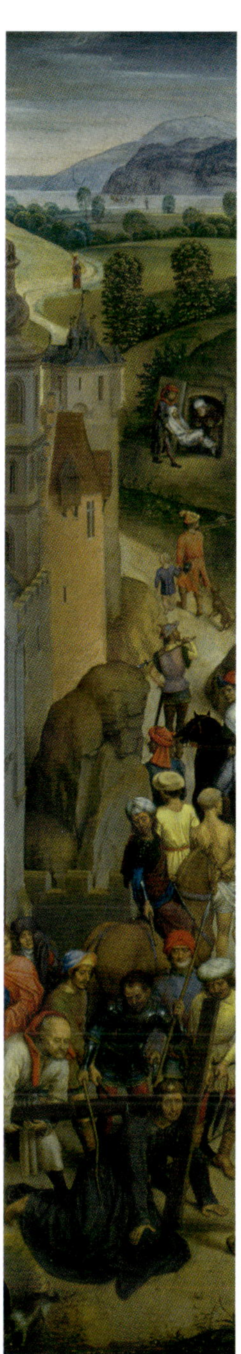

ently from left to right, but he places all his night scenes on the lower left, in the dark, with the picture getting progressively lighter as the sun rises over the hill on the upper right. He also locates the narratives so that on each side of the image, where the donors kneel, a scene unfolds which places Christ in close proximity to their view, as the object of their devotions. This work shows Memling's inventiveness and extraordinary narrative ability at its best.

A very different visual strategy, which limited all extraneous narrative detail, was also used increasingly in the late fifteenth century by many artists to heighten the sense of participation and aid contemplation. This can be seen expertly deployed in a small panel (39 × 30 centimetres) painted by Jean Hey (*fl.* 1494–1504), an artist praised by Jean Lemaire de Belges in *Le Plainte du Désiré* [**204**].[10] Hey was probably of Netherlandish origin, but was active in France in the last decade of the fifteenth century and has been plausibly identified with the Master of Moulins.[11] His name is inscribed on the back of this work, which states, in beautiful, formal letters spaced to cover most of the panel (implying that the reverse was intended to be seen), that 'Master Jean Cueillette, aged 40 years, notary and secretary to King Charles VIII, caused this outstanding work to be produced by Master Jean Hey, the illustrious Teutonic painter, in 1494'.

In this panel Jean Hey has depicted a precise narrative moment in Christ's Passion, made clear by the inscription above His head: *Ecce Homo* (behold the man). These were Pilate's words to the Jews when he presented Christ to them following His having been scourged, bound at the wrists, crowned with thorns and given a reed as a mock sceptre, all of which are evident in the image. He was also, however, given a red cloak—not depicted but possibly alluded to in the parted red curtains that reveal the image of His body to us. By presenting Christ naked, without the cloak, the image may also have been intended to evoke images of the Man of Sorrows—that is, Christ after the Crucifixion, as He appeared in a vision to St Gregory the Great, and as depicted in a famous mosaic icon in Rome, which was much copied (an engraved version was issued by Israhel van Meckenem, **205**) and which, by this period, had many indulgences attached to it. By showing this moment without any extraneous detail—no crowds shouting for Christ's death, no tormentors, no Pilate, and indeed no substantive setting, as well as with very limited colours (white, red, and green alone) all the attention is focused on the body of Christ: His expression, flesh and blood, and therefore His humanity. Placing Christ in front of the curtains (made evident from the reed He holds which juts over them), while the ropes seem to spill over the picture plane itself, makes His painted form even more tangible and immediate, heightening the sense of His presence. In many ways, this image follows the expected conventions of a royal portrait—in its format and in the revelatory curtains—and gains further meaning and impact by its allusion to that form; immediately prior to the moment depicted here Christ was mocked as 'King of the Jews' by His tormentors. Some of the most useful images for contemplation and imagination must have been those which, like this, depicted one moment in narrative time while alluding to events just past, and those still to happen.

It was not only Passion images that made use of these visual tools to engage the viewer and to convey a sense of immediacy and presence. An image of

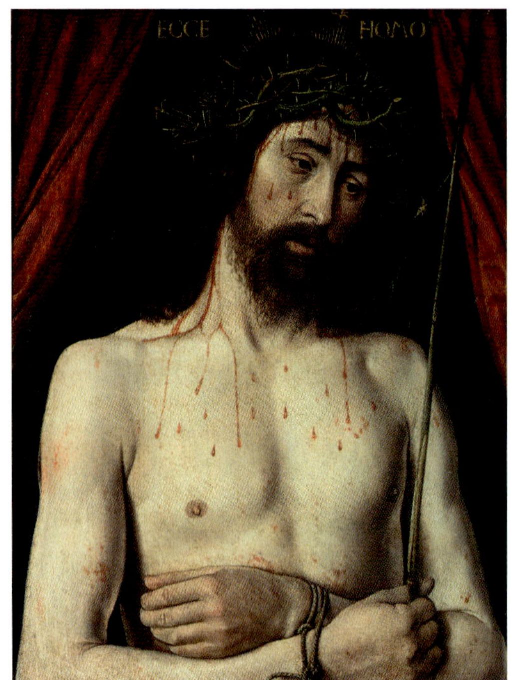

204 Jean Hey (the Master of Moulins)

Ecce Homo, oil on wood, dated 1494.

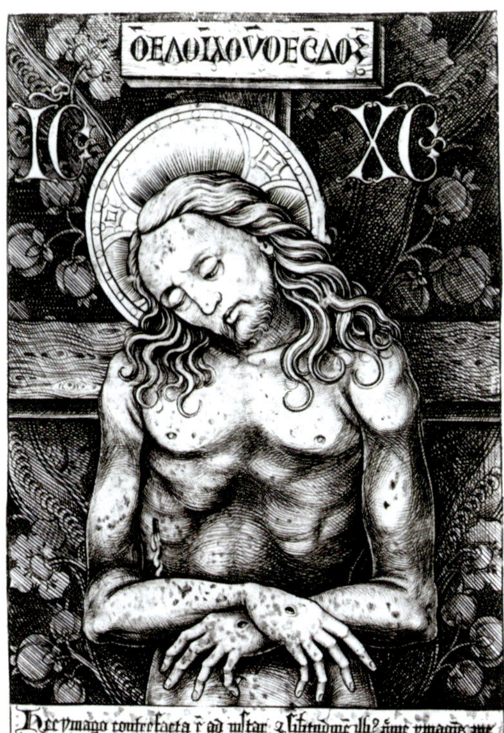

205 Israhel van Meckenem

Imago Pietatis, copperplate engraving on paper, *c.*1495–1500.

The inscription claims it to be a 'true copy' of the icon owned by the Carthusians of Santa Croce in Rome, an indulgenced image; the benefits of the original had been extended to copies of it by Urban IV in the mid-fourteenth century, which in part accounts for the increase in popularity of this subject (**158** and **138** are versions of it). Israhel's engraving reproduces the form of the icon, as it claims, but the figure of Christ has been made more three-dimensional, and thus 'real', by what must have been his own invention: setting it against a brocade cloth. Israhel used the same device for his self-portrait [**105**], possibly for related reasons.

206 Follower of Simon Marmion

St Anthony Abbot, from a book of hours, possibly made for Antonine Rolin, parchment, 1490s.

Like **22**, this miniature depends in part for its effect on an absence of any border decoration. It heads a suffrage to St Anthony, one of two to this saint and the only illustrated suffrage in the manuscript; it seems probable that the book was made for someone called Antonine, possibly Antonine Rolin, son of the famous chancellor Nicolas Rolin [**207**], who was married to Marie d'Ailly (the initials A and M are found elsewhere in the manuscript).

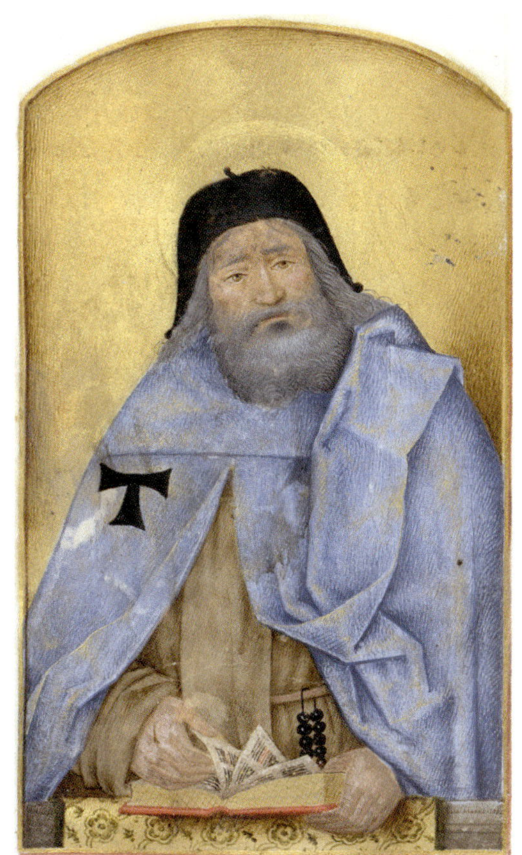

St Anthony [**206**] from a book of hours, painted by an artist in the circle of Simon Marmion (who was instrumental in experimenting with and popularizing close-up half-length figures), shows a similar range of devices used to great effect.[12] The saint is shown as if standing behind a ledge on which he has rested his prayer book; he appears either to have been momentarily distracted from his text, or to be contemplating something he has read in it; the book itself is foreshortened so that it seems to come out into the space of the viewer—the artist uses the parapet and book here like Jean Hey used the curtains, reed and rope. As in the *Ecce Homo* image, the advantage of the half-length form in attaining a portrait-like quality, with the face and its expression the central conveyor of meaning and effect, is evident. But this put demands on an artist, who had to be very good at painting faces, indeed portraits, even if imagined; only the more talented artists adopted this visual form with success.

Verisimilitude in images designed for meditation must have been an important aid to devotional contemplation. The immediacy of works like Hey's *Ecce Homo* or the crown of thorns on the reverse of the *Small Round Pietà* [**162**] must have increased their sensual impact and potential to convey the sufferings of Christ. Devotional portrait diptychs, like the one attached to Philip the Good's fabric oratory, played particularly on this potential, not

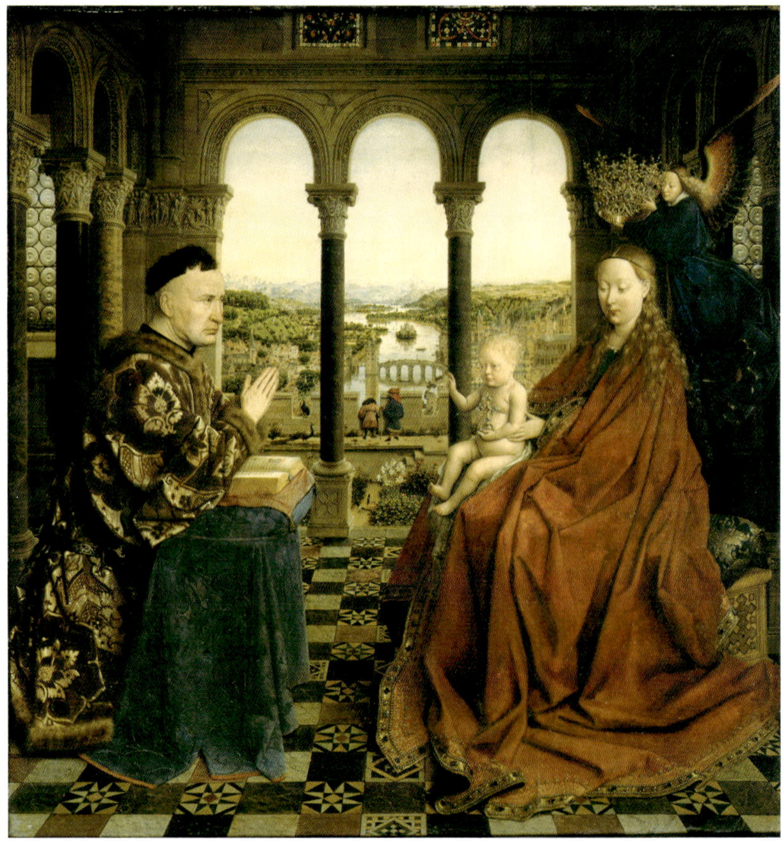

207 Jan van Eyck

Madonna of Chancellor Nicolas Rolin, oil on Baltic oak, *c.*1435.

only in the apparent reality of the sacred figures, but also in the likeness, and thus tangible presence, of the donor.

One of the most famous images of this type, although not actually in diptych form, is the panel made for the Burgundian Chancellor Nicolas Rolin (1376–1462) by Jan van Eyck around 1435, now in the Louvre [**207**].[13] This work, its painted surface measuring 65 × 62.3 centimetres, is not of the intimate, very small scale of many of van Eyck's devotional paintings. However, its imagery suggests that the primary purpose of Rolin's panel, at least during Rolin's lifetime, was as an aid for meditation. Rolin is depicted kneeling in prayer before the Virgin and Child in a defiantly unreal space which is neither necessarily Rolin's on earth nor a heavenly sphere: indeed, this ambiguity is evident in the way the image dissects horizontally down the centre line of tiles in a manner suggesting that the left half is Rolin's world, the right that of Christ and the Virgin. Set behind Rolin is a town and many vineyards, the source of his wealth, while above him in the carved arches vines allude to his earthly wealth as well as to Christ's sacrifice; on the Virgin's side we have a city that is made almost entirely of churches, and as such is clearly not a real place but a symbol of the Virgin herself. The landscape may include other references or allusions; it is clearly not an actual place.

That the practice of devotional contemplation was considered in the decisions made by patron and painter about this image is indicated by the texts inscribed around the Virgin's robe, which are excerpts from the text Rolin most probably has in front of him: the Little Office of the Virgin, the basis of the Book of Hours. One way of reading this image is therefore that, through prayer, the Virgin has materialized to Rolin, at least in the form of a visualization. The distant landscape with mountains (see the quote from Nicolas Oresme heading this chapter) which occupies the centre of the picture could have been designed with such meditational practices in mind, helping to move Rolin from contemplating an image evoked by prayer (the Virgin and Child), to the ideal of imageless devotion, that is contemplation of the abstract qualities of the divine, embodied by nature, his creation, as advocated by Jean Gerson and others.

Because this work was recorded hanging on the wall of Rolin's funerary chapel in the church of Notre-Dame-du-Châtel at Autun in the eighteenth century, it is usually presumed that it was designed for a semi-public, non-domestic purpose. However, it is painted with fictive marbling on the back, which would be a waste of time and effort if the work were to be fixed to the wall from the start, and this alone indicates that a more flexible role for this work was envisaged. Perhaps it was intended, eventually, to have a commemorative function, set near the altar and presumably in some physical relation to his tomb. The original frame, with its inscription, is now lost, but it is tempting to speculate whether the work might have subsequently functioned as an epitaph in Rolin's burial chapel. This could explain its visual complexity and ambiguity: what was needed was an image that worked as a devotional tool, showing Rolin in the act of prayer, but which might also imply Rolin's acceptance into the presence of the Virgin and Child, and thus the heavenly realm, as would be suitable for an epitaph. Van Eyck translated both these needs into one image, which could both inspire contemplation and suitably ensure the commemoration of Rolin in the setting of his funerary chapel.

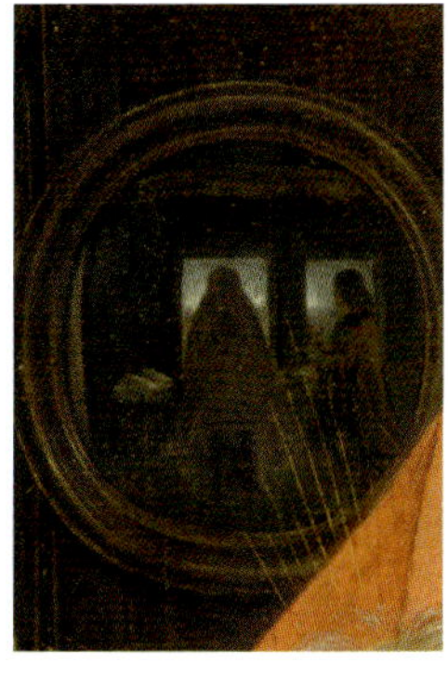

208 Hans Memling
Diptych of Maartin van Nieuwenhove, oil on Baltic oak, 1487.

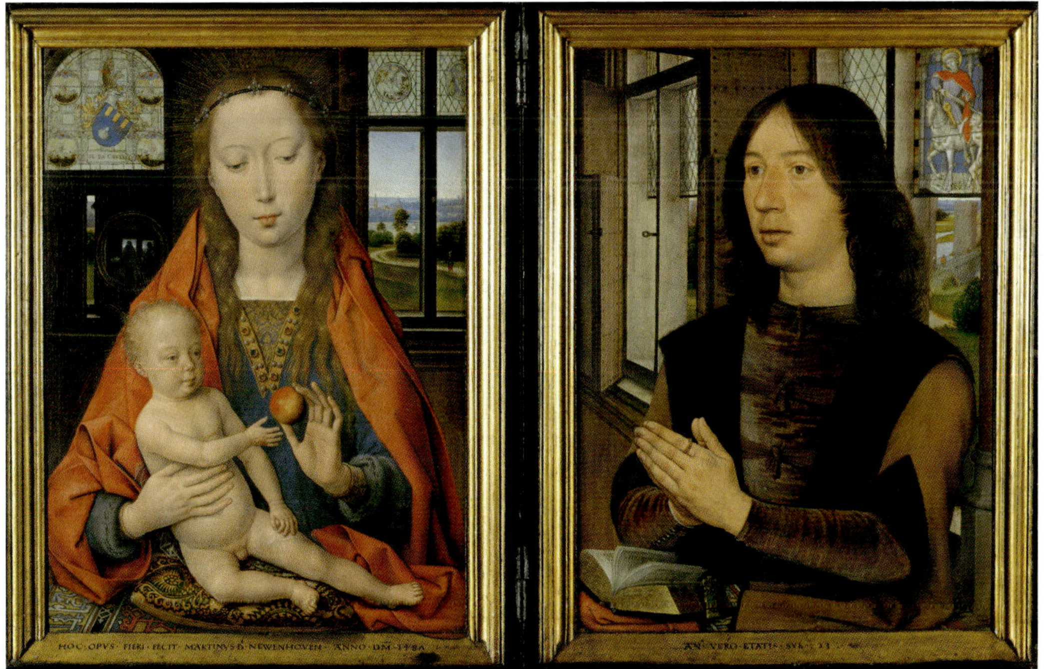

In a diptych painted around fifty years later, also in Bruges, for the councillor and captain of the civic guard, Maarten van Nieuwenhove (1463–1500) [208], we are left in no doubt that the Virgin has appeared to Maarten in his own space: the room in which he is shown has his patron saint and coats of arms in the stained glass window and is a recognizable reality (if not an actual one) in terms of a fifteenth-century interior in a way that Rolin's is not.[14] The apparent verismilitude of the vision—so real in fact that both he and the Virgin are reflected in the mirror of the room—must have helped the devotee to visualize such an image. What is often overlooked when we consider these works is that in most cases the principal, or at least first, user was the person portrayed in the image, so that when Maarten opened his diptych he was looking at an image of himself looking at an image of the Virgin. What this visual strategy achieves is not absolutely clear, but perhaps patrons like Maarten could more easily imagine themselves having such a visualization of the Virgin when they can see an image of it happening in front of them, like the visualization process athletes use today, picturing themselves winning to help them achieve victory. In that case such images might help speed up the process of visualization, which would be of great benefit to a man as busy as the chancellor of Burgundy, and other secular men and women with more limited time to pray than the members of religious orders like the Carthusians whose practice of prayer was an ideal to be emulated.

Although Nieuwenhove and Rolin may have been the primary viewers of their panels, such images were clearly intended for posterity too. Maarten's family members would presumably continue to use this work and would pray for Maarten in doing so—it would be hard for them to do otherwise with such a vivid likeness of him present. We have already seen how Rolin's was intended to function for posterity, next to the altar in his burial chapel in Autun, where he would be in perpetual devotion to the Virgin in the painting as well as, given the work's likely position, to the altar in the chapel, the images set on it, and the services held in front of it. We have other documented examples of images which combined portraits and devotional imagery beginning their life as private objects and changing their function on the owner's death, being moved physically to a new, more public setting. These works then had functions that became primarily commemorative. This is evident from the documentation concerning a lost panel, probably a diptych, owned by the famous composer Guillaume Dufay, which showed not himself but his friend and fellow canon, Simon le Breton. This he willed to the cathedral at Cambrai, where he specified it was to be brought out and placed on the altar in the chapel where he (Dufay) was to be buried, on feast days and on the anniversaries of his death and that of his friend Simon.[15]

That these often intimate and apparently private portraits of men and women in prayer before images of the Virgin or other saints (the term donor is not quite the right one here) were intended to be used in this way—as reminders for their families to pray for their them—is further explicated in two contemporary texts: the first is written in a book of hours made for a French nobleman, Macé de Prestesaille. It is placed on the folios directly following an image of Macé with his (deceased) wife and numerous children (some also deceased) in prayer before the Pietà [209]. The text indicates that the book was made 'for the memory and remembrance of the dead,

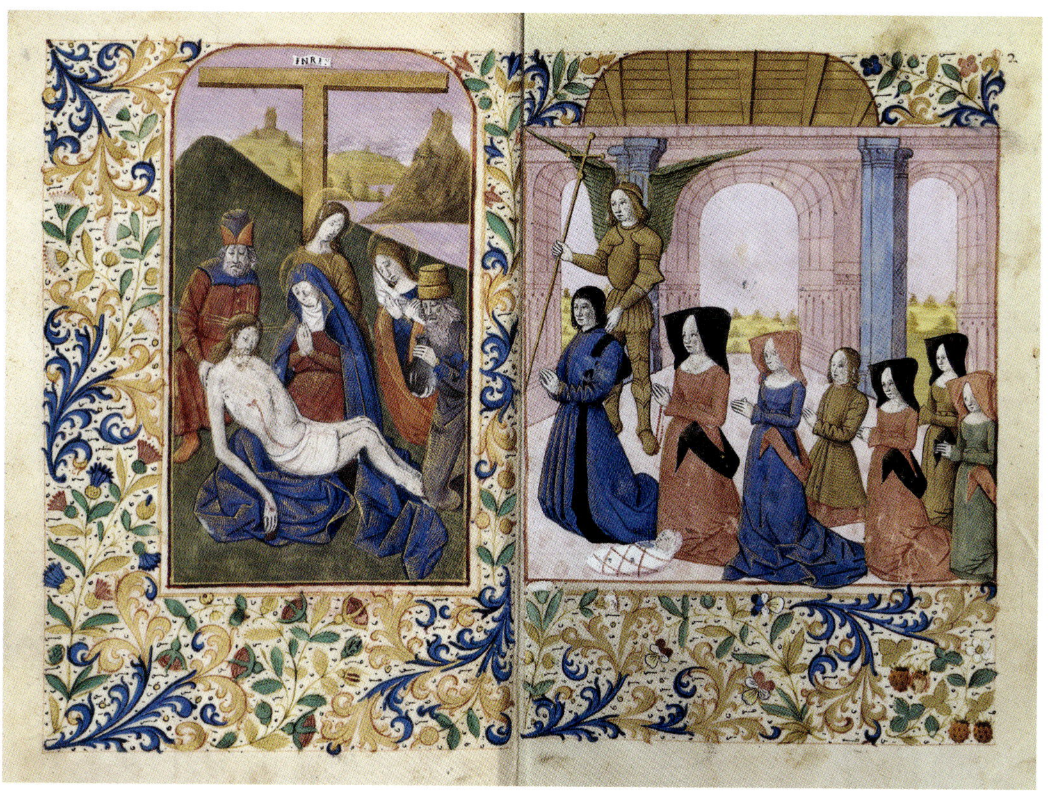

209 Anonymous French illuminator working in Tours
Macé de Prestesaille, his Wife Jeanne and their Children kneeling in Prayer to the Pietà, from the Hours of Macé de Prestesaille, parchment, dated 1475.
These are the opening folios in this book of hours: designed without text, they work like a devotional diptych. Their intention was also commemorative: turning the page reveals an inscription giving the patron's name and the date this book was made, along with a text requesting prayers for him, his dead wife, and their children (some of whom were also deceased). In order to fit in all six children (including one babe in swaddling), the artist expanded this miniature across the space usually reserved for the border.

and principally for the memory of Jeanne ... in her lifetime wife of Macé de Prestesaille, and also for the memory of their children, which Jeanne had had or had conceived during the time of their marriage'. The text goes on to ask that 'all lords, ladies, priests, clerics, secular and otherwise, who read or hear this text read, will pray for the soul of the deceased [Jeanne], and all the other deceased [her children] by each saying an Our Father and a Hail Mary'. Clearly it was envisaged that this apparently private book might have a wider audience than we might suppose and would act like a more public memorial eliciting prayers for the souls of the departed.[16]

The second example relates to versions of a more famous image, Jan van Eyck's *St Francis* panels, discussed in Part IV [**130, 131**]; two such images were owned in 1470 by Anselm Adornes, a Genoese merchant whose family had long been established in Bruges.[17] On leaving for a pilgrimage to the Holy Land, Adornes made a will in which he specified that the two paintings were to be given to his two daughters, both of whom were in convents near Bruges, and that the daughters must then have 'portraits of me and my wife made on the little shutters which close off these little paintings. They have to be good likenesses so that they [his daughters] and other pious persons may remember us [in their prayers].' That such reminders should be as vivid as possible is made clear in the specification that they have to be good likenesses. In both these instances, despite the small and private nature of the works, a larger audience of potential future viewers was envisaged, as we have also postulated for Chancellor Rolin's and Maartin van Nieuwenhove's paintings. All these examples show that portable works, in particular, could have varied

210 Jean Fouquet
Etienne Chevalier presented to the Virgin and Child by St Stephen (the 'Melun Diptych'), oil on panel, *c.*1455–60.

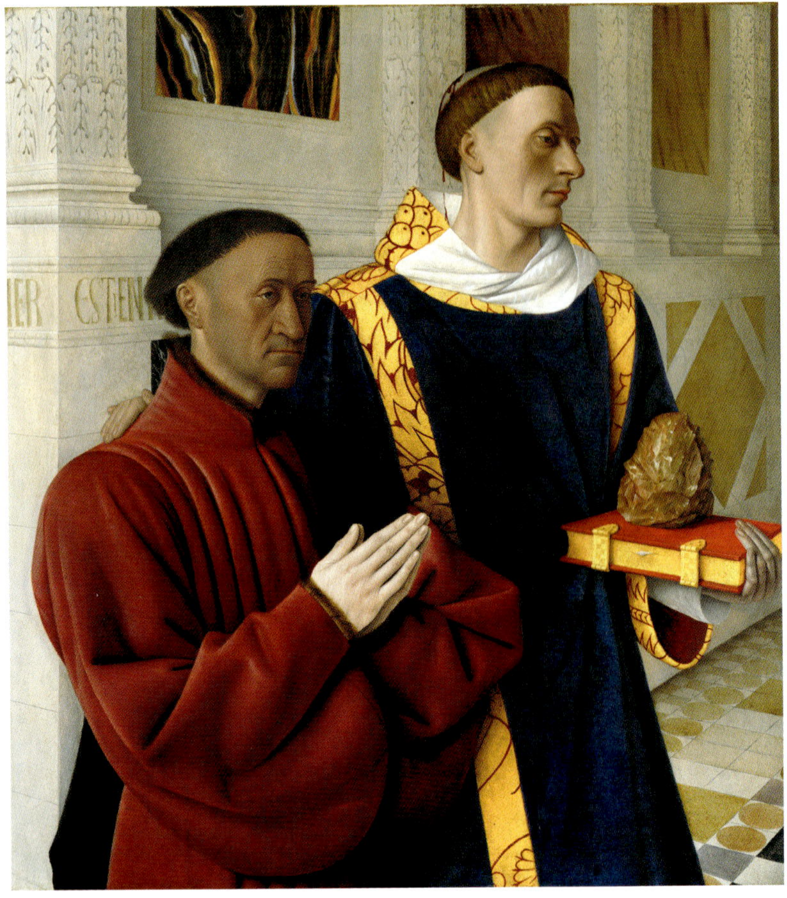

and changing functions and be seen by a range of different viewers in different spaces, even within the lifetime of their owner.

Perhaps the most extraordinary and mysterious of all diptychs, indeed, of any work of our period, is that made for the treasurer to Charles VII of France, Etienne Chevalier [**210**], by the painter to the king, Jean Fouquet.[18] This is a large work (each panel measures about 94 × 85 centimetres), and may well have been an altarpiece, as has recently been shown to be the case for several other diptychs of this size and form.[19] We know it was in the collegiate church of Notre-Dame at Melun, where Chevalier and his wife were buried, in 1661 when it was described by Denys Godefroy as 'two pictures closing one unto another'.[20] He also described the (lost) frame of Etienne Chevalier's diptych, which was covered with blue velvet, decorated with love knots and the chancellor's initials formed in pearls; it was also set with 'medals of silver gilt', one of which may be the gold and enamel self-portrait of the painter [**211**], though this is produced in a material in which the artist himself did not routinely work.

This diptych combines a conventional image of the donor at prayer, presented by St Stephen, with a remarkable image of the Virgin and Child, set on a throne and surrounded by blue and red cherubim and seraphim. The figure of the Virgin is what startles us and demands explanation: she is dressed as a highly fashionable queen of the period, with an ermine-lined cloak, plucked

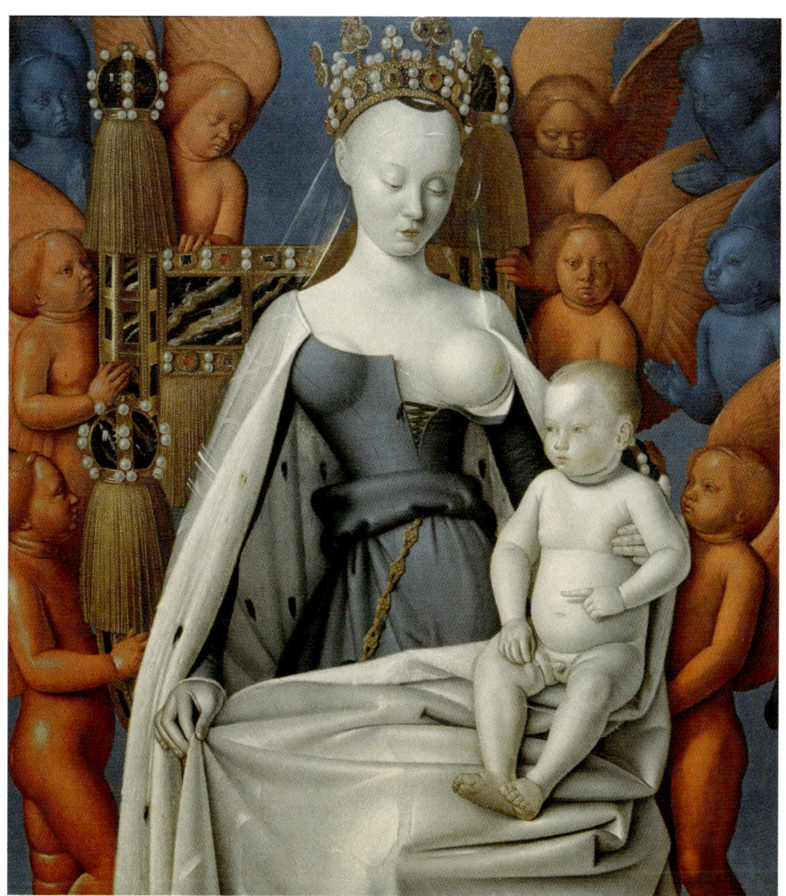

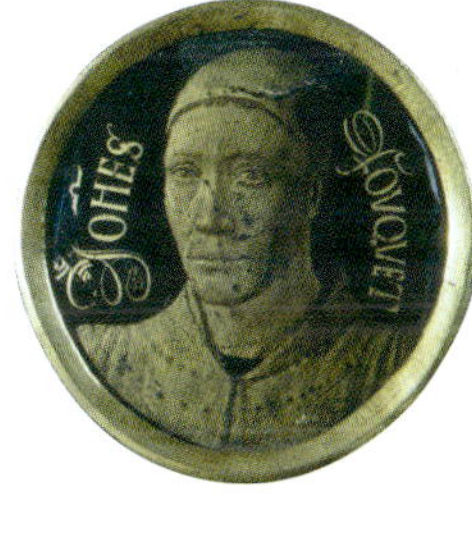

211 Jean Fouquet

Self-portrait, once set around the frame of **210**, copper, dark blue enamel, and gold paint, 7.5 cm diameter with frame.

The portrait is built up using two different tones of gold laid directly over the dark blue enamel, applied in long thin strokes with a very fine brush; some of the gold was then scratched away with a very thin stylus to create further remarkable detail in the facial features, especially the eyes.

eyebrows and hair-line, and a high-waisted dress, which is undone to reveal her breast. The latter in itself is not unusual—this is a common way of depicting the Virgin and refers to her special (and thus powerful) relationship with Christ, who she breast-fed, unlike, indeed, mothers of high social status at the period.[21] However, the child ignores the breast, and both He and the Virgin are unnaturally white. He points, to the treasurer or perhaps to the womb of the Virgin, which is visually emphasized by her belt and the unusual form of her dress, with the band of fabric rolled up around the waist. The image becomes even harder to 'read' when we realize that this Virgin is, as the visual evidence and long-standing tradition tell us, a portrait of the mistress of King Charles VII, Agnès Sorel, with whom Etienne Chevalier was in close contact at court. Agnès had died in 1450, under mysterious circumstances, apparently poisoned while pregnant with the king's child (she had already borne him two girls), some time before this work was made: dendrochonology of the panel suggests a date after 1456. What this work shows, then, is something that never could be: Agnès as queen and Agnès as mother to a son, a future king, all in the guise of the Virgin. Etienne Chevalier's Virgin may, however, be a repetition of a version already in existence: x-rays reveal that an identical Virgin and Child, to the same dimensions, was begun on a panel which was then painted over, in Fouquet's workshop, with a portrait of Charles VII himself (Paris, Louvre). That a pattern existed for this Virgin suggests the workshop was involved in reproducing versions of it—one that was abandoned and one that was completed for Chevalier—but neither of these is necessarily the primary one. Indeed, it seems plausible that the demand for this extraordinary image came initially from the king, who was desolate at the death of his mistress, and that Fouquet invented this Agnès-Virgin for him. Etienne, in adopting it for his diptych, is perhaps reiterating, besides his devotion to the Virgin, his very firm devotion to Agnès (he was one of the executors of her will), to her faction at court, and thus to the king. Although it might seem extraordinary to us today, the intense identification with holy and historical figures was not unfrequently made visually emphatic by giving them the features of contemporary people: Philip the Bold had himself depicted as Jeremiah on the *Well of Moses*; Charles the Bold frequently cast himself as Alexander the Great; Mary of Burgundy and Margaret of Austria had themselves depicted as the Magdalene, and perhaps most pertinent here, Charles VII was depicted as one of the Magi in another work made for Etienne Chevalier and painted by Jean Fouquet, his book of hours.[22]

The complexity of the Melun Diptych, as memorial, devotional image, altarpiece, and portrait, is not in itself so extraordinary. As we have seen, the more sophisticated artists of the period produced images that worked on many levels, that could potentially fulfil several, sometimes changeable purposes, conveying meaning and encouraging identification and emotional engagement through a range of visual strategies and allusions. Painters, in particular, evoked other media and materials in their works, creating images which were both true to life and entirely unreal, rendering utterly believable objects in utterly unreal combinations and conjunctions [**18, 33, 20, 37, 174, 207, 208**]. Thus while painting may not have been the most materially valuable, or indeed the most highly coveted of media, it was perhaps, when expertly worked, the most effective in achieving an impact on both memory and emotions, and was to increasingly become the dominant mode of artistic production across Europe in the subsequent centuries. Its potential was something Dürer, the only northern artist of our period to write down his thoughts on the purpose of his art, clearly recognized, despite his own increasing focus on the making of prints rather than paintings. He should have the last word:

> 'The art of painting is employed in the service of the church and by it the sufferings of Christ and many other profitable examples are set forth. It preserves also the likeness of men after their death. By aid of delineation in painting the measurements of the earth, the waters, and the stars have come to be understood, and many things will become known unto men thereby. The attainment of true, artistic and lovely painting is hard to come unto. It needs long time and a hand most free and practiced. Whosoever, therefore, is not gifted in this manner, let him not undertake it; for it comes by inspiration from above. The art of painting cannot be truly judged save by such as are themselves good painters; from others it is verily hidden even as a strange tongue.'[23]

Notes

Chapter 1: Introduction

1. A view implicit in the date range of another book in this series, V. Sekules, *Medieval Art* (Oxford 2001); for historical arguments against a strict division of our view at this point see S. Hindman, 'The Illustrated Book: An Addendum to the State of Research in Northern European Art', *The Art Bulletin*, 68 (1986), 536–42. J. Huizinga in *The Autumn of the Middle Ages*, tr. R. J. Peyton and U. Mammitzsch (Chicago 1996), takes a related view in seeing this period as the declining moment of the previous centuries.
2. For this see F. Piponnier and P. Mane, *Dress in the Middle Ages* (London 1997); M. Scott, *The History of Dress Series: Late Gothic Europe, 1400–1500* (London 1980); M. Scott, 'The Role of Dress in the Image of Charles the Bold, Duke of Burgundy', in E. Morrison and T. Kren (eds), *Flemish Manuscript Painting in Context: Recent Research* (Los Angeles 2006), 43–56.
3. See the Bibliographic Essay.
4. E. Welch, *Art and Society in Italy 1350–1500* (Oxford 1997).
5. P. Tafur, *Travels and Adventures 1435–1438*, ed. M. Letts (London 1926), 198–204.
6. 'Pel millor i més apte pintor que pogués ésser trobat'; deliberations of the Barcelona councillors, 4 September 1443; quoted in J. Berg Sobré, *Behind the Altar Table: The Development of the Painted Retable in Spain, 1350–1500* (New York 1989), 293.
7. '... zway cöstliche maysterliche werk'; quoted in E. Oellermann, 'Die Schnitzaltäre Friedrich Herlins im Vergleich der Erkenntnisse neuerer kunsttechnologischer Untersuchungen', *Jahrbuch der Berliner Museen*, 33 (1991), 213–38.
8. 'Bauduin de Bailleul ou par un autre meilleur paintre qu'ilz pourront finer'. Published in E. Soil, *Les tapisseries de Tournai: Les tapissiers et les hautelisseurs de cette ville, Recherches et documents sur l'histoire, la fabrication et les produits des ateliers de Tournai* (Tournai and Lille 1892), 374–5, quoted in T. P. Campbell, *Tapestry in the Renaissance: Art and Magnificence*, exh. cat. (New York 2002), 44.
9. Original text in W. H. J. Weale, *Hubert and John van Eyck: Their Life and Work* (London 1908), xlii–xliii, translated in E. G. Holt, *A Documentary History of Art, Volume I: The Middle Ages and the Renaissance* (New York 1957), 304–5. On the interpretation of 'science' see C. Reynolds, 'The King of Painters', in S. Foister, S. Jones, and D. Cool (eds), *Investigating Jan van Eyck* (Turnhout 2000), 1–16.
10. For discussion of the history and use of this term see M. Belozerskaya, *Rethinking the Renaissance: Burgundian Arts across Europe* (Cambridge 2002), 7–46; M. L. King, *The Renaissance in Europe* (London 2003), viii–xii; E. Panofsky, '"Renaissance"—Self-Definition or Self-Deception?', in *Renaissance and Renascences in Western Art* (London 1965), 1–35.

Chapter 2: Dispersal and Destruction

1. M. van Vaernewijck, *Den Spieghel der Nederlandscher Audtheyt* (Ghent 1568), published in French as M. de Smet de Naeyer (ed.), *Mémoires d'un patricien gantois du XVI siècle: Troubles religieux en Flandre et dans les Pays-Bas au XVI siècle*, 2 vols (Ghent 1905–6), I, 126.
2. The various lines of argument on the Ghent Altarpiece are summarized in E. Dhanens, *Art in Context—Van Eyck: The Ghent Altarpiece* (London 1973), and more recently B. Ridderbos, 'Objects and Questions', in B. Ridderbos, A. van Buren, and H. van Veen (eds), *Early Netherlandish Paintings: Rediscovery, Reception and Research* (Amsterdam 2005), 42–59.
3. L. Guicciardini, *Descrittione di tutti i Paesi Bassi* (Antwerp 1567); K. van Mander, *Het Schilder-boeck* (Haarlem

1604), English trans. H. Miedema (ed.), *Karel van Mander: The Lives of the Illustrious Netherlandish and German Painters* (Doornspijk 1994–9); M. J. Friedländer, *Early Netherlandish Painting*, 14 vols (original German publication 1924–7; trans. Leiden and Brussels 1967–76). This is still a fundamental reference work for Netherlandish painting of the period.

4. For Dürer's comment see W. M. Conway, *Literary Remains of Albrecht Dürer* (Cambridge 1889), 117; for de Beatis see J. R. Hale (ed.), *The Travel Journals of Antonio de Beatis: Germany, Switzerland, the Low Countries, France and Italy, 1517–1518* (London 1979), 96; de Heere's ode was published by van Mander, and can be found in translation in Carel van Mander, *Dutch and Flemish Painters, Translated from the Schilder-boeck and Introduction by C. van de Wall* (New York 1936), 10–12. For Vasari, G. Vasari, *Lives of the Painters, Sculptors and Architects*, tr. G. du C. de Vere, intro. and notes D. Ekserdjian, 2 vols (London 1996), II, 862.

5. For its technical examination, P. Coremans, *L'Agneau mystique au laboratoire: Examen et traitement* (Antwerp 1953), which includes a contribution on the history of its tribulations, 21–68; J. R. J. van Asperen de Boer, 'A Scientific Re-examination of the Ghent Altarpiece', *Oud Holland*, 93 (1979), 141–214, for the underdrawings; for its frame see H. Verougstraete and R. van Schoute, 'Le cadres de l'Agneau mystique de Van Eyck', *Revue de l'art*, 77 (1987), 73–6; for recent dendrochronology on its wings J. Vynckier, 'Analyse dendrochronologique de quelques panneaux du retable de l'Agneau mystique de Van Eyck', *Bulletin de l'Institut Royal du Patrimone Artistique*, 28 (1999–2000), 237–42.

6. De Smet de Naeyer (ed.), *Mémoires d'un patricien gantois*, I, 132.

7. Letter of 7 July 1817, quoted in Coremans, *L'Agneau mystique au laboratoire*, 43–5.

8. On Rogier's painting see L. Campbell, *National Gallery Catalogues: The Fifteenth Century Netherlandish Schools* (London 1998), 407–27.

9. For Halle see J. W. Steyart, *The Sculpture of St Martin's in Halle and Related Netherlandish Works*, PhD, University of Michigan (Ann Arbor 1974); for Zoutleeuw, C. Englen, *Zoutleeuw: Jan Mertens en de laatgotiek: confrontatie met Jan Borreman* (Leuven 1993).

10. A notable example is the high altar of the cathedral in Strasbourg, dismantled in 1642 when the town returned to Catholicism; over the next 100 years all but small parts were dispersed and destroyed. C. Dupeux, P. Jezler, and J. Wirth (eds), *Iconoclasme: Vie et mort de l'image médiévale*, exh. cat. (Berne and Strasbourg 2001), 388–9.

11. L. Flavigny and C. Jablonski-Chauveau (eds), *D'Angleterre en Normandie: Sculptures d'albâtre du Moyen Âge*, exh. cat. (Rouen 1998); N. Ramsay, 'Medieval English Alabasters in Rouen and Evreux', *Apollo*, 147 (1998), 50–1.

12. Dupeux, Jezler, and Wirth (eds), *Iconoclasme*, 350–1.

13. For the destruction in Brussels at this period see A. Smolar-Meynart (ed.), *Autour du bombardement de Bruxelles de 1695: Désastre et relèvement* (Brussels 1997); for Rogier's paintings see E. Dhanens and J. Dijkstra, *Rogier de la Pasture van der Weyden* (Tournai 1999), 113–24, and D. de Vos, *Rogier van der Weyden: The Complete Works* (Antwerp 1999), 345–54. For the tapestries see A. Cetto, *Der Berner Traian- und Herkinbald-Teppich* (Berne 1966) and E. Cleland, *More than Woven Paintings: The Reappearance of Rogier van der Weyden's Designs in Tapestry*, PhD, Courtauld Institute of Art (Univ. London, 2002), 82–115.

14. For the Chartreuse de Champmol see S. Lindquist, *Agency, Visuality and Society at the Chartreuse de Champmol* (Aldershot 2008); R. Prochno, *Die Kartause von Champmol: Grablege der burgundischen Herzöge 1364–1477* (Berlin 2002); S. Jugie and S. Fliegel (eds), *Art from the Court of Burgundy 1364–1419*, exh. cat. (Dijon 2004). C. Monget, *La Chartreuse de Dijon d'après les documents des archives de Bourgogne*, 3 vols (Montreuil-sur-Mer 1898–1905), III, 6–181, is still the most extensive discussion of the events during the French Revolution.

15. For Prindale see M. Beaulieu and V. Beyer, *Dictionnaire des sculpteurs français du Moyen Âge* (Paris 1992), 250–2.

16. For these and other works in foreign treasuries see *Paris 1400: Les arts sous Charles VI*, exh. cat. (Paris 2004), 165–80.

17. Miedema (ed.), *Karel van Mander*; J. B. Descamps, *Voyage pittoresque de la Flandre et du Brabant* (Paris 1769); E. Fromentin, *Les Maîtres d'Autrefois: Belgique—Holland* (Paris 1876).

18. N. MacGregor, *A Victim of Anonymity: The Master of the Saint Bartholomew Altarpiece* (London 1993), 15–17.

19. Contract translated in W. Stechow, *Northern Renaissance Art: Sources and Documents* (Evanston 1989), 10–11. For its iconography M. Smeyers, 'The Living Bread: Dirk Bouts and the Last Supper', in *Dirk Bouts (ca 1410–1475) een Vlaams primitief te Leuven*, exh. cat. (Leuven 1998), 35–58.
20. On this issue of names and their implications see MacGregor, *A Victim of Anonymity*, 16–19; on the Master of the Embroidered Foliage see F. Gombert and D. Martens, *Primitifs flamands: Le maître au feuillage brodé, secrets d'ateliers*, exh. cat., Lille, Palais des Beaux-Arts (Paris 2005); on the Vienna Master of Mary of Burgundy see T. Kren and S. McKendrick, *Illuminating the Renaissance: The Triumph of Flemish Manuscript Painting in Europe*, exh. cat. (London 2003), 126–57, 227–9.
21. On the issue of documentation relating to Hugo van der Goes see E. Dhanens, *Hugo van der Goes* (Antwerp 1998), especially 15–22.
22. For Lochner see J. Chapuis, *Stefan Lochner: Image Making in Fifteenth-Century Cologne* (Turnhout 2004). The identification of the artist was questioned by M. Wolfson, 'Hat Dürer das "Dombild" gesehen? Ein Beitrag zur Lochner-Forschung', *Zeitschrift für Kunstgeschichte*, 48 (1986), 229–335; the uncertainty has led to him being termed the Dombild Master in some recent literature, notably B. Corley, *Painting and Patronage in Cologne, 1300–1500* (London 2000).
23. The fundamental study setting out the evidence and reassessing the stylistic groups is L. Campbell, 'Robert Campin, the Master of Flémalle, and the Master of Mérode', *The Burlington Magazine*, 116 (1974), 634–46; technical evidence in S. Foister and S. Nash (eds), *Robert Campin: New Directions in Scholarship* (Turnhout 1996); for the recent state of the debate L. Nys and D. Vanwijnsberg (eds), *Campin in Context* (Valenciennes 2007), especially the essays by S. Kemperdick, 'The Flémalle-Campin-van der Weyden Problem: Still Existing', 3–14, and L. Campbell, 'Brussels and Tournai', 113–23.
24. Campbell, *The Fifteenth Century Netherlandish Schools*, 20.
25. J. Sanchis y Sivera, *Pintores medievales en Valencia: Archivo de Arte Valenciano* (Valencia 1930), 16–21.
26. On Italian writers see M. Baxandall, *Giotto and the Orators: Humanist Observers of Painting in Italy and the Discovery of Pictorial Composition* (Oxford 1971).
27. J. Stecher (ed.), *Oeuvres de Jean Lemaire de Belges*, 4 vols (Leuven 1882–91).

Chapter 3: Italian Perspectives

1. F. de Holanda, *Four Dialogues on Painting*, tr. A. F. G. Bell (Oxford and London 1928), 15–16; the Portuguese wording of the line on 'external exactness' is: 'Pintam em Flandres propriamente para enganar a vista exterior, ou coisas que vos alegrem ou de que não possais dizer mal ...'; see F. de Holanda, *Diálogos em Roma*, ed. J. da Felicidade Alves (Lisbon 1984), 29–30.
2. I. Villela-Petit, 'Propositions for Jean d'Arbois', in *La création artistique en France autour de 1400: actes du colloque international 2004* (Paris 2006), 319.
3. R. Krautheimer, 'Ghiberti and Master Gusmin', *The Art Bulletin*, 29 (1947), 25–35.
4. M. Baxandall, 'Bartholomaeus Facius on Painting', *Journal of the Warburg and Courtauld Institutes*, 27 (1964), 90–107.
5. For this translation, P. Nuttall, *From Flanders to Florence: The Impact of Netherlandish Painting, 1400–1500* (New Haven and London 2004), 37 and 269, n.49.
6. Recent literature has returned to this idea in the light of new technical evidence, see E. Hall, 'The Detroit St Jerome in Search of its Painter' and B. Heller, 'St Jerome in the Laboratory: Scientific Evidence and the Enigmas of an Eyckian Panel', both in *The Bulletin of the Detroit Institute of Arts*, 72 (1998), 10–37; 39–55.
7. For a discussion of these nudes, J. Paviot, 'Les tableaux nus profanes de Jan van Eyck, *Gazette des Beaux-Arts*, 135 (2000), 265–82.
8. C. M. Richardson, K. W. Woods, and M. W. Franklin (eds), *Renaissance Art Reconsidered: An Anthology of Primary Sources* (Oxford 2007), 186–7.
9. H. Fierens-Gevaert, *La Renaissance septentrionale et les premier maîtres des Flandres* (Brussels 1905). For Beauneveu and the tomb of Charles V, S. Nash, with contributions by T.-H. Borchert and J. Harris, *'No Equal in Any Land': André Beauneveu Artist to the Courts of France and Flanders* (London 2007).
10. For example Dhanens, *The Ghent Altarpiece*, 103–9.
11. E. Panofsky, *Early Netherlandish Painting: Its Origins and Character*, 2 vols (Cambridge MA 1953), 272–6, and C. Harbison, *The Art of the Northern Renaissance* (London 1995), also published as *The Mirror of the Artist: The Art of the Northern Renaissance*

(New York 1995), 157; both see Rogier's trip as having an impact on his art.

12. See R. White, 'Analyses of Norwegian Medieval Paint Media: A Preliminary Report', in M. Malmanger, L. Berczelly, and S. Fuglesang (eds), *Norwegian Medieval Altar Frontals and Related Material* (Rome 1995), 127–35; A. Massing (ed.), *The Thornham Parva Retable: Technique, Conservation and Context of an English Medieval Panel Painting* (Cambridge 2003); R. White and J. Kirby, 'Some Observations on the Binder and Dyestuff Composition of Glaze Paints in Early European Panel Paintings', in J. Nadolny (ed.), *Medieval Painting in Northern Europe: Techniques, Analysis, Art History: Studies in Commemoration of the 70th Birthday of Unn Plahter* (London 2007), 215–22; M. Presca, R. Bruquetas, and M. Connor, 'Oil Painting in the Late Middle Ages in Spain: The Relationship of Style to Technique in the Epiphany Altarpiece of St Paul's Convent in Toledo', and M. T. Doménech et al., 'Analytical Study of the Evolution of Panel Painting Technique in Valencian Workshops from the Fourteenth to the Seventeenth Century', both in A. Roy and P. Smith (eds), *Painting Techniques: History, Materials and Studio Practice: Contributions to the Dublin Congress 7–11 September 1998* (London 1998), 22–34, 77–81.

13. As technical studies are increasingly showing, e.g. E. M. Gifford, S. Halpine, and S. Quillen Lomax, 'Interpreting Analyses of the Painting Medium: A Case Study of a Pre-Eyckian Altarpiece', in M. Faries and R. Spronk (eds), *Recent Developments in the Technical Examination of Early Netherlandish Painting: Methodology, Limitations and Perspectives* (Turnhout 2003), 107–16.

14. See D. Brine, *Piety and Purgatory: Wall-Mounted Memorials from the Southern Netherlands, c.1380–c.1520*, PhD, Courtauld Institute of Art (Univ. London, 2006), 210–52.

15. For the Descent see de Vos, *Rogier van der Weyden*, for its patronage, see M. Trowbridge, 'The *Stadschilder* and the *Serpent*: Rogier van der Weyden's Deposition and the Crossbowmen of Louvain', *Dutch Crossing* 23 (1999), 5–28. For the technical analysis, J. R. J. van Asperen de Boer, R. van Schoute, M. C. Garrido, and J. M. Cabrera, 'Algunas cuestiones técnicas del *Descendimiento de la Cruz* de Roger van der Weyden', *Boletín del Museo del Prado*, 4 (1983), 39–50; and M. T. Davila and C. Garrido, 'Proceso de restauración del Descentimento de la Cruz', in *X Congreso de Conservación y Restauración de Biens Culturales* (Cuenca 1994), 231–50; for its copies, A. Powell, 'The Errant Image: Rogier van der Weyden's Deposition from the Cross and its Copies', *Art History*, 29 (2006), 707–28.

16. See note 1 in this chapter.

17. C. Reynolds, 'Reality and Image: Interpreting Three Paintings of the *Virgin and Child in an Interior* Associated with Campin', in Foister and Nash (eds), *Robert Campin: New Directions in Scholarship*, 183–95.

18. The Gillebert de Metz text is published in A. J. Le Roux de Lincy, *Description de la Ville de Parisau XVe siècle par Guillebert de Metz* (Paris 1855), 233. The use of the term 'engin' is also explored in relation to descriptions of famous legendary women artists by S. Perkinson, 'Engin and Artifice: Describing Creative Agency at the Courts of France, ca. 1400', *Gesta*, 41 (2002), 51–68.

19. Conway, *Literary Remains*, 117. The German is 'ein über köstlich, hoch verständig gemähl ...', H. Rupprich, *Dürer: Schriftlicher Nachlass*, 3 vols (Berlin 1956–69), I, 168.

20. For the epitaph, C. Dehaisnes, *Recherches sue le retable de Saint-Bertin et sur Simon Marmion* (Lille and Valenciennes 1892), 72–4; for this manuscript and others like the Visions of Tondal with similarly inventive depictions, see Kren and McKendrick, *Illuminating the Renaissance*, 199–202 and 111–16.

21. 'D'inuention i'ay pleines corbeillettes / I'ay ce que i'ay, i'ay plus qu'il ne me faut', Stecher (ed.), *Oeuvres de Jean Lemaire de Belges*, II, 162. This point about invention is made most eloquently in Campbell, *The Fifteenth Century Netherlandish Schools*, 31–2.

Chapter 4: Sources and Documents

1. J. Labarte, *Inventaire du mobilier de Charles V* (Paris 1879), 2–3.

2. The 1363 inventory is published by D. Gaborit-Chopin, *L'inventaire de trésor du dauphin future Charles V, 1363* (Nogent-le-Roi 1996); the 1379–80 by Labarte, *Inventaire du mobilier de Charles V*.

3. J. Guiffrey, *Inventaires de Jean, duc de Berry (1401–1416)*, 2 vols (Paris 1894–6).

4. H. Moranvillé, *Inventaire de l'orfèvrerie et des joyaux du Louis Ier, duc d'Anjou* (Paris 1903).

5. B. Prost, *Inventaires mobiliers et extraits des comptes des ducs de Bourgogne de la maison de Valois (1363–1477)*, 2 vols (Paris 1902–8); C. Dehaisnes, *Documents et extraits diverse concernant l'histoire de l'art dans la Flandre, Artois et le Hainaut avant le XVe siècle* (Lille 1886), II, 825–54.
6. L. Douet-d'Arcq, *Choix de pièces inédites relatives au règne de Charles VI publiées pour la Société de l'histoire de France*, 2 vols, Paris (1863–4); P. Henwood, *Le trésor royal sous Charles VI: L'inventaire de 1400* (Paris 2004).
7. Dehaisnes, *Documents et Extraits*, II, 855–920.
8. All in L. E. S. J. de Laborde, *Les ducs de Bourgogne: Études sur les lettres, les arts et l'industrie pendant le XVe siècle—preuves*, 3 vols (Paris, 1849–52), II, 235–78; the tapestry inventory of *c.*1430 is in E. van Drival, *Les tapisseries d'Arras—Étude artistique et historique* (Arras 1864), 124–32; manuscripts in G. Doutrepont, *Inventaire de la librairie de Philippe le Bon, 1420* (Brussels 1906); J. B. J. Barrois, *Bibliothèque prototypique, ou librairies des fils du Roi Jean, Charles V, Jean de Berri, Philippe de Bourgogne et le siens* (Paris 1830) (1467–9 library inventory).
9. C. Leber, *Collections des meilleurs dissertations, notices, et traités particuliers relatifs à l'histoire de France*, 19 (Paris 1838), 120–69.
10. F. M. Graves, *Deux inventaires de la Maison d'Orléans (1389 et 1408)*, 2 vols (Paris 1926); A. Champillion-Figeac, *Louis et Charles, duc d'Orléans* (Paris 1844); J. Roman, *Inventaires et documents relatifs aux joyaux et tapisseries des princes d'Orléans-Valois, 1389–1481* (Paris 1896).
11. F. Palgrave, *The Ancient Kalendars and Inventories of the Treasury of His Majesty's Exchequer* (London 1836), III, 313 ff; forthcoming publication in full by J. Stratford.
12. J. Stratford, *The Bedford Inventories: The Worldly Goods of John, Duke of Bedford, Regent of France (1389–1435)* (London 1993).
13. M. Michelant, 'Inventaire des vaiselles, joyaux, tapisseries, peintures, manuscrits, etc. de Marguerite d'Autriche, dressé en son palais de Malines, le 9 juillet 1523', *Compte rendue des séances de la Commission royale d'histoire*, 12 (1871), 5–78, 83–136; M. Debae, *La bibliothèque de Marguerite d'Autriche: essai de reconstitution d'après l'inventaire de 1523–1524* (Leuven 1995); D. Eichberger, *Leben mit Kunst, Wirken durch Kunst: Sammelwesen und Hofkunst unter Margarete von Österreich, Regentin der Niederlande* (Turnhout 2002); F. J. Sánchez Cantón, *Libros, tapices y cuadros que coleccionó Isabel la Católica* (Madrid 1950); A. and E. A. de la Torre, *Testamentaría de Isabel la Católica* (Barcelona 1974); D. Starkey, *The Inventory of Henry VIII* (London 1998). For a fuller list of published examples from the sixteenth century, see F. Falk, *Edelsteinschliff und Fassungsformen im späten Mittelalter und im 16. Jahrhundert* (Ulm 1975), 145–7.
14. Moranvillé, *Inventaire de l'orfèvrerie*, 190–1 (item 479). For a discussion of some of the objects in this inventory see F. Robin, 'L'Orfèverie, art de cour: Formes et techniques d'après l'inventaire de Louis I d'Anjou', *Gazette des Beaux-Arts*, 12 (1983), 60–74.
15. Guiffrey, *Inventaires de Jean, duc de Berry*, I, 235, 253–4, 275; II, 340–1.
16. On the *Goldenes Rössl*, R. Baumstark (ed.), *Das Goldenes Rössl: Ein Meisterwerk der Pariser Hofkunst um 1400*, exh. cat. (Munich 1995), with extensive illustrations documenting its restoration, and J. Stratford, 'The Goldenes Rössl and the French Royal Collections', in E. M. Tyler (ed.), *Treasure in the Medieval West* (Woodbridge 2000), 109–33.
17. Original text in Henwood, *Le trésor royal sous Charles VI*, 92.
18. On these techniques see *Paris 1400*, 165–80, 380–7.
19. One *marc* was equivalent to 244.75 grammes or 8 ounces.
20. B. Buettner, 'Past Presents: New Year's Gifts at the Valois Courts, ca. 1400', *The Art Bulletin*, 83 (2001), 598–625.
21. Labarte, *Inventaire du mobilier de Charles V*, items 2622 'deux grans beaulx tableaux d'yvire des troys Maries que fist Jehan le Braellier en ung estuy de cuir', and 2626 'ungs tableaux de boys de quarter pieces, que Girard d'orleans fist'. For the third item, a painted silk altar hanging, see S. Nash, 'The Parement de Narbonne: Context and Technique', in C. Villers (ed.), *The Fabric of Images: European Paintings on Textile Supports in the Fourteenth and Fifteenth Centuries* (London 2000), 81.
22. For these see Nash, *'No Equal in Any Land'*, 133.
23. They have not been fully transcribed; extracts in de Laborde, *Les ducs de Bourgogne*; Dehaisnes, *Documents et Extraits*; C. Dehaisnes, *Inventaire sommaire des archives départementales antérieures à 1790: Nord, Archives civiles, Série B, IV* (Lille 1881); for Brussels see E. d'Hondt, *Extraits des comptes*

du domaine de Bruxelles des XVe et XVIe siècles concernant les artistes de la cour (Brussels 1989).

24. Extracts from the archives relating to many Belgium towns now found in the Archives Générale du Royaume in Brussels are published by A. Pinchart, *Archives des arts, sciences et letters*, 3 vols (Ghent 1860, reprint Brussels 1994). For Bruges: L. Gilliodts-Van Severen, *Inventaire des Archives de la ville de Bruges*, 8 vols (Bruges 1871–85). Amiens: G. Durand, *Inventaire sommaire des archives communales antérieures à 1790, ville d'Amiens* (Amiens 1891–1901); for further references to the town accounts and other documents for Netherlandish towns, see L. Campbell, 'The Art Market in the Southern Netherlands in the Fifteenth Century', *The Burlington Magazine*, 118 (1976) 188–98.

25. For the payment accounts relating to the Feast of the Pheasant, de Laborde, *Les ducs de Bourgogne*, I, 422–6; Dehaisnes, *Inventaire sommaire*, 195–7, and for the Bruges wedding, de Laborde, *Les ducs de Bourgogne*, II, 293–381.

26. Published extensively in Prochno, *Die Kartause von Champmol*, 253–348.

27. The fullest chronicle accounts of the Feast of the Pheasant and the Bruges wedding are by Olivier de La Marche, see H. Beaune and J. d'Arbaumont, *Mémoires d'Olivier de La Marche*, 4 vols (Paris 1883–8) II, 340–80; III, 101–201, and IV, 97–144.

28. For these see D. Eichberger, 'The Tableau Vivant—an Ephemeral Art Form in Burgundian Civic Festivities', *Parergon*, 6 (1988), 37–64.

29. A bibliography of 79 published contracts from the southern Netherlands dating between 1419 and 1551 is given by J. Dijkstra, *Origineel en Kopie: Een onderzoek naar de navolging van de Meester van Flémalle en Rogier van der Weyden* (Amsterdam 1990), 295–303; several Spanish contracts, translated, in Berg Sobré, *Behind the Altar Table*, 267–337; for southern French examples, H. Requin, *Documents inédits sur les peintres, peintres-verriers et enlumineurs d'Avignon au XVe siècle* (Paris 1889); for German examples, H. Huth, *Künstler und Werkstatt der Spätgotik* (Darmstadt 1967), 108–39, and H. Rott, *Quellen und Forschungen zur südwestdeutschen und schweizerischen Kunstgeschichte im 15. und 16. Jahrhundert* (Stuttgart 1933–8).

30. For example, A. Louant, 'Un retable en polychromie et plat peinture de Nicaise Barat', *Revue Belge d'archéologie et d'histoire de l'art*, 9 (1939), 11–19.

31. Z. Véliz, 'Wooden Panels and their Preparation for Painting from the Middle Ages to the Seventeenth Century in Spain', in K. Dardes and A. Rothe (eds), *The Structural Conservation of Panel Paintings: Papers Given at a Symposium at the J. Paul Getty Museum*, 1993 (Los Angeles 1998), 136–7.

32. Document in Pinchart, *Archives des Arts*, I, 42–8; see also R. Hanke, 'Art religieux et création artistique au XVe siècle: les retables sculptés de l'abbaye cistercienne de Flines', *Les amis de Douai: revue du syndicat d'initiative de Douai et de l'arrondissement*, 9 (1984), 105–11.

33. M. Guigue, 'Jacques Morel sculpteur de Montpellier', *Archives de l'art français: Recueil des documents inédits relatifs a l'histoire des arts en France* (1856), 313–20.

34. 'semblable et non moins, tant de taille, de dorure et estoffure come de pourtraiture'. Document in Pinchart, *Archives des arts*, III, 192–3.

35. A. S. Fuchs, 'The Virgin of the Councillors by Lluís Dalmau (1443–1445): The Contract and its Eyckian Execution', *Gazette des Beaux-Arts*, 99 (1982), 45–54.

36. Original and translation in Berg Sobré, *Behind the Altar Table*, 288–92; translated here slightly differently.

37. For an example in stained glass, see the contract of 1474 between Pieter van den Dike, glazier, and Garcia de Contreras for five windows for the cloister of the Observants Friars, Bruges, published in M. P. J. Martens, *Artistic Patronage in Bruges Institutions, ca. 1440–1482*, PhD (University of California, Santa Barbara 1992), 531–2; in sculpture, that between Riquart of Valenciennes and the Abbess of Flines, Pinchart, *Archives des arts*, I, 43–7.

38. R. de Lespinasse and F. Bonnardot, *Le livre des métiers d'Etienne Bolieau* (Paris 1879), 127–32, 168–73 (the 1269 regulations); C. Leber, *Collections des meilleurs dissertations, notices et traités particuliers relatifs à l'histoire de France*, 19 (Paris 1838), 453–8 (those of 1391).

39. W. Englefield, *The History of the Painter-Stainers Company of London* (London 1950), 28–31, 49–52.

40. J. B. van der Straelen, *Jaerboek der vermaerde en kunstryke Gilde van Sint Lucas binnen de stad Antwerpen* (Antwerp 1855), 1–35; the 1470 regulations translated in Richardson, Woods, and Franklin (eds), *Renaissance Art Reconsidered*, 71–3.

41. Those for Brussels have not been published in full but see F. Favresse, 'Les premiers statuts connus des métiers bruxellois du duc et de la ville', *Bulletin de la Commission royale d'histoire*, 111 (1946), 37–91; C. Mathieu, 'Le métier des peintres à Bruxelles aux XIVe et XVe siècles', in *Bruxelles au XVme siècle* (Brussels 1953), 221–35. The tapestry weavers' statutes of 1450–1 are translated in Richardson, Woods, and Franklin (eds), *Renaissance Art Reconsidered*, 198–203.
42. D. van de Casteele, 'Documents divers de la Société S. Luc, à Bruges: Première partie, Keuren', *Annales de la Société d'émulation de Bruges*, 3rd series, I (1866), 5–60. Not strictly a trade guild, see Reynolds, 'Illuminators and the Painters' Guilds', in Kren and McKendrick, *Illuminating the Renaissance*, 18–19.
43. A. Goovaerts, 'Les ordonnances données en 1480 à Tournai, aux métiers des peintres et des verriers', *Compte rendue des séances de la Commission royale d'histoire de Belgique*, 5th series, 6 (1896), 97–182, reprinted in D. Vanwijnsberghe, *'De fin or et d'azur': Les commanditaires de livres et le métier de l'enlumininure à Tournai à la fin du Moyen Age (XIVe-XVe siècles)* (Leuven 2001), 247–63.
44. L. Devillers, 'Le passé artistique de la ville de Mons', *Annales du cercle archéologique de Mons*, 16 (1880), 404–19.
45. E. van Even, 'Monographie de l'ancienne école de peinture de Louvain', *Messager des sciences historiques* (1867), 443–5.
46. P. Charron, 'Les peintres, peintres-verriers et enlumineurs lillois au début du XVI siècle d'après les statuts inédits de leur corporation', *Revue du Nord*, 82 (2000), 723–38.
47. L. Nys and A. Salamagne (eds), *Valenciennes aux XIVe et XVe siècles: Art et Histoire* (Valenciennes 1996), 418–25.
48. A. de Montaiglon, 'De la corporation des peintures de Rouen et de leur confrérie de Saint Luc dans l'église Saint-Herblard', *Archives de l'Art français*, 11 (1859), 179–212.
49. Comte de Pastoret, *Ordonnances des roys de France de la troisiéme race, recueillies par ordre chronologique, etc*, 23 vols (Paris 1723–1849), XX (1840), 562–71.
50. B. Prost, 'Statuts des peintres et des verriers de Dijon (1466)', *Archives historiques, artistiques et littéraires*, 1 (1889–90), 315–18.
51. A. Thierry, *Recueil des monuments inédits de l'historie du Tiers-Etat: Région du Nord* (Paris 1853–70), II, 4–7, 447–9 (for Amiens); IV, 341–7 (for Abbeville).
52. J. Chapuis, *Stefan Lochner: Image Making in Fifteenth-Century Cologne* (Turnhout 2004), 301–7.
53. O. Rüdiger (ed.), *Die ältesten Hamburgischen Zunftrollen und Brüderschaftsstatuten* (Hamburg 1874), 90–6.
54. C. Wehrmann, *Die älteren Lübeckischen Zunftrollen* (Lübeck 1872), 326–30.
55. B. Schmidt, *Frankfurter Zunfturkunden bis zum Jahre 1612*, 2 vols (Frankfurt am Main 1914), I, 423.
56. V. Liedke, 'Die Münchner Tafelmalerei und Schnitzkunst der Spätgotik', part 1, *Ars Bavarica*, 17/18 (1980), 123–5.
57. P. P. Weissenberger, 'Die Künstlergilde St. Lukas in Würzburg', *Archiv des historischen Vereins von Unterfranken und Aschaffenburg*, 70 (1936), 182–5.
58. Baxandall, *Limewood Sculptors*, 108–10.
59. H. Rott, *Quellen und Forschungen zur südwestdeutschen und schweizerischen Kunstgeschichte im 15. und 16. Jahrhundert* (Stuttgart 1933–8), I (Quellen), 71–2, 82–8, 131–3.
60. R. Wackernagel, 'Erneuerung der St Lucas-Bruderschaft zu Basel, 21 Sept., 1437', *Baseler Zeitschrift für Geschichte und Altertumskunde* (1913), 391–4.
61. H. Pátaková (ed.), *Cechovní Kniha Prazskych Malíru (Das Buch der Prager Malerinnung), 1348–1527*, (Prague 1996).
62. B. Bucher, *Die alten Zunft- und Verkehrsordnungen der Stadt Krakau* (Vienna, 1889), 57–9; F. Winkler, *Der Krakauer Behaim-Codex* (Berlin 1941), 103–24.
63. For references to the published guild regulations of these Spanish towns, see R. Kasl, 'Painters, Polychromy and the Perfection of Images', in S. L. Stratton (ed.), *Spanish Polychrome Sculpture 1500–1800 in United States Collections*, exh. cat. (New York 1993). The Córduba regulations are translated by Z. Veliz, 'Appendix: The 1493 *Ordenanzas de Córdoba* for regulating the profession of painting', *Hamilton Kerr Institute Bulletin*, 3 (2000), 35–40.
64. Veliz, 'Appendix: The 1493 *Ordenanzas de Córdoba*', 37.
65. For extracts of regulations and other documentary evidence relating specifically to gilding: J. Nadolny, *The Techniques and Use of Gilded Relief Decoration by Northern European Painters*, PhD, Courtauld Institute of Art (Univ. London 2000).
66. Document in Richardson, Woods, and Franklin (eds), *Renaissance Art Reconsidered*, 205–6.

Chapter 5: Physical Evidence and Technical Examination

1. W. G. Constable, *The Painter's Workshop* (London 1954), 4.

2. Methods are considered and findings surveyed most extensively and recently by M. Faries, 'Technical Studies of Early Netherlandish Painting: A Critical Overview of Research', in Faries and Spronk (eds), *Recent Developments*, and J. Dijkstra, 'Technical Examination', in Ridderbos, van Buren, and van Veen (eds), *Early Netherlandish Paintings*, 292–328.

3. Discussion of these painted surfaces in H. Verougerstraete and R. van Schoute, 'Frames and Supports of Some Eyckian Paintings', in Foister, Jones, and Cool (eds), *Investigating Jan Van Eyck*, 107–17.

4. For the Seilern Triptych C. Villers and R. Bruce Gardner, 'The *Entombment* Triptych in the Courtauld Institute Galleries', in S. Foister and S. Nash (eds), *Robert Campin: New Directions in Scholarship* (Turnhout 1996), 27–35, and S. Nash, *Robert Campin, the Master of Flémalle and the Entombment Triptych in the Courtauld Institute Gallery* (forthcoming, London 2009).

5. See the various essays in K. Dardes and A. Rothe (eds), *The Structural Conservation of Panel Paintings: Papers Given at a Symposium at the J. Paul Getty Museum*, 1993 (Los Angeles 1998), especially those by Klein, Véliz, Wadum, and Walker.

6. For explanation of the method and some of its results with the most recent estimates concerning drying time and sapwood rings see P. Klein, 'Dendrochronological Analyses of Netherlandish Paintings', in Faries and Spronk, *Recent Developments*, 65–81.

7. The steps in the process of an understanding of the relationship between these panels and their connections to Juan de Flanders are outlined in M. Ainsworth, 'What's in a Name? The Question of Attribution in Early Netherlandish Painting', in Faries and Spronk, *Recent Developments*, 140–1; the technical investigation is fully documented in R. Grosshans, 'Rogier van der Weyden: Der Marienaltar aus der Kartause Miraflores', in *Jahrbuch der Berliner Museen*, 23 (1981), 49–112; R. Grosshans, 'Infrarotuntersuchungen zum Studium der Unterzeichnung auf den Berliner Altären von Rogier van der Weyden', *Jahrbuch Preussischer Kulturbesitz*, 19 (1982), 137–77.

8. For this reconstruction, S. Kemperdick, *Der Meister von Flémalle: die Werkstatt Robert Campins und Rogier van der Weyden* (Turnhout 1997), discussed in Ridderbos, 'Objects and Questions', in Ridderbos, van Buren, and van Veen (eds), *Early Netherlandish Paintings*, 5–9.

9. H. Verougstraete and R. van Schoute, 'Frames and Supports in Campin's time', in S. Foister and S. Nash (eds), *Robert Campin: New Directions in Scholarship* (Turnhout 1996), 87–93: 91.

10. Traces of marbling on both reverses of this work show, however, that it cannot have been fixed to a wall: see J. O. Hand, C. A. Metzger, and R. Spronk (eds), *Prayers and Portraits: Unfolding the Netherlandish Diptych*, exh. cat. (New Haven and London 2006), 292–3.

11. For x-rays, J. Lang and A Middleton (eds), *Radiography of Cultural Material*, 2nd edn (Amsterdam and London 2005).

12. For this see Nash, *The Entombment Triptych*.

13. Most lucidly for this method and some of its results D. Bomford (ed.), *Art in the Making: Underdrawings in Renaissance Paintings*, exh. cat. (London, National Gallery 2002).

14. This type of examination is referred to as infrared reflectography to distinguish it from the less sensitive infrared photographic methods.

15. R. Billinge, 'Examining Jan van Eyck's Underdrawings', in Foister, Jones, and Cool (eds), *Investigating Jan van Eyck*, 84–5.

16. M. L. Koster, 'New Documentation for the Portinari Altar-Piece', *The Burlington Magazine*, 145 (2003), 164–79; for the Dombild see Chapuis, *Stefan Lochner*, 126–37.

17. R. Billinge and L. Campbell, 'The Infra-red reflectograms of Jan van Eyck's Portrait of Giovanni (?) Arnolfini and his Wife Giovanna Cenami (?)', *National Gallery Technical Bulletin*, 16 (1995), 47–60; R. Billinge, 'Examining Jan van Eyck's Underdrawings', in Foister, Jones, and Cool (eds), *Investigating Jan van Eyck*, 83–100.

18. For example, E. M. Gifford, 'Van Eyck's Washington *Annunciation*: Technical Evidence for Iconographic Development', *The Art Bulletin*, 81 (1999) 108–16.

19. Most notably E. Panofsky, 'Jan van Eyck's Arnolfini Portrait', *The Burlington Magazine*, 64 (1934), 117–27; for a recent reinterpretation of the picture with a similar method but different conclusions see
M. Koster, 'The "Arnolfini Double Portrait": A Simple Solution', *Apollo*, 158 (2003), 3–14. The fundamental work on this painting

remains the entry in Campbell, *The Fifteenth Century Netherlandish Schools*, 174–211.
20. For GCMS see J. Mills and R. White, *Organic Chemistry of Museum Objects*, 2nd edn (Oxford 1994).
21. As is demonstrated effectively by E. Effmann, 'Theories about the Eyckian Painting Medium from the Late Eighteenth to the Mid-Twentieth Centuries', *Reviews in Conservation*, 7 (2006), 17–26; see also Gifford et al., 'Interpreting Analyses of the Painting Medium', in Faries and Spronk (eds), *Recent Developments*, 107–16, and M. Spring and C. Higgitt, 'Analysis Reconsidered: The Importance of the Pigment Content of Paint in the Interpretation of the Results of Examination of Binding Media', in Nadolny (ed.), *Medieval Painting in Northern Europe: Techniques, Analysis, Art History*, 223–9.
22. J. Dunkerton and R. Billinge, *Beyond the Naked Eye: Details from the National Gallery* (London 2005).

Chapter 6: Centres

1. '... la plus renommée de tout le monde par le fait de marchandise qui se y haute', in a letter of 1450 concerning the abolition of tax on goods traded by the Catalonian merchants in that town; L. Gilliodts-van Severin, *Cartulaire de l'ancien Consulat d'Espagne à Bruges* (Bruges 1901), 42.
2. Tafur, *Travels and Adventures*, 204.
3. P. Spufford, *Power and Profit: The Merchant in Medieval Europe* (London, 2002), 65–7.
4. For immigrants, W. Blockmans, 'The Creative Environment: Incentives to and Functions of Bruges Art Production', in M. W. Ainsworth (ed.), *Petrus Christus in Renaissance Bruges: An Interdisciplinary Approach* (New York and Turnhout 1995), 11–20; for wages, M. P. J. Martens, 'The Position of the Artist in the Fifteenth Century: Salaries and Social Mobility', in W. Blockmans and A. Janse (eds), *Showing Status: Representations of Social Positions in the Late Middle Ages* (Turnhout 1999), 387–414.
5. For the Bible Historiale see most recently A. Korteweg, *Splendour, Gravity and Emotion: French Medieval Manuscripts in Dutch Collections* (The Hague 2002), 98–101; C. Sterling, *La Peinture médiévale à Paris, 1300–1500* (Paris 1987), I, 187–92.
6. M. Whiteley, 'Le Louvre de Charles V, dispositions et fonctions d'une résidence royale', *Revue de l'Art*, 97 (1992), 60–71; M. Whiteley, 'Public and Private Space in Royal and Princely Chateaux in Late Medieval France', in A. Renoux and P. Contamine (eds), *Palais royaux et princiers au Moyen Age: Actes du colloque international tenu au Mans les 6–7 et 8 octobre 1994* (Le Mans 1996), 71–5.
7. R. C. Gibbons, 'The Queen as "Social Mannequin": Consumerism and Expenditure at the Court of Isabeau of Bavaria, 1393–1422', *Journal of Medieval History*, 26 (2000), 371–95.
8. *Paris 1400*, 125.
9. R. H. Rouse and M. A. Rouse, *Manuscripts and their Makers: Commercial Book Producers in Medieval Paris, 1200–1500* (Turnhout 2000), esp. the biographical register in vol. II.
10. On the Boucicaut Hours see M. Meiss, *French Painting in the Time of Jean de Berry: The Boucicaut Master* (London 1968), 7–22; C. de Mérindol, 'Les Heures du Maréchal de Boucicaut: Mise au point et nouvelles lectures—Réflexions sur les manuscrits à caractère officiel ou davantage privé', in M. Smeyers and B. Cardon (eds), *Flanders in a European Perspective: Manuscript Illumination around 1400 in Flanders and Abroad* (Leuven 1995), 61–74.
11. On the identification of Jacques Coene see Meiss, *The Bouciaut Master*, 60–2; more recently on the Boucicaut problem see C. G. Andrews, 'The Boucicaut Masters', *Gesta*, 41 (2002), 29–38.
12. Published in M. Merrifield, *Original Treatises Dating from the XIIth to the XVIIIth Centuries on the Art of Painting*, 2 vols (London 1849, repr. New York 1999), I, 3–14, 258–91; see also 'An International Exchange among Miniaturists: Alcherius and Lèbegue', in Rouse and Rouse, *Manuscripts and their Makers*, 211–16.
13. For this artist and foreign illuminators in Paris: *Paris 1400*, 262–75.
14. Payments to these artists in the Burgundian accounts are published by J. Duverger and J. Versyp, 'Schilders en borduurwerkers aan de arbeid voor een vorstenduel te Brugge in 1425', *Artes textiles: Bijdragen tot de geschiedenis van de tapijt-, borduur-, en textielkunst*, II (1955), 3–17.
15. For the list of artists paid in 1468 see de Laborde, *Les ducs de Bourgogne*, I, 526–8, 530.
16. Blockmans, 'The Creative Environment', in Ainsworth (ed.), *Petrus Christus*, 14.
17. Quality was now to be maintained by means of spot-checks of workshops not less than three times a year; A. Wauters, *Les tapisseries bruxelloises* (Brussels 1878), 43–5.

18. Campbell, *Tapestry in the Renaissance*, 279.
19. P. Rombouts and T. van Lerius, *De liggeren en andere historische archieven der Antwerpsche Sint-Lucasgilde* (Antwerp 1864–72), publishes the registrations in the Antwerp Guild; the figures are from N. Peeters and M. P. J. Martens, 'A Cutting Edge? Wood Carvers and their Workshops in Antwerp 1453–1579', in C. van de Velde, H. Beeckman, J. van Acker, and F. Verhaeghe (eds), *Constructing Wooden Images* (Brussels 2005), 75–92, and N. Peeters and M. P. J. Martens, 'Masters and Servants: Workshop Assistants in Antwerp Artists' Workshops (1453–1579), A Statistical Approach to Workshop Size and Labour Division', in H. Verougstraete, R. van Schoute, and A. Dubois (eds), *La peinture ancienne et ses procédés: Copies, répliques, pastiches—Le dessin sous-jacent et la technologie dans la peinture, Colloque XV* (Leuven 2006), 115–20.
20. Guicciardini, *Descrittione di tutti i Paesi Bassi*, 114–15; B. Dubbe and W. Vroom, 'Patronage and the Art Market in the Netherlands in the Sixteenth Century', in *Kunst voor de beeldenstorm: noordnederlandse kunst 1525–1580*, exh. cat. ('s-Gravenhage 1986), 9.
21. A. van Buren, 'Willem Vrelant: Questions and Issues', *Revue belge d'archéologie et d'histoire de l'art* 58 (1999), 22–3. On women artists and painters' guilds see Reynolds, 'Illuminators and the Painters' Guilds', in Kren and McKendrick, *Illuminating the Renaissance*, 22.
22. Comte de Pastoret, *Ordonnances des roys de France*, XX, 563, Item 2.
23. Vanwijnsberghe, *'De fin or et d'azur'*, 251, 261–2.
24. D. Wolfthal, 'Agnes van den Bossche: Early Netherlandish Painter', *Women's Art Journal*, 6 (1985), 8–11; all the documents relating to her are transcribed in D. Lievois, 'Werklist van Agnes vanden Bossche', in *Agnes vanden Bossche: Een zelfbewuste vrouw en een merkwaardige kunstenares uit het 15de-eeuwse Gent* (Ghent 1996), 77–90.
25. For the ducal palace, P. Saintenoy, *Les arts et les artistes à la cour de Bruxelles: Le palais des ducs de Bourgogne sur le Coudenberg à Bruxelles du règne d'Antoine de Bourgogne à celui de Charles-Quint* (Brussels 1934); K. de Jonge, 'Het Paleis op de Coudenberg te Brussel in de vijftiende eeuw', *Revue belge d'archéologie et d'histoire de l'art*, 60 (1991), 5–38; for Dürer's account, Conway, *Literary Remains*, 101.
26. Martens, *Artistic Patronage in Bruges Institutions*, 50–2.
27. Tafur, *Travels and Adventures*, 182.
28. For these figures and what follows, see H. van der Velden, *The Donor's Image: Gerard Loyet and the Votive Portraits of Charles the Bold* (Turnhout 2000), esp. 14–16 and 155–65.
29. See F. Deuchler, *Die Burgunderbeute: Inventar der Beutestücke aus den Schlachten von Grandson, Murten und Nancy, 1476/1477* (Berne 1963).
30. As is fully explicated in van der Velden, *The Donor's Image*.
31. In 1468 Willem Vrelant in Bruges was paid for illuminating the second volume, and Loyset Liédet, also based in Bruges, the third: C. van den Bergen-Pantens (ed.), *Les Chroniques de Hainaut, ou les ambitions d'un prince bourguignon*, exh. cat. (Brussels 2000).
32. For the methods of production of large secular volumes, see S. McKendrick, 'Reviving the Past: Illustrated Manuscripts of Secular Vernacular Texts 1467–1500', in Kren and Mckendrick, *Illuminating the Renaissance*, 59–78; for manuscripts more generally J. J. G. Alexander, *Medieval Illuminators and their Methods of Work* (London, 1992).
33. L. Campbell, 'Rogier van der Weyden and Manuscript Illumination', in Morrison and Kren (eds), *Flemish Manuscript Painting in Context*, 87–102.
34. Spufford, *Power and Profit*, 84–5.
35. D. Wolfthal, *The Beginnings of Netherlandish Canvas Painting: 1400–1530* (Cambridge 1989); C. Reynolds, 'The Function and Display of Netherlandish Cloth Paintings', in Villers (ed.), *The Fabric of Images*, 89–98.
36. J. A. Goris, *Étude sur les colonies marchandes meridionales (portugais, espagnols, italiens) a Anvers de 1488–1567* (Leuven, 1925), 295–306.
37. L. F. Jacobs, *Early Netherlandish Carved Altarpieces, 1380–1550: Medieval Tastes and Mass Marketing* (Cambridge 1998), 156, 160.
38. J. M. Montias, *Artists and Artisans in Delft: A Socio-Economic Study of the Seventeenth Century* (Princeton 1982), 12–13.
39. Tafur, *Travels and Adventures*, 198–204.
40. D. Ewing, 'Marketing Art in Antwerp, 1460–1560: Our Lady's Pand', *The Art Bulletin*, 72 (1990), 558–84.

Chapter 7: Products

1. Quoted with the original text in Campbell, *Tapestry in the Renaissance*, 131 and 145.
2. G. Baldwin Brown (ed.), *Vasari on Technique*, tr. L. S. Maclehose (New York 1960), 267.
3. Conway, *Literary Remains*, 114.
4. For the gifts given at Arras see J. Dickinson, *The Congress of Arras, 1435* (Oxford 1955); for the gifts by Philip to the popes see Campbell, *Tapestry in the Renaissance*, 13–27.
5. For these see M. García Calvo, 'Dos tapices Flamencos "de cruzades" en la iglesia parroquial de Pastrana', *Goya: Revista de Arte*, 293 (2003), 81–90.
6. For the Trojan tapestries see S. McKendrick, 'The *Great History of Troy*: A Reassessment of the Development of a Secular Theme in Late Medieval Art', *Journal of the Warburg and Courtauld Institutes*, 54 (1991), 43–82, and Campbell, *Tapestry in the Renaissance*, 55–64.
7. For these marks and their interpretation see H. Nieuwdorp, 'De oorspronkelijke betekenis en interpretatie van de keurmerken op Brabantse retabels en beeldsnijwerk (15de—begin 16de eeuw)', *Archivum Artis Lovaniense*, VII (1981), 85–98 (with English summary); J. van der Stock, 'De organisatie van het beeldsnijders- en schildersatelier te Antwerpen: Documenten 1480–1530', in H. Nieuwdorp (ed.), *Antwerpse retabels 15de–16de eeuw: II Essays*, exh. cat. (Antwerp 1993), 47–53; Jacobs, *Early Netherlandish Carved Altarpieces*, 157–61.
8. For the Ternant retables see R. Didier, 'Les retables de Ternant', *Congrès archéologique de France*, 125 (1967), 258–76; for the Strängnäs and Västerås Altarpieces, see J. de Borchgrave d'Altena, *Les retables Brabancons conservés en Suède* (Brussels 1948), 13–16, 24–6, 39–49.
9. For this retable, Jacobs, *Early Netherlandish Carved Altarpieces*, 188–90.
10. 'Unes Horas de Madona Santa Maria, obra de Flandes, de pergami'; G. Llompart, 'Mallorca-Flandes: linea directa y costa arriba', in *Bartolomeo Bermejo y su época. La pintura gotica hispano flamenco*, exh. cat. (Barcelona and Bilbao, 2003), 69–75. Examples in A. Arnould, 'Flemish Books for English Readers', in A. Arnould and J. M. Massing, *Splendours of Flanders: Late Medieval Art in Cambridge Collections*, exh. cat. (Cambridge 1993), 113–31.
11. J. J. G. Alexander, *The Master of Mary of Burgundy: A Book of Hours for Engelbert of Nassau* (Oxford 1970), and Kren and McKendrick, *Illuminating the Renaissance*, 134–7.
12. For Sluter at Mechelen, document in Prochno, *Die Kartause von Champmol*, 344; for Utynam, C. Reynolds, 'England and the Continent: Artistic Relations', in Marks and Williamson (eds), *Gothic: Art for England*, 82.
13. Baldwin Brown (ed.), *Vasari on Technique*, 270.
14. T. B. Husband et al., *The Luminous Image: Painted Glass Roundels in the Lowlands, 1480–1560*, exh. cat. (New York 1995), 52–3.
15. J. Squilbecq, 'Les Lutrins dinantais de Venise et de Gênes', *Bulletin de l'Institut l'historique belge de Rome*, 21 (1940–1), 347–56.
16. Reynolds, 'England and the Continent', in Marks and Williamson (eds), *Gothic: Art for England*, 82.
17. R. Krautheimer and T. Krautheimer-Hess, *Lorenzo Ghiberti* (Princeton 1956, repr. 1982), 418, doc. 254.
18. P. Ciselet and M. Delcourt (eds), *Monetarius: Voyage aux Pays-Bas (1495)* (Brussels 1942), 57.
19. Nuttall, *From Flanders to Florence*, 78; for further examples of the ownership of brass chandeliers see Campbell, *The Fifteenth Century Netherlandish Schools*, 187–8; Marks and Williamson (eds), *Gothic: Art for England*, for an example now in Bristol Cathedral, 423, no. 314.
20. M. Norris, *Monumental Brasses: The Craft* (London 1978), 44–51; H. K. Cameron, *A List of Monumental Brasses on the Continent of Europe* (London 1970).
21. J. W. Steyaert, *Late Gothic Sculpture: The Burgundian Netherlands*, exh. cat. (Ghent 1994), 205–7.
22. M. de Ruette et al., 'Étude technologique des dinanderies coulées: L'oeuvre de Renier van Thienen et la restauration du chandelier pascal de Léau (1483)', *Bulletin de l'Institut Royal du Patrimone Artistique*, 25 (1993), 171–210.
23. F. Benito Doménech and J. Gómez Frechina, *La Clave Flamenca en los Primitivos Valencianos*, exh. cat. (Valencia 2001), 328–33.

Chapter 8: Patrons: Importing Art and Artists

1. For the Medici collections of Netherlandish art and what follows see Nuttall, *From Flanders to Florence*, 105–17.

2. Campbell, *The Fifteenth Century Netherlandish Schools*, 38–45.
3. Full text of the letter in Gilbert, *Italian Art: Sources and Documents*, 117–18.
4. P. Nuttall, '"Panni Dipinti de Fiandri": Netherlandish Painted Cloths in Fifteenth-Century Florence', in Villers (ed.), *The Fabric of Images*, 109–17.
5. B. Hatfield Strens, 'L'arrivo del trittico Portinari a Firenze', *Commentari*, 19 (1968), 315–19. On the Portinari Altarpiece in general see E. Dhanens, *Hugo Van der Goes* (Antwerp 1998), 250–301, and M. Koster, *Hugo van der Goes and the Procedures of Art and Salvation* (Turnhout 2008).
6. For this triptych see de Vos, *Hans Memling*, 82–9, and P. Nuttall, 'The Patrons of the Chapel at the Badia of Fiesole', *Studi di Storia dell'Arte*, III (1992), 97–112.
7. For this correspondence see Campbell, *Tapestry in the Renaissance*, 88–9. The letters are published in full in A. Grunzweig (ed.), *Correspondance de la filiale de Bruges des Medici* (Brussels 1931), 26–31, 38–43, 78–84, 98–103.
8. Vespasiano da Bisticci, *The Vespasiano Memoirs: Lives of Illustrious Men of the XVth Century*, tr. W. George and E. Waters (Toronto 1997), 101.
9. The letters in original and translation are in Belozerskaya, *Rethinking the Renaissance*, 194–6.
10. Fuchs, 'The Virgin of the Councillors', 48, n.8.
11. For Boteram see V. Baesens, 'Boteram, Rinaldo', in *Nouvelle Biographie Nationale*, I, Brussels 1988, 15–18. L. Campbell, 'Cosmè Tura and Netherlandish Art', in S. J. Campbell, *Cosmè Tura: Painting and Design in Renaissance Ferrara*, exh. cat. (Boston 2002), 71–5.
12. Possibly a work by the Brussels painter, the Master of the Legend of St Catherine, for which she is reported to have paid 26,810 marvadis, see D. Martens, 'Identificación del "Quadro" flamenco de la Adoración de los Reyes, antiguamente en la Cartuja de Miraflores', in *Actas del Congresso Internacional sobre Gil Siloe y la Escultura de su época* (Burgos 2001), 71–89.
13. For this work see J. Trizna, *Michel Sittow: Peintre revalais de l'école brugeoise* (Brussels 1976) 31–3, 96; the wording is 'Que mejor y mas cierta y perfectamente las pintura Michel', 31, n.6.
14. For these works see A. H. Wethey, *Gil de Siloe and his School: A Study of Late Gothic Sculpture in Burgos* (Cambridge MA 1936), 24–55; J. Yarza Luaces, 'El retablo mayor de la Cartuja de Miraflores', in *Actas del Congreso internacional sobre Gil Siloe*, 207–38; M. José Martinez Ruiz, 'Las aventuras labores de restauracion de Conde de la Almenas en la Cartuja de Miraflores', *Goya*, 313 (2006).
15. L. Reis-Santos, 'Olivier de Gand, sculpteur du XVIe siècle au Portugal', *Miscellanea Prof. Dr D. Roggen* (Antwerp 1957), 229–47.
16. M.-J. Baptista-Neto, 'Os portais principais da cartuxa de Champmole da igreja de Sta Maria de Belem: influencia, semelhancas e divergencias', *Cudermos de arte e iconografia*, 6 (1993), 43–51.
17. For Valladolid, J. Ara-Gil, 'Las fachadas de San Gregorio y San Pablo de Valladolid en el contexto de la arquitectura europea', in C. Freigang (ed.), *Gotische Architektur in Spanien: Akten des Kolloquiums der Carl Justi-Vereinigung und des Kunstgeschichtlichen Seminars der Universität Göttingen, Göttingen, 4–6. Februar 1994* (Frankfurt and Madrid 1999), 317–34.
18. C. Périer-d'Ieteren, *Dieric Bouts: The Complete Works* (Antwerp 2006), 240–9.
19. B. Fransen, 'El retablo de Belén en la Iglesia de Santa María de la Asunción de Laredo: Exponente de las innovaciones en la escultura tardogótica de Bruselas en torno a 1440', *Clavis: Boletín del Museo Diocesano de Santillana del Mar*, 3 (1999), 70–98.

Chapter 9: The de Limbourgs in the Service of Jean de Berry

1. M. Meiss, *French Painting in the Time of Jean de Berry: The Limbourgs and their Contemporaries* (London 1974), 77; the documentary evidence published and translated there, 71–81.
2. On the *Très Riches Heures* see R. Cazelles and J. Rathofer, *Illuminations of Heaven and Earth: The Glories of the Très Riches Heures du Duc de Berry* (New York 1988). For its complex subsequent history see most recently C. Reynolds, 'The "Très Riches Heures", the Bedford Workshop and Barthélemy d'Eyck', *The Burlington Magazine*, 147 (2005), 526–33.
3. 'Item un livre contrefait d'une pièce de bois paincte en semblance d'un livre, ou il n'a nulls fueillets ne rien escript ...': Meiss, *De Limbourgs*, 76.
4. The portrait side is lost, although the Virgin side may be identified as a medal now in Berlin. For these medals see

S. K. Scher, *The Currency of Fame: Portrait Medals of the Renaissance*, exh. cat. (New York 1994), 31–7.
5. For the psalter, Nash, *'No Equal in Any Land'*, 107–43.

Chapter 10: Hans Memling Painting Panels in Bruges

1. H. Dussart, *Fragments inédits de Romboudt de Doppere découverts dans un manuscript de Jacques de Meyere: Chronique brugeoise de 1491 à 1498* (Bruges 1892), 49.
2. T.-H. Borchert, 'Memling—Life and Work', in T.-H. Borchert et al., *Memling's Portraits*, exh. cat (Madrid, Bruges, and New York 2005), 10–47.
3. Vasari, *Lives of the Painters*, tr. G. du C. de Vere, I, 426, II, 862.
4. Her family name was van Brugghen; Périer-d'Ieteren, *Dieric Bouts*, 17–18.
5. On Rogier's investments see Campbell, 'Brussels and Tournai', in Nys and Vanwijnsberghe (eds), *Campin in Context*, 113–23; for Marmion's investments see Dehaisnes, *Recherches sur le Retable de Saint-Bertin*, 59–77, 129–49, and M. Hénault, 'Les Marmion (Jehan, Simon, Mille et Colinet): Peintres amiénois du XVe siècle', *Revue archéologique*, 9 (1907).
6. M. Ryckaert, 'Het huis van Memling in Brugge', in D. de Vos (ed.), *Hans Memling: Essays* (Bruges, 1994), 104–8.
7. For these works by Memling see D. de Vos, *Hans Memling: The Complete Works* (London 1994), cats 31, 63, 81, 90.
8. On his assistants, ibid., 393–401.
9. The evidence is circumstantial and technical, see M. Faries, 'The Underdrawing of Memling's *Last Judgement Altarpiece* in Gdańsk', in H. Verougstraete, R. van Schoute, and M. Smeyers (eds), *Memling Studies: Proceedings of the International Colloquium (Bruges, 10–12 November 1994)* (Leuven 1997), 243–59, and J. Dijkstra, 'On the Role of Underdrawings and Model Drawings in the Workshop Production of the Master of Flémalle and Rogier van der Weyden', in R. van Schoute and H. Verougstraete-Marcq (eds), *Le dessin sous-jacent dans la peinture: Colloque VII* (Leuven 1989), 37–53.
10. M. P. J. Martens, 'Hans Memling and his Patrons: A Cliometrical Approach', in Verougstraete et al. (eds), *Memling Studies*, 35–41.
11. On Memling's inscriptions, de Vos, *Hans Memling*, 375–1, for his frames see H. Verougstraete and R. van Schoute, 'Cadres et supports chez Memling', in Verougstraete et al. (eds), *Memling Studies*, 269–86.
12. On which see Campbell, *The Fifteenth Century Netherlandish Schools*, 374–91.
13. For example, panels in New York (Metropolitan Museum of Art), London (National Gallery), Vienna (Kunsthistorisches Museum); see cats 35, 51 and 53 in de Vos, *Hans Memling*.
14. On Memling's technique, M. Spring, 'The Technique and Materials of the Paintings attributed to Memling in the National Gallery, London', in Verougstraete et al. (eds), *Memling Studies*, 213–19.
M. W. Ainsworth, 'Minimal Means, Remarkable Results: Memling's Portrait Painting Technique', in *Memling's Portraits*, 93–111.
15. M. Rohlmann, 'Memling's "Pagagnotti Triptych"', *The Burlington Magazine*, 137 (1995), 438–45.
16. L. Campbell, 'Memling and the Netherlandish Portrait Tradition', P. Nuttall, 'Memling and the European Portrait Tradition', both in *Memling's Portraits*, 48–61; 62–86.

Chapter 11: Printmakers in the Rhine Valley Inventing, Marketing, and Distributing Images

1. D. Landau and P. Parshall, *The Renaissance Print, 1470–1550* (New Haven and London 1994), 52.
2. See Koerner, *The Reformation of the Image* (London 2004).
3. For the issue of origins, most recently P. Parshall and R. Schoch, *Origins of European Printmaking: Fifteenth-Century Woodcuts and Their Public*, exh. cat. (Washington 2005).
4. Landau and Parshall, *The Renaissance Print*, 20, who do the calculation in relation to the *Melancolia I*, a print of similar dimensions and workmanship to the *St Jerome*.
5. Ibid., 8.
6. These figures are compiled from Dürer's diary of his journey to the Netherlands, translated in Conway, *Literary Remains*, 92–126.
7. For northern engravings in use in Florentine workshops see M. Holmes, *The Influence of Northern Engravings on Florentine Art during the Second Half of the Fifteenth Century*, MPhil, Courtauld Institute of Art (Univ. London 1983); D. Ekserdjian, 'A Print Source for Botticelli: A Devil by

the Master ES', *Apollo*, 148 (1998), 15–16; Nuttall, *From Flanders to Florence*, 140–3; for their use elsewhere in Italy see, for example, M. Evans, 'German Prints and Milanese Miniatures: Influences on- and from- Giovan Piietro Birago', *Apollo* 153 (2001), 3–12. For prints by Master IAM Zwolle, Schongauer, and Meckenem in Spain and Mallorca, see M. P. McDonald, *The Print Collection of Ferdinand Columbus: A Renaissance Collector in Seville*, 2 vols (London 2004), M. Pilar Silva Maroto, 'Influencia de los grabados nórdicos en la pintura Hispanoflamenca', *Archivo español de arte*, 61 (1988), 271–90, and A. Galilea Anton, 'Martin Schongauer y su importancia en la pintura hispanoflamenca', in *Bartolomeo Bermejo y su epoca*, 87–97; for Master IAM Zwolle in Florence, see M. Evans, 'Pollaiuolo, Dürer and the Master IAM van Zwolle', *Print Quarterly*, 3 (1986), 109–16; for Schongauer's prints in Poland, see A. Labuda, 'Les gravures de Schongauer et l'art gothique tardif en Pologne', in A. Châtelet (ed.), *Le beau Martin: études et mises au point* (Colmar 1994), 285–97.

8. Landau and Parshall, *The Renaissance Print*, 31.

9. See J. Campbell Hutchinson, 'Schongauer Copies and Forgeries in the Graphic Arts', in Châtelet (ed.), *Le beau Martin: études et mises au point*, 115–25.

10. 'novem printe lignee ad imprimendas ymagines': J. W. Enschedé, 'Een Drukkerij buiten Mechlen voor 1466', *Het Boek*, 7 (1918), 286–92. For a discussion of this convent and its production see U. Weekes, *Early Engravers and their Public: The Master of the Berlin Passion and Manuscripts from Convents in the Rhine-Maas Region, ca. 1450–1500* (Turnhout 2004), 163.

11. Recently refuted in Parshall and Schoch, *Origins of European Printmaking*, 92–4; for the 'picture panel' see ibid., 169–9, and P. Schmidt, 'The Use of Prints in German Convents of the Fifteenth Century: The Example of Nuremberg', *Studies in Iconography*, 24 (2003), 43–69.

12. The finds are published in H. Appuhn and C. von Heusinger, 'Der Fund kleiner Andachtsbilder des 13. bis 17. Jahrhunderts im Kloster Wienhausen', *Niederdeutsche Beiträge zur Kunstgeschichte*, 4 (1965), 157–238; H. Appuhn, *Kloster Wienhausen: Der Fund vom Nonnenchor* (Hamburg 1973); also *Krone und Schleier: Kunst aus Mittelalterlichen Frauenklöstern*, exh cat. (Essen and Bonn 2005), esp. 437–41. E.-M. Haenlein, *Traces of Spirituality: Analysis of Thirteen Papier-Mâché Reliefs from the Fifteenth Century Found in the Nunnery at Wienhausen*, MA, Courtauld Institute of Art (Univ. London 2002).

13. J. F. Hamburger, *Nuns as Artists: The Visual Culture of a Medieval Convent* (Berkeley, Los Angeles, and London 1997); Weekes, *Early Engravers*, 167–85.

14. For this see Weekes, *Early Engravers*, 81–97, 145–66, and McDonald, *The Print Collection of Ferdinand Columbus*, I, 146.

15. For Master W with the Key see U. Mayr-Harting, *Early Netherlandish Engraving c.1440–1540*, exh. cat. (Oxford 1997), 18–21; J. Filedt-Kok, 'Meester W met de sleutel, Gotisch kerkinterieur, ca. 1490', *Bulletin van het Rijksmuseum*, 37 (1989), 166–8 and 283–4 (English summary); for his proposed identification as the Bruges goldsmith Willem vanden Cruce see A. Wegener Sleeswyck, 'De Graveur WA: Een Speurtocht', *Gens Nostra*, 49 (1994), 1–13.

16. For mother-of-pearl see R. A. Koch and C. Sommer, 'A Mother-of-Pearl Carving after the Master ES', *Journal of the Walters Art Gallery*, 5 (1942), 119–24; for engravings as sculptors' models in Germany see Huth, *Künstler und Werkstatt der Spätgothik*, 35–6; J. Bier, 'Riemenschneider's Use of Graphic Sources', *Gazette des Beaux-Arts*, 50 (1957), 203–22; for the use of Master ES's works by other artists in general see Shestack, *Fifteenth Century Engravings*. Lehrs lists hundreds of copies after Schongauer in the decorative arts and German sculpture, see M. Lehrs, *Geschichte und kritischer Katalog des deutschen, niederländischen und französischen Kupferstichs im XV. Jahrhundert*, 9 vols (Vienna 1908–34): vols 5 and 6.

17. P. Lacroix and A. Renon, 'Apôtres gravés de Schongauer et Credo apostolique: des stalles d'Aoste aux peintures de Walbourg', in Châtelet (ed.), *Le beau Martin: études et mises au point*, 165–73; as models for a leather triptych see G. Morello and G. Wolf, *Il Volto di Cristo*, exh. cat. (Rome 2000), 195–6.

18. E. W. Hoffman, 'Some Engravings Executed by the Master ES for the Benedictine Monastery at Einsiedeln', *The Art Bulletin*, 43 (1961), 231–7, and B. Welzel, 'Die Engelweihe in Einsiedeln und die Kupferstiche vom Meister E.S.', *Städel Jaarboek*, 15 (1995), 121–44. Master ES may have produced more engravings for this event.

19. A. Shestack, *Fifteenth Century Engravings of Northern Europe from the National Gallery of Art, Washington*, exh. cat. (Washington 1967), nos 154–249, and Landau and Parshall, *The Renaissance Print*, 56–63.
20. Shestack, *Fifteenth Century Engravings*, no. 236.
21. By Landau and Parshall, *The Renaissance Print*, 53.

Chapter 12: Declaring Authorship and Expertise: Signatures and Self-Portraits

1. On van Eyck's inscriptions generally see M. Smeyers, 'Jan van Eyck, Archaeologist? Reflections on Eyckian Epigraphy', in M. Lodewijckx (ed.), *Archaeological and Historical Aspects of West-European Societies* (Leuven 1996), 403–14, and for the use of Greek and Hebrew in his paintings and others from his circle J. Paviot, 'Les inscriptions grècques et hébraïques dans les tableaux eyckiens', *Revue Belge d'archéologie et d'histoire de l'art*, 75 (2006), 53–73.
2. Campbell, *The Fifteenth Century Netherlandish Schools*, 200–1.
3. On the *Saint Barbara* see R. Billinge, 'The Saint Barbara', *Investigating Jan Van Eyck*, 41–8, and Koreny et al., *Early Netherlandish Drawings*, 39–43.
4. Brine, *Piety and Purgatory*, 240–7.
5. Examples at Brussels, Tongeren, and Wijk-Maastricht, R. Didier, 'Lutrins et statuaire en laiton du pays mosan au Moyen Age', in J. Toussaint (ed.), *Art du Laiton Dinanderie* (Namur 2005), 63–94; for a signed brass sacrament tower at Lübeck see U. Albrecht, 'Auf den Spuren eines verlorenen Deukmalensembles: die spätgotische Chorausstatfung der lübecker Marienkirche', in A. Moraht-Fromm, *Kunst und Liturgie: Choranlagen des Spätmittelalters-ihre Architektur, Ausstattung und Nutzung* (Ostfildern 2003), 113–39.
6. M. de Ruette et al., 'Étude technologique des dinanderies coulées: L'oeuvre de Guillaume Lefèvre (Synthèse)', *Bulletin de l'Institut Royal du Patrimone Artistique*,
22 (1988–9), 104–60; M. de Ruette et al., 'Etude technologique des dinanderies coulées 1: Le chandelier pascal de Saint-Ghislain', *Bulletin des Musées royaux d'art et d'histoire*, 55 (1984), 24–54.
7. G. Weilandt, *Die Sebalduskirche in Nürnberg: Bild und Gesellschaft im Zeitalter der Gotik und Renaissance* (Petersberg 2007), 363–418 and 526–55.
8. For these see C. Tracy and H. Harrison, *The Choir Stalls of Amiens Cathedral* (Reading 2004); C. Charles, *Stalles sculptés de XVe siècle: Genève et le duché de Savoie* (Paris 1999); P. Lacroix and A. Renon (eds), *Pensée, image et communication en Europe médiévale: À propos des stalles de Saint-Claude* (Besançon 1993).
9. S. Roller and M. Roth, *Michel Erhart und Jörg Syrlin d.Ä.: Spätgotik in Ulm*, exh. cat. (Stuttgart 2002).
10. K.-U. Hogg, 'Die Inschriften am Chorgestühl des Ulmer Münsters', *Ulm und Oberschwaben*, 45/46 (1989), 103–61. D. Gropp, *Das Ulmer Chorgestühl und Jörg Syrlin der Ältere: Untersuchungen zu Architektur und Bildwerk* (Berlin 1999).
11. For this see J.-C. Klamt, 'Artist and Patron: The Self-Portrait of Adam Kraft on the Sakramenthaus of St. Lorenz in Nuremberg', *Visual Resources*, 13/3–4 (1998), 393–42. W. Schmid, 'Strategien künstlenscher Sebiltdantellung in Nürnberg um 1500: zum Selbstbildnis des Adam Kraft am Sakramentihaus in St Lorenz', in F. M. Kammel (ed.), *Adam Kraft: Die Beiträge des Kolloquiums im Germanischen Nationalmuseum* (Nuremberg 2002), 231–70.
12. For the contract see B. Daun, *Adam Krafft und die Künstler seiner Zeit* (Berlin 1897), 5–18; extracts are translated in Stechow, *Sources and Documents*, 81–2; H. K. Röthel, *Das Sakramentshaus von Adam Kraft* (Berlin 1946).
13. Inscriptions in E. Oellermann, 'Das Triumphkreuz von Bernt Notke im Dom zu Lübeck: Ein Fundbericht', *Kunstchronik*, 26 (1973), 93–6: 94, and E. Oellermann, 'Das Triumphkreuz von Bernt Notke im Dom zu Lübeck: Zweiter Fundbericht', *Kunstchronik*, 27 (1974), 419–27.
14. For the relics, K. Petermann, *Bernt Notke: Arbeitsweise und Werkstattorganisation im späten Mittelalter* (Berlin 2000), 46–7.
15. For van Eyck's, Campbell, *The Fifteenth Century Netherlandish Schools*, 212–17; for Dürer's, J. L. Koerner, *The Moment of Self-Portraiture in German Renaissance Art* (Chicago and London 1993).
16. H. Maier, 'Jan van Eyck, sein Motto als Chiffre', *Belvedere*, 2 (2003), 4–19 (English translation 80–7).
17. Document in Stechow, *Sources and Documents*, 10–11.

Chapter 13: Workspace and Equipment

1. The original in full in Stecher (ed.), *Oeuvres*, IV, 158.
2. C. J. Purtle (ed.), *Rogier van der Weyden, Saint Luke drawing the Virgin: Selected Essays in Context* (Turnhout 1997).
3. M. Mende, *The Dürer House in Nuremberg: Its Past and Present in Views from 1714 to 1990* (Nuremberg 1991), esp. 11–12.
4. Cranach's house is extensively investigated in *Lucas Cranach d. Ä. und die Cranachhöfe in Wittenberg* (Halle 1998); G. Heydenreich, *Painting Materials, Techniques and Workshop Practice of Lucas Cranach the Elder*, PhD, Courtauld Institute of Art (Univ. London 1998), 242.
5. On the restoration of these works see K. Stoll, E. M. Vetter, and E. Oellermann, *Triumphkreuz im Dom zu Lübeck:Ein Meisterwerk Bernt Notkes* (Wiesbaden 1977), and A. von Ulmann, 'Die Restaurierung des Triumphkreuzes im Lübecker Dom, 1971–77', in S. Bjarnhof and V. Thomsen (eds), *Polykrom skulptur og maleri på træ* (Copenhagen 1982), 134–41.
6. For the inventory see A. Vidier, 'Un tombier liégeois à Paris au XIV siècle, inventaire de la succession de Hennequin de Liège (1382–1383)', *Mémoire de la société de l'histoire de Paris et de l'Île-de-France,* 30 (1903), 280–308.
7. For these C. Stroo, P. Syfer-d'Olne, A. Dubois, and R. Slachmuylders, *The Flemish Primitives II: The Dirk Bouts, Petrus Christus, Hans Memling and Hugo van der Goes Groups (*Brussels 1999), 56–100. The documentation is reviewed in J. Wisse, 'Distinguishing Between Bouts and Stuerbout as Official City Painters', in M. Smeyers (ed.), *Dirk Bouts (ca.1410–1475) een Vlaams primitief te Leuven*, exh. cat. (Leuven, 1998), 19–33.
8. L. Campbell, 'Rogier van der Weyden and his Workshop', *Proceedings of the British Academy*, 84 (1993 Lectures and Memoirs) (1994), 1–24: 4; for a revised estimate of the size and original location of the *Justice* panels see Dhanens and Dijkstra, *Rogier de la Pasture van der Weyden*, 118–24.
9. Rouse and Rouse, *Manuscripts and their Makers*, I, 305, and Map 5 for the plan of the street and its houses.
10. For Notkte's properties and workshop see Petermann, *Bernt Notke*, 19–24.
11. For painters' shops in Strasbourg see P. Lorentz, *Jost Haller, le peintre des chevaliers et l'art en Alsace au XVe siècle* (Colmar 2001), 48–50.
12. Devillers, 'Le passé artistique de la ville de Mons', 408; van de Casteele, 'Documents divers de la Société S. Luc, à Bruges', 30–2.
13. Van de Casteele, 'Documents divers de la Société S. Luc, à Bruges', 28–30.
14. Theophilus, *On Divers Arts,* tr. J. G. Hawthorne and C. S. Smith (New York 1979), 81.
15. Conway, *Literary Remains*, 65.
16. Heydenreich, *Painting Materials*, 241; for Malouel, see the document in Prochno, *Die Kartause von Champmol*, 334.
17. De Laborde, *Les ducs de Bourgogne*, I, 173, and 172–7 for further payments to painters for this event. See also L. Campbell, 'Artists' Supplies', in J. Cannon, J. Kirby, and S. Nash (eds) *European Trade in Artists' Materials to 1700* (forthcoming, London 2009).
18. For the tapestry makers see Richardson, Woods, and Franklin (eds), *Renaissance Art Reconsidered*, 200; for the Bruges sculptors see Jacobs, *Early Netherlandish Carved Altarpieces*, 156.
19. 'Nus ne puet ne ne doit ouvrer ... ne de nuiz, car la clartez de la nuit ne souffist pas a ouvrer de leur mestier: car leur mestier est de taille', de Lespinasse and Bonnardot, *Le livre des metiers*, 128.
20. J. van der Stock, *Printing Images in Antwerp: The Introduction of Printmaking in a City, Fifteenth Century to 1585,* tr. B. Jackson (Rotterdam 1998), 350.
21. Inventory in Sanchis y Sivera, *Pintores medievales en Valencia*, 16–21.
22. Documentation in D. Roggen, 'Hennequin de Marville en zijn atelier te Dijon', *Gentsche Bijdragen tot de Kunstgeschiedenis* (1934), 173–205, and D. Roggen, 'Rekeningen betreffende het atelier van Klaas Sluter', *Gentsche Bijdragen tot de Kunstgeschiedenis*, IV (1937), 151–71; brief extracts translated in T. G. Frisch, *Gothic Art 1140–c.1450: Sources and Documents* (Toronto 1987), 117, 124.
23. The Ghent regulations and related disputes are most fully discussed and interpreted by Reynolds, 'Illuminators and the Painters' Guilds', in Kren and McKendrick, *Illuminating the Renaissance*.
24. Van der Stock, *Printing Images in Antwerp*, doc. 3, 305–6, and doc. 18, 331.

25. P. J. Goetshalckx, 'Vier ongekende schilders der XVe eeuw', *Bijdragen tot de Geschiedenis, bijzonderlijk van het aloude Hertogdom Brabant*, II (1903), 240–1; Campbell, *The Fifteenth Century Netherlandish Schools*, 24–5.

26. Sanchis y Sivera, *Pintores medievales*, 16–21.

27. Some have been found with traces of paint in archaeological sites, see H. Howard, 'Shells as Palettes and Paint Containers in England', in Nadolny (ed.), *Medieval Painting in Northern Europe: Techniques, Analysis, Art History*, 202–14.

28. C. Cennini, *The Craftsman's Handbook: The Italian 'Il libro dell'arte'*, tr. D. V. Thompson (New York 1960), 40–1.

29. 'pour Ic de creusequins de terre pour metre les couleurs dont ledit paintre fait son ouvrage', document in Prochno, *Die Kartause von Champmol*, 328. Their value was low but not insignificant: they cost about the same as 5 pints of oil or half a pound of vermillion; they appear to have been worth itemizing in inventories and passing on with the rest of your tools.

30. 'sis olletes de tenir colors' and 'dues dotzensde scudelletesde tenir colors'. Sanchis y Sivera, *Pintores medievales*, 17–18.

31. Vanwijnsberghe, *Le métier de l'enluminure à Tournai*, 262 (article 44); this article partially translated in Stechow, *Sources and Documents*, 24–5.

32. See van der Stock, *Printing Images in Antwerp*, documents in Appendix 3; Reynolds, 'Illuminators and Painters Guilds'.

33. Conway, *Literary Remains*, 122; the reference to 'porpoise hair brushes' presumably a translation error.

34. For Cranach's accounts see Heydenreich, *Painting Materials*; for the Tournai regulations, Vanwijnsberghe, *Le métier de l'enlumininure à Tournai*, 262 (article 44).

35. 'pour soyes de porc pour faire broisses, et fil pour loyler lesdites broisses' and 'pour Ic de tuyaux de plumes de cigne pour faire pinceaux'. Document in Prochno, *Die Kartause von Champmol*, 334.

36. For the full text of this poem see D. Yabsley (ed.), *Jean Lemaire de Belges: La Plainte du Désiré* (Paris 1932), 68–76, 71: 'j'ay pinceaulx mille, et brosses, et outilz'.

37. Heydenreich, *Painting Materials*, 147–8.

38. J. Ayers, *The Artist's Craft: A History of Tools, Techniques and Materials* (Oxford 1985), 176–202, for tools and techniques of stone and wood carving.

39. Roggen, 'Rekeningen betreffende het atelier van Klaas Sluter', 164.

40. For this work, see F. Koreny, 'Drawings by Vranke van der Stockt', *Master Drawings*, 41 (2003), 276–9.

41. A. de la Grange, 'Choix de testaments tournaisiens antérieurs au XVIe siècle', *Annales de la Société historique et archéologique de Tournai*, 2 (1897), 287.

42. Full text in N. Coste, 'Recherches sur l'art provençal: Liste des peintres, sculpteurs, architectes, enlumineurs ayant séjourné en Provence depuis le Moyen-Age jusqu'au XIXème siècle', *Revue historique de Provence* (1901–2), 296.

43. Document published in R. A. Parmentier, 'Bescheiden omtrent Brugsche schilders van de 16e eeuw, I: Ambrosius Benson', *Annales de la Société d'émulation de Bruges*, 80 (1937), 92–4; Campbell, 'The Early Netherlandish Painters and their Workshops', 53–4, and M. W. Ainsworth, '"Diverse Patterns Pertaining to the Crafts of Painters or illuminators": Gerard David and the Bening Workshop', *Master Drawings*, 41 (2003), 241–65.

44. J. J. Martín González, 'La vida de los artistas en Castilla la Vieja y Léon durante el siglo de oro', *Revista de archivos, bibliothecas y museos*, 67/1 (1959), 404.

45. Sanchis y Sivera, *Pintores medievales*, 18: 'Item una caxa de pi ab mostres vella en la qual atrobam los bens e coses seguents. Primo moltes e diverses mostres pintades e figurades en diverses papers.'

46. For the drawing see Arnould and Massing, *Splendours of Flanders*, 64–5; a painted copy of the lost work it relates to is in Liverpool, Walker Art Gallery, inv. no. 39.

47. S. Buck, 'The Impact of Hugo van der Goes as a Draftsman', *Master Drawings*, 41 (2003), 229–33.

48. For these works see de Vos, *Rogier van der Weyden*, 217–25, 276–84.

49. Scheller, *Exemplum*, 21, 226–32 (cat. 20); B. Drake Boehm and J. Fajt (eds), *Prague: The Crown of Bohemia, 1347–1437*, exh. cat. (New York and Prague 2005), cat. 117, 274–6.

50. On David's drawings M. Ainsworth, *Gerard David: Purity of Vision in an Age of Transition* (New York 1998), 7–55.

51. See A. L. Dierick, 'Jan van Eyck's Handwriting', in Foister, Jones, and Cool (eds), *Investigating Jan van Eyck*, 79–82.

52. For this practice see H. Marijnissen and G. Van de Voorde, 'Un procede enigmatique des primitifs flamands: annotations concernant l'oeuvre de Joos van Wassenhouve, Hugo van der Goes, Roger van der Weyden et Hans Memling', *Le Dessin sous-jacent dans la peinture*, V, 1983 (Louvain-la Neuve, 1985), 23–4; L. Campbell, 'Publications Received', *The Burlington Magazine* 126 (1984), 303–5.
53. C. Lemaire, 'Un dessin d'exécution pour un chapiteau historié de l'hotel de ville de Bruxelles (vers 1444): histoire, philologie et jeu de mots: Le "Scupstoel"', *Revue Belge d'archéologie et d'histoire de l'art*, 73 (2004), 3–16; Koreny, *Early Netherlandish Drawings*, 101–3.
54. R. Koechlin, *La Sculpture à Troyes et dans la Champagne méridionale au seizième siècle* (Paris 1900), 26: 'lesquelz personages lesit fondeur [Henri le serrurier] n'attandoit a faire pour ce que'il disoit de la cherte des patrons combine que ilz en parent et ambellissemt fort l'oeuvre'.
55. See the examples illustrated in Huth, *Künstler und Werkstatt der Spätgotik*, 36–54.
56. D. Gropp in Roller and Roth, *Michael Erhart und Jörg Syrlin*, 66–71.
57. 'Item die matery sol sin ain crucifix mit maria und sancto johanne.'
58. 'feray de ma proper manufaiture, sans ce que autre y touche que moy, les patrons de terre cuite'. P. Vitry, *Michel Colombe et la sculpture française de son temps* (Paris 1901), 487–8.
59. R. Baumstark (ed.), *Das Goldenes Rössl*, 226–9, where the specifications concerning the monument in Ludwig's will are transcribed.

Chapter 14: The Workforce

1. W. H. J. Weale, 'Documents inédits sur les enlumineurs de Bruges', *Le Beffroi*, 4 (1872–3), 249.
2. Roggen, 'Hennequin de Marville en zijn atelier te Dijon', 177.
3. Heydenreich, *Painting Materials*, 255–6.
4. For these regulations see notes 38, 43, 48, and 49 to Chapter 4.
5. Heydenreich, *Painting Materials*, 252.
6. Peeters and Martens, 'A cutting edge?', 84.
7. For all these guild regulations see notes 38, 40, 43, 48, 58 and 63 to Chapter 4.
8. The phrasing is found in the Cologne painters', glaziers', and woodcarvers' regulations, Chapuis, *Stefan Lochner*, 304.
9. Rouse and Rouse, *Manuscripts and their Makers*, I, 313–14.
10. For apprentice enrolment in Tournai see A. de la Grange and L. Cloquet, 'Études sur l'art à Tournai et sur les anciens artistes de cette ville', *Mémoires de la Société historique et littéraire de Tournai*, 21 (1888), 76–8. For Truffin see G. Hulin de Loo, 'Truffin (Philippe)', in *Biographie nationale de Belgique*, XXV (Brussels 1930–2), 692–6.
11. Berg Sobré, *Behind the Altar Table*, 12.
12. Prochno, *Die Kartause von Champmol*, 311.
13. For gilding see Nadolny, *The Techniques and Use of Gilded Relief Decoration*.
14. See notes 43, 56 and 59 to Chapter 4.
15. For a discussion of this issue see Nash, '*No Equal in Any Land*', 45–9.
16. For the document see de la Grange and Cloquet, 'Etudes sur l'art à Tournai', 263.
17. Jacobs, *Early Netherlandish Carved Altarpieces*, 85–8; L. Smets, 'Notes on the Technique, Conservation, and Restoration of Polychrome Sculpture', in Steyaert, *Late Gothic Sculpture*, 31–5; P. Philippot, 'Jalons pour une histoire de la sculpture polychrome médiévale', *Revue belge d'archéologie et d'histoire de l'art*, 53 (1984), 21–42.
18. Veliz, 'Appendix: The 1493 *Ordenanzas de Córdoba*', 36.
19. Thierry, *Recueil des monuments inédits*, II, 6.
20. For these guild regulations see notes 59 and 63 to Chapter 4.
21. Comte de Pastoret, *Ordonnances des roys de France*, XX, 567.
22. Comte de Pastoret, *Ordonnances des roys de France*, XX, 570. The subject of St George and Notke's image in particular is discussed in J. Svanberg, *Saint George and the Dragon* (Stockholm 1998).
23. The document is in Sanchis y Sivera, *Pintores medievales en Valencia*, 69–70. For a discussion of van Eyck's picture and its impact on Italian painters, notably Cosmè Tura, see Campbell, 'Cosmè Tura and Netherlandish Art', in Campbell, *Cosmè Tura*, 93–9.
24. Vasari, *Lives of the Painters*, I, 426.
25. The full text of Summonte's letter is translated in Richardson, Woods, and Franklin (eds), *Renaissance Art Reconsidered*, 194–6.
26. For this work and its recent restoration see *El cavalleri la princesa: El Sant Jordi de Pere Nisard i la Ciutat de Mallorca*, exh. cat. (Palma 2001).

27. For these panels see J. R. J. van Asperen de Boer et al., *Jan van Eyck: Two Paintings of 'Saint Francis Receiving the Stigmata'* (Philadelphia 1997), especially P. Klein, 'Dendrochronological Analyses of the Two Panels of "Saint Francis Receiving the Stigmata" ', 47–50, and J. R. J. van Asperen de Boer, 'Some Technical Observations on the Turin and Philadelphia Versions of "Saint Francis Receiving the Stigmata" ', 51–63; for the tracing of compositions within van Eyck's workshop, S. Jones, 'The Use of Patterns by Jan van Eyck's Assistants and Followers', in Foister, Jones, and Cool (eds), *Investigating Jan van Eyck*, 197–207.
28. For these guild regulations (and those which follow) see Part I.
29. Baxandall, *Limewood Sculptors*, 108–9.
30. M. Hasse, 'Lübecker Maler und Bildschnitzer um 1500: Zweiter Teil', *Niederdeutsche Beiträge zur Kunstgeschichte*, 4 (1965), 137–8; for the Munich regulations, Liedke, 'Die Münchner Tafelmalerei', 123–5.
31. For *Zubereiters* see M. Hasse, 'Maler, Bildschnitzer und Vergolder in den Zünften des späten Mittelalters', *Jahrbuch der Hamburger Kunstsammlungen*, 21 (1976), 31–42.
32. Conway, *Literary Remains*, 64; the German is: 'Vnd hab sie zu ainem zubereiter gethan, der hat sie geweist, geferbet, vnd wirdt sie die ander wochen vergulten.'
33. For the document see de Vos, *Rogier van der Weyden*, 398.
34. J.Campbell Hutchinson, *Albrecht Dürer: A Biography* (Princeton 1990), 83.
35. Comte de Pastoret, *Ordonnances des roys de France*, XX, 570.
36. The original text is published in P. Vitry, *Michel Colombe et la sculpture française de son temps* (Paris, 1901), 487–90; English translation in Stechow, *Sources and Documents*, 146–50. The extensive correspondence concerning this project between Colombe, his patron, and Jean Perreal is published in M. Bruchet, *Marguerite d'Autriche* (1927). For a discussion of the documents see P. Pradel, *Michel Colombe* (Paris 1953).
37. Monget, *La Chartreuse de Dijon*, I, 395–6, has a table listing its membership year by year. For more systematic publication of records of payments and activities of the members of the shop see H. Drouot, 'L'atelier de Dijon et l'exécution du tombeau de Philippe le Hardi', *Revue belge d'archéologie et d'histoire de l'art*, 2 (1932), 11–39; Roggen,'Hennequin de Marville en zijn atelier te Dijon' and Roggen, 'Rekeningen betreffende het atelier van Klaas Sluter'. The workshop of Marville and Sluter is also discussed by K. Morand, *Claus Sluter: Artist at the Court of Burgundy* (London 1991), 60 ff.
38. For the tomb see Jugie and Fliegel, *Art from the Court of Burgundy*, 223–34; S. Jugie, 'La restauration des tombeaux des ducs de Bourgogne au musée des Beaux-Arts de Dijon', *La revue des musées de France*, 55 (2005), 5–8.
39. For this document see Hasse, 'Lübecker Maler und Bildschnitzer um 1500', 137–40.
40. J. van de Stock, 'Flemish Illuminated Manuscripts: Assessing Archival Evidence', in Morrison and Kren (eds), *Flemish Manuscript Painting in Context*, 117–21; translated in full in Richardson, Woods, and Franklin (eds), *Renaissance Art Reconsidered*, 124–7.
41. For a detailed discussion see Campbell, 'Rogier van der Weyden and his Workshop', 1–24. R. Billinge, L. Campbell, and M. Spring, 'The Materials and Techniques of Five Paintings by Rogier van der Weyden and his Workshop', *National Gallery Technical Bulletin*, 18 (1997), 68–86.
42. For works with such changes and publication of the reflectograms revealing them see J. R. J. van Asperen de Boer, J. Dijkstra, and R. van Schoute, 'Underdrawing in Paintings of the Rogier van der Weyden and Master of Flémalle Groups', *Nederlands Kunsthistorisch Jaarboek*, 41 (1990) (Zwolle 1992).

Chapter 15: Materials, Methods, and Technical Virtuosity

1. 'que nul du dit mestier de tailleur d'images ne pourra livrer ouvrage de Pierre de la carrière de Pont-Remy pour Pierre de Longue, ne Pierre de Longue pour Pierre de Braumetz, car entre les dites pierres il y a difference de bonté, l'une meilleur que l'autre', Thierry, *Recueil des monuments inédits*, IV, 344.
2. On the retable see M. C. Lacarra Ducay et al., *El retablo mayor de San Salvador de Zaragoza* (Zaragoza 2000); X. Barral I Altet and M. R. Manote, 'Le sculpteur et l'oeuvre en albâtre au XVe siècle: Pere Joan et le retable de la cathédrale de Saragosse', in X. Barral I Altet (ed.), *Artistes, artisans et production artistique au Moyen Âge* (Paris 1986–90), II, 575–82.

3. For this see K. W. Woods, 'Centres of Excellence', in van de Velde et al. (eds), *Constructing Wooden Images*, 53.
4. See the essays on these centres in Cannon, Kirby, and Nash (eds), *European Trade in Artists' Materials*.
5. For these and what follows on prices in German pharmacies, A. Burmester and C. Krekel, 'The Relationship between Albrecht Dürer's Palette and Fifteenth/Sixteenth-Century Pharmacy Price Lists: The Use of Azurite and Ultramarine', in A. Roy and P. Smith (eds), *Painting Techniques: History, Materials and Studio Practice: Contributions to the Dublin Congress 7–11 September 1998* (London 1998), 101–5.
6. Campbell, 'Suppliers of Artists' Materials to the Burgundian Court', in Cannon, Kirby, and Nash (eds), *European Trade in Artists' Materials*.
7. S. Nash, 'Supplying Artists' Materials to the Chartreuse de Champmol', in Cannon, Kirby, and Nash (eds), *European Trade in Artists' Materials*.
8. De Laborde, *Les ducs de Bourgogne*, I, 176–7, 183–4, 245–6.
9. Of sixty panels dating from 1450 to 1550 tested at the Doerner Institut in Munich, only one featured ultramarine; similarly at the National Gallery in London, it was found in only two paintings, one of which is a work by Lochner and thus made in Cologne, the other a Tyrolean school work (NG 4190); see Campbell et al., 'Methods and Materials'; see also the findings by H. Kühn published in table form in F. G. Zehnder, *Katalog der Altkölner Malerei: Kataloge des Wallraf-Richartz-Museums, XI* (Cologne 1990), 568–666.
10. J. Kirby and R. White, 'The Identification of Red Lake Dyestuffs and a Discussion of their Use', *National Gallery Technical Bulletin*, 17, (1996), 56–80.
11. In *La Plainté du Désiré*, 1505, Stecher (ed.), *Oeuvres*, III, 162–3.
12. Campbell, *The Fifteenth Century Netherlandish Schools*, 24–5.
13. For Grünewald, see the inventory of his studio, where large quantities (pounds rather than ounces) of pigments are listed: W. K. Zülch, *Der historisches Grünewald: Mathis Gothardt Neithardt* (Munich 1938), 373–5.
14. E.-L. Richter and H. Harlin, 'The Stuttgarter "Kartenspiel": Scientific Examination of the Pigments and Paint Layers of Medieval Playing Cards', *Studies in Conservation*, 21 (1976), 18–24; for the regulations, see Vanwijnsberghe, *Le métier de l'enluminure à Tournai*, 259 (article 34).
15. The Paris regulations, for example, specify about monstrances and altarpieces, Leber, *Collections des meilleurs dissertations*, 454, as do those of Lyon (Comte de Pastoret, *Ordonnances des roys de France*, XX, 565: 'que nulls tables d'ostel ne seront dorées que de fin or et argent brun doré de tainte, et ce qui sera de colleurs sera de fines coulleurs') and Rouen (de Montaiglon, 'De la corporation des peintures de Rouen ' 194).
16. For the trade in Baltic oak see T. Wazny, 'The Origin, Assortments and Transport of Baltic Timber', in Van de Velde et al., *Constructing Wooden Images*, 115–26; I. Tyers, 'The European Trade in Boards 1200–1700', in Cannon, Kirby, and Nash (eds), *European Trade in Artists' Materials*.
17. For these panels and their documentation see note 7 to Chapter 13 above.
18. Campbell, *The Fifteenth Century Netherlandish Schools*, 80, 83.
19. Z. Véliz, 'Wooden Panels and their Preparation for Painting from the Middle Ages to the Seventeenth Century in Spain', in *The Structural Conservation of Panel Paintings*, 136–7.
20. These regulations are translated in Richardson, Woods, and Franklin (eds), *Renaissance Art Reconsidered*, 71–3.
21. Leber, *Collections des meilleurs dissertations*, XIX, 453–5, items 3, 5, 11.
22. Spufford, *Power and Profit*, 280, and D. Gaborit-Chopin, *Ivoires médiévaux, Ve-XVe siècle* (Paris 2003); for ivories see also P. Barnet (ed.), *Images in Ivory: Precious Objects of the Golden Age*, exh. cat. Detroit Institute of Arts (Princeton 1997).
23. Conway, *Literary Remains*, 65.
24. It is particularly evident in Spanish contracts for painted retables and sculpted works; see the contracts published and translated in Berg Sobré, *Behind the Altar Table*, 267–337, and the discussion in Nadolny, *The Techniques and Use of Gilded Relief Decoration*. See L. Watteeuw, 'Flemish Manuscript Production, Care and Repair: Fifteenth-Century Sources', in Morrison and Kren (eds), *Flemish Manuscript Painting in Context*, 75–86, for preparation of parchment for manuscript illumination and its implications.
25. R. Billinge, L. Campbell, and M. Spring,'The Materials and Techniques of Five Paintings by Rogier van der Weyden and his Workshop', *National Gallery Technical Bulletin*, 18 (1997), 72.

26. Van Asperen de Boer, van Schoute, Garrido, and Cabrera, 'Algunas cuestiones técnicas', 48–9.
27. Villers and Bruce Gardner, 'The *Entombment* Triptych', in Foister and Nash (eds), *Robert Campin*, 30. For other examples of the *imprimatura* playing an important visual role in the final work see C. A. Metzger and M. Palmer, 'The Washington *Portrait of a Lady* by Rogier van der Weyden Reconsidered in Light of Recent Investigations', in Roy and Smith (eds), *Painting Techniques: History, Materials and Studio Practice*, 94–7.
28. L. Campbell, S. Foister, and A. Roy (eds), 'Methods and Materials of Northern European Painting in the National Gallery, 1400–1550', *National Gallery Technical Bulletin*, 18 (1997), 41.
29. Gifford, Halpine, and Quillen Lomax, 'Interpreting Analyses of the Painting Medium', in Faries and Spronk (eds) *Recent Developments*, 107–16, underscore the potential for false results in some methods for testing for protein; a good review of the debate concerning the use of protein binding agents by early Netherlandish painters is Effmann, 'Theories about the Eyckian Painting Medium'.
30. For the use of walnut oil see Campbell, Foister, and Roy (eds), 'Methods and Materials', 40–1, 53–5.
31. For a table of occurrences of heat-bodied oil in National Gallery paintings see Campbell, Foister, and Roy (eds), 'Methods and Materials', 53–5.
32. Billinge, Campbell, and Spring, 'The Materials and Techniques of Five Paintings by Rogier van der Weyden', 78.
33. Lakes, of course, could fade especially when mixed with lead white, and their stability depended on their source, see J. Kirby, D. Saunders, and M. Spring, 'Proscribed Pigments in Northern European Renaissance Paintings and the Case of Paris Red', in D. Saunders, J. H. Townsend, and S. Woodcock (eds), *The Object in Context: Crossing Conservation Boundaries, Contributions to the IIC Munich Congress, 28 August – 1 September 2006* (London 2006), 236–43.
34. On van Eyck's technique see A. Roy, 'Van Eyck's Technique: The Myth and the Reality, I' and R. White, 'Van Eyck's Technique: The Myth and the Reality, II', both in Foister, Jones, and Cool (eds), *Investigating Jan van Eyck*, 97–100 and 101–5.
35. For the manufacture of tapestries at this period see A. S. Cavallo, *Medieval Tapestries in the Metropolitan Museum of Art* (New York 1993), esp. 17–25; Campbell, *Tapestry in the Renaissance*, esp. 29–39.
36. For these see Campbell, *Tapestry in the Renaissance*, 41–2, 55–64; F. Avril and N. Reynaud, *Les manuscrits à peintures en France 1440–1520*, exh. cat. (Paris 1993), 64–6.
37. P. Henwood, 'Peintres et sculpteurs parisiens des années 1400: Colart de Laon et les statuts de 1391', *Gazette des Beaux-Arts*, 98 (1981), 95–102.
38. P.-P. Guignard, 'Mémoires fournis aux peintres chargés d'éxecuter les cartons d'une tapisserie destinée à la collégiale St-Urbain de Troyes, représentant les Légendes de St Urbain et de Ste Cécile', *Mémoires de la Société académique de l'Aube* (Troyes 1851), ix–xiii.
39. On the Angers *Apocalypse* see F. Muel et al., *La tenture de l'Apocalypse d'Angers* (Nantes 1987); D. King, 'How Many Apocalypse Tapestries?', in V. Gervers (ed.), *Studies in Textile History in Memory of Harold B. Burnham* (Toronto 1977), 160–7; F. Joubert, 'L'Apocalypse de Angers et les débuts de la tapisserie historiée', *Bulletin Monumental*, 139 (1981), 125–40; F. Joubert, 'Création à deux mains: l'élaboration de la tenture de l'apocalypse d'Angers, *Revue de l'art*, 114 (1996), 45–68.
40. For the manuscript, which survives, see G. Henderson, 'The Manuscript Model of the Angers "Apocalypse" Tapestries', *The Burlington Magazine*, 127 (1985), 209–18.
41. Guignard, *Mémoires fournis aux peintres*.
42. J. Lestocquoy, 'L'atelier de Bauduin de Bailleul et la tapisserie de Gédéon', *Revue belge d'archéologie et d'histoire de l'art*, 8 (1938), 119–37.
43. For Bataille and his career see J. Guiffrey, 'Nicolas Bataille, tapissier parisien du XIVe siècle: Sa vie, son oeuvre, sa famille', *Mémoires de la Société de l'Histoire de Paris et de l'Ile-de-France*, 10 (1883), 268–317, and Lestocquoy, 'L'atelier de Bauduin de Bailleul'; for the problems of localizing tapestries see Cavallo, *Medieval Tapestries in the Metropolitan Museum of Art*, 59–61.
44. For madder red see R. Chenciner, *Madder Red: A History of Luxury and Trade* (Richmond 2000); also J. H. Munro, 'The Medieval Scarlet and the Economics of Sartorial Splendour', in N. B. Harte and

K. G. Ponting (eds), *Cloth and Clothing in Medieval Europe: Essays in Memory of Professor E. M. Carus Wilson* (London 1983), 13–70; for woad see M. Pastoureau, *Blue: The History of a Colour* (Princeton 2001); a large proportion of the expensive lake pigments used by painters at this period were produced from the selvage of the cloth production industry.

45. Figures given by Campbell, *Tapestry in the Renaissance*.

46. R. Vaughan, *Philip the Good: The Apogee of Burgundy* (Woodbridge 2002), 154, and Campbell, *Tapestry in the Renaissance*, 33.

47. Nuttall, *From Flanders to Florence*, 81.

48. See Muel (ed.), *La tenture de l'Apocalypse*, 63–73.

49. These figures are drawn from the entries in Campbell, *Tapestry in the Renaissance*.

50. For the Great Cross and what follows here see S. Nash, 'Claus Sluter's Well of Moses at the Chartreuse de Champmol in Dijon Re-considered: I', *The Burlington Magazine* (2005), 798–809; Part II, *The Burlington Magazine* (2006), 456–67; Part III, *The Burlington Magazine* (forthcoming 2008).

51. The complex construction of the pillar was first demonstrated by M. Chateignère, 'Problèmes poses par la restauration du Puits de Moïse: Aspects techniques', *Actes des Journées internationals Claus Sluter*, (Dijon 1992), 85–96; see also M. Chateignère and J. Fanton, 'Polémique autour d'un chef-d'oeuvre de l'art médiéval: Le Puits de Moïse', *L'Objet d'art*, 2000, 72–82.

52. For a full discussion of this alignment and the way the prophets are designed to work with it see Nash, 'Claus Sluter's Well of Moses', II, 466–7, and III (forthcoming).

53. For these documents see W. Loose, *Anton Tuchers Haushaltbuch* (Tübingen, 1877), 144; Baxandall, *Limewood Sculptors*, 271. For the technical examination of Stoss's *Annunciation*, see J. Taubert, 'Der Englische Gruß des Veit Stoss in Nürnberg', in Johannes Taubert (ed.), *Farbige Skulpturen: Bedeutung—Fassung—Restaurierung* (Munich 1978).

54. *Vasari on Technique: Being the Introduction to the Three Arts of Design, Architecture, Sculpture and Painting, Prefixed to the Lives of the Most Excellent Painters, Sculptors and Architects*, ed. and trans. L. S. Maclehose (New York 1960), 174–5.

55. For the qualities of limewood see Baxandall, *Limewood Sculptors*, 32–6.

56. H. Beeckman, 'The Impact of Forest Management on Wood Quality: The Case of Medieval Oak', in Van de Velde et al., *Constructing Wooden Images*, 93–113.

57. D. Eckstein, 'Wood Science and Art History: Interdisciplinary Research Illustrated from a Dendrochronological Point of View', in Van de Velde et al. (eds), *Constructing Wooden Images*, 19–26.

58. For Notke's methods in the *Triumphal Cross* and the *St George*, see Petermann, *Bernt Notke*, 45–55, 124–126, and 153–7; for the polychromy of the *Triumphal Cross* see Stoll, Vetter, and Ollermann, *Triumphkreuz im Dom zu Lübeck*.

59. For the debate see Petermann, *Bernt Notke*, 24–5.

60. For Herlin's altarpiece see K.-W. Bachmann, E. Oellermann, and J. Taubert, 'The Conservation and Technique of the Herlin Altarpiece (1466)', *Studies in Conservation*, 15 (1970), 327–69; M. Broekman-Bokstijn et al., 'The Scientific Examination of the Polychromed Sculpture in the Herlin Altarpiece,' *Studies in Conservation*, 15 (1970), 370–400; R. Kahsnitz, *Carved Altarpieces: Masterpieces of the Late Gothic* (London 2006), 57–8; for the translated contract of Pacher's altarpiece, see Stechow, *Sources and Documents*, 77–8, and for the altarpiece in general, Kahsnitz, *Carved Altarpieces*, 76–105.

61. Documents published in full in M. Comblen-Sonkes and N. Veronee-Verhaeghen, *Musée des Beaux-Arts de Dijon* (*Primitifs flamands 14*), 2 vols (Brussels 1986), 70–158; see also Jugie and Fliegel (eds), *Art from the Court of Burgundy*, 193–7.

62. See Berg Sobré, *Behind the Altar Table*, 267–337.

Chapter 16: Moving Images

1. Baxandall, *Limewood Sculptors*, 48.

2. Labarte, *Inventaire du mobilier de Charles V*, 289 (item 2700).

3. Moranvillé, *Inventaire de l'orfeverie et des joyaux du Louis Ier*, 589 (item 3574).

4. On the *Libretto* see *Les fastes du gothique: le siècle de Charles V*, exh. cat. (Paris 1981), 260–2, F. Geens, *Ungs très petiz tableaux à pignon, qui cloent et ouvrent, esmaillez dehors et dedens: A Study of Small Scale, Folding Pieces of Goldsmiths' Work in Fourteenth Century Europe*, PhD, Courtauld Institute of Art (Univ. London 2002), 29–35, and Kovács, *L'Âge d'or*, 174–9.

5. 'Item, ungs tableaux d'or, pains d'enlumineure par dedans de Nostre Seigneur despendu de la croix d'un costé, et Nostre Dame, saint Jehan et saint Andry, de l'autre, neelez au doz des armes de monseigneur de Berry', Labarte, *Inventaire du mobilier de Charles V*, 287–8 (item 2681). It weighed close to a kilo, so was not a very small object.
6. P. Henwood, 'Jean d'Orléans, peintre des rois Jean II, Charles V et Charles VI (1361–1407)', *Gazette des Beaux-Arts*, 95 (1980), 137–40.
7. B. Jestaz, 'Le reliquaire de Charles V perdu par Charles VIII à Fornoue', *Bulletin Monumental*, 147/1 (1989), 7–10.
8. Prost, *Inventaires*, II, 225 (item 1409).
9. Lille Arch. Dept. Nord. B 1923, accounts for 1420–1.
10. F. Deuchler, *Die Burgunderbeute*, no. 42.
11. For the Choques Triptych see H. W. van Os et al., *The Art of Devotion in the Late Middle Ages in Europe, 1300–1500*, exh. cat. (Amsterdam and London 1994), 122–3, and *Paris 1400*, 170–1 (cat. 90).
12. De Vos, *Rogier van der Weyden*, 409; T. Lüttenberg, '"Je he ce que mord": Die Bedeutung von Motto und Emblem auf einem Rogier van der Weyden zugeschriebenen Porträt', *Zeitschrift für Kunstgeschichte* 63 (2000), 558–61.
13. For this painting, *Paris 1400*, 200 (cat. 116).
14. Guiffrey, *Inventaires de Jean, duc de Berry*, I, 24 (items 38 and 39).
15. '... quil fait mettre tous les jours devant lui en son oratoire', M. Picard, 'La devotion de Philippe le Hardi et de Marguerite de Flandre', *Mémoires de l'académie des sciences, arts et belles-lettres de Dijon*, 11 (1907–10), 1–116, 4.
16. Labarte, *Inventaire du mobilier de Charles V*, 282–326 (items 2635–3140).
17. Labarte, *Inventaire du mobilier de Charles V*, 86 (item 556).
18. Douet-d'Arcq, *Choix de pièces*, II, 282.
19. Prost, *Inventaires*, I, 131 (no. 788).
20. One was embroidered, its weight counted in with the (heavy) panel and its metal attachments; one was red cloth, covering a large image of the Virgin and Child, which a later note stated had mysteriously disappeared during a visit of the Duke of Guienne; and one was green, covering an image of the Virgin holding a blood-covered crown of thorns. None of these panels had wings or are described as folding in any manner: Guiffrey, *Inventaires de Jean, duc de Berry*, I, 19, 33, 39 (items 15, 64, 77).
21. For these panels C. Ishikawa, *The Retablo de la Reina Católica by Juan de Flandes and Michel Sittow* (Turnhout 2004).
22. Hand, Metzger, and Spronk, *Prayers and Portraits*, 82–7.
23. For Lenten choir hangings see M. Ranacher, 'Painted Lenten Veils and Wall Coverings in Austria: Technique and Conservation', in N. S. Bromelle, G. Thomson, and P. Smith (eds), *Conservation within Historic Buildings, IIC Pre-prints of the Vienna Congress, 7–13 September 1980* (London 1980), 142–8, and U. Schiessl, S. Wülfert, and R. Kühnen, 'Technical Observations on the So-called "Grosses Zittauer Fastentuch": A Lenten Veil Dating from 1472', in Villers (ed.), *The Fabric of Images*, 99–108; also *Krone und Schleier: Kunst aus Mittelalterlichen Frauenklöstern*, exh. cat. (Essen 2005), 369–70.
24. Conway, *Literary Remains*, 107, 118.
25. For the Delft handbook see G. Verhoeven, 'Kerkelijke feestdagen in de late middeleeuwen: Utrechtse en Delftse kalendars', *Holland: regionaal-historisch tijdschrift*, 25 (1993), 156–73; for the St Lorenz handbook see W. Haas, 'Die mittelalterliche Altaranordung in der Nürnberger Lorenzkirche', in H. Bauer, G. Hirschmann, and G. Stolz (eds), *500 Jahre Hallenchor St. Lorenz zu Nürnberg 1477–1977* (Nuremberg 1977), 63–108; the Freising handbook is referred to in Kahsnitz, *Carved Altarpieces*, 16.
26. A. Gümbel, *Das Mesnerpflichtbuch von St. Lorenz in Nürnberg vom Jahre 1493* (Munich 1928), and P. Crossley, 'The Man from Inner Space: Architecture and Meditation in the Choir of St. Laurence in Nuremberg', in R. G. Owen-Crocker and T. Graham (eds), *Medieval Art: Recent Perspectives, A Memorial Tribute to C. R Dodwell* (Manchester and New York 1998), 165–82. On the altarpieces in St Lorenz see C. Schleif, *Donatio et memoria: Stifter, Stiftungen und Motivationen au Beispielen aus der Lorenzkirche in Nürnburg* (Munich 1990) and B. Heal, *A Woman Like Any Other? Images of the Virgin Mary and Marian Devotion in Nuremberg, Augsberg and Cologne, c.1500–1600*, PhD, Courtauld Institute of Art/Royal Holloway (Univ. London 2001).
27. Although rarer in the Netherlands, they were a form increasingly popular there around 1500, seen in works by Jan Borman (now Brussels, Musées Royaux d'Art et

d'Histoire, painted wings lost) and Jean Bellegambe (altarpiece at Douai, Musée de la Chartreuse).

28. B. Heise and H. Vogeler, *Die Altäre des St Annen-Museums* (Lübeck 1993), 74–8; U. Albrecht (ed.), *Corpus der mittelalterlichen Holzskulptur und Tafelmalerei in Schleswig-Holstein*, vol. I (Kiel, 2005), no. 83, 248–57.

29. For this altarpiece R. Budde and R. Krischel (eds), *Genie ohne Namen: Der Meister des Bartholomäus-Altars*, exh. cat. (Cologne 2001), 376–7; for the Master of St Bartholomew, MacGregor, *A Victim of Anonymity*.

30. Kahsnitz, *Carved Altarpieces*, 222–37; Baxandall, *Limewood Sculptors*, 172–90, 262, including part of the contract.

31. For this work most recently Hand, Metzger, and Spronk, *Prayers and Portraits*, 70–7.

32. For the *liber ordinarius* see M. Hamann, 'Die Liturgie am Neuen Stift in Halle unter Albrecht Kardinal von Brandenburg', in A. Tacke (ed.), *Der Kardinal: Albrecht von Brandenburg: Renaissancefürst und Mäzen*, exh. cat. (Halle 2006), II, *Essays*, 323–39.

33. H. J. Krause, '"Imago ascensionis" und "Himmelsloch": Zum Bildgebrauch in der spätmittelalterlichen Liturgie', in F. Möbius and E. Schubert (eds), *Skulptur des Mittelalters: Funktion und Gestalt* (Weimar 1987), 281–353.

34. Gümbel, *Das Mesnerpflichtbuch von St Lorenz*.

35. J. F. Hamburger, *Nuns as Artists: The Visual Culture of a Medieval Convent* (Berkeley, Los Angeles, and London 1997), and *Krone und Schleier*.

36. Identified as such by the present author in relation to a drawing made in the eighteenth century, see *An Album of Medieval Art*, cat. (Sam Fogg Gallery) (London 2007); for this drawing and other paraphernalia associated with the rituals of the relic of the Holy Blood in Bruges and its confraternity, see J. Koldeweij, *Foi et bonne fortune: parue et devotion en Flandre médiévale*, exh. cat. (Bruges 2006), 177–80.

37. J. Tripps, *Das handelnde Bildwerk in der Gotik: Forschungen zu den Bedeutungsschichten und der Funktion des Kirchengebäudes und seiner Ausstattung in der Hoch- und Spätgotik* (Berlin 2000), 145.

38. Dupeux, Jezler, and Wirth (eds), *Iconoclasme*, 132.

39. L. Weigert, *Weaving Sacred Stories: French Choir Tapestries and the Performance of Clerical Identity* (Ithaca 2004), 55, 201.

40. The documents on the Tonnerre *Entombment* are published in B. Prost, 'Le Saint Sépulcre de l'hôpital de Tonnerre', *Gazette des Beaux-Arts*, 9 (1893), 492–501, and W. H. Forsyth, *The Entombment of Christ: French Sculptures of the Fifteenth and Sixteenth Centuries* (Cambridge MA 1970), 200–1.

41. Documents in Forsyth, *The Entombment of Christ*, 195–6.

42. 'pour ce que ledit lieu ne doit pas ester grant et cler, mais petit et obscure pour devocion', T. Leuridan, 'Epigraphie ou recueil des inscriptions du Departement du Nord ou du Diocese de Cambrai V', *Mémoires de la société d'Études de la province de Cambrai*, 21 (1914), 238–9.

43. For the Adornes chapel in Bruges see N. Geirnaert and A. Vandewalle, *Adornes en Jeruzalem: Internationaal leven in het 15de- en 16de- eeuwse Brugge* (Bruges 1983).

Chapter 17: Settings, Vistas, and Accoutrements for Mass and Prayer

1. Autrand, *Charles V*, 754.

2. Christine de Pisan, *Le Livre des fais et bonnes meurs du sage roy Charles V*, ed. S. Solente (Paris 1936–40), I, 42–4.

3. See J. Fajt (ed.), *Magister Theodoricus, Court Painter to Emperor Charles IV: The Pictorial Decoration of the Shrines at Karlštejn Castle*, exh. cat. (Prague 1998), 25, and Drake Boehm and Fajt (eds), *Prague: The Crown of Bohemia*.

4. 'Quant en hault furent, la sainte chace ouverte, l'Empereur osta son chaperon, et joint les mains, et comme en lermes fist son oroison longuement et à grant devocion': Christine de Pisan, *Le Livre des fais et bonnes meurs*, II, 109–10.

5. B. de Chancel-Bardelot and C. Raynaud (eds), *La Sainte-Chapelle de Bourges: Une fondation disparue de Jean de France, duc de Berry*, exh. cat. (Bourges 2004).

6. A. Vallet de Viriville, 'Journal ou relation envoyée par les Florentins à Louis XI, du 27 octobre 1461 au 13 mars 1462: son passage en Berry', *Comptes rendus des travaux de la Société du Berry à Paris* (1864–5), 240–7.

7. Nash, *'No Equal in Any Land'*.

8. For the palace and chapel of Jacques Coeur see J. Favier, *L'Hôtel de Jacques Coeur* (Paris 1992) and J.-Y. Ribault, *Le palais de Jacques Coeur* (Paris 2001).

9. For the chapel at Brou see A. Carpino, 'Margaret of Austria's Funerary Complex at Brou: Conjugal Love, Political Ambition, or Personal Glory', in C. Lawrence (ed.), *Women and Art in Early Modern Europe: Patrons, Collectors, and Connoisseurs* (University Park PA 1997), 37–52; for the connecting chapel at Saint-Pol see M. Whiteley, 'Deux vues de l'hôtel royal de Saint Pol' *Revue de l'Art*, 128 (2000), 49–53.
10. For Louis of Gruuthuse see M. P. J. Martens, *Lodewijk van Gruuthuse: mecenas en Europees diplomaat ca. 1427–1492* (Bruges 1992), and M. Vale, 'An Anglo-Burgundian Nobleman and Art Patron: Louis de Bruges, Lord of la Gruthuyse and Earl of Winchester', in C. Barron and N. Saul (eds), *England and the Low Countries in the Late Middle Ages* (New York and Stroud 1995), 115–31.
11. For the Champmol oratory see Jugie and Fliegel (eds), *Art from the Court of Burgundy*, 183–7.
12. On the tombs of Charles V see P. Pradel, 'Les tombeaux de Charles V', *Bulletin Monumental*, 109 (1951), 273–96, and 'Art et politique sous Charles V', *Revue de l'Art*, 1 (1951), 89–93; Nash, *'No Equal in Any Land'*, 31–65.
13. For the documentation and the political aims of this tomb see A. M. Roberts, 'The Chronology and Political Significance of the Tomb of Mary of Burgundy', *The Art Bulletin*, 71 (1989), 376–400.
14. For Berry's funeral and its visual apparel see F. Lehoux, *Jean de France, Duc de Berri, sa vie, son action politique, 1340–1416* (Paris 1966–8), III, 406–18.
15. J. Mayo, *A History of Ecclesiastical Dress* (London 1984) for the use of these items.
16. For these see M. J. Garnier, 'Inventaire du trousseau de Marie de Bourgogne mariée à Adolphe, comte de Clèves', *Revue de société des savants*, 1 (1875), 612–19.
17. On French royal fabric *chapelle* sets see Stratford, *Bedford Inventories*, 73–83, and Nash, 'The *Parement de Narbonne*', in Villers (ed.), *The Fabric of Images*, 77–87.
18. For the embroidered Golden Fleece vestments see J. von Schlosser, *Der Burgundische Paramentenschatz des Ordens vom goldenen* Vliesse (Vienna 1912); the most recent and useful discussion in English is by H. Trnek et al., *Kunsthistorisches Museum Vienna. The Secular and Ecclesiastical Treasuries* (Salzburg 1991), 208–23, for the documents on Thierry du Chastel, F. de Gruben, *Les chapitres de la Toison d'Or à l'époque bourguignonne (1430–1477)* (Leuven 1997), 450–1, 485–6.
19. For the prayer book of Philip the Good see A. S. Korteweg, 'The Book of Hours of Philip the Good, Duke of Burgundy, in the Hague and its Later Adaption', in B. Cardon (ed.), *'Als ich can': Liber Amicorum in Memory of Professor Dr. Maurits Smeyers* (Paris 2002), 757–71; C. Reynolds, 'The Undecorated Margin: The Fashion for Luxury Books without Borders', in Morrison and Kren (eds), *Flemish Manuscript Painting in Context*, 9–26.
20. For these paintings see M. Gill, 'The Wall Paintings in Eton College Chapel: The Making of a Late Medieval Marian Cycle', in P. Lindley (ed.), *Making Medieval Art* (Donington 2003), 173–201.

Chapter 18: Meditation and Imagination

1. The best discussion of these ideas and their development in relation to the use of images at our period is S. Ringbom, *Icon to Narrative: The Rise of the Dramatic Close-up in Fifteenth-Century Devotional Painting*, 2nd edn (Doornspijk 1983); van Os et al., *The Art of Devotion in the Late Middle Ages in Europe*; J. F. Hamburger, *The Visual and the Visionary: Art and Female Spirituality in Late Medieval Germany* (New York 1998); E. Duffy, *Marking the Hours: English People and Their Prayers, 1240–1570* (New Haven and London 2006); R. Marks, *Image and Devotion in Late Medieval England* (Stroud 2004).
2. For this manuscript see most recently Kren and McKendrick, *Illuminating the Renaissance*, 371–3 (cat.110). For books of hours, their form and use see R. S. Wieck, *Painted Prayers: The Book of Hours in Medieval and Renaissance Art*, exh. cat. (New York 1997), R. S. Wieck et al., *The Book of Hours in Medieval Art and life* (London 1988).
3. Most recently Kren and McKendrick, *Illuminating the Renaissance*, 37–41 (cat. 19). E. Inglis, *Hours of Mary of Burgundy: Codex Vindobonensis 1857, Vienna, Österreichische Nationalbibliothek* (London 1995) is a facsimile, although at a reduced size.
4. A. van Buren, 'A Window on Two Duchesses of Burgundy', in J. F. Hamburger and A. S. Korteweg (eds), *Tributes in Honor of James H. Marrow: Studies in Painting and Manuscript Illumination of the Late Middle Ages and Northern Renaissance* (Turnhout 2006), 505–20, reads this figure as Margaret of York.

5. A. Clark Bartlett and T. H. Bestul (eds), *Cultures of Piety: Medieval English Devotional Literature in Translation* (Ithaca and London 1999), 90–1.
6. For devotion to the Magdalene see S. Haskins, *Mary Magdalen: Myth and Metaphor* (London 1993) and K. L. Jansen, *The Making of the Magdalene: Preaching and Popular Devotion in the Later Middle Ages* (Princeton 2000).
7. Parshall and Schoch et al., *Origins of European Printmaking*, 173–4 (cat. 43).
8. See de Vos, *Hans Memling*, 112–14; the most recent discussion is in Finaldi and C. Garrido (eds), *El trazo oculto*, 78–91.
9. De Vos, *Hans Memling*, 105–9; more recently Nuttall, *Flanders to Florence*, 64–5.
10. Richardson, Woods, and Franklin (eds), *Renaissance Art Reconsidered*, 349–52.
11. For this painting and its author's identification as the Master of Moulins see E. Panofsky, 'Jean Hey's Ecce Homo: Speculations about its Author, Its Donor and Its Iconography', *Bulletin des Musées royaux des beaux-arts de Belgique*, 5 (1956), 95–138; N. Reynaud, 'Jean Hey, peintre de Moulins, et son client, Jean Cueillette', and C. Sterling, 'Jean Hey, le Maître de Moulins', both in *Revue de l'art*, 1–2 (1968), 34–7, 26–33.
12. For this work see Kren and McKendrick, *Illuminating the Renaissance*, 334–5.(cat. 94).
13. On van Eyck's Rolin Madonna see M. Comblen-Sonkes and P. Lorentz, *Corpus de la peinture des anciens Pays-bas méridionaux et de la principauté de Liège au quinzième siècle: 17: Musée du Louvre Paris*, 2 vols (Brussels 1995), I, 11–80; also A. H. van Buren, 'The Canonical Office in Renaissance Painting, Part II: More about the Rolin Madonna', *The Art Bulletin*, 60 (1978), 617–33, P. Lorentz,'The Virgin and Chancellor Rolin and the Office of Matins', in Foister, Jones and Cool (eds), *Investigating Jan van Eyck*, 49–57, and B. Rothstein, 'On Devotion as Social Ornament in Jan van Eyck's Virgin and Child with Chancellor Nicolas Rolin', *Dutch Crossing*, 24 (2000), 96–132.
14. For this diptych see most recently Hand, Metzger, and Spronk, *Prayers and Portraits*, 178–85, 292–3 (cat. 26), and R. L. Falkenburg, 'Hans Memling's Van Nieuwenhove Diptych: The Place of Prayer in Early Netherlandish Devotional Painting', in J. O. Hand and R. Spronk (eds), *Essays in Context: Unfolding the Netherlandish Diptych* (New Haven and London 2006), 92–109.
15. For this case see Brine, *Piety and Purgatory*, 71, 81–2, and most recently the essays by L. Campbell and H. van der Velden in Hand and Spronk (eds), *Essays in Context*, 33, 125.
16. S. Nash, 'Le livre d'heures de Jacques II de Chastillon, chef d'oeuvre acquis par la BnF', *Art de l'Enluminure*, 2 (2002), 93–4.
17. For the documentation on these paintings see N. Geirnaert, 'Anselm Adornes and his Daughters: Owners of Two Paintings of Saint Francis by Jan van Eyck?', in Foister, Jones, and Cool (eds), *Investigating Jan van Eyck*, 163–8.
18. F. Avril (ed.), *Jean Fouquet: Peintre et enlumineur du XVe siècle*, exh. cat. (Paris 2003), 121–7. On the x-ray of the portrait of Charles VII see N. Reynaud, 'La radiographie du portrait de Charles VII par Fouquet', *Revue du Louvre*, 33 (1983), 97–9.
19. H. van der Velden, 'Diptych Altarpieces and the Principle of Dextrality', in Hand and Spronk (eds), *Essays in Context*, 124–55.
20. D. Godefroy, *Histoire de Charles VII, roy de France* (Paris 1661), 885–6.
21. Reynolds, 'Reality and Image', in Foister and Nash (eds), *Robert Campin*, 183–95.
22. For this image, Avril (ed.), *Jean Fouquet*, 193–217. That Jeremiah on the *Well of Moses* is a portrait of Philip the Bold has not previously been recognized. For this see Nash, 'Claus Sluter's Well of Moses', Part III, forthcoming in *The Burlington Magazine*, 2008
23. Stechow, *Sources and Documents*, 112.

List of Illustrations

The publisher would like to thank the following individuals and institutions who have kindly given permission to reproduce the illustrations listed below.

1. Michelangelo, *The Virgin and Child* ('The Bruges Madonna'), 1503–6, marble, H 128 cm including base. Onze-Lieve-Vrouwekerk, Bruges. Photo Author.
2. Hans Memling, *The Virgin and Child with Angels* (the 'Pagagnotti Triptych'), *c.* 1480, oil on Baltic oak, 57 × 42 cm. Galleria degli Uffizi, Florence/© 1990. Photo Scala, Florence, courtesy of the Ministero Beni a Attività Culturali.
3a. Hubert and Jan van Eyck, The Ghent Altarpiece (closed), dated 1432, oil on Baltic oak, 351 × 229 cm. St Bavo's Cathedral (formerly collegiate church of St John the Baptist), Ghent. Photo © IRPA-KIK, Brussels.
3b. Interior of the Ghent Altarpiece [**3a**], 365 × 487 cm. Photos Giraudon/Bridgeman Art Library, and photo Lukas-Art in Flanders (detail facing p. 11).
4. The discovery of panels from the Ghent Altarpiece by American troops in the Alt Ausee Mines in 1945. Hugh Craig Smyth/ Collection L.H. Nicholas.
5. Copy by Heinrich Thomann of Heinrich Bullinger's *Reformationgeschichte*, ('History of the Reformation'), 'How the mass and images were suppressed in Berne', 1605–6, pen and watercolour on paper, 10 × 15 cm. Zentralbibliothek (Ms. B 316, f. 321), Zurich.
6. Rogier van der Weyden and workshop, *The Exhumation of St Hubert*, *c.* 1435–40, oil with some egg tempera on oak panel, 88.9 × 81.2 cm. National Gallery (NG783), London.
7. The city gate of Berne, *c.* 1864, showing [**8**] intact and in situ, figure 990 × 130 cm. Photo Historisches Museum (inv.33319), Berne.
8. Albrecht of Nuremberg (?), Fragment of a colossal St Christopher, 1496–8, limewood, 271 cm high. Historisches Museum (inv.652), Berne.
9. Brussels tapestry workshop, after Rogier van der Weyden, *Justice of Trajan and Herkinbald*, wool, before 1461, whole tapestry 461 × 1053 cm. Historisches Museum (inv.2), Berne.
10. Jacques-Philippe Gilquin, *Tomb of Philip the Bold, Duke of Burgundy*, 1736, pen and wash, 74.5 × 52.5 cm. Bibliothèque Nationale (MS nouv. acq. fr. 5916), Paris.
11. Aimé Piron, View of the Chartreuse de Champmol, Dijon, 1686, Bibliothèque Municipale, Dijon/photo Author.
12. Jacques de Baerze (sculpture) and Melchior Broederlam (painted wings and polychromy)
Crucifixion Altarpiece, 1391 -99, polychromed and gilded wood, oil and tempera on panel, 167 × 502 cm (fully open). Musée des Beaux Arts, Dijon/photo Author.
13. Dieric Bouts, Altarpiece of the Holy Sacrament, 1464–8, oil on Baltic oak, centre 180 × 150 cm, wings 88.5 × 71.5. Sint-Pieterskerk, Leuven/photo akg-images.
14. Stefan Lochner, The Dombild Altarpiece, *c.* 1445, oil on panel, 261 × 569 cm when open. Cologne, Cathedral/photo © Rheinisches Bildarchiv.
15. Follower or workshop of Jan van Eyck (?), *St Jerome in his study*, *c.* 1435, oil on paper glued to Baltic oak panel, 19.9 × 12.5 cm. Detroit Institute of Art, City of Detroit Purchase/photo Bridgeman Art Library.
16. Frontispiece to Hyppolyte Fierens-Gevaert, *Études sur l'art flamand. La Renaissance septrinonale et les premiers maîtres des Flandres*, Brussels 1905, Photograph of the Head of Charles V of France. Photo Author.
17. André Beauneveu, Tomb effigy of Charles V of France, 1364–66, marble, 180

× 50 × 30 cm. St Denis, Paris/photo Hugo Martens/© Sam Fogg.

18. Jan van Eyck, *Virgin and Child with Saints Donatian, George and Canon Joris van der Paele*, oil on Baltic oak panel, dated 1436, 141 × 176.5 cm (including frame). Groeninge Museum, Bruges.

19. Anonymous Netherlandish sculptor (Jean Delemer?), Epitaph (memorial tablet) of Michel Ponche, 1431–6, Tournai limestone with 19th-century polychromy, 133 × 99 cm. St Omer/photo Author.

20. Rogier van der Weyden, *Descent from the Cross*, before 1443, oil on Baltic oak, 220 × 262 cm. Prado, Madrid/photo Bridgeman Art Library.

21. Southern Netherlandish weavers, probably after a cartoon by Pierre Spicre, *Scenes from the Life of the Virgin*, wool tapestries around the Choir of the collegiate Church of Notre Dame, Beaune, designed 1474, woven 1500, H 186 × W *c.* 600 cm. Photo Author.

22. Simon Marmion, *The Last Judgement*, miniature from the Hours of Charlotte de Bourbon-Montpensier, after 1474 and before March 1478, parchment, 21.5 × 15.5 cm (whole folio).
Collection of the Duke of Northumberland (Ms. 482, f. 171v), Alnwick Castle.

23. Jean Perréal, *Charles VI Enthroned*, frontispiece to a late fifteenth-century copy of the Inventory of Charles V, *c.* 15 × 19 cm. Bibliothèque Nationale (Ms. fr. 2705, f.1r), Paris.

24. Anonymous Parisian goldsmith, The *Goldenes Rössl*, 1405, gold, silver gilt, *email en ronde bosse*, pearls, rubies and sapphires, 61.85 × 45.45 × 26 cm. Schatzkammer der Heiligen Kapelle, Altötting (Bavaria)/ photos Bayerisches Nationalmuseum, Munich and Author (detail).

25. Accounts of Amiot Arnaut, Receiver General of Burgundy, recording yearly expenses at the Chartreuse de Champmol, Folio showing entries for lights, torches and pigments for 1398, parchment. Archives Municipale, Dijon/photo Author

26. Jean Fouquet, *Martyrdom of St Apollonia*, from the Hours of Etienne Chevalier, *c.*1452–60, parchment, 15.9 × 12.1. Musée Condé (Ms. Fr.71, f.39), Chantilly/photo akg-images.

27. Lluís Dalmau, *Virgin of the Councillors*, 1443, oil on Baltic oak panel, 285 × 310 cm. Museu Nacional d'Art de Catalunya, Barcelona, © MNAC/photo Calveras/ Mérida/Sagristà.

28. For or by Lluís Dalmau, *Mostra* for the altarpiece of the Virgin of the Councillors, 1443, ink on parchment, 47 × 42.5 cm. Arxiu Històric de la Cuitat (Ms. 1G.50), Barcelona.

29. The Flémalle panels being removed from the wall for reframing by curators and staff at the Städel, Frankfurt/photo Author

30. Circle of the Master of Flémalle (Robert Campin?), Reverse of [**31**], the 'Seilern Triptych'/photo Courtauld Institute of Art Gallery.

31. Circle of the Master of Flémalle (Robert Campin?), *The Entombment and Ressurection of Christ with a kneeling donor* (the 'Seilern Triptych'), *c.* 1425, oil with some egg tempera on Baltic oak, 65.2 × 107.2 cm. Courtauld Institute of Art Gallery, London.

32. Circle of the Master of Flémalle (Robert Campin?), X-ray of [**31**]. Photo Courtauld Institute of Art Gallery, London.

33. Rogier Van der Weyden, Triptych of the Virgin ('Miraflores Altarpiece'), *c.* 1442–5, oil on Baltic oak, each panel 74 × 45. Staatliche Museen Berlin/photo BPK.

34. Spanish copy after Rogier van der Weyden (Juan de Flandes?), Reduced copy of [**33**], oil on Baltic oak, *c.* 1490–1500, *Nativity* and *Pieta*, 37 × 50 cm, Granada, Capilla Real/photos Bridgeman Art Library, and *Christ appearing to his Mother*, 63.5 × 38 cm. Metropolitan Museum of Art, New York, The Bequest of Michael Dreicer, 1921 (22.60.58). Image © the Metropolitan Museum of Art.

35. Master of Flémalle, The *Trinity, Virgin and Child*, and *St Veronica*, (the 'Flemalle panels'), *c.* 1440, oil on Baltic oak. Photo Author.

36. Diagram of construction of the three panels in [**35**] (by Joachim Sander) and reconstruction of altarpiece (by Stefan Kemperdick).

37. Jan van Eyck, *Portrait of Giovanni (?) Arnolfini and his Wife*, 1434, oil on Baltic oak, 84.5 × 62.5 cm. National Gallery (NG186), London.

38. Jan van Eyck, Infra-red reflectogram of [**37**]. Photo National Gallery, London.

39. Master of Flémalle (Robert Campin?), Details of the eyes of the Christ Child and St Veronica from [**35**]. Photo Author.

40. Jan van Eyck, detail of cope of St Donation from [**18**]. Photo Author.

41. Jan Boudolf, *Jean de Vaudetar presents his book to King Charles V*, Bible Historiale of Jean de Vaudetar, 1372, parchment, 29.5 × 21.5 cm (each folio). Museum Meermanno-

Westreenianum (Ms.10 B. 23, f. 1v-2r), The Hague.

42. The October Master (Barthélemy d'Eyck?), *The Palace of the Louvre*, Detail of the October miniature from the calendar of the Très Riches Heures, *c.* 1440, showing the medieval Louvre palace, parchment, 29 × 21 cm (whole folio). Musée Condé (Ms. 65, f.10v), Chantilly/photo akg-images.

43. Cité des Dames Master, *Christine de Pisan presents her book to Isabeau of Bavaria*, miniature heading Christine de Pisan's *Cité des Dames*, Christine de Pisan, *Œuvres*, 1414, parchment, 37 × 28.5 cm (whole folio). British Library (Ms. Harley 4431, vol. 1, f. 3r), London.

44. Boucicaut Master, *Marshal Jean le Meingre de Boucicaut praying before St Catherine*, miniature from the Boucicaut Hours, *c.* 1401–8, parchment, 27.4 × 19 cm. Institut de France, Musée Jacquemart-André (Ms. 2, f. 38v), Paris.

45. Agnes van den Bossche, Flag of the city of Ghent, 1481–2, oil on cloth, 277 × 104 cm. Bijokemuseum (inv.787), STAM Ghent/photo Studio Claerhout.

46. Diebold Schilling, *Chronique de Lucerne*, 1507–13. pen and wash on paper. Zentralbibliothek (Hs.S.23, f. 100v), Lucerne/Eigentum der Korporation Luzern.

47. Gerard Loyet, Votive Image of Charles the Bold, 1467–71, gold, silver-gilt and enamel, 53 × 17 × 13 cm. Treasury of the Cathedral, Liège,/photo © IRPA-KIK, Brussels.

48. Rogier van der Weyden, *Philip the Good receiving Jean Wauquelin's translation of the Chroniques de Hainaut*, 1448, parchment, 43.9 × 31.6 cm (whole folio). Bibliothèque royale de Belgique (Ms. 9242, f. 1r), Brussels.

49. Antonius Sanderus, The Beursplein, Bruges, From *Flandria Illustrata*, 1641. Photo Author.

50. Marcus Gheeraerdts, *Panoramic plan of Bruges*. Stedelijke Musea, Steinmetzkabinet, Bruges/photo Author

51. Librado Romero, photographer, A Tapestry being carried up the main staircase of the Metropolitan Museum of Art in 2002. © Librado Romero/New York Times/Redux/Eyevine.

52. Netherlandish weavers organized by Pasquier Grenier(?), design by Nuño Gonclaves (?), *The Capture of Arzila and Tangier*, from the *Expedition of the Portuguese in North Africa in* 1471, 1470s, wool and silk, 400 × 1110 cm (whole piece). Museo Parroquial de los Tapices, Pastrana/photo Bridgeman Art Library.

53. Netherlandish weavers organized by Pasquier Grenier, *The Tent of Achilles*, sixth tapestry from an eleven-piece set of the *Story of the Trojan War*, *c.* 1475–95, 481 × 942 cm (whole piece). Museo Catedralicio, Zamora/photo Author.

54. Marks of Brussels and Antwerp on carving and polychromy of sculptures (left to right): mark guaranteeing the painting and gilding of Antwerp altarpieces, from retable of the Virgin, Vasteras church, Sweden/photo Author; mark of the Brussels joiners' guild; mark of the Brussels sculptors' guild; mark of the Brussels painters' guild/all from Retable for Bishop Rogge, as in 55. Photos © IRPA-KIK, Brussels.

55. Brussels Workshop, circle of Jan Borman (?), Retable for Bishop Rogge, called Strängnäs I, oak with original polychromy, *c.* 1490, W 582 × H 252 × D 30 cm. Cathedral, Strängnäs, Sweden/photo Author.

56. Brussels Workshop, Passion Altarpiece of Claudio Villa (?) and Gentina Solaro (?), *c.* 1470, oak, with original polychromy, 253 × 252 × 26.5 cm. Musées Royaux d'Art et d'Histoire, Brussels/photo © IRPA-KIK, Brussels.

57. Vienna Master of Mary of Burgundy, *Death of the Virgin* and *Coronation of the Virgin*, from the Hours of Englebert of Nassau, *c.* 1475, parchment, 13.8 × 9.7 cm (each folio). Bodleian Library (Mss. Douce 219–220, ff. 170v-171r), Oxford/photo The Art Archive.

58. Master of the Houghton Miniatures and Ghent Associates (?), *Annunciation to the Shepherds*, parchment, 12.5 × 9 cm, J. Paul Getty Museum (Ms.95.ML.53.r), Los Angeles, and *Adoration of the Shepherds*, parchment, 14.5 × 10.2 cm, Department of Printing and Graphic Arts (Typ. 443–443.1, f. 157r), Houghton Library, Harvard College Library, Cambridge, Mass., from the Emerson-White Hours, *c.* 1475–80.

59. Anonymous Netherlandish glass painter, *Entombment of Christ*, window in the church of the Charterhouse of Miraflores, Burgos, stained glass, *c.* 1500. Photo Author

60 After a design by Hugo Van der Goes, *Rebecca Taking Leave of her Parents*, *c.* 1480–1500, yellow-stained glass, diameter 21.6 cm. Rijksmuseum (inv.NM12242), Amsterdam.

61. Anonymous Bruges brass founder, Brass of Kateine Daut, *c.* 1461, brass, 152 × 90 cm. St Jacobs, Bruges/photo Author.

62. Renier van Thienen, Pascal candelabrum, 1483, brass, 560 cm high. St Leonard's church, Zoutleeuw/photo Author.
63. Circle of Renier van Thienen and Pieter de Backere, *St Martin and the Beggar*, 1492, bronze, 260 × 230 × 75 cm. San Martín Obispo parish church, Valencia/photo Author.
64. Petrus Christus, *Portrait of a Young Woman*, *c.* 1460–70, oil on Baltic oak, 28 × 21 cm.
Gemäldegalerie, Berlin/photo akg-images.
65. Dieric Bouts, *Resurrection*, *c.* 1470, glue size on cloth, 90 × 74.5 cm. The Norton Simon Foundation, Pasadena.
66. Hugo van der Goes, *Annunciation*, exterior of the Portinari Altarpiece, *c.* 1474–8 (?), arrives in Florence in 1483, oil on Baltic oak panel, closed 253 × 141 cm. Galleria degli Uffizi, Florence. © 1990. Photo Scala, Florence, courtesy of the Ministero Beni e Attività Culturali.
67. Interior of **66**, *Tommaso and Maria Portinari and their children presented by Saints Anthony, Thomas, Mary Magdalene and Margaret to the Nativity*, open 253 × 586 cm. Galleria degli Uffizi, Florence. © 1990. Photo Scala, Florence, courtesy of the Ministero Beni e Attività Culturali, and photo The Art Archive (detail facing p. 101).
68. Domenico Ghirlandaio, Altarpiece of the Adoration of the Shepherds with portraits of Francesco Sassetti and his wife Nera Corsi, 1485, from the Sassetti Chapel in Sta. Trinita, Florence, panel and fresco, altarpiece panel 167 × 167. Photo Alinari, Florence.
69. Michel Sittow, *Portrait of Catherine of Aragon*, daughter of Isabella of Castile, 1503–4, oil on oak panel, 29 × 20.5 cm. Kunsthistorisches Museum (inv.GG 5612), Vienna.
70. Gil de Siloé, Tomb of Juan II of Castile and Isabella of Portugal, 1489–93, alabaster. Carthusian monastery of Miraflores, Capilla Mayor, Burgos/photos Oronoz, Madrid, and Author (detail).
71. Gil de Siloé (sculpture) and Diego de la Cruz (polychromy), High Altarpiece polychromed wood, 1496–99. Carthusian monastery of Miraflores, Capilla Mayor, Burgos/photo Author.
72. Olivier de Gand (sculpture) and Jean d'Ypres (polychromy), Retable of the high altar of Sé Velha de Coïmbra, wood, painted and gilded, 1499–1501/2. Photo Instituto dos Museus e da Conservação, I.P. (Divisão de Documentação Fotográfica), Lisbon.
73. Anonymous Brussels workshops, *The Annunciation, the Virgin and Child and the Crucifixion* (the 'Laredo Altarpiece'), *c.* 1440, oak and walnut with polychromy, much of which is not original. Laredo, near Santander, Northern Spain/photos Author.
74. Pol, Jean and Herman de Limbourg, *Ego Sum*, miniature from the *Très Riches Heures*, 1411–16, parchment, 29 × 21 cm (whole folio). Musée Condé (Ms. 65, f. 142v), Chantilly/photo Giraudon/Bridgeman Art Library.
75. Pol, Jean and Herman de Limbourg, January miniature from the calendar of the *Très Riches Heures*, 1411–16, parchment, 29 × 21 cm (whole folio). Musée Condé (Ms. 65, f. 2v),
Chantilly/photos akg-images, and Bridgeman Art Library (detail facing p. 115).
76. Pol, Jean and Herman de Limbourg, *The Meeting of the Magi* and the *Adoration of the Magi* from the *Très Riches Heures*, 1411–16, parchment, 29 × 21 cm (each folio). Chantilly, Musée Condé (Ms. 65, ff. 51v-52r)/photos Giraudon/Bridgeman Art Library.
77. Artists in the circle of Jean de Berry, *Constantine the Great*, silver, obverse of medal made from two repoussé plates soldered together, *c.* 1410, diameter 8.8 cm. © Trustees of the British Museum (inv. MO269), London.
78. André Beauneveu, *Amos* and *Matthew*, miniatures from the Psalter of Jean de Berry, *c.* 1390, parchment, 25 × 17. 7 (each folio). Bibliothèque Nationale (Ms. Fr. 13091), Paris.
79. Hans Memling, Altarpiece of Saint John the Baptist and Saint John the Evangelist ('Two Saint Johns Altarpiece'), 1479, oil on Baltic oak, 1.93 × 3.89 m open (including frame). Sint-Janshospitaal, Memlingmuseum, Bruges/photo Bridgeman Art Library.
80. Hans Memling, Detail of the painted frame on the exterior wings of the Triptych of Jan Floreins, 1479, oil on Baltic oak panel, whole, including case 78 × 80 × 18 when closed. Sint-Janshospitaal, Memlingmuseum, Bruges.
81. Hans Memling, *The Virgin and Child with Saints and Donors* ('The Donne Triptych'), 1478, oil on Baltic oak, 72.3 × 133.8 fully open. National Gallery (NG6275), London.
82. Hans Memling, *Christ as Salvator Mundi with music-making Angels*, panels from an altarpiece made for the Dominican church in Nájera, Northern Spain, *c.* 1487–90, 164 ×

636 (each panel 164 × 212) cm. Koninklijk Museen voor Schone Kunsten, Antwerp/ photo © Lukas-Art in Flanders.
83. Hans Memling, *Portraits of Tommaso and Maria Portinari*, *c.* 1470, oil on Baltic oak, each 44 × 34 cm. The Metropolitan Museum of Art, New York, Bequest of Benjamin Altman, 1913 (14.40.626). Image © The Metropolitan Museum of Art.
84. Albrecht Dürer, *St Jerome in his Study*, 1514, copperplate engraving on paper, 24.8 × 18.9 cm. Trustees of the British Museum, London.
85. German, found at Wienhausen, *Head of Christ*, papier-mâché roundel, *c.* 1500, diameter 10 cm. Convent of Wienhausen (inv.WienKc3), near Celle.
86. Master of the Berlin Passion, *Arrest of Christ*, copperplate engraving on paper stuck onto parchment, gilded and painted, c. 1470. Trustees of the British Museum, London.
87. Master W with the Key (Willem vanden Cruce?), *Design for a Monstrance*, copperplate engraving on paper, 49.1 × 11.1 cm. Trustees of the British Museum, London.
88. Master W with the Key (Willem vanden Cruce?), *Design for an Altarpiece with Eight Niches*, engraving on paper, 31.9 × 25.2 cm (whole sheet). Ashmolean Museum (WA. OA.1441), University of Oxford.
89. Master ES, *St Philip Seated*, copperplate engraving on paper, 19.7 × 9.7 cm. Trustees of the British Museum, London.
90. Martin Schongauer, *St Judas Thaddeus*, copperplate engraving on paper, 9.3 × 6 cm. Trustees of the British Museum, London.
91. Martin Schongauer, *Death of the Virgin*, *c.* 1480, copperplate engraving on paper, 25.8 × 17 cm. Trustees of the British Museum, London.
92. Master ES, *Large Virgin of Einsiedeln*, copperplate engraving on paper, 20.6 × 12.3 cm. Trustees of the British Museum, London.
93. Master ES, *Small Virgin of Einsiedeln*, hand coloured copperplate engraving on paper, 13.3 × 8.7 cm. Kupferstichkabinett, Berlin/photo BPK.
94. Master ES, *Smallest Virgin of Einsiedeln*, copperplate engraving on paper, 9.7 × 6.5 cm.
Trustees of the British Museum, London.
95. Israhel van Meckenem, The *Dissimilar Couple*, *c.* 1495–1503, copperplate engraving on paper, 16.1 × 11 cm. Rosenwald Collection, 1943.3.158.(B-2713), Image courtesy of the Board of Trustees, National Gallery of Art, Washington DC.
96. Martin Schongauer, The *Way to Calvary*, *c.* 1480–85, copperplate engraving on paper, 28.4 × 42.6 cm. Whitworth Gallery, University of Manchester/photo Bridgeman Art Library.
97. Jan van Eyck, *St Barbara*, brush with brown-grey pigment, silverpoint, white body colour and pigment on Baltic oak panel, dated 1438, 41.2 × 27.5 cm (including frame). Koninklijk Museum voor Schone Kunsten, Antwerp/photo © Lukas-Art in Flanders.
98. Jan van Eyck, *Portrait of Margaret van Eyck*, oil on Baltic oak, dated 1439, 41.2 × 34.6 cm. Groeninge Museum, Bruges.
99. Guillaume Lefèvre, Baptsimal font, 1446, in St Martin's church, Halle, H 238 cm. Photo Author.
100. Peter Vischer the Elder, Self-portrait from the shrine of St Sebaldus, Nuremberg, bronze, 1507–19. Photo Author.
101. Jörg Syrlin the Elder, Choir stalls in Ulm Minster, oak, 1469–74. Photo Author.
102. Jörg Syrlin the Elder, Detail of 101 showing the inscription giving Syrlin's name and marking the completion of the work (photo Author) and bust of Virgil (akg-images/photo Erich Lessing).
103. Adam Kraft, Sacrament House in St Lorenz, Nuremberg, 1493–96, sandstone, partially polychromed, H *c.* 20 m. Photo Author.
104. Adam Kraft, Self portrait of the sculptor in [**103**]. Photo Author.
105. Israhel van Meckenem, *Self portrait with his Wife Ida*, 1490, copperplate engraving on paper, 12.9 × 17.4 cm. Trustees of the British Museum, London.
106. Jan Van Eyck, *Portrait of a Man (self-portrait?)*, 1433, oil on Baltic oak, 33.1 × 25. 9 cm (including frame). National Gallery (NG222), London.
107. Albrecht Dürer, *Self-portrait of 1500*, oil on panel, 1500, 67 × 49 cm. Alte Pinakothek, Munich/photo akg-images. Detail facing p. 157 and in margin, Conrad Witz, *Saint Catherine and the Magdalene*, *c.* 1440, oil on panel, 161 × 131 cm. Musée de l'Oeuvre de Notre Dame, Strasbourg/photo Musées de la Ville de Strasbourg/N. Fussler,
108. Rogier van der Weyden, *St Luke drawing the Virgin*, *c.* 1440, oil on Baltic oak panel, 137.5 × 110.8 cm. Museum of Fine Arts, Boston, Gift of Mr and Mrs Henry Lee Higginson/
photo Bridgeman Art Library.

109. Dürer's house in the former Zisselgasse, Nuremberg, photographed in 1896. Photo akg-images.
110. Figures by Bernt Notke and workshop from the Triumphal Cross in restoration *c.* 1971.
Photo Author.
111. Dieric Bouts, *The Justice of Emperor Otto III: The Beheading of the Innocent Count* (left) and *The Ordeal by Fire* (right), 1468–75, oil on Baltic oak, 324.5 × 182 and 323.5 × 181.5 cm. Musées Royaux des Beaux-Arts de Belgique, Brussels/photo Bridgeman Art Library.
112. Brussels painter c. 1500, *St Luke painting the Virgin*, wing from a carved retable, Sala, Sweden, parish church, oil on Baltic oak, *c.* 1500. Photo Author
113. German c. 1480, *Marcia Varronis carving an Image*, woodcut *c.* 1480. Photo Author.
114. Niklaus Manuel Deutsch, *St Luke painting the Virgin*, 1515, oil on panel, 122 × 83 cm. © Kunstmuseum (inv.G 0324), Bern.
115. Vranke van der Stockt(?), *Two sculptors at work*, *c.* 1445, pen and brown ink over black chalk on paper, 17.8 × 19.8 cm. The Hermitage, St Petersburg.
116. After the Master of Flémalle, *Descent from the Cross*, late fifteenth century, brush drawing in ink with white body colour and red chalk, on paper, 27.5 × 15.9 cm. Fitzwilliam
Museum, Cambridge/photo Bridgeman Art Library.
117. Netherlandish artist (after Rogier van der Weyden), *The Exhumation of St Hubert*, *c.* 1480–1500, pen and brown ink on paper, 22.1 × 19.1 cm. Museum Boijmans Van Beuningen (inv.N-8), Rotterdam.
118. Associate of Hugo van der Goes, Seated royal female saint, *c.* 1475, brush and ink with white bodycolour on green prepared paper, 23 × 18.9 cm. Courtauld Institute of Art Gallery, London.
119. Bohemian *c.* 1400, Modelbook drawings of heads of figures and animals, silverpoint, pen and brush on green-tinted paper, mounted on maplewood tablets, held together by strips of parchment, 9.5 × 9 cm. Sammlung für Plastik und Kunstgewerbe (inv.KK 5003), Kunsthistorisches Museum, Vienna.
120. Gerard David, Four girls' heads and two hands, *c.* 1500–05, silverpoint over black chalk on prepared paper, 8.9 × 9.7 cm. Musée du Louvre (RF3812r), Paris/photo RMN/© Michèle Bellot.
121. Jan van Eyck, *Cardinal Niccolò Albergati* (?), 1435, silverpoint on prepared paper, 21.4 × 18.1 cm. Kupferstichkabinett, Staatliche Kunstsammlungen, Dresden/akg-images/ photo Erich Lessing.
122. Workshop of Rogier van der Weyden, Drawing for a capital on Brussels Town Hall (the 'Scupstoel'), *c.* 1440, pen and grey-brown ink on paper, 29.8 × 42. 6 cm. The Metropolitan Museum of Art, New York, Robert Lehman Collection, 1975 (1975.1.848) Image © The Metropolitan Museum of Art.
123. Nineteenth century copy of capital from Town hall, Brussels, carved after the drawing in [**122**]. Photo Author.
124. Hans Schuchlin (?), for the use of Jörg Syrlin the Elder and Michael Erhart Viserung for the High Altarpiece of Ulm Minster, ink on parchment, H 231 cm. Württembergisches Landesmuseum (inv.E 743), Stuttgart.
125. Hans Multscher, Model for the Tomb of Ludwig of Bavaria, 1430, limestone, 85 × 31 cm. Bayerisches Nationalmuseum, Munich.
Detail facing p. 179, Parisian illuminator of *c.* 1400, *Thamar painting as an Assistant grinds Colours*, from Boccaccio's *Des cleres et nobles femmes*, parchment, 1403. Bibliothèque Nationale (Ms. Fr. 12420, f. 86r), Paris/photo Bridgeman Art Library.
126. Anonymous Brussels sculptor, *Christ on the Cold Stone*, polychromed wood, *c.* 1500, church of St Leonard, Zoutleeuw/photo Author.
127. Bernt Notke, *St George and the Dragon*, completed 1489, wood, parchment, paint, metal, hair, bone, string and polychromy, main group *c.* 600 cm high. City Church, Stockholm/photo Author.
128. Johannes Stradanus (Jan van der Straet), engraved and published by Philips Galle
Color Olivi (Oil Colour), engraving from *Nova Reperta* ('Modern Inventions'), designed in the 1580s, published 1600. Bibliothèque Nationale (CC-9-FOL, no.317), Paris.
129. Pedro Nisart, *St George and the Dragon*, 1468, oil on wood panel, 284 × 187 cm. Museo Catedralico, Palma de Mallorca/ photo Oronoz, Madrid.
130. Workshop of Jan van Eyck, *St Francis receiving the Stigmata*, *c.* 1440, oil on Baltic oak, 29.2 × 33.4 cm. Galleria Sabauda, Turin/© 1992. Photo Scala, Florence,

courtesy of the Ministero Beni e Attività Culturali.

131. Workshop of Jan van Eyck, *St Francis receiving the Stigmata*, reduced copy of [**130**], *c.* 1440, oil on parchment stuck onto Baltic oak, 12.4 × 14.6 cm, Philadelphia Museum of Art, John G. Johnson Collection.

132. Michael Colombe and workshop,Tomb of François II of Brittany and Marguerite of Foix, begun 1499, completed 1507, white and red Italian marble, black Dinant marble, L 390 × W 233 × H 127. Cathedral of St Pierre, Nantes/photo Conway Library, Courtauld Institute of Art, University of London.

133. Jean Marville, Claus Sluter, Claus de Werve and workshop, Tomb of Philip the Bold, 1384–1411, Italian marble, Dinant marble, alabaster and polychromy. Musée des Beaux Arts, Dijon/photo Author.

134. Pere Johan and Hans de Suabia, High retable of La Seo cathedral, Zaragoza, 1435–1444 and later fifteenth century. Photo Oronoz, Madrid.

135. Lucas Moser (?), Playing card of the *Lady in Waiting of Stags*, *c.* 1420, paint and gilding on cardboard. Landesmuseum Württemberg (inv.KK grau 17), Stuttgart/ photo P. Frankenstein/H. Zwietasch.

136. Workshop of the Master of Flémalle, *Portrait of a Franciscan* (?), *c.* 1430, oil on Baltic oak, 22.7 × 15.3 cm. National Gallery (NG6377), London.

137. Workshop of the Master of Flémalle (Jacques Daret?), *Virgin and Child in an Interior*, *c.* 1430, oil on Baltic oak, 22.5 × 15.4 cm. National Gallery (NG6514), London.

138. South Netherlandish sculptor, *Man of Sorrows with Angels*, *c.* 1470, alabaster, H 39.9 cm. Museum Mayer van den Bergh, Antwerp/photos © IRPA-KIK, Brussels.

139. Hugo van der Goes or follower, *St Luke drawing the Virgin*, *c.* 1480, oil on panel, 104 × 62.4 cm. Museu Nácional de Arte Antiga, Lisbon/photo Instituto dos Museus e da Conservação, I.P. (Divisao de Documentação Fotografica).

140. Detail of red robe of the Virgin and blue brocade velvet robe of St Donatian, both from the *Van der Paele Madonna* [**18**]. Photo Author.

141. Cross-sections taken from Rogier van der Weyden, *The Exhumation of St Hubert* [**6**]. Photos National Gallery, London.

142.Attributed to the Coëtivy Master, *The Sack of Troy*, *petit patron* (design) for tapestry 11 of the *Trojan War*, *c.* 1475, pen and wash on paper, 31 × 57.5 cm. Musée du Louvre (Département des arts graphiques, inv.RF2146), Paris/photo RMN © Thierry Le Mage.

143. Designed by Jan Boudolf, partly woven by Robert Poinçon, coordinated by Nicolas Bataille, 1377–81, wool, each piece *c.* 450 × 2300 cm, general view of the full set of six Angers *Apocalypse* tapestries. Château, Angers/photo Région Pays de la Loire, Inventaire général/P. Giraud/F. Lasa.

144. Detail of [**143**], Scene from the first piece showing the *Pale Horse of Death*. Château, Angers/photo Région Pays de la Loire, Inventaire général/P. Giraud/F. Lasa.

145. Detail of [**143**], Scene from the fifth piece, showing the *Whore of Babylon*. Château, Angers/photo Lauros/Giraudon/ Bridgeman Art Library.

146. Claus Sluter, Claus de Werve and workshop, The 'Well of Moses' (the Great Cross), with figures of prophets and angels, 1395–1404, Asnières stone, traces of original polychromy and gilding. Photo Author.

147. Author's reconstruction drawing showing the original appearance of the Great Cross [**146**]. Author.

148. Claus Sluter and Claus de Werve, Detail of angel between Jeremiah and Zachariah, from the base of the Great Cross (the 'Well of Moses'). Photo Author.

149. Veit Stoss, *Annunciation of the Rosary*, 1517–18, limewood, original polychromy, overall height 5m, width 3.2 m; Virgin and Gabriel 218 cm high. St Lorenz, Nuremberg/photo Author.

150. Veit Stoss, *St Roche*, *c.* 1510–20, limewood, unpainted, H 170 cm. Church of the Annunziata, Florence/photo Author.

151. Bernt Notke, *Triumphal Cross* in the Cathedral of Lübeck, oak, polychormy and other materials, consecrated 1477, H 1700 cm; figure of Christ 370 cm. Cathedral, Lübeck/photo Author.

152. Detail of Head of the Virgin in [**149**]. Photo Author.

153. Friedrich Herlin, shrine and caisse by Hans Waidenlich, High Altarpiece for the parish church of St Jakob, Rothenburg ob der Tauber, dated 1466, caisse, shrine and painted panels oak; figures limewood, original gilding and polychromy, H 854 cm, W 731 cm when open. Photo Author.

154. Michael Pacher, High Altarpiece for the parish and pilgrimage church of St Wolfgang, Salzkammergut, Upper Austria, completed 1481, stone pine (*caisse*, shrine and sculptures), spruce (wing frames and panels), gilding, polychromy and painting,

H 1088 cm, W 660 cm when open. Photo Achim Bednorz, Cologne.
Detail facing p. 229, Veit Stoss, High Altarpiece in process of being opened, St Mary's Church, Krakow, limewood and polychromy, 1477–89, overall H 1395 × W 1068 cm. Photo Author.
155. Parisian Goldsmith *c.* 1380, Reliquary called the *Libretto*, *c.* 1380, gold, enamel, pearls, rubies and parchment, H 7.5 cm, W 24.4 cm fully open, parchment plaque H 6.5 cm. Museo dell'Opera del Duomo, Florence.
156. Parisian Goldsmith *c.* 1380, Reverse of [155].Photo Museo dell'Opera del Duomo.
157. Anonymous Italian, Drawing of *Libretto* made for Charles V and lost by Charles VIII at Fornoue, 1495, pen and ink, 19.5 × 17 cm. Archivio di Stato (Commemoriali, reg.17, f.186v), Venice, courtesy Ministero per I Beni e le Attività Culturali.
158. Paris *c.* 1390–1400, *Man of Sorrows with the Virgin and St John the Evangelist*, above, the *Coronation of the Virgin*; exterior wings, *St Catherine and St John the Baptist* on a grey-blue enamelled ground, gold, *baisse-taille* enamel and *email en ronde bosse* *c.* 1400, H 12.7 cm, L when open 12.5 cm. Rijksmuseum (BK-17045), Amsterdam.
159. Parisian Goldsmiths *c.* 1400, Reverse of [158], the *Assumption of the Virgin* and the *Holy Face* in pointillé decoration on gold.
160. Circle of Rogier van der Weyden, Portrait of Guillaume Filastre(?), *c.* 1440, front and reverse showing holly and motto, oil on Baltic oak, 44.3 × 34.2 cm (including frame). Courtauld Institute of Art Gallery, London.
161. Parisian painter, The 'Small Round Pieta', *c.* 1400, paint and gilding on walnut panel, diameter 12.7 cm. Musée du Louvre (RF2216), Paris/photo RMN/© Jean-Gilles Berizzi.
162. Crown of thorns and nails, reverse of [157]. Musée du Louvre (RF2216), Paris/ photo RMN/© Jean-Gilles Berizzi.
163. Parisian *c.* 1400, *Last Judgement*, *c.* 1400, polychromed ivory set into silver gilt, *c.* 6cm diameter. New York Metropolitan Museum of Art.
164. Juan de Flandes, *Christ appearing to the Virgin with the Redeemed of the Old Testament, c.* 1500 oil on oak panel, 21.4 × 16 cm, part of the *Retablo* of Isabella of Castile. National Gallery (NG1280), London.
165. Michel Sittow, *Assumption of the Virgin*, *c.* 1500, oil on oak panel, 21.3 × 16.4 cm, part of the *Retablo* of Isabella of Castile. National Gallery of Art, 1965.1.1.(1928), Washington, Ailsa Mellon Bruce Fund, Image courtesy of the Board of Trustees, National Gallery of Art, Washington.
166. Nicolas Froment, *Diptych of Jean de Matheron*. Interior: portraits of René of Anjou and Jeanne de Laval,. *c.* 1480, Exterior: mottos and devices of Jean de Matheron, oil on poplar, each panel 17.7 × 13.4 cm. Musée du Louvre (RF665), Paris/ photo RMN/© Thierry Le Mage.
167. Velvet bag in which [166] was kept. Museé du Louvre (RF665), Paris/photo RMN/© Franck Raux.
168. Anonymous Utrecht painter, *Apparition of the Virgin to the Dominicans of Utrecht*, *c.* 1520, oil on panel, 105.5 × 66 cm with frame. Museum Catharijneconvent (inv. ABMs71),Utrecht.
169. Hermen Rode, St Luke Altarpiece, painted panels, gilded and polychromed wood, dated 1484, produced 1485–90, 174 × 115 × 44 (closed). St Annenmuseum, Lübeck/photo Author.
170. Hermen Rode, [169] in the process of opening the second set of wings to reveal the interior, 174 × 239 × 22 (open). Photo Author.
171. Master of the Altarpiece of St Bartholomew, *The Annunciation with Sts Peter and Paul*, exterior of the Holy Cross Altarpiece, 1490s/1500, oil on panel, 107 × 68 (closed). Wallraf-Richartz Museum (WRM 180), Cologne/photo © Rheinisches Bildarchiv.
172. Master of the Altarpiece of St Bartholomew, *The Crucifixion with Saints*, interior of [171]. Wallraf Richartz Museum (WRM 180), Cologne/photo © Rheinisches Bildarchiv.
173. Tilman Riemenschneider, Altarpiece of the Holy Blood, fir (superstructure) limewood (figurative work), 1499–1505. Church of St Jacob's, Rothenberg. Photos Author.
174. Jan van Eyck, *Annunciation*, diptych, *c.* 1435, oil on Baltic oak panel, each panel 38.8 × 23.3 cm (including frame). Museo Thyssen-Bornemisza (inv.137), Madrid/ photo © Museo Thyssen-Bornemisza.
175. Workshop of Hans Multscher, *Christ on a Donkey*, *c.* 1430, wood, polychromy, 247 × 108 × 202 cm. Museum, Ulm.
176. Martin Gramp, *Christ Ascending*, 1503, limewood, polychromy. Musée d'Art et d'Histoire (inv.2448), Fribourg.
177. Michael Erhart, Blessing Christ Child with jointed arms, polychromed wood, *c.* 1480. Museum, Ulm.

178. Bruges (?) sculptor, 'Pareerkersse' (banner) of the confraternity of the Holy Blood, *c.* 1480, oak, with remains of gilding and polychromy. Photos Sam Fogg.
179. Southern Netherlandish weavers, probably after a cartoon by Pierre Spicre, *Scenes from the Life of the Virgin*, wool tapestries around the Choir of the collegiate Church of Notre Dame, Beaune, designed 1474, woven 1500. Photos Author.
180. Jean Michel and Georges de la Sonnette, *Entombment*, viewed as approached from the entrance to the chapel in the Hospital of Notre-Dame des Fontenilles, Tonnerre, stone, 1453–4. Photo Author.
181. Jean Michel and Georges de la Sonnette, [**180**] viewed from inside the chapel. Photo Author.
182. Bohemian architect and builders, Karlštejn Castle, 30 km south-west of Prague, Exterior, 1348- *c.* 1365. Photo Archives of the National Monuments Institute, Regional Office of Central Bohemia, Prague.
183. Master Theodoric, Interior of the Holy Cross Chapel, Karlštejn Castle, view of south wall, walls set with painted panels, hard stones, and murals, vaults gold leaf and gilded glass, 1365–67. Photo Archives of the National Monuments Institute, Regional Office of Central Bohemia, Prague.
184. Etienne Martellange, View of Jean de Berry's Sainte Chapelle at Bourges, drawing of c. 1615. Bibiothèque Nationale (Estampes, Res. Ub-9-FT 5, Pl.46), Paris.
185. Designed by André Beauneveu (?), *Apostle and Prophet*, stained glass from the Sainte Chapelle, Bourges, 1395–1400, now crypt of the Cathedral, Bourges. Photo Author.
186. Chapel of the Hôtel of Jacques Coeur, Bourges, 1448–50, view showing the oratory of Jacques Coeur; nineteenth century polychromy. Photo Author.
187. Eastern façade of Hôtel of Jacques Coeur, showing exterior of chapel. Photo Author.
188. Interior of the oratory of Louis of Gruuthuse, spanning his palace and the Church of Our Lady, Bruges, Stone, painted wood panel, constructed 1472. Photo Author.
189. Jean Jacques Gaillard (d. 1867), Oratory of Louis of Gruuthuse, coloured drawing on paper from the *Album met Brugse grafmonumentem*, c. 1850. Bruges, Groeningemuseum.
190. Jan Borman (wooden model) Renier van Thienen (casting), Pieter de Backere (gilding), Hubert Nonon (stonework and polishing) Jacques and Lieven van Lathem (heraldry), Tomb of Mary of Burgundy, gilt bronze, enamel and black Dinant marble, 1488–96, Church of Our Lady, Bruges, figure of Mary of Burgundy 190 cm long including cushion. Photo Author.
191. Jean le Tavernier, *Philip the Good at Mass*, miniature from the Treatise on Our Lords Prayer, 1454, parchment, 34.5 × 29 cm (whole page). Bibliothèque royale de Belgique (Ms. 9092, f. 9), Brussels.
192. Thierry du Chastel, after designs by Jan van Eyck or an artist in his circle, Cope of the Virgin, part of the full chapel set made for the Order of the Golden Fleece, *c.* 1430–1445, embroidered gold and silk threads, pearls. Kunsthistorisches Museum (inv.KK 21), Vienna.
193. Detail of [**192**]
194. Parisian painter (Girard de Orleans?), The 'Parement de Narbonne', ink on silk, 286 × 78 cm *c.* 1370, Musée du Louvre (Departement des Arts Graphiques MI1121), Paris.
195. Jean le Tavernier, *Adoration of the Magi*, miniature from the Hours of Philip the Good, *c.* 1450, parchment, 26.8 × 18.7 (whole folio). Koninklijke Bibliotheek (Ms. 76 F2, f. 143v), The Hague.
196. Anonymous Netherlandish (?) artists, *Miracles of the Virgin*, wall painting in Eton College chapel, 1480s. Reproduced by permission of the Provost and Fellows of Eton College.
197. Master of James IV of Scotland, *James IV of Scotland presented by St James, in prayer to an altarpiece of the Salvator Mundi*, from the Hours of James IV of Scotland, *c.* 1502–3, parchment, 20 × 14 cm. Österreichische Nationalbibliothek (Ms. 1897, f. 24v), Vienna.
198. Master of James IV of Scotland (?), *Margaret Tudor in prayer to an image of the Virgin and Child*, from the Hours of James IV of Scotland, *c.* 1502–3, parchment, 20 × 14 cm. Österreichische Nationalbibliothek (Ms. 1897, f. 243v), Vienna.
199. Vienna Master of Mary of Burgundy, *Mary of Burgundy (?) in prayer at a window*, from the Vienna Hours of Mary of Burgundy, *c.* 1480, parchment, 22.5 × 32.6 cm (whole opening). Österreichische Nationalbibliothek (Ms. 1857, f. 14v), Vienna.
200. Vienna Master of Mary of Burgundy, *Christ Nailed to the Cross*, from the Vienna

Hours of Mary of Burgundy, *c.* 1480, parchment, folio size 22.5 × 16.3 cm. Österreichische Nationalbibliothek (Ms. 1857, f. 43v), Vienna.
201. Southern Germany *c.* 1450, The *Crucifixion*, coloured woodcut with frame printed from separate block, *c.* 1450, 19.6 × 14 cm. Germanisches Nationalmuseum (inv.H.20), Nuremberg.
202. Hans Memling, Epiphany Triptych, *c.* 1470–72, oil on Baltic oak, 95 × 271 cm. Museo del Prado, Madrid/photo Bridgeman Art Library.
203. Hans Memling, *The Passion of Christ*, *c.* 1470, oil on Baltic oak panel, 56.7 × 92.2 cm. Galleria Sabauda, Turin/photo Bridgeman Art Library.
204. Jean Hey (the Master of Moulins), *Ecce Homo*, oil on wood panel, dated 1494, 39 × 30 cm. Musées Royaux des Beaux Arts, Brussels/photo akg-images/Joseph Martin.
205. Israhel van Meckenem, *Imago Pietatis*, *c.* 1495–1500, copperplate engraving on paper, 17.5 × 11.9 cm. Albertina (inv.DG1926/1016), Vienna,.
206. Follower of Simon Marmion, *St Anthony Abbot*, from a book of hours, possibly made for Antoine Rolin, 1490s, parchment, 17.1 × 11.8 cm. The Walters Art Museum (Ms. W. 194, f. 102v), Baltimore.
207. Jan van Eyck, *Madonna of Chancellor Nicolas Rolin*, *c.* 1435, oil on Baltic oak, 66 × 62 cm. Musée du Louvre (INV1271), Paris/photo RMN/© Hervé Lewandowski.
208.Hans Memling, Diptych of Maartin van Nieuwenhove, 1487, oil on Baltic oak, each panel 52 × 41.5 cm including frame. Sint-Janshospitaal, Memlingmuseum, Bruges/photo akg-images/Erich Lessing.
209. Anonymous French illuminator working in Tours, *Macé de Prestesaille, his wife Jeanne and their children kneeling in prayer to the Pieta*, from the Hours of Macé de Prestesaille, dated 1475, parchment, 19 × 13 cm (each folio). Bibliothèque Nationale (Ms. Lat. 1179, ff. 1v-2r), Paris.
210. Jean Fouquet, *Etienne Chevalier presented to the Virgin and Child by St Stephen* (the 'Melun Diptych'), *c.* 1455–60, oil on panel, (left panel), 93 × 85 cm Gemäldegalerie, Berlin/photo BPK, and (right panel), 94.5 × 85.5 cm Musées Royaux des Beaux Arts, Antwerp/photo akg-images.
211. Jean Fouquet, Self portrait, once set around the frame of [**210**], copper, dark blue enamel and gold paint, 7.5 cm diameter including frame. Musée du Louvre, Paris/photo Bridgeman Art Library/Peter Willi.

The publisher and author apologize for any errors or omissions in the above list. If contacted they will be pleased to rectify these at the earliest opportunity.

Bibliographic Essay

This essay provides direction to some of the most significant literature on northern art of this period, as far as possible works in English. For reasons of space and because this study is not organized biographically, it does not, on the whole, include works on specific artists, for which the reader is directed to entries in the *Grove Dictionary of Art*. References to material on the individual objects discussed in the text, and to primary sources essential for any serious study of the period, are also to be found in the endnotes, which should be used in conjunction with this essay, since an attempt has been made here not to overtly reproduce material cited there.

General

There are few surveys that cover the whole geographical area or a full range of media in English in detail. A traditional chronological survey, somewhat outdated and focused mostly on painting, is provided by J. Snyder, *Northern Renaissance Art* (New York 1985), while Jeffry Chipps Smith, *Art of the Northern Renaissance* (London 2004) balances the coverage of media more evenly; both these also extend their enquiry well into the sixteenth century, and their focus and depth is necessarily different from this volume. The volumes published to accompany the Open University Renaissance course, K. W. Woods (ed.), *Making Renaissance Art*; C. M. Richardson (ed.), *Locating Renaissance Art*; K. W. Woods, C. M. Richardson, and A. Lymberopoulou (eds), *Viewing Renaissance Art* (all New Haven and London 2007), provide a reliable and up-to-date overview although the weight of the discussion is biased towards Italy. There are several good introductory texts which focus on specific media or regions: for paintings, highly recommended is J. Dunkerton, S. Foister, D. Gordon, and N. Penny, *Giotto to Dürer: Early Renaissance Painting in the National Gallery, London* (New Haven and London 1991). Northern European sculpture is surveyed in T. Müller, *Sculpture in the Netherlands, Germany, France and Spain 1400–1500* (Harmondsworth, 1966) and with better illustrations but without footnotes in G. Duby (ed.), *Sculpture: From Antiquity to the Present Day* (London 2002).

For **Early Netherlandish painting** the introductory essay in L. Campbell, *The Fifteenth Century Netherlandish Schools* (London 1998) is essential. Complementary material is in M. W. Ainsworth and K. Christiansen (eds), *From Van Eyck to Bruegel: Early Netherlandish Paintings in the Metropolitan Museum of Art*, exh. cat. (New York 1998). R. van Schoute and B. de Patoul (eds), *Les Primitifs Flamands et leurs temps* (Tournai 2000) is well illustrated and comprehensive. Good up-to-date summaries of the state of research are M. W. Ainsworth (ed.), *Early Netherlandish Painting at the Crossroads: A Critical Look at Current Methodologies* (New York 2001) and B. Ridderbos, A. van Buren, and H. van Veen (eds), *Early Netherlandish Paintings: Rediscovery, Reception and Research* (Amsterdam 2005). E. Panofsky, *Early Netherlandish Painting: Its Origins and Character*, 2 vols (Cambridge MA 1953) remains relevant mostly in relation to historiography of the field; his arguments, as well as his method, have often been superseded by closer investigations of the objects themselves; by contrast, M. J. Friedländer, *Early Netherlandish Painting*, 14 vols (original German publication 1924–7; trans. Leiden and Brussels 1967–76) is still a fundamental reference work for Netherlandish painting of the period. M. Belozerskaya, *Rethinking the Renaissance: Burgundian Arts across Europe* (Cambridge 2002) and *Flanders in the Fifteenth Century: Art and Civilization*, exh. cat. (Detroit 1960) both consider a wider range of artistic production from the Netherlands than paintings alone. Although in large part concerned with one metalwork object, H. van der Velden, *The Donor's Image: Gerard Loyet and the Votive Portraits of Charles the Bold* (Turnhout 2000) is one of the best books on early Netherlandish art, drawing with sophistication on primary sources, and addressing wider issues about the production and use of images. **Netherlandish manuscript illumination and tapestry production** are well served by the magisterial catalogues of T. Kren and S. McKendrick, *Illuminating the Renaissance: The Triumph of Flemish Manuscript Painting in Europe* (Los Angeles and London 2003) and T. P. Campbell, *Tapestry in the Renaissance: Art and Magnificence* (New Haven and London 2002). For **Netherlandish sculpture**, J. W. Steyaert, *Late Gothic Sculpture: The Burgundian Netherlands*, exh. cat. (Ghent 1994) considers a wide range of materials and types; for carved wooden retables, most useful are the introductory chapter in K. Woods, *Imported Images: Netherlandish Late Gothic Sculpture in England, c. 1400–1550* (Donington 2007), and L. F. Jacobs, *Early Netherlandish Carved Altarpieces, 1380–1550: Medieval Tastes and Mass Marketing* (Cambridge 1998).

General, up-to-date texts in English which survey the field of French, Spanish, German, Eastern European, or English art are more scarce. For **French painting**, G. Ring, *French Painting 1400–1500* (London 1949) remains useful; C. Sterling, *La peinture médiévale à Paris* (I, 1987, II, 1990) is well illustrated, but the attributions are optimistic. For **French sculpture, metalwork, stained glass, and tapestry**, *Les Fastes du Gothique*, exh. cat. (Paris 1981) admirably covers the period *c*.1320–1400, and *Paris 1400: les arts sous Charles VI*, exh. cat. (Paris 2004) overlaps with this and goes up to the 1420s. Artistic production in and for Dijon *c*.1370–1420 is most recently brought together in S. Fliegel and S. Jugie (eds), *Art from the Court of Burgundy 1364–1419*, exh. cat. (Dijon and Cleveland 2004). C. Prigent (ed.), *Art et Société en France au XVe siècle* (Paris 1999) has a wide-ranging remit and a useful glossary at the back. For French sculpture M. Beaulieu and V. Beyer, *Dictionnaire des sculpteurs français du Moyen Âge* (Paris 1992) has detailed entries for both French and Netherlandish sculptors, and full further bibliography. The most extensive study on Parisian goldsmiths' work, which includes transcriptions of payments and other evidence, is E. Kovács, *L'Âge d'or de l'orfèverie parisienne au temps des princes de Valois* (Dijon 2004); see also R. W. Lightbown, *Secular Goldsmiths' Work in Medieval France: A History* (London 1978). The standard work on **French manuscript illumination** of the fifteenth and early sixteenth centuries is the monumental exhibition catalogue by F. Avril and N. Reynaud, *Les manuscrits à peintures en France 1440–1520* (Paris 1993).

For **Spanish painting**, J. Berg Sobré, *Behind the Altar Table: The Development of the Painted Retable in Spain, 1350–1500* (New York 1989) is the most extensive compilation of material on Spanish retables in English, but is poorly illustrated; better illustrations and a useful overview also are in J. Berg Sobré and L. M. F. Bosch (eds), *The Artistic Splendour of the Spanish Kingdoms: The Art of Fifteenth Century Spain*, exh. cat. (Boston 1996). The exhibition catalogues *La Clave Flamenca en los Primitivos Valencianos* (Valencia 2001) and *La pintura gotica hispano flamenca: Bartolomé Bermejo y su época* (Bilbao and Barcelona 2003) have English translations accompanying them and provide more recent material with good reproductions; M. Natale (ed.), *El Renacimiento Mediterráneo: Viajes de artistas e itinerarios de obras entre Italia, Francia y España en el siglo XV*, exh. cat. (Madrid 2001) considers artistic interchange across the Mediterranean; for Spanish sculpture, see B. G. Proske, *Castilian Sculpture: Gothic to Renaissance* (New York 1951).

For **German painting** Cologne and Nuremberg are the only centres covered by studies in English: see J. Chapuis, *Stefan Lochner: Image Making in Fifteenth-Century Cologne* (Turnhout 2004), B. Corley, *Painting and Patronage in Cologne 1300–1500* (London 2000), and *Gothic and Renaissance Art in Nuremberg 1300–1550*, exh. cat. (New York 1986). M. Baxandall, *The Limewood Sculptors of Renaissance Germany* (New Haven and London, 1980) remains the fundamental text for **German sculpture**, considering the subject with the widest range of possible evidence; a review article by G. Lutz, 'Recent Research on Late Gothic Sculpture in Germany', *Speculum*, 80 (2005), 494–502, gives an overview of more recent literature in this area. German sculpted altarpieces are fabulously illustrated and informatively discussed in R. Kahsnitz, *Carved Altarpieces, Masterpieces of Late Gothic* (London, 2006). See also the excellent exhibition catalogue J. Chapuis (ed.), *Tilman Reimenschneider: Master Sculptor of the Late Middle Ages*, exh. cat. (New York and Washington 2000). For the artistic production of two key centres in **Eastern Europe** see B. Drake Boehm and J. Fajt (eds), *Prague: The Crown of Bohemia, 1347–1437*, exh. cat. (New York and Prague 2005) and I. Takács (ed.), *Sigismundus Rex et Imperator: Art et culture à l'époque de Sigismond de Luxembourg 1387–1437*, exh. cat. (Budapest 2006). The German edition, however (eds J. Fiat, M. Hörsch, and A. Langer), is far more extensive. For the production of **art in and for England** at the period, R. Marks and P. Williamson (eds), *Gothic: Art for England 1400–1547*, exh. cat. (London 2003).

There are several useful compilations of specialist bibliographies covering material in this book: J. Mundy, *Painting in Bruges, 1470–1550: An Annotated Bibliography* (Boston 1985); B. Lane, *Flemish Painting outside Bruges, 1400–1500: An Annotated Bibliography* (Boston 1986); H. Mund and C. Stroo, *Early Netherlandish Painting (1400–1500): A Bibliography (1994–1998)* (Brussels 1998); C. Madelaine Harrison, *Stained Glass before 1540: An Annotated Bibliography* (Boston 1983); C. Lord, *Royal French Patronage in the Fourteenth Century: An Annotated Bibliography* (Boston 1985); a recent and expert survey of the field and bibliography of French art *c.*1400 is provided by M. Tomasi, 'L'art en France autour de 1400: elements pour un bilan', *Perspective: Revue de l'INHA* (2006), 97–120.

Sources and Documents in English Translation

The most extensive compendium of translated documentary sources is C. M. Richardson, K. W. Woods, and M. W. Franklin (eds), *Renaissance Art Reconsidered: An Anthology of Primary Sources* (Oxford 2007); this can be supplemented by W. Stechow, *Northern Renaissance Art: Sources and Documents* (Evanston 1989) and T. G. Frisch, *Gothic Art 1140–c.1450: Sources and Documents* (Toronto 1987). The volume by C. E. Gilbert, *Italian Art 1400–1500: Sources and Documents* (Englewood Cliffs 1980) includes various documents relating to northern art such as letters from the Medici agents in Bruges. Translations of contracts for some retables made in Spain at the period can be found in Berg Sobré, *Behind the Altar Table*. Baxandall, *Limewood Sculptors* has translations of documentary material relating to German sculpture, including the Ulm guild regulations and a number of contracts. The Antwerp guild regulations and various guild disputes are translated in Richardson, Woods, and Franklin (eds), *Renaissance Art Reconsidered*; the Cologne regulations are translated in Chapuis, *Stefan Lochner*; and those of Córdoba are in Z. Veliz, 'Appendix: The 1493 *Ordenzas de Córdoba* for Regulating the Profession of Painting', in *Hamilton Kerr Institute Bulletin*, 3 (2000), 35–9. A number of contracts and some guild disputes are translated by M. P. J. Martens, *Artistic Patronage in Bruges Institutions, ca. 1440–1482*, PhD (University of California, Santa Barbara 1992). Fazio's writings concerning Jan van Eyck and Rogier van der Weyden are translated in full in M. Baxandall, 'Bartholomaeus Facius on Painting', *Journal of the Warburg and Courtauld Institutes*, 27 (1964), 90–107. For the writings of Albrecht Dürer, see W. M. Conway, *Literary Remains of Albrecht Dürer* (Cambridge 1889); the travel diary of Pero Tafur is translated in full in *Travels and Adventures 1435–1438*, ed. M. Letts (London 1926); van Mander's works have been the subject of a complete translation and full study: H. Miedema (ed.), *Karel van Mander: The Lives of the Illustrious Netherlandish and German Painters*, tr. D. Cook-Radmore (Doornspijk 1994–9).

Introduction

For historical background, the most stimulating view of Europe at this period is that presented through patterns of trade and trade routes by P. Spufford, *Power and Profit: The Merchant in Medieval Europe* (London 2002), complemented by H. van der Wee, *The Low Countries in the Early Modern World* (Aldershot 1993) and M. Vale, 'The Civilization of Courts and Cities in the North, 1200–1500', in G. Holmes (ed.), *The Oxford Illustrated History of Medieval Europe* (Oxford and New York 1988), 297–351; the most recent English edition of J. Huizinga, *The Autumn of the Middle Ages* (1997), tr. R. Payton and U. Mammitzsch, presents this influential and evocative text in full: earlier English translations are partial, without references, and with material rearranged. Changing styles of dress and the way clothing can convey meaning are discussed in M. Scott, *Late Gothic Europe 1400–1500*, History of Dress series (London 1980). For religious history, see B. Hamilton, *Religion in the Medieval World* (London 1986); E. Duffy, *The Stripping of the Altars: Traditional Religion in England c.1400–c.1580* (New Haven and London 1992) is rich in evidence.

Challenges to the view of Florentine dominance are done most deftly by

Campbell in *The Fifteenth Century Netherlandish Schools* and P. Nuttall, *From Flanders to Florence* (London 2004); Belozerskaya, *Rethinking the Renaissance* attacks the problem head on with gusto. The demand for Netherlandish painting across Europe and the impact of its style and techniques are also explored in I. Alexander-Skipnes (ed.), *Cultural Exchange between the Low Countries and Italy (1400–1600)* (Turnhout 2007); T.-H. Borchert et al., *The Age of Van Eyck: The Mediterranean World and Early Netherlandish Painting 1430–1530*, exh. cat. (Bruges 2002); V. Schmidt (ed.), *Italy and the Low Countries: Artistic Relations* (Florence 1999); B. Aikema and B. L. Brown (eds), *Renaissance Venice and the North: Crosscurrents in the Time of Dürer, Bellini and Titian*, exh. cat. (Venice 1999).

Part I

On iconoclasm and its effects see most recently J. L. Koerner, *The Reformation of the Image* (London 2004). See also the treasure trove of objects and information in C. Dupeux, P. Jezler and J. Wirth (eds), *Iconoclasme: Vie et mort de l'image médiévale*, exh. cat. (Berne and Strasbourg 2001). On war damage, see N. Lambourne, *War Damage in Western Europe: The Destruction of Historic Monuments during the Second World War* (Edinburgh 2001). On the historiography of and changing taste for early Netherlandish paintings see J. Chapuis, 'Early Netherlandish Painting: Shifting Perspectives', in Ainsworth (ed.), *From Van Eyck to Bruegel*, 3–21; T.-H. Borchert, 'Collecting Early Netherlandish Paintings in Europe and the United States', and W. Krul, 'Realism, Renaissance and Nationalism', both in Ridderbos et al. (eds), *Early Netherlandish Paintings*, 173–216; 252–289; the chapter on 'Huizinga and the Flemish Renaissance' in F. Haskell, *History and its Images: Art and the Interpretation of the Past* (New Haven and London 1993), 431–95, is particularly insightful; the latter work also considers the development of the taste for white marble sculpture, as opposed to polychromed wood.

For inventories and their contents see the exhaustive study of the Duke of Bedford's goods by J. Stratford, *The Bedford Inventories: The Worldly Goods of John, Duke of Bedford, Regent of France (1389–1435)* (London 1993). For gift giving see B. Buettner, 'Past Presents: New Year's Gifts at the Valois Courts, ca. 1400', *The Art Bulletin*, 83 (2001), 598–625. For the archives of the Burgundian Netherlands, M. Martens, 'Approaches to the Heuristics of Early Netherlandish Art', in *Early Netherlandish Painting at the Crossroads*, discusses the relative reliability of the archivists of the nineteenth and early twentieth centuries, with further bibliography concerning publications of primary sources. An essential discussion of archival sources relating to Netherlandish painting with full further references is L. Campbell, 'The Art Market in the Southern Netherlands in the Fifteenth Century', *The Burlington Magazine*, 118 (1976), 188–98; see also his essay 'Approaches to Petrus Christus', in M. Ainsworth (ed.), *Petrus Christus in Renaissance Bruges* (Turnhout and New York 1995), 1–10, which discusses some recent documentary findings and their implications, supplemented by his insightful 'Reflections on Sources and Reconstructions', in M. Clarke, J. H. Townsend, and A. Stijnman (eds), *Art of the Past: Sources and Reconstructions; Proceedings of the First Symposium of the Art Technological Source Research Study Group* (London 2005), 33–8. For *tableaux vivants* and entries at this period see in general G. Kipling, *Enter the King: Theatre, Liturgy and Ritual in the Medieval Civic Triumph* (Oxford 1998) and more specifically M. P. J. Martens, 'Art and Politics: Festive Decorations for Triumphant Entries in the Burgundian Netherlands', in H. T. van Veen, V. M. Schmidt, and J. M. Jezler (eds), *Polyptiek: een veelluik van Groninger bijdragen aan de kunstgeschiedenis* (Zwolle 2002), 27–31, 219–20; P. Arnade, *Realms of Ritual: Burgundian Ceremony and Civic Life in Late Medieval Ghent* (London 1996); D. Eichberger, 'The Tableau Vivant—An Ephemeral Art Form in Burgundian Civic Festivities', *Parergon*, 6 (1988), 37–64. On the Feast of the Pheasant see R. Vaughan, *Philip the Good: The Apogee of Burgundy* (reprint Woodbridge 2002), 143–5; on the 1468 wedding see R. Vaughan, *Charles the Bold: The Last Valois Duke of Burgundy* (reprint Woodbridge 2002), 48–53. For religious dramas see K. Young, *The Drama of the Medieval Church* (Oxford 1933).

On painters' guilds see L. Campbell, 'The Early Netherlandish Painters and their Workshops', in D. Hollanders-Favart and R. van Schoute (eds), *Le dessin sous-jacent dans la peinture: Colloque III 6–7–8 septembre 1979: Le problème Maître de Flémalle—van der Weyden* (Louvain-la-Neuve 1981), 43–61; for German painters' and sculptors' guilds, Baxandall, *Limewood Sculptors*, esp. 106–22, and H. Huth,

Künstler und Werkstatt (Darmstadt 1967). On the painters' trade in Spain in general, see M. R. Katz, 'Architectural Polychromy and the Painters' Trade in Medieval Spain', *Gesta*, 61 (2002), 3–13, and Berg Sobré, *Behind the Altar Table*, 12–26.

A very good introduction to and explication of the full range of methods used in the examination of paintings is A. Kirsch and R. S. Levenson, *Seeing Through Paintings: Physical Examination in Art Historical Studies* (New Haven and London 2000), supplemented by J. R. J. van Asperen de Boer and J. P. Filedt Kok (eds), *Scientific Examination of Early Netherlandish Painting: Applications in Art History*, *Nederlands Kunsthistorisch Jaarboek*, 26 (1976). On infra-red reflectography and underdrawings see D. Bomford (ed.), *Art in the Making: Underdrawings in Renaissance Paintings*, exh. cat. (London 2002); some of the most legible reflectograms of paintings from Spain and Italy as well as the Netherlands are in G. Finaldi and C. Garrido (eds), *El trazo oculto: dibujos subyacentes en pinturas de los siglos XV y XVI,* exh. cat. (Madrid 2006). See also the many studies on underdrawings in the proceedings of the conferences held bi-annually on this topic, published as *Le dessin sous-jacent dans la peinture*, by the Université catholique de Louvain, Louvain-la-Neuve. For the wood, frames, and construction of early Netherlandish paintings see H. Verougstraete-Marcq and R. van Schoute, *Cadres et supports dans la peinture flamande aux 15e et 16e siècles* (Heure-le-Romain 1989).

For studies surveying the results of technical examination in the field of early Netherlandish painting see M. Faries and R. Spronk (eds), *Recent Developments in the Technical Examination of Early Netherlandish Painting: Methodology, Limitations and Perspectives* (Cambridge MA and Turnhout 2003). Another useful overview but with some different examples is to be found in J. Dikstra, 'Technical Examination', in Ridderbos, van Buren, and van Veen, *Early Netherlandish Paintings*, 292–328.
Four compilations of essays from various international conferences provide some of the most useful and up-to-date technical evidence and discussion of individual artists: these are M. Ainsworth (ed.), *Petrus Christus in Renaissance Bruges* (Turnhout and New York 1995); S. Foister and S. Nash (eds), *Robert Campin: New Directions in Scholarship* (London 1996); C. Purtle (ed.), *Rogier van der Weyden's St Luke Drawing the Virgin: Selected Essays in Context* (Turnhout 1997); S. Foister, S. Jones, and D. Cool (eds), *Investigating Van Eyck* (Turnhout 2000).

Part II

For the relative wealth of European rulers at this period and population figures, see Spufford, *Power and Profit*. The formation of the Burgundian state is most fully discussed by R. Vaughan, *Valois Burgundy* (London 1975) and *Philip the Bold* (Woodbridge 2002); for the political and economic situation of the Netherlandish towns and their relative economic importance, see W. Blockmans and W. Prevenier, *The Promised Lands: The Low Countries Under Burgundian Rule, 1396–1530* (Philadelphia 1999), which provides a useful chronology and genealogical table. For a discussion of the economic crisis in the Netherlands and its impact, R. van Utyven, 'Splendour or Wealth: Art and Economy in the Burgundian Netherlands', *Transactions of the Cambridge Bibliographical Society* (1992), 101–24; J. H. Munro, 'Economic Depression and the Arts in the Fifteenth Century Low Countries', *Renaissance and Reformation* (1983), 235–50.

For Paris and its history at this period see J. Favier, *Paris au XVe siècle, 1380–1500* (Paris 1974); for Charles V, F. Autrand, *Charles V* (Paris 1994) and his patronage, most recently F. Pleybert (ed.), *Paris et Charles V: Arts et architecture* (Paris 2001).
For Isabeau of Bavaria, see S. Hindman, 'The Iconography of Queen Isabeau de Bavière (1410–1415): An Essay in Method', *Gazette des Beaux-Arts*, 102 (1983), 102–10; R. C. Gibbons, 'The Queen as "Social Mannequin": Consumerism and Expenditure at the Court of Isabeau of Bavaria, 1393–1422', *Journal of Medieval History*, 26 (2000), 371–95. The exhibition catalogues *Les Fastes du Gothique* and *Paris 1400* gather together most of the significant movable (and some immovable) objects made in Paris at this period. For the Paris book trade and *libraires*, R. H. Rouse and M. A. Rouse, *Manuscripts and their Makers: Commercial Book Producers in Medieval Paris, 1200–1500* (Turnhout 2000). For the English in Paris, G. L. Thompson, *Paris and its People under English Rule: The Anglo-Burgundian Regime 1420–1436* (Oxford 1991) and for their patronage of art, C. Reynolds, '"Les Angloys, de leur droicte nature, veullent toujours guerreer": Evidence for Painting in Paris and Normandy, c.1420–1450', in C. T. Allmand (ed.), *Power, Culture,*

and Religion in France c.1350–c.1550 (Woodbridge 1989), 37–55.

On the Burgundian ducal residences in general see W. Paravicini, 'Die Residenzen der Herzöge von Burgund, 1363–1477', in H. Patze and W. Paravicini (eds), *Fürstliche Residenzen im spätmittelalterlichen Europa* (Sigmaringen 1990), 207–63. The exhibition catalogue *Charles the Bold (1433–77): Burgundy in its Glory and Decline* (Bern 2008) is the most extensive and up-to-date study of this Burgundian ruler and his artistic patronage. For the merchant communities of Bruges see A. Vandewalle et al., *Les marchands de la Hanse et la Banque de Médicis: Bruges, marché d'échanges culturels en Europe*, exh. cat. (Bruges 2002); for Florentines most recently Nuttall, *From Flanders to Florence*; for Spaniards, Gilliodts-van Severin, *Cartulaire de l'ancien Consulat d'Espagne à Bruges*; J. Maréchal, 'La colonie espagnole de Bruges du XIVe au XVIe siècle', *Revue du Nord*, 35 (1953), 5–40. For those in Antwerp see J.-A. Goris, *Étude sur les colonies marchandes méridionales (portugais, espagnols, italiens) à Anvers de 1488–1567* (Leuven 1925).

For the Bruges and Antwerp fairs see D. Ewing, 'Marketing Art in Antwerp, 1460–1560: Our Lady's Pand', *The Art Bulletin*, 72 (1990), 558–84; J. C. Wilson, *Painting in Bruges at the Close of the Middle Ages: Studies in Society and Visual Culture* (University Park 1998), 171–87; J. C. Wilson, 'The Participation of Painters in the Bruges *Pandt* Market, 1512–1550', *The Burlington Magazine*, 125 (1983), 476–9. For the art market more generally, L. Campbell, 'The Art Market in the Southern Netherlands in the Fifteenth Century', *The Burlington Magazine*, 118 (1976), 188–98, and M. North and D. Ormrod (eds), *Art Markets in Europe, 1400–1800* (Brookfield 1998).

For the production and export of cloth painting in the Netherlands, see the essays by Nuttall and Reynolds in C. Villers (ed.), *The Fabric of Images: European Paintings on Textile Supports in the Fourteenth and Fifteenth Centuries* (London 2000), and the survey by D. Wolfthal, *The Beginnings of Netherlandish Canvas Painting: 1400–1530* (Cambridge 1989). For Burgundian metalwork, manuscripts, tapestries, and sculpture see the works cited above, under 'General, early Netherlandish art'; for glass roundels, P. C. Ritsema van Eck, *Painted Glass Roundels from the Netherlands 1480–1560* (Zwolle 1999), T. B. Husband et al., *The Luminous Image: Painted Glass Roundels in the Lowlands, 1480–1560*, exh. cat. (New York 1995); on brass manufacture see S. Collon-Gevaert, *Histoire des arts du métal en Belgique* (Brussels 1951), M. Norris, *Monumental Brasses: The Craft* (London 1978), H. K. Cameron, 'Technical Aspects of Medieval Monumental Brasses', *The Archaeological Journal*, 131 (1974), 215–37, J. Toussaint (ed.), *Art du Laiton—Dinanderie* (Namur 2005).

The literature on Medici patronage is vast, but for our purposes Nuttall, *From Flanders to Florence*, is the most useful and relevant study. There is little in English on Isabella of Castile although her patronage is considered in J. Brown, 'Spain in the Age of Exploration: Crossroads of Artistic Cultures', and J. J. Martín González, 'Sculpture in Castile c.1492', both in J. A. Levenson (ed.), *Circa 1492: Art in the Age of Exploration*, exh. cat. (Washington 1991), 41–9 and 51–4; see also *Reyes y mecenas: Los Reyes Católicos, Maximiliano I y los inicios de la casa de Austria en España*, exh. cat. (Toledo 1992); J. Yarza Luaces, *Isabel La Católica: promotora artistica* (León 2005).

Part III

For the de Limbourgs, see M. Meiss, *French Painting in the Time of Jean de Berry: The Limbourgs and their Contemporaries* (London 1974), and R. Dückers and P. Roelofs (eds), *The Limbourg Brothers: Nijmegen Masters at the French Court, 1400–1416*, exh. cat. (Nijmegen 2005). For Jean de Berry's patronage and collection see M. Meiss, *French Painting in the Time of Jean de Berry: The Late Fourteenth Century and the Patronage of the Duke*, 2 vols (London 1967). For Memling, see D. de Vos, *Hans Memling: The Complete Works* (London 1994); H. Verougstraete, R. van Schoute, and M. Smeyers (eds), *Memling Studies: Proceedings of the International Colloquium (Bruges, 10–12 November 1994)* (Leuven 1997) and T.-H. Borchert et al., *Memling's Portraits*, exh. cat (Madrid, Bruges, and New York 2005). Printmaking at this period is surveyed in some detail in D. Landau and P. Parshall, *The Renaissance Print, 1470–1550* (New Haven and London 1994); this is well supplemented by F. Koreny, '"Per Universam Europam": German Prints and Printmaking before 1500', in M. P. McDonald, *The Print Collection of Ferdinand Columbus, 1488–1539: A Renaissance Collector in Seville*, 2 vols (London 2004), I, 168–74; also rich in documentary evidence is J. van der Stock, *Printing Images in Antwerp: The Introduction of Printmaking in a City: Fifteenth Century to 1585* (Rotterdam 1998);

P. Parshall and R. Schoch et al., *Origins of European Printmaking: Fifteenth-Century Woodcuts and Their Public*, exh. cat. (Washington 2005) provides a new, polemical direction for the field; U. Weekes, *Early Engravers and their Public: The Master of the Berlin Passion and Manuscripts from Convents in the Rhine-Maas Region, ca. 1450–1500* (Turnhout 2004) considers prints inserted or pasted into manuscripts. A wide range of issues concerning printmaking and collecting are covered in M. P. McDonald, *The Print Collection of Ferdinand Columbus (1488–1539): A Renaissance Collector in Seville* (London 2004). A. Shestack, *Fifteenth Century Engravings of Northern Europe from the National Gallery of Art, Washington*, exh. cat. (Washington 1967) remains useful. For Dürer's prints, most recently G. Bartrum, *Albrecht Dürer and his Legacy: The Graphic Work of a Renaissance Artist*, exh. cat. (London 2002).

For a discussion of some self-portraits in German sculpture, see C. Schleif, 'Nicodemus and Sculptors: Self Reflexivity in Works by Adam Kraft and Tilman Riemenschneider', *The Art Bulletin*, 75 (1993), 599–626, and in painting J. L. Koerner, *The Moment of Self-Portraiture in German Renaissance Art* (Chicago and London 1993). On van Eyck's inscriptions see M. Smeyers, 'Jan van Eyck, Archaeologist? Reflections on Eyckian Epigraphy', in M. Lodewijckx (ed.), *Archaeological and Historical Aspects of West-European Societies* (Leuven 1996), 403–14. A range of sculptors' signatures are illustrated or transcribed in J. Baudoin, *La sculpture flamboyant: Les grands imagiers d'occident* (Nonette 1983), 91–100.

Part IV

The British Museum's *Medieval Craftsmen* series provides introductions to particular media; most relevant here are P. Binski, *Painters*, K. Staniland, *Embroiderers*, S. Brown and D. O'Connor, *Glass-Painters* (all London 1991), C. de Hamel, *Scribes and Illuminators* (London 1992). The essays in P. Lindley (ed.), *Making Medieval Art* (Donington 2003), especially that by A. Timmermann, 'The Workshop Practice of Medieval Painters', 42–53, also provide an overview; more specialized contributions are in the conference proceedings X. Barral I Altet (ed.) *Artistes, artisans et production artistique au Moyen Age*, 3 vols (Paris 1986–90); A. Roy and P. Smith (eds), *Painting Techniques: History, Materials and Studio Practice, Contributions to the Dublin Congress 7–11 September 1998* (London 1998); K. Dardes and A. Rothe (eds), *The Structural Conservation of Panel Paintings: Papers Given at a Symposium at the J. Paul Getty Museum, 1993* (Los Angeles 1998).

Insights into practical aspects of creating images are provided by J. Ayers, *The Artist's Craft: A History of Tools, Techniques and Materials* (Oxford 1985). For focused studies on the techniques of early Netherlandish and German paintings, see L. Campbell, S. Foister, and A. Roy (eds), 'Methods and Materials of Northern European Painting in the National Gallery, 1400–1550', in *National Gallery Technical Bulletin*, 18 (1987) (special issue: *Early Northern European Painting*). For the making of Netherlandish wood sculpture see C. van de Velde, H. Beeckman, J. van Acker, and F. Verhaeghe (eds), *Constructing Wooden Images: Proceedings of the Symposium on the Organization of Labour and Working Practices of Late Gothic Carved Altarpieces in the Low Countries* (Brussels 2005); S. Guillot de Suduiraut (ed.), *Retables Brabacons des XVe et VXIe siècles: Actes du colloque 18–19 March 2001* (Paris 2002); for polychromy see also S. Boldrick, D. Park, and P. Williamson, *Wonder: Painted Sculpture from Medieval England*, exh. cat. (Leeds 2002) and M. Serk-Dewaide, 'Support and Polychromy of Altarpieces from Brussels, Mechlin and Antwerp: Study, Comparison and Restoration', in V. Dorge and F. Carey Howlett (eds), *Painted Wood: History and Conservation* (Los Angeles 1998), 82–99, and for Spain, R. Kasl, *Painters, Polychromy and the Perfection of Images in Spanish Polychrome Sculpture 1500–1800 in United States Collections* (Los Angeles 1994), 33–52. The most extensive investigations of the techniques of German sculpture and its polychromy are in H. Meurer et al. (eds), *Meisterwerke Massenhaft: Die Bildhauerwerkstatt des Nicklaus Weckmann und die Malerei in Ulm um 1500* (Stuttgart 1993). For sculptors' tools, M. Rief and S. Giesen, 'Mittelalterliche Bildhauer und ihre Werkzeuge in zeitgenössischen Darstellungen', *Restauratorenblätter* (1997–8), 43–51; for methods and tools of limewood carving, see Baxandall, *Limewood Sculptors*. For manuscript illumination the essays by N. K. Turner, 'The Suggestive Brush: Painting Techniques in Flemish Manuscripts from the Collections of the J. Paul Getty Museum and the Huntington Library', and L. Watteeuw, 'Flemish Manuscript Production, Care and Repair: Fifteenth Century Sources', both in Morrison and Kren (eds), *Flemish Manuscript Painting in Context: Recent Research*, 57–74, 75–86, are highly recommended. Most recently on drawings see F. Koreny et al., *Early Netherlandish Drawings from Jan van Eyck to Hieronymus Bosch*, exh. cat. (Antwerp 2002); the 2005 issue of *Master Drawings* is devoted to northern drawings of the period; on model books, R. W. Scheller, *Exemplum: Model-Book Drawings and the Practice of Artistic Transmission in the Middle Ages (ca. 900–ca. 1470)* (Amsterdam 1995).

For underdrawings, see publications listed under Part I above.

Apprentices, journeymen, and workshops are discussed in Campbell, 'The Early Netherlandish Painters and their Workshops', 43–6; for German sculptors' and painters' workshops, Huth, *Künstler und Werkstatt*, and Baxandall, *Limewood Sculptors*, especially 106–16; for Antwerp woodcarvers, N. Peeters and M. P. J. Martens, 'A Cutting Edge? Wood Carvers and Their Workshops in Antwerp 1453–1579', in Van de Velde et al., *Constructing Wooden Images*, 75–92; for illuminators, Rouse and Rouse, *Manuscripts and their Makers*, and Reynolds, 'Illuminators and the Painters Guilds', in Kren and McKendrick, *Illuminating the Renaissance*, 15–33. For the trade in artists' materials, pigments, and their prices, J. Cannon, J. Kirby, and S. Nash (eds), *European Trade in Painters' Materials to 1700* (forthcoming 2009) and J. Kirby, 'The Price of Quality: Factors Influencing the Cost of Pigments during the Renaissance', in G. Neher and R. Shepherd (eds), *Revaluing Renaissance Art* (Aldershot 2000), 19–33.

For the characteristics and history of individual pigments see N. Eastaugh, *The Pigment Compendium: Optical Microscopy of Historical Pigments* (Oxford 2004). On the qualities and handling properties of oil and egg, J. Dunkerton, 'Observations on the Handling Properties of Binding Media Identified in European Painting from the Fifteenth to the Seventeenth Centuries', *Bulletin de l'Institut royal du patrimoine artistique*, 27 (1996–8), 287–92. For van Eyck's technique see A. Roy, 'Van Eyck's Technique: The Myth and the Reality, I' and R. White, 'Van Eyck's Technique: The Myth and the Reality, II', in Foister, Jones, and Cool (eds), *Investigating Van Eyck*, 97–100, 101–6. For Rogier van der Weyden's technique see R. Billinge, L. Campbell, and M. Spring, 'The Materials and Techniques of Five Paintings by Rogier van der Weyden and his Workshop', *National Gallery Technical Bulletin*, 18 (1997), 68–86.

For stonecarving, see S. Nash, *'No Equal in Any Land': André Beauneveu Artist to the Courts of France and Flanders* (London 2007), esp. Chapter 2 on artistic practice, and P. Lindley, 'Gothic Sculpture: Studio and Workshop Practice', in Lindley (ed.), *Making Medieval Art*, 25–34. The making of a large German carved retable is investigated in detail with regard to Friedrich Herlin's Rothenburg altarpiece by K.-W. Bachmann, E. Oellermann, J. Taubert, M. Broekman-Bokstijn et al. 'The Conservation and Technique of the Herlin Altarpiece (1466)' and 'The Scientific Examination of the Polychromed Sculpture in the Herlin Altarpiece', both in *Studies in Conservation*, 15 (1970), 327–400.

Part V

The taste for folding objects has been explored by D. Eichberger, 'Devotional Objects in Book Format: Diptychs in the Collection of Margaret of Austria and her Family', in M. Manion and B. J. Muir (eds), *The Art of the Book* (Exeter 1998), 291–323, and at greater length in J. O. Hand, C. A. Metzger, and R. Spronk (eds), *Prayers and Portraits: Unfolding the Netherlandish Diptych*, exh. cat. (New Haven and London 2006) and the essays in J. O. Hand and R. Spronk (eds), *Essays in Context: Unfolding the Netherlandish Diptych* (New Haven and London 2006); see also the wide range of objects of this type in H. W. van Os et al., *The Art of Devotion in the Late Middle Ages in Europe, 1300–1500*, exh. cat. (Amsterdam and London 1994); for metalwork objects of this sort, F. Geens, *Ungs très petiz tableaux à pignon, qui cloent et ouvrent, esmaillez dehors et dedens: A Study of Small Scale, Folding, Pieces of Goldsmiths' Work in Fourteenth Century Europe*, PhD, Courtauld Institute (Univ. London 2002). For a discussion of the leather boxes made for plate at this period see Lightbown, *Secular Goldsmiths' Work*, 34–40; on covers and containers for portraits see L. Campbell, *Renaissance Portraits* (London 1990), 65–7, 254, n. 121.

For an overview of the literature on the functions of altarpieces at this period see B. Williamson, 'Altarpieces, Liturgy, and Devotion', *Speculum*, 79 (2004), 341–406, where altar dedications and relics are also discussed; see also J. Gardner, 'Altars, Altarpieces and Art History: Legislation and Usage', in E. Borsook and F. S. Gioffredi (eds), *Italian Altarpieces 1250–1550: Function and Design* (Oxford 1994), 5–39; and P. Humfrey and M. Kemp (eds), *The Altarpiece in the Renaissance* (Cambridge 1990), especially the essay by K. Woods, 'The Netherlandish Carved Altarpiece *c.*1500: Type and Function', 76–89; Jacobs, *Early Netherlandish Carved Altarpieces*, 12–18, provides a useful discussion of issues of function in relationship to Netherlandish carved retables, and D. Eichberger, 'The Winged Altarpiece in Early Netherlandish Art', in Lindley (ed.), *Making Medieval Art*, 152–70. On the altarpieces in St Lorenz see C. Schleif, *Donatio et memoria: Stifter, Stiftungen und Motivationen au Beispielen aus der Lorenzkirche in Nürnburg* (Munich 1990); also B. Heal, *A Woman Like Any Other? Images of the Virgin Mary and Marian Devotion in Nuremberg, Augsburg and Cologne, c.1500–1600*, PhD, Courtauld Institute (Univ. London 2001).

On the functions of grisaille see M. Teasdale Smith, 'The Use of Grisaille as a Lenten Observance', *Marsyas*, 8 (1959), 43–54; on its potential meaning and appeal see C. Itzel, *Der Stein trügt: die Imitation von Skulpturen in der niederländischen Tafelmalerei im Kontext bildtheoretischer Auseinandersetzungen des frühen 15: Jahrhunderts*, PhD (Univ. Heidelberg 2003); for its employment in Netherlandish altarpieces see H. Belting and C. Kruse, *Die Erfindung des Gemäldes: das erste Jahrhundert der niederländischen Malerei* (Munich 1994) and P. Philippot, 'Les Grisailles et 'les degrés de réalité' de l'image dans la peinture flamand des XVe et XVIe siècle', *Bulletin des Musées royaux des beaux-arts de Belgique*, 15 (1966), 225–42, and C. Itzel, 'Peinture et Hétérodoxie: La Peinture Flamande à la lumière du débat sur les images', in *Campin in Context* (2007), 140–54. The question of competition between sculpture and painting is addressed in R. Preimesberger, 'Zu Jan van Eycks Diptychon der Sammlung Thyssen-Bornemisza', *Zeitschrift für Kunstgeschichte*, 54 (1991), 459–89. Polychromy in Riemenschneider's work is discussed in the essays by Oellermann, Marincola, Göbel, and Fischer in J. Chapuis (ed.), *Tilman Riemenschneider c.1460–1531*, Studies in the History of Art 65, Center for Advanced Studies in the Visual Arts Symposium Papers XLII (Washington 2004).

On the opening of altarpieces at St Lorenz see P. Crossley, 'The Man from Inner Space: Architecture and Meditation in the Choir of St. Laurence in Nuremberg', in R. G. Owen-Crocker and T. Graham (eds), *Medieval Art: Recent Perspectives, A Memorial Tribute to C. R. Dodwell* (Manchester and New York 1998), 165–82. There is little in English on the use of sculpture in liturgical rituals; the fundamental study is J. Tripps, *Das handelnde Bildwerk in der Gotik: Forschungen zu den Bedeutungsschichten und der Funktion des Kirchengebäudes und seiner Ausstattung in der Hoch- und Spätgotik* (Berlin 1998); see also his contributions to Dupeux, Jetzler, and Wirth (eds), *Iconoclasme*. For figures of Christ with movable arms see G. Taubert, 'Mittelalterliche Kruzifixe mit schwenkbaren Armen', in J. Taubert (ed.), *Farbige Skulpturen: Bedeutung—Fassung—Restaurierung* (Munich 1978), 38–50. On ascending Christ figures, J. Krause, '"Imago ascensionis" und "Himmelsloch", Zum Bildgebrauch in der spätmittelalterlichen Liturgie', in F. Möbius and E. Schubert (eds), *Skulptur des Mittelalters: Funktion und Gestalt* (Weimar 1987), 281–353. On nuns' devotional and artistic practices see J. F. Hamburger, *Nuns as Artists: The Visual Culture of a Medieval Convent* (Berkeley, Los Angeles, and London 1997) and *Krone und Schleier: Kunst aus Mittelalterlichen Frauenklöstern*, exh cat. (Essen and Cologne 2005).

For choir tapestries, L. Weigert, *Weaving Sacred Stories: French Choir Tapestries and the Performance of Clerical Identity* (Ithaca 2004) and C. Arminjon (ed.), *Saints de chœurs tapisseries du Moyen Âge et de la Renaissance*, exh. cat. (Toulouse 2004). For Entombment groups W. H. Forsyth, *The Entombment of Christ: French Sculptures of the Fifteenth and Sixteenth Centuries* (Cambridge MA 1970); M. Martin, *La Statuaire de la Mise au Tombeau du Christ des XVe et XVIe siècles en Europe occidentale* (Paris 1997); for early Rhenish and Swabian examples, S. Abelléa, *Les saints sépulcres monumentaux du Rhin supérieur et de la Souabe (1340–1400)* (Strasbourg 2003). On devotion to the Holy Sepulchre more generally see C. Morris, *The Sepulchre of Christ and the Medieval West: From the Beginning to 1600* (Oxford 2005). On tomb sculpture A. McGee Morganstern, *Gothic Tombs of Kinship in France, the Low Countries and England* (University Park 2000) and E. Valdez de Almo (ed.), *Memory and the Medieval Tomb* (Aldershot 2000); on commemorative monuments and practices more generally, see T. van Buren and A. van Leerdam, *Care for the Here and the Hereafter: Memoria, Art and Ritual in the Middle Ages* (Turnhout 2005).

For Jean Gerson and his writings see B. P. McGuire, *Jean Gerson and the Last Medieval Reformation* (University Park 2005); for the Brethren of the Common Life see R. R. Post, *The Modern Devotion: Confrontation with Reformation and Humanism* (Leiden 1968). For Pseudo-Bonaventura's *Meditations on the Life of Christ* see I. Ragusa and R. B. Green (tr. and eds), *Meditations on the Life of Christ: An Illustrated Manuscript of the Fourteenth Century by Saint Bonaventure* (Princeton 1961); for Ludolph of Saxony see C. Abbott Conway Jr, *The Vita Christi of Ludolph of Saxony and Late Medieval Devotion centered on the Incarnation: A Descriptive Analysis* (Salzburg 1976) and Sister M. I. Bodenstedt, *The Vita Christi of Ludolphus the Carthusian* (Washington 1944).

The best discussion of the use of devotional images remains S. Ringbom, *Icon to Narrative: The Rise of the Dramatic Close-up in Fifteenth-Century Devotional Painting*, 2nd edn (Doornspijk 1983); see also H. W. van Os et al., *The Art of Devotion in the Late Middle Ages in Europe, 1300–1500*, exh. cat. (Amsterdam and London 1994); J. Hamburger, *The Visual and the Visionary: Art and Female Spirituality in Late Medieval Germany* (New York 1998); R. Marks, *Image and Devotion in Late Medieval England* (Stroud 2004); B. Rothstein, *Sight and Spirituality in Early Netherlandish Painting* (Cambridge 2005). For the imagery of Christ's Passion and its use see J. H. Marrow, *Passion Iconography in Northern European Art of the Late Middle Ages and Early Renaissance: A Study of the Transformation of Sacred Metaphor into Descriptive Narrative* (Kortrijk 1979); A. A. MacDonald, B. Ridderbos and R. Schlüsemann (eds), *The Broken Body: Passion Devotion in Late-Medieval Culture* (Groningen 1998); and G. Finaldi, *Seeing Salvation: The Image of Christ*, exh. cat. (London, National Gallery 2000).For books of hours see R. S. Wieck, *Painted Prayers: The Book of Hours in Medieval and Renaissance Art*, exh. cat. (New York 1997) and E. Duffy, *Marking the Hours: English People and Their Prayers, 1240–1570* (New Haven and London 2006). For painted diptychs, see Hand, Metzger, and Spronk, *Prayers and Portraits* and Hand and Spronk, *Essays in Context*, the entries and contributions to which include important technical evidence as well as analysis of function, ownership, and viewing angles.

Index

Note: References to illustrations are in *italic*. There may also be textual references on the same page.